PRAISE FOR THIS BOOK

"*The Internet Kids & Family Yellow Pages* is an excellent reference for a household with a computer and kids."
John Frazer Dobson
Computer Shopper

"Jean Armour Polly makes the Internet a lot more kid-friendly."
Ira Flatow, host of public radio's Science Friday

"It's a jungle out there on the Internet, and for families needing guidance to steer them to suitable Web sites for children, *The Internet Kids & Family Yellow Pages* is a great resource."
San Francisco Chronicle

"*The Internet Kids & Family Yellow Pages* gives you summaries of the sites so your kids will really know where they're going, and it's also a place for you and your kids to begin a dialogue about what's out there. Besides, they list some REALLY cool sites."
Krissy Harris
Los Angeles Times

"...a totally cool—and useful—guide."
Disney Adventures

"A great book for kids and parents....More than just a collection of sites, it's full of ideas."
Independent Web Review

"Whether your child needs a copyright-free map of Afghanistan, help with quadratic equations, or just wants to spend time with the Power Rangers, this book will save hours of connect time and arguments."
New York Newsday

"Jean Armour Polly is the perfect Internet guide for kids and families."
Cheryl Kravetz
Lake Worth Herald

"One of the most thorough collections of Web sites that are safe for kids."
Melinda Miller
Buffalo New York News

"*The Internet Kids & Family Yellow Pages* will help almost any teacher quickly locate quality Web pages on student interests and will help any teacher find the Web resources they need to support lessons."
Joyce Kasman Valenza
Philadelphia Inquirer

NET-MOM®'S INTERNET KIDS & FAMILY YELLOW PAGES

2002 EDITION

ABOUT THE AUTHOR

Jean Armour Polly is Net-mom® and the author of
*Net-mom®'s Internet Kids & Family Yellow Pages, 2002
Edition* (Osborne McGraw-Hill, now in its sixth edition),
a family-friendly directory to 3,500 of the best children's
resources the Internet has to offer.

Author, librarian, and mom, Jean has tinkered with
Internet accounts since 1991 and has participated in online
telecommunities for over 18 years. She wrote the original
"Surfing the Internet" back in 1992, and, in 1993, became
one of the first two women elected to the Internet Society
Board of Trustees.

Under her Net-mom® brand, Jean is a private consultant,
writer, and speaker. Past clients include America Online,
The Bertelsmann Foundation, Children's Television
Workshop, Disney Online, MCI Foundation, The Morino
Institute, and TCI.Net. She has also been a television and
radio product spokeswoman for GuardiaNet, Ask Jeeves
for Kids, and Ameritech.net. She appeared in video and
voice-over on *Cruise Control*, an online safety CD-ROM
produced jointly by Ameritech.net, the Urban League,
TechCorps, and The National Center for Missing and
Exploited Children. Jean also writes a column for *Becoming Family* magazine and a weekly column for the
Ask Jeeves for Kids Web site. Her work also appears on FamilyClick.com as well as other sites. Jean is also
the publisher of Net-mom® News, a free electronic newsletter.

Jean serves on the Board of the Internet Content Rating Association, a group promoting rating of Internet
resources by their authors. She has also functioned as a finals judge in the international ThinkQuest Internet
Challenge competition, sponsored by Advanced Network and Services, Inc. In 2001, she was the emcee for
the Cable and Wireless Childnet Awards.

Before becoming a full-time author, Jean worked for an Internet service provider for three years and before
that, was a public librarian for sixteen years. Jean was also the co-founder and moderator emerita of PUBLIB,
the oldest and largest Internet discussion list for public librarians. She is a member of the American Library
Association and is a former director of the Library and Information Technology Association's Board. Jean
received her BA in Medieval Studies at Syracuse University in 1974, and her Master's in Library Science from
the same University in 1975.

She lives on a hill in Central New York, above a forest full of raccoons, fox, and deer. Mom to a teenage son,
Stephen, Jean also enjoys her cats and a garden pond full of goldfish and water lilies. Her husband Larry
works in Web development at SUNY Upstate Medical University and is system administrator of the
netmom.com and pollywood.com domains. More about Jean is available at her current home page,
<http://www.netmom.com/>.

To send communications about this book, kindly use the form at *<http://www.netmom.com/feedback.htm>*.

Photos of author & family courtesy of Ron Trinca Photography.

NET-MOM®'S INTERNET KIDS & FAMILY YELLOW PAGES

2002 EDITION

Jean Armour Polly

Osborne/McGraw-Hill

Berkeley New York St. Louis San Francisco Auckland Bogotá Hamburg
London Madrid Mexico City Milan Montreal New Delhi Panama City
Paris Sáo Paulo Singapore Sydney Tokyo Toronto

NET-MOM®'S INTERNET KIDS & FAMILY YELLOW PAGES

2002 EDITION

OSBORNE/MCGRAW-HILL
2600 TENTH STREET
BERKELEY, CALIFORNIA 94710
U.S.A.

For information on translations or book distributors outside the U.S.A., or to arrange bulk purchase discounts for sales promotions, premiums, or fund-raisers, please contact Osborne/**McGraw-Hill** at the above address.

234567890 QPD QPD 901987654321

ISBN 0-07-219247-X

This book was composed with Corel VENTURA™ Publisher.

Publisher
Brandon A. Nordin

Vice President and Associate Publisher
Scott Rogers

Acquisitions Editor
Megg Bonar

Acquisitions Coordinator
Alex Corona

Project Editor
Lisa Wolters-Broder

Proofreader
Linda Medoff

Indexer
James Minkin

Computer Designers
Tara A. Davis & Roberta Steele

Illustrators
Michael Mueller & Lyssa Wald

Series Design
Peter F. Hancik

For our son, Stephen,
and our parents.

Jean and Larry Polly

Put it before them briefly so they will read it, clearly so they will appreciate it, picturesquely so they will remember it, and, above all, accurately so they will be guided by its light.

Joseph Pulitzer

Table of Contents

Acknowledgments

You wouldn't be holding this book in your hands if it weren't for my husband, Larry Polly. He developed the custom database for this project, he runs the servers, and he manages the Web site. I write the prose and organize the book, but Larry manipulates the data back out of the database and makes it into a real chapter to be sent to the publisher. Doing a book like this is always a mammoth task, and Larry never loses his sense of perspective and humor.

And to my teenage son, Stephen, a big hug and thanks for giving Dad and me the time to do something for kids all over the world. I hope everyone likes Stephen's section of the book, too.

At Osborne/McGraw-Hill, I would like to thank Brandon Nordin, publisher, for believing in ruby slippers and happy endings. Scott Rogers, editor-in-chief, deserves praise for his continued support of the book and other Net-mom projects. Many thank yous to my acquisition editor, Megg Bonar, whose uncanny abilities in tracking down information may rival my own. This year's Project Editor, Lisa Wolters-Broder is lauded as well for her unfailing taste, sense of humor, and supportive attitude.

Syndicated columnist Jayne Lytel worked hard on this edition, too. Her work was wonderful, on time, and it was truly a pleasure to work with her. Find out more about Jayne in the Research Team section.

To Vicki, Diane, Peg, and all the girlfriends, thanks again for the support.

To Nora , sidekick Monty Moose, and all the kids at Nestor Elementary School, Coquitlam, British Columbia, thanks for loaning me a furry friend and suggesting sites about Canada.

To Melinda and Harry, thanks for luring us out of the computer room and into the sunshine to help you on your quest for the ultimate antique Griswold cast iron cookware and the quintessential vintage Royal Canadian Mounted Police memorabilia.

Stephen wants to thank his former English teacher Mrs. Jennifer Kirchoff, Jedi Master Mangram, and the entire sophomore class of Manlius Pebble Hill school. In addition, he credits his favorite research associates, T.J. and Tyler.

I also want to thank Mom for providing outstanding moral support services, including cooking a few random dinners and washing the occasional dish.

I also credit the interfaith teachings of His Holiness Baba Virsa Singh Ji, of Gobind Sadan, South Delhi, India. His inspiring work and words, and those of Jesus Christ and the Sikh Guru Gobind Singh Ji, helped me to complete this book. Truth is eternal. <http://www.GobindSadan.org/>.

Finally, thank you to the parents, families, teachers, and librarians who bought the first five editions of the book and made it a best-seller. Kids do belong on the Net.

Respectfully,

Jean Armour Polly
Jamesville, New York
August 2001

About the Research Team

Jayne Lytel has been exploring and explaining the Internet to readers since before the invention of the World Wide Web. She created one of the first newsletters to cover commercialization of the Internet, and she writes Internet911.com, an Internet advice column syndicated by United Feature Syndicate Inc. She says, "Despite my lack of qualification in either category, I am listed in *E-mail Addresses of the Rich and Famous*."

Larry M. Polly is a Web developer for the Upstate Medical University at Syracuse, New York. He created their original campus gopher and now manages their main Web servers and creates custom Web programs for the University. He also manages www.netmom.com and volunteers his time in the creation and maintenance of www.gobindsadan.org, official Web site of an interfaith center near New Delhi, India. Travel and gardening are also indulged in at regular intervals.

Stephen Jade Polly, 15, served as the Official Kid Advisor and arbiter of humor in the book. He also designed the "rubber ducky" symbol appearing before the preschool sites, and invented the term "Net File" for the trivia questions in the book. He is occasionally introduced at bookstore book signings as Net-mom's Vice President of Marketing, since he likes to hand out bookmarks and T-shirts and encourage people to buy the book. He likes to use the Net to learn things about science, and his favorite season is Hawaii. In the future he is interested in developing a bionic plant with speakers that can talk back. But currently, his main hobby is growing mass quantities of hot peppers, and of course, talking with his friends on mIRC on his homebrew computer. He has memorized the entire script of *Monty Python and the Holy Grail*. His cat, Pooshka, is incredibly large. And, helping his Mom with this book has given him a new respect for the word "Alphabet."

Introduction

Welcome! This book is a labor of love for us, and we are happy it seems to have fulfilled a need for so many readers worldwide.

Here's what you'll find in this sixth, 2002 edition:

■ More than 3,500 educational and entertaining Internet sites, all handpicked and family-friendly. Sites are arranged in broad subject headings, organized alphabetically. The main A—Z section is written for kids in grades K—12, although many general reference works for all ages are included.

★ Star symbols highlight important sites worthy of special mention.

🦆 "Rubber Ducky" symbols draw attention to sites best for preschoolers.

■ In "C" we now offer expanded coverage of CANADA. Visit official sites for all the provinces and territories, plus museums, historic sites, and online fun.

■ In "F" there is a large FAMILY FUN section, which has lots of things a mixed age group can do together. The whole family will enjoy these sites.

■ In "H" you'll find a new section called HELP. It's for kids in crisis. It contains toll-free hotlines, safe houses, and counseling services for runaways and troubled teens.

■ In "W" there is an expanded section called WHY? In that area you'll find Internet sites where kids (and parents) can go to find out answers to such things as

Why is the sky blue?

Why is the sunset red?

Why do the leaves change color in the fall?

What makes a cat's eyes glow in the dark?

Why is the ocean salty?

What color is snow?

■ More than 200 "Net Files" trivia questions are scattered throughout the book to encourage interest in Net exploration. Don't worry, the answers are there, too!

■ We've identified more than 140 sites that are "Too Good to Miss." You'll find them under their correct subject headings, of course, but we have also highlighted them under a special magnifying glass throughout the book.

■ Check the newly updated hotlist section featuring 100 "Best of the Net" sites in categories like homework help, sports, and science, plus sites for preschoolers, family fun, and more!

■ Back by popular demand, Son-of-Net-mom® returns with an additional list of surefire sites kids love (including some their parents might consider yucky, such as the Belch Page). New this year, Son of Net-mom has added his own Net Safety Tips for teens. They focus on chat room safety and go far beyond the usual rules.

■ We offer free online updates at <http://www.netmom.com/>. We track changes to the addresses in this book and post them online to help our readers stay up-to-date. We also offer a free e-mail newsletter; see the Web site for details.

■ Looking for information on individual countries? Just visit <http://netmom.com/world/> to find its new home. Explore the globe through official government sites, embassies, departments of tourism, and more. In the book, we offer a general COUNTRIES OF THE WORLD section. In addition to the chapter on CANADA and UNITED STATES. We believe you'll find it very helpful for school reports!

WELCOME HOME TO THE NET

Because of my unique background as a public librarian, Internet pioneer, and mom, I wrote this book because I believe kids belong on the Net. It's not just because of the treasure chest of resources they can access, but because children themselves can become publishers of their own sites. What we can learn from them is at least as important as what they can learn from us. Still, I know that there are places on the Net that I would not want my son to go without me. There are places in the city where I live that I wouldn't let him go to alone, either.

So, I set out to find places on the Net that were built expressly for children or where people of any age could find real value and answers to their questions. You're holding in your hands the addresses to thousands of such locations. You'll visit the Library of Congress, NASA, the British Museum, the Vatican, a research station in Antarctica, a zoo in Colorado, and even some school and family home pages.

SELECTION POLICY: WHAT YOU WILL FIND IN THIS BOOK

Every good library needs a selection policy, so naturally, we have one. Here it is.

I collect for preschoolers through adults. I select educational and recreational Web sites based on how they measure up against my selection policy guidelines. Although the perfect site will have all these features, most of my choices are based on high points, but not full points. Here are things I look for:

1. Sites need to be age appropriate for my readers: families, usually with high school kids to preschoolers.

2. Sites need to be current. In general, if it hasn't been updated in a year, it's out. (That said, some sites are "timeless." Example of timeless content: directions for making a paper airplane.)

3. Sites should have some real-world authority— for example, from NASA, or the Smithsonian, or National Geographic.

4. Sites should have good organization and interior navigation. They should be consistent in their interfaces and not confuse the user.

5. Sites should be on a stable server; they shouldn't be unreachable every other time.

6. Sites shouldn't have gratuitous Java or overblown graphics (too much noise, not enough signal). They shouldn't have too many distractions, especially music I can't turn off.

7. I don't require privacy policies, but if there is one I read it, and if it's arrogant or suspect I either note it in my annotation or leave the site out.

8. The site should teach me something and ideally get me excited about the subject. If it suggests things for me to do offline, so much the better.

9. Sites have to offer something of value for free.

10. There can be advertising but it can't be so pervasive that I can't find the content anymore. In addition, if there was a pop-up casino ad, I left.

11. No material inappropriate for kids, in my personal opinion, on the day or days I explored it. If something's borderline, or there were too many links to check, I put a "parental advisory" note in the annotation. No adult stuff, no bad language. No hate speech. Nothing too gross (Son of Net-mom's page of picks notwithstanding.)

In addition, I had to *like* the site!

If I think a site shows potential but I've disallowed it for a particular reason, sometimes I write to the webmaster and explain that they have off-color jokes in their collection, or that their "preschool" game collection might stand another look, since it includes realistic Gulf War military violence. Occasionally I have written to inform a company that although their site targets elementary school kids, their banner ad exchange company is sending them ads for alcoholic beverages. Sometimes I write to explain that their site crashes Macintosh browsers.

I choose everything in the book. I am the only one applying my selection policy and I believe that this is the main reason I achieve consistent high quality in my collection. My readers get my personal view of what is great on the Net for kids and families. I want people to think of Net-mom® as the trusted Internet brand for families.

Recently we estimated how many sites I have personally explored since the first edition of the book. We were stunned to discover that I have visited about 185,000 Web sites. Even if I looked at only eight subpages for each site, that works out to about 1.5 million Web pages I have personally inspected since 1996.

The Internet is always in motion, and resources may change. Something I found appropriate for inclusion in the book today may be inappropriate tomorrow. So, I cannot guarantee that your Internet experience, based on my recommendations, will always meet your needs.

I strongly recommend that parents, caregivers, and teachers always use the Internet alongside their children and preview sites if at all possible.

TROUBLESHOOTING: WHEN THE ADDRESSES DON'T WORK

Unfortunately, I can't help you with connectivity problems. Contact your Internet service provider and ask them to help you with setting up your browser or configuring other Internet software applications. They may also be able to help you with modem settings or other hardware-related concerns.

However, I can help you with the following:

I typed in the address, but it doesn't work. I got "404 Not Found," "Not found on this server," "No DNS entry exists for this server," or some other cranky-sounding message. What should I do?

If you come across this situation, just follow these steps:

1. Try it again. The Internet isn't perfect. Along the way, from where the information lives to your computer, something may have blinked. On my Netmom.com Web site, there is a section called "Ask Net-mom: What Parents Ask Me About Kids and the Internet." Here is the direct address < *http://www.netmom.com/ ikyp/samples/ask_index.shtml*>. In it, and among other things, I explain how Web pages get from host computers to your desktop, and what can go wrong in-between.

2. Check your spelling. Many of these addresses are long and complex, so it's easy to make a mistake. You might try having another person read you the address while you type it. Make sure you are careful to use capital letters or lower case when they are printed in this book. They are not interchangeable, and the computer won't recognize its file called "foo.html" if you have typed "FOO.HTML."

3. Check to see if I have found where the page has gone. The free updates to this book are all at <*http://www.netmom.com/*>. Be sure to look for the "Updates" section.

4. The location or file name may have changed since I visited the page. That means its address will be different. Computer files (making up the pages you see on the World Wide Web) are stored in directories on remote servers all over the world. Sometimes people move these files to different places, so you need to find where they have been moved.

5. And if you're pretty smart (and you are, because you've got this book), you'll know three tricks to help you find pages that have moved.

Trick #1: Solve File Name Change Problems

The first trick is to shorten the address and look there. Say that you've been looking for Dorothy and Toto's home page. It used to be at:

http://land.of.oz.gov/munchkinland/mainstreet/ dorothy.html

Perhaps Dorothy has changed the name of her home page. Try going "back" a level and look around there. Let's try:

http://land.of.oz.gov/munchkinland/mainstreet/

That takes you "higher" in the directory path, and you may be able to find where Dorothy has moved from there. On the "mainstreet" Web page, we might see several new choices:

/the.scarecrow.html
/the.tin.man.html
/the.cowardly.lion.html
/dorothy.and.toto.html

Great! Dorothy's just changed the name of her home page to include her little dog, too. Choose that one, and make a note of it for future visits. Write the changes directly into this book, I won't mind. Another mystery solved!

If you still can't find what you're looking for, try going "back" yet another level. You may have to try several levels back until you locate what you want.

Trick #2: Solve Server Name Change Problems

It's also possible that the Wizard of Oz has ordered that the new name of the World Wide Web server containing everyone's home page will now be called "www.land.of.oz.gov" instead of "land.of.oz.gov." That creates a problem for people looking for home pages under the *old* server name, which isn't there anymore. How are you supposed to find it?

Fortunately, the crafty old Wizard chose a common name change. If a computer server's name is going to be changed, it's often given a prefix to reflect the type of services it runs. If you don't know what the new server name might be, try *guessing*. For a Web server, try putting "www." in front of whatever name it originally had (unless it already had that prefix). For example, here's the old name:

http://land.of.oz.gov

Here's your guess at the new name:

http://www.land.of.oz.gov

Bingo! That was it! Be sure to make a note of the change in this book, so you won't have that problem again

Trick #3: Check with Us

When all else fails, don't forget to look on my home page at <http://www.netmom.com/>. While you were trying the first two tricks, we may have already found where the page has been moved. You can search our database yourself. Just look for the "Updates" section and follow the directions. In the event that you still can't find the site you need, please write to me at feedback@netmom.com. I will usually respond promptly and track down the site for you.

These are just some tips to help you find where Dorothy's gone. I know they will help!

NET-MOM(R)'S
10 SPECIAL DON'T-MISS HOTLISTS

FOR KIDS WHO LOVE ARTS AND CRAFTS

On the Internet, virtual crayons never break, and you never have to clean the paint brushes!

♨ Arthur: Welcome to D.W.'s Art Studio

Select your online brush, choose a color, and you're good to go have fun with the coloring book pages here. Based on Marc Brown's "Arthur" series characters, your artist in residence is D.W. She'll explain how you can use the paint features as well as the rubber stamping tools. You can also choose to clear the canvas and "draw" on a blank screen.

http://www.pbs.org/wgbh/arthur/dw/paint/

★ Donna's Day Activities

There's always something fun to do when Donna's around! She knows how to make play clay out of baking soda, how to make butter, and how to make soap out of oatmeal! She's shared some of her favorite "recipes" at this page, yum!

http://www.donnasday.com/donna/creativefun/
    activities.shtml

★ Hands-On Crafts

No more messy glue, broken crayons, or dried out markers. This site is a treasure-trove of virtual craft activities that you can do with the click of a mouse.

http://www.handsoncrafts.org/

★ Hands-On Crafts for Kids - Projects

This site gives clear instructions for making milk carton birdhouses, sand cast sea treasures, seed topiary trees, bumble bee mobiles, and lots more. Over 50 terrific craft project ideas are collected here.

http://www.crafts4kids.com/projects.htm

★ Kaleidoscope Painter

We won't spoil the surprise! Just click and drag your mouse slowly across the screen and watch what happens. If you just want to relax and watch, click on Auto. Note that you can select your brush size.

http://www.permadi.com/java/spaint/spaint.html

★ A Lifetime of Color

Explore color mixing and matching activities and learn how the "mood" of a painting changes if you magically switch to different colors. Learn about proportions and portrait techniques. Little children will enjoy the color wheel game, while bigger ones (and adults, too) will be fascinated with chasing down the evil Dr. Gray and his Dechromatizers.

http://www.sanford-artedventures.com/

★ Lizzy Visits the Sculpture Garden

Lizzy is dragged to the National Gallery of Art because her pesky brother Gordon has to do a school assignment. "Stretch your mind," says mom. Gordon is more interested in lunch than artistic expression. Lizzie's bored until she discovers a sculpture can speak to her. In fact, this Web site speaks to you as you read the story, exploring the sculpture garden right along with the children.

http://www.nga.gov/kids/lizzy/lizzy.html

★ The @rt Room

Explore art "sparkers"—activities to jump start your brain into its most creative thinking. For example, draw a storm, or a picture of your favorite hero. You can learn to "think like an artist" by exploring "@rtageous" ways to make the familiar strange, and see the world in a completely new light.

http://www.arts.ufl.edu/art/rt_room/

★ Snowflake Designer

Around the holidays it's fun to fold little squares of paper and snip them here and there to make a lacy snowflake. The trouble is, you can never visualize what all your cutting will look like before the paper is unfolded. Now you can! Try this array of snowflake designers, and make a whole blizzard!

http://www.explorescience.com/activities/
    activity_list.cfm?categoryID=4

★ What is a Print?

Did you know some artworks are made using a printing process? Visit this interactive site to try making a virtual woodcut, an etching, a lithograph, and a screen print. You'll have to manipulate the online tools in order to see the print take shape right before your eyes!

http://www.moma.org/whatisaprint/

FOR FAMILY FUN

Looking for a site the whole family can enjoy? There is something for everyone at the following Net destinations.

★ Bonus.com - The SuperSite for Kids

This way to find family-safe places to visit. Head in any direction and play a game, enter a contest, find homework help, or learn about dinosaurs, the United States, or what's under the sea. For rainy-day fun, remember this site!

http://www.bonus.com/

★ CBC4kids

Don't miss the action-intensive Kids Club games. Blast into space to attack asteroids. Think quickly (and creatively) to help save Mr. Snoozleberg—a sleepwalking diplomat. And did you ever get a tune into your head and you can't remember what it is? The "hum line" will help.

http://www.cbc4kids.ca/

★ Funschool.com

How much interaction can you stand? Expect LOADS of fun, engaging, and educational Java games here. There are separate sections for each age group, preschoolers through sixth grade. Don't miss the Stone City adventure—can you solve the puzzles and retrieve all the gemstones?

http://www.funschool.com/

★ Harcourt School Publishers - The Learning Site

Click here for a spectacular collection of entertaining and educational games for all age levels. There are spelling, reading, math, science, social studies, art, health, and other challenges and activities that you can use for free.

http://www.harcourtschool.com/

★ HBO Magnet

Nothing to do? Try this graphically engaging site and its wide variety of games and activities. One of the more challenging is Toon Beats. It turns your keyboard into a musical instrument and lets you record, save, and play back songs you compose.

http://www.hbomagnet.com/hbo_family/

★ Kids' Space

This internationally recognized and award-winning site will become one of your favorite Internet destinations. Toddlers will love the detour to HPT (Hop Pop Town) to try out the many interactive musical experiences.

http://www.kids-space.org/

🦆 Knowble

There are a number of cool things to do here, such as explore an ocean. Click on some seaweed and a scary shark pops out! Don't worry—his false teeth pop out, too! Look for coloring books, paper airplane directions, online and offline activities, and more.

http://www.knowble.com/

★ Lycos Zone

The Lycos Zone selections for kids are arranged in several big areas: Fun, Games, Alfy's Playground, Homework, and Comics. It's one-stop if you're shopping for many of the best games on the Net!

http://lycoszone.lycos.com/

★ MaMaMedia

This jazzy site offers lots of fun activities and games. You do have to sign in (it's free, and they notify your parents), but after that, you can design, play, and interact all day. Create your own online town and invite other kids in to play.

http://www.mamamedia.com/

★ Noggin

Explore and enjoy clever and fun games (we loved Flood Control). You can make your own animation, which might be added to the daily animation "quilt" for everyone to admire. There's also a special Noggin just for little kids; look for and click on that button.

http://www.noggin.com/

FOR KIDS WHO LOVE GAMES AND INTERACTIVE STUFF

Online gizmos, games, and activities from the Net's leading edge of fun.

★ Ask Yoda

Be cool you must. And also chill out you should. Only the truth does Yoda speak. Carefully you must listen; important things tell you he will. Come to him sooner you should have.

http://www.sun-sentinel.com/graphics/entertainment/
  yoda.htm

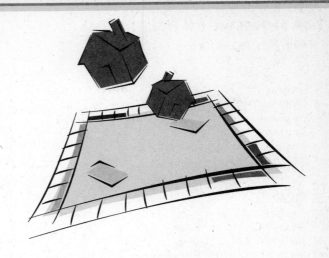

★ Castlemouse 2000

EEK! There's a mouse in the castle and the king says it's up to you to chase it out. The mouse will always run away from your cat. However, the cat is afraid of your dog. The dog is frightened by the bear, and so on. Knowing all these relationships, you can construct a formidable chain reaction!

http://www.castlemouse.com/

★ The Double J Files

Try this fun detective game to learn about some of the inventions of the First Nations in North America. Who invented sunglasses? Who dreamed up lacrosse? Click on the right clues, and you'll discover the answers.

http://www.tvokids.com/doublej/

★ Lights, Puppets, Action!

Don't miss this activity! You're the director: choose your performers, tell them what to do, then sit back and enjoy your play. Will you write a drama, a documentary, a comedy, or a rock video?

http://www.childrensmuseum.org/artsworkshop/
  puppetshow.html

★ Nature Puzzles and Fun

Don't miss this terrific collection of interactive animal games. Test your knowledge of Mongolian horses and culture as you race across the steppe, learn sign language with Koko the gorilla, try dogsledding 101, and check out the life-forms in the virtual tide pool.

http://www.pbs.org/wnet/nature/fun.html

★ Rooney Design

This is a rather strange site with offbeat, quirky games. In Mr. Leakey's House, your job is to find all the ways that water is being wasted—and do something about it. There's also an interactive advent calendar and an Overtime at Santa's Factory game if you happen to be in a holiday mood.

http://www.mother.com/~prdesign/
  FlashGamesFrame.html

★ Rumpus Games

The Skwertz family tries to take out the arcade ducks by—ahem—spitting at them. The sound effects are particularly juicy. If you'd like something a little more refined, try Herschel Hopper, who needs you to clear a path to the Easter eggs, or Benny Blanket who'll take you back to the '60s in search of flower power.

http://rumpus.com/news_games.html

★ Science U

Try Kali—choose a wallpaper "seed pattern" and a color, move your mouse to the drawing screen, and click. Now drag your mouse. Satisfied with the pattern? Click to freeze it into place. Now start off in another direction to add more. When you're happy with your design, click twice to lock it in.

http://www.ScienceU.com/geometry/

★ Sodaplay

Create a little onscreen two-dimensional model made out of "masses and springs." They are easy to make, and may be endlessly tinkered with by adjusting various items like wave speed, amplitude, "muscles," and more.

http://www.sodaplay.com/

★ Spark Island

Play a handful of games for ages 3 to 11 and study math and science without even knowing it. In Find the Sun, you'll learn to identify the position of the sun by examining the shadows it casts on a make-believe town.

http://www.sparkisland.com/public/free_activities/
  for_home/?view=generic

FOR HOMEWORK HELP

Just the facts, just in time!

★ DiscoverySchool.com The Student Channel

You might be able to complete all your homework using just this one site! Look up answers to science, geography, and history questions, browse the dictionary, take a side trip to create your own word search and other puzzles, and even learn how to attack your science fair project (before it attacks you!).

http://school.discovery.com/students/

★ e-nature

Wow—it's the *Audubon Field Guides* online! There are pictures and information on over 4,800 animals and plants here, drawn from the well-known print guidebooks. The content includes: Amphibians, Birds, Butterflies, Fishes, Insects, Mammals, Reptiles, Seashells, Seashore Creatures, Spiders, Trees, and Wildflowers.

http://www.enature.com/

★ Fact Monster

Just type in "highest waterfall" or "Britney Spears' birthday," and—BAM! There's the answer. Don't forget to take a break. How stupendous will your score be on the Harry Potter quiz? Don't miss this site.

http://www.factmonster.com/

★ KidsClick! Web Search

Browse educational and fun Web sites in 15 different categories. All of them have been selected, categorized, and described by a team of librarians who know what kids want. How do they know? Because kids come into their libraries and ask!

http://sunsite.berkeley.edu/KidsClick!/

★ KidsClick! Worlds of Web Searching

Learn the secrets of searching the Web from the Web-savvy librarians of KidsClick. This site is a must-see!

http://www.worldsofsearching.org/

★ LibrarySpot

Acronym dictionaries, biographical dictionaries, inventions, virtual math and science calculators—all are here for your use. Explore numerous magazines and newspapers, phone books, mapping programs, and more.

http://www.libraryspot.com/

★ Merriam-Webster's Collegiate Dictionary

Look up words, get the definitions, and even hear the word pronounced! One of the coolest online features is that if you spell the word wrong, it quickly gives you a list of possible alternative spellings.

http://www.m-w.com/netdict.htm

★ NoodleBib - The MLA Bibliography Composer

Creating a bibliography for your school paper is a breeze with this free bibliography generator. A handy pull-down menu lets you select the type of reference you need to cite (book, magazine, Web page, etc.). Just fill in the blanks. Once you press submit, presto—your bibliography citation is created online and in the proper format. It couldn't be easier.

http://www.noodletools.com/noodlebib/

★ Quia!

At this site, anyone can create a quiz or an activity to be enjoyed by others. You can take a quiz about French verbs, computer systems, or state capitals. Try Science Stumpers if you like *Jeopardy*-style games.

http://www.quia.com/

★ Study Buddy: Your School Survival Connection

A wonderful collection of tips on everything from memorizing lines in a play to dealing with procrastination is in store for you at this site. You'll find lots of study "survival" information here, too.

http://studybuddy.com/

FOR KIDS WHO LOVE MATH

These sites all add up to fun.

★ A+ Math

Loads of math drills are found at this site; one of our favorites is Matho—it's like playing bingo, except you have to know your multiplication tables and other math facts to win. You'll also discover interactive flash cards and homework helper tips.

http://www.aplusmath.com/

★ Absurd Math

The Powers2B are holding the DVine PImander in an unknown location. You'll have to know (or learn) some pre-algebra skills, and the way is treacherous. Can you meet the challenge? (Don't forget to talk to the Vorpal Rabbit.)

http://www.learningwave.com/abmath/

★ Coolmath.com - An Amusement Park of Mathematics . . . and More!

This is the greatest math site ever. Really, it has no equal. Want to multiply your fun on the Net—as far as arithmetic, geometry, algebra, trigonometry, or calculus goes? See for yourself! We don't want to take away the surprise.

http://www.coolmath.com/

🦆 Cynthia Lanius' Lessons: Let's Count! Activities

Spinning cars, dancing frogs, bouncing puppies—can you count moving things? If that's too hard, try the other games: Which is more?, What comes next? There's also a "counting machine" that shows you how to count by twos, threes, fives, and tens.

http://math.rice.edu/~lanius/counting/

★ Figure This! Math Challenges for Families

Work on interesting problems that encourage the whole family to do the math. There's also a list of questions to help you to figure out your homework, and hints on how to get the most out of your math class.

http://www.figurethis.org/

★ FunBrain.com - Numbers

Can you use your arithmetic and pre-algebra skills to help build a pyramid? Maybe you can guess a hidden pattern and discover the missing number in a series. Or maybe you just want to kick back and eat some fresh-baked fractions. Much more than drill and practice, these games are also fun!

http://www.funbrain.com/numbers.html

★ Math Advantage

Marvelous math games may be manipulated here: sort numbered bumper cars in Carnival Cars or graph coordinates to make a robot Elvis dance.

http://www.harcourtschool.com/menus/
    math_advantage.html

★ Math Cats

Practice with pattern building in "Tessellation Town," start a collection of paper polyhedrals, and try more math games as curious kittens follow you around the site.

http://www.mathcats.com/

★ Maths File - BBC Education

The Builder Bob game cracked us up. We even won a virtual Pythagorus doll in Late Delivery (about a postman in a rather odd town where all the house addresses are in algebraic terms). There are also games you can print for later.

http://www.bbc.co.uk/education/mathsfile/

★ Powers of Ten

Imagine a special camera that would take pictures of the same scene from ten meters away, 100 meters away, 1,000 meters (one kilometer) away, and so on. Not only that, this camera would be able to look at the scene microscopically, too. This site simulates that kind of a camera. Within a small number of photos, you'll see a flower bed from the perspectives of both the farthest reaches of the universe and the interior of a proton.

http://cern.web.cern.ch/CERN/Microcosm/P10/
    english/welcome.html

FOR KIDS WHO LOVE MUSIC

Forget surfing. Sing, play, or dance the Internet.

★ Becky's Campfire Songbook

Every silly song you ever learned at camp is in this collection, plus a few yells, clapping games, and skits. This is a must before you go on a long road trip with your parents. They will love hearing these songs over, and over, and over, and . . . .

http://www.geocities.com/EnchantedForest/Glade/
8851/

★ Boom Thang

Simply click the record button, and select the instrument you want to play. You can choose from four different categories of sound: drums, bass, keyboard/guitar, and special effects. When you've finished, the site lets you play back your creation.

http://www.kaboose.com/shockWin2.cfm?infoID=
boomthang&shockType=fl

★ Continental Harmony

The Sound Lounge will blow you away. Explore how we create and manipulate music "and how it manipulates us." In six interactive activities, you can experiment with melody, rhythm, instruments and harmony, and play the role of composer.

http://www.pbs.org/harmony/soundlounge/

★ Essentials of Music

This terrific page outlines the six major periods in music history: the Middle Ages, Renaissance, Baroque, Classical, Romantic, and Twentieth Century. In each, you'll learn about cultural and other forces of the time period and discover the major composers of the era. There are more than 70 composer biographies included, many containing audio clips.

http://www.essentialsofmusic.com/

★ Juice Bottle Jingles

Have you ever tapped a half-filled glass and made a musical note? Behold a virtual six-bottle xylophone, and a tunebook for your playing (and listening) pleasure. Just follow the notes to tap out such all-time favorites as "Jingle Bells" and "Mary Had a Little Lamb."

http://www.lhs.berkeley.edu/shockwave/jar.html

★ Play Music

Meet other kids involved in playing and writing music, learn parts of the orchestra, and take the suggested links to other musical sites. One is Creating Music <http://www.creatingmusic.com/> where you can try out a musical sketch pad. Did you know you can "draw" in notes and tones?

http://www.playmusic.org/

★ Popular Songs in American History

Find out what songs were popular during various periods in American history. This unique collection contains audio files, lyrics, and historical notes. "Greensleeves" was popular in sixteenth-century America. "The Drinking Gourd" was from the Civil War era. "I've Been Working on the Railroad" was what the forty-niners sang as they searched for gold in California.

http://www.contemplator.com/america/

★ Steel Drum

Bang on the virtual steel drum and hear all the notes, or listen to some recorded steel drum music. You can even record your own little melody and play it back.

http://www.mathsyear2000.org/museum/gallery1/
steeldrum/

★ Turntables

Think you'd make a phat DJ? Here's your chance to find out! Select a beat, choose a scratch, and rock on. Click to activate the lights and be sure to tell the "shouting man" what lyrics to yell. Hint: touch his sneakers to make him go backstage.

http://www.turntables.de/start.htm

★ WholeNote - The On-Line Guitar Community

Guitar basics, free lessons, tablature, and lots more await you at this portal to the guitar-playing community. There's even an online tuner (just click on the tuning fork on the bottom left).

http://www.wholenote.com/

FOR PRESCHOOLERS

These engaging sites will amuse, excite, amaze, educate, and entertain little ones as well as others who are kids at heart.

🦆 BBC Online - Little Kids

In Picture Perfect you need to identify shapes in a picture of a boat, a house, and a castle in order to win fish, flowers, and swans. Play the "easy" version until you get the idea. There are also Teletubbies games, painting and coloring activities, and several audio storybooks.

http://www.bbc.co.uk/littlekids/

🦆 Bookworm Bunch

Can you find Corduroy bear? He's hiding somewhere in the street scene; you'll just have to keep clicking until you find him. He moves around each time, so you can play again. The Seven Little Monsters section offers finger puppets you can print, or a fun addition game you can play online.

http://www.pbs.org/bookwormbunch/

🦆 Clifford the Big Red Dog

Now you can read online stories about Clifford the Big Red Dog, plus play matching games with sounds and letters. Don't miss the link to Birdwell Island for more Big Dog fun. Who's under the sand castle? Click and see!

http://teacher.scholastic.com/clifford1/

★ GameGoo - Learning That Sticks

There's kangaroo confusion all over the amusement park! Some of the kiddy 'roos have misplaced their parents. Luckily, each child is wearing a shirt with a letter of the alphabet on it. Click on the dad with the matching clothing, and they'll get on the Ferris wheel together. There are loads of other reading games, plus don't miss the "Fun Goo" for still more interactive monkey business.

http://www.cogcon.com/gamegoo/gooeylo.html

🦆 Julia's Rainbow Corner

We were charmed by this site, designed for pre-readers. Help Julia the octopus find her crown. Then "decorate" the day, or try the night—how many stars can you put in the sky? There is so much to do here, you'll want to return to this rainbow often.

http://www.juliasrainbowcorner.com/

🦆 The Little Animals Activity Centre

Follow Foxy Dancer onto the dance floor and see if you can imitate his musical steps, then play a rhyming word game with Digby Mole (hope you like to eat worms). Mike Maker offers craft and activity suggestions, while other Little Animals hop up and down and try to get you to play with them too!

http://www.bbc.co.uk/education/laac/

🦆 The Otto Club

Visit Otto the car and his interactive town. Sing along with the Seat Belt Song by pressing the radio buttons on Otto's dashboard. Play the traffic light game, and see if you can compare the two pictures and decide who's stopped for red, based on the signals YOU can see.

http://www.ottoclub.org/

🦆 Paw Island

It's shaped like a paw print, it's inhabited by dogs and cats, and it's called—can you guess?—Paw Island! We landed at Howlin' Hills, but your arrival may be at a different spot; just click on the map to explore. Wherever you go, be sure to look for (and click on) hidden smiley faces in each picture. There are online games, coloring pages, activities, and lots more fun on this tropical isle.

http://www.pawisland.com/

🦆 PBS Kids

It's the home of the *Teletubbies*, as well as *Clifford*, *Barney*, *Arthur*, and many more favorite TV shows. Often there are educational activities associated with each program, such as the animal games in *Zoboomafoo*.

http://www.pbs.org/kids/

🦆 StoryPlace: The Children's Digital Library

Here's a fabulous collection of preschool stories and activities in both English and Spanish. Animated stories read themselves to you, plus there are activities you can try online as well as away from the computer.

http://www.storyplace.org/

FOR KIDS WHO LOVE READING, WRITING, CHAT, OR PEN PALS

Have you read these URLs? They are on Net-mom's "best seller" list.

★ BBC - KS2 Revisewise English

Can you solve the mystery of the missing jewelry? You'll have to read very carefully, then question the witnesses. Who is telling the truth and who is lying? Other parts of this rollicking good-fun site teach you how to write a great story, spell well, and more.

http://www.bbc.co.uk/education/revisewise/english/

★ Book Adventure

Do you like to read? Do you like to win cool prizes? You might be able to do both at the same time if you visit this site. Select some books here first, go to the library, take a quiz, and collect points.

http://www.Bookadventure.com/

★ BookHive: Your Guide to Children's Literature & Books

Looking for a great book to read? Why not ask the librarians of the Public Library of Charlotte & Mecklenburg County in North Carolina? They have been as busy as bees combing their bookshelves to find just the book for you. They have found some "real honeys," too!

http://www.bookhive.org/bookhive.htm

★ ePals Classroom Exchange

Would your whole class or homeschool like to write to another class of kids on the other side of the world? Search for kids by city, state, country, grade/age, or language. There are also free real-time, password-protected chat facilities offered.

http://www.epals.com/

★ Golden Books Fun Factory!

If you do only one thing on this site, go to the Road to Reading Ramblin' Road trip. Make sure you take Amusement Avenue and stop at Super Sleuth. Here you'll be able to play Kid Detective. If you're clever enough, you'll be able to solve the mystery of the missing pooch.

http://www.goldenbooks.com/fun/

★ Headbone Zone

There are several chat rooms here, including some for teens and some for younger kids. Before you sign on, remember to read their rules: don't give out personal information in chat (addresses, last names, school names, ICQ#s, phone numbers).

http://www.headbone.com/

★ The Neverending Tale

Just start reading a story, and when you get to the bottom of the page you'll find a number of choices about what to do next. You can follow a path someone else has written, or you can easily add your own series of choices.

http://www.coder.com/creations/tale/

★ Penpal Box

Looking for a penpal? Browse through the boxes for various age groups. There's also a box for classes that want to exchange e-mail. Read the FAQ for safety tips, and remember not to give your home address to anyone.

http://www.ks-connection.org/penpal/penpal.html

★ The Prince and I

The teenage prince lives in a beautiful castle, but there's a small problem. How can he be king someday if he can't read? He needs some friends to help him learn!

http://www.nfb.ca/Kids/

★ Write on Reader

Learn about the history of writing, the writing process, and how you can make and "publish" your own book. There are also some fascinating interviews with authors, librarians, and editors, as well as kid-approved book reports.

http://library.thinkquest.org/J001156/

FOR KIDS WHO LOVE SCIENCE

Are you building a rocket out of old pieces of junk? Are you growing mold cultures in your sock drawer? Then experiment with these sites at home.

★ BBC Education - The Essential Guide to Rocks

What's for lunch today? At this site, it's "Sedimentary Sandwiches"! Use layers of bread and specific foods to create your own slice of the past. If that doesn't grab you, try The Geology of the Bathroom or the Graveyard Rockwalk.

http://www.bbc.co.uk/education/rocks/

★ BrainPOP

Watch over 130 entertaining and educational animated cartoons that explain lots of scientific things, such as how your eyes work and how your sense of smell operates. Try some experiments with "Bob, the Ex-lab Rat" or register (it's free) to ask questions of your own.

http://www.brainpop.com/

★ The Exploratorium

Do you know what makes a fruit fly grow legs out of its head? Want to explore the science of sports? Care to slog through a creepy virtual swamp, looking for frogs? San Francisco's huge hands-on science laboratory is for kids of all ages.

http://www.exploratorium.edu/

★ Geo-Mysteries @ The Children's Museum of Indianapolis

Rex, the dino detective, has a big problem on his claws. All sorts of strange things are happening. There's a rock that floats, an assortment of stone beads, and a golden cube. Follow the clues to learn about volcanic processes, fossils, and mineral crystals.

http://www.childrensmuseum.org/geomysteries/

★ Journey North

Journey North is a project where the Internet really shines. Report your local signs of seasonal change. The results of your observations will be combined with other reports from all over the U.S., and a map will be created to show where Spring's sprung and Fall's fallen.

http://www.learner.org/jnorth/

★ NASA Kids

Get ready for touchdown at this terrific site! Learn about space pioneers and astronauts, rockets and airplanes, plus space and beyond. And if you see The Mole—click on him to "dig deeper."

http://kids.msfc.nasa.gov/

★ On the Prairie: Prairie Ecology

Choose to restore a tallgrass or a shortgrass prairie. Then add plants and animals, but be careful! If you choose the wrong things, your prairie will not survive. Use the virtual field guide to help you decide. If you're right, you'll see an animated prairie grow right before your eyes.

http://www1.umn.edu/bellmuse/mnideals/prairie/

★ Reeko's Mad Scientist Lab

It sure is dusty here in Reeko's basement science lab. Fun, educational experiments in astronomy, chemistry, physics, and earth science may be found here if you look around a bit.

http://www.spartechsoftware.com/reeko/

★ Sky View Cafe

Was the moon full when you were born? What constellations and planets will be visible over your house tonight? This site allows you to plug in time, location, and other selections to "see" what's up, even during the daylight hours. Check the Sample Views area to get the idea.

http://www.skyviewcafe.com/

★ Try Science

The content at this site changes from time to time as it is all contributed by science museums around the Web. You might try to build and test a paper bridge, investigate the best way to clean up an oil slick, or measure your own lung capacity.

http://www.tryscience.com/

FOR KIDS WHO LOVE SPORTS AND OUTDOOR FUN

Somebody had to make the call. Net-mom says these sites are "safe at home," and they are all winners!

★ BoatSafe.com and BoatSafeKids

Learn a lot about personal flotation devices, running lights, knots and how to tie them, and all sorts of boating information. You can even take an online boating safety course.

http://boatsafe.com/nauticalknowhow/

★ Exploratorium's Science of Baseball!

Do you think you could hit a 90-mph fastball, coming straight for you? You can test your reaction time online. There are more activities for you to try, and don't miss the scientific slugger and his quest for a home run.

http://www.exploratorium.edu/baseball/

★ The Exploratorium's Science of Hockey

Join the San Jose Sharks as they explore the science of hockey, one of the most exciting sports. Did you know there is a difference between fast ice and slow ice? Follow the Sharks as you learn about the ice, the skills, the equipment, and more.

http://www.exploratorium.edu/hockey/

★ Geocaching - The Official GPS Stash Hunt Site

Is there any treasure near your house? Worldwide, geocache game players have hidden small waterproof boxes filled with inexpensive gadgets and goodies. On this page, they give sketchy directions and GPS readings to assist would-be treasure hunters. Be sure to bring an adult along to help, as well as a trinket of your own to trade.

http://www.geocaching.com/

★ Horse-country.com

Horse history, care, stories, sounds, images, and associations are all here. There's an International Pen Pal List for horse lovers. "Call a check" at the simulation games—why not open your own virtual stable? Don't miss the online gymkhana or the equestrian paper dolls.

http://www.horse-country.com/

★ The National Baseball Hall of Fame

Visit the Baseball Hall of Fame in Cooperstown, New York. You'll read about Babe Ruth's bat, Mickey Mantle's locker, and the special displays on women in baseball. You can also discover the baseball greats who have been inducted into the Hall of Fame, as well as see pictures of this year's class of inductees.

http://www.baseballhalloffame.org/

★ Salt Lake Organizing Committee for the Olympic Winter Games of 2002

Everybody knows about the XIX Olympic Winter Games held in Salt Lake City, Utah, February 8–22, 2002. Learn about the sports and the mascots—their names are Powder, Copper, and Coal. Can you guess what animals they are?

http://www.slc2002.org/

★ Sports ID Instructional Videos for Every Sport

This site offers video instruction in sports like bodyboarding, bowling, fly fishing, football, hockey, martial arts, and on and on. Your favorite sport is probably listed. Choose from movies in several different formats, based on your Internet connection speed.

http://www.sportsid.com/sid2000/

★ Sports Illustrated for Kids

When was the last time you sailed around the world, or picked up some tips from the world's best skateboarders— all without leaving your computer? Don't miss the interviews with sports heroes, games, and a whole lot more. Hint: Buzz Chat isn't, really.

http://www.sikids.com/

★ Streetplay.com

From hopscotch to jacks, to stickball to double Dutch jumprope, this site has the rules (were there rules?), the moves, and the dish on what's plain fun on the playground today.

http://www.streetplay.com/thegames/

SON-OF-NET-MOM'S
TOP SITES

You've seen the sites that my Mom thinks you'll like, but now you'll see the ones I know you will like! These sites are Son-Of-Net-mom approved!

Why didn't my mother tell me about "The Internet Kids & Family Yellow Pages" sooner?

Ambrosia Software, Inc.
http://www.ambrosiasw.com/Ambrosia.html

This page is for people with a Macintosh (New games are in production for PCs). It has all kinds of shareware games that you can download and play. Personally, my favorite games are "Escape Velocity," "EVO," and "Barrack," but there are many others. Ambrosia also has mailing lists to tell you about upcoming games and such. Some of the games they have can be enhanced by the addition of downloadable plug-ins. And, like any good game maker, they have hidden cheats and Easter eggs. Also check out some of the new games they are working on , including a third game in the Escape Velocity series.

The Belch Page
http://www.rahul.net/renoir/belch/index.html

Do you like the pleasant sound of a burp? Do you wish you did not have to hurt yourself trying to get just the right tone? And do you want the assurance that when your mother comes to yell at you, you can truthfully say it was not your fault? Well, this site is for you! It contains five high quality burps that you can listen to, and one "Grade A" snore! CAUTION: In the interest of good taste and possible regurgitation, do not have your volume up too loud. The Belch Page: still your key source for the gut-wrenching sounds of other people burping.

The Codebook
http://www.codebook.pp.se/

CAUTION—MACINTOSH SPOILERS! This site has more cheats than you can shake a computer game at! Extra lives, unlimited funds, hints, walkthroughs, Easter eggs, it's all there! Codebook is constantly updated, so if you just got a new game and Codebook doesn't have the cheats for it yet, don't worry, it will! A word from Son-Of-Net-mom: This is the only program I use to get cheats, but my Mom lists more codes in the VIDEO AND COMPUTER GAMES section of the book.

Digital Blasphemy
http://www.digitalblasphemy.com/

Are you bored with that turquoise blue desktop background you've had ever since you bought your PC? Or perhaps those desktop patterns that came with your iMac have started to get old. If any of this has got you thinking, let me give you some advice before you make a wrong move: go check out Digital Blasphemy. Ryan Bliss works full time making unbelievable desktop art. From city scenes and oceans, to blue planets in purple nebulas, it's the best stuff I've ever seen. But what's really nice about it is that every now and again he adds one of the pictures from the members area into the free area for everyone to download. Ever since I discovered this site, Ryan's art is all I have had on my desktop.

The Exploratorium
http://www.exploratorium.edu/

This is the official page for one of my favorite museums: the Exploratorium in San Francisco. Here you can find out what an aurora is, or play memory games (JAVA required). If I had to choose one section to go to, I'd pick the Observatory section. The cool part is that you can see a movie of an eclipse—from space! Or if you like, you can look at past online exhibits. For example, check the dissection of a cow's eye (something I saw live when I was there!). From space to sheep brains, this site has everything.

Grossology, the Science of Really Gross Things

http://www.grossology.org/yuck.shtml

Welcome to Grossology, where all of your gross questions can be answered. You can look at the gross fact of the moment or research grossness. You can even get your virtual diploma by taking Gross 101. Like I said before, you can search for a gross fact and find out about tons of gross things. Oh, and did I mention that there are recipes for "Fake Snot," and "Fake Blood"? Grossology has all this and more, but you may not want to go there at all if you want to continue to believe you're the only living thing in your bed ;-).

The Hitch Hiker's Guide to the Galaxy - The Adventure Game

http://www.douglasadams.com/creations/
    infocom.html

If you like books, and this series contains quite possibly the best books ever written in time and space, then you will love this site. If you have read the books in question, you will probably agree with me. I feel as though I've left something out, oh yes, the title of these books: The Hitch Hiker's Guide to the Galaxy series. As far as Son-Of-Net-mom is concerned, these are the best books ever written. Enough with the books, what about this site? It contains the game version that author Douglas Adams made with Infocom. This game is basically a compilation of the first few books in the series; it is very amusing and can keep anyone entertained for hours. The only problem with the Internet version is that you cannot save your game. Oh, one other thing: this was made before games had graphics (it was actually first published in 1984). Consequently, this game is just text. But that's OK, it just means you have to exercise your imagination :). On a more solemn note, Douglas Adams passed away in 2001. So long, and thanks for all your work.

KidsClick! Weird & Mysterious

http://sunsite.berkeley.edu/kidsclick!/topweir.html

Have you ever wondered what your dreams meant? Maybe you need to get a really good scary story for your next camping trip? Perhaps you've always wanted to learn about Astrology? Well, you've found the right place: KidsClick! From Aliens to Werewolves, and Vampires too, this site has lots of goodies. It also has a terrific kids' search engine with lots of great info. Check it out!

Name That Candybar

http://www.sci.mus.mn.us/sln/tf/c/crosssection/
    namethatbar.html

Do you like candy bars? Do you like them so much that you could recognize them anywhere? At this site you can test your skills! There are 24 pictures of candy bars that have been cut in cross- section so you can see what is inside them. Twelve of these are harder and in a different section of the site. See if you can beat Son-Of-Net-mom! I was able to get 18 of them right. Most of the ones I got wrong were some sort of local generic brand candy. If you beat me, well, give yourself a pat on the back!

Space Camp

http://www.spacecamp.com/main.htm

Ah, Space Camp—the ultimate place for all kids to go to be trained for their off-planet futures (the aliens are coming, you know). Well, even if that last part wasn't true—at least, not yet—Space Camp is an awesome place. I actually visited Space Academy for five days with some of my class mates and my math teacher Mr. Herbert. The guides are very cool and you learn (a little bit) about how an astronaut lives and a lot about how they are trained. However, if you go, I offer you a word of caution: before going in the Multi- Axis-Trainer, make sure you have nothing in your pockets ;-).

Tasty Insect Recipes

http://www.ent.iastate.edu/misc/insectsasfood.html

Have you heard your friends talk about chocolate covered ants, and thought—YUCK! Would you ever purposely eat a bug? Whether you want to eat bugs or not, this site is filled with recipes containing common insects ("Chocolate Chirpie Chip Cookies"), to not- so-common ones (like the rootworm beetles in "Beetle Dip"). If you try to make any of these and your parents seem confused, tell them that bugs give you protein!

Tom's Hardware Guide

http://www.tomshardware.com/

I visit this site almost daily. It's a news site for computer technology. Just about every day there's an article about a new type of processor, or advances in hard drive sizes, and information on all kinds of consumer electronics. They do comparisons of different brands of equipment, and tell you which one works the best, and also tell you about ways to overclock your processor to its limits.

Wizards of the Coast

http://www.wizards.com/

Wizards of the Coast produces the best customizable card games ever made: games like Pokémon, and my personal favorite, Magic: The Gathering. It includes official rules and notes about game play, and best of all, it's free. So head on over to Wizards of the Coast...right now!

★ Yucky Gross & Cool Body

http://yucky.kids.discovery.com/body/

Everything you've ever wondered about the science of sweat, pimples, burps, ear wax, and unseemly bodily noises is here. There are even audio recordings of stuff like a stomach growling—but it's not the real thing, and you get to guess what they used to make the sounds. It's not really disgusting, but it is gross, so if you're over 13 or so, don't even think of visiting this site! Those that do will learn a lot about digestion, the circulatory system, and other things about the human body and its mysteries.

§ØÑ ØF Ñ€†-MØM'Z S4F3TY T|PS

Can you read what's written above? It's in something called "leet" (or, if written in leet: 1337). It's a style of writing using different characters that look something like their corresponding English letters. Leet, short for "elite," means that the user is "clueful" or at least trying to appear that way. It is often used on the Net, especially in chat rooms.

In this list of tips, I sometimes use words like "prolly" (short for probably) and "gonna" (short for going to) just because that's the way I type online in IRC chat, and it makes things go faster. But I'll limit myself to those two. If I wrote this all in online shorthand it would be hard to read, even for me! ;) Oh, and that's a wink. It means I'm joking.

Chat rooms. Bad people. Privacy. Porn. The Internet's only dangerous if you don't know what you're doing. But I'm gonna tell you what to look out for so that you do know.

Just remember one thing. Well, two things. You meet people online who seem too good to be true. They ARE. They prolly aren't the age or sex they claim to be. Part two: don't believe everything you see on the Net.

Only You Can Protect Your Privacy

It's fun to talk to your friends and meet people in chat rooms. But be careful. In chat room conversation, people ask for personal information all the time. They type "A-S-L" which means they want everyone in the chat room to say their age, sex, and location. I think it's OK to give this information out as long as you keep it general. If you live in a big city, it's OK to say you live there. But if you live in a small town, make your location more general than that, like "Near Boston" or "in central Massachusetts."

People may ask you where you go to school. I think it's OK to tell them that too, but use common sense. Don't give out your locker number, or your team number if you play sports. Just be aware of what you are saying to people and protect your privacy!

Another thing you should know is that chat rooms are not all alike. Some are entertaining but others seem to focus on bullying, taunting, and making fun of other people; others are just plain stupid. If you find yourself in one, and the conversation makes you feel uncomfortable, just leave, and go to a different one. There are a lot of chat rooms out there and something for everyone. Look for a topic you want to discuss, and try to find a chat room where people are talking about it. Don't type a lot right away but sit back and watch the others and get a feeling for what's going on.

Password Scams

Most chat rooms ask you to pick a user name and sometimes a password before you can get in. In gaming chat, like on Battle.net, your game characters are stored in your username account. If you have a good character that you've worked hard on, people may try to access your account and shift your stuff to their own accounts. This is bad. So what you'll see are people posing as official Web site administration operators. They will tell you all sorts of reasons why they need your username and password, but don't fall for that trick. Trust me, the admin people already know your username and password, although it's probably encrypted. There is NO reason to ever disclose your password in an online chat room.

Profiles

Most chat rooms let you click on a username to find out more info about the person using that name. This is sometimes called a profile. It's amazing the personal information people will put in there. Don't do it. Have you ever heard the expression "less is more"? It means that being a little mysterious is often better or more interesting than telling every single thing about yourself. It's safer too.

I like to change my profile daily, and I don't even put any contact information in there. But I do like to show my personality. If you've ever seen the movie *Fight Club*, you would get the joke, but every day, I change this part of my profile: I am Jack's _____. The blank is what I change. It's a simple way to let my friends know what I'm up to, without putting in too much. An example would be: "I am Jack's insomnia," if I can't get to sleep, or: "I am Jack's lack of inspiration," if I can't think of anything new to write. ;)

Living in a Fantasy World

You might say, "So Steve, is it ever OK to put in any information about myself?" To which I would reply, "Yes, but be careful."

If you're buying something online my advice would be different, but sometimes a site will ask you for your address in order to let you play a game or download something. Don't give up your privacy just to play a game!

Consider doing what I do: make up a fake persona you can use all the time. Have fun with it. Give yourself a different name and address and use it consistently. A tip: the ZIP code 12345 is for Schenectady, NY ;)

Don't give your "real" e-mail address unless your parents say it is OK. You're just opening up your mailbox to spam (the junk mail, not the tasty (?) meat product).

Get your alter ego an e-mail address. You can get a free account at Yahoo! <http://mail.yahoo.com/> or Hotmail <http://www.hotmail.com>. Then you use this "disposable" e-mail account instead of your "real" e-mail address. You'd only go to this alternate account when you had to. Otherwise, just let it fill up with spam. Yahoo! is particularly good because it offers some anti-spam protection.

Many sites ask for your date of birth. There are lots of reasons for this, but one is that in the U.S. there are special rules that sites have to use if you happen to be under 13. These rules help protect your privacy.

You've Got . . . Chain Letters!

Something else you'll see in your mailbox besides spam is chain mail. Not the kind from medieval times—the kind of letter that asks you to send a copy to all your friends. Do the Internet a favor and DON'T. Trust me, no one ever got a million dollars because they sent a chain letter on to the next mailbox. If you think the chain letter is particularly witty, you might send it to a friend or two who might appreciate the humor, but please don't send it to your whole address book. Although the letter prolly predicts lifelong bad luck if you "break the chain" and don't send it on, be brave. There is no truth to this sort of thing, and anyway some are illegal. I can't say this enough: chain mail is stupid, and none of it is true.

You've Got . . . Viruses!

Other things people love to forward to other people are virus warnings, most of which are bogus. When you get one of these, stop for a minute and go to a Web site where you can learn the truth. I like the Computer Emergency Response Team's site *<http://www.cert.org/>* and Hoaxbusters *<http://HoaxBusters.ciac.org>*/. Also, the Symantec site *<http://www.symantec.com/avcenter/>* is particularly good. They offer excellent virus protection software, too.

One more thing about viruses, though. If you get unexpected mail with an attached file—you have to be suspicious FIRST. Don't just open it and ask questions later. If you have a PC and you get a file with the filename extension .EXE or .DLL, don't open or run them at all. The .DLL one is most likely a virus and the .EXE one may be one as well.

Did you get the mail and the file from someone you don't know? DON'T open it. Just delete the whole thing; it's prolly a virus. If it's important, the person will send it to you again.

If you got the mail from someone you do know, you still should not open it. Contact your friend and ask what it was. If you are going to send someone a file, you should send them e-mail beforehand and say that you're going to be sending them an attached file. That way they will know what it is.

To those of you with Macs instead of PCs: no worries, mate. Writing a virus for a Mac is a long and tedious process and most people just don't bother. Those .EXE or .DLL PC files won't infect your computer, either.

You've Got . . . Hoaxes!

The Hoaxbusters site mentioned above will also clue you in on some of the common e-mail hoaxes you'll come across. By the way, Craig Shergold has recovered from cancer and doesn't want any more business cards, and Bill Gates won't be sending you a check for $1,000.00 although I hope he sends me one for helping to set you guys straight.

Stupid Net Tricks

Sooner or later you will probably stumble into something on the Internet that is pornographic, disturbing, or both. The good news: this is becoming harder to do by accident, but it is not impossible.

Just hit the "Back" button on your browser, if you can. Some sites will not let you do this and will keep opening up window after window after window, each one with more bad stuff displayed. On a PC, the easiest way to get rid of it all is to just shut down the computer. But first, be sure to save your work in any open applications (wouldn't want to lose your homework!).

If you don't want to shut off the computer, you could try this tip. Type another URL (like yahoo.com) in the address bar, and go there. That defeats the other Web site because it's checking to see if you're hitting the back button, or trying to close the window. It's not expecting you to just try going to another site.

It wasn't your fault that you got to this Internet site. If you are worried about it, or if you feel really disturbed about whatever you saw, definitely talk to a friend, your parents, teacher, or other trusted adult. Don't let this stuff haunt you; it's not worth it.

Web Diaries: Growing Trend or Growing Stale?

Many people keep a public diary on the Web, and invite strangers and friends to comment on it. Would you write your innermost thoughts and feelings and post them on the school cafeteria wall? I thought not. So, why people are obsessed with keeping public Web diaries is beyond me. I think they are a colossal waste of time and I don't promote them. I think by exposing your life like that you open yourself up to having your feelings hurt, or losing your self-esteem, which is something we all need more of, not less of.

If you must try a Web diary, write it for your alter ego (remember him, the guy in Schenectady?) You could have some creative fun dreaming up adventures for him, without risk to your own privacy.

I'll prolly be adding to these tips from time to time. You'll be able to find the most current version at <http://www.netmom.com/steve/>

AFRICAN AMERICANS

Afro-American Almanac

Start off with some traditional folk tales, such as "Why the Sun Lives in the Sky." Then head for the Biography section to learn about individuals like Frederick Douglass, and groups, such as the Buffalo Soldiers. In the Historical Documents area you can read everything from the Emancipation Proclamation to the principles of the Black Panthers. Don't stop now—information about Juneteenth and Kwanzaa is available at this site, as well.

http://www.toptags.com/aama/

HISTORICAL FIGURES

A Black History Treasure Hunt

This is a fun and educational Black History Month activity—a treasure hunt that will take you all over the Web to find the answers. Don't worry, there are suggested Web sites for you to try first. Be sure to choose the right hunt for your grade level. There are four different treasure hunts: one for fourth grade and below, one for fifth and sixth graders, one for seventh and eighth graders, and one for ninth graders and above. Sample question for fourth graders: "This person refused to give up a seat on the bus. That led to a 382-day bus boycott by black people in Montgomery, Alabama." Do you know the answer? Find out here.

http://www.education-world.com/a_lesson/
    lesson052.shtml

The Faces of Science: African Americans in the Sciences

This site gives you biographical information on more than 100 African Americans who have made important contributions to science. The articles are well documented, and their sources are cited. You can also see a selection of patents issued to some of these scientists.

http://www.princeton.edu/~mcbrown/display/
    faces.html

Great African Americans

In celebration of Black History Month, The History Channel offers brief biographical sketches of celebrities, scientists, sports figures, and politicians. You'll find out what Oprah Winfrey's dad did for a living, discover Alex Haley's Coast Guard career, and learn what medals Colin Powell received after the Vietnam War, among other things.

http://www.historychannel.com/exhibits/blackhist/

The Internet African American History Challenge

Learn about 12 famous African American men and women from the nineteenth century; then see if you can score high on the quiz. Did you know that Mary Church Terrell was the first president of the National Association of Colored Women or that Mary Ann Shadd was the first black woman editor of a North American newspaper? Read about other African American pioneers at The Internet African American History Challenge.

http://www.brightmoments.com/blackhistory/

Seattle Times: Martin Luther King Jr.

In a thoughtful and moving Web site, the *Seattle Times* commemorates the life and legacy of Dr. Martin Luther King, Jr. You'll find a time line of his life, along with many photos and audio files. You'll be able to hear part of his famous "I Have a Dream" speech, as well as others. Check the sections on the history of the civil rights movement, and read about how the Martin Luther King, Jr., Day national holiday was created in memory of this great leader, called "America's Gandhi."

http://www.seattletimes.com/mlk/

Bring an umbrella, we're going to explore WEATHER AND METEOROLOGY resources!

A
B
C
D
E
F
G
H
I
J
K
L
M
N
O
P
Q
R
S
T
U
V
W
X
Y
Z

★ Stamp on Black History

Some of the most important African American historical figures have been pictured on U.S. postage stamps. See who's who in many fields, including art, science, medicine, and sports. Browse this site by the name of the person, such as Louis Armstrong. Or check the field for which the person is known, such as Physical Education or History. You'll see a picture of each stamp and read a little about each individual. This resource was built by students for the ThinkQuest competition.

http://library.thinkquest.org/10320/

Tuskegee Airmen

Overcoming prejudice and discrimination during World War II, more than 1,000 black fighter pilots were trained in Tuskegee, Alabama. They achieved an impressive record. None of the bombers they escorted was lost to enemy aircraft. They collectively won more than 850 medals during their tours of duty. At this site you can see pictures of the aircraft they flew and learn more about these American heroes.

http://sun.kent.wednet.edu/KSD/SJ/TuskegeeAirmen/
   Tuskegee_HomePage.html

HISTORY

★ The African American Journey

This excellent site from the editors of *World Book Encyclopedia* traces the history of African Americans from slavery to freedom. It offers information on the civil rights movement, as well as a brief history of Black History Month itself. The idea began all the way back in 1926, with the observance of Negro History Week. It was originally proposed by Carter G. Woodson, among others. Woodson was a black historian who is now known as the "Father of Black History." Black History Week began during the early 1970s, and Black History Month was first celebrated in 1976. It is sponsored each year by the Association for the Study of Afro-American Life and History in Washington, D.C., which Woodson founded in 1915.

http://www.worldbook.com/fun/aajourny/html/

The African-American Mosaic Exhibition (Library of Congress)

The Library of Congress is in Washington, D.C., and it has a huge collection of materials, some of which cover about 500 years of African history throughout the Western Hemisphere. The materials include books, periodicals, prints, photographs, music, film, and recorded sound. This exhibit samples these materials in four areas: Colonization, Abolition, Migrations, and the Work Projects Administration period. You'll be able to look at pages from original materials, such as an abolitionist children's book. Sometimes it's useful to look at these original materials, also called primary sources, for yourself, rather than use books other people have written about these same sources—this way, you're closer to what really happened. This site has lots to use for school reports.

http://lcweb.loc.gov/exhibits/african/intro.html

Africans in America

This Web site is the online companion to the Public Broadcasting System's television series of the same name. It chronicles the history of the slave trade in the United States from the sixteenth century, through the end of the Civil War in 1865. The story comes alive through personal narratives, historical documents, engravings, and other artworks. If some of the texts look a little odd, because of their archaic words and misspellings, take a look at "How to Read a 200-Year-Old Document" at <*http://www.earlyamerica.com/earlyamerica/howto.html*>. There's also a teacher's guide, and one for students, too, including suggested links to more information.

http://www.pbs.org/wgbh/aia/

AFRO-Americ@: The Black History Museum

Enter this site to learn about several fascinating subjects: black resistance during the times of slavery, famous figures like Jackie Robinson and the Tuskegee Airmen, and historic events such as the Million Man March. The illustrated essays also feature the disturbing story of the trial of "the Scottsboro boys."

http://www.afroam.org/history/history.html

Anacostia Museum

Explore many examples of the contributions of African Americans to U.S. history and culture. You will discover online exhibits of African American–influenced inventions, art, music, and more. The museum, part of the Smithsonian Institution, is located in Washington, D.C., but you can visit it by clicking on Exhibitions and Programs.

http://www.si.edu/anacostia/

Born in Slavery

In the 1930s, the Federal Writers' Project collected personal stories from ordinary Americans in order to preserve unwritten history. Some of the people interviewed were ex-slaves. Read their reminiscences of life under slavery and the hardships they endured. You might have a little trouble at first as you read the articles. The writers tried to preserve the sound of the words as spoken by the interviewees, so the text is written in dialect form. Be aware that some of the words used in these selections are considered racial slurs today.

http://lcweb2.loc.gov/ammem/snhtml/snhome.html

Education First: Black History Activities

This comprehensive and thoughtful collection of links will take you all over the Web on a treasure hunt to find the answers to some very big questions. What was the medical experimentation tragedy known as the Tuskegee Study? Who were the Little Rock 9? This site has study questions and activities for classes as well.

http://www.kn.pacbell.com/wired/BHM/AfroAm.html

The Encyclopedia Britannica Guide to Black History

Music history question—what's the difference between "boogie-woogie" and a cakewalk? Maybe you'd better "phone a friend!" Who to call? Muddy Waters might know, but what about Tiger Woods, Paul Robeson, or Jesse Owens? Learn about famous African Americans and important events in Black History at this media-rich Web site.

http://blackhistory.eb.com/

Exploring Amistad at Mystic Seaport

What has come to be known as the Amistad Revolt began in 1839 as a shipboard slave uprising off the coast of Cuba. It intensified into a debate on slavery, race, Africa, and the foundations of American democracy itself. Popularized by a contemporary movie, you can read the original accounts of the story at this informative site. The schooner the slaves took over was named *Amistad*, which means "friendship."

http://amistad.mysticseaport.org/main/welcome.html

Free at Last: The Civil Rights Movement in the United States

If the Civil Rights movement is new to you, try this site, if only for the glossary of terms such as "Jim Crow" and "Sit-in." Study a time line and learn about important Civil Rights leaders and issues. When you think you're ready, try the "Free at Last!" quiz game or one of the crossword puzzles or word searches offered. This Web page was created by students for the ThinkQuest Junior competition.

http://library.thinkquest.org/J0112391/

Lissa Explains It All—HTML Help for Kids

Lissa's a teen who was born to code HTML. She's gotten so many questions about her Web pages that she decided to put up some brief tutorials. Learn everything from basic tags to more advanced tricks like how you get that cool rippling lake effect on your graphics. You'll also see how changing color or graphics on mouseovers is done, and you can check out lots of resources for finding free graphics.
http://www.lissaexplains.com/

A B C D E F G H I J K L M N O P Q R S T U V W X Y Z

Harriet Tubman and the Underground Railroad

An escaped slave could work his way north to Canada and gain his freedom, but the journey was often hundreds of miles long. He had to remain hidden, his route secret. Along the way, he would be helped by a loose organization of sympathetic people who provided a hot meal, shelter, and, often, help traveling to the next "station" on the so-called "Underground Railroad." You'll also find links to other Web resources on the Underground Railroad and the brave "conductors" who made it run, without regard to their own personal risk. One of the most famous was Harriet Tubman. A second-grade class created this page so you could learn all about her.

http://www2.lhric.org/pocantico/tubman/
    tubman.html

★ Living Under Enslavement

What was it like to live as a slave? Visit re-created slave quarters at the Hermitage Plantation in Georgia and find out. Click on items inside the house and discover their use and meaning. One of the best parts is the audio retelling of slave escapes, but if you don't have sound capabilities, there is a written transcript version.

http://www.hfmgv.org/smartfun/hermitage/tocfr.html

NET FILES

How many people are on Earth?

Answer: Quite a few—over six billion! For the latest estimate, check the world population clock at *http://www.census.gov/cgi-bin/ipc/popclockw/*

National Civil Rights Museum

Take the Interactive Tour to discover what it was like when African Americans had to sit at the back of the bus and avoid "whites only" restaurants, swimming pools, and drinking fountains. As bizarre as this seems to us now, before the civil rights movement of the 1960s, this was standard, everyday life in many places in the U.S. The Freedom Summer of 1964 included student sit-ins, boycotts, and protest marches. This museum in Memphis, Tennessee, re-creates some of the sights, sounds, and scenes of that era. Remember, the struggle for civil rights continues around the world today, and it involves people of many races.

http://www.civilrightsmuseum.org/

North by South

Between the years 1900 and the 1960s, almost 5 million African Americans left the South seeking better lives and better jobs in the northern states and cities of the U.S. Along with their families, they brought along their culture: music, foods, social customs, and more. Trace these influences in cities such as Chicago and Cleveland.

http://www.northbysouth.org/

Roots

During the winter of 1977, a powerful miniseries appeared on television. It was a dramatization of Alex Haley's Pulitzer Prize–winning book, *Roots*. The series of programs traced Haley's ancestors back to the days of slavery. The compelling story made it one of the most-watched miniseries of all time, with 130 million viewers during its initial telecast. Although Americans had learned about slavery in school, this was the first time it was portrayed in such close and personal detail, and adults and kids all over the country couldn't wait until the next show to see what happened to Kunta Kinte and the other characters. This online exhibit gives a chronological background and introduction to slavery in America, as well as a listing of inventions by African Americans.

http://www.historychannel.com/exhibits/roots/

Sojourn Project

High school students can participate in this innovative travel/study tour called "Sojourn to the Past," aimed at teaching civil rights lessons that just can't be learned via a textbook. Kids start their journey on the steps of the Lincoln Memorial in Washington, D.C., as they listen to a tape of Dr. Martin Luther King's famous "I Have a Dream" speech, which was delivered there in 1963. Other stops along the historic route include Atlanta, Selma, Montgomery, and Memphis. If you can't make the trip yourself, you can read other students' impressions at the Web site.

http://www.sojournproject.org/

Time for Kids Black History Month

Retrace the famous 1965 civil rights march from Selma to Montgomery, Alabama. Try to answer trivia questions about African American history to walk the walk for yourself. Explore a brief but terrific illustrated time line; listen to famous speeches; and try to pick out Oprah Winfrey, Eddie Murphy, and other celebrities from their baby pictures.

http://www.timeforkids.com/TFK/specials/
0,6709,97217,00.html

★ The Underground Railroad

Using stunning graphics and sound effects, this site explores the people, places, and history of the Underground Railroad. Put yourself in the role of a slave facing a choice: escape with "Moses" to possible freedom in Canada, or face continued slavery. What would you do? Choose your own path and see if you can become "free at last!"

http://www.nationalgeographic.com/features/99/
railroad/

Understanding Slavery

Although slavery still exists in the world today, the very idea of buying and selling human beings is hard for us to imagine. Go back in time to 1845 in Richmond, Virginia. Witness a slave auction yourself, and "step into the shoes" of several onlookers. What would your reaction be? Will you try to stop the sale? What options, if any, are open to the slaves?

http://school.discovery.com/schooladventures/
slavery/

AMERICAN SAMOA

See UNITED STATES—TERRITORIES

AMPHIBIANS

See also ANIMALS; PETS AND PET CARE; and REFERENCE WORKS

Amphibian Checklist and Identification Guide

Tired of guessing whether that creature under the woodpile is a tiger salamander or an eastern newt? Unable to distinguish a western toad from a spadefoot variety? Puzzled over differences between a mink frog and a pickerel frog? This terrific field guide offers color photos and range maps to help you arrange your amphibians and know them all by their proper names.

http://www.npwrc.usgs.gov/narcam/idguide/
specieid.htm

★ Virtual Exhibit on Canada's Biodiversity: Focus on Amphibians

Scoop up something interesting in the pond? What on earth is it? Visit this site to identify many amphibians by reading the extensive descriptions of both their adult and larval phases. You'll also find photos and information on the habitat and conservation of many species. The most fun part of this site is the Life History section. There you will see animated life cycles and metamorphoses, such as how a pollywog becomes a frog. The Virtual Habitats part of the site is interesting, too. Explore a pond, a stream, a woodland, and a meadow and see what species thrive there. Click on one to bring up more information.

http://collections.ic.gc.ca/amphibians/

A
B
C
D
E
F
G
H
I
J
K
L
M
N
O
P
Q
R
S
T
U
V
W
X
Y
Z

A
B
C
D
E
F
G
H
I
J
K
L
M
N
O
P
Q
R
S
T
U
V
W
X
Y
Z

FROGS AND TOADS

★ Exploratorium: Frogs

I hope you brought a flashlight. That's the only way we're going to be able to track frogs in this swamp tonight. Shine your light over THERE. Oh, it's a carpenter frog. Hear how his call sounds like a person hammering or chopping wood? Hold on, what's THAT? Whew, just a Pine Barrens tree frog. Um, was that your foot I just stepped on? No? I hope it wasn't a bullfrog!

http://www.exploratorium.edu/frogs/

Frog and Toad Photographs and Calls

Get your frog sounds right here! We've got your spring peeper, your squirrel tree frog, even your American toad. Step right up, no waiting, plenty of high-quality frog songs for all.

http://www.naturesound.com/frogs/frogs.html

NET FILES

What are the six major food groups? (Isn't one of them chocolate?)

Answer: The Food Pyramid lists six food groups:
❖ Bread, cereal, grains, pasta
❖ Fruit
❖ Vegetables
❖ Meat, poultry, fish, dry beans
❖ Milk, cheese, yogurt
❖ Oils, fats, sweets (yes, that's chocolate, but eat only a little!)
Find out more at http://www.nal.usda.gov:8001/py/pmap.htm

FrogWeb

This site has all the latest scientific news on how amphibian populations are declining, but it also suggests ways you can help. How about adopting a nearby frog pond? Monitor your local frog activities and report them to this national watch dog (or should that be "watch frog"?) organization. Be certain you follow the "Rules of Froggy 'Hunting'" <http://www.frogweb.gov/froghunt.htm> to make sure both you and the frogs stay safe. There's also a fun section with coloring pages, froggy games, and lots of links.

http://www.frogweb.gov/

Habitat Hints for Backyard — Project - Pond

Wouldn't it be great to build a frog pond or maybe a toad abode? Learn how at this fun site from the National Wildlife Federation. Marvel at froggy facts, and find out what you can do to help frogs and their kin.

http://www.nwf.org/habitats/backyard/beyondbasics/
   hints/frogpond.cfm

Netfrog - The Interactive Frog Dissection

Did you ever wonder what's inside a frog? Now you can look for yourself. Scientists learn about dead animals using a technique called dissection. Learn to identify the locations of a frog's major organs. Click on one button and watch movies of dissections. Click on another button and practice what you've learned. Only one frog had to lose its life for this Web page, and many simulated dissections can be performed over and over, by kids all over the world.

http://curry.edschool.Virginia.EDU/go/frog/

The Somewhat Amusing World of Frogs

This Australian page offers many intriguing froggie facts, such as "Frogs don't drink, but absorb water from their surroundings through their skin (by osmosis)." You'll love the illustrations and sounds, but the jokes on this page may make you croak. Example: "Why are frogs normally so happy? They eat whatever bugs them."

http://www.csu.edu.au/faculty/commerce/account/
   frogs/frog.htm

A Thousand Friends of Frogs

Are you a friend of frogs? If so, you can join 999 others and celebrate all that is green or brown and croaks or sings. From the Center for Global Environmental Education in Minnesota, you can learn fantastic frog facts and help them by answering questions about frogs in your area.

http://cgee.hamline.edu/frogs/

AMUSEMENT PARKS

See also DISNEY

★ Carousel! Your Carousel Information Center

Everyone has seen carousel horses, but did you know that some carousels also have frogs, roosters, and fantastic creatures like sea monsters on them? Find out about the history of carousels, see some detailed wooden horses, and listen to carousel music—this site is guaranteed to make you smile! Learn where antique carousels can still be found and ridden (look in the History section, under Census). They are something of a rarity, since many old carousels have been taken apart and sold to collectors. Maybe you can help save an old carousel in your town.

http://www.carousel.org/

iFairground

Want to operate an amusement park of your own someday? What's it like to work in one of the Disney parks? What if your great-grandfather had invented the Ferris wheel? Find out here! This site was created by students for the ThinkQuest competition, who interviewed a park owner, a park employee, and a ride manufacturer, among others in the family entertainment field. You'll also find material on amusement park history, ride design, and safety.

http://library.thinkquest.org/C002926/

ROLLER COASTERS

Build a Coaster

Part of a larger site on amusement parks, this applet lets you design your own roller coaster. It doesn't seem to have much to do with actual physics or real-world safety, so go ahead and make the most outrageous coaster you can. Then hit the submit button and see how it performs against Vince's "scream" rating.

http://www.discovery.com/exp/rollercoasters/
    build.html

Roller Coasters

Trace the history of "scream machines" at this thrilling site from *Encyclopedia Britannica*. From the "Russian Mountain" rides of the 1800s to the stomach-churning monster rides of tomorrow, you'll learn all about the invention and development of roller coasters through the text and multimedia offered at this site.

http://coasters.eb.com/

ANCIENT CIVILIZATIONS AND ARCHAEOLOGY

See also HISTORY

Ancient Greece

Not only can you find out about the daily life, language, and sports of ancient Greece, but you can also read the complete text of Greek classics such as the *Iliad* and the *Odyssey*. Get to know the Greek gods and heroes; then ponder the history (and spelling) of the Peloponnesian war. This site was created by students for the ThinkQuest competition.

http://library.thinkquest.org/17709/

A B C D E F G H I J K L M N O P Q R S T U V W X Y Z

Archaeological Pieces of the Past

What's it like to be a real archaeologist? Get your equipment together, because you're about to find out! Canada's Royal Ontario Museum invites you to visit a simulated "dig" on the site of an old farmstead. Examine various artifacts, puzzle over their meaning, and emerge with a clearer understanding of the past.

http://www.rom.on.ca/digs/munsell/

Archaeology's Dig

How's this for a fantastic factoid? In 1996, at a dig site in Sweden, archaeologists found what they think is the world's oldest piece of chewing gum! It was made of birch bark tar and might be over 6,500 years old. For some reason, no one checked to see if it had lost its flavor. Brief articles like this are featured at this site. For lots of intriguing information, be sure to read the answers to questions people have asked Dr. Dig.

http://www.dig.archaeology.org/

Be an Archaeologist

Are you good at jigsaw puzzles? We hope so because we've just found a pile of Maya pottery pieces and we think maybe they can be put back together. If you've got the right plug-in, would you care to try? This is part of a larger site on archaeology.

http://www.pbs.org/wgbh/nova/laventa/
    archaeologist.html

Collapse: Why Do Civilizations Fall?

One minute it seems like your community's going pretty well, and the next minute your entire civilization's just a footnote in a dusty old history book. It happened to the Maya in what is now Honduras and also to the Anasazi in what's now the American desert southwest. But they are not the only ones. This also happened to many other cultures. What causes empires to fall? Some take many years to decline, while others experience a more rapid failure. There are many reasons: disease, war, natural disasters, economic collapse, and more. What do the lessons of the past have to teach the civilizations of the future? Find out here.

http://www.learner.org/exhibits/collapse/

★ Daily Life in Ancient Civilizations

What would your daily routine be like if you lived in ancient China, India, Greece, or Rome? In the section on China, follow the cheat sheet to learn about life under many dynasties, including that of Hu the Tiger. Find out what he had in common with a famous *Star Wars* villain! Check fashion in ancient India, breakfast in Rome, and school in Greece.

http://members.aol.com/Donnclass/indexlife.html

★ Kids Dig Reed

With the help of a talking cow, you'll participate in a "dig" on a mid-1800s West Virginian farm site using the latest virtual archaeological methods. Survey the site, use a metal detector, screen for artifacts, and try to put it all together into a picture of the Reed's family life. Don't miss the games area. Can you match the old-time artifact with its modern-day equivalent?

http://www.kidsdigreed.com/

★ Mr. Donn's Ancient History

Look no further for information on ancient Mesopotamia, Egypt, Greece, Rome, China, India, and more. Online resources, games, lesson plans, quizzes—they're all here!

http://members.aol.com/donnandlee/

Mummies Unwrapped

If you think that all mummies are stiff-legged movie monsters walking around in tattered bandages, you need to unwind at this site. Learn about bog mummies, ice mummies, and mud mummies, to name a few. If you are hungry after that, try the Yummy Mummy cookies.

http://library.thinkquest.org/J003409/

Curl up with a good URL in BOOKS AND LITERATURE!

A
B
C
D
E
F
G
H
I
J
K
L
M
N
O
P
Q
R
S
T
U
V
W
X
Y
Z

NOVA Online - Secrets of Easter Island

On remote Easter Island stand almost 900 giant stone statues. No one knows who carved them or what they mean. One of the biggest questions archaeologists ask is, "How were they built?" The average figure, called a *moai*, stands over 13 feet tall and weighs over 13 tons! Follow along as scientists attempt to construct a modern moai using methods suggested by several different theories. You can also play Move the Megalith and see how well you'd do at the simulated task.

http://www.pbs.org/wgbh/nova/easter/

NOVA Online - Secrets of Lost Empires

If you liked the previous site, try the others in this series. See historians try to build a medieval siege engine, a Roman bath, a Chinese bridge, and even an Egyptian obelisk.

http://www.pbs.org/wgbh/nova/lostempires/

★ Odyssey Online

Explore the ancient cultures of the Near East, Greece, Rome, and Egypt via cool puzzles and games. For example, click on Greece and find out all about famous Greek heroes, rulers, and athletes. Discover what daily life was like, and learn about their death and burial customs. Examine artifacts and see if you can guess which ones relate to athletic events or prizes. In other games, you try to put fragments of statues back together—don't forget to bring your superglue on this adventure!

http://www.emory.edu/CARLOS/ODYSSEY/

Welcome to the Dig

What do archaeologists do? What techniques do they use to sift through the rubble of civilizations? Meet several real-life archaeologists and discover some famous dig sites. If you want to get your hands dirty with virtual soil, try the virtual dig game. How many Greek vases can you discover without breaking one? The Baroness de Badger acts as your furry guide to the underworld of archaeology. Why? Because nobody digs better than a badger! This site was created by students for the ThinkQuest competition.

http://library.thinkquest.org/J001645/

Oatbox Crystal Set Project

It's easy and fun to build your own "crystal" radio set using only some simple components. You will need a soldering iron, some stuff from Radio Shack or your favorite electronics parts store, a Quaker oatmeal box (or other round, tall box), and some time. All the directions are explained at the URL listed below. If you want a more elaborate project, you can find an old cigar box and build a radio with a simple tuner. Cigar stores may have empty boxes; just ask. The directions for that project are at *http://www.midnightscience.com/project.html*

ANCIENT EGYPT

★ Ancient Egypt

Ancient Egyptians believed in many gods and goddesses, and worship was very important. Explore a catalog of Egyptian deities, and learn (among other things) whose laughter could start an earthquake! Before you leave, try to help Jane: she's lost inside the museum. The statues will help, but first you'll have to find and return some lost articles.

http://www.ancientegypt.co.uk/menu.html

Cleveland Museum of Art Pharaohs Exhibition

See kings and queens, pharaohs, and their treasures. Marvel at statues and carvings from long ago. While you're there, learn some fun facts about the ancient pharaohs. Did you know that some of them were women? Follow your guide, Rosetta Stone, and learn how to construct a paper model of a pharaoh (the pattern is printable). Or join Sahara the scarab beetle on an expedition to find out more about animals of ancient Egypt. Hut, hut, go King Tut!

http://www.clemusart.com/archive/pharaoh/

A B C D E F G H I J K L M N O P Q R S T U V W X Y Z

★ CMCC - Mysteries of Egypt

Tutankhamun's tomb, discovered by Howard Carter in 1922, contained over 3,000 "wonderful things," including a golden mask of the boy king himself. Although he became king at age 9, he was dead by about age 17. What really happened to Tutankhamun? What was his life like? Was he murdered? Find out possible answers here. Gaze in awe at the treasures found, displayed for you in the virtual galleries. If you have the right plug-ins, you can manipulate artifacts to see them better, or take a virtual reality tour of a tomb. There are also many additional links collected at this excellent site.

http://www.civilization.ca/membrs/civiliz/egypt/
   egypt_e.html

EgyptWorld

You may be familiar with the Pyramids at Giza, but did you know these monuments are spread throughout Egypt? Take a tour of them as you explore this graphically rich site. Along the way there's a time line, various media kiosks, and games. Learn about the Rosetta stone, which gave the key to unlock the secrets of hieroglyphics. This site was created by students for the ThinkQuest competition.

http://library.thinkquest.org/15924/

NOVA Online - Pyramids - The Inside Story

Who built the pyramids? How old are they? These are common questions you may have, and they are answered here—but here's a new question: if it took 100,000 people to build these giant structures—where's the city in which the workers lived? Follow along as archaeologists search for it. Don't miss the QuickTime virtual reality tours to the pyramids so you can really experience the "inside story."

http://www.pbs.org/wgbh/nova/pyramid/

Secrets of the Pharoahs

Join PBS on a virtual "flythrough" of the famous Great Pyramid in Egypt. What might be hidden beyond the Queen's chamber? In other parts of this site, find out how mummies are prepared, and carefully explore King Tut's tomb to locate and learn about 14 hidden treasures.

http://www.pbs.org/wnet/pharaohs/

See Your Name in Hieroglyphic Language (Egypt's Tourism Net)

If you want to know how you'd have to sign your homework if you were in ancient Egypt, go here. "Net-mom" looks like a squiggle, an arm, a half circle, a couple of falcons, and a baby chick. What does your name look like?

http://www.tourism.egnet.net/cafe/tor_trn.htm

ANCIENT EUROPE

★ The Anglo-Saxons

Try writing in Anglo-Saxon runes, see if you can guess the answers to some puzzling riddles, and help Hild find five objects she must bring to the village feast. Along the way you will learn about daily life in A.D. 800. If you successfully gain entrance to the great hall, you can print several activity sheets.One gives instructions to make a musical lyre out of a shoe box.

http://www.bbc.co.uk/education/anglosaxons/

NET FILES

When was the first camera made available to consumers?

Answer: The first consumer camera was marketed all the way back in 1888. The Kodak camera was priced at $25 and included film for 100 exposures. It was a little inconvenient to get your pictures developed, though. The whole camera had to be returned to Kodak in Rochester, New York, for film processing. For more on the history of photography, click over to
http://www.eastman.org/5_timeline/1899.htm

Flints and Stones

Everyone thinks cavemen were big, hairy guys who carried clubs and dragged women around by the hair. This site explodes that myth and others. Could you survive in Stone Age times? Meet the shaman, who will show you what life is like in his village of Ice Age hunters and gatherers. You'll also meet the archaeologist, who will show you how he interprets the lives of the village folk from the objects, art, and other signs they have left behind. You'll also be able to take a Stone Age food quiz—hmmm, should you eat that mushroom or not?

http://museums.ncl.ac.uk/flint/menu.html

Hunt the Ancestor

Ah, the troubles of an archaeologist! Can you locate an ancient burial site without overspending your research budget? You'll have to check old county records, consult crumbling maps, and arrange for some aerial photography. Try to extract the artifacts before the quarry blasting destroys everything. Other parts of this site give details on marine archaeology, carbon dating, and more.

http://www.bbc.co.uk/history/ancient/archaeology/
index.shtml

The Viking Network Web

Experience the Viking way of life: raiding, trading, and exploration. This site is aimed at kids and teachers all over the world who are interested in Viking heritage and culture. This site has information on Viking musical instruments to explore, along with notes on clothing and daily life. For extra fun, check out the Viking math quiz.

http://www.viking.no/

The Vikings

Don't forget the Vikings! Learn about daily life in a Viking village, explore Viking beliefs, and try a few activities to see if you've got the right Viking stuff. Speaking of stuff, help Thorkel locate five gifts for a sea captain's family, then go along on a voyage!

http://www.bbc.co.uk/education/vikings/

ANCIENT ROME

Discovery.com - Pompeii

Until it was destroyed by the eruption of Mt. Vesuvius on August 24 A.D. 79, Pompeii was a prosperous Roman trading city with 20,000 citizens. In 1748, archaeologists began uncovering the layer of ash that buried the ruins. This site offers QuickTime movies of what the destruction must have been like, as well as many illustrations and artifacts from the period.

http://www.discovery.com/news/features/pompeii/
pompeii.html

The Romans

According to this site, "Most children did not go to school. Parents had to pay for their children to go and they would only teach boys!" Other facts: Romans liked to eat mice, and they are credited with the invention of concrete. Keep exploring. There's a whole legion of ideas, crafts, and activities to make your study of the Roman empire less "Gaul"-ing.

http://www.bbc.co.uk/education/romans/

Travel to the Roman Empire

How much do you know about Roman emperors? You have heard of Julius Caesar, and maybe Nero—but did you know there were almost 80 more of them? The last one was a woman named Irene; in fact, she is considered a saint by the Greek Orthodox church. Explore this site to learn about 800 years of Roman rule. But the coolest thing on this site is watching "yesterday's" pictures of famous Roman sites morph into those of "today." This site was created by students for the ThinkQuest competition.

http://library.thinkquest.org/17740/

You won't believe how the PLANTS, TREES, AND GARDENS section grew!

A
B
C
D
E
F
G
H
I
J
K
L
M
N
O
P
Q
R
S
T
U
V
W
X
Y
Z

NET FILES

In your travels you meet a gandy dancer, a grease monkey, and a gumshoe. What mode of transportation are you using?

Answer: You're on a train. Those are all terms associated with railroads. A gandy dancer is a track laborer, a grease monkey oils cars and track parts, while a gumshoe is a railroad detective. Find out more rail jargon at *http://www.rrb.gov/funfacts3.html*

MESOPOTAMIA

Write Like a Babylonian

In ancient Babylonia they didn't have pen and ink, so they inscribed symbols in wet clay whenever they wanted to write something down. This language is called cuneiform, and it was used for about 3,000 years prior to the first century B.C. The clay tablets were baked in order to make them permanent. (Wouldn't it be funny to tell your teacher your homework was "still in the oven!") Type in your initials and have the ancient scribes translate them into cuneiform.

http://home.korax.net/~websiter/cgi-bin/
   cuneiform.cgi

You Be the Judge on Hammurabi's Code

Whenever people decide to form a community, they have to agree on acceptable social behavior in order for things to work smoothly. Hammurabi, the "Priest-King," ruled ancient Babylon (ca. 1792–1750 B.C.) and united Mesopotamia under a code of law. There were 282 laws dealing with a variety of crimes and abuses. Solve some of the problems Hammurabi faced; for example, what should happen if a boy slaps his father?

http://members.nbci.com/pmartin/hammurabi/
   homepage.htm

ANIMALS

See also species of animals, such as BIRDS; CATS; DINOSAURS; DOGS; FISH; HORSES; and SHARKS; and also see animal categories such as AMPHIBIANS; FARMING AND AGRICULTURE; INSECTS AND SPIDERS; INVERTEBRATES; MAMMALS; REPTILES; and also ENDANGERED AND EXTINCT SPECIES; PETS AND PET CARE; and ZOOS. Check the animal's name in the index at the back of this book if you're not sure in which category to look.

Alaska Wildlife Notebook Series

Here's a great reference resource of pictures and facts about animals, birds, fish, and other creatures found in Alaska, including polar bears, moose, eagles, otter, and salmon. Many of the animals are also common in other states.

http://www.state.ak.us/adfg/notebook/notehome.htm

🦆 Animaland! from The ASPCA

The American Society for the Prevention of Cruelty to Animals has a warm, fuzzy Web site for you to enjoy! Read stories about how kids like you are helping animals every day. You might volunteer at an animal shelter, or assist in capturing stray cats so that they can be neutered. If you'd like to have a career working with animals, you could always become a veterinarian or a zookeeper, or perhaps an arachnologist. What's that? Visit this Web site and see!

http://www.animaland.org/

BillyBear4Kids.com Animal Scoop

Everything at this site involves animals. Print the bear domino tiles for a fun matching game you can play over and over. Make some cute animal bookmarks. Then try some of the online activities. Can you guess which animal wants you to tickle his toes? When you've giggled through that one, and brayed at the virtual pin the tail on the donkey game, help Clarence clean up the barnyard (watch where you walk!).

http://www.billybear4kids.com/animal/scoop.htm

Casting Animal Tracks

A few years ago we discovered raccoons had made tracks in the mud near our house. They were clear tracks, and we could see every detail of their pads and claws. We thought it would be fun to make plaster of Paris casts of these tracks so we could look at them forever. This Web site shows you how to do it. If you don't have a wild animal about, make a cast of your own footprint or hand print, or your dog's.

http://freeweb.pdq.net/headstrong/track.htm

🐦 Davis' Farmland

Besides farm mazes, crosswords, and coloring pages, our favorite part of the site is the section on animal sounds. Click to hear the dog bark, the pig oink, and the kitty meow. There are 15 other sounds for you to enjoy—well, maybe 14, it's hard to enjoy the screaming peacock! Click on "More animal sounds" to hear animals you won't see at Davis' Farmland.

http://www.davisfarmland.com/fun/funpages.htm

Kids Go Wild at the Wildlife Conservation Society

Try the online coloring book—you don't have to stay within the "lions." Other parts of the site include wild animal facts, wildlife news, and information for those who want to join the club.

http://wcs.org/5675/kidsgowild

Nature: Inside the Animal Mind

When you go to school, does your cat miss you? Or does she just roll over and go to sleep? You love your dog, but is he capable of loving you back? Explore animal intelligence, emotions, and instincts at this fascinating multimedia site.

http://www.wnet.org/nature/animalmind/

★ Nature Puzzles and Fun

Don't miss this terrific collection of interactive animal games. Test your knowledge of Mongolian horses and culture as you race across the steppe, learn sign language with Koko the gorilla, try dogsledding 101, and check out the life-forms in the virtual tide pool. If that's not enough of a challenge, try the three-sided jigsaw puzzle.

http://www.pbs.org/wnet/nature/fun.html

★ Natureworks

Animals use many different methods of communication. You can hear a wolf howl, or listen to a cat purr. You know something's amiss when you see a horse put his ears back, and you can tell by a splendid wagging tail that a dog is excited and happy. Animals also use scent to spread their messages. An angry skunk can really make his feelings known, but did you know when a cat rubs against you, she's really "marking" you as her territory? Scent glands around the cat's mouth and forehead leave a residue warning competing cats to stay away. Natureworks is chock-full of interesting tidbits like this. Learn about animals, plants, ecology, and lots more at this terrific site.

http://www.nhptv.org/natureworks/nw4.htm

What did grandma do when she was a kid? There is a list of questions to ask in GENEALOGY AND FAMILY HISTORY.

A
B
C
D
E
F
G
H
I
J
K
L
M
N
O
P
Q
R
S
T
U
V
W
X
Y
Z

A
B
C
D
E
F
G
H
I
J
K
L
M
N
O
P
Q
R
S
T
U
V
W
X
Y
Z

Sounds of the World's Animals

Everybody knows that a dog's bark is "woof-woof," right? Well, not everybody knows that! A French dog says, "ouah ouah," while a Japanese dog says, "wanwan." In Sweden, the dogs say, "vov vov," and in the Ukraine, you'll find them saying, "gaf-gaf." This is a Web page full of what the world thinks various animals sound like. There's an audio sound file for some animals, so you can hear and decide for yourself which language "says it best."

http://www.georgetown.edu/cball/animals/
  animals.html

★ Virtual Wildlife

Just opening this page may startle you if the computer's volume is turned up! But there's no need to be frightened. The animals here just want you to learn more about them. In the Remarkable Animals section, visit twelve strange creatures, including the "climbing perch"—a fish that doesn't really climb trees but can walk to the next pond if his water source evaporates! Check out the Wild Places area for information about ten different habitats and what animals you might spy there. The Animal List features pictures and loads of facts about even more animals, from zebras to whales. This site is hosted by the World Wildlife Fund.

http://www.panda.org/kids/wildlife/wildlife.htm

Yellowstone's Antler & Horn Match Game for Kids

Whose horns are these, anyway? Match the antlers to their rightful owners and you'll win. Watch out you don't create a "jackalope" by mistake!

http://www.nps.gov/yell/kidstuff/AHgame/

If you forgot the words to "gopher guts" try lyrics in MUSIC AND MUSICIANS.

Zoobooks Kids Menu

Here's a question from the animal quiz: "I swim and feed in the kelp beds off the coast of California. It's rare that I come to shore; I even sleep at sea. So we do not get swept away by ocean currents, I twist myself and my baby in the kelp. I use 'tools' to open shells; crabs are one of my favorite foods. Who am I?" The answer choices are pilot whale, dolphin, sea otter, seal, or whale. What do you think? You "otter" know the answer if you spend a little time around this site!

http://www.zoobooks.com/gatewayPages/
  gateway1Kids.html

ANTARCTICA

See EARTH SCIENCE— LAND FEATURES—POLAR REGIONS

AQUARIUMS

See also FISH

Aquaria

Can you raise native fish and minnows in your fish tank? Is your aquarium getting smothered by too many snails? Interested in finding out about African clawed frogs? Wondering about the lighting in your tank, but don't know how to spell "fluorescent"? (This site explains how: "u" comes before the "o." Just remember there is no flour in fluorescent lights.) Some of these answers are otherwise hard to find on the Net, but here they are collected all in one place.

http://www.geocities.com/CapeCanaveral/4742/
  aquaria.html

The Sun never sets on the Internet.

Cathy's Homepage of Tropical Fishkeeping

A tank of colorful fish can be an educational and fun hobby, but keeping the aquarium looking nice can be a lot of work. How much work? Check out the beginner information and the answers to frequently asked questions, and then send some fishy electronic postcards to your friends. The annotated list of links alone is well worth your visit.

http://www.tropicalfishkeeping.com/

🐢 The Monterey Bay Aquarium

Visit the Monterey Bay Aquarium page and get a diver's-eye view of the fish in the kelp forest tank. Maybe you'll see sharks, rockfish, and eels that inhabit the underwater seaweed forests. Don't miss the interactive exhibit called Splash Zone. It offers lots of online fun, and you'll learn about rock and reef homes for sea creatures, too. The Learning Center features the kids' E-Quarium where you can just choose a habitat and explore. Will you select the sandy sea floor, the deep sea, or the rocky shore?

http://www.mbayaq.org/

★ National Aquarium in Baltimore - Animals

The National Aquarium in Baltimore, Maryland, offers this wonderful Web page on some of their more popular species. See animated jellyfish, learn about horseshoe crabs, and bone up on invertebrates such as sea anemones. You'll also find a good deal of information on poison dart frogs and venomous fish, if you dare to read it! There's a fun matching game, too; and if you're a real fish fanatic, visit the section on setting up a home saltwater aquarium.

http://www.aqua.org/animals/

★ The New England Aquarium

Perched on the wharf in Boston Harbor is the New England Aquarium. You can join Stefan on a virtual whale watch—maybe you'll see some humpbacks on your day trip out on the water. Inside the building, there's a giant ocean tank containing more than 200,000 gallons of water! The 50-ish sea turtle, Myrtle, can usually be found snoozing on the bottom, so be sure to look for her if you visit Boston. In the Learn section of this site, there are some science projects for you to try—how about making your own miniature deep-sea vent?

http://www.neaq.org/

The North American Native Fishes Association

The sailfin shiner, the lyre goby, and the tesselated darter are all native North American fishes. Read about conservation efforts to protect them and many other native species at this site. Some stream-dwelling fishes may be successfully kept in a riffle tank, which is a special aquarium with a flowing current. You can learn how to set up one at this site (look in the Information Resources area).

http://www.nanfa.org/

Model T Road Trip

Follow along in Jenny's 1919 diary as her parents decide to purchase a Model T automobile and go on a road trip vacation. Learn about the history of the Ford Motor Company and enjoy the family's adventures as they drive along rural dirt roads. Sooner or later you'll have to help start the Model T, among other interactive activities (it sure was hard to do).

http://www.hfmgv.org/smartfun/welcome.html

A B C D E F G H I J K L M N O P Q R S T U V W X Y Z

SeaWorld/Busch Gardens Animal Information Database

Do you ever wish you could visit SeaWorld in Florida, Ohio, Texas, or California? You can find out about all kinds of fish here and also learn about parrots, polar bears, gorillas, lions, and more. Interested in setting up a tropical saltwater aquarium? This page tells you how to keep an aquarium as a hobby. Write, e-mail, or phone Shamu the Killer Whale to ask questions about the ocean and marine animals. From the Animal Resources area, don't miss the SeaWorld Songbook—the whale rap is hilarious! Check out the wide variety of educational programs and curriculum materials on endangered rain forests, ecosystems, and habitat. Surprise your grandmother with her very own pet "coral reef"—find out how to grow one at the top of the coral reef area of this site. New this year: give a listen to the animal sounds library!

http://www.seaworld.org/

NET FILES

What year was the first commercial radio broadcast?

Answer: Although experimental radio broadcasts took place in the early 1900s, formal "broadcasting" is usually considered to have begun on November 2, 1920, when Westinghouse's KDKA-Pittsburgh broadcast the Harding-Cox presidential election returns (Harding won).

http://www.pbs.org/wgbh/aso/databank/entries/dt20ra.html

★ Tetra

Tetra makes fish food, as well as lots of other supplies for aquarists. Even if you don't have a tank of your own, you can still experience playing with the Virtual Aquarium at this site. You don't even have to get wet! Just choose what type of tank and decorations you want, and the site will recommend some friendly fish. Then make your selections, and watch the fun. There is also information about maintaining a classroom fish tank, and links to the home pages of major public aquaria around the United States.

http://www.tetra-fish.com/va/

ARCHITECTURE

See also HISTORY—HISTORIC SITES

Arches

Have you ever wondered how medieval masons built those wonderful stone arches? This site explains it all in detail, with animations to make sure you understand the unfamiliar terms. Be sure you go through the brief tutorial; then play the game to see if you, too, can build a perfect arch.

http://www.bbc.co.uk/history/games/arches/arches.html

Architecture Through the Ages

Punch your own ticket and you're off to see some of the world's greatest architectural wonders. Choose from Mesoamerican, European, Chinese, District of Columbian, Islamic, or Egyptian architectural history. You can also explore castles and cathedrals. Learn about gothic vaults, flying buttresses, and building materials. This site was created by students for the ThinkQuest competition.

http://library.thinkquest.org/18778/

Be an Architect! Design a House with Carmine Chameleon

Learn about how site selection affects the ultimate design of a house. Draw your own floor plan and elevations, and choose your building materials. Try it yourself! Along the way you'll discover a lot about architects and how they go about designing beautiful spaces in which we can live, work, and play.

http://www.sanford-artedventures.com/play/arch2/

The Great Buildings Collection

Visit architecture's greatest hits through the ages. You'll gasp in awe at the elevation drawings of the Brooklyn Bridge, shake your head in amazement at a 3-D walkthrough of Stonehenge, and smile with pleasure when you realize that this database can be sorted in many different ways. Locate all the cool buildings in a particular city. Find all the famous buildings by a certain architect. Identify examples of airport terminals, churches, or factories. This is a fun way to learn about architectural history.

http://www.greatbuildings.com/

BRIDGES, ROADS, TUNNELS, AND DAMS

See also ARCHITECTURE

★ Discovery Online, Buildings, Bridges, and Tunnels

Spires count, but tall antennas don't when it comes to measuring the world's tallest buildings. Which one is tallest this year? It's the Petronas Towers in Kuala Lumpur, Malaysia, soaring to 1,483 feet. Follow a twentieth century time line of the world's tallest buildings and learn how high we may be able to build the next ones. Other parts of this site reveal how bridges and tunnels are constructed. Check the How to Build a Tunnel game and see if you can match famous tunnels with the techniques used to engineer them.

http://www.discovery.com/stories/technology/buildings/buildings.html

Golden Gate Bridge, Highway, and Transportation District

San Francisco's most beautiful bridge is the Golden Gate. It's not painted gold; it's painted a color called international orange. The name of the bridge comes from the location it spans: the Golden Gate Strait, which is the entrance to the San Francisco Bay from the Pacific Ocean. This site offers history, photos, and answers to trivia questions such as "Has the bridge ever been closed?" The answer is yes: it was closed several times due to 70 mph winds and again a few times for visiting dignitaries.

http://www.goldengate.org/

Hoover Dam - A National Historic Landmark

Built to tame the flooding of the Colorado River, Hoover Dam was completed in 1935. A wonder of clever engineering, the dam is 726 feet tall—much higher than the Washington Monument, which is 555 feet tall. At this site you can take a virtual tour and also learn about the people who built it.

http://www.hooverdam.usbr.gov/

NOVA Online - Super Bridge

Deadlines, deadlines. You're an expert bridge-building civil engineer, charged with spanning four different gaps, from 120 to 5,000 feet. What type of bridge will you propose for each location? Play the Shockwave matching game and see how well you do. There's also a terrific set of links for further study.

http://www.pbs.org/wgbh/nova/bridge/

CHURCHES, TEMPLES, MOSQUES, AND SYNAGOGUES

See also RELIGION AND SPIRITUALITY

Looking for the State Bird or the State Motto? It's in the UNITED STATES—STATES section.

A
B
C
D
E
F
G
H
I
J
K
L
M
N
O
P
Q
R
S
T
U
V
W
X
Y
Z

A
B
C
D
E
F
G
H
I
J
K
L
M
N
O
P
Q
R
S
T
U
V
W
X
Y
Z

NET FILES

What plants attract butterflies?

Answer: Many flowering plants attract butterflies, and others help feed their caterpillars. Some of these are milkweed, lantana, lilac, cosmos, goldenrod, and zinnia. If you flutter by, you can find out more at http://www.butterflies.com/guide.html

Cathedral Calls

The layout of a Christian cathedral is usually in the form of a cross. The long nave is perpendicular to the crossing transept. Improve your knowledge of these architectural elements and find out how Medieval stonemasons rocked their world. Fly though a 3-D cathedral (if you have the right plug-in) and try "painting" the exterior of Wells Cathedral in the online game. There are also links to major British cathedral Web sites.

http://www.bbc.co.uk/history/programmes/cathedral/

Washington National Cathedral

On the highest point in Washington, D.C., is a beautiful interfaith cathedral. It is decorated with 107 carved stone gargoyles and untold numbers of grotesques. A grotesque is like a gargoyle in that it redirects rainwater, except it has no pipe inside and the water runs over the outside of the carving. The cathedral also has wonderful stained glass windows inside. The western rose window contains over 10,500 pieces of glass! Along the inside aisle is another window commemorating the flight of Apollo 11. It holds a real piece of moon rock. In addition to many U.S. presidents, Dr. Martin Luther King, Jr., and Indira Gandhi have spoken from the pulpit. Helen Keller is among the famous Americans buried beneath the cathedral.

http://www.cathedral.org/cathedral/

★ Westminster Abbey - Place of Worship and House of Kings

This London landmark has been the site of every British coronation since 1066. Many kings and queens are entombed at the Abbey, notably Elizabeth I. You'll also find Chaucer's grave in the Poets' Corner, along with those of other famous English authors, including Lewis Carroll. The Abbey has been the scene of numerous royal ceremonies, royal weddings, and other important events. The funeral of Diana, Princess of Wales, was held at Westminster Abbey on September 6, 1997. Admire the inspiring Gothic architecture as you wander around with the other tourists at this site.

http://www.westminster-abbey.org/

GOVERNMENT AND PUBLIC BUILDINGS

Discovery Online, Secrets of the Great Wall

Stretching 4,500 miles, the Great Wall of China is one of only a few man-made structures visible from space. In fact, check the satellite photo at this site to see it for yourself! More than 2,000 years old, the wall was built to keep out enemies from the north. Nowadays, it's a popular tourist attraction. Who built the wall? Find out here!

http://www.discovery.com/stories/history/greatwall/
greatwall.html

★ Empire State Building - New York City

It's big, it's historic, it's got a big gorilla climbing up it! OK, we were just kidding about that last part—that only happened in the movies. Besides the monkeyshines you remember in King Kong, about 90 other movies have featured the Empire State Building. In case you were wondering, the building is about 1,454 feet (OK, exactly 1,453 feet, 8 9/16 inches), or 443.2 meters, tall, to the top of the lightning rod. There are 1,860 stairs from street level to the 102nd floor. Every year a race is held to see who can climb them the fastest. The course distance is .2 miles. In 2001, the winning time was 9 minutes 37 seconds.

http://www.esbnyc.com/html/
empire_state_building.html

★ The Official Site of the Eiffel Tower

Symbol of Paris, the Eiffel Tower was finished on March 31, 1889. How tall is it? Well, in 1889 it was 1,024.5 feet (312.27 meters) high, including the flagpole. But in 1994, it grew an antenna and got taller: now it's 1,045.6 feet (318.7 meters) high. Visit this site to learn all about the history of the tower and activities and things you can see at each level. Don't like the color of this famous landmark? Choose to Play with the Tower (in the Summary section) and try various fashion statements of your own. We like the giraffe look, or perhaps the cloud camouflage. Check the QuickTime streaming video of the fireworks on January 1, 2000!

http://www.tour-eiffel.fr/indexuk.html

★ The Tower of London

The Traitor's Gate. The Bloody Tower. The Ceremony of the Keys. The Crown Jewels. The Tower of London has been a treasury, a prison, and a government building for a thousand years. It is said that if the ravens that inhabit the Tower green ever leave, the Commonwealth of Great Britain will fall. You can take a tour of the Tower and its grounds right here. But don't scare the ravens!

http://www.camelot-group.com/tower_site/

★ U.S. Capitol Virtual Tour - A "Capitol" Experience

Tour the U.S. Capitol in Washington, D.C. There are some virtual reality views of areas such as the Old Supreme Court Chamber, and you can press the space bar to locate "hot spots" to click for more information. You'll learn the history of the building, too. On September 18, 1793, George Washington laid the first cornerstone for the Capitol. The dome is made of cast iron and was erected during the Civil War. The pictures of the building's construction are fascinating.

http://www.senate.gov/vtour/

The truth is out there in UFOS AND EXTRATERRESTRIALS. Maybe.

LIGHTHOUSES

Lighthouse Getaway

It's a foggy night, and a ship is lost amid the black waves, with shoals and rocks somewhere out ahead. Suddenly, the darkness is pierced by a friendly light in the distance. It's the lighthouse! Checking the navigational map, the ship's captain notes the location of the lighthouse on shore and is able to steer clear of danger. Part of American lore and legend, lighthouses all over America (and now, Ireland) can be visited via this home page. You'll find pictures and descriptions of lights from New England, through the Great Lakes, around the South Atlantic, and to the West Coast. There are also links to Lighthouse Societies and something about the history of the Fresnel lens, which produces the powerful light needed.

http://lighthousegetaway.com/

Lighthouse Heritage

Many lighthouses and historic ships may be seen at America's national parks. This site offers photos of the buildings and provides interesting information about each one. For example, the current Boston Harbor lighthouse was first lit in 1783 and is still operational. Its original light source was tallow candles, but now it has a "second order Fresnel lens." As old as it is, this lighthouse is not the first at this location. The original stone tower was built in 1716, but it was blown up by the British in 1776.

http://www.cr.nps.gov/maritime/lt_index.htm

UNUSUAL

Lucy the Elephant, Margate, NJ

Lucy is a famous elephant-shaped building in Margate City, New Jersey. She dates back to 1881, built by a realtor to advertise his business development plans. It took one million pieces of lumber for the structure and 12,000 feet of tin for the elephant's skin. You can climb up spiral staircases inside the legs to get to the rooms inside. She is 65 feet high—as tall as a six-story building. From the top, you get a great view of the beach. Remember to keep your cool souvenir ticket to prove you walked through an elephant!

http://www.lucytheelephant.org/

A
B
C
D
E
F
G
H
I
J
K
L
M
N
O
P
Q
R
S
T
U
V
W
X
Y
Z

A
B
C
D
E
F
G
H
I
J
K
L
M
N
O
P
Q
R
S
T
U
V
W
X
Y
Z

NOVA Online - Fall of the Leaning Tower

The famous Leaning Tower of Pisa may have been saved by a group of engineers who can actually "steer" the tower in any direction by removing some of the soil underneath the foundation. Early tests have been quite successful. Read about how this method works and find out how other monuments around the world are being stabilized and preserved.

http://www.pbs.org/wgbh/nova/pisa/

ART

See also CLOTHING; COLOR AND COLORING BOOKS; COMICS, CARTOONS, AND ANIMATION; and CRAFTS AND HOBBIES

Art Safari

Would you like to go on a safari to see some animals? You don't even have to leave the room! These animals aren't real, they live only in artworks, and your job is to look carefully and describe what you think is happening in the picture. You can save your story for others to read later. Some of the stories are very imaginative! There is also a fun drawing activity for you to try. Use "rubber stamp" shapes to create a fantastic animal of your own, and then color the picture using your electronic paints.

http://artsafari.moma.org/

The Incredible Art Department

A shifty-eyed Mona Lisa welcomes you to explore this intriguing toolbox of art lessons, projects, cartoons about art, and art news. But don't mind her, jump right in and explore. In the Art Lesson section you'll find projects for everyone, from preschoolers all the way up to college kids. Try some of these: Q-Tip painting, cool flip books, or aboriginal bark painting.

http://www.artswire.org/kenroar/

KinderArt

Tired of coloring books and crayon drawings? Get ready for a whole new artist's palette of ideas, techniques, and tools at this site. Lots of hands-on projects, holiday activities, and tips on how to make your own chalk, clay, and painted sand! There's a glossary of art terms and even a virtual fridge to display your work alongside the work of others from around the globe.

http://www.kinderart.com/lessons.htm

★ A Lifetime of Color

Explore color mixing and matching activities and learn how the "mood" of a painting changes if you magically switch to different colors. Learn about proportions and portrait techniques. Little children will enjoy the color wheel game, while bigger ones (and adults, too) will be fascinated with chasing down the evil Dr. Gray and his Dechromatizers.

http://www.sanford-artedventures.com/

Virtual HandsOn

Have you ever wanted to try a potter's wheel to shape a clay pot, vase, or goblet? This Shockwave game will let you see how it works, without the mess. Drag your mouse up to create more clay coils, then right or left to help shape the pot. There's also an electric kiln to fire, an experiment in dry clay mixing, and an electric chalkboard. Some of these games are quite large and require a lengthy download time.

http://www.handsonsite.com/handson/virtual/hol.html

ART HISTORY AND MUSEUMS

★ Artcyclopedia: The Guide to Museum-Quality Art on the Internet

If you only had more Monet to buy Degas to make the Van Gogh, you might be able to get to a museum to see art like this. But until then, visit a spectrum of museums online. Searchable by the name of the artist or museum, this site Rubens, er, rules!

http://www.artcyclopedia.com/

> **What time is it, anyway? Check with the atomic clock in TIME.**

ArtLex - Dictionary of Visual Art

From Baroque to Pop Art, from Realism to Renaissance—all those confusing art terms are defined here, along with notes on how to pronounce them. Included are over 3,100 techniques, styles, and art history words. Here's the best part: the dictionary is illustrated; and not only that, there are links to other Web pages with more information.

http://www.artlex.com/

★ Ghost of the de Young

If you think visiting an art museum sounds more boring than, say, sorting out the letters in your bowl of alphabet soup, then you should read this online comic book. Seems Irene and Farley are trying to take Irene's daughter, Olive, to the de Young art museum in San Francisco's Golden Gate Park. Olive wants to go to Disneyland instead. Mom and Farley leave Olive on a lobby bench (with a guard nearby) while they visit a special exhibit. Suddenly, the ghost of Mr. de Young himself appears and takes Olive on a very special tour of some of the museum's masterpieces! Follow along on this humorous 72-page story. (Hint: Load all the pictures first, and then read them with the family.)

http://www.thinker.org/fam/education/publications/ghost/

Impressionism

Lessons on the art movement called impressionism are featured here. They will help you learn to look closely at a painting and its shapes, colors, and objects. Included are works by Van Gogh, Cézanne, Renoir, and others. Go to the Experience Impressionism section for a quick and entertaining tour to this style of art, considered radical and revolutionary in its time.

http://www.impressionism.org/

The Impressionists

Explore the colors, brushwork, and themes of several magnificent impressionist paintings, and then try to re-create one yourself. Select an outline canvas, a brush, and your color palette, and then try to stay within the lines. When you're done, you can even select your favorite frame and print it. Will your masterpiece ever hang in the Louvre?

http://www.biography.com/impressionists/

★ Inside Art: An Art History Game

You're being dragged around the art museum with your parents. It's hot, your feet hurt, and you're simply bored, bored, bored. Wait—the colors in that artwork: they seem to be moving. The swirling vortex leaps off the wall and inches towards you. Suddenly, you're sucked in, and now you're caught up and trapped inside the painting! You'll have to ask the help of a fish named Trish and learn some things about art technique and art history before you can escape. If you manage to get out of this dilemma, there are other adventures available—just follow Carmine the chameleon.

http://www.eduweb.com/insideart/

Miami Museum of Science - The pH Factor

Is something an acid or a base? You need to know that if you're going to the lab! Use the online "pH panel" machine to explore the pH of common household solutions such as virtual lemon juice, borax, vinegar, and Lava soap. Then check out the real kitchen chemistry experiments you can try with an adult. Some involve toothpicks and gumdrops, while others require more elaborate preparations. http://www.miamisci.org/ph/

A
B
C
D
E
F
G
H
I
J
K
L
M
N
O
P
Q
R
S
T
U
V
W
X
Y
Z

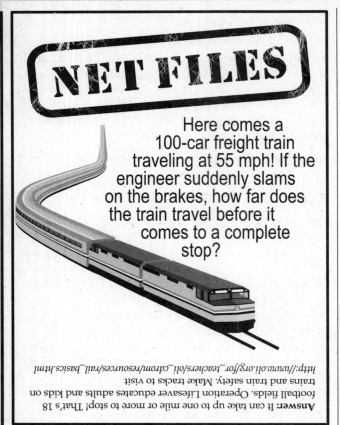

NET FILES

Here comes a 100-car freight train traveling at 55 mph! If the engineer suddenly slams on the brakes, how far does the train travel before it comes to a complete stop?

Answer: It can take up to one mile or more to stop! That's 18 football fields. Operation Lifesaver educates adults and kids on trains and train safety. Make tracks to visit

http://www.oli.org/for_teachers/oli_cdrom/resources/rail_basics.html

The Metropolitan Museum of Art

Let's read the tour brochure: "In formation since 1870, the Metropolitan Museum's collection now contains more than two million works of art from all points of the compass, ancient through modern times. About 3,500 objects are reproduced here as a first installment, as well as the entire Department of European Paintings—with the online equivalent of wall labels." Hmmm, maybe we should think about spending the whole day exploring this one site! This world-class art museum is located in New York City. If you visit the virtual version, you'll see suits of armor, Egyptian antiquities, Asian art, twentieth century art, sculpture, and lots of famous art masterpieces. Don't miss the Explore & Learn section, which is especially for kids. In it, you can search for animals woven into an Indian carpet, wander around an interactive time line of art history, or ponder what color "celadon" might happen to be.

http://www.metmuseum.org/

★ Monet at Giverny

Turn-of-the-century French artist Claude Monet is famous for his dreamy, misty garden and water lily paintings. His garden at Giverny has been reproduced online so you can stroll about and see where some of Monet's works were created. Select either the flower or water garden and begin your exploration. As you move the miniature Monet around, photographs, paintings, and facts will appear. See if you can find a painting of a Japanese bridge.

http://www.mmfa.qc.ca/visite-vr/anglais/

National Museum of American Art

Browse these pages and take a walk through American history. Or, if you're in a playful mood, stop in at the Education section and select the Kid's area. There you'll meet Cappy, a very unusual giraffe, who will take you on a special museum tour he calls Bottlecaps to Brushes. It will give you a whole new appreciation of art and artists, plus some great ideas for activities you can do at home.

http://www.nmaa.si.edu/

★ Sanford & A Lifetime of Color: Study Art

Stroll through a time line of art history, and explore famous art movements or styles such as baroque, gothic, impressionism, abstract, art deco, and many more. There's also a quick encyclopedic tour to the elements of art (color, form, line, shape, space, texture, and value) as well as its principles, such as balance, contrast, and emphasis. Finally, if you don't want to mix your media, there's a section explaining the differences among acrylic, oil paint, tempera, and other types of art materials.

http://www.sanford-artedventures.com/study/study.html

Vincent Van Gogh

Do you know Van Gogh? You will after you visit this site. Discover his artworks and learn the facts about his life, "the ear incident," and his struggle with epilepsy. There's a quiz and a word search game, too. This site was created by students for the ThinkQuest Junior competition.

http://tqjunior.advanced.org/6382/

DRAWING AND PAINTING

Art Studio Chalkboard

Have you ever heard of "one point perspective"? What type of paintbrush offers which effect? Confused by color theory? This excellent tutorial focuses on the technical fundamentals of perspective, shading, and color in drawing and painting.

http://www2.evansville.edu/studiochalkboard/

Big Brush Watercolor Lessons by Peter Humeniuk

If you've ever wondered how watercolor artists get those beautiful blended and muted colors, take the free lesson offered here. See how the artist uses really big brushes and cut-up credit cards to create a realistic-looking grove of birch trees.

http://www.Bigbrush.com/

🦆 Flipper

You'll need Java enabled on your browser to get this fun drawing tool to work. Run your mouse over the drawing board, and all the little flippers will turn over. By manipulating the flippers up or down, you can make four different color values, and some very cool drawings.

http://www.mowa.org/kids/art/X3/flipperfr2.html

Kali

Is it art or is it math? It doesn't matter, let's just call it fun! Kali is a geometry program that makes cool symmetrical patterns based on your instructions, which are easily entered by clicking on pictures and buttons. The designs are suitable for framing or just coloring.

http://www.geom.umn.edu/apps/kali/about.html

🦆 Learn to Draw With Billy Bear - A Project 4 Kids

Grab your colored pencils, crayons, or your computer drawing software and join Billy Bear's art class. Step by step, you'll learn how to draw several perky animals, including a funny frog and a sleepy lion. There are also coloring sheets if you don't want to make your own outlines.

http://www.billybear4kids.com/Learn2Draw/
Learn2Draw.html

Mark Kistler's Imagination Station

The real world is in three dimensions: objects have width, length, and depth. In a drawing, you have only two dimensions to work with: length and width. You have to use special techniques to simulate the third dimension of depth. No problem—Mark's here to give you 3-D drawing lessons. You say you can't even draw a straight line? Mark claims it doesn't matter. Soon you'll be talking about the 12 Renaissance secrets of 3-D drawing right along with him.

http://www.draw3d.com/

🦆 NIEHS Kids Page - Shapes & Patterns/ Spirograph & 3D Models

Do you love to draw patterns? At this site there's an electronic toy that will draw complicated patterns for you. When your parents were kids, they had to draw this type of design using clumsy toys that were actually mechanically geared tools. Their pens and gears were always slipping, and it took forever to draw the final image. Now you can "draw" them by moving the slider buttons on this Web page. Isn't technology wonderful? We also loved the interactive chemical models and other features on the page.

http://www.niehs.nih.gov/kids/jvspiro.htm

If you feel funny, think what we went through when we wrote the JOKES AND RIDDLES section!

A B C D E F G H I J K L M N O P Q R S T U V W X Y Z

Not everything on the Net is true.

★ The @rt Room

Explore art "sparkers"—activities to jump start your brain into its most creative thinking. For example, draw a storm, or a picture of your favorite hero. You can learn to "think like an artist" by exploring "@rtrageous" ways to make the familiar strange, and see the world in a completely new light. Play artist scrabble and art trivia, or view artwork from kids around the world. You can also find out all about the greatest art theft of the twentieth century: the day the *Mona Lisa* was stolen!

http://www.arts.ufl.edu/art/rt_room/

★ Van Gogh at Etten

This beautiful, appealing site was created by students for the ThinkQuest competition. It details not only Van Gogh's early career as an artist, but a special billboard project in 1990. Students created huge copies of famous Van Gogh paintings and installed them alongside the highway in celebration of Van Gogh's 100th birthday.

http://library.thinkquest.org/C001734/

★ What Is a Print?

You know what a fingerprint is. Press your finger against a mirror or a window and see what your own fingerprint looks like. Of course, your parents will want you to clean it off afterwards! Did you know some artworks are made using a printing process? Visit this interactive site to try making a virtual woodcut, an etching, a lithograph, and a screen print. You'll have to manipulate the online tools in order to see the print take shape right before your eyes!

http://www.moma.org/whatisaprint/flash.html

GLASS

Glass Works: The Story of Glass and Glass-Making in Canada

This virtual exhibit from the Canadian Museum of Civilization may shatter any preconceived notions you have about the history of glassmaking. You will clearly see how glass is made and how it is used. In "panestaking" detail, you will learn about everything from industrial to inspirational glass. This site offers a window into the glittering realm of glass: come see!

http://www.civilization.ca/membrs/canhist/verre/veint00e.html

Kokomo Opalescent Glass

Visit a stained glass factory, where they create beautiful glass shimmering with opalescent colors. Take the virtual tour to see this process. A mixture of glass is shoveled, by hand, into the "twelve-pot furnace," which is heated to a temperature exceeding 2400 degrees Fahrenheit. Over a 17-hour period, all the glass melts into a liquid. The "table man" rings a bell every minute and a half, which means it's time to pour another sheet of glass. The men use large ladles to scoop up the fiery hot glass. Then, "ladles full and cooling fast, the ladlers run to the mixing table. They keep the glass in constant motion to keep it from cooling unevenly on the way. Trailing molten threads behind them, as many as five people (one for each color in the sheet) converge on the mixing table. Tread carefully, assume everything is hot, and if you smell rubber burning you better check your own shoes first!" Visit the site to learn the rest of the process, see many samples of colors and patterns, and be inspired by the windows displayed in the online gallery.

http://www.kog.com/

Mr. Spock agrees it is highly logical to want to know all about STAR TREK, STAR WARS, AND SPACE EPICS.

A Resource for Glass

No one knows who first made glass. Pliny, the Roman historian, said the first glass was made by mistake. According to his account, Phoenician sailors landed on a beach to make a cooking fire. They propped up their pot using a block of natron, a naturally occurring alkali used in the mummification process, that they were carrying as cargo. As the fire got hotter, the sand beneath it melted. When it later cooled, the material hardened into glass. This site, from the Corning Museum of Glass, will tell you about the history of glassmaking and the properties of glass. Learn how making fudge can teach you about the making of glass!

http://www.cmog.org/page.cfm?page=77

MASKS

Faces of the Spirits

Doctors wear masks so they won't spread germs. Kids celebrating Halloween wear masks for a different reason: they want you to believe they are someone or something else! Sometimes masks have religious or sacred meaning, while others are worn just for fun. Explore some African masks at this colorful site. A caution to parents: some of these masks may be frightening (but then, sometimes that's the idea).

http://cti.itc.virginia.edu/~bcr/
   African_Mask_Faces.html

Maskmaking

If you'd like to make a really special mask, why not try this activity? You need the type of plaster bandages commonly used to make casts for broken bones, plus a few other supplies. Also, you can't make this type of mask on yourself, so you'll need a trustworthy assistant to help. After the mask is dry, it can be carved, painted, or otherwise decorated. Check this site for ideas and links to more magical masks.

http://www.artlex.com/ed/Maskmaking.html

SCULPTURE
Christo & Jeanne-Claude

Most sculptors make artwork from stone, metals, or other substances. Christo and Jeanne-Claude make artwork out of landscapes. For example, there was the *Running Fence*. Made of shimmering white fabric, it was 5.5 meters (18 feet) high and ran 40 kilometers (24.5 miles). It began north of San Francisco and followed rolling hills until at last it dropped down to the Pacific Ocean at Bodega Bay. It was completed on September 10, 1976, and remained in place for two weeks. More recent projects include fabric panels above the Arkansas River (Colorado) and a special wall made of 13,000 oil barrels (Germany). What do you think these artistic statements mean? Visit the Web site to be astounded by more of Christo and Jeanne-Claude's impressive and thought-provoking large-scale sculptures.

http://christojeanneclaude.net/

★ Lizzy Visits the Sculpture Garden

Lizzy is dragged to the National Gallery of Art because her pesky brother Gordon has to do a school assignment. "Stretch your mind," says mom. Gordon is more interested in lunch than artistic expression. Lizzie's bored until she discovers a sculpture can speak to her. In fact, this Web site speaks to you as you read the story, exploring the sculpture garden right along with the children.

http://www.nga.gov/kids/lizzy/lizzy.html

NET FILES

What is Earth's oldest living tree?

Answer: As far as we know, it's a bristlecone pine tree named "Methuselah," in the White Mountains of California. It is more than 4,700 years old. Read more at http://www.sonic.net/bristlecone/intro.html

It never rains in cyberspace.

Sculpture

You might think sculptures are made only out of carved stone, but this site introduces you to four artists who use different materials. One uses old machines and gears to create sculptures, while another produces art from sand, wood, and glass. Find out what sculptors do, how they work, and what they hope to communicate through their creations.

http://www.childrensmuseum.org/artsworkshop/sculpture/

SETI@home: The Search for Extraterrestrial Intelligence

Now you can use your Win, Mac, or Unix computer to help look for alien signals! Just download the free screen saver (gee, it looks really cool while it is running). Then leave your computer on when you are not using it, and the SETI@home screen saver will come on and do its work. It does not need to be connected to the Internet. It uses your spare computer cycles to check the backlog of radio astronomy data sets, looking for signals that seem odd. When it completes a data set, it does need to connect to the Internet to transfer results. It's all explained in the FAQ. Here at Pollywood Farm, we are part of the SETI project, and you might consider joining too. You'll be doing some real science, and wouldn't it be cool if YOUR computer found the signal pattern that means off-Earth intelligence?
http://setiathome.ssl.berkeley.edu/

ASIAN AMERICANS

See also HOLIDAYS—ASIAN HOLIDAYS

AskAsia

Here's a site on Asia designed especially for K–12. There's an Information/News section, with news events about Asia, and a What's New area for recent additions to the site. For teachers, there are instructional resources, as well as a directory to other institutions. The student section offers several games and puzzles, and don't miss Teenage Tokyo, an anime-style story with some surprising plot twists!

http://www.askasia.org/

CULTURE

Chinese Calligraphy

This beautiful site explains the tools and techniques used in traditional Chinese writing, or calligraphy. You'll also learn a lot about Chinese lettering and what the various characters mean. This site was built by kids and is a ThinkQuest Junior contest finalist.

http://tqjunior.thinkquest.org/3614/

Dim Sum: A Connection to Chinese-American Culture

Could you draw the flag of China just from following written instructions, without seeing a picture of it first? Try this activity at this Web site! You can also choose to read Chinese folk tales; maybe you will be inspired to write your own. Learn about Asian animals, Chinese inventions, and lots more in this cultural cornucopia.

http://www.newton.mec.edu/Angier/DimSum/chinadimsumaconnection.html

Kid's Window

This little window on things Japanese will bring a smile to your face. Learn several origami folded figures, select items from a Japanese restaurant menu, and hear some Japanese letters and words.

http://www.jwindow.net/KIDS/

★ Living in Tokyo Is . . .

This excellent winning site from a past Cyberfair was created by over 40 kids from a school in Japan. They will tell you from experience that living in Tokyo is fun, delicious, interesting, challenging, and inspiring! You'll discover the fascinating material they present on Japanese customs, theater and music, sumo wrestling, foods, and more.

http://cyberfair.gsn.org/smis/contents.html

HISTORY

See also HISTORY—HISTORIC SITES—CALIFORNIA

Asian Pacific American Heritage Month

Did you know May is Asian Pacific American Heritage Month? It was conceived by Jenny Jew, a Chinese American woman who, with the help of friends, managed to get Congress and President George Bush to first authorize the observance in 1992. You can learn about suggested historical and cultural celebrations at this site. There is an excellent selection of links about Asian Americans in New York and elsewhere.

http://www.familyculture.com/apamonth.htm

Asian Pacific American Heritage Month Site

How many famous Asian Americans can you name? Kristi Yamaguchi (Olympic skater), Vera Wang (fashion designer), and Ann Curry (news anchor) are a few. At this site, you can read about these people and others, including Robert Nakasone, CEO of Toys 'R' Us!

http://www.abcflash.com/apa/

Bring your shovel and meet us in the TREASURE AND TREASURE-HUNTING section.

The Manzanar National Historic Site

In 1942, President Roosevelt signed an executive order authorizing the eviction and detainment of Japanese Americans. More than 120,000 were forced from their homes to be relocated and kept in remote concentration camps under harsh conditions. Although it is shocking to think that this could have happened at all, it was due to war hysteria and the belief that anyone of Japanese heritage could be a spy. Read about this chapter in America's history, and see many photographs.

http://www.nps.gov/manz/

ASTRONOMY, SPACE, AND SPACE EXPLORATION

★ Amazing Space Web-Based Activities

The Hubble Space Telescope folks offer a whole spectrum of fun Web-based activities at this site. In Star Light, Star Bright you can explore the nature of light waves and prisms. Don't miss the brain teasers in this section. Try Make a Comet and see how different "ingredients" affect the outcome. Learn fast facts about planets to collect virtual Solar System Trading Cards. Try matching photos of galaxies to their classification system names. If none of those are challenging enough, fasten your seat belts and enter the Hubble Deep Field Academy for some advanced training. Still think you're pretty good? Help plan a Hubble Space Telescope mission.

http://amazing-space.stsci.edu/

Astronomy: Our Place in Space

What's your address? You probably know your house number, street, city, and state, but that won't mean much when you meet, say, a Martian! Visit this site to learn a little song to help you remember your full address in space terms. Other activities include matching Hubble telescope pictures to their descriptions, a closer look at Mars, and a question: what would happen if gravity were suddenly turned off? Hint: many of these pages scroll sideways instead of down.

http://www.ology.amnh.org/astronomy/

A B C D E F G H I J K L M N O P Q R S T U V W X Y Z

A B C D E F G H I J K L M N O P Q R S T U V W X Y Z

Campaign for Dark Skies

"The light from the rest of the Universe takes hundreds, thousands, or millions of years to reach our eyes. What a pity to lose it on the last moment of its journey!" Yet, that's what happens when light from Earth "pollutes" the night sky. Instead of stars, we see a glowing sky, as light from cities, street lamps, and other terrestrial sources streaks upwards instead of down on the ground where we need it. This useless light is scattered by moisture and dust particles in the atmosphere, which produces the glowing effect. This is important to astronomers, who need as much darkness as possible, but it's also important to everyone else. A dark night sky, spangled with stars, is our heritage as humans. Read all about the various campaigns that say "Let there be dark!" A particularly good introduction may be found at <http://www.dark-skies.freeserve.co.uk/cfds/info/inf003.htm>.

http://www.dark-skies.freeserve.co.uk/

★ Cosmic Dust: Mankind's Journey into the Unknown

Just like you, the first humans looked up at the starry night sky and said, "Wow!" Early cultures such as the Babylonians, Egyptians, Greeks, and others developed calendars from astronomical observations and calculations. Find out more about these early astronomers and how their discoveries helped future astronomers. Explore an illustrated time line of space research from the 1950s to the present, and then learn about space objects and cosmic phenomena. This beautifully designed site was created by students for the ThinkQuest competition.

http://library.thinkquest.org/17445/

Frequently Asked Questions About NASA

Can you "buy" a star? Is the U.S. government investigating UFOs? What's the "face" on Mars? Maybe you just want to get those cool space mission patches to sew onto your backpack. You might say that NASA (National Aeronautics and Space Administration) has the mother ship of all space pages. The answers are here!

http://www.nasa.gov/qanda/

How to Make Red Flashlights

If you ever go to a nighttime outdoor star party sponsored by a local astronomy society, you'll find no lights on anywhere. Whatever you do, don't use a flashlight to see where you're going! The bright light impairs people's "night vision"—that's when your eye pupils are open widest to admit the most light from distant stars. Show everyone you care. You can either put red cellophane over your regular flashlight lens, or to be really cool, make this simple electronic project using a red LED.

http://people.aero.und.edu/~nordlie/astronomy/redlight.html

Imagine the Universe

The High-Energy Astrophysics Learning Center has a hot page aimed at kids 14 and up. This is not your kid brother's astronomy Web page with cute sound effects and animated astronauts; this is serious stuff. It's got X-ray astronomy satellites, dark matter, pulsars, light curves—even a Scientist of the Month. The material is presented in such a way that you'll be sucked in from the start. . . . or is that the black hole on page four?

http://imagine.gsfc.nasa.gov/docs/

★ NASA Kids

Get ready for touchdown at this terrific site! Learn about space pioneers and astronauts, rockets and airplanes, plus space and beyond. Each section is divided into basic informational articles (called "Brain Terrain") and brand new cutting-edge stuff (called "New Frontiers"). There are suggested links for each story, and a handy pronunciation guide that pops up next to words that are marked with a little mouth. And, if you see The Mole—click on him to "dig deeper."

http://kids.msfc.nasa.gov/

NASA Multimedia Gallery

Over the years, NASA has snapped a lot of pictures. Not only that, but astronauts have shot miles of videotape, created hundreds of animations, and made thousands of audio recordings. Here's where you can find links to many of them!

http://www.nasa.gov/gallery/

★ NASA Spacelink - An Aeronautics & Space Resource for Educators

You could visit the NASA Home Page at <*http://www.nasa.gov/*>, but for kids and teachers, we like this jumping-off place better. Did you read a space-related story in yesterday's newspaper? Chances are there is something about it here, in the Hot Topics area. For more general topics, you can browse some of the most popular sites on the Web in the Cool Picks area. International Space Station stuff? Current location of launched spacecraft? If it's about space and it's the latest and greatest, then this site is a convenient shortcut to it all.

http://spacelink.nasa.gov/

NASA Television

How would you like to see pictures live from space? NASA Television has a slew of video cameras taking pictures of Earth, of weather in the vicinity of the Kennedy Space Center, and more. This site explains how you can watch over satellite TV or via several Web page locations. If there is a mission going on, you can view the shots as they come in. You will also find a large archive of past webcasts. Want your NTV? It's out of this world!

http://www.nasa.gov/ntv/

NASA's K–12 Quest Project

If you'd like to chat with NASA scientists involved in space exploration or aeronautic design, talk your teacher into signing up at this site. Frequent webcasts, chat sessions, contests, and other interactive elements help kids know firsthand what it's like to work for NASA. There's also a special section on the Women of NASA.

http://quest.arc.nasa.gov/

There's some funny business going on in the CIRCUSES AND CLOWNS section!

The Planetary Society

This nonprofit group was founded by the late astronomer Carl Sagan and others. Its mission is to encourage planetary exploration and the search for extraterrestrial life. Naturally, the Web site has links to the SETI (Search for ExtraTerrestrial Intelligence) pages, and now you can use your computer to help look for ET! You'll be doing some real science, and wouldn't it be cool if YOUR computer found the signal pattern that means off-Earth intelligence? But there's more. How about building your own Mars rover, which distant kids can control (don't worry, you can also drive their rovers). The Planetary Society also sponsors occasional contests for kids.

http://www.planetary.org/

Sky & Telescope Magazine

If you really want to know what's up in the sky this week, today, NOW!, then you've got to visit this site. It's from the publisher of *Sky & Telescope* magazine and other magazines, books, star atlases, and much more. Included are tips for backyard astronomers, including how to find and see satellites and spacecraft in the night sky overhead. You can also track the latest comet sightings, meteor forecasts, and eclipse data. There is a fabulous collection of links, too. If it's happening in space or astronomy this week, you'll find something about it here.

http://www.skypub.com/

NET FILES

In what sport would you find the following terms: bump and run, fried egg, and smothered hook?

Answer: They are all golfing terms. Find out what they mean at http://www.pga.com/instruction/glossary/

A
B
C
D
E
F
G
H
I
J
K
L
M
N
O
P
Q
R
S
T
U
V
W
X
Y
Z

Hop Pop Town

Preschoolers who love music, march right this way! Click on objects and animals to experiment with noises, sounds, and instruments. Record your own tune and play it back online. This rollicking site is fun and easy to use—with a little help from an adult or older brother or sister.
http://www.kids-space.org/HPT/

★ Sky View Cafe

Was the moon full when you were born? What constellations and planets will be visible over your house tonight? How different are the stars in another part of the world, or in another part of time? This site allows you to plug in time, location, and other selections to "see" what's up, even during the daylight hours. Check the Sample Views area to get the idea.

http://www.skyviewcafe.com/

★ Space Day

Every year, Space Day is celebrated on the Thursday before the anniversary of President John F. Kennedy's May 1961 challenge to "land a man on the moon and return him to the Earth." There are loads of related online events that day, but the official Web page is fun anytime. Try the Night Watchman and see if you can click and drag the constellations to the correct place in the sky (if you've got sound, you'll even hear the crickets!). In The Phaser, you'll learn all about the phases of the Moon (hope you know your waxing from your waning gibbous; if not, this site will teach you). And don't forget to send your friends some space postcards to show that you really get around.

http://www.spaceday.com/

★ Space Place Launch Pad

Care for some El Niño pudding? Or perhaps some Asteroid potatoes? Want to make a meat tray nanorover? Or a super sound cone? You've come to the right place: the Space Place from the Jet Propulsion Lab. Discover galaxies of cool crafts, puzzles, and information that is really "out there." We loved it.

http://spaceplace.jpl.nasa.gov/

Space Weather

Better bring your umbrella, the geomagnetic storms will be quite heavy later today. There's a chance of solar flares as well, with an expected rising solar wind. The closest asteroid to pass by us this week will miss us by more than 12 lunar distances. On a lighter note: Did you know Earth has a tail? That's what our plasma trail looks like to an outside observer. Take a space weather tutorial and find out more at this fascinating site.

http://spaceweather.com/

★ Spacekids.com

Best for elementary and middle school kids, this site offers everything from current space news to fun games and puzzles. Want to be more grown up? See how old you'd be on other planets. (Hint: on Mercury, you'd be an old geezer!) Learn about the planets, space travel, and lots more on this really cool site.

http://www.spacekids.com/

**DID YOU KNOW WRITING IN ALL CAPITAL LETTERS IS CONSIDERED YELLING?
See, isn't this nicer?
Use upper and lower-case letters in mail and chat rooms.**

★ StarChild: A Learning Center for Young Astronomers

This is a wonderful beginner's guide to astronomy. It's written for younger children and is presented in easy-to-read text. This site includes sections on general astronomy, Earth, planets, stars, galaxies, the Sun, and more. Use these pages to introduce a child (or brother or sister) to the wonders of space. You may even learn some new stuff yourself. There are two levels; Level One is for younger kids, and you can choose to have the material read to you—or sung to you, in the case of the Doppler shift song! If the material on this level is too basic for you, just click into Level Two.

http://starchild.gsfc.nasa.gov/docs/StarChild/
　StarChild.html

AURORA BOREALIS

★ Auroras 2000.com: Presented by the Exploratorium

What's the probability of seeing aurora in tonight's sky? See current photos of the Earth's auroral activity from satellites aimed at the North and South poles. Check the custom forecast for your location. Other gems at this site include activities (Make Your Own Aurora!), luminous photos and movies, and the answer to the question, "Are aurora found on other planets?"

http://www.exploratorium.edu/auroras/

★ Auroras: Paintings in the Sky

The Exploratorium science museum in San Francisco is famous for its outstanding online exhibits, and this one is no exception. View spectacular photos of aurora from Earth and from space. Find out why no two aurora are alike and why they come in different colors. One of the neat features of this site is the audio explanations, so you don't have to read; you can just listen and enjoy the dazzling pictures.

http://www.exploratorium.edu/learning_studio/
　auroras/

Be an angel and check what we've found in RELIGION AND SPIRITUALITY.

COMETS, METEORS, AND ASTEROIDS

Asteroid Comet Impact Hazards

Fueled by recent blockbuster disaster movies, worries about the possibility of a huge chunk of space rock crashing into Earth are on our minds. Will this occur in the future? If it does, what happens to us? This site helps separate the facts from the hype. Check the very complete Links section for more.

http://impact.arc.nasa.gov/

★ Asteroids: Deadly Impact @ Nationalgeographic.com

Can you solve the mystery in this adventure? Were the craters left by comets, meteors, or something else? Log in and see what you can discover. Here's your mission: "TOP SECRET — LEVEL 4 CLEARANCE REQUIRED — CLASSIFIED DATA. Welcome back, Agent Your Name Here. Sorry to clutter your desk in your absence, but I need you on these mysterious cases. All involve extraterrestrial perpetrators. You know the drill: examine the evidence in the files and on your desk, and then finger the most probable culprits. Close every case correctly and you'll get to download a clip from National Geographic Television's classified videotape of 'Asteroids: Deadly Impact.' I know you'll get to the bottom of these cases. Click here to destroy this message. —The Director."

http://www.nationalgeographic.com/features/97/
　asteroids/

A
B
C
D
E
F
G
H
I
J
K
L
M
N
O
P
Q
R
S
T
U
V
W
X
Y
Z

A
B
C
D
E
F
G
H
I
J
K
L
M
N
O
P
Q
R
S
T
U
V
W
X
Y
Z

Blast from the Past

Sixty-five million years ago, it was a very bad day for dinosaurs and a lot of other living things on Earth. That day, a huge asteroid crashed into the Gulf of Mexico, near what is now known as the Yucatan Peninsula. The hypothesis is that the asteroid, which was about 10 kilometers (6 miles) wide, vaporized on impact, but the collision blasted trillions of tons of debris into the atmosphere. All this stuff, plus ash and soot, managed to create a dark day. In fact, there were so many dark days in a row that plants couldn't get sunlight to grow, the plant eaters didn't have anything to nibble on, and lots of them couldn't survive. Read why we know what we think we know here.

http://www.nmnh.si.edu/paleo/blast/

Build Your Own Comet

If your parents won't let you stay up late to look for comets and meteors on a school night, maybe you can get your teacher to help you make one during the day, in class! This "comet recipe" includes dry ice and ammonia, so you'll need some help working with these materials, which need careful handling. You'll also find tips for introducing this activity to the classroom, along with comet facts and other links to educational resources.

http://www.noao.edu/education/igcomet/
   igcomet.html

Comets and Meteor Showers

Are any comets currently visible? Find out at this page, which gives you the latest news about sightings around the world. There's a nice selection of links, too, one of which explains the difference between a comet and a meteor. Comets are made of ice and dust, and it's important to realize that they are not on fire. As they get close to the Sun, some of the ice melts and the released dust particles form the comet's distinctive tail. Meteors are tiny dust specks that orbit the Sun and come to our attention only when they hit our atmosphere and burn up. Comets can be tracked, meteors cannot.

http://comets.amsmeteors.org/

Make Asteroid Potatoes

This activity explains where asteroids come from and gives a recipe to make edible asteroids, complete with realistic-looking craters. If you don't want to eat the result of this experiment, you can always keep your new asteroid as a pet. It won't eat much, we guarantee!

http://spaceplace.jpl.nasa.gov/ds1_ast.htm

The Natural History Museum, London - The Cosmic Football

Scientists often explore the ice of Antarctica for micrometeorites. These tiny space travelers are so small, you need a microscope to see them! They have to be collected and studied under very special conditions so that they are not contaminated. This is the story of one very unusual micrometeorite and the British scientist who unraveled its mystery. See if you can follow the clues and make the correct hypothesis about how it got its distinctive shape.

http://www.nhm.ac.uk/interactive/science-casebooks/
   cf/cf13x.html

STARDUST

The STARDUST spacecraft was launched in February 1999. Its mission: to visit Comet Wild-2, collect particles, and return them to Earth for analysis. The Jet Propulsion Lab invited kids to send their names along for the ride. The names were placed on two microchips, which will be carried back to Earth after the dance through the comet. This won't be until 2006. Until then, maybe you can find your name on the microchips—check it out! You can also find out where STARDUST is now on its three-billion-mile journey.

http://stardust.jpl.nasa.gov/

Stay skeptical—people in chat rooms aren't always who they say they are.

ECLIPSES

Espenak's Eclipse Home Page

Have you ever seen an eclipse? It's certainly an eerie event. It takes the Moon, the Sun, and Earth to make an eclipse. A solar eclipse happens when the Moon gets between Earth and the Sun and casts a shadow on Earth. A lunar eclipse occurs when Earth gets between the Moon and the Sun and casts a shadow on the Moon. All three objects have to be lined up just right in the sky for this to happen. Read about eclipses and discover the special words astronomers use to describe the event. Did you know that it's dangerous to look directly at a solar eclipse? The infrared and ultraviolet light can be very bad for your eyes! Visit the Eclipse Resources section of this site to learn how you can safely watch a projected image of an eclipse using a straw hat, a big leafy tree, or even your interlaced fingers.

http://sunearth.gsfc.nasa.gov/eclipse/eclipse.html

Total Eclipse of the Sun

When's the next solar or lunar eclipse? Where is the best place in the world to see it? Check this site! You'll also find a calendar of space events, a mailing list so you can keep up on eclipses, meteor showers, occultations, sightings, sunspots, rumors, and more. Lots of eclipse Web pages have great photography, and this one is no exception. But how many sites offer audio files? No, you can't hear the Sun say, "Hey Moon! Get out of my way!"; but the assembled crowd of astronomers and spectators does have a reaction, and you can hear it here if you use Internet Explorer.

http://eclipse.span.ch/total.htm

SOLAR SYSTEM AND PLANETS

Astronomy for Kids

No boring stuff here! It's just the facts you want to know about each planet: Where is it?; Can I see it?; What's it made out of?; and lots more. Don't miss the sky maps; they will show you the constellations as they will appear this month in the central U.S.

http://www.dustbunny.com/afk/

Astronomy Online - Explore the Mysterious Universe

This site's stunning opening sequence will leave you breathless! Once you recover, you'll be able to explore photos of many of the solar system's greatest hits. There's also a huge fact file per planet, plus a discussion board, and more links than we could count. This site was created by students for the ThinkQuest competition.

http://library.thinkquest.org/15200/

How Big Is the Solar System?

Let's say you had a bowling ball to represent the Sun and a peppercorn to represent Earth, and you chose other objects to stand in for the other planets. Do you think you could make a scale model of the solar system that would fit on a tabletop? No. Well then, would it fit in your classroom? Still no. OK, how about your school playground? Truth is, you would need 1,000 yards (or slightly less than 1 kilometer in the metric version) to perform this fascinating and unforgettable "planet walk." This is a great activity for a family picnic, too, since it's fun for both children and adults. Complete instructions are provided here.

http://www.noao.edu/education/peppercorn/pcmain.html

NET FILES

You can't go to the bank and ask for a pound of money, but if you could, how many U.S. bills would tip the scales at a pound of cash?

Answer: According to the Bureau of Engraving and Printing, "The approximate weight of a currency note is .032 troy ounces (12 ounces to a pound). There are 490 notes in a pound." Find more worthy facts at http://www.bep.treas.gov/faqforum.cfm

Is Pluto a Planet?

Wow, things are really heating up on icy Pluto! Its status as the ninth planet is under attack. Some people say Pluto isn't a planet at all, just a minor chunk of ice in the Kuiper comet belt. This page looks at the question from both sides. Get the latest word right here.

http://www.studyworksonline.com/cda/content/
    article/0,1034,NAV4-42_SAR920,00.html

The Nine Planets

Here's a site with pictures of all the planets and their moons and much, much more. How did they get their names? Find out what planets are made of and which are most dense, brightest in the sky, and so on. Many of the words are linked to a glossary; just click on a highlighted word for an explanation. Also find out which planets have the best prospects for supporting life. Earth is listed first!

http://seds.lpl.arizona.edu/nineplanets/nineplanets/
    nineplanets.html

The Nine Planets for Kids

If you thought the previous site was just a little, well, boring, try this version. It's much of the same information, but with a snazzy, much cooler wrapper.

http://www.staq.qld.edu.au/k9p/intro.htm

Solar System Exploration Home Page

If NASA's ever sent a spacecraft there, or is planning to send a spacecraft there, you'll find information about it here. You'll discover why we bother to explore space, how we overcome design challenges, and what new discoveries have been made.

http://sse.jpl.nasa.gov/

Virtual Solar System @ Nationalgeographic.com

If you have a Windows system running the Viscape SVR plug-in (free download here) you can see an amazing 3-D visualization of the solar system. If you're a Mac user, or don't want to download the plug-in, you can content yourself with the less thrilling 2-D version. At either rate, there's plenty of planetary information here.

http://www.nationalgeographic.com/solarsystem/

Weight on Different Planets

Do you know how many kilograms you weigh on Earth? (Hint: To convert pounds to approximate kilograms, take the number of pounds and divide by 2.2.) What would your weight be on other planets? Use this Shockwave simulation to experience the unbearable lightness of being on Pluto; then experiment with the others.

http://www.questacon.edu.au/html/weight.html

SOLAR SYSTEM AND PLANETS—MARS

See also ASTRONOMY, SPACE, AND SPACE EXPLORATION—SPACE EXPLORATION AND ASTRONAUTS

Mars Academy

If it were up to you to design a space mission to Mars, how would you start? You'd have to make a lot of decisions. Where will you land? Who will be your crew and what kinds of skills will they have? What sort of propulsion system will your spacecraft use? When should you launch and what should your trajectory be? Follow along as kids make these decisions, guided by scientists. This site was created by students for the ThinkQuest competition.

http://library.thinkquest.org/12145/

Mars Exploration

Since ancient times, the red planet Mars has fascinated astronomers. Only in recent years have some of the ongoing questions been answered, largely as a result of NASA's *Pathfinder*, *Surveyor*, and other missions. At this site, you will read about past, current, and future visits to Mars, including plans for human exploration. If you're too busy to go yourself, just sign up to send your name. It will travel to Mars on the *Rover*-2003 mission.

http://mars.jpl.nasa.gov/

Mission to Mars

This exemplary site, entirely built by kids, won the 1998 ThinkQuest competition's Math and Science category. You can learn all sorts of information here at Mars Academy. But the real fun starts when you can outfit and fly your own mission! You have to know a lot to design your mission, so you'd better go back to the Academy and make sure you did all the assigned homework. This site takes a long time to explore, and your mission may take many visits to complete.

http://library.thinkquest.org/11147/

SOLAR SYSTEM AND PLANETS—MOON

★ Inconstant Moon

A multimedia "tour" to this evening's Moon offers information on its current phase, prominent features you might be able to spot, and a wealth of other facts. You'll discover animations and further explanations as you explore. And that music you hear? It's the "Moonlight Sonata" of course! But if you don't like that, choose to listen to other moon-related tunes from rock, country, or other musical styles.

http://www.inconstantmoon.com/

> **Know your alphabet?
> Now try someone else's in
> LANGUAGES AND ALPHABETS.**

Parenting WebSmart Kids

How do you know if the information you find on the Internet is true? There are many ways to evaluate resources, and this Web site shows you how. Get your parents up to speed too by exploring these activities together. *http://www.websmartkids.org/*

Sky and Telescope - Touring the Moon with Binoculars

If you have a pair of binoculars, you can take a good look at the Moon and explore the dusty "seas," the rocky craters, and the craggy mountain ranges. This site offers a good lunar map, viewing instructions, and more. Watch out for the Terminator!

http://www.skypub.com/sights/moonplanets/
moontour.html

Sky & Telescope - What's a Blue Moon?

We've always heard that if there are two full moons in the same calendar month, the second is called the blue moon. *Sky & Telescope*, the authority on astronomy, has investigated the source of this popular belief. Turns out that in the past, blue moons were figured a different way. Read about the controversy here, and then celebrate blue moons both ways! For even more information about Blue Moons, visit Once in a Blue Moon <*http://www.obliquity.com/astro/bluemoon.html*>.

http://www.skypub.com/sights/moonplanets/
9905bluemoon.html

A
B
C
D
E
F
G
H
I
J
K
L
M
N
O
P
Q
R
S
T
U
V
W
X
Y
Z

SOLAR SYSTEM AND PLANETS—SUN

Primer on the Solar Space Environment

How well do you know our nearest star? Have you ever wondered how long the Sun will last before it burns out? How big are sunspots? Are they bigger than your school? Visit this site for a comprehensive description of the Sun as an energy source and its effects on life on Earth. Did you know that geomagnetic storms on the Sun can alter current flow in pipelines and really confuse homing pigeons?

http://www.sec.noaa.gov/primer/primer.html

Solar Learning Activities

You don't even need a sunny day to try some of these projects! Make your own color wheel out of paper plates and different colored cellophane, and discover why scientists use color filters to examine space. Figure out how high a satellite's orbit is, examine the rotation of the Earth, and make a sundial you can wear around your neck.

http://solar.physics.montana.edu/YPOP/Classroom/

★ Solar Max 2000.com: Presented by the Exploratorium

If it's been raining for days and you're beginning to forget what the Sun looks like, check the images at this site! See current photos of the Sun as taken from Extreme Ultraviolet Imaging Telescopes and an X-ray telescope located on satellites out in space. Or you might prefer the White Light image as seen from Big Bear Solar Observatory in New Jersey, or any of a handful of other images. There are also links to activities and Sun fun.

http://www.exploratorium.edu/solarmax/

The Sun: Man's Friend & Foe

The Sun: should it stay or should it go? Most people would say STAY, but the Sun is also a force behind terrible weather conditions and other disruptions. Find out science facts about our nearest star, as well as cultural influences the Sun has had over the centuries. This site was created by students for the ThinkQuest competition.

http://library.thinkquest.org/15215/

SPACE EXPLORATION AND ASTRONAUTS

Biosphere 2

Did you know there is a rain forest in the middle of the Arizona desert? There's also an ocean. It's true, and the most amazing part: they are both indoors! Biosphere 2 is a 7,200,000-cubic-foot sealed glass and space frame structure, and inside are seven wilderness ecosystems, or biomes, including a rain forest and a 900,000-gallon ocean. The idea was to find out how people could survive inside a sealed environment, in case we wanted to colonize other planets. Could they grow all their own food? Manufacture their own air? Recycle their own waste? The first crew of biospherians (four women and four men) entered Biosphere 2 on September 26, 1991. They remained inside for two years, emerging again on September 26, 1993. Biosphere's original experiments were very controversial, but the results were undisputed: we don't know how to successfully accomplish this mission—yet. Columbia University now operates the facility as a learning center about the greenhouse effect. See what they are up to and take a virtual tour.

http://www.bio2.edu/

Cassini-Huygens: Mission to Saturn and Titan

It was launched back in 1997, and it's begun a scenic tour of the solar system. So far, the *Cassini* spacecraft has had a couple of flyby visits to Venus and Jupiter, but its ultimate destination is Saturn in 2004. Find out its current location, check status reports, and enjoy the accompanying Travel Guide. In the Kids' section, there are models of the spacecraft for you to print and build.

http://www.jpl.nasa.gov/cassini/

★ CosmicQuest @ The Children's Museum of Indianapolis

Could you design a comfortable habitat for living and working in space? Try the Design a Space Station simulation and see! You'll need to provide water, power, food, and don't forget the bathroom! Other parts of this fun site include a Field Guide to the Universe, an expedition to the magnetic North pole, and more.

http://www.childrensmuseum.org/cosmicquest/

★ Exploring Space

The NASA Ames Research Center says this site is "As close as you can get without being a rocket scientist!" Click on Pressure Girl to explore air pressure in different earthly environments plus several that are out of this world! Not to be outdone, Gravity Boy shows off his jumping skills on Earth, the Moon, and Mars. Speaking of Mars, don't miss the Mars Virtual Landing Sites virtual reality panoramas. (Spot any Martians? Call NASA!) You can also try the Lunar prospector simulation and maneuver the craft into orbit around the Moon. (Hint: attend the "Mission Briefing" session before launch (or dinner).

http://www.exploringspace.arc.nasa.gov/

Galileo - Journey to Jupiter

This spacecraft's mission to Jupiter began upon launch in 1989. *Galileo* reached the planet in 1995 and spent several years in orbit, collecting data. These days, the plucky little craft is touring Jupiter's moons. This site offers spectacular pictures, animations, and mission updates so you'll always know where *Galileo* is located.

http://www.jpl.nasa.gov/galileo/

GPS: A New Constellation

Global Positioning System (GPS) satellite navigation systems determine your position on Earth. No, they don't say whether you're standing or sitting; they pinpoint your location on Earth. Well, maybe not pinpoint, exactly—the accuracy is about 65 feet in either direction. Still, that's plenty good enough for navigating ships and planes, fertilizing and planting specific areas of fields, hiking, mapping, and lots of other uses. A newer system, Differential GPS (DGPS), now has accuracy to about 3 feet. There are three components to the system: a ground control station, a "constellation" of satellites to provide data, and receivers carried around by the user. Find out how it all comes together at this site. If you need a more in-depth tutorial, try the one at the Trimble site <http://www.trimble.com/gps/>.

http://www.nasm.edu/galleries/gps/

International Space Station

It's finally happening—the International Space Station (ISS) is being built! Read current updates on the construction, the crews, and the mission as it proceeds.

http://spaceflight.nasa.gov/station/

Kennedy Space Center

Attention! Your space shuttle is boarding! Visit the starting place for all NASA flights involving humans. Find out how you can view launches in person (or over the Web). The site has the current countdown for the next shuttle mission and tons of information on the shuttle and its payloads. There's also a terrific time line of past manned flights.

http://www.ksc.nasa.gov/

NET FILES

Dad says I can eat dessert first "once in a blue moon." What's a Blue Moon, and when is the next one?

Answer: Calendar months are either 30 or 31 days long. But the lunar month is 29 1/2 days. Every now and again, there are two full moons in the same month. The second full moon in the same month is called a blue moon. This site at *http://www.obliquity.com/astro/bluemoon.html* will calculate blue moons in a given year. BUT—remember to correct for time zones; the times and dates given are in GMT.

Liftoff to Space Exploration

OK, so you can't track *Mir* anymore, but what about all those other satellites and spacecraft spinning around in the sky? Where would you look to see, say, the current position of the Hubble Space Telescope, or one of those NOAA weather satellites? Right here! But that's not all. This comprehensive NASA site includes information on space exploration and spacecraft, and features on cool concepts like microgravity.

http://liftoff.msfc.nasa.gov/

The Mars Millennium Project

Your mission is to design an off-world community to support 100 humans arriving on Mars in 2030. Got any ideas? This might make a great family, class, or club project. Registration will also make you eligible for additional collaborative events.

http://www.mars2030.net/

MESSENGER

This spacecraft's acronym stands for MErcury Surface, Space ENvironment, GEochemistry and Ranging. It won't launch until 2004, but you can find out about the best-laid plans for the close encounter with the innermost planet: Mercury.

http://sd-www.jhuapl.edu/MESSENGER/

Discovery Online - Live Cams

The view of the world varies here. As we look at the selection of cams on the Web today, we see weddings in Las Vegas, a California beach, puppies, and naked mole-rats. So many cams, so little bandwidth.
http://www.discovery.com/cams/cams.html

NASA Astronauts

Being an astronaut must be a cool job. How do you get to be one? Good eyesight and excellent physical condition are a must. This page tells you all about astronauts past, present, and future (maybe you!). Find out about living in space, how to contact an astronaut for an appearance at your school, and lots more.

http://www.jsc.nasa.gov/Bios/more.html

★ NASA Human Spaceflight

Looking for the latest on the International Space Station? It's at this site, as well as current info on any recent space shuttle flights. Real-time data, video feeds, and viewing opportunities for satellites and shuttle spotting are also available. Check the History section for details on *Mercury, Gemini, Apollo, Skylab,* and other past missions. Official status reports and NASA News make this site a must!

http://spaceflight.nasa.gov/

Near Earth Asteroid Rendezvous Mission

The Near Earth Asteroid Rendezvous mission was launched in 1996. Its destination? An asteroid named 433 Eros, located 160 million miles away. It finally got there in 1999, after a long circuitous voyage. The "long way around" was necessary because of the low-power rocket used to launch the NEAR Shoemaker mission. Scientists piloted the spacecraft to take advantage of the "slingshot effect" offered by the longer path around Earth. In February, 2001, NEAR Shoemaker actually landed on Eros. Eros is small: only 21 miles long and 8 wide, so why go there? Some people think asteroids are debris left over from the formation of the solar system. Find out what scientific equipment is on NEAR, and what scientists are learning and hope to learn.

http://near.jhuapl.edu/

Outer Planets/Solar Probe Project

What are the outer planets like? And what's beyond them? This resource offers a convenient spot to find information on several missions at once: the *Europa* orbiter (to launch 2003); the *Pluto-Kuiper Express* (was scheduled to launch 2004, but NASA halted the project; now there's a letter-writing campaign to restart the mission); and even the *Solar Probe* mission (scheduled to launch in 2007).

http://www.jpl.nasa.gov/ice_fire/

Tech Museum - The Satellite Site

Communications satellites let us make phone calls and see TV signals from everywhere, even from the other side of the world. Weather satellites show us where the storms are and where the sun is shining. What other types of satellites are there? What do they look like? Did you know there are different types of satellite orbits? Learn about them at this site from the Tech Museum in California. Then try designing your own satellite using the construction set provided (don't forget to add the thermal protection!).

**http://www.thetech.org/exhibits_events/online/
satellite/**

Voyager: The Grandest Tour

Both *Voyager 1* and *Voyager 2* were launched in 1977, aimed in opposite directions. Like the Energizer bunny, the *Voyager* spacecraft just keep going, and going, and going! Meant to last about five years, they are now expected to last until about 2020! By that time, *Voyager 1* will be 12.4 billion miles from the Sun and *Voyager 2* will be 10.5 billion miles away. At this site, you'll learn all about the Grand Tour they have made, and continue to make. There's also quite a bit of information on the "Golden Discs" carried on each spacecraft. They contain sights and sounds of Earth, including everything from Bach to Chuck Berry! Find out lots more about the disc at the main project home page, *<http://vraptor.jpl.nasa.gov/voyager/record.html>*.

http://www.jpl.nasa.gov/voyager/

STARS AND CONSTELLATIONS
SEDS Messier Database

This would definitely make E.T. feel homesick: 110 images of the brightest and most beautiful objects in the night skies. This is the Messier catalog of star clusters, galaxies, and nebulae. Charles Messier started this catalog in the eighteenth century as a collection of objects that were most often mistaken for comets. It serves as an excellent reference list for both beginner and seasoned astronomers. You'll also find the celestial position for each object, which will help you locate it in the sky. If you can locate all 110 objects in one night, or even over a lifetime, you become a "Messier Marathoner." Find out the details here.

http://seds.lpl.arizona.edu/messier/Messier.html

Stars and Constellations

Brilliant Java applets pinpoint the constellations for you in an interactive star chart. Learn about the closest stars and the brightest ones, find out what months are best to see which constellations, read myths about the stars, and explore the links suggested for more information.

**http://www.astro.wisc.edu/~dolan/constellations/
constellations.html**

TELESCOPES AND OBSERVATORIES
★ Chandra X-ray Observatory Center

In 1895, Wilhelm Roentgen, a German physicist, discovered something really strange. It was so strange he called it X-radiation. It was sort of like light, except it went right through things. These days, we have found many uses for X-radiation. X-rays are useful to see if bones are broken or if your teeth have cavities. Did you know X-ray astronomy is really hot? Scientists know X-rays are emitted from things like black holes, neutron stars, and other interesting stellar objects. The only problem is, the Earth's atmosphere absorbs X-rays coming in from space. So, astrophysicists have to use special off-Earth telescopes in order to study these more exotic locales. The Chandra telescope is the premier X-ray observatory to date. Follow Chandra's mission here. You can also play some Chandra-related games and even Ask an Astrophysicist a question.

http://xrtpub.harvard.edu/pub.html

A B C D E F G H I J K L M N O P Q R S T U V W X Y Z

A
B
C
D
E
F
G
H
I
J
K
L
M
N
O
P
Q
R
S
T
U
V
W
X
Y
Z

Exploratorium: Origins: Hubble a Vew to the Edge of Space

How do scientists tell Hubble where to look? How does the information get back to Earth? Find out what the spectacular photos are telling us about the birth of the universe. And who was this Hubble guy, anyway? The answers are here.

http://www.exploratorium.edu/origins/hubble/

★ HubbleSite

They say on a clear day, you can see forever. However, astronomers would rather do without the air, no matter how clear. Light waves become distorted as they travel through the air, and it's hard to get a good picture when you're trying to see very far away. That's the idea behind the Hubble Space Telescope (HST). With this powerful telescope now in orbit above the atmosphere, scientists have been able to get spectacular pictures of our universe. Be sure to check out the fun and games section to learn about galaxies, comets, and more with some really fun Shockwave games.

http://hubble.stsci.edu/

NET FILES

YOU'VE MADE IT INTO THE FORBIDDEN CITY, HOME OF CHINESE EMPERORS OF LONG AGO. NOW, CAN YOU FIND YOUR WAY OUT? HOW MANY ROOMS ARE THERE?

Answer: Beijing is the capital city of China. At its center is the Forbidden City, which was the home and audience hall of the Ming and Qing Emperors. The Forbidden City contains 9,999 rooms! It was originally built in the early 1400s. Read more at http://www.museumca.org/exhibit/exhib_forbiddencity.html

★ MicroObservatory Online Telescopes

If you're an educator, you can send in a proposal to use this network of automated telescopes. The day we visited there were four of them online, located in spots as far away from each other as Arizona and Australia. The lines to use the 'scopes weren't long either—there was only one person waiting. You can see who is in line ahead of your job, and what they are going to be photographing. This is fun to visit Even If You're Not Going To Sign Up To Use The Telescopes.

http://mo-www.harvard.edu/MicroObservatory/

Mount Wilson Observatory

Located above Los Angeles, California, this observatory has been at the forefront of astronomy for many years. The lights in nearby L.A. are about as bright as a full moon, so observations are limited to bright objects such as nebulae or star clusters. Still, scientific competition to use the telescopes at this facility is fierce! On the virtual tour, you'll visit all the 'scopes on the mountain. Plus, you'll get a tour of the Monastery, which is the building where scientists sleep when not performing their duties. The building is divided into two parts: the "day" side (for scientists who sleep at night and work the solar towers during the day) and the "night" side (for those who sleep during the day and use the telescopes at night).

http://www.mtwilson.edu/

★ NASA's Visible Earth

Go ahead and search on something like "New York," or "city lights." Be amazed at the fascinating satellite photos NASA has taken over the years. If a volcano erupted, a tanker spilled oil, or a hurricane formed, there's probably a full-color photo of it here.

http://visibleearth.nasa.gov/

Telescopes

Telescopes need to magnify light from weak, distant sources and make the images visible to the observer. This Shockwave demonstration shows you how refractive, Newtonian, and Smith-Cassegrain telescopes work. Remember to use the interactive focus knobs!

http://www.sprocketworks.com/shockwave/
load.asp?SprMovie=telescopesweb

UNIVERSE

Black Holes

You can check in, but you can't check out! As far back as 1793, astronomer Rev. John Mitchell reasoned that if something were big enough, its gravity would be so strong that even light could not escape. Since then, Einstein's theory of relativity has helped explain how this is possible. These objects are now called black holes. Some scientists think that black holes are formed from stars that collapse into themselves when they burn out. That's hard to imagine, but we're finding out more and more about black holes all the time. Maybe you'll be the one who makes a big discovery someday about the mystery of black holes.

http://www.aspsky.org/education/tnl/24/24.html

Our Universe

Dark matter. Wormholes, black holes, white holes. Superstrings. What about the "Theory of Everything"? This site provides nice concise explanations of these astronomy puzzlers and more. Plus, there's a "defend the earth" arcade game for fun. This site was created by students for the ThinkQuest competition.

http://library.thinkquest.org/20632/

Steven Hawking's Universe

What's the deal with the universe, anyway? Where did it come from? Where is it going? Stephen Hawking, a British physicist, has spent most of his life thinking about these questions. The answers he's come up with are here. Two of the answers are, "Yes" and "Maybe, if you use exotic matter." (Oh, you want the questions? OK, here they are: Do black holes really exist? Do wormholes really exist?) But there is a lot more here, including a galaxy of links and reading suggestions.

http://www.pbs.org/wnet/hawking/html/

AVIATION AND AIRPLANES

See also MILITARY AND ARMED FORCES

Aeronautics Learning Laboratory

If you don't know your ailerons from your fuselage, you should make for a landing at this site. Learn about the parts of an airplane and the principles of flight. There are some fun experiments in airfoil design you can try, using simple household materials. Don't miss the history of flight in the History section, chock-full of details on early planes and aviators.

http://www.allstar.fiu.edu/

AeroNet

Explore aerodynamics, from the physical forces involved in flight to the importance of design. Then test what you've learned by using a battery of airfoil experimentation applets. This site even offers a look at aviation pioneers. This site was created by students for the ThinkQuest competition.

http://library.thinkquest.org/25486/

Reeko's Mad Scientist Lab

It sure is dusty here in Reeko's basement science lab. Better put on this lab coat to keep your clothes clean, and a pair of goggles might not be a bad idea, either. Fun educational experiments in astronomy, chemistry, physics, and earth science are categorized by subject and level of difficulty. Reeko has a fun sense of humor, too. Consider the description for Rocket Powered Pennies: "O.K., so maybe the term rocket powered is taking it a little too far. But we still get to propel an object. All we need for this simple experiment is an empty soda bottle and a penny (unless you are getting your Mad Scientist supplies from Dad, in which case—ask for a quarter)."
http://www.spartechsoftware.com/reeko/

A
B
C
D
E
F
G
H
I
J
K
L
M
N
O
P
Q
R
S
T
U
V
W
X
Y
Z

NET FILES

Happy Maewyn Succat's Day! You probably celebrate this holiday under another name—what is it?

(Hint: It's in March.)

http://www.nando.net/toys/stpaddy/stpaddy.html

Answer: It's Saint Patrick's Day! Maewyn Succat is believed to be his original name. He changed his name to Patricus, or Patrick, when he became a priest. Did you know he was not Irish? He was born either in Scotland or Roman Britain. Read more at

The American Experience: WayBack - Flight

Meet ten aviation personalities you'd love to know. One of them is a commercial airline pilot who also performs in a stunt plane on her day off. There are also feature stories on the Wright Brothers and their early flights in Kitty Hawk. Read some "Scare Mail" about early airmail pilots and the hazards they faced in 1918. And let's mention the aviation jokes. Sample: Rebecca: Did you hear about the duck that was flying upside down? Ricardo: No! What happened? Rebecca: It quacked up!

http://www.pbs.org/wgbh/amex/kids/flight/

Aviation: The Science of Flight

The history of flight, from Leonardo da Vinci's early drawings to today's avionics, is covered here in an engaging presentation. Discover the principles of lift and other forces that make flying possible. You'll also learn how to become a civilian, military, or commercial pilot. This site was created by students for the ThinkQuest competition.

http://library.thinkquest.org/20174/

👋 Boeing Kids Page: "Let's Fly!"

Select a background, choose a set of colorful planes, and print a page full of aircraft. You can also try mazes, connect-the-dots pictures, and word searches involving flight and planes. There's also a fairly extensive coloring book section.

http://www.boeing.com/companyoffices/aboutus/kids/

Flights of Inspiration

Did you know that the Wright Brothers' first flight, on December 17, 1903, lasted only 12 seconds? Orville was at the controls, and ten years later he remembered it like this, ". . . I would hardly think today of making my first flight on a strange machine in a twenty-seven mile wind, even if I knew that the machine had already been flown and was safe. After these years of experience I look with amazement upon our audacity in attempting flights with a new and untried machine under such circumstances. Yet faith in our calculations and the design of the first machine, based upon our tables of air pressures, secured by months of careful laboratory work, and confidence in our system of control developed by three years of actual experiences in balancing gliders in the air had convinced us that the machine was capable of lifting and maintaining itself in the air, and that, with a little practice, it could be safely flown." At this site you can yourself be inspired by learning about planes and what makes them fly. There are several hands-on activities and experiments you can try with paper airplanes and other materials.

http://www.fi.edu/flights/

History of Flight

Click anywhere on The Runway of Flight to explore various milestones in aviation history. You'll start with the dreams of Leonardo da Vinci, whose ideas were ahead of available technology. Keep going up the runway to learn about test pilot Chuck Yeager, military aircraft, and commercial flight service. Along the way, you can test your knowledge with some fun simulations. This site, built by kids, is a ThinkQuest Junior contest finalist.

http://tqjunior.advanced.org/4027/

A B C D E F G H I J K L M N O P Q R S T U V W X Y Z

How Things Fly?

It sounds weird, but spacecraft don't actually fly, they fall around the Earth! In space, astronauts just have to contend with two forces: thrust and gravity. There are a couple other minor details, such as getting to space in the first place, and staying there, but this Web site deals with those problems, too.

http://www.nasm.edu/galleries/gal109/NEWHTF/
HTF030.HTM

Howstuffworks - How Airplanes Work

Loads of pictures help you understand the various parts of the plane and how wings, flaps, and ailerons work together to make it fly. Some suggested experiments and a carefully selected list of links make this resource take off.

http://www.howstuffworks.com/airplane.htm

Howstuffworks - How Helicopters Work

They land and take off vertically—how do they do that? Wonder no more—climb in; you'll feel like you're right in the cockpit, running your hands over the controls. Get close-up views of the rotors and other components at this multimedia-laden site. You won't even get dust in your eyes!

http://www.howstuffworks.com/helicopter.htm

The K–8 Aeronautics Internet Textbook

How much do you know about the principles of aeronautics? That's the science of how planes, balloons, and other aircraft fly. Knowing how airfoils work can also help you throw a baseball or improve your tennis game—visit this site to learn how this works! You can also explore careers in aviation—from flying airplanes to fixing them.

http://wings.ucdavis.edu/

Kids Corner

The Federal Aviation Administration page offers instructions for making several different types of paper aircraft. There's a 1903 Wright flyer (you'll need some Styrofoam meat trays, some toothpicks, and glue), or you could try a really unusual plane that looks like a drinking straw with two loops of paper at each end. Will it really fly? They say so!

http://www.faa.gov/education/resource/kidcornr.htm

Science Fun with Airplanes

Have you got some scissors, a piece of tape, 15 paper clips, and a printer? Then you can make and experiment with a paper glider. Just download the PDF file and get ready to soar. Other parts of this site teach you about airplane controls and the science of flight. There are even some suggested science fair projects.

http://www.ag.ohio-state.edu/~flight/

Smithsonian National Air and Space Museum

See pictures and learn about milestones in aviation. For example, Charles Lindbergh was one of the most famous pilots in history. In his plane, Spirit of St. Louis, he was the first to cross the Atlantic alone. He took off from Roosevelt Field, in New York state, early on the morning of May 20, 1927. After 33 hours, Lindbergh landed at *Le Bourget* Field, near Paris, welcomed by a cheering crowd. This was the first solo crossing of a major ocean by air, and it was a very big deal at the time. Come in for a landing at this online museum, where you'll also see famous spacecraft and even a real moon rock! The National Air and Space Museum is part of the Smithsonian Institution, and it is located in Washington, D.C.

http://www.nasm.edu/

To Fly Is Everything

Some of the first experiments in airplane flight didn't get off the ground. Others did, and this resource offers an archive of photos, films, and simulations to round out your study of aviation history. There are even more simulations at the First Flight site <*http://firstflight.open.ac.uk/*>.

http://hawaii.psychology.msstate.edu/invent/
air_main.shtml

A
B
C
D
E
F
G
H
I
J
K
L
M
N
O
P
Q
R
S
T
U
V
W
X
Y
Z

Lycoszone

Look no further than this site for the best collection of online games and fun we've seen. All of our favorite games from Billy Bear, Alfy, Bonus.com, and other hot sites are gathered here for your playing pleasure. You'll find games for little kids, big kids, and everyone in between. There's even a musical karaoke machine so you can sing favorites like "Alice the Camel" and "The Cat Came Back." *http://www.lycoszone.com/*

Two Legends of Aviation

Charles Lindbergh's solo flight across the Atlantic made him a great American hero in 1927. It had never been done before. The flight took just over 33 hours and was considered the wonder of its day. At this site you can learn about Lindbergh's life, his plane, and his record-breaking flights. You can compare and contrast his experiences with those of Amelia Earhart, the famous pilot who disappeared over the Pacific in 1937, on the last leg of her round-the-world trip. Her story is here as well.

http://www.worldbook.com/fun/aviator/html/
twolegnd.htm

BALLOONING, BLIMPS, AND AIRSHIPS
Goodyear Blimp Information

The first Goodyear blimp took off in 1925; today there are three in the U.S., one in Europe, and another in South America. At this site, you'll learn about blimp basics, see inside a cockpit, and find out how they got that strange name in the first place.

http://www.goodyear.com/us/blimp/

Hot Air Balloon Cyber-Ride

Up, up, and away! What happens when you take a balloon ride? This little adventure will let you experience it all on a virtual trip. Will you fly over the barn or make for that big mountain in the distance? The choice is up to you. Remember, although champagne is traditional at the end of a balloon journey, you'll have to stick to a nonalcoholic beverage!

http://www.hot-airballoons.com/cybride.html

MetLife Online®: The Blimp

Have you ever noticed that large sporting events tend to attract blimps, like flies around a picnic? The blimp carries a joystick-controlled camera, which gets a live overhead shot of the playing field. You may have seen the MetLife blimp—it has everyone's favorite beagle, Snoopy, on it. But is it Snoopy One or Snoopy Two? There are two MetLife blimps, one based on each coast. While they normally are tasked to help televise sporting events, the western Snoopy recently helped track some whales as part of an environmental research project. This site will tell you all about the blimp's construction, its history, and how the heck they park it!

http://www.metlife.com/Blimp/

MODEL ROCKETRY
Let's Make a Rocket!

There are two sets of directions here for basic rockets, but we particularly liked the one made out of a "plug-type" film canister and some antacid tablets. It's "Guaranteed to make a mess!" Get an adult and some supplies (try Fuji print film) and head for a big open space.

http://www.alaskascience.com/rocketmain.htm

I wonder what the QUEENS, KINGS, AND ROYALTY are doing tonight?

BAKER ISLAND

See UNITED STATES—TERRITORIES

BIOLOGY

See also SCIENCE—EXPERIMENTS; SCIENCE—SCIENCE FAIRS

★ The Cell

Biology, the study of living things, begins with a look at life's most basic unit: the cell. Learn about cell components—called organelles—and how each one helps the cell eat, breathe, and in general keeps the cell healthy. Put a lot of cells together and what have you got? A plant or an animal, perhaps? You may be able to tell a cow from an oak tree, but how are you at identifying different kinds of oak trees? Scientists have a special way of categorizing and organizing living things. It's called taxonomy, and you can learn all about it here. Other parts of the site explore ecosystems, food chains, and biomes.

http://www.kapili.com/c/cell.html

Cellupedia

Did you know that cells can talk? That's how your brain tells you it's time to eat or sleep. Cells have their own chemical "language." Sometimes the cells are too far away to contact directly, so the blood system delivers the messages. That's a simplified version of how cells communicate, but you can get a more scientific explanation as you delve into this rich resource on cell biology. This site was created by students for the ThinkQuest competition.

http://library.thinkquest.org/C004535/

Wolves are a howl in MAMMALS.

Life in Extreme Environments

Way under the sea, there are thermal vents in the ocean floor. Minerals and scalding water spew from them constantly. You wouldn't think anything could live there—but giant tube worms do! That's just one of the mysterious species living in extreme environments around the planet. This resource covers things that creep in the dark, thrive in the desert, and survive radiation. You can also learn about the seemingly impossible: living bacteria in 30 million-year-old amber.

http://www.astrobiology.com/extreme.html

Life Science Safari

Sally's your adventure guide, and she's ready to take you on a virtual safari throughout the five kingdoms: bacteria, protists, fungi, animals, and plants. Her job is to describe what's inside each organism. But you won't see a boring slide show of cells and cell structures. Instead, Sally uses animated pictures—like a wrecking ball hitting a brick wall—to explain how lysosomes digest waste and break down food.

http://www.vilenski.com/science/safari/

NET FILES

"Don't linger too long at the pewter wash basin at the station. Don't grease your hair before starting or dust will stick there in sufficient quantities to make a respectable 'tater' patch. Tie a silk handkerchief around your neck to keep out dust and prevent sunburns. Don't imagine for a moment you are going on a picnic; expect annoyance, discomfort and some hardships. If you are disappointed, thank heaven."

What is going on here?

Answer: These are some of the hints given to passengers traveling by stagecoach from St. Louis, Missouri, to San Francisco, California, in 1877. The trip generally took about 24 days! Read more about it at
http://www.wellsfargo.com/about/stories/ch1.jhtml

Living Things

Spirogyra might sound like the name of the latest band to top the Billboard charts, but it's really a microbe. A what? A microbe is an organism too small to be seen without a microscope. This site will tell you more about how small organisms like spirogyra live and grow. When you're ready to explore bigger life forms, check out the Circle of Life section for the story about the vine that ate the South.

http://www.fi.edu/tfi/units/life/

The Microbe Zoo - Dirtland

Did you know that you have a fabulous microbe zoo running wild in your yard, in your food, even on your clothes? Microbes are so small, you can't see them without a microscope; but they affect your life daily, in a big way. Zoom in on the invisible world of these small creatures and learn how they interact with the larger world around them. And don't forget to thank them for that last chocolate bar you ate or root beer you drank—they helped make it!

http://commtechlab.msu.edu/sites/dlc-me/zoo/zdmain.html

How Stuff Works

Have you ever wondered how your television set works? Or how cell phones get a message from here to there without any wires? And CDs—how does all that music get written onto those shiny discs? Don't forget those See 'N' Say toys—how do they keep talking without using batteries? And while we're at it, let's look at How Airplanes Work, and How Toilets Work. There's even a dissection of the crazy Singing Fish. Haven't you always wanted to know what's inside?
http://www.howstuffworks.com/

BACTERIA (MONERA)

Bacteria Rule @ Nationalgeographic.com

According to this site, at any given time you probably have about a billion bacteria on every tooth in your mouth. If that fact doesn't make you want to run for the mouthwash, read on. You'll find lots more bacteriological details to gross out your mom, as well as a splendid list of links for still more dirt on microbes.

http://www.nationalgeographic.com/world/0010/bacteria/

★ Infection, Detection, Protection

Meet the microbes! They are among the oldest life forms on Earth. At this site you'll learn about bacteria, viruses, and protozoa. Some of these can cause diseases, but over 95 percent of them are harmless. Use the Size-o-Meter to get a sense of how small these critters actually are; then go on a microbe quest in the cafeteria and try to solve the microbe riddle. Learn how Lou got the flu, and try playing detective in the Case of the Mixed-Up Microbes.

http://www.amnh.org/nationalcenter/infection/

Introduction to the Bacteria

Have you hugged a bacterium today? Chances are, you have, and didn't even know it! Learn all about friendly (and not so friendly) bacteria. They are everywhere, and different types can do everything from making delicious yogurt to making you ill. Did you know that some can lie dormant for years?

http://www.ucmp.berkeley.edu/bacteria/bacteria.html

FUNGI

★ Bread Bag Nightmares

Explore the exciting world of molds by experimenting with various types of bread and common household items like lemon juice and sugar water. Soon, a colorful and fuzzy mold farm will be yours. Other cool projects at this site include Fun with Fomites, Biosphere in a Bottle, and Yeast on the Rise. You can also help Sam Sleuth Stalk the Mysterious Microbe.

http://www.microbe.org/experiment/nightmares.asp

Introduction to the Fungi

It's more than just mushrooms! Discover the mysterious world of the fungus kingdom, which also includes molds, yeasts, and that odd fungus/algae friendship: lichens.

http://www.ucmp.berkeley.edu/fungi/fungi.htm

Lichens of North America

"Lichens are fungi that have discovered agriculture!" says the quote on this page. This refers to the fact that lichens are actually organisms combining two, sometimes three, different kingdoms. The main host organism is a fungus. It attracts food-producing partner organisms that can be algae (Kingdom Protista) or blue-green algae (Kingdom Monera). They all get along quite well. At this site you will learn about the special biology of lichens and how people and animals use them.

http://www.lichen.com/

Tom Volk's Fungi

Friends of Fungi everywhere should make this site their first stop. Applaud the fungus of the month and browse through a virtual encyclopedia of fungi portraits (by the way, the huge one on the main page isn't real). You can also discover why we have fungi to thank for the "merry" in Christmas.

http://tomvolkfungi.net/

GENETICS, CLONES, AND BIOTECHNOLOGY

Clone o' Matic

Your goal: create a genetically altered cow that gives chocolate milk! Use virtual lab equipment to splice a gene from the cacao tree into a strand of cow DNA. Once you've mastered the basic idea, try the Clone o' Matic machine just for fun. Collect five sheep or five cow DNA samples. Oops, did you grab the wrong petri dish? Hey, that was DNA from a monkey! Oh no, now you've added genetic material from a lobster! We don't even want to tell you what happens next, except that there are more than 3,000 possible combinations. Thank goodness this is just a game.

http://www.sun-sentinel.com/graphics/science/
  clone.htm

DNA for Dinner?

Care for a little bacteria with your vegetables? Right now, scientists are splicing genes from bacteria and other unlikely sources into the genetic material of such staple food products as corn. The idea is to make the crops more resistant to diseases, or to increase the yield per plant. According to this site, one third of the American corn crop has been genetically modified. Half of the soybeans, and half of the cotton plants are also altered. Some people aren't so sure this is a good idea. Should products containing these laboratory-built genes be labeled so that consumers can seek them out or avoid them altogether? Explore the question here.

http://www.gis.net/~peacewp/webquest.htm

★ DNA from the Beginning

This multimedia tutorial starts with the very simple premise, "Children resemble their parents." From that jumping-off point you'll quickly learn how Gregor Mendel, the "father of modern genetics" experimented with cross-pollination of pea plants in the mid-1800s. From there, you're off on a tour to the history of genetics research. Meet geneticists who explain their experiments and results to you. Each section is illustrated with colorful animations, audio, and video. It's all so interesting and presented in such an engaging way, we have to give it high marks!

http://vector.cshl.org/dnaftb/

★ DNA Is an Instruction Manual

DNA, the building block of life, is in almost every cell of your body. At this site, you can zoom in for a closer look at someone's hand until you get to the cell level. See The Nucleus? That's The Control Tower For Everything that goes on in the cell. It's also where you'll find the DNA "spaghetti." Check it out, and then explore this excellent site to learn all about the double helix, as well as ethical concerns about genetic testing.

http://www.thetech.org/exhibits_events/online/
  genome/

A
B
C
D
E
F
G
H
I
J
K
L
M
N
O
P
Q
R
S
T
U
V
W
X
Y
Z

A B C D E F G H I J K L M N O P Q R S T U V W X Y Z

NET FILES

How many Hershey's Kisses are produced in one day?

Answer: According to this site, "Today's wrapping machines can wrap up to 1,300 Hershey's Kisses a minute. Manufactured at both the Hershey, PA, and the Oakdale, CA, plants, Hershey Chocolate U.S.A. has the capacity to make approximately 33 million Hershey's Kisses per day, or more than 12 billion a year.
http://www.hershey.com/products/kisses/

★ Genetic Science Learning Center

You don't need fancy equipment to extract DNA from cells. This site shows you a method using only a test tube (or jar), a little detergent, and some rubbing alcohol. (Hint: extract the DNA from wheat germ, not your big toe.) This resource also explains gene mapping and reveals what scientists do for fun: they think up clever names for genes! Surely you can do better. Give it a try here.

http://gslc.genetics.utah.edu/students.html

Mouse Genetics - Multimedia Activities

Learn about genetics using cute little virtual mice! This simulation requires Shockwave. First, you'll have to answer some questions about statistics and probability; but don't worry, there's a cool little tutorial that will have you flipping virtual coins in no time. When you think you know a gene from a chromosome, just enter the Simple Mouse House and breed some critters. When you've got that one figured out, move on to the trickier Advanced Mouse House. Can you discover how to make a pink-eyed black mouse?

http://www.explorescience.com/activities/
   Activity_page.cfm?ActivityID=39

MICROSCOPES
Scanning Electron Microscope

The Scanning Electron Microscope (SEM) uses electrons, rather than light, to create a magnified image. Very detailed 3-D microscopic images can be created this way. If you've ever wondered how this process works, there's a quick tutorial and loads of fascinating pictures to explore at this site.

http://www.mos.org/sln/SEM/

PROTOZOA AND ALGAE (PROTISTS)
★ The Smallest Page on the Web

A drop of green pond water hides a tiny microscopic world. In it, you might find water bears, hydra, and beautiful crystalline diatoms. This page in praise of protozoa offers a quick identification guide to what's on your slide as you look through the lens. If you'd like to farm your own paramecium, or enjoy a little aquarium of protozoa, the directions are here <http://www.microscopy-uk.org.uk/pond/collect.html>.

http://www.microscopy-uk.org.uk/mag/wimsmall/
   smal1.html

Virtual Ocean

Imagine attaching your body to one spot and not moving for the rest of your life. Believe it or not, that's what a sea squirt does. This microscopic creature lives in the ocean and begins life looking something like a tadpole. When it grows up, it turns into what looks like a plant. But it's really still an animal! You can learn more about sea squirts and other tiny creatures of the sea when you dive into this site.

http://www.euronet.nl/users/janpar/virtual/
   ocean.html

Want a snack? Learn to make one in COOKING, FOOD, AND DRINK.

BIRDS

See also FARMING AND AGRICULTURE—POULTRY; PETS AND PET CARE; REFERENCE WORKS

🐦 All About Birds

Learn about the functions of feathers, discover why there are few bird fossils, and see pictures of birds used as national and state symbols. Take loads of links to pages about different species, and chuckle over bird jokes such as this: Why does a flamingo stand on one leg? A: Because if he lifted that leg off the ground, he would fall down! You'll also learn about Bird Extremes, like, "How fast can a bird fly?" The peregrine falcon has been clocked at 90 mph, and the spine-tailed swift is right up there, too, at 90 to 100 mph. The fastest land bird is the ostrich, which can speed along at 43 mph on a good day. If you want to know the biggest, smallest, or highest birds ever, this is a good place to start!

http://www.EnchantedLearning.com/subjects/birds/

Audubon WatchList for Kids

Did you know that the greatest threat to wild birds is the loss of habitat? Learn how to make your backyard "bird friendly" by putting up feeders, providing nesting material, and—here's an important one—keeping your cat indoors! There's a list of threatened species the Audubon Society wants kids to watch for and monitor. The idea is, "If we can watch them now, maybe we won't have to rescue them later!" Do explore the rest of the Audubon site <http://www.audubon.org/> for lots of bird information and more educational activities.

http://www.audubon.org/bird/watch/kids/

Flapping Flight

If you're a bird, there's a lot more to flying than just moving your wings up and down. It turns out that your wings are also twisting and folding. At this site, kids can admire animations of all three motions, as well as learn to build their own ornithopter, a flapping-wing model aircraft. All the directions and plan drawings are online.

http://www.catskill.net/evolution/flight/

Never give your name or address to a stranger.

Patuxent Bird Identification InfoCenter

Basic information on a variety of birds can be found at this site. Look for photographs, songs, identification tips, maps, and life history information for North American birds.

http://www.mbr.nbs.gov/id/framlst/framlst.html

Virtual Birding - Educational Materials

Have you ever noticed that all birds don't have the same size and shape of bill? That's because they eat different types of things: some peck at seeds while others gobble down insects. This resource offers a series of lessons that will teach you how to discover a bird's diet by inspecting its beak. Besides that, you'll learn how birds are classified, how they build nests, and how they communicate. This is a simple and informative beginner birding guide.

http://www.inhs.uiuc.edu/chf/pub/virtualbird/educational.html

BIRD WATCHING

American Birding Association: Young Birders

Are you fascinated by birds? You might like to draw them or look for them. You might want to join a flock of other young birders here and compete for Young Birder of the Year! You might win a scholarship to bird camp or other prizes. You don 't need to be an expert birder with a "life list" as long as your arm, but you do need to be able to take careful field notes, or draw birds, or write an essay about them. There's also a chat room for teen birders, plus announcements of other contests and lots more.

http://www.americanbirding.org/programs/ygbgen.htm

A B C D E F G H I J K L M N O P Q R S T U V W X Y Z

A
B
C
D
E
F
G
H
I
J
K
L
M
N
O
P
Q
R
S
T
U
V
W
X
Y
Z

Audubon's Birds of America

This multimedia edition of John James Audubon's comprehensive guide to birds was converted from his mid-nineteenth century seven-volume edition. It contains 500 color illustrations and interesting text outlining Audubon's observations about each species. In Volume V, for example, Audubon speaks of the passenger pigeon. "In the autumn of 1813, I left my house at Henderson, on the banks of the Ohio, on my way to Louisville. In passing over the Barrens a few miles beyond Hardensburgh, I observed the Pigeons flying from north-east to south-west, in greater numbers than I thought I had ever seen them before, and feeling an inclination to count the flocks that might pass within the reach of my eye in one hour, I dismounted, seated myself on an eminence, and began to mark with my pencil, making a dot for every flock that passed. In a short time finding the task which I had undertaken impracticable, as the birds poured in in countless multitudes, I rose, and counting the dots then put down, found that 163 had been made in twenty-one minutes. I traveled on, and still met more the farther I proceeded. The air was literally filled with Pigeons; the light of noon-day was obscured as by an eclipse, the dung fell in spots, not unlike melting flakes of snow; and the continued buzz of wings had a tendency to lull my senses to repose." Although this bird appeared in great numbers in Audubon's time, it is extinct today. Find out why in the article on passenger pigeons in the ENDANGERED AND EXTINCT SPECIES section of this book.

http://employeeweb.myxa.com/rrb/Audubon/

Bird Pamphlets

The bird food store has so many choices: black oil sunflower, safflower seed, niger seed, or maybe peanut hearts. How do you sort it all out? The good news is that you don't have to sort the various seeds—the birds do that for you! You'll find a handy guide to what species of birds like which foods. There are also tips about feeders and how to place them in the right spots to attract the most birds. Other pamphlets describe how to build nesting boxes and bird houses.

http://migratorybirds.fws.gov/pamphlet/pamplets.html

Bird Song

When you go on a bird watching hike, odds are you'll hear a lot more birds than you'll see. Wouldn't it be cool to be able to identify a bird by the sounds it makes? For example, you're out for a walk in the woods and you hear a bird that seems to be singing, "Sweet Canada, Canada, Canada"—instantly, you know that's a white-throated sparrow. Or maybe you're walking in the meadow and hear a high-pitched "Chortle-deeeeee," drawn out on that last syllable. You recognize at once that's a red-winged blackbird. How did you get so smart? You've memorized a list of birds and little hints to help you remember what their songs sound like. One's available on this home page! The fancy word for memory-joggers like these is mnemonics.

http://www.1000plus.com/BirdSong/

Bird Song Central: Birding by Ear - Spring Tune-Up

Have you ever heard a bird's song and wondered who wrote the music? You might find its composer here, where they have many of the latest bird tunes on file for your listening pleasure. If you can't go out in the woods and fields to look for birds, this site also offers virtual birding in many types of habitat. Play the Bird Song Matching game. Click on Bird Song Central at the bottom of the page, or go to <http://www.virtualbirder.com/vbirder/matcher/matcherDirs/SONG/>.

http://www.virtualbirder.com/bbestu/

★ Bird Sounds Digitally Recorded

If you haven't found the bird song you're looking for at the previous sites, it's probably in this excellent collection. Besides birds, this intrepid adventurer records insects, animals, and other sounds. Find them all at this site, along with links to recordings of bird songs all over the world.

http://www.naturesongs.com/birds.html

BirdSource

Sponsored by the National Audubon Society and the Cornell Laboratory of Ornithology, BirdSource attempts to chart the large-scale movements of bird populations over time. Where is the first robin of spring? These folks know. Occasionally, they ask for your help. Identify what birds are in your area, and then add them to the database at this site. You'll also find links to Cornell's classroom bird watch project so you can get your whole class involved.

http://birdsource.cornell.edu/

Help . . . I Found a Baby Bird!

What would you do if you found a baby bird that had been blown out of a nest by the wind? This site explains what you have to know. Keep it warm, but your first call should be to a licensed wildlife rehabilitator. Sometimes they are listed in the phone book, or you can call the wildlife regulatory agency in your area. They will have a list of who takes care of birds in your region.

http://www.webbedworks.com/messingerwoods/babybirds.htm

★ OnLocation Virtual Birding

Have you memorized your field guide to birds, including even the exotic species that don't even live in your area? Tired of birding in your backyard and seeing only the same old robins, blue jays, and crows? Why not take a virtual bird hike in a different environment? Wander around a Florida marsh or try the Cape May hawk version. It's like an adventure game because you get points for every bird you know. You can also participate in contests and win prizes for your virtual birding skills.

http://www.virtualbirder.com/vbirder/onLoc/

There's a real gem of a site in EARTH SCIENCE—GEOLOGY—GEMS AND MINERALS!

NET FILES

Where is the smallest area administered by the National Park Service? (Hint: It is a national memorial.)

Answer: It's in Pennsylvania. The Thaddeus Kosciuszko National Memorial is 0.02 of an acre. He was a Polish-born Revolutionary War patriot and helped to fortify both Saratoga and West Point. Read more about him at http://www.nps.gov/thko/

Peterson Online

Peterson's field guides are world-famous for their detail and ease of use. The Web site is no exception to the quality we've come to expect. You can get a sample in the Bird Identification section, where complete information is provided for about 25 species. The Peterson's Perspective part of the site is a bird watcher's tutorial for the beginner. Learn about bird shapes, identifying field marks, and lots more. A clutch of selected and annotated links rounds out the site.

http://www.petersononline.com/

Wild Birds Unlimited Bird FeederCam

If you don't have your own bird feeder to watch, take a peek at what's chowing down at the FeederCam. You might spot a northern cardinal, a bluejay, or a black-capped chickadee. Of course, you might also see a number of squirrels. The feeder is located in Indianapolis, Indiana.

http://www.wbu.com/feedercam_home.htm

A
B
C
D
E
F
G
H
I
J
K
L
M
N
O
P
Q
R
S
T
U
V
W
X
Y
Z

A B C D E F G H I J K L M N O P Q R S T U V W X Y Z

NET FILES

Just before the justices enter the Supreme Court, they are announced by the marshall. What does the marshall say? (Hint: He repeats the word three times.)

Answer: "Oyez, oyez, oyez!" (pronounced "o-yay" or "o-yez" or "o-yes"). It's an old word from Middle English that means "listen up—I'm calling for silence and attention!" Read the story of why this phrase is used to open court of law at *http://oyez.nwu.edu/other/faq.html*, where you can also hear the marshal's announcement.

BIRDHOUSES
The BirdHouse Network

Find out how to build and place bird houses at this site from the Cornell University Lab of Ornithology. Then wait to see who moves in. When you have identified the bird, send in your report and post your data online. Even if you're not going to build a birdhouse, stop by to check the nest box cams and see what's hatching today. When we visited, we watched baby bluebirds, although we had to look at archived shots of the barn owlets, who had flown.

http://birds.cornell.edu/birdhouse/

Homes for Birds

Home, home on a metal pole? Sure, if you're talking about a birdhouse! Did you know that more than two dozen North American birds will nest in birdhouses? Visit this Web site, and you will discover very complete advice about how to design a birdhouse to attract different types of birds to your neighborhood.

http://www.bcpl.lib.md.us/~tross/by/house.html

PET BIRDS

Kaytee: Companion Birds

Confused about cockatiels? Puzzled over parakeets? If you're thinking of getting a pet bird, you should start here. Canaries are best kept in pairs, and they don't like to be handled. Parakeets are good with young children, easy to keep, and sometimes can be trained to talk. A healthy 'keet can live for 25 years! Cockatiels need a large cage and prefer to be hand fed. Lovebirds are fun and make good pets for families. Learn about the rest of the cage bird species and their care here. Another good source is *Bird Talk Magazine* <http://www.animalnetwork.com/birds/default.asp>.

http://www.kaytee.com/companion/

SPECIES: BATS

BATS are not birds, they are mammals. Visit Web resources about them under MAMMALS—CHIROPTERA—BATS

SPECIES: EAGLES, FALCONS, VULTURES, AND HAWKS

American Bald Eagle Information

According to this site, an eagle can spot a rabbit from over a mile away. Their sharp vision is at least four times better than any human's! Learn about the natural history of this majestic bird, and find out why Ben Franklin opposed the choice of the bald eagle as the national symbol of the United States.

http://www.baldeagleinfo.com/

SPECIES: HUMMINGBIRDS AND SWIFTS
The Hummingbird Web Site

You know why hummingbirds hum? It's because they have forgotten the words to the song! This nifty site offers information on 17 hummingbird species, loads of factual information, and answers to questions like, "My husband says he saw a ruby-throated hummingbird with a yellow belly? Is there any such thing?" The answer is yes! The bird's belly gets covered with yellow pollen as it sips nectar from flowers!

http://www.portalproductions.com/h/

★ Hummingbirds

Did you know that in the spring, male hummingbirds start heading north as early as three weeks ahead of the females and immature birds? This is so the male can scout ahead for food for the females and young during migration. For more information on attracting hummingbirds to your yard, hummingbird feeders, the natural history of hummingbirds, and more, visit this hobbyist's outstanding page. Don't miss the hummingbird webcams!

http://www.hummingbirds.net/

SPECIES: OWLS
Owling.com

To an Apache Indian, dreaming of an owl meant approaching death. To the ancient Greeks, the owl was the symbol of Athena, goddess of wisdom. Learn about owls at this excellent site, which features species descriptions; photos; and screeches, hoots, and calls from owls all over North America.

http://www.owling.com/

What do you want to be when you grow up? JOBS AND CAREERS has some ideas!

SPECIES: PENGUINS
Pete & Barb's Penguin Pages

Why aren't there any penguins in the Northern Hemisphere? Why can't penguins fly? Why are they white on one side and black on the other? The answers to these questions and more are available on this site. You can learn about penguin species and threats to their habitat, and find out who's trying to save them.

http://ourworld.compuserve.com/homepages/
    peter_and_barbara_barham/Pengies.htm

SPECIES: PERCHING BIRDS
North American Bluebird Society

The bluebird is one of North America's most beloved birds. One way to help these beautiful creatures is to establish a "bluebird trail" of nest boxes. Plans for constructing these are at this site, along with "raccoon baffles" to keep the nestlings safe. If you can't build your own box, you can "adopt a box" along the transcontinental bluebird trail, and monitor it for activity. This does cost money, which goes to the organization to help more bluebirds. Discover why everyone loves bluebirds at this site.

http://www.nabluebirdsociety.org/

The Underground Railroad

Using stunning graphics and sound effects, this site explores the people, places, and history of the Underground Railroad. Put yourself in the role of a slave facing a choice: escape with "Moses" to possible freedom in Canada, or face continued slavery. What would you do? Choose your own path and see if you can become "free at last!"
http://www.nationalgeographic.com/features/99/rail road/

A
B
C
D
E
F
G
H
I
J
K
L
M
N
O
P
Q
R
S
T
U
V
W
X
Y
Z

A
B
C
D
E
F
G
H
I
J
K
L
M
N
O
P
Q
R
S
T
U
V
W
X
Y
Z

SPECIES: PHEASANTS, TURKEYS, AND QUAIL
Newton Central on Prairie Chickens

Third and fourth graders wrote these reports. They became interested in the prairie chicken when they found the once-abundant bird was now an endangered species. In the mid-1800s, there were 10 to 14 million prairie chickens in Illinois. In 1990, there were less than 50 left. What happened? Mostly, it was loss of habitat. The good news is that prairie chicken sanctuaries have been set aside, and the birds are starting to repopulate them. These fascinating birds have a winter habit called "snow roosting." At night, they let the snow cover them up, and this insulates and keeps them warm. In the morning, they burst out of their "igloo"—which must startle passersby! You will also read about what types of grasses are found in a prairie and be surprised to learn that Illinois has an official prairie grass: the big bluestem.

http://www.museum.state.il.us/mic_home/schools95/newton/project/

NET FILES

Every August, kids from all over the world can't wait to get to Akron, Ohio, and go as fast as they can down a 954-foot hill.

Why?

Answer: They're in the World Championships of the All-American Soap Box Derby. You won't find any motorized vehicles here—these are gravity powered! Three division winners get to wear the traditional gold championship jackets at the end of Derby Day. Read more about it at http://aasbd.org/

Have you written to your PEN PALS lately?

The Return of the Wild Turkey

Down the road by Potter's farm, Net-mom saw a pair of wild turkeys with nine curious baby turkeys—called poults—clustered around them. The babies were about as big as cats! In recent years, the wild turkey population hereabouts has really surged. If you want to see a picture and learn more about wild turkeys, which are found in all of the lower 48 states and Hawaii, try this link.

http://www.esf.edu/pubprog/brochure/turkey/turkey.htm

SPECIES: PIGEONS AND DOVES
Project Pigeon Watch

Have you ever noticed the variety of color patterns in pigeons? The original wild pigeons from Africa and Europe are of a coloration called "blue bar." Now, there are almost 30 different variations of that, and you can see a number of them at this page! Scientists don't understand it, and they want kids to help them figure it out. There is a nominal cost for your classroom or family to get an official research kit. You'll need to make observations of pigeons in your area and send in reports to Cornell's Laboratory of Ornithology. Even if you don't plan on joining, you can learn about pigeon color variations here.

http://birds.cornell.edu/ppw/

Staring off into space? Discover ASTRONOMY, SPACE, AND SPACE EXPLORATION!

BOATING AND SAILING

See also KNOTS; SHIPS AND SHIPWRECKS

★ BoatSafe.com and BoatSafeKids

At this site you can learn a lot about personal flotation devices, running lights, knots and how to tie them, and all sorts of boating information. There's a special area just for kids where you can ask questions like "How far is the horizon?" and "Why are life jackets orange?" You can even take an online boating safety course that's approved by the National Association of State Boating Law Administrators (NASBLA) and recognized as acceptable by the U.S. Coast Guard Recreational Boating Program. To get your official Boating Safety ID card and certificate, you must pass the final exam with a score of at least 80 percent and pay a small fee. Good luck!

http://boatsafe.com/nauticalknowhow/

The Great Cardboard Boat Regatta

Here's something interesting. You make a human-sized boat out of corrugated cardboard, strong enough to do several laps around a short water course. There's competition in many categories, and some people wind up with very odd boats. There's one that looks like a dragon, and another that resembles a submarine sandwich. According to this site, "Regattas are enjoyed by more than 1,500 participants and more than 100,000 spectators across the USA each summer, and more communities join the Circuit each year." They also claim it's "yachts" of fun.

http://www.gcbr.com/

You can always count on the info in MATH AND ARITHMETIC.

International Signal Flags

You want to say "Hi" to your buddy in a boat across the bay, but it's too far to yell. You could use the semaphore alphabet and two flags to send messages. How? Boaters spell words by holding a flag in each hand and moving them into different positions. An "H" is made by holding the right-hand flag out straight to your right side in the 9 o'clock position, and the left-hand flag down and across the body at about 7 o'clock. For the "I," leave your left hand in the same position and raise the right-hand flag to about the 10 o'clock mark. You can learn the whole semaphore alphabet from the pictures and descriptions you'll find at this page. Get your flags, and practice! Would you like to learn more about the maritime signal flag system, or the semaphore flag code? At this site you can have your name spelled out in either one, or both! If you think you're ready, take the test and see how well you do.

http://www.envmed.rochester.edu/WWWRLP/ flags/ flags.htm

★ Kids in Boats

Welcome aboard this great little tutorial from the Australia-New Zealand Safe Boating Education Group. There's a lot to learn about buoyancy, tides, swells, and winds if you're going out on the ocean. This page covers it all with engaging illustrations and a useful glossary.

http://www.anzsbeg.org.au/kids.html

NET FILES

The comic strip "Peanuts" was first printed on October 2, 1950. In what year did Snoopy the beagle first appear standing on two legs instead of four?

Answer: Snoopy first stood on two legs in 1958. You'll find more Snoopy facts at http://www.snoopy.com/ comics/peanuts/d_history/html/date/1958.html

A
B
C
D
E
F
G
H
I
J
K
L
M
N
O
P
Q
R
S
T
U
V
W
X
Y
Z

NOS MapFinder

Even though waterways don't have roads, you still need a map if you want to visit unknown waters. There are underwater hazards like cables and shoals you'll want to avoid. Plus, you need to follow navigational buoys and channel markers to stay safe. Where on the Net can you get a navigational chart? Right here, but the way to get to them is rather complicated. Choose Search for Maps, and then click the box to the left of the words "Nautical Charts." If you are using Internet Explorer and don't see a box, try Netscape instead. Then click the state or island for which you want to find a chart. On the next map screen, find the little box in the lower right that says "Enable Fast Jump to Results Page" and put a check in the box. Then click on the map itself. On the next screen, click on GIF to see the actual chart. Try an unusual one, like Palmyra Atoll.

http://mapfinder.nos.noaa.gov/

NOVA Online - Lost at Sea: The Search for Longitude

Where would navigators be without longitude? Lost, probably! In ancient times, sailors just followed the coastlines and didn't venture into the open sea. Other early navigators found their way by reading ocean currents and swells, or following clouds, which often formed above islands, or birds, that knew where "home" was. Later, they learned to steer by the stars, measuring the star's distance above the horizon and then consulting charts or measurements for that specific time of the year. That was great for knowing latitude north or south, but how to know the distance east and west remained a mystery. That is, until the 1700s, when a clock maker solved the problem. Read this amazing story, and then try the game to figure out where in the world you are. There's also a great simulation of how GPS (Global Positioning System) satellites work.

http://www.pbs.org/wgbh/nova/longitude/

Catch a ride on a Carousel in AMUSEMENT PARKS.

Opening and Closing of Lock Gates

Ever see locks in operation? They allow boats to go around waterfalls or rapids by providing a water "elevator" for the boat to climb or descend the river. Here's an animated version. We wonder if the fish use it too.

http://www.wrsc.usace.army.mil/ndc/animlock.htm

The Paper Boat Page

From the world's most acclaimed expert on cellulose-based naval architecture (that's paper boat building) comes this quirky page describing a forgotten nineteenth century art. Sure, you can find little folded boat instructions here, but you'll also discover how to make a full-sized paper canoe and other watercraft. Keep in mind that Net-mom recommends you stick to building boats no larger than your bathtub!

http://www.home.eznet.net/~kcupery/

Recent Marine Data

This site falls into the category of the truly amazing. A network of sea buoys and C-MAN (Coastal Marine Automated Network) stations is maintained by the National Data Buoy Center (NDBC), a division of NOAA (National Oceanic and Atmospheric Administration). The observations are updated continuously, and an eight-hour history is usually available for each station. They report temperature, dew point, wind (sustained and gust) direction and speed, surface pressure, wave heights, and the period between waves. How are the waves off Maui, Hawaii? What's the temperature off Anchorage, Alaska? What's the visibility in the English Channel? You can check even closer to home, if you're going boating in the coastal waters of the U.S. or maritime Canada. Do take the link to the virtual tour of the NDBC center <http://www.ndbc.noaa.gov/Tour/ virtr1.shtml> to find out how all those buoys are moored in the deep sea.

http://www.ndbc.noaa.gov/Maps/rmd.shtml

Rowing Frequently Asked Questions

"Stroke! Stroke! Stroke!" That's the call of the coxswain as the rowers propel the shell (that's what those sleek racing vessels are called) ahead in a race for the finish line. Rowing is a sport particularly enjoyed by college and university teams around the world, with many amateur clubs as well. There are several variations on the sport, and the boats, equipment, and rowers are different in many cases. Did you know that rowers are grouped in heavyweight and lightweight classes? Learn all about the sport of rowing here.

http://www.ruf.rice.edu/~crew/rowingfaq.html

Sailing Terms

Where's the bow? What if your scupper is plugged? How do you know when to luff? If you're going to be talking to boaters or sailors (or if you're going to be one), then you'll have to check out this site. And you thought you were a sailor because you knew your port (left) from your starboard (right)! Sail on over and find the definition of any sailing word.

http://www.eddystone.com/maritime/
  home.htm?boatdict.htm

StudyWorks! Online: Navigation and Mapping

The King's asked you to sail around the world and explore new lands. How good are your navigation skills? Specifically, how can you tell how far east or west you are? Better keep checking that chronometer, and hope the skies stay clear enough for you to see the north star at night!

http://www.studyworksonline.com/cda/content/
  explorations/0,1035,NAV2-5_SEP364,00.html

DINOSAURS AND PREHISTORIC TIMES are in the past, but they are under "D."

United States Power Squadrons

Can you pass the online navigation quiz offered by the Power Squadron? Try it! You'll be asked which color running light is on the port side, and similar questions. You can compare your scores with others, and no, you don't have to sign your name. If your score could use some improvement, check to see if there is a local Power Squadron group near you. They offer free classes in boating and sailing safety and navigation. You can preview what will be taught in the classes here.

http://www.usps.org/

CANOEING AND KAYAKING
GORP - Paddling Skills & How-To

Tired of surfing the Net? Why not try kayaking the keyboard or canoeing the computer? This resource is a great casting-off point from which to paddle Net resources about canoeing, kayaking, rafting, and similar water vehicles. Parental advisory: not all links have been checked, and GORP has numerous advertisements.

http://www.gorp.com/gorp/activity/paddling/
  pad_how.htm

NET FILES

TIME magazine's annual "Man of the Year" isn't always male. Who was the first woman to be honored this way? (Hint: A king loved her so much that he gave up his throne to marry her.)

Answer: Wallis Warfield Simpson was TIME magazine's first "Woman of the Year" for the year 1936. Find out more at http://www.pathfinder.com/time/special/moy/1936.html

A
B
C
D
E
F
G
H
I
J
K
L
M
N
O
P
Q
R
S
T
U
V
W
X
Y
Z

A
B
C
D
E
F
G
H
I
J
K
L
M
N
O
P
Q
R
S
T
U
V
W
X
Y
Z

The River Wild: Running the Selway @ Nationalgeographic.com

Some people love to ride down a wild river, working their way through the rapids, braving the dangers of unknown waters. Others just like to read about such a trip. We'll take yet another route—riding the waters on the Internet. "Holy Smokes," "Galloping Gertie"—we're in some mighty fast waters here! They give these rapids some pretty interesting names. Watch it, here we come to "Ping Pong Alley"! That one was "No Slouch"! Don't know about you, but we think it is time for a rest. You forge on ahead if you wish; we'll be there later!

http://www.nationalgeographic.com/features/96/selway/

BOOKS AND LITERATURE

See also NEWS, NEWSPAPERS AND MAGAZINES; READING AND LITERACY; and WRITING

★ Book Adventure

Do you like to read? Do you like to win cool prizes? You might be able to do both at the same time if you visit this site. First, you need a parent, teacher, or guardian to sign up with you (it's free). Then key in the titles of some of your favorite books. The computer will suggest new books you might enjoy. Go to the library and read some of these books. When you're done, visit this site again, log in, and take the quiz associated with the book you read. There will be between 4-10 questions, based on your age. All questions are multiple choice. You can take a quiz twice, and only the highest score counts towards winning prizes. Some of the prizes require parental permission; read the complete rules at this site.

http://www.Bookadventure.com/

Lots of monkey-business in MAMMALS.

Carol Hurst's Children's Literature Site

Sometimes it's fun to learn about a topic by reading a story about it rather than slogging through a regular textbook. For example, there is something called "historical fiction." Here's how it works. Instead of reading about, for example, the Revolutionary War in a fact-after-fact, date-after-date history book, you can read a novel written about that time period. By following the story of the characters and how they interact with events and their environment, you can really learn a lot about the time period at hand. This Web site lists stories on historical periods, themes, topics, and lots more. An added bonus for teachers: activities and discussion questions are suggested for many titles.

http://www.carolhurst.com/

Amazing Space Web-Based Activities

The Hubble Space Telescope folks offer a whole spectrum of fun Web-based activities at this site. In Star Light, Star Bright you can explore the nature of light waves and prisms. Don't miss the brain teasers in this section. Try Make a Comet and see how different "ingredients" affect the outcome. Learn fast facts about planets to collect virtual Solar System Trading Cards. Try matching photos of galaxies to their classification system names. If none of those are challenging enough, fasten your seat belts and enter the Hubble Deep Field Academy for some advanced training. Still think you're pretty good? Help plan a Hubble Space Telescope mission.
http://amazing-space.stsci.edu/

Fairrosa Cyber Library of Children's Literature

You'll find lots of links to online kids' books, such as A Little Princess, Peter Pan, and *A Journey to the Center of the Earth*. One of the coolest things, though, is the selection of links to authors' home pages. Need some biographical author info to complete your book report? Try here!

http://www.dalton.org/libraries/fairrosa/

Historical Fiction by Date

This is a great little resource you're going to need someday, if not today. Say your teacher has given you an assignment to read a novel set in the 1800s. This site lists more than one hundred of them! But don't stop there. You'll also be ready if the teacher says to pick a book set in 1861, or 1590, or 1944. Years covered span from prehistoric times to 1989.

http://www.fcps.k12.va.us/FranklinMS/research/
    hisfic.htm

How a Book Is Made

These pages give you an inside look at how a book is published. Illustrations from Aliki's book, *How a Book Is Made*, help to tell the story. Cats pose variously as a book's illustrator, author, and editor, as well as workers in production, advertising, and sales. They show the steps involved in the writing and publishing of a book. You can also see how a pop-up book is made in other areas of this site.

http://www.harperchildrens.com/hch/picture/
    features/aliki/howabook/book1.asp

★ IPL Youth Collection: Reading Zone

Welcome to the Internet Public Library, or IPL! Click on Picture Books to read (and sometimes hear) stories from all over the Web. Got a book report coming up soon? You'll find TONS of author information at this site, as well as links to their home pages.

http://www.ipl.org/cgi-bin/youth/
    youth.out.pl?sub=rzn0000

Lit Cafe

Need a quick guide to biographies of leading thinkers throughout the ages? Want some spelling hints or a grammar refresher? Maybe you'd like an overview of William Shakespeare and his works. Try the "adventure" game that allows you to try to publish your own book—look in the Publisher's Corner for this one. This site was created by students for the ThinkQuest competition.

http://library.thinkquest.org/17500/

Make an Artist Book

Want to publish your own book? Make one yourself! This page explains how to make a cool book out of a brown paper bag! Other links lead to instructions on constructing "concertina" books, a page on Japanese bookbinding (it's easier than it sounds), and more.

http://www.arts.ufl.edu/art/rt_room/sparkers/
    artist_book/artist_bk.html

StoryQuest

Make your way inside the stone castle and begin with some funny Mad-Libs. That's where you supply a few words and a story is written for you. Looking for the perfect book to read? Check the book reviews and the selected booklists. There are also links to popular authors' Web pages and hints on both writing and proofreading stories. This site was created by students for the ThinkQuest competition.

http://tqjunior.advanced.org/5115/

Find your roots in GENEALOGY AND FAMILY HISTORY.

A
B
C
D
E
F
G
H
I
J
K
L
M
N
O
P
Q
R
S
T
U
V
W
X
Y
Z

A
B
C
D
E
F
G
H
I
J
K
L
M
N
O
P
Q
R
S
T
U
V
W
X
Y
Z

BOOKS

American Girl

Have you already met Felicity, Josefina, Kirsten, Addy, Samantha, and Molly? They lived long ago and you can explore their worlds through a wonderful series of books. This site tells you all about each of these heroines and their stories, but that's not all. Look at the site map and notice that there are historical Web paper dolls you can play with online or print to play with later. You'll find online games, too. If you're ever in Chicago, visit American Girl Place, with exhibits and performances galore! Until then, you can peek at photos of it online. There's also an online store if you need some American Girl gear.

http://www.americangirl.com/

Anne of Green Gables

This site is dedicated to the works and life of Lucy Maud Montgomery (or LMM, for short), the Canadian author of the *Anne of Green Gables* series. Here you will find information about Cavendish, Prince Edward Island, which is the model for Avonlea. There is also a virtual reality tour of Green Gables and a comprehensive list of LMM's works. You can download text versions of several of them, too.

http://www2.gov.pe.ca/lucy/

How fast is a "snail's pace"?

Answer: According to the Conchologists of America, "*Helix aspersa,* a common garden snail, can travel about two feet in three minutes. At that rate, it would travel one mile in five and a half days!" For more on snails, read *http://coa.acnatsci.org/conchnet/facts.html*

Charlotte's Web

This classic tale of Charlotte the spider and her good friend Wilbur the pig is summarized and illustrated by a class of talented second-graders. There is also a quiz, a crossword puzzle, and more. We say, "Some swell page; it's terrific!"

http://www2.lhric.org/pocantico/charlotte/

Goosebumps!

Are you a fan of R. L. Stine? His *Goosebumps* series is the subject of this home page. Follow creepy links that lead you to Stine's biography, his photo, and the transcript of an online Halloween chat with Stine. Also read a ghoulish chapter from recent books in his series. Did you know you can get Goosebumps from TV? A link includes synopses of the TV episodes, identifying the featured book. Did you hear a noise? We're sure we heard something . . . did it come from the Field of Screams?

http://www.scholastic.com/goosebumps/

HarperChildrens.com

This Web site gives you the latest news from this publisher of children's books. Read how classics such as *If You Give a Mouse a Cookie* were developed. There's a lot at this site, including games, activities, and news on upcoming titles. Don't miss the links to the home pages of beloved authors, such as Beverly Cleary (*Ramona* and more), Jean Craighead George (*My Side of the Mountain* and many more) and Eric Carle (*The Very Hungry Caterpillar,* and many, many more). Newer titles include the dismal *A Series of Unfortunate Events* books and R.L. Stine's *Nightmare Room* series.

http://www.harperchildrens.com/

Narnia

Net-mom is always peeking behind coats in large wardrobes to see if there's a door leading into the magical land of Narnia, so richly imagined by C.S. Lewis, author of the *Chronicles of Narnia*. If you, too, are a fan of these books, this is your page. There's an interactive map of Narnia, descriptions of all the characters, sample chapters from the books, a time line, background reading on Lewis, and lots more.

http://www.narnia.com/

Project Gutenberg

Parental guidance is very strongly suggested, since Project Gutenberg is a very large archive. Most of the complete children's books you will find below will be retrieved as text files.

Aesop's Fables
Alcott, Louisa May   *Little Women*
Barrie, Sir James Matthew   *Peter Pan*
Baum, Lyman Frank   *The Wonderful Wizard of Oz* series
Burnett, Frances [Eliza] Hodgson   *The Secret Garden, Sarah Crewe*
Burroughs, Edgar Rice   *Tarzan* series
Carroll, Lewis [Dodgson, Charles Lutwidge]   *Alice in Wonderland* series
Dickens, Charles   *Oliver Twist* and many other titles
Doyle, Arthur Conan   Sir Sherlock Holmes stories
Hope, Laura Lee   *The Bobbsey Twins* series
Lang, Andrew   Many fairy tales
London, Jack   *White Fang, The Call of the Wild*
Montgomery, Lucy Maud   *Anne of Green Gables* series
Potter, Beatrix   Many favorite tales of Peter Rabbit and other animals
Pyle, Howard   *Robin Hood* and other titles
Sewell, Anna   *Black Beauty*
Stratton-Porter, Gene   *A Girl of the Limberlost* and others
Twain, Mark [Clemens, Samuel Langhorne]   *Adventures of Tom Sawyer* and other favorites
Verne, Jules   *Around the World in 80 Days* and other titles
Wiggin, Kate Douglas Smith   *Rebecca of Sunnybrook Farm*

http://www.promo.net/pg/

Scholastic Kids

Animorphs, The Magic School Bus series, the Harry Potter series, Captain Underpants, Baby-sitter's Club, Goosebumps, even Clifford the Big Red Dog—all of these books are published by Scholastic. At this site you can play games inspired by these books and find out which series will be releasing new titles soon. Teachers will like the lesson plan and activity ideas, and families will enjoy the feature articles.

http://www.scholastic.com/

Treasure Island

It's a tale of adventure, pirates, tropical islands, and murder! "If this don't fetch the kids, why, they have gone rotten since my day," said Robert Louis Stevenson, when he wrote this book in 1881. The book is available online at this site. Besides a biography of the author, you'll find links to sites about pirates, islands, and buried treasure. This finely designed site also has some rainy-day suggestions for things to do—besides reading, of course.

http://www.ukoln.ac.uk/services/treasure/

BOOKS—HARRY POTTER

Harry Potter

The Harry Potter series, as everyone probably knows, is all about a very odd student at an even-odder wizardry school called Hogwarts. Now, Net-mom herself is a Muggle, but she has definite sympathies towards Harry and his friends and their great battle against evil. At this site you can test your knowledge of Hogwarts, Diagon Alley, quidditch, and lots more.

http://harrypotter.warnerbros.com/home.html

Harry Potter Lexicon

This site is like the "Cliffs Notes" version of Harry Potter's world. Always forgetting the names of the various magical spells Harry learns? They are all here in the Encyclopedia of Spells. Confused by the sheer number of rules from the Ministry of Magic? Check the official list of departments and regulations here. Trying to puzzle out just when He Who Must Not Be Named first came to power? Consult the time line. Warning: if you have not read the books, this site contains "spoilers" that give away the plot.

http://www.i2k.com/~svderark/lexicon/

Kidwizard

Scientific "spells," unusual "potions," and interactive games are some of the fun choices a Hogwarts student might select once her homework is done. You can, too! There are also wizard-related coloring pages, crosswords, mazes, and a story to keep you in a magical mood.

http://www.kidwizard.com/

A B C D E F G H I J K L M N O P Q R S T U V W X Y Z

Sidebar alphabet: A B C D E F G H I J K L M N O P Q R S T U V W X Y Z

★ The Official Harry Potter Web Site

This is it! The one, the only official Harry Potter site! Step right up and enroll, then go through the sorting hat ritual (Net-mom's in Gryffindor!). Look over the list of books and magical items you'll need for your first year at Hogwarts, then head off to Ollivander's wand shop to select your . . . oops, we mean, let your wand select you! Dawdle at Bertie Botts and choose an Every Flavor Bean (will you get ice cream or smelly feet?), then head back to campus. Are you ready for some quidditch? You can also download the trailer for the new Harry Potter movie!

http://harrypotter.warnerbros.com/web/

BOOKS—LITTLE HOUSE SERIES

The Definitive Laura Ingalls Wilder Pages

Whether you're a fan of the book or the television series, you need to visit this little house on the cyberprairie to find out everything about Laura Ingalls Wilder and her life. You'll be able to track her travels from the big woods to the prairie, chronicled in her book series about Ma, Pa, Mary, and, of course, herself. You can visit the Heritage Sites, which are now located in the places Wilder describes in her novels. There are even some suggested activities and picnic recipes!

http://www.vvv.com/~jenslegg/

NET FILES

What's the world's longest insect?

Answer: According to The Encyclopedia Smithsonian, the longest insect in the world is the giant stick insect with a body length of 13 inches! That's not all. With its legs outstretched, the critter is 20 inches long! To find out more incredible facts, check http://www.si.edu/resource/faq/nmnh/buginfo/incredbugs.htm

Little House Home

You know of Laura Ingalls Wilder and her series of "Little House" books. Now the series has been expanded to tell the stories of Laura's mother's girlhood, as well as her grandmother's and great-grandmother's. Even Laura's daughter, Rose, has her own books. Check this site to learn more about these five generations and try some suggested activities and recipes.

http://www.littlehousebooks.com/

BOOKS—OZ SERIES

Oz Encyclopedia

Jump on this page and prepare to be swept away by a Kansas twister and totally immersed in Oziana. Piglet Press has gone way beyond the call of duty in promoting their small collection of Oz audiotapes by putting together a most thorough collection of pictures, descriptions, and notes to the beloved series of books by L. Frank Baum. There are pages devoted to each and every Baum book, as well as material on those done by Ruth Plumly Thompson and other successors. Look up specific characters, places, and things from the books and the movies (several have been made). Get details about Baum himself, and find out about international Oz Clubs. There are also sample sound files from the Piglet tapes, sections on Baum's songs and short stories, and a bibliography. To exit from the page, just click your heels together and say, "There's no place like home . . ."

http://www.halcyon.com/piglet/

The Wizard of Oz

Visit this site for the fabulous illustrations by the kindergarten and first-grade kids at Carminati Elementary School in Tempe, Arizona. They retell *The Wonderful Wizard of Oz* in a way that will delight you. Notice that Dorothy sometimes has ruby slippers (as in the movie) and other times has silver slippers (as in the original book)!

http://seamonkey.ed.asu.edu/oz/wizard1.html

BOOKS—WINNIE THE POOH

The Page at Pooh Corner

Somewhere in the Internet's Hundred-Acre Wood is The Page at Pooh Corner. It's the home of information about A. A. Milne's Winnie-the-Pooh books. Find general information about Pooh and facts about author Milne and the illustrator, E. H. Shepard. Learn about the area in England where the Pooh stories are based and the real Christopher Robin. Sing along with your favorite Disney Pooh songs or download pictures of Pooh and his companions. This page also gives you links to more sites that feature Pooh, that "tubby little cubby all stuffed with fluff."

http://www.pooh-corner.org/

Winnie the Pooh - An Expotition

Click on The Original Expotition to explore an interactive map of the "100 Aker Wood"—then try to find and visit all 20 wonderful places. Check out the Bee Tree, Rabbit's house, and the ever-popular Heffalump Trap. You'll find little stories at each site.

http://www.worldkids.net/pooh/

LITERARY CRITICISM AND REVIEWS

★ BookHive: Your Guide to Children's Literature & Books

Looking for a great book to read? Why not ask the librarians of the Public Library of Charlotte & Mecklenburg County in North Carolina? They have been as busy as bees combing their bookshelves to find just the book for you. They have found some "real honeys," too! Look for reviewed suggestions in the following topics: Fantasy; Humor; Mystery; Science Fiction; Sports; and many more. There are also a few coloring pages featuring the site's mascot, Zinger.

http://www.bookhive.org/bookhive.htm

★ Kid-Lit

This is one great little resource. Use the easy fill-in-the-blanks form to find books, say, for a 12-year-old about the Gold Rush. Or how about something for a ten-year-old about wizards (NOT Harry Potter). You can also browse the listings by title and author. Once you've found something interesting, you're just one click away from a brief review and further information about the book.

http://www.kid-lit.com/

On-Lion for Kids

The New York Public Library's children's librarians deserve a raise and a vacation! They must have spent weeks picking out the 100 Favorite Children's Books (in ten popular categories) plus 100 Picture Books Everyone Should Know. Each title offers a one-sentence annotation: just enough to make you want to run to the library to read more about the book! You'll also find suggested holiday reading for 11 different festivities, from Christmas to Asian-Pacific American Heritage Month. Other parts of the site offer links to author home pages and lots more.

http://www2.nypl.org/home/branch/kids/

★ Stories from the Web

This attractive site invites you to share reviews of your favorite books with other kids around the world. You don't have to write pages and pages, just a sentence is enough. Want some samples to get you started? There are plenty of them here, written by kids in libraries in the United Kingdom. You'll also find word search puzzles, contests, and links to similar sites and author pages.

http://hosted.ukoln.ac.uk/stories/

★ World of Reading

There are at least two reasons you'd want to visit this site: you want to tell everyone about the great book you've just read; or you want to find and read a book another kid recommends! Read kid-written reviews in lots of genre types: Scary Stories; Fantasy; History; Suspense; and many more. Recently read a wonderful book? Tell other kids about it at this site!

http://www.worldreading.org/

A
B
C
D
E
F
G
H
I
J
K
L
M
N
O
P
Q
R
S
T
U
V
W
X
Y
Z

A
B
C
D
E
F
G
H
I
J
K
L
M
N
O
P
Q
R
S
T
U
V
W
X
Y
Z

MYSTERIES
Mystery

What is a mystery? Did you know there are different kinds of mysteries? They include hard-boiled detective mysteries and those by amateur sleuths, among others. At this site there are story starters to help you create your own mysterious stories, as well as several completed ones you can try to solve. This site was created by students for the ThinkQuest Junior competition.

http://tqjunior.advanced.org/5109/

★ Mystery!: Games

Pollyanne Fishenchips has disappeared from the cursed Hollyshock Manor. As Chief Inspector, your job is to find her body and nab the murderer. Clues point to Miss Squeezy Bittles and a dastardly doctor, but you'll need to click your way through Hollyshock Manor to reveal other clues that point to the doer of this dire deed. If you're sharp as a dart you can solve this murder mystery, and then check out the others.

http://www.pbs.org/wgbh/mystery/game.html

MysteryNet's Kids Mysteries

Do you like collecting clues to solve a mystery? If you do, you'll love this site! Mysteries are in abundance here; each one should take you three to five minutes to complete. Every month you'll find contests, too, as well as magic tricks and other goodies. Mysteries are a ton of fun, but did you know they also teach you critical thinking skills?

http://kids.mysterynet.com/

PICTURE BOOKS
Alex's Scribbles - Koala Trouble

Alexander Balson wanted to write some stories about Max, a koala bear who's always getting into trouble. At the time, Alex was only five years old, so he got some help from his parents. Together they created a fine Web page for your enjoyment. Alex's illustrations really make the interactive story come alive. (Hint: When you go to this page, it asks your name. They just want to greet you with your name, but you can click cancel or make one up if you like.)

http://www.scribbles.com.au/max/

Candlelight Stories - Kids' Zone

Storybooks right on the Web! The illustrations are beautifully done by the author of this site. It's amazing how kids can learn to use the mouse when they are reading these stories. Try "Sally Saves Christmas" for a look at what happens when a little girl travels on a moonbeam. As you look at each page, try asking your little brother or sister what will happen next—will Sally decide to follow the Moon Queen? You can also get your own stories published on this site. If you have the right media, you can hear many of these stories read out loud. If you're over 13, there's also an opportunity to get a pen pal at this site, but be sure to read the online safety tips section first. Alternative sites are in the PEN PALS area of this book.

http://www.CandlelightStories.com/kidsMemA.asp

Disney Books: Story Time

Everyone knows Disney makes terrific movies. Did you know they also publish books? Some of them are online here. Currently, some of the titles you can read are *Aladdin*, *Toy Story*, *A Bug's Life*, *The Lion King*, *101 Dalmatians*, *Mulan*, *Pocahontas*, and more.

http://asp.disney.go.com/DisneyBooks/StoryTime.asp

Fabler Fox's Reading Room

Fabler Fox has seen many things Under the Big Blue Sky. Best yet, he can really spin a story! Everyone in the meadow wants to hear them, and you can too. Read about Buster the Robin, Eeny-Miney the Mole, Kyoko Peacock, and more. Just bring him a blueberry muffin, stretch out on the comfortable grass, and enjoy!

http://www.bookgarden.com/fox.html

How to Tell the Birds from the Flowers

Think you know the difference between a bird and a flower? Can you spot a crow among the crocus? Can you tell a tern from a turnip? How about a clover from a plover? These clever pictures are taken from a book originally published in 1907—and although they may not fool you, they are fun to read!

http://www.geocities.com/Vienna/2406/cov.html

IPL Story Hour

Just want to read something new? Point your browser towards the IPL (Internet Public Library) Story Hour. Many traditional stories are available, as well as newer ones. Some are illustrated by kids, too!

http://www.ipl.org/youth/StoryHour/

★ Jan Brett's Home Page

Jan Brett illustrates the most magical picture books, giving us a window into her fairy-tale world of big rumbley bears, little apple-cheeked girls, and cunning pen and brush work. Her Web site gives some details about how she tackles a new project. For example, before starting on the illustrations for the beloved poem "The Owl and the Pussycat," Brett visited the Caribbean Island of Martinique to get some ideas for landscapes, boats, island colors, and other items. You can download a current calendar, print out some cool T-shirt transfers, and explore activities connected with her many books.

http://www.janbrett.com/

Kids' Corner

View an online audio slide show of the classic Beatrix Potter book, *The Tale of Peter Rabbit*, and listen as it is read to you. Some of the other audio stories at this site include the beautifully illustrated *The Tale of Squirrel Nutkin* and *The Story of Miss Moppet*, and you'll find *Cecil Parsley's Nursery Rhymes*, also illustrated by Potter.

http://www.tcom.ohiou.edu/books/kids.htm

Merpy

Merpy looks a little blue today—but guess what, that's her normal complexion! Merpy is a lovable child who gets into all sorts of interesting adventures with her friends Jeremy Dragonfly, Rufus the Firefly, and some—argh!—monsters. Tag along as she celebrates holidays, deals with getting up grumpy, and searches for monsters under her bed. The animations, sounds, and other multimedia will give you the giggles!

http://www.merpy.com/

NET FILES

What takes place every February on the hilltop of Gobbler's Knob, Pennsylvania?

Answer: That's where Punxsutawney Phil, America's most famous groundhog, reveals his official weather forecast for an early spring—or a late winter. Find out all about Groundhog Day and Phil at *http://www.groundhog.org/*

The Official Berenstain Bears Website

Roll your mouse over the welcoming neighborhood on the screen and see what happens! A bird pops out of its birdhouse, windows and door fly open invitingly, and all sorts of odd things take place. Enter the Bear's treehouse and explore, or line up for a ticket to the Movie Theater—where you can see some brief cartoons. In the Activities area, try some mazes and slider puzzles or print out the Bear family paper dolls.

http://www.berenstainbears.com/

Storyplace - The Children's Digital Library

The Public Library of Charlotte & Mecklenburg County in North Carolina has produced a fabulous collection of stories and activities. Available in Spanish as well as English, the stories are arranged in several libraries for different age groups. Click on the Preschooler's collection. You'll find an animated story that reads itself to you, plus activities you can try online as well as away from the computer. It's guaranteed fun by your friends, the librarians.

http://www.storyplace.org/

A
B
C
D
E
F
G
H
I
J
K
L
M
N
O
P
Q
R
S
T
U
V
W
X
Y
Z

❧ The Theodore Tugboat Online Activity Centre

Here's a tugboat with a smile and appealing eyes, straight from the Canadian TV series. Toddlers will love the interactive stories, in which they get to choose what happens next. Downloadable coloring book pages sail via the Net to your printer or graphics program. Beginning readers will enjoy the rebus story "Hank and the Hug," which uses some pictures instead of big words! Don't miss the construction photos—they have just launched a life-size replica of Theodore himself!

http://www.theodoretugboat.com/theodore.html

❧ The World of Peter Rabbit and His Friends

Beatrix Potter really did own a pet rabbit called Peter. After she published the book in 1902, she was surprised at its overnight success. Peter has appeared in several of her books besides the original. At this site, you can meet all the characters, hear some stories, play some very nice games, send animated greeting cards, and enjoy the many colorful bees and butterflies that flutter throughout the pages. And do you think the "click" sound on this site is Peter crunching a carrot? We do! Note: if you have a Macintosh computer, use Netscape to view this site. It does not work properly under Internet Explorer.

http://www.peterrabbit.co.uk/templates/

PLAYS AND DRAMA

Children's Creative Theatre Guide

Take a trip through time as you explore the history of theater from the times of the ancient Greeks through today. If you're unfamiliar with theatrical terms, there is a handy glossary where you can discover, for example, that the apron is the part of the stage that projects towards or into the auditorium. There are some drama warm-up exercises you can try, and when you're ready, your family can put on the skit that's provided. This site was created by students for the ThinkQuest Junior competition.

http://tqjunior.advanced.org/5291/

The Complete Works of William Shakespeare

Ah, the Bard himself comes to the Net! Visit this site for the complete works of Shakespeare. You can search the texts, find lists of his plays (chronologically and alphabetically), and read Bartlett's familiar Shakespearean quotations, as well as find a picture of William himself. The list of Shakespeare's works is divided into comedy, history, tragedy, and poetry. After you choose a play, you will move to a Web page where you can read one scene per page.

http://tech-two.mit.edu/Shakespeare/

Domenic and Josh's World of Shakespeare

Did Shakespeare really write all those plays? Or was it someone else—or maybe several someone elses! Learn about the controversy here as you explore this most interesting site. Did you know many of our everyday expressions come from Shakespeare's plays? Read about some of them here. The real fun is in the Games section, where you play Hamlet or experiment with online magnetic poetry. This site was created by students for the ThinkQuest competition.

http://tqjunior.advanced.org/6337/

Reader's Theater Editions

Looking for a play you can perform with the rest of your class? This site has 25 complete plays for grades two through eight. A wide range of subjects is covered, from folktales to science fiction. Most are adapted from short stories by Aaron Shepard.

http://www.aaronshep.com/rt/RTE.html

POETRY

★ The Academy of American Poets

If the words don't sound right when you read a poem out loud, the Listening Booth will set you straight. It's an audio archive of poems, many read by their authors. But your poetry lesson doesn't need to stop there. Test your reading skills by clicking through the verses of more than 1,000 poems. There are also biographies and photos of more than 200 poets.

http://www.poets.org/

A B C D E F G H I J K L M N O P Q R S T U V W X Y Z

★ Favorite Poem Project

Do you have a favorite poem? A lot of people do, and at this site, you will see and hear them read their special poem and tell why it has made a difference in their lives. President Clinton reads "Concord Hymn," and a student recites "Casey at the Bat." The stories (and poems) are fascinating. Perhaps you could organize a "Favorite Poem" reading at your school or public library. This site, sponsored by a grant from the National Endowment for the Arts, will tell you how.

http://www.favoritepoem.org/

Funny Poetry for Children

What would you call a computer nerd from Athens? If you guess "Greek Geek," you'd not only be a computer know-it-all but also a poet! This site offers many more Rhyme-Time Riddles, fill-in-the-blank poetry, and even Poetry Class lessons for those who want to write a "sound poem" or a haiku.

http://www.gigglepoetry.com/

Glossary of Poetic Terms from Bob's Byway

Your teacher has assigned a poetry project that's just gone from bad to "verse." There are many unfamiliar words and lots of confusing jargon! Do you know the difference between a sestina and a sonnet? Can you write a poem in iambic pentameter? Visit this site to learn all these terms and more. Many are also illustrated with examples.

http://shoga.wwa.com/~rgs/glossary.html

Online Poetry Class

This site from the American Academy of Poets is focused on how to teach poetry in the classroom, but it's great for basic information, too. Hundreds of poets are listed at this site, many with a photo, a biography, and a collection of annotated links. There's an interactive U.S. map, too. Click on any state and see what famous poets lived there once or live there now.

http://www.onlinepoetryclassroom.org/

Poets' Corner

Some of your favorite poems are collected on the Web, but you'll have to search through these archives to find such works as "Hiawatha," "Jabberwocky," and other classics. Try this site first—it has over 6,500 famous poems, loads of authors' pictures, and best of all—it's easy to use.

http://www.geocities.com/~spanoudi/poems/

The Poets Read

Not all great poets are dead. Honest. The PBS series *Fooling with Words with Bill Moyers* dispels that myth by giving you a chance to hear—and see—some of today's great contemporary poets read their prose. If that motivates you to tap a few verses out on your keyboard, there's a style sheet on the do's and don'ts of poetry writing.

http://www.pbs.org/wnet/foolingwithwords/main_video.html

Where on Earth can you climb *inside* a huge elephant and live to tell your friends about it?

Answer: Lucy is a famous elephant-shaped building in Margate City, New Jersey. She dates back to 1888, built by a realtor to advertise his business development plans! It took one million pieces of lumber for the structure and 12,000 feet of tin for the elephant's skin. You can climb up spiral staircases inside the legs to get to the rooms inside. See a picture of Lucy at
http://www.levins.com/lucy.htm

A
B
C
D
E
F
G
H
I
J
K
L
M
N
O
P
Q
R
S
T
U
V
W
X
Y
Z

Strike up the bandwidth in MUSIC AND MUSICIANS.

POETRY—HAIKU

The Shiki Internet Haiku Salon

Poet Shiki Masaoka was born in Japan in 1867 and helped popularize the arts, as well as haiku—Japan's short poem form. Haiku consists of three lines of five, seven, and five syllables each, and it usually includes a special word to evoke the season. Here is a haiku we made up about the Internet:
The Net's a garden.
See, my modem light is on.
Netscape slowly blooms.

http://mikan.cc.matsuyama-u.ac.jp/~shiki/

POETRY—NURSERY RHYMES

The Mother Goose Pages

Everyone loves these gentle rhymes of childhood. The rhymes are subdivided by subject, including animals, bedtime, folks and things they do, food, places to go, and weather and things around us. An alphabetical listing is available, as well as a list of recommended books. The rhymes chosen are favorites of the collector and her children. This is a useful site for finding those elusive words you can't quite remember from a long-forgotten nursery rhyme. Please note the site author's caution that many are no longer "politically correct." Coming soon: historical notes on all the rhymes.

http://www-personal.umich.edu/~pfa/dreamhouse/
nursery/rhymes.html

♨ Mother Goose Rebus Rhymes - Enchanted Learning Software

Beginning readers will be charmed by these rebus retellings of classic nursery rhymes. Pictures replace many of the words so that even very young children can "read" along.

http://www.EnchantedLearning.com/Rhymes.html

The Real Mother Goose

She doesn't honk or have feathers, and her name was really Elizabeth Foster Vergoose. The real Mother Goose was indeed a real person, buried, some believe, in Boston, Massachusetts, in 1757. That "slightly credible" story is part of a big collection of links about Mother Goose and her nursery rhymes. No, Elizabeth Foster Vergoose didn't actually write any of the rhymes. She just collected them. And yes, you can find the texts of the poems here, too.

http://www.amherst.edu/~rjyanco/literature/
mothergoose/

BULLIES

See PEACE

LibrarySpot

You may not need this today, but believe Net-mom, you'll need it in the future, as term paper season approaches. Acronym dictionaries, biographical dictionaries, inventions, useful calculators (how much grass seed to buy, how to convert cooking measurements) all are here for your use. There are also links to hundreds of library card catalogs all over the world. Explore numerous magazines and newspapers, phone books, mapping programs, and more. If you like Library Spot, you'll love its sister site, Book Spot <http://www.bookspot.com/> with links to the bestseller lists, authors, publishers, and what's new and old in award-winning books for kids and adults. http://www.libraryspot.com/

CANADA

★ Canada Information Office - Kids Canada

One-stop homework help, right here! Find facts on each province and territory and learn about Canadian symbols and anthems, the Royal Family, and Canadian holidays. You can study the Canadian system of government, gaze at the country's natural wonders, and visit Kids Canada to find educational links and games and quizzes.

http://www.cio-bic.gc.ca/kce.html

★ Canada's SchoolNet

Explore this site and its many educator-selected resources for K–12 students, teachers, and parents. There are also feature stories, headlines about new Canadian Web sites, and lots more.

http://www.schoolnet.ca/

★ The Canadian Encyclopedia Online

This multimedia-rich site offers interactive everything: articles, maps, graphs, and games. Read about the 100 most important events in Canadian history, take the "Canucklehead Quiz," and check out biographies of famous Canadians. In the Interactive Maps area there's a fascinating look at more than 40 of Canada's natural wonders, including the "singing sands" of Prince Edward Island.

http://www.thecanadianencyclopedia.com/

★ Canadian Heritage Information Network

The Virtual Museum of Canada includes online exhibits from many different Canadian museums. We loved the multimedia look at "Hockey: a Nation's Passion" with its hockey puck cursor and animated Zamboni ice machine. The "Endangered Species in Endangered Spaces" is very informative, and you can even play the virtual musical instruments at this exhibit <*http://www.virtualmuseum.ca/ Exhibitions/ Instruments/Anglais/ compositionmusicale.html*>. (Hint: move your mouse to where the arrows point, don't just click on the arrows. You will find you are able to strum each string of the guitar, for example.)

http://www.chin.gc.ca/

CBC4Kids: Being Canadian

What does "Canadian culture" mean? It's more than just hockey and maple leaves! Explore the answers to this quesion at this site from the Canadian Broadcasting Corporation.

http://www.cbc4kids.ca/general/time/ beingcanadian/

Environment Canada Weather

Find out if it's hazy in Halifax, wet in Winnipeg, or very nice in Victoria today. One cool thing to try is in the monthly and seasonal forecast area. Compare past forecasts to the weather conditions as observed. How right are the weather forecasters? Check this site to see!

http://weatheroffice.ec.gc.ca/

First Nations in Canada

Imagine yourself living thousands of years ago. You're traveling across a land bridge from Asia to North America and coming into the vast wilderness we now know as Canada. Maybe you would have hunted buffalo, moving your tipi and following the herds as they crossed the plains. Maybe you would have established a permanent village along the Pacific coast and fished for salmon and whales. Read all about the six distinct Canadian Indian cultures and the main tribes in each. Find out how they lived and hunted, what their dwellings looked like, and what they wore. This site takes you through the centuries of change the native populations have experienced, including progress in the last 30 years. The Kids' Stop section offers audio of several native languages, an interactive map of aboriginal place names, and more. For additional sites, see the section of this book under NATIVE AMERICANS AND FIRST NATIONS–CANADA.

http://www.inac.gc.ca/pr/pub/fnc/indexe.html

Hinterland Who's Who

Put on your snowshoes and follow the animal tracks across northern Canada, where you'll find interesting information about more than 80 mammals and birds native to Canada's hinterlands. There are also video clip close-ups on more than 30 species.

http://www.cws-scf.ec.gc.ca/hww-fap/engind.html

A B C D E F G H I J K L M N O P Q R S T U V W X Y Z

A
B
C
D
E
F
G
H
I
J
K
L
M
N
O
P
Q
R
S
T
U
V
W
X
Y
Z

The National Anthem of Canada

This resource is a music and history lover's delight. Not only do you get the official lyrics and sheet music for "O, Canada," Canada's national anthem, but you can also listen to the music, too. Then you can read the full history of this anthem, from its beginnings as a patriotic poem written by Sir Adolphe-Basile Routhier to when it was put to music by Calixa Lavallée in 1880. "O, Canada" was rewritten in 1908 by Robert Stanley Weir, in honor of the 300th anniversary of the founding of Quebec City. Despite the many English versions that have appeared over the years, the French lyrics have remained unaltered.

http://www.halhinet.on.ca/oreillyj/anthem.html

The National Atlas of Canada Online

You'll find maps of all kinds at this interactive learning site about the geography of Canada—in both English and French. Make your own custom map of Canada, and then print it and use it in your report, or frame it and put it on your wall. Be sure to read the instructions, as the interface is not easily understood. Choose a theme for your map: physical geography, people, economic impact, or other. We had problems using this site under Internet Explorer, so we used Netscape instead. But there are "Quick Maps," too, and they worked just fine under Internet Explorer. Try your hand at the Interactive Geography Quiz, but don't think you have mastered it all just yet. Make sure you don't overlook the Canadian Land of Superlatives section—the ultimate Canadian trivia test—to find weird and wonderful answers to questions you never knew you wanted to know!

http://atlas.gc.ca/english/

The National Flag of Canada

This site presents a complete history of the first Canadian flags, right up through the final selection of today's single maple leaf design. You'll also find flag etiquette rules and information about other national symbols.

http://www.pch.gc.ca/ceremonial-symb/english/
    embflagintro.html

National Gallery of Canada - Virtual Tour

Wander through virtual galleries of Canadian art with a knowledgeable CyberMuse guide by your side. If you have Real Audio, you will be able to hear the guide's narration. But even if you want to take a silent tour, the vibrant pictures will astound you.

http://national.gallery.ca/

Parks Canada - Parcs Canada

Learn about Canada's historic sites, such as Pier 21 in Halifax, Nova Scotia. It was the major port of entry for thousands of immigrants after World War II. Besides learning about these landmarks, take a walk on the wild side of Canadian National Parks. From the windy headlands of Cape Breton to the tranquil coves of Pacific Rim, explore them all via this easy-to-use resource. You'll discover each park's history and resources, as well as information on visiting.

http://parkscanada.pch.gc.ca/

The Royal Canadian Mint / Monnaie Royale Canadienne

In 1996, the Royal Canadian Mint introduced a two-dollar coin. The reasoning was simple: they last longer than paper money. A metal coin can survive circulation for about 20 years! The two-dollar bill was very popular, but the government had to replace them every year as they wore out! It costs more to make a coin, but over the coin's lifetime, Canadians will save millions. It's a very cool-looking coin, too. There is a smaller circle in the center, made of gold-colored aluminum bronze, while the outer ring is silver-colored nickel. There's a polar bear on the back. Kids call these coins "Twonies." Why? Just for fun, and to differentiate them from the one-dollar coins. The one dollar coin has a loon on it, and those coins are called "Loonies." Learn a lot about the Royal Canadian Mint and the history of currency here! Coming soon: a kid's zone!

http://www.rcmint.ca/

> "Use the source, Luke!"
> and look it up in
> REFERENCE WORKS.

The Royal Canadian Mounted Police

The Musical Ride of the Royal Canadian Mounted Police developed from a desire of early members to display their riding ability and entertain the local community. The series of figures that form the basis of the Musical Ride was developed from traditional cavalry drill movements. The Ride is performed by 32 regular member volunteers (male and female) who have had at least two years of police experience. The Ride contingent consists of 36 horses. It travels throughout Canada and sometimes into the U.S.

http://www.rcmp-grc.gc.ca/musicalride/

Statistics Canada

How many people live in Canada? What is the unemployment rate? Which one of the Great Lakes is the deepest? Which animals are threatened or endangered? If you're looking for any kind of official statistic from Canada, begin at this site.

http://www.statcan.ca/

Teaching and Learning About Canada

Teachers and students alike will love this convenient collection of links and information about all of Canada's provinces and territories. You'll also easily find quality links on geography, history, culture, climate, and much more. There are even a few games!

http://www.canadainfolink.ca/

HISTORY
The Canadian Museum of Civilization

If you think museums are b-o-r-i-n-g, this one will change your mind! Click on the Virtual Museum and then hop the elevator to Level 2 to see the displays of folk art and fine crafts. Visit the Treasures Gallery to see why Canada is truly a cultural mosaic. Canadian History Hall is on Level 3. Take the voyage through all the regions of Canada and see a prairie curling rink, an Alberta oil rig, and lots more. Take a snack break if you need to, but don't leave the museum before venturing up to Level 5 to see the History in a Box Exhibit and find out what the colors and symbols on a mailbox can tell about the history of a country. Cool! Learning history was never so much fun.

http://www.civilization.ca/cmc/cmceng/
    welcmeng.html

Tenement Museum

What do you think an "urban log cabin" would be like? The Lower East Side Tenement Museum thinks it has a pretty good idea. They say that between the years 1870 and 1915, over 10,000 people moved in and out of the apartments at 97 Orchard Street in New York City. This building was abandoned in 1935 and boarded up until 1987. When it was reopened, it was like stepping into a time machine. Everything was as it had been left in 1935. See what was found in the rooms and what has been excavated in the courtyard. Click on the windows in the virtual tenement house to meet some of the residents and learn their stories. Touch the wall and click through 13 layers of wallpaper! *http://www.wnet.org/archive/tenement/*

A
B
C
D
E
F
G
H
I
J
K
L
M
N
O
P
Q
R
S
T
U
V
W
X
Y
Z

A
B
C
D
E
F
G
H
I
J
K
L
M
N
O
P
Q
R
S
T
U
V
W
X
Y
Z

Confederation for Kids

Canada is made up of ten provinces and three territories. It became a country in 1867, but its history goes back much farther than that. Learn about the history of the First Nations tribal groups, British North America, and the challenges of "Confederation:" joining all the colonies together into one country. There's also a terrific look at some of the famous people who helped shape this process.

http://www.nlc-bnc.ca/2/2/index-e.html

Historica

The Heritage Minutes project helps bring to life historic moments in Canadian history, as well as offering mini-biographies of notable Canadians. You can view some of the mini-movies here. In other parts of the site, you can try games with Canadian themes and visit an excellent set of annotated links.

http://www.histori.ca/

PROVINCES AND TERRITORIES

ALBERTA

About Alberta

Alberta's emblems include the official stone (petrified wood), mammal (Rocky Mountain bighorn sheep), flower (wild rose), tree (lodgepole pine), bird (great horned owl), and fish (bull trout). Read about them all, as well as the official tartan, flag, and coat of arms.

http://www.gov.ab.ca/aboutalberta/emblems.cfm

Travel Alberta

If you love outdoor recreation and the thrill of caving, hang gliding, white-water rafting, or downhill skiing in the Rockies, then here is a place you won't want to miss. Banff National Park, Canada's oldest national park, was established in 1855. Jasper National Park is home of the Columbia Icefields, the largest chunk of ice in the Rocky Mountains. Learn about them both, as well as many other tourism destinations in Alberta. It is no wonder that the motto of this Canadian province is "*Fortis et Liber*" ("Strong and Free").

http://www.travelalberta.com/

BRITISH COLUMBIA

The British Columbia Outdoors

Here you can venture into the beautiful and fascinating wilderness areas of British Columbia and learn about the creatures that inhabit its forests and coasts. From badgers to wolverines, bald eagles to wood ducks, from Alpine fir to yellow cedar, practically everything you might want to know about the animals, birds, fish, forests, and wildflowers of this Canadian province is all right here. You can learn how to tell the difference between a bobcat and its larger cousin, the lynx. Peer into the eyes of the great horned owl. Wade right in and take a look at some weird-looking fish that you may never have seen before. If you're more of a land rover, learn to identify the wildflowers and plants that paint this Canadian province with such spectacular color.

http://bcadventure.com/adventure/wilderness/

NET FILES

If you were stuck in a room with only a calendar, how would you survive?

Answer: Eat the dates and the "sundaes" and drink from the spring! Visit the Calendar Zone at *http://www.calendarzone.com/* for calendar poetry, lore, and jokes—of course.

Lost your sheep? Find them in FARMING AND AGRICULTURE.

Government of British Columbia

Did you know that British Columbia, or B.C., is bigger in land area than France and Germany combined? This official site explains all about B.C. government, including the official emblems: dogwood (provincial flower), Steller's jay (provincial bird), jade (provincial gemstone), and western red cedar (provincial tree).

http://www.gov.bc.ca/

MANITOBA

Explore Manitoba

This official site is your gateway to information about Manitoba's government. Discover links to tourism and business, as well as living and working in Manitoba. We wish they had a kid's version of this site. Maybe next year!

http://www.gov.mb.ca/cgi-bin/choosehome.pl

Travel Manitoba: Manitoba Official Emblems

This official site offers information on Manitoba's fishing and other outdoor activities, but you'll also find material on urban attractions and historical sites. You can also learn about the official emblems. The great grey owl is the official bird, the crocus is the flower, and the white spruce is the official tree. The province has an official tartan cloth; according to this site: "Each colour has its own significance: Dark Red Squares—natural resources of the province; Azure Blue Lines—Lord Selkirk, founder of Red River Settlement (Winnipeg); Dark Green Lines—the men and women of many races who have enriched the life of the province; and Golden Lines—grain and other agricultural products."

http://www.travelmanitoba.com/quickfacts/
   emblems.html

NEW BRUNSWICK

Government of New Brunswick

New Brunswick has some of the highest tides in the world, as it is bordered by the Bay of Fundy. The Bay of Fundy has its own Web page, and you can find it if you click on Tourism from the main page of this official government site. Looking for the official emblems? They are here <http://www.gnb.ca/cnb/nb/nb-e.htm>. The purple violet is the official flower, and the black-capped chickadee is the provincial bird. The official tartan cloth is described this way: "These are represented in the design by the forest green of lumbering, the meadow green of agriculture, the blue of coastal and inland waters, all interwoven with gold, a symbol of the province's potential wealth. The red blocks represent the loyalty and devotion of the early Loyalist settlers, the Royal New Brunswick Regiment and all of our people. The red block also contains the grey and gold of the province's coat of arms and the regimental crest. Because the first weaving of the design was commissioned for Lord Beaverbrook, the province's eminent benefactor, the red blocks are highlighted by 'beaver' brown."

http://www.gov.nb.ca/

NEWFOUNDLAND

Government of Newfoundland and Labrador

Visit this official site and find out lots of interesting facts. For example, ever heard of "Iceberg Alley"? That's where the icebergs drift south from Greenland, sometimes all the way into the north Atlantic shipping channels. That's what happened to the *Titanic* in 1912. See some pictures, and find out where you can spot icebergs along the coasts. The Provincial flag and symbols are found here <http://www.gov.nf.ca/nfld&lab/>.

http://www.gov.nf.ca/

The Sun never sets on the Internet.

A
B
C
D
E
F
G
H
I
J
K
L
M
N
O
P
Q
R
S
T
U
V
W
X
Y
Z

A
B
C
D
E
F
G
H
I
J
K
L
M
N
O
P
Q
R
S
T
U
V
W
X
Y
Z

NORTHWEST TERRITORIES

Government of the Northwest Territories

This site takes you to Canada's Northwest Territories, which encompasses one-third of the land mass of Canada, about 1.3 million square miles. It is a land firmly rooted in the cultural past and old traditions of the Inuit, Inuvialuit, Dene, and Metis; it is a land of adventure and exploration, where some of the wildlife and scenery are like nowhere else on earth. The direct link to the official symbols is at *<http://www.gov.nt.ca/research/facts/>*.

http://www.gov.nt.ca/

NOVA SCOTIA

The Playground

This official site is chock-full of kid-approved fun, facts, and trivia about Nova Scotia. As you look around, you'll learn that the Coat of Arms includes a rearing unicorn, thistles, and a First Nations warrior. These are the oldest arms (granted in 1625) in the commonwealth, outside of Great Britain. Keep exploring, there is much to do at this site. Can you beat the Bluenose Brain Buster quiz?

http://www.gov.ns.ca/playground/

Titanic - The Unsinkable Ship and Halifax

After the maritime disaster that befell the *Titanic* on April 15, 1912, ships from Halifax, Nova Scotia, were sent to recover many of the bodies. They are buried in Halifax's city cemeteries, and at this site you can find a list of those who were identified. There is a J. Dawson, but it's not Jack—it's James. He was a 23-year-old "trimmer." At this site you can learn about artifacts and recovery efforts, as well as see interesting photos and find a series of links to related sites.

http://titanic.gov.ns.ca/

Explore underwater archaeology in SHIPS AND SHIPWRECKS.

NUNAVUT

Leo Ussak Elementary School

These kids go to a cool school—we really mean it's cool there. This school is way up north. They live in Nunavut, above the 60th parallel. At this site, you can learn about Inuktitut, the language of the Inuit people, and you can get a lot of information about what life is like in an Arctic village. Although the school is very Net-savvy (read about how they videoconference with a school in Hawaii) and modern, they honor the elders and their traditional ways; you 'll find a good deal of cultural information here. For example, what kinds of foods do kids eat there? "Here in Rankin Inlet you can eat caribou (a lean, nutritious, delicious meat), delectable arctic char, lake trout, or grayling. In the fall you can pick ripe, juicy berries growing all over the tundra. You can sample seal, *mukta* (yes it's true, Inuit do consider it a delicacy to eat whale blubber!) and goose. You can also have a Pizza Hut pizza or Kentucky Fried Chicken if you want!" And how do people sleep when the sun stays above the horizon all "night"? "On June 21st, it is light almost all of the time. People sometimes put cardboard, plastic garbage bags or aluminum foil on their windows to help make it dark enough to sleep. It is darkest on December 21st when the sun rises at 9:45 in the morning and goes down at 2:45 in the afternoon. Sleeping is no problem then! "

http://www.arctic.ca/LUS/

NET FILES

How many mosquitoes can one little brown bat catch in one hour?

Wet or dry, give AMPHIBIANS a try!

Nunavut Government Directory

Until fairly recently, Canada had ten provinces and two territories—the Yukon Territory and the Northwest Territories. These two territories together made up more than one-third of the entire country's land area. On April 1, 1999, the northern and eastern portion of the Northwest Territories became Nunavut, Canada's third territory. Read all the background details of the establishment of Nunavut and see what the plans are for the future. Looking for the official symbols? One place to find them is <*http:// www.canadainfolink.ca/nunavut.htm*>.

http://www.nunavut.com/government/english/

ONTARIO

Canada's Capital

Ottawa is the national capital of Canada. It's located in the province of Ontario. Stroll through this site to visit Parliament Hill and other historic and noteworthy attractions. If you're visiting in the winter, make sure to bring your sweater for ice skating on the Rideau Canal. And when you get too cold, you can take a virtual tour of some of Ottawa's historic museums: the Canadian Museum of Civilization, the Canadian War Museum, the National Library, and the National Aviation Museum, just to name a few. While you're there, stop by the Fun Zone for some Canadian-themed puzzles, games, and trivia.

http://www.capcan.ca/english/about/intro/

The Premier's Kid Zone

Find out about Ontario's symbols, its history, and how its government works. Your host is the very hip and cool Max the Moose. Follow him on an adventure tour around the province, but you'd better study the rest of the site a little bit first, because there's a quiz.

http://www.kids.premier.gov.on.ca/english/

PRINCE EDWARD ISLAND

Prince Edward Island Information Centre

What do Avonlea, Kindred Spirits, and Lover's Lane all have in common? You can find them all on Prince Edward Island, the birthplace of Lucy Maud Montgomery, who wrote the universally beloved book, *Anne of Green Gables*, first published in 1908. Her story was inspired by the land, the sea, and the people around her. Anne of Green Gables is so popular with young (and old) readers that it has been translated into many different languages and put on film. You'll enjoy all the stops on the " Anne " tour at this site, especially the Green Gables Farmhouse in Cavendish, which is preserved as a national museum. Check out the L. M. Montgomery literature links, and before you leave, don't forget to look through the IslandCam, Prince Edward Island's mobile digital camera located in Charlottetown. The provincial symbols are located at <*http:// www.gov.pe.ca/infopei/ Reference/ProvincialSymbols/*>.

http://www.gov.pe.ca/

QUÉBEC

Government of Québec

This official site is quite extensive if you speak French. If you speak only English, much of the site is unavailable to you. The tourism section contains beautiful photos of the region.

http://www.gouv.qc.ca/Indexen.html

SASKATCHEWAN

Government of Saskatchewan

If you think that Saskatchewan is "one big wheat field," then it's time for you to learn more. Facts and figures may be found here, as well as this link to information on the official emblems and symbols <*http://www.iaa.gov.sk.ca/protocol/html/Emblems/ coatarms.htm*>.

http://www.gov.sk.ca/

A B C D E F G H I J K L M N O P Q R S T U V W X Y Z

A
B
C
D
E
F
G
H
I
J
K
L
M
N
O
P
Q
R
S
T
U
V
W
X
Y
Z

Saskatchewan - Land of Living Skies

Sure, you'll find lots of information about tourism in this province, but if you're looking for emblems, go to <http://www.sasktourism.com/info/ emblems.shtml>. The sharp-tailed grouse is the official bird, and the western red lily is the flower. How did this province get its name? According to this site: "Plains Indians are credited with originating the name Saskatchewan. Their word was 'kisiskatchewan'—meaning the river that flows swiftly—in reference to the most important waterway running through their territory."

http://www.sasktourism.com/

Time Service Dept

The U.S. Naval Observatory in Washington, D.C., is the official timekeeper for the United States. This site is tied into the master clock—clocks, actually. U. S. Naval Observatory timekeeping is based on several unusual clocks: cesium beam and hydrogen maser atomic clocks. You can find out more about these at this site. They also use a network of radio telescopes to make sure they are always right on time. Why is that so important? Well, if a rocket engine burns a second too long, the rocket may end up miles from where it should be. Or if one computer sends a message but the other computer isn't "on" to receive it yet, that's a problem. These clocks are correct to the nanosecond level, which is a billionth of a second! At this site, you can also calculate the sunrise, sunset, twilight, moon rise, moon set, and moon phase percentages and times for a U.S. location.
http://tycho.usno.navy.mil/time.html

YUKON

Ghosts of the Klondike Gold Rush

It's 1898, and we're going to join the 100,000 others stampeding towards Canada's mysterious Yukon hoping to fulfill their dreams. We've survived avalanches and beat starvation, and we've made it as far as Dawson City. Now we're ready to pan for gold and strike it rich! You may not find "real" gold here, but you'll pick up nuggets of fact and fiction about this memorable time in history. Find out what motivated some of these prospectors by hearing what the grandchildren of a Klondike stampeder have to say.

http://www.gold-rush.org/

Government of Yukon

From this official government site you can take a link to the travel and tourism area. You'll find all kinds of info about visiting this section of the country. Read about its climate, and get vital statistics such as birthrate, employment, and population.

http://www.gov.yk.ca/

Yukon Virtual Tour

QuickTime virtual reality panoramas will make you feel you are right in Carcross desert, "the smallest desert in the world," or hiking along one of Crestview's lovely trails. Kids made these "movies" with the help of their teachers! You can also take a virtual visit to their schools and look around the classrooms. Check Grade 5P in the Jack Hulland school tour. They appear to be having a good deal of fun!

http://www.yesnet.yk.ca/vrtour/

We like the INVERTEBRATES best. —The Nields

CARS

★ Rockets on Wheels: Build Your Own Online Race Car

Why not try to design your own online race car? First pick your wheels. There's a no-tread variety, one with a deep tread, and one that seems to be made out of stone. Which will go faster? Now pick the rest of the car's parts and features, and see how well you do! There is a lot about the science of racing here, too, so start your engine and zoom on over.

http://www.pbs.org/tal/racecars/

Under the Hood

Welcome to new car owner's night! The donuts and fruit punch are right over there, please help yourselves. Now those of you who are beginners at engines and all this other stuff under the hood, please sit down and work on the novice tutorials. Anyone here know a fuel injector from a brake drum? Then please line up by the advanced class sign. Just here for the donuts? You can find some cool games over there in the corner. This site was created by students for the ThinkQuest competition.

http://library.thinkquest.org/19199/

★ Vince & Larry's Safety City

Larry and Vince are real dummies—crash test dummies, that is. They have been in over 10,000 car crashes through the years, in order to test car safety. What happens at the Car Testing Grounds? What's the correct way to wear a seat belt? Are air bags more trouble than they are worth? What's the best way to be safe around school buses? What's up with bicycle safety? Larry and Vince give you the answers. They also give you the questions in the Safety Challenge Trivia game—can you beat the current high score?

http://www.nhtsa.dot.gov/kids/

WebINK: Auto Tour: So You Want to Make a Car . . .

Have you ever wondered how cars are made? This site takes you through all the steps, saving you from walking the 16 miles of conveyors that transfer car bodies from start to finish. That's more than 230 football fields in length! At this auto factory, over 260 programmable robots install, weld, and paint in order for those shiny new vehicles to roll off the line. Look over their shoulders (or whatever robots have) and see how cars are built. There are also some great links on car history, solar cars, and race cars.

http://www.ipl.org/autou/

ALTERNATIVE FUEL

See also ENERGY

Introduction to Alternative Fuels and Alternative Fueled Vehicles

We know, we know. It's a PDF file you have to open with Adobe Acrobat. In general, we hate to list these. But really, this workbook developed by Miramar College, San Diego, is worth the effort. You'll learn all about alternative-fueled vehicles in a colorful, fun way. Why are we experimenting with fuels other than gasoline? For one thing, other types of fuels may be more friendly to the environment and not produce so many harmful emissions. Plus, other fuels may be renewable, that is, we can make more of them any time (unlike the gas and oil underground—when it's gone, it's gone).

http://www.transportationtech.com/Resources/pdfs/afv99.pdf

A Student's Guide to Alternative Fuel Vehicles

Besides electric cars, there are lots of other alternative fuels. There's ethanol; methanol; propane; natural gas; and, of course, solar power. No dilithium crystals yet, but somebody somewhere is probably working on it; and when there is news about it, that news will be here! The California Energy Commission also has an excellent series of pages on energy.

http://www.energy.ca.gov/education/AFVs/

A B C D E F G H I J K L M N O P Q R S T U V W X Y Z

A
B
C
D
E
F
G
H
I
J
K
L
M
N
O
P
Q
R
S
T
U
V
W
X
Y
Z

HISTORY

★ Mileposts

What was new in 1900? Kodak cameras, the Scholastic Aptitude Tests, baseball's American League was formed, and Ford Motors was founded. In those days there were only ten miles of paved roads, and the latest cars could travel at a top speed of eight miles per hour. They also got 35 miles per gallon—something your parents would like to get now! Travel through time in automotive history, enjoying the landmarks along the way.

http://www.aaca.org/bntc/mileposts/mileposts.htm

★ Model T Road Trip

Follow along in Jenny's 1919 diary as her parents decide to purchase a Model T automobile and go on a road trip vacation. Learn about the history of the Ford Motor Company and enjoy the family's adventures as they drive along rural dirt roads. Sooner or later you'll have to help start the Model T, among other interactive activities (it sure was hard to do).

http://www.hfmgv.org/smartfun/welcome.html

NET FILES

WHERE IS THE WORLD'S LARGEST URBAN (THAT MEANS "IN A CITY") COLONY OF BATS?

Answer: The largest known colony is in a city in Austin, Texas, under the Congress Avenue bridge. The Austin bats eat 10,000 to 30,000 pounds of insects per night, including mosquitoes and numerous agricultural pests. According to Bat Conservation International, "This is the largest urban bat colony in North America. With up to 1.5 million bats spiraling into the summer sunset, Austin now has one of the most unusual and fascinating tourist attractions anywhere." See the bats at
http://www.batcon.org/discover/congress.html

Sloan Museum - Flint, Michigan

Take a tour of the Sloan Car Museum. Start with the 1902 Flint Roadster and look at 15 more, ending with an Indianapolis 500 pace car. There's also a neat history of how cars were made, focused on the vehicles produced by General Motors in Flint, Michigan.

http://www.ipl.org/exhibit/sloan/

CATS

See also ANIMALS; MAMMALS—CAT FAMILY; and PETS

The Cat Fanciers' Association (CFA)

This page comes straight from the source: the Cat Fancier's Association. Learn what happens in cat shows and see who the top winners are. There are 35 pedigreed breeds recognized by this organization, plus five more with either provisional or miscellaneous status. There is also very detailed information on cat health and cat care.

http://www.cfainc.org/

★ Cats @ Nationalgeographic.com

Chuck's given you a task: design the best, most effective predator you can. Choose a skeletal base; a muscle structure; and various other goodies, such as senses, behavior, and bitey, scratchy parts. What will your predator look like?

http://www.nationalgeographic.com/features/97/cats/

KittyCam

Kitty is a real working cat. Her job involves holding down office conference room chairs and sleeping in sunny spots all day long. You can often view her blistering pace on her live webcam, but if she's out at the cappuccino machine on a break, you can see the Best of KittyCam. Naturally, she has collected some links you might enjoy, and you can "paws" to drop her a note or join her newsletter if you wish.

http://www.kittycam.com/

CHEMISTRY

See also SCIENCE—EXPERIMENTS;
SCIENCE—SCIENCE FAIRS

BrainPOP - Matter and Molecules

Tim and Moby tackle the MASSive puzzle of learning about chemistry. Even Moby, who is usually pretty DENSE, manages to learn VOLUMES. Everyone should visit this page PERIODICALLY.

http://www.brainpop.com/science/matter/

★ Carbon is 4 Ever

Your name is Bond . . . Carbon Bond. Your mission is to learn about carbon and its components. So, spend some time doing that before playing Atom Casino and the other games. If you don't, you won't be able to pit your skills against the final game. Every mission will teach you something new about carbon, and the game that follows tests your knowledge. If you complete a mission, you get a code word. Once you've finished all four missions, you're ready for Mission Omega, the final challenge. Don't try to skip ahead. You need the code words to play Mission Omega. This site was created by students for the ThinkQuest competition.

http://library.thinkquest.org/C005377/

Chem4Kids!

Where, exactly, are the states of matter? Are they anywhere near Cleveland? Does it matter? Of course, you know that anything that takes up space or weight is also called matter. You've got your solids, your liquids, and your gases, but did you know there's also something called plasma? It has nothing to do with the type of plasma associated with blood, though. Examples of this kind of plasma include ball lightning and the aurora borealis, or northern lights. You can also view plasma in the electrically charged matter contained in a fluorescent light or a neon sign. Find out lots about matter, elements, atoms, ions, and reactions at this fascinating site.

http://www.chem4kids.com/

Chemical Carousel: A Trip Around the Carbon Cycle

Welcome to the interactive tour to the carbon cycle. I'm your host, Captain Carbon, man of steel (well, only 1.5 percent steel, but you get the idea . . .). On the tour today you'll learn that carbon recycles through the food chain and other processes you may have heard about, such as photosynthesis in plants. In fact, it's hard to separate chemistry from biology when it comes to carbon! The carbon atoms in your body today may have once been a tree, a chicken, or . . . well let's just get started on the tour. It's sure to be an eye-opener! This site was created by students for the ThinkQuest competition.

http://library.thinkquest.org/11226/

ChemWeb 2000

One-stop high school chemistry, this way! Acids and bases, balancing equations, gas laws—it's all here. There are also several multimedia movies of various chemistry experiments. For example, what is that gel-like absorbent material used in diapers? What's elephant toothpaste? Check the handy calculators to convert a gram to a mole and back, or to help you with your titrations. And don't miss the mad-lib (called a Chemlib here)! This site was created by students for the ThinkQuest competition.

http://library.thinkquest.org/19957/

★ Common Molecules

According to this site, "Molecules are the smallest collection of atoms of a compound which retains the properties of that material." Everybody knows that the formula for a molecule of water is H_2O (two hydrogen atoms joined to one of oxygen). X-ray crystallography is one way to study the structure of molecules. The ones illustrated here range from minerals like quartz to really bizarre stuff like buckyballs. What's really fun is that you can drag your mouse around to manipulate the molecules in space. Look at them from all sides. Did you notice that diamond looks like a bee's honeycomb?

http://www.iumsc.indiana.edu/common/
  common.html

A
B
C
D
E
F
G
H
I
J
K
L
M
N
O
P
Q
R
S
T
U
V
W
X
Y
Z

A
B
C
D
E
F
G
H
I
J
K
L
M
N
O
P
Q
R
S
T
U
V
W
X
Y
Z

★ HyperChemistry on the Web

Do you think early humans knew anything about chemistry? Even fire—the simple process of fuel, air, and spark called combustion—is considered a chemical reaction. Learn about the history of chemistry from those early times right up to the Nobel Prize winners of the twentieth century. There's a nice section on chemical experiments you can try at home (with an adult). Visit the Periodic Table to learn about the history of each element, as well as its physical properties. This site was created by students for the ThinkQuest competition.

http://library.thinkquest.org/2690/

★ Miami Museum of Science - The pH Factor

Is something an acid or a base? You need to know that if you're going to the lab! Use the online "pH panel" machine to explore the pH of common household solutions such as virtual lemon juice, borax, vinegar, and Lava soap. Then check out the real kitchen chemistry experiments you can try with an adult. Some involve toothpicks and gumdrops, while others require more elaborate preparations.

http://www.miamisci.org/ph/

NET FILES

You are very hip to the latest fashions: Your front teeth have inlaid pyrite, obsidian, or jade gemstones, and you wear a lot of quetzal feathers and a big hat. You can't wear jaguar sandals, though, since they are reserved for the chief only. You're a member of an ancient civilization. Who are you?

Answer: You're a Maya. Discover more classic Maya beauty tips at http://www.halfmoon.org/beauty.html

★ Mr. Guch's Calvalcade o' Chemistry

It's true that back in the day, Net-mom could never understand how to convert atoms to moles to grams and back again. So she was not expecting much when she examined Mr. Guch's lesson on the subject. Imagine her surprise when, in the comfort and safety of her own home, she was able to perform these calculations at last. Thank you, Mr. Guch. This quirky page includes tutorials and practice worksheets for everything you'll need in high school chem class.

http://www.acs.org/vc2/

VC2: Your Virtual Chemistry Club

Discover the science behind "magic" color-changing pens, get some advice on your science fair project, and see how scientists solved some "chemistry mysteries." This site from the American Chemical Association even offers some molecular origami!

http://www.acs.org/vc2/

PERIODIC TABLE OF THE ELEMENTS

The Comic Book Periodic Table of the Elements

Why should you bother knowing anything about the elements or their arrangement in the periodic table? One reason is the frequent occurrence of elements in—comic books. After all, you need to know things like what's radioactive, what blows up when you add water, and what's really valuable. Is there really such a thing as kryptonite, destroyer of Superman's powers? Check it out.

http://www.uky.edu/Projects/Chemcomics/

It's Elemental - Element Flash Card Game

If you draw a blank when confronted with the Periodic Table of Elements, you're not alone. This site offers a way to change all that with that tried and true system: flash card drill and practice. You can decide to be challenged by all the elements or just the naturally occurring ones. The computer will choose an element and you have to provide the name, or symbol. (Don't worry, you can peek at the table if you want.)

http://www.jlab.org/services/pced/elementflashcards/

★ Visual Elements

This site takes you way beyond the colorful chart on the wall and helps you understand the relationships among the elements and why they are grouped the way they are. Read up on the history of the periodic table. Check the electronic postcards section to see the periodic table visualized as ethereal landscapes. You can also download some of them as screen savers or desktop patterns. It's fascinating stuff! One caution: although this resource is supported by the Royal Society of Chemistry, it is only current to 109 elements known in 1997.

http://www.chemsoc.org/viselements/

WebElements Periodic Table

You can learn a lot about chemistry at the WebElements Periodic Table. Just click on any element and you'll be transported to all the info you need. Note that elements 114, 116, and 118 have been reported in 1999, and 113, 115, and 117 have not yet been discovered as of this writing, but there are placeholders in the table for them.

http://www.webelements.com/webelements/scholar

CIRCUSES AND CLOWNS

See also JUGGLING

Animal Protection Institute's Circus Campaign

Circuses are a controversial topic due to their use of animals in the shows. Some organizations want to educate people that "circuses aren't fun for the animals." This site is one to visit to learn about that view, but the material presented here is not for the sensitive. Another like resource is sponsored by the People for the Ethical Treatment of Animals, at <http://www.circuses.com/>. For still more on this topic, visit the RIGHTS AND FREEDOMS— ANIMAL RIGHTS section of this book.

http://www.api4animals.org/default.asp?ID=61

CircusWeb! Circus Present and Past

As a new circus employee, there is so much to learn. For example, there are a lot of superstitions. If you're walking in a circus parade, it's bad luck to look behind you. And don't even think about whistling in the dressing room! After the show, if you're hungry, don't ask where the kitchen is—you want the "Pie Car." This page gives a glimpse of circus life, including how the heck they get those big tents up. There are also links to circuses and performers all over the world. Parental advisory: preview them, and caution kids not to try these tricks at home.

http://www.circusweb.com/circuswebFrames.html

Cirque du Soleil

Since its beginning in 1984, millions of people have been enchanted and delighted by a Cirque du Soleil show. They have performed all over the world, and often several of their circus companies are touring at any one time. What makes Cirque du Soleil so different? For one thing, there are no animal acts. For another, this is a reinvented circus—one that is part theater, part magic, part imagination, and mostly just plain fun! To see the impossible become reality, visit this site and find out where they will be performing next.

http://www.cirquedusoleil.com/

★ The Great Circus Parade - Wisconsin's National Treasure

Hey, look at this poster. It reads: "Come to the Great Circus Parade! A two-hour processional over a three-mile route, authentically re-creating turn-of-the-century circus street parades. Features 60 historic wagons, 700 horses, cavorting clowns, wild animals in cage wagons, and the fabulous 40-Horse Hitch." Sounds like fun! Look over there—isn't that Buffalo Bill Cody in his beaded buckskin jacket? You can learn something about circus history, including circus trains, at this colorful, animated site.

http://www.circusparade.com/

A B C D E F G H I J K L M N O P Q R S T U V W X Y Z

A
B
C
D
E
F
G
H
I
J
K
L
M
N
O
P
Q
R
S
T
U
V
W
X
Y
Z

★ Ringling Bros. and Barnum & Bailey Circus

It's billed as The Greatest Show on Earth, and now you can visit it whenever you choose! The first performance of the Ringling Bros. and Barnum & Bailey Circus was held in New York City's Madison Square Garden, on March 29, 1919. Do you have what it takes to perform in the circus? It takes ability, grace, skill, and did we mention nerves of steel? Take the online aptitude test and see how well you do. In the Arcade section there's also a loads-of-laughs "create a clown" game for little kids, as well as other online games. Some are also available as downloads, and there are free screen savers and wallpaper in the Souvenir Stand area, too. In the links section, look for pointers to clown organizations and lots more.

http://www.ringling.com/

CLOTHING AND COSTUME

See also HOLIDAYS—HALLOWEEN

Fabric Online

According to this site, people wear clothing for three basic purposes: protection, communication, and decoration. Learn about fashions developed for each of these reasons as you explore this site. Find out what wearing black says about you, and what fashion trend (other than wearing black) was started by Queen Victoria.

http://library.thinkquest.org/C004179/

NH Extra: Fashion

What is fashion, anyway? Who gets to say what colors and styles are "in" this year? If you dye your hair pink, are you doing it because you want to be "different" or because everyone else in your crowd has multicolored locks? Track down a few fashion fads at this trendy Web site.

http://www.pbs.org/newshour/on2/fashion.html

HISTORY

The Costume Page

Digging through this resource is like exploring an old clothing trunk you found in Grandma's attic. The deeper you go, the more interesting things you discover! Want to know what was fashionable in Roman times, Elizabethan times, or any other time? There is probably a link here. You can also find great ideas for Halloween costumes or other dress-up fancy wear for imaginative play. There's even a link to "How to tie a tie" (in the Schools and Instructions area). If you're looking for anything to do with fashion and its history, try here first! Parental advisory: we have not checked all links.

http://members.aol.com/nebula5/costume.html

The History of Costume by Braun & Scheider

Your school is having an Ancient Rome day, and you don't know how to tie your toga? No problem, just drop in here, where there are 500 costumes pictured, from ancient times through the nineteenth century. The original German text was written in the Victorian period. This page concentrates on the pictures, which are detailed. Whether you intend to dress as a fourteenth-century German knight or a late-nineteenth-century Swiss Heidi, you'll find a model here! (Hint: Choose the TEXT version, which loads faster, and then focus on the time period you need to explore.)

http://www.siue.edu/COSTUMES/history.html

Hold onto Your Hats! History and Meaning of Headwear in Canada

What kind of hat do you wear? Sometimes hats are worn to keep your head warm, or to keep the sun out of your eyes. Other hats have sports, religious, or other ritual meanings. Still other hats are just plain fun! Can you learn about history and culture just by studying styles and trends in headgear? You bet.

http://www.civilization.ca/membrs/canhist/hats/hat00eng.html

People are the true treasures of the Net.

The Invention of Jeans

Levi's jeans have been around for over 125 years. They proudly say that theirs is the only nineteenth-century garment still in active use today. At this site you can read about how the idea of riveted blue denim revolutionized both work clothing and the fashion industry.

http://www.levistrauss.com/about/history/jeans.htm

★ The Regency Fashion Page

If you were a girl living in the Regency Period (ca. 1790–1829) in England, you would have needed a big closet. That's because of all the clothing girls wore to be proper in the social circles of the times. In the morning you'd have had to wear "morning dress," which was supposed to be plain and unadorned. Later, you might have put on your walking attire, or your promenade dress. Then there's the semiformal half dress for the afternoon tea parties and such, and later on, dinner, opera, or evening dresses (they were all different). Ah, should you be called to attend a party at the royal court, there were special clothes for that, too. Wait until you see the bathing suits, er, "seaside bathing dresses!"

http://locutus.ucr.edu/~cathy/reg3.html

★ Solemates: The Century in Shoes

Experience great moments in twentieth-century shoe history, from Dorothy's ruby slippers to platform shoes of the 90s. "Dial a Decade" to see what kind of footwear was popular when. Period advertisements and QuickTime movies add to this informative history of what people danced in, worked in, and hung around in throughout time. There's also a shoe time line that stretches from 4,000 B.C. to the late 1800s.

http://www.centuryinshoes.com/

Traditional Costumes

What's the national costume for American kids? It may well be blue jeans and a T-shirt! If you have another tradional costume, you might send a photo in to this site, perhaps it will be featured. When we visited, we learned about clothing in China, Vietnam, Austria, Tanzania, Turkey, Mongolia, Ethiopia, Japan, Sweden, and England. There's a fun matching game, too. Can you match the right country to its national dress?

http://www.kids-space.org/CTC/

Victorian and Tudor Costume

In the years between 1600 and 1880, fashion changed dramatically. At this site, you can select "Dress the Men." To "Dress the Ladies" go to <http://www.bbc.co.uk/history/games/costumes/costume1.html>. You'll be presented with two different models and an article of clothing: for example, a pair of stockings. Is this something worn by a Tudor man or a Victorian one? Keep guessing until the models are fully dressed. You'll learn about each garment as you play the game.

http://www.bbc.co.uk/history/games/costumes2/costumes2.html

Space Place Launch Pad

Care for some El Niño pudding? Or perhaps some Asteroid potatoes? Want to make a meat tray nanorover? Or a super sound cone? You've come to the right place: the Space Place from the Jet Propulsion Lab. Discover galaxies of cool crafts, puzzles, and information that is really "out there." We loved it. *http://spaceplace.jpl.nasa.gov/*

A
B
C
D
E
F
G
H
I
J
K
L
M
N
O
P
Q
R
S
T
U
V
W
X
Y
Z

A
B
C
D
E
F
G
H
I
J
K
L
M
N
O
P
Q
R
S
T
U
V
W
X
Y
Z

CODES AND CIPHERS

See also RADIO—AMATEUR RADIO; and WORDS. Are you looking for game codes? They are in the VIDEO AND COMPUTER GAMES section.

Morse Code and the Phonetic Alphabets

Morse code was invented by Samuel Finley Breese Morse as a way to send messages over telegraph lines. Morse is known as the inventor of the "electromagnetic recording telegraph," although he had help from others. The first message was transmitted over a telegraph line in 1844. "What hath God wrought" went 36 miles, from Washington, D.C., to Baltimore, Maryland, in code sent by Morse himself. What happens if you make a mistake in sending code? You can't erase or backspace, so to indicate that a mistake has been made and tell the receiver to delete the last word, send . . . . (eight dots). This site offers a few Morse code translators (listen to your name in Morse!), as well as a section on phonetic alphabets.

http://www.soton.ac.uk/~scp93ch/morse/

NET FILES

How do you say, "Where is the bathroom?" in Klingon?

Answer: nuqDaq 'oH puchpa' e'? Say that six times fast! If you need help with your pronunciation, go to http://www.kli.org/tlh/phrases.html

NOVA Online - Decoding Nazi Secrets

The ENIGMA code machine was used by the Germans before and during WWII. This site explains how this ingenious device worked. It could be set in any of 159,000,000,000,000,000,000 possible ways, which kept code breakers puzzled for a very long time until its secrets were finally cracked. This resource lets you follow the thought processes of a code breaker, plus try a virtual online ENIGMA machine.

http://www.pbs.org/wgbh/nova/decoding/

The Riddle of the Beale Treasure

The Beale ciphers hold the key to one of the greatest unsolved puzzles of all time. The story goes that around 1820, a fellow named Beale hid two wagon loads of silver, gold, and jewels someplace near Roanoke, Virginia. He left three coded letters, supposedly detailing the location of the treasure, with a trusted friend. Then he left for the West and was never seen again. One of the letters, describing the treasure, has been deciphered. It is in a code based on the Declaration of Independence. It is believed the other letters are similarly coded to the same document or other public documents. You can read about the status of the Beale ciphers, and you might want to try solving them yourself (if you find this treasure, please let us know!).

http://www.unmuseum.org/beal.htm

Secret Language

Psssst! Want to send a secret message to a friend, one that nobody else can possibly decipher? Head on over to this page at San Francisco's Exploratorium, where you can print out a copy of some substitution cipher wheels. Put one inside the other, twirl them around a little bit, and you're in the spy biz!

http://www.exploratorium.edu/ronh/secret/secret.html

Thunk.com - Secret Messages for Kids Only!

Now send a secret e-mail message to your friend! Visit this site, type in your message, and then hit the "Scramble" button. Copy and paste the resulting text into your e-mail message, and then be sure to tell your friend to go to Thunk.com to unscramble the message! There are also links to other sites on ciphers and spies, plus encrypted jokes.

http://www.thunk.com/

COLLECTORS AND COLLECTING

See also EARTH SCIENCE—GEOLOGY—GEMS AND MINERALS; GAMES; TOYS; and other subjects.

Cracker Jack Collectors Association

Although Cracker Jack was invented in 1871, prizes weren't put into the boxes until 1912. Since then, over 17 BILLION toys have been dug out from underneath the sticky popcorn and peanut confection everyone loves. Do you collect Cracker Jack toys? These folks do! There's a section on where to get toys and how to keep them in their best condition. The site also reminds kids that the whole point of the toys is to play with them and have fun—so, you might want a "good" set you trade with, and another set to play with. Visit the official Cracker Jack site for more history and fun <http://www.crackerjack.com/>.

http://www.collectoronline.com/CJCA/

KidZone Olympic Pin Collecting Page

Ashley has it all figured out, and she's letting you in on her secrets of Olympic pin collecting. One of her tricks is to find out all the Olympic sponsors and get their addresses. Then send them each a polite letter saying how old you are, what you like to do, and how much you would love to have one of their pins. She says she always offers to pay, but most places will send them for free. She says she's gotten hundreds of pins this way! Read her other suggestions; then go for the gold yourself.

http://www.pinfever.com/kidszone.html

PEZ Candy, Inc.

Have you ever had PEZ? This "interactive candy" is best known for its famous collectible dispensers. There are hundreds of different models; this site offers a checklist of which ones have been sold in the U.S. For detailed pictures of most of the dispensers, often with the date of manufacture for each one, try <http://www.pezworld.com/>.

http://www.pez.com/index.htm

Soft Drink Cans

Here's a person who is easily amused. He collects soft drink cans from around the world. You won't believe the diversity. Who knew, for example, that so many soft drink cans have pictures of animals on them? He also archives candy bar wrappers, scans them, and puts them on the Web. Apparently, he's not the only one: he has links to people who do the same thing.

http://members.nbci.com/bclairoux/cans.html

Starting a Banana Label Collection

Did you think you were the only one with a collection of banana stickers? Oh, no, my friend. There's a whole world of kids and grown-ups out there, all of them peeling off banana stickers and sticking them on the refrigerator, on their computer monitor, on their little brother's back, etc. If you haven't started a collection, this site gives you the basics of beginning this appeeling hobby.

http://www.geocities.com/napavalley/1702/

Wheaties and the Hobby of Collecting Sport Cereal Boxes

Did you eat your Wheaties today? If they are all gone, you might think about saving the box! Some of the boxes are very collectible and command high prices from people interested in them. This page tells you how to get started in collecting these boxes, many of which are released only in certain regions of the U.S. (that's what makes some Wheaties boxes rare).

http://pages.prodigy.net/funnybusiness3/cbox.htm

A
B
C
D
E
F
G
H
I
J
K
L
M
N
O
P
Q
R
S
T
U
V
W
X
Y
Z

A
B
C
D
E
F
G
H
I
J
K
L
M
N
O
P
Q
R
S
T
U
V
W
X
Y
Z

COIN COLLECTING

See also MONEY

American Coin Online

What's your coin worth? First, you have to identify it. This site pictures many old U.S. coins, and provides a convenient way to figure out what you've got. Then you need to decide what condition the coin is in and find its mint mark, if any; this site explains how that's done, too. Finally, research what other people are willing to pay for the coin. There are links to current coin prices from this site. You'll also find a wealth of valuable information on everything from cleaning old coins (don't!) to foreign currency and bills.

http://www.acoin.com/

Coin Collecting FAQ Part 1

Have you already put together a nice collection of coins, or did you just stumble onto a few old ones in your change? Not really sure what to do with them? Roll on over to this page and get some of the more basic coin collecting questions answered. "How can I determine what a coin is really worth?" and "How can I sell my coins?" are two questions that are answered here, clearly and with logic and detail.

http://www.telesphere.com/ts/coins/faq.html

★ Coin World Online

Whether you're a beginner or a pro at collecting coins, Coin World will have something of interest. There is a history of the U.S. Mint, including information on coin goofs and mint errors. Sometimes coins are struck in the wrong metal, and other times they are struck twice (double die) with the second strike slightly offset. These rarities can be worth a lot of money! Check this site to find out what to look for; then ask Mom if you can look through her pocket change. This site also offers some coin-related trivia games and crossword puzzles. Don't miss the section on State Quarters. If you're the first in your state to find a new one, you can get your name listed at this site.

http://www.coinworld.com/

SPORTS TRADING CARDS

Baseball Card Collecting

Most baseball card collectors settle into one type of category or another. Some collect only new cards, some collect old cards, some try to find only the players they like, and others attempt to complete sets of cards. All of these choices are described at this page along with the pros and cons of each. There's also a terrific section on the best ways of storing your cards so that the corners don't get bent and your dog doesn't walk off with one.

http://www.baylor.edu/~JefferyHuett/Page3.html

Collecting Baseball Cards, a Detailed Hobby

Card collecting has been popular since the late 1800s, when tobacco companies printed cards with sports figures on them. They thought maybe they'd sell more of their products if people liked the cards. They were right, but it wasn't until 1933 that a bubble gum manufacturer came up with the idea of enclosing baseball cards with the gum. Or is it the other way around? This resource will get you up to speed on the hobby of sport card collecting: how cards are made, what to look for, and what's valuable.

http://www.communityonline.com/local/sports/base-
    ball/ballcard.htm

STAMP COLLECTING

Junior Philatelists of America

What's a philatelist? That's a person who really, really likes to collect stamps, postal markings, and other pieces of postal history. If you're under 18 and you'd like to know more about this very popular hobby, here's a great place to start. One online pamphlet you can read is called "How to Avoid Common Mistakes As a Beginning Stamp Collector." One very important hint involves getting the used stamp off the envelope—you don't just peel it off. There's a lot to know!

http://www.jpastamps.org/

Surf, and you shall become empowered (or wet).

National Postal Museum

Check out one of the Smithsonian Institution's newest museums! Its exhibits are organized into several major galleries that tell the story of postal history, and it includes a great collection of rare and wonderful stamp images. In many ways, the study of U.S. postage stamps is the study of American history and tradition. Special online collections include how the Titanic and the gold rush are connected to postal history. Whether you collect stamps or just use them to mail letters, you'll find a visit to this site well worth the time.

http://www.si.edu/postal/

Stamp Collecting Basics

Stamps can be graded by their condition. The better condition a stamp is in, the more valuable it is. But the words used are so confusing: "Superb," "Extra Fine," "Very Fine," and others. How do you judge condition? This site explains it all—look in "Collecting Basics." There's also a list of upcoming new stamp releases, sometimes with pictures of the stamps and information on how to order them. Don't miss the Zillions of Stamps section, which includes a price guide.

http://www.linns.com/reference/basics.asp

Get on board, little children, in RAILROADS AND TRAINS.

COLOR AND COLORING BOOKS

See also ART—DRAWING AND PAINTING

★ Carmine's Introduction to Color

It doesn't matter whether you're picking up crayons for the first time or you're a portrait painting pro, you will find something of interest at this Web page. Explore color mixing and matching activities and learn how the "mood" of a painting changes if you magically switch to different colors. Learn about proportions and portrait techniques. Little children will enjoy Carmine's color wheel game, while bigger ones (and adults, too) will be fascinated with chasing down the evil Dr. Gray and his Dechromatizers!

http://www.sanford-artedventures.com/play color1/color1.html

Inside Art: An Art History Game

You're being dragged around the art museum with your parents. It's hot, your feet hurt, and you're simply bored, bored, bored. Wait—the colors in that artwork: they seem to be moving. The swirling vortex leaps off the wall and inches towards you. Suddenly, you're sucked in, and now you're caught up and trapped inside the painting! You'll have to ask the help of a fish named Trish and learn some things about art technique and art history before you can escape. If you manage to get out of this dilemma, there are other adventures available, just follow Carmine the chameleon.
http://www.eduweb.com/insideart/

A
B
C
D
E
F
G
H
I
J
K
L
M
N
O
P
Q
R
S
T
U
V
W
X
Y
Z

A
B
C
D
E
F
G
H
I
J
K
L
M
N
O
P
Q
R
S
T
U
V
W
X
Y
Z

Color Matters

Red means "stop" and green means "go"—everyone knows that without giving it much thought. But did you know that color can affect the way you feel? It can make you feel relaxed or jumpy. It can make you feel interested or bored, even make you feel warmer or colder! And color sometimes means different things in different countries: for example, black is the color of grief and mourning in the U.S., while in some Asian countries the appropriate color is white. Find out more about the fascinating world of color here.

http://www.colormatters.com/

Crayola

What's your favorite Crayola color? In 1903, the Binney & Smith company manufactured the first box of Crayolas. Explore the history of Crayolas and learn about Crayola trivia. Make sure you visit the activities section for lots of craft ideas. How do they make crayons anyway? There's an online factory tour here <http://www.crayola.com/factory/preview/factoryfloor/crayonmfg.htm>.

http://www.crayola.com/

★ Make a Splash with Color

San Jose's The Tech Museum has a nifty online exhibit about color. You'll learn how to describe a color based on its hue, saturation, and brightness. As they explain it, hue helps you tell which bananas in the bunch are ripe. Saturation is the color difference between your chocolate milk and your sister's. And brightness tells us the difference between plain white bread and burnt toast.

http://www.thetech.org/exhibitsevents/online/color/
   teaser/

🦆 Mixing Colors

Click the rainbow to begin, and follow the audio directions to create color-mixing adventures of your own. You will need Shockwave to play the games.

http://www.harcourtschool.com/activity/color/
   color.html

COLORING BOOKS

🦆 Arthur: Welcome to D.W.'s Art Studio

Select your online brush, choose a color, and you're good to go have fun with the coloring book pages here. Based on Marc Brown's "Arthur" series characters, your artist in residence is D.W. She'll explain how you can use the paint features, as well as the rubber stamping tools. You can also choose to clear the canvas and "draw" on a blank screen.

http://www.pbs.org/wgbh/arthur/dw/paint/

★ Kaleidoscope Painter

We won't spoil the surprise! Just click and drag your mouse slowly across the screen and watch what happens. If you just want to relax and watch, click on Auto. Note that you can select your brush size.

http://www.permadi.com/java/spaint/spaint.html

🦆 Kendra's Coloring Book

Coloring used to be so hard. There's that "stay within the lines" thing. Plus, it can be tough to find the right color crayon or marker. When you do find it, it's always broken or out of ink. If you make a mistake, you might as well start over. Your worries are over at this site. All you have to do is pick a picture, select a color, and click where you want the color to go. No more wondering where you left the "peach." If you do want to print the picture and use real paints, there's a button to choose that option, too.

http://www.geocities.com/EnchantedForest/7155/

🦆 Paint Kit

Crayons all broken? Not to worry. This online coloring book lets you click and color your way through six drawings. When you're through, you can either print out your masterpieces or click the Reset button to start over.

http://www.kaboose.com/shockWin2.cfm?infoID=
   painting&shockType=fl

♣ Theodore Tugboat Activities

We loved the online coloring book at this site. Select the tugboat you want to color, choose a crayon, and click the area you want to fill. Magically, you'll hear a sound and the color will be right where you want it. Change your mind? Just pick another crayon and click in the same area!

http://www.cochran.com/theodore/activities/

COMICS, CARTOONS, AND ANIMATION

See also DISNEY; PUPPETS AND MUPPETS; and TELEVISION—NETWORKS

Cartoon Network.com

Bugs, Daffy, Fred, Scooby Doo, Powderpuff Girls, and lots of your favorites await you at this site. There's also an online tour to Hanna-Barbera, as well as an introduction to animation. You'll find loads of games, but unfortunately, loads of advertisements, too.

http://www.cartoonnetwork.com/

★ Clay Animation Station

If you've ever wondered how they make those animated movies using clay figures, wonder no more. At this site you'll discover tips, tricks, and techniques to help you make your first animated movie starring—CLAY! You will need a camera (the site suggests a digital one is best) and other supplies, but the results pictured here are fabulous. This site was created by students for the ThinkQuest competition.

http://library.thinkquest.org/22316/

★ Comics.com

Every week they make families around the world laugh. They have names like Snoopy, Dilbert, and Marmaduke. Who are these wacky characters? They are the drawings that make up the comic strips in your newspaper. Catch up on your favorite comic strip characters, and see what they are doing on the Internet. More than 90 comic strips are listed. Find out about the artists and how they thought up the characters. Sometimes there are games or screen savers based on the comics, too.

http://www.unitedmedia.com/comics/

★ DC Comics for Kids

DC Comics is the home of such superhero greats as Superman and Batman, along with many others. We wonder if they ever go out for lunch together. If you want to know what's new at their comic book company, stop in here. You will find some coloring pages, a quiz, and more. Don't miss the special Internet Safety edition of The Daily Planet.

http://www.dckids.com/

NET FILES

Research scientists say we have five basic tastes. You probably know four of them: sweet, salty, sour, and bitter. What is the fifth? (No, it is not chocolate!)

Answer: It's called umami ("you-mommy"), which is a Japanese word variously translated as savory, essence, deliciousness—although apparently even that's not a very good explanation. Find out more at http://faculty.washington.edu/chudler/questions.html#q4 and at http://archives.seattletimes.nwsource.com/cgi-bin/texis/web/vortex/display?slug=wats&date=19980804&query=umami

Discovery: Animation Maker

Think you could be an animator, given the chance? Now's the time to give that theory a try! Select a space-related plot, choose a background and starring characters, write dialogue ("All your bases belong to us!"), and watch the cartoon you have created. You can e-mail it to a friend, too.

http://apps.discovery.com/animaker/animaker.html

★ Draw and Color with Uncle Fred

"Uncle Fred" Lasswell has been drawing the "Barney Google and Snuffy Smith" comic strip since 1934, and he still stays on the cutting edge of today's technology. His Web page includes numerous fun cartoon drawing lessons and features from his videodisk of the same name. Even the youngest of Web surfers will have no trouble drawing these characters.

http://www.unclefred.com/

★ Lee's (Useless) Super-Hero Generator

Wouldn't it be great to have superpowers? You could just snap your fingers and your homework would do itself! You need a cool superhero name first, and this site will make one up for you. Net-mom herself is now going to turn into the wondrous Spyder Arrow, taking off on her space stilts.

http://home.hiwaay.net/~lkseitz/comics/herogen/

The Official Wallace and Gromit Homepage

Wallace is an eccentric inventor, while Gromit is his faithful dog. Their adventures are depicted in Claymation, a special animation technique that uses clay figures as actors. You can learn more about this process, plus relive the plots of the W&G movies from the links at this site. There are also cool W&G downloads, sounds, and other fun in Wallace's Workshop. The Fashion Follies game allows you to change the head, middle, and bottom of an unsuspecting Wallace. You may have to use Internet Explorer rather than Netscape to play, however.

http://www.aardman.com/wallaceandgromit/

❧ Thomas the Tank Engine

Do you know Thomas the Tank Engine & Friends? If you're a fan of the TV show or the book series, then you'll love the coloring book pictures and information on Thomas and the whole gang. There are some cute games waiting for you down the track, too.

http://www.thomasthetankengine.com/

COMMUNICATION

See also BOOKS AND LITERATURE; INTERNET; LANGUAGES AND ALPHABETS; RADIO; TELEPHONE; TELEVISION; and WRITING

Global Networking Timeline

If you ever need to write a report on the history of communication from the beginning of time to the present day, you'll really be glad we found this site. It starts off at 30,000 B.C. with cave drawings. Lots and lots of entries later we come to 1040 or so, when movable type was invented in China. Many decades later, Marconi received the first telegraph signal across the Atlantic. It's fascinating reading, and you'll get lots of facts for your assignment.

http://www.ciolek.com/PAPERS/milestones.html

The Many Faces of Communication

Explore the world of communication, from the silence of body language to speaking; print; writing; advertising; TV; and, of course, the Internet. There's even an ad jingle to promote the World Wide Web. This site was created by students for the ThinkQuest competition.

http://library.thinkquest.org/17844/

Messages

Decode alien messages. Listen to people from six different countries say the same words. Interpret a scene from a movie clip by listening to five different soundtracks. This site is chock-full of Shockwave activities that aim to explain all of the ways animals and humans communicate. So, the next time you want to make your Mom happy, pick a bouquet of flowers. She'll get the message.

http://aries.mos.org/

COMPUTERS

BrainPOP - Computers

What's a CPU? If it megahertz do you put a bandage on it? Can you serve dip with your RAM and ROM chips? The BrainPOP crew examine what's inside a computer and how the components interact. Another part of this site explains how a computer mouse works.

http://www.brainpop.com/tech/computeranddigital/
computer/index.weml

Click 'n' Learn

Have you ever looked inside your computer? There is quite an interesting world in there. There are little dust bunnies that move the data around . . . and elves who spin the disk drive, and, no—only kidding! With the help of this site, you'll soon be able to tell a heat sink from a power supply, and even a PCI slot from the ISA ones. We didn't spot any elves; maybe you will.

http://www.kids-online.net/learn/cnl.html

A Complete Illustrated Guide to the PC Hardware

You've got to respect a review article that comes right out and says it: "Choosing the right video card is hard." This source explains, pictures, and reviews interfaces, chip sets, drives, and more. The opinions expressed by the webmaster may help you get a better understanding of your own PC.

http://www.karbosguide.com

Computers Can Be a Real Pain

Everybody knows that sometimes computers can be a real pain. Not just because they lock up, or because they don't do what you want them to—but because of the way you sit at them when you use them. This site explains why it's important to sit square in your chair, use a wrist rest, and not stay at the keyboard (or the mouse) too long.

http://kidshealth.org/kid/watch/house/
kergonomics.html

Dave's Guide to Buying a Home Computer

How do you figure out which computer is the right one for you? What size and speed of microprocessor do you need? You don't want to waste your allowance money on a computer that is more than you need, but you do want a system that will be usable for a number of years. Read these guides for tips and suggestions on purchasing and installing a PC. Find out what to ask the store salesperson and what to look for in features. The opinions expressed here are just that—opinions—but you'll find some valuable information. One of the most useful sections is the one on how to buy a used PC.

http://www.css.msu.edu/pc-guide.html

Spacekids.com

Best for elementary and middle school kids, this site offers everything from current space news to fun games and puzzles. Want to be more grown up? See how old you'd be on other planets. (Hint: on Mercury you'd be an old geezer!) Learn about the planets, space travel, and lots more on this really cool site.
http://www.spacekids.com/

A B C D E F G H I J K L M N O P Q R S T U V W X Y Z

★ Intel® The Journey Inside

Did you know you can learn something about computers just by making breakfast? This site compares a computer to a toaster: you put in the bread (input); then there's an area where the bread is stored (storage); it awaits the heating element (the processor); and finally, your toast is done (output). Enjoy this multimedia look at how computers make toast, er, well, you get the idea. Just don't get any jelly on the keyboard.

http://www.intel.com/education/journey/

❧ IPL Youth Division: Do Spiders Live on the World Wide Web?

Take your baby sister to story time at the University of Michigan's Internet Public Library. This picture book dictionary will help her learn the difference between the mouse on your desk and the mouse in your barn. In case you were wondering, the one in the barn eats up all the corn, while the one on your desk eats up all your time.

http://www.ipl.org/youth/StoryHour/spiders/
    mousepg.html

The Jargon File

In the beginning, computers were understood by only a small group of insiders. These insiders developed their own language and made up their own words, all of which served to further isolate them from the rest of the world, which was, after all, a distraction from computers and programming. ;-) For years, hacker lore and legend has been collected into this file. Now it has made it to the Web, and you will laugh at the funny computing terms and lingo heard daily in machine rooms all over the Net. Some have even made it into popular conversation! You can search the file for specific terms or just browse for fun. Parental advisory: some of these terms have mildly adult origins.

http://www.tuxedo.org/~esr/jargon/

PC Hardware Primer

Whether you want to buy your family's first computer, or are trying to update one you already have, visit this site. The array of confusing gear at the store will suddenly become clear after you've studied the material about interfaces, protocols, and more. You'll also get some interesting advice, such as why you should think twice before overclocking your processor.

http://www.help.com/cat/1/618/hto/14199/1.html

ZDNet: Quick Start Guides

This is the first place you should go if you are a new owner of a computer or peripheral. Everything from PCs to digital cameras, from virus protection software to MP3 players, it's all covered. Learn more about your new device, and try some suggested first projects.

http://www.zdnet.com/quickstart/

ARTIFICIAL INTELLIGENCE

Artificial Intelligence

Alan Turing (1912–1954) was a British computer scientist who believed that one day a machine would be designed that would be "intelligent" enough to fool a human into thinking he was talking to another person. The Turing Test is only one part of this very informative site on A-life, AI, or artificial intelligence. How far have we come? Where are we going? This site was created by students for the ThinkQuest competition.

http://library.thinkquest.org/2705/

Intelligent Agents - Agentland

Someday soon you may not interact with the Net yourself—you'll have a "bot" or "agent" to go out on the Web for you and bring back what you want. This resource helps you track the latest news in intelligent agents, and we don't mean Fox Mulder.

http://www.agentland.com/

A B C D E F G H I J K L M N O P Q R S T U V W X Y Z

HISTORY

★ One Digital Day - Created by Photojournalist Rick Smolan

In what ways has our world been transformed by the invention of the computer chip? Photojournalist Rick Smolan decided to find out. Famous for such projects as *A Day in the Life of America*, Smolan sent photographers off to the far reaches of the world to capture one digital day. This Web site shows many of the results, which include helping kids who can't go out in the daytime, working to save endangered species, and body sensor research to help bicycle racers go faster. You can also see how a silicon chip is made at this most interesting site.

http://www.intel.com/OneDigitalDay/

The Triumph of the Nerds

You know the nerds, those geeky technology-types who wore plastic pocket protectors and really thick glasses. In the 70s they were ridiculed, but they ignored all that, put away their slide rules and went ahead to build Silicon Valley. They founded computing and software companies, made themselves millionaires, and in doing so changed the world as we knew it! This Web site tells their story.

http://www.pbs.org/nerds/

MACINTOSH

Apple Computer

This is the computer "for the rest of us" that launched the mouse, the Graphical User Interface, and the networked laser printer into the consumer mainstream. Apple's home page has product information to help you choose a system and a technical support area to help answer questions. You'll also find downloadable upgrades to Apple software and information on what Apple is working on to improve their products for the future. You can also use something called iDisk to store your own files on Apple's server, and share them with your friends.

http://www.apple.com/

MacFixIt.com: Troubleshooting for Your Mac

Eventually, every Macintosh computer owner will run across a problem and will need some kind of support. We like the info at this site, which is constantly updated. If you have a bizarre problem you just can't seem to troubleshoot, search here on keywords describing the situation. You may strike gold!

http://www.macfixit.com/

The Ultimate Macintosh

Hundreds of Macintosh-related links are piled on this one page, making it possible to conduct a search using your browser's Find command (on Lynx, use the / command). The best thing about this page is the What's HOT! section, which provides up-to-the-minute news and links to the latest information (including promotions from Apple and major vendors) and software updates. Not all links have been viewed.

http://www.ultimatemac.com/

NET FILES

There are AAA, AA, C, and D batteries. What happened to sizes A and B?

Answer: According to The Last Word, "The AA, C, and D size designations originated in the U.S. at a time when battery-operated valve radio receivers were widely used. These receivers had already laid claim to the A and B designations: the A battery (usually a lead-acid accumulator) heated the filaments of the valves, while the B battery provided the high-voltage supply for the anodes. Therefore, new cells could not use the same names, and AA, C, and D sizes were adopted." Find out more battery cell history at http://www.last-word.com/lastword/answers/lwa110gadgets.html

A
B
C
D
E
F
G
H
I
J
K
L
M
N
O
P
Q
R
S
T
U
V
W
X
Y
Z

PC COMPATIBLES, MICROSOFT WINDOWS

Annoyances.org

Does using Microsoft Windows make you annoyed? Well, you're not alone. In fact, there's a series of books about reducing clutter, improving performance, and learning to cope with Windows Me, Windows 95, and 98. There are companion Web sites that will help you, too. Find the one you need via this page.

http://www.annoyances.org/

Dell Computer Corporation

According to their Web site, "Dell is the world's No. 1 computer systems company." Dell computers are cropping up in more and more K–12 classrooms, and here's the best place to see the latest and greatest.

http://www.dell.com/

Gateway.com

Did you know Gateway computers are shipped in boxes that look like they are part dairy cow? What's with those cows, anyway? Ted Waitt's family had been in the cattle business for many generations. When he created a new computer company, he brought some of his heritage with him. Find out what's new down on the Gateway farm right here.

http://www.gateway.com/

IBM Corporation

Here's where the personal computer (PC) all started. IBM introduced the PC in 1983. Before the PC, and even now, IBM's stronghold has been with big-business computers that run governments, corporations, banks, and other institutions. Now schools are installing wireless labs and "learning village" solutions. Explore this Web site to see what this computer giant is up to these days.

http://www.ibm.com/

Intel in Education

Intel doesn't make computers, but it does make the chips inside them. Now you can see what's going on inside Intel and K–12 education. This site clues you in on Intel-sponsored research, invites you to enter the Intel Science and Engineering Fair, and offers a wonderful online museum featuring the history of the transistor, the microprocessor, and more. There are also resources on using technology in education, and a list of available grants and donations sponsored by Intel. Don't miss the section on PC Parents with tips on cyber-parenting. It's in the Education section.

http://www.intel.com/education/

Microsoft in Education

Visit these K–12 pages and see what Microsoft is doing in the way of sponsoring programs to promote education, computers, and networking. There are also plenty of online tutorials in the Instructional Resources section. Learn how to use PowerPoint, Outlook Express, Internet Explorer, and several others.

http://www.microsoft.com/education/

NET FILES

Everyone's heard of the 4-H Club. What are the four Hs?

Answer: In 1911, they stood for "Head, Heart, Hands, and Hustle . . . head trained to think, plan and reason; heart trained to be true, kind and sympathetic; hands trained to be useful, helpful and skillful; and the hustle to render ready service, to develop health and vitality . . ." Now, however, they signify Head, Heart, Hands, and Health. Read about this and more 4-H history at http://www.fourhcouncil.edu/market/4hinfo/NHISTORY.HTM

PERSONAL DIGITAL ASSISTANTS

Yahoo! Handheld and Palmtop Computers

We don't remember what we did before we got a PDA (Personal Digital Assistant). Although we originally thought it would be just another high-tech toy, we quickly became proficient in using the stylus writing device for booking appointments; sketching quick maps; looking up phone numbers; and, yes, playing Wheel of Fortune while waiting for the dentist. Now we go everywhere with it. To find out what's new and on the horizon in PDA products and technology, try this site.

http://fullcoverage.yahoo.com/FullCoverage/Tech/
   HandheldandPalmtopComputers/

PROGRAMMING

Dr. Dobb's

If you're really into computers, you might think of writing your own program—maybe even a cool new game! How do you get started? One way is here. Check the tutorials on everything from C and C++ to JavaScript.

http://www.ddj.com/

Programming 4 Kids

Find out how to take free programming classes right over the Web. There's also a site for teens interested in programming games, and several suggestions on how to prepare for the College Board's AP computer exams.

http://www.gomilpitas.com/homeschooling/explore/
   programming.htm

RECYCLED EQUIPMENT

Computers for Learning

The federal government uses lots of computers in its offices all over the U.S. When they upgrade to new systems, sometimes the old computers and peripherals become available for schools (yes, even home schools) and other educational or nonprofit purposes. Find out if your organization qualifies, and maybe you can get some free recycled computers!

http://www.computers.fed.gov/

★ Share the Technology

These folks find new homes for recycled computers and peripherals. Look through the requests and you'll find inquiries from all over the world. Does your mom's company periodically upgrade its computers? If you find out the old ones are headed for the trash, see if you can get the company to consider a recycling project instead.

http://sharetechnology.org/

SOFTWARE ARCHIVES

See also GAMES AND FUN—ONLINE GAMES; VIDEO AND COMPUTER GAMES

CNET.com - Shareware.com

Thousands of shareware files are available via the metasearch engine here, if you happen to own any or all of the following computer platforms: PC; Mac; Linux; Windows CE; or Palm Pilot. You can search in several different software archives all at the same time; we like to see what's new. In some of them, you can also browse through the most popular downloads or choose to try what the editor suggests.

http://shareware.cnet.com/

Yucky Roach World

Visit the yuckiest site on the Internet, where you can find out all about cockroaches and other bug stuff. Check out roach anatomy. Learn what they do for fun. You'll also discover that cockroaches spend 75 percent of their time resting up for those late-night snack runs. There are links to Worm World, too, if you haven't gotten your fill of yucky yet. *http://www.yucky.com/flash/roaches/*

A B C D E F G H I J K L M N O P Q R S T U V W X Y Z

Info-Mac HyperArchive

Over the years, Info-Mac has become the master list for Macintosh software archives, with mirror sites around the world. Now you can use your browser to search this mirror collection at MIT. This is a great way to find shareware, demos, clip art, help, and information about Macintosh. If you own a Mac, this will become one of your favorite links.

http://hyperarchive.lcs.mit.edu/HyperArchive.html

Jumbo!

Shareware? What's that? It means you can try out software files before you buy them. Sometimes the shareware version will do everything that the full version will do. Jumbo also has lots of shareware and free programs for most computers and operating systems. It's easy to find what you want, since everything is classified by subject. The short descriptions will help you find that arcade game, er, math tutorial you want! Don't miss the games and MP3 sections for fun, skins, and screen savers.

http://www.jumbo.com/

NET FILES

Who are **Nahuelito, Champ,** and **Ogopogo?**

(Hint: If you can find them at all, they will be in water.)

Answer: Like Nessie of Loch Ness, they are all legendary lake monsters. Nahuelito supposedly inhabits Nahuel Huapi Lake (Argentina), while Champ is from Lake Champlain (between New York and Vermont). Ogopogo has been spotted in the waters of Lake Okanagan in British Columbia, Canada. Read more about them at http://www.strangemag.com/nessie.home.html

★ Kid's Domain

Families who drop in on this site will find it a severe test of the storage capacity of their hard drives. :-) A wealth of kids' software is available on the Internet, and this is the place to look. This extensive, fully annotated collection gives each program its own page, including age recommendations; program sizes; and shareware fees, if any. The page is divided between Mac and PC archives, and another section is devoted to online games.

http://www.kidsdomain.com/

NoNags Freeware Shareware World Center

Freeware, shareware—this site has it all—that is, as long as you're looking for 32-bit Windows software. They promise "no disabled features, nags, time limits, or any other tricks." Some of the site is available only to members, but a large portion is free to all. They plan to add Linux software in the future.

http://www.nonags.com/

Simtel.Net Worldwide Shareware and Freeware Software Distribution

Check out the legendary Simtel archives for access to just about all known public domain, shareware, and freeware software for DOS and Windows. The Simtel collection goes back to the early DOS years, and it is one of the largest collections of PC programs and information in the world.

http://www.simtel.net/simtel.net/

★ Tucows Network

Tucows says it is the world's most popular collection of Internet software for Windows, Linux, PDA, BeOS, and Macintosh software—and we believe it! This collection is mirrored all around the globe, so pick a site close to you. (Another suggestion is to pick a server located where the local time is in the middle of the night—that server will probably not be overloaded.) This is your source for plug-ins, helper applications, screens, themes, and games. Don't miss the section called TuKids, chock-full of super downloads, online games, crafts, and lots more.

http://www.tucows.com/

> ## RAILROADS AND TRAINS
> ### are on track.

SOFTWARE REVIEWS
Best Educational Software

Nobody wants to spend a lot of money on a piece of software and find out later that it doesn't work, or that it's too easy (or too hard), or that it's no fun! This site gives you details about each program: how it works, what skills are taught, who will enjoy it, and lots more. Focus on the software that will do what you want, and not just on whatever looks like fun at the store.

http://school.discovery.com/parents/reviewcorner/
 software/

Children's Software Revue

There's so much new software coming out, how do you know which ones are worth your time and money? The *Children's Software Revue* magazine is one terrific way to keep up with this ever-growing marketplace. Many features from the print version are also available here, and you can search a database of thousands of reviews. Also quite valuable is the selection of links to other qualified review resources on the Web.

http://www2.childrenssoftware.com/
 childrenssoftware/

SuperKids Educational Software Review

This site is aimed at parents and teachers, but you can use it, too! Find out if that new software title you've seen advertised on TV is really any good. Each month, a team of reviewers (parents, teachers, kids) checks out a selection of the newest programs in a specific subject area, such as math, reading, or science. What do they really like? What really made them yawn? Find out here.

http://www.superkids.com/

TUTORIALS
In and Out of the Classroom

So, your classroom has come up with a great idea for a Web site. Now what? Take a cue from Microsoft and delve into the Front Page tutorial on designing and building a site. This and other practical guides will get your site up and running even if you don't know the difference between a body tag and a head tag. The site also offers other tutorials on Microsoft software—PowerPoint, Excel, Windows 98, Encarta—and their use in the classroom.

http://www.microsoft.com/education/tutorial/
 classroom/

UNIX AND LINUX
Linux Central

Although Microsoft Windows may seem to be the operating system of choice for those with PCs, a popular new system is gaining ground. PowerPC Mac users, there's a version for you, too. Find out about the wonderful world of open source Linux at this site.

http://linuxcentral.com/linux/

Linuxnewbie.org - Wanna Learn Linux?

The "Newbieized Help File" comes in two favors: click on Intel, Solaris, or Mac to learn how to install the Linux operating system on your computer. Join those whose mascot is a penguin!

http://www.linuxnewbie.org/nhf/

Unix Is a Four-Letter Word

Unix is cool. Because of its power, Unix is the operating system that is most often used by engineers and networking professionals. Unix systems don't have to add TCP/IP to plug into the Internet—it's their native networking language. Now try to guess what operating system was used to expand the Internet into what it is today. You're right, it's Unix. Unix was even used to run Jurassic Park in the movie! This nicely designed site gives beginners a good feel for the Unix operating system. There is also a good introduction to the vi text editor for you purists out there.

http://www.msoe.edu/~taylor/4ltrwrd/

A B C D E F G H I J K L M N O P Q R S T U V W X Y Z

UNIXhelp for Users

Excuse me, but you "grepped" my file while I was "rm"-ing it! Unix geeks like to talk that way a lot. At this site you can learn basic Unix commands and be able to translate what the Unix wizards are saying.

http://www.geek-girl.com/Unixhelp/

CONSUMER INFORMATION

See also MONEY

Consumer Reports for Kids

With so many toys to choose from, it's often hard to tell the good from the bad. Now, Consumer Reports, which tests appliances, cars and other things for adults, is rating toys, using kids and their families as toy testers. But the advice doesn't stop there. Get tips on water guns, radio controlled toys, and bicycle and skating safety. Another fun section is the Ad Patrol, which features the latest ads aimed at kids. Like did you know there's really a Don't Do the Dishes Day? Yep, and it's sponsored by a paper plate company.

http://www.zillions.org/

Consumer Reports® Online

Consumer Reports is a nonprofit organization that tests appliances, audio and TV equipment, cameras, cars, and all sorts of other things. They issue their opinions on which items are the best, based on the results of the tests they run on competing products. They accept no advertising in their magazine, so you can really trust what they have to say. Next time you want to buy something, see if it has been reviewed lately. You'll be glad you did. By the way, be sure to tell your parents this is online.

http://www.consumerreports.org/

Street Cents Online

Young people make money, save money, and spend money, just like everyone else! But sometimes there just isn't much advice for young people about handling their money. Do you spend money on entertainment, sports, music, and food? What's the deal on dental gum? Does Duracell really outlast the Energizer bunny? All of these topics and more are covered by *Street Cents*, a popular Canadian television show. And now it's online in an informative and fun Web page. Many of these topics may be found in the archives section. Spend some time here!

http://www.halifax.cbc.ca/streetcents/

What's the most common mineral on Earth?

Answer: Quartz. It occurs in many different forms and colors. Find out more at http://www.minerals.net/mineral/silicate/tecto/quartz/quartz.htm. Some people classify water as a mineral, so we'll accept that answer, too. See http://www.minerals.net/mineral/oxides/water/water.htm for an explanation of this.

COOKING, FOOD, AND DRINK

See also COLLECTORS AND COLLECTING

SpiceGuide

Once, spices were as precious as gems. The demand for spices drove expeditions and opened up new trade routes. You can discover the history of spices at this nicely designed site. A spice encyclopedia tells you where the spice grows, what its uses are, and more. For example, according to its entry, spearmint and peppermint are both native to Asia. Peppermint was used by Egyptians, and spearmint is mentioned in the Bible. Spearmint grew wild in the United States after the 1600s, and peppermint was cultivated commercially before the Civil War. You'll also find recipes and a list of must-have spices for the average kitchen. The Kid's Sugar and Spice section will tell you some interesting facts about a highlighted spice.

http://www.spiceguide.com/

COOKING FOR BEGINNERS

Big Top's Fun Recipes

If you're having a party or other special occasion, why not take a chance and try some Keroppi Frozen Treats or some Hello Kitty Chocolate Truffle Hearts? The Big Top Frozen Krazy Punch sounds delicious, and the Wacky Popcorn would be a great snack for watching TV.

http://www.bigtop.com/kids/recipes1.html

Cooking with Blondee - Kids

Check Blondee's easy pizza recipes, porcupine salad, and butter graham crackers. These nutritious snacks and finger foods are fun to make and delicious, too. There's also a play-dough recipe if you want to play and not eat!

http://www.familyinternet.com/cooking/kids/

Donna's Day Recipes

It would be great to have lunch with Donna, because it would be like taking a trip around the world! How about some British ribbon sandwiches, or maybe some African groundnut stew? Don't forget the garnish—learn how to make a radish mouse or a hard-boiled egg bunny. For dessert, it's back to the states for American cherry pie! Some of these recipes are easy enough for kids, while others will require adult assistance.

http://donnasday.com/donna/creativefun/
cooking.shtml

Idea Box: Recipes

Visit this site to find over 70 easy recipes for kids (and interested adults) or anyone who is just learning to cook! You'll find recipes for holidays and regular days, breakfasts, lunches, and dinners. Some of the recipes include Chocolate Graduation Caps, Funny Faced Bagels, and Nine Patch Toast.

http://www.theideabox.com/ideas.nsf/recipe

OnLocation Virtual Birding

Have you memorized your field guide to birds, including even the exotic species that don't even live in your area? Tired of birding in your backyard and seeing only the same old robins, blue jays, and crows? Why not take a virtual bird hike in a different environment? Wander around a Florida marsh or try the Cape May hawk version. It's like an adventure game because you get points for every bird you know. You can also participate in contests and win prizes for your virtual birding skills. *http://www.virtualbirder.com/vbirder/onLoc/*

A
B
C
D
E
F
G
H
I
J
K
L
M
N
O
P
Q
R
S
T
U
V
W
X
Y
Z

A
B
C
D
E
F
G
H
I
J
K
L
M
N
O
P
Q
R
S
T
U
V
W
X
Y
Z

FOOD—BREAD, CEREAL, RICE, AND PASTA

The Popcorn Board

There's more to popcorn than movie theaters! It's believed the first use of wild corn was for popping. Although it probably originated in what is now Mexico, it was grown in China, Sumatra, and India long before Columbus arrived in the New World. At this site you can get more popcorn history, as well as popping tips (there's a way to save, re-hydrate, and use the kernels that don't pop).

http://www.popcorn.org/

Riceweb

In many places around the world, rice is considered a gift from God, and it is treated with reverence and has a special place in ritual and worship. At this site, you'll learn all about the cultivation and production of rice—one of the world's food staples. There's quite a research push to find ways to grow rice without using so much water. New varieties will be needed. Read how biotechnology and crop modeling are helping.

http://www.riceweb.org/

FOOD—FRUITS AND VEGETABLES

★ Chiquita Banana

We're here to say that bananas may be the world's most perfect food. Loaded with vitamin B6, they are also a good source of vitamin C, potassium, and dietary fiber. At this kicked-up site, you'll meet Chiquita Banana herself and find out what all the singing is about! (You can find the lyrics to the famous song here, too.) Take the link to ChiquitaKids <http://www.chiquitakids.com/> to find games. Can you beat the Chiquita Challenge?

http://www.chiquita.com/

Be dazzled by the laser shows in PHYSICS.

Dole 5 a Day: Just for Kids

Do you mind your peas and carrots? Learn the nutritional values of the fruits and vegetables that you eat every day. Then fun stuff awaits when you meet Lucy Lettuce, Bobby Banana, and their friends. Try the 5 A Day Game along with them, as they point out how important they are to your well-being. There are some snappy songs to learn and plenty of lesson plans for teachers to share with health-minded kids.

http://www.dole5aday.com/

Mann's Broccoli

From seed to your dinner plate, follow the virtual path of broccoli, the healthy dark green vegetable. In the Kid's Club you can play some neat games (none involving broccoli, crown jewel of nutrition), but you'll have to visit the Mann's Farm section to learn that broccoli has as much calcium per ounce as milk. You can also get some vegetable clip art and recipes at this leafy green site.

http://www.broccoli.com/

Produce Oasis

Don't be like comedian Jerry Seinfeld and roll the melons down the supermarket aisle to see if they are ripe! You can get the inside scoop on selecting all kinds of fruit, vegetables, and specialty produce right here. You'll also find nutritional information for these products, as well as recipes and fun facts. For example, according to this page, "Carrots spread westward, introduced into England from Holland in the fifteenth century. At that point, carrots were coveted for their tops, and no well-dressed English gentlewoman would be seen without lacy carrot leaves decorating her hair."

http://www.produceoasis.com/

The State of Florida Department of Citrus

Did you know that citrus fruit must be picked ripe? It will not continue to ripen after it leaves the tree. Here's another interesting fact: although mechanical tree shakers are sometimes used, 98 percent of Florida oranges are picked by hand. Follow the story of tree-to-juice at this sunny delight of a site.

http://www.floridajuice.com/floridacitrus/ whereojbar.htm

Computers are dumb, people are smart.

Sunkist Growers Incorporated

Are oranges sweeter at one end? Try the experiment here to find out. Then check the Welcome to Sunkist area to discover more: how oranges are propagated and grown; what's the difference between a navel and a valencia; and more. You'll also find information about grapefruit, lemons, and tangerines. You'll also learn about a woman known as "Mother Navel" because she planted the first California oranges.

http://www.sunkist.com/

Washington Apples - Just the Thing

Granny Smith, Jonagold, Gala, Delicious—how many varieties of apple can you name? This site describes them all, as well as the best uses for each type. Did you know that the average American eats almost 20 pounds of apples per year? But that's nothing. Residents of some European countries each eat more than 45 pounds annually! Learn all about apples at this site.

http://www.bestapples.com/

FOOD—MEAT, POULTRY, FISH, DRY BEANS, EGGS, AND NUTS
Butterball

Which do you prefer: light or dark meat? ("Hey!" says the turkey, "It's all the same meat to me!") Not only is turkey a very popular food during the holiday season, it's also a great meal any time of the year. ("Yeah, well so is vegetarian pizza!") Turkey is great, because after the first meal, the leftovers are good for a zillion sandwiches and a delicious soup. ("Ever heard of falafel, pita, and hummus?") At this page, you will find great stuffing recipes, gravy recipes, carving tips, and creative garnishing ideas. ("I'm outta here!")

http://www.butterball.com/

Canadian Egg Marketing Agency

We could say this page is *eggciting*. We could say it's *eggzactly* what you're looking for. We don't think that would be an *eggzaggeration*. Here's an *eggzample* of what you'll find: egg nutrition, egg recipes, information on egg farming, grading eggs, and lots of eggtivities. Here's an egg yolk, er, joke: Question: If a rooster laid an egg on the top of a barn, which way would it roll? Answer: Neither, roosters don't lay eggs. We *eggspect* you'll have fun here!

http://www.canadaegg.ca/

Green Eggs and Ham: Recipes

Learn how to make three different versions of this traditional Dr. Seuss fan's breakfast. No, you don't have to go out and find green chickens first!

http://www.randomhouse.com/seussville/titles/greeneggs/recipes.html

Picture a snail shell. Most snail shells coil in one direction—which way?

Answer: According to the Conchologists of America, "Ninety-nine percent of all snail species have shell whorls that coil in a clockwise direction." For more on snails, read http://coa.acnatsci.org/conchnet/facts.html

A
B
C
D
E
F
G
H
I
J
K
L
M
N
O
P
Q
R
S
T
U
V
W
X
Y
Z

★ Oscartown

If you wish you were an Oscar Mayer wiener, you'll want to spend a lot of time at this site. There are the usual games, recipes, contests, and company jabbering, but what caught our eye was the interactive History of the Wienermobile. The first hot dog on wheels toured the streets of Chicago in 1936. It was only 13 feet long. By the 1950s, the Wienermobile had grown to 22 feet. It had a sound system and a sunroof. By 1958, though, it finally got what it had been lacking all these years. No, it wasn't mustard—it was a bun! Six "Wienebagos" were touring the world by 1988, with the comforts of onboard microwave ovens and other conveniences. In 2001, the latest model is 27 feet long. Hot dog! Don't miss playing the interactive wiener whistle.

http://www.kraftfoods.com/oscar-mayer/
omindex.html?B=*&L=3

Peanut Butter Lovers Club

Did you know that about one-third of the U.S. peanut crop goes toward making that famous American staple: peanut butter? Runner peanuts, grown primarily in Georgia, Alabama, and Florida, are the preferred type to use. This is because they are uniform in size and it's easier to get them all evenly roasted. At this site you can find out how peanut butter is made, discover how nutritious peanut butter is, and play a fun trivia game.

http://www.peanutbutterlovers.com/

FOOD—SWEETS

Ben & Jerry's Ice Cream

If you still grieve over the discontinuation of your favorite Ben & Jerry's ice cream flavor, make sure to visit the flavor graveyard and find peace of mind knowing that at least they have gone to the great Web page on the Net. If you get a craving for the real thing, don't even try to lick the screen—just go to the store like everyone else. Funny thing, though. They make over 50 products, but only 34 of them are available in supermarkets. For the rest, you have to go to one of their Scoop Shops. Their hottest ice cream flavor is Cherry Garcia. Run to the store right now to try their newest "2 Twisted" flavors.

http://www.benjerry.com/

Bob's Candies

Haven't you always wondered how those stripes get on candy canes? The answer's here! Visit the candy cane factory to see how it's done. You'll also discover the origin of the distinctive hooked shape and its association with Christmas.

http://www.bobscandies.com/

Exploratorium: Exploring Chocolate

This traces the story of chocolate from the cacao bean right to your mouth! Along the way you'll learn about the science of chocolate, because the site is from a science museum, after all. Who discovered chocolate and how did it spread around the world? Find out here.

http://www.exploratorium.edu/exploring/
exploringchocolate/

★ Hershey's KidzTown

Crunchy, creamy, drippy (like hot fudge) or steaming (like cocoa)—what could be more delicious than chocolate? Where do they make chocolate? Lots of places, but one of them is in Hershey, Pennsylvania, at Hershey's Chocolate Town, U.S.A. This site has fun facts about chocolate and a tour of the largest chocolate factory in the world. And did we mention the games? Flavor Farm and Milky Business are habit-forming! There's also a lot of cool info about the Hershey Kissmobile—check the schedule to see when it's coming to your town. The direct link is <http://www.hersheys.com/kissmobile/>.

http://www.hersheys.com/kidztown/

Jell-O: 100 Years and Still the Coolest

Wow—in a year, 413,997,403 packages of Jell-O gelatin dessert are produced. According to this site, "if you laid the boxes end to end, they would stretch three-fifths of the way around the globe with plenty of room to spare!" Trace the cool history of America's favorite dessert and find recipes, as well as a place to buy special molds online.

http://www.kraftfoods.com/jell-o/history/

★ Jelly Belly Online

There are over 40 different flavors of Jelly Belly jelly beans, and some of them can be combined in "recipes" to make still more flavors. For example, chew a Peanut Butter candy and a Grape one to taste Peanut Butter and Jelly. Jelly Bellys have flown on the space shuttle and were served at former President Reagan's inaugural festivities. At this site you can take a factory tour and check out some fabulous art made entirely of—you guessed it. You can also order some of Harry Potter's favorites: Bertie Bott's Every Flavor Beans (along with lemon, you might get sardine!).

http://www.jellybelly.com/

★ M&M's® Industrial Candy & Magic

When you eat M&M's, which colors do you eat first? Which colors do you eat last? Take a tour of the M&M factory, and find out how they get all those tiny "m's" on there. Then play some funny Shockwave games like Melt 'Em (it involves a powerful magnifying glass, the sun, and Brand X chocolate bars). Remember, virtual M&M's don't melt in your hand or your mouth, but you'll be hungry for some serious chocolate after you visit this site!

http://www.m-ms.com/factory/

NabiscoWorld

Are you a twister or a dunker? Any way you eat Oreos, they are America's favorite sandwich cookie treat. Discover the stories behind how your favorite snacks came to be—like Fig Newtons, Barnum's Animal Crackers, and Chips Ahoy cookies. Nabisco also offers a section for healthy living, cooking tips, and recipes, and they challenge you to lots of fun games.

http://www.nabiscoworld.com/

Have an order of pi in MATH AND ARITHMETIC.

★ Planet Twinkie

How do you feel about Twinkies—you know, those delectable cream-filled sponge cakes? Most people either love them or hate them, but the company must be doing something right because millions are sold each year. Here you'll find a whole "planet" dedicated to this snack food, including games about Twinkies, Web sites about Twinkies, and even wacky scientific experimentation with, what else: Twinkies! You'll also be able to explore a few other places, like Cup Cake Island and Ding Dong Kingdom.

http://www.twinkies.com/

The Story of Chewing Gum

The first patent for chewing gum was granted in 1869—to an Ohio dentist. The most popular flavors are cinnamon, spearmint, and peppermint. Are those your favorites, too? Kids in North America spend approximately half a billion dollars on bubble gum every year. This site lets you chew on gum history and provides hints on how to get gum out of your hair and off clothing and carpet.

http://www.nacgm.org/consumer/consumer.html

NET FILES

How many quills does the average porcupine have?

Answer: How would you like to be the one who has to count? It's been estimated that most have about 30,000 quills, and new ones grow back in when others have been lost in an enemy attack. Read more at

http://www.canadianforestry.com/nature/porcupine.html

A
B
C
D
E
F
G
H
I
J
K
L
M
N
O
P
Q
R
S
T
U
V
W
X
Y
Z

A
B
C
D
E
F
G
H
I
J
K
L
M
N
O
P
Q
R
S
T
U
V
W
X
Y
Z

HISTORY

★ The Food Timeline

Ever wonder what medieval knights ate at their farewell meal before setting off to the crusades? Did you ever need to write a report on cookery in the 1800s? Maybe you just have to know some good recipes from Civil War times. Remember the food time line! Stretching from information on grains back in 17,000 B.C. to the details on foods of the 1990s, this site provides entertaining and educational fare.

http://www.gti.net/mocolib1/kid/food.html

NUTRITION

Dairy Council of Wisconsin Nutrition Activities

This is a great site to get reproducible "blackline masters" to hand around in class. You'll find material in the site's Food Pyramid, Lunch in Any Language, Breakfast Around the World, and Nutritious Nibbles sections. There are also some very tasty links to other nutrition sites on the Net.

http://www.DCWnet.org/nutritionactivities.html

Healthy Choices for Kids Online

Produced by the growers of Washington state apples, this site offers stories, plays, and lesson plans about the food groups. You'll learn about choosing healthy snacks plus find lots of tips for healthy eating. There are also lesson plans and activities to promote good nutrition.

http://www.healthychoices.org/

Mrs. P's Toast Two-somes!

OK, so it's not really about nutrition. But it IS a fun game! Match the sandwich components and see if your mouth is big enough to snack on the results!

http://www.tvokids.com/mrsp/

★ Nutrition Cafe

Try the Grab a Grape game to see how you'll do playing nutrition Jeopardy. Then try to pick a good breakfast, lunch, or dinner in the Have-a-Bite Cafe. This site is a joint project of the Pacific Science Center and the Washington State Dairy Council.

http://www.exhibits.pacsci.org/nutrition/

Nutrition on the Web

Written by teens for other teens, this site won an award in the ThinkQuest competition. The site is in Spanish, German, and English. It has two parts: the Informative section and the Interactive section. In the first part, you'll read some nutrition horror stories, find out what makes up a good diet, and explore some myths. For example, some kids believe that eating a vegetarian diet is always more healthy. The fact is that "vegetarian diets, which contain absolutely no animal products, are very low in vitamin B-12 and, unless carefully planned, may be deficient in vitamin B-6, riboflavin, calcium, iron, and zinc. Strict macrobiotic diets, which include everything except grains, are extremely hazardous. More moderate vegetarian diets that include milk and eggs, and perhaps fish and/or poultry, meet the nutritional needs of growing teenagers if carefully planned. This is why many adolescents that are vegetarians are also anemic." The interactive section of this resource asks you to input your weight, height, and age, and it will tell you how many calories you need to eat per day to maintain your weight. There's also a diet planner, a nutrition database, and more. Some things require an account (free!), but you don't have to give your real name.

http://library.thinkquest.org/10991/

Rate Your Plate

Compose a virtual menu for yourself by choosing an entrée, a dessert, beverage and side dishes. Then, as the title of this site implies, rate your plate. Once you do, you'll get the nutritional values for what you eat. So, if your parents think you're eating too many chicken nuggets and not enough fruits and vegetables, now's your chance to see who's right.

http://www.sp.uconn.edu/~cthompso/

Have a whale of a time in MAMMALS.

The Vita-Men!

Meet the vitamins: superheroes of your body. They help you stay healthy and help support many basic body functions. Check out the Vita-Men (and women) online trading cards to learn about each of them and how they help you. It's a fun way to learn about six vitamins and eight B-complex "heroes."

http://www.vita-men.com/

RECIPES

Parents: We get so many requests for recipes, we're including a few large sites. However, be advised they may contain links or recipes involving alcohol as an ingredient. You may want to stick to the COOKING FOR BEGINNERS sections.

All Recipes.com - The Recipe Network

The title pretty much says it all. This site tries to collect all recipes for baking, soups, chicken dishes, pasta, and holiday meals, and more. They are arranged in such a way that you can visit the site and find just the right recipe for Cafeteria Macaroni and Cheese, or whatever comfort food you crave. The Special Diets section (see Recipe Index) caters to vegans and vegetarians, plus those on diabetic, gluten-free, sugar-free, or egg-free diets.

http://www.allrecipes.com/

Cookie Recipe.com - Cookie Recipes

What's your favorite kind of cookie? Chocolate chip? Sugar or sugar free? Peanut butter? Or do you prefer those luscious holiday cookies, or filled cookies, or no-bake cookies, or maybe some ethnic recipes? The cookie of your dreams is here. Take a bite.

http://www.cookierecipe.com/

Epicurious

You still can't find that extra-special recipe for your doll's dinner party? Check the recipe file to locate those hard-to-find holiday cookies. If you're looking for a recipe from another country, search here for some delicious meal suggestions. Click on Recipe File Main Page; then choose Browse, and then Cuisine, to select from 16 choices—including African, Caribbean, Greek, Indian, and others. You can even choose to find recipes that match what's in your pantry! And don't miss the detour to kid-friendly recipes. A tip: visit the video techniques section to watch how to make a perfect pie crust, roast a turkey, and perform several other kitchen skills.

http://food.epicurious.com/

Gross (But Fun!) Recipes

Now here are some tempting recipes: Boogers on a Stick; Brain Cell Salad; Cat Litter Casserole; Dead Sea Soup; and many more. These won't be the hit of your formal garden party, but they might be fun fare for a Halloween bash.

http://www.melborponsti.com/kids/gross/

The Tower of London

The Traitor's Gate. The Bloody Tower. The Ceremony of the Keys. The Crown Jewels. The Tower of London has been a treasury, a prison, and a government building for a thousand years. It is said that if the ravens that inhabit the Tower green ever leave, the Commonwealth of Great Britain will fall. You can take a tour of the Tower and its grounds right here. But don't scare the ravens! *http://www.camelot-group.com/tower_site/*

A
B
C
D
E
F
G
H
I
J
K
L
M
N
O
P
Q
R
S
T
U
V
W
X
Y
Z

A
B
C
D
E
F
G
H
I
J
K
L
M
N
O
P
Q
R
S
T
U
V
W
X
Y
Z

Mama's Cookbook

Do you want to be a great cook? Mama's Italian cookbook is a great place to start. It has recipes for all your favorite Italian meals, plus cooking and pasta glossaries for beginners. There is also a searchable database of recipes if you know what you want and don't want to hunt through the list to find it.

http://www.eat.com/cookbook/

RECIPES—SPECIAL DIETS

In a Vegetarian Kitchen

If you can't find the vegetarian recipe you're looking for in the Recipes Galore section, try the terrific collection of links. "Fight Fear of Tofu," learn how to simmer a Soulful Soup, and plan a veggie barbecue and holiday meals.

http://www.vegkitchen.com/

International Vegetarian Union

It's not just about tofu! This site offers a history of vegetarianism, a list of famous vegetarians, and a special section just for teens. There's a great FAQ ("How do you pronounce 'vegan'?") and, oh yes, more than 1,700 recipes!

http://www.ivu.org/

Veggie Kids

Sometimes kids don't like the same tastes their older brothers and sisters do. Here are some kid-approved vegetarian meals that you might ask your parents to try. There's a lentil dish with alphabet pasta, "corny" mini-muffins, and a special party "Hummm!us" dip made out of peanut butter! There are also tips for raising kids to love their veggies.

http://www.execpc.com/~veggie/tips.html

COUNTRIES OF THE WORLD

See also CANADA; TRAVEL; and UNITED STATES Welcome to the Countries of the World! Below, we've listed large general educational, entertaining, interesting, and fun Web pages about countries and regions of the world. If you're looking for the Arctic or the Antarctic, also check the EARTH SCIENCE—LAND FEATURES—POLAR REGIONS section in this book. In addition, hundreds of selected Web sites about individual countries may be found online at the NetMom.com home page <http://www.netmom.com/>.

★ A-to-Z Geography - Discovery Channel School

Look up information on world cities, countries, rivers, lakes, and other geographical features at this easy-to-use site. Powered by World Book encyclopedia, the country articles feature a color flag plus maps and photos. Subsections cover the country's government, people, and way of life. There are usually links to related articles, study questions, and a suggested bibliography.

http://school.discovery.com/homeworkhelp/
    worldbook/atozgeography/

★ African Voices

Explore themes common to the many nations of Africa: family, work, wealth, history, and more. As you scroll through the virtual Smithsonian exhibits, you will find exhilarating objects illuminated by fascinating facts and details. This site is a must-see!

http://www.mnh.si.edu/africanvoices/

Chiefs of State and Cabinet Members of Foreign Governments

What's the name of the President of Austria? How is the King of Tonga's name spelled? Who is the Nepalese ambassador to the United States? Check this site for the answers. This resource covers the movers and shakers for all the world's countries and it is always right up to date.

http://www.odci.gov/cia/publications/chiefs/

May the force be with you in PHYSICS.

CIA World Factbook

It's the job of the Central Intelligence Agency (CIA) to know what's going on in the world. This involves gathering information about each country's government, its people, economy, and transportation facilities, including maps of each country. Check the Notes and Definitions area for a handy list of Independent States, Dependencies and Areas of Special Sovereignty (Hey—Greenland is part of the Kingdom of Denmark!), and Miscellaneous (Gaza Strip, West Bank). There's also a category called Other, holding only one entry: Taiwan, which the U.S. recognizes as part of China, though the Taiwanese consider themselves independent.

http://www.odci.gov/cia/publications/factbook/

Countries of the World

Besides the usual factual information, this resource gives information on world religions, languages, and ethnicity and race. You can also examine lists of countries with nuclear weapons or the death penalty, or which ones are currently under armed conflict. On a lighter note, check the national holidays section or the one on the 50 most commonly spoken languages. Which language is spoken by the most people around the world? It's Mandarin Chinese, followed by Spanish and then English.

http://www.infoplease.com/countries.html

Countrywatch

This resource offers much the same information as the CIA World Factbook, but you may prefer this site's layout. One nice feature is that you can choose to browse an entire region at once, such as the Middle East and North Africa. Supplementing the usual facts are current news links about each country, as well as a handy currency converter (all the way at the bottom of the page).

http://www.countrywatch.com/

Database Europe

Browse through a geographical database that includes Statistics, History, Politics, Culture, Climate, And Weather of all the European countries. It has been compiled by the students and teachers at the Albert Schweitzer Gymnasium in Erlangen, Germany. We hope they each got an A+ because they did a great job of gathering all sorts of information. There are wonderful maps of all the countries and of Europe. In addition, they link to many other sites filled with helpful information for a student working on a term paper or a family planning a vacation.

http://www.asg.physik.uni-erlangen.de/europa/
　indexe.htm

NET FILES

What's the surface speed record—for the Moon?

Answer: According to http://www.minervatech.u-net.com/ moon/cyc_triv.htm, it's "10.56 miles per hour. It was set in an Apollo lunar rover."

A
B
C
D
E
F
G
H
I
J
K
L
M
N
O
P
Q
R
S
T
U
V
W
X
Y
Z

A
B
C
D
E
F
G
H
I
J
K
L
M
N
O
P
Q
R
S
T
U
V
W
X
Y
Z

The European Union

According to this site, "The ultimate goal of the European Union is 'an ever closer union among the peoples of Europe, in which decisions are taken as closely as possible to the citizen: the objective is to promote economic and social progress which is balanced and sustainable, assert the European identity on the international scene and introduce a European citizenship for the nationals of the Member States." The European Union currently has 15 member states and is preparing to expand. It has its own flag, anthem, and "day" (May 9).

http://europa.eu.int/abc-en.htm

Footnotes to History

Don't take the information at this site and turn it into a term paper. Most of the entries here cover "Nations you didn't learn about in high school geography." Consider Sealand, which is located solely on a World War II vintage radar platform in the North Sea. Independent state or pirate hangout? You decide.

http://users.mcleodusa.net/j/jlerwin/index.htm

Geographica Homepage

The Interknowledge Corporation presents this professional-looking site containing country-specific pages on many regions around the world. Each country site is both a pleasure to look at and a treasure chest of comprehensive information. This is a don't-miss site for worldly info-seekers.

http://www.geographia.com/

★ Infonation

This very interesting site lets you compare statistics on up to seven different countries at a time. Select the countries you want. Then click on up to four data sets. These can be things like population, unemployment, life expectancy, or more than 40 other choices. Then click on View Info to see how your countries compare with each other. Amazing! Hint: you may have to use Netscape to get the checkboxes to appear.

http://www.un.org/Pubs/CyberSchoolBus/infonation/
   einfonation.htm

Islands of the Pacific

Visit this collection of pages dedicated to over two dozen islands around the Pacific. Each island page contains links to various sites specific to that island, and most links have a brief note on the purpose or content of the site. Check the bottom of the main page for a Newspapers, News, and Media section and a Flags of the Pacific Islands page. The Te Puna Web Directory <http://tepuna.natlib.govt.nz/webdirectory/pacislandslist.htm> is also a rich source of information on these locations.

http://www.escapeartist.com/pacific/pacific.htm

Latin American Network Information Center (LANIC)

The Institute of Latin American Studies at the University of Texas at Austin has compiled this site of information on and from the Caribbean, Central America, Mexico, and South America. Browse through categories such as Countries, Education, Government, Science, and Society & Culture. Within Countries, each country is subdivided into additional sections. Within the remaining top categories, information is subdivided by country where appropriate. In all, this is a comprehensive collection of sites. There is also a search function that spans all collected resources. If it's Latin, it's in LANIC.

http://www.lanic.utexas.edu/

The Living Africa

Did you know that blue duikers, a small antelope, returns to the same area each night to sleep—a rare habit unique to this species? Or that the people in Dibouti are Muslim, while many in Malawi are Catholics? There's much more to discover about Africa at this site, including info about its cities, schools (a typical day at school), ethnic groups, and languages. Don't miss the wildlife conservation game. This site was created by students for the ThinkQuest competition.

http://library.thinkquest.org/16645/

★ Mr. Dowling's Electronic Passport

Somewhere in Florida there's a real Mr. Dowling, teaching sixth grade students during the day and adding to his Web pages at night. His country and world region overviews are a must. They simplify learning and make the process fun! Some sections include the Middle East and North Africa; Africa Today; India to the Himalayas; China; Southeast Asia; Canada; Europe; South America; the Caribbean; and Mexico and Central America.

http://www.mrdowling.com/

Nations of the World

Here's another site with much the same data as the CIA World Factbook, but this one offers a few different, and useful, touches. Alongside each country's flag, map, and facts, you'll find an audio file of its national anthem and a text file of its lyrics. Also, you can click on Related Links to find a small selection of additional country Web pages.

http://www.emulateme.com/preview.htm

Summary of the Peri-Antarctic Islands

Here's an interesting collection of materials on the islands surrounding Antarctica. These 19 islands and archipelagos include the somewhat familiar South Georgia and the South Sandwich islands, and some not so familiar—like Iles Crozet and Iles Kerguelen. This site provides brief information about each of the islands.

http://www.spri.cam.ac.uk/bob/periant.htm

Tourism Offices Worldwide Directory

Where do you want to go on vacation? You have a lot of possible choices; where can you go to get information on each? You want official material, too, not just brochures from hotels and resorts. The same thing applies if you're doing a report on a state or a country: you want information from some authoritative source. Here it is! Just select the country or state you want, and the contact information (and sometimes, the Web page location) will appear on your screen. It will also tell you the last time the address was verified.

http://www.towd.com/

★ United Nations CyberSchoolBus

It won't take you 80 days to go around the world at this site, but you'd find plenty here to keep you busy if you did want to take that long! Besides learning all about the United Nations and how and why it began, you could check Resource Source and learn about special celebration activities for days that are relevant to the entire world, such as World Environment Day. The City Profile section includes descriptions of cities around the world and an urban fact game. The Country At A Glance section contains information about all member countries of the United Nations. Test your knowledge of flags with the Flag Tag game or take quizzes from the Health Game. Periodically, the Professor goes on a seven-week tour of historically and culturally significant sites around the world. Based on the hints from the postcards, you have to figure out where the professor has been. If you uncover all seven destinations, you'll win a prize and get your name listed on the Photo Quiz site. You'll also find lots of info on Model UN activities here.

http://www.un.org/Pubs/CyberSchoolBus/

Walk Through Time - BBC Education History - Age 7-9

Let's try "Odd One Out." Hmm, seems to be a street scene from Victorian times. Wait—something's not quite right. The gentleman is dressed rather strangely for this time period, isn't he? And doesn't the fire-fighting apparatus look positively medieval? Click what doesn't belong, and try to drop it in the time tunnel. If you're right, the item will disappear, to be replaced by its timely equivalent. If you drag the wrong thing, it will come back, along with a short explanation. Try scenes from many different time periods. *http://www.bbc.co.uk/history/walk/*

A
B
C
D
E
F
G
H
I
J
K
L
M
N
O
P
Q
R
S
T
U
V
W
X
Y
Z

A
B
C
D
E
F
G
H
I
J
K
L
M
N
O
P
Q
R
S
T
U
V
W
X
Y
Z

World Heritage Center

What do the Grand Canyon, the Galápagos Islands, Moenjodaro, Völklingen Ironworks, the Island of Gorée, and the Citadel of Haiti all have in common? Though each of these sites is located in a different part of the world, they share a common heritage as unique treasures. If environmental or political situations cause them to disappear, it would be a loss for each and every one of us. UNESCO (United Nations Educational, Scientific, and Cultural Organization) believes that preservation of this common heritage concerns us all. They have established a list of these sites, recognized as exhibiting "outstanding universal value." At press time, the World Heritage List included 690 cultural and natural sites. Find out if your country has any special sites on this list. Maybe your school can become part of the World Heritage Youth Project. Check the Just for Kids section, where you'll find out What Makes a Site and what a World Heritage site manager does, and take some Virtual Tours in the Let's Visit section.

http://www.unesco.org/whc/nwhc/pages/home/pages/

Yahoo! - Countries

Brazil has its rain forests, Morocco has its desert, Chile has its mountains, and Yahoo has them all. Browse the world's countries here to your heart's content. Each country's links are sorted into many categories, such as government, health, libraries, culture, and more.

http://dir.yahoo.com/regional/countries/

CRAFTS AND HOBBIES

See also FAMILY FUN; PRESCHOOLERS

★ DLTK's Printable Crafts for Kids

If you've got a color or black-and-white printer, and a large supply of empty toilet paper roll tubes, you've got a whole toy store! You don't believe it? Neither did we until we saw this site. Explore its pages and print out adorable cows, firemen puppets, Pokémon characters, and lots more. There are also calendars and other printable crafts for you to try.

http://www.dltk-kids.com/

Early Childhood Art Lessons

There are a lot of crafty activities at this site, for example, how about painting without a paintbrush? Even the littlest artists will love dipping popcorn, lettuce, cotton balls, and other objects into the paint. The results can be astounding, and messy, so put on some old clothes first!

http://www.artswire.org/kenroar/lessons/early/
    early.html

NET FILES

What are the historical origins of the Frisbee toy?

Answer: It depends on whether you go with the "Pie Plate" theory or the "Cookie Tin" theory. But everyone agrees that the Frisbie Pie Company, operating in New Haven, Connecticut, in the early 1870s, had a lot to do with the origin of the game. Yale college students had a lot to do with it, too. You can learn about the history of the disk at
http://www.upa.org/~upa/upa/frisbee-hist.html

**Something fishy going on?
Visit AQUARIUMS.**

Earlychildhood.com: Arts & Crafts

Bioputty, colored spaghetti, goofy goop, and cornstarch concoctions are only a few of the "squishy fun" projects collected here. Other, less clean-up intensive activities include handprint paperweights, a wax paper autumn leaf collage, and paper bag pumpkins. There's sure to be something here to interest you, too!

http://www.earlychildhood.com/Crafts/

Eileen's Camp Crafts and Other Fun Things

Eileen is full of exciting ideas! Check this huge resource for instructions on everything from braiding plastic lace lanyards to making candles, from knotting friendship bracelets to creating beadie creatures. Who knew there were so many crafts one can make from empty baby food jars?

http://www.chadiscrafts.nu/fun/siteindex.html

FamilyPlay - Activities

Whether you're looking for rainy day fun or travel games, try this site for creative and fun ideas. Make a dragonfly out of a clothespin, a drum out of an oatmeal box, or a treasure chest from an old shoe box. Use the scroll boxes on the left to select Art Projects, At Home, or Gift Ideas, among other options.

http://www.familyplay.com/activities/

Friendship Bracelets

With some colorful threads and beads and directions from this site, you'll have all you need to make a friendship bracelet. Step-by-step instructions are given for 10 bracelet patterns, including Zig Zag, Rag Rug, and Swirl and Braids. If you can learn the basic knot, you can make other cool things with your bracelets. Hair ties, shoelaces, chokers, and key chains are a few ideas.

http://www.singnet.com.sg/channel/kidcorner/bracelet/

Gimp

Gimp is that colorful flat plastic lacing you played with at summer camp. First, you have to learn how to braid or weave it together, and all the directions are right here at this page. You can use gimp to make bracelets, necklaces, and everyone's favorite: the lanyard. Never lose your keys again!

http://www.cam.com/gimp/

★ Hands On Crafts

No more messy glue, broken crayons, or dried out markers. This site is a treasure-trove of craft activities that you can do with the click of a mouse. The thrill of throwing a virtual pot just might tempt you to run to the backyard and scoop up a bucket of mud. But you'll learn from the online instructions that you'd better stick with real artist's clay if you want to make a lasting pot. When you're done with your pot project, try building a face jug or learn what slabbing is all about.

http://www.handsoncrafts.org/

★ Hands On Crafts for Kids - Projects

This site gives clear instructions for making milk carton birdhouses, sand cast sea treasures, seed topiary trees, bumble bee mobiles, and lots more. More than 50 terrific craft project ideas are collected here.

http://www.crafts4kids.com/projects.htm

Kid's Domain Craft Exchange

Looks like it's another great resource from Kid's Domain, this time with hundreds of craft ideas. Choose from scout crafts, easy jewelry, crafts made from natural materials, things that would make nice gifts, and many more. Don't miss the suggested links to other crafty places.

http://www.kidsdomain.com/craft/

A
B
C
D
E
F
G
H
I
J
K
L
M
N
O
P
Q
R
S
T
U
V
W
X
Y
Z

A
B
C
D
E
F
G
H
I
J
K
L
M
N
O
P
Q
R
S
T
U
V
W
X
Y
Z

Kids' Clubhouse

Opening a lemonade stand soon? Print all the signs you'll need using the patterns here. If you don't have a color printer, just print them in black and get out your crayons. Other projects include snazzy bedroom door signs ("Don't Even Think About It!" is one of them), as well as party hats and binder decorations.

http://www.hp.com/printingideas/kidsclub/k00.html

Making Friends and Other Crafts for Kids

Although this site has a lot of advertising, they do offer many wonderful free patterns for all sorts of crafts. There are super pony bead projects, paper dolls, magnets, rainsticks, and a whole section on making swaps for scout camp exchanges!

http://www.makingfriends.com/

Which large, plated dinosaur is known for having a brain the size of a walnut?

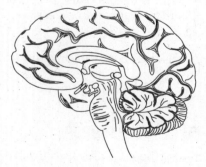

Answer: The stegosaurus. Its brain power was so limited that the animal needed a "second brain" in its hips in order to control its legs. Check out all the dinos at http://kids.infoplease. com/ipka/A0770763.html

Michaels Kids Club Online

Michaels is a huge craft store chain, and they are always dreaming up new ways for you to use their materials. At their Web site, though, you are just using recycled electrons, and there is never a mess to clean up. There are instructions for zillions of craft projects like spoon puppets and refrigerator magnets. The Click-N-Print online coloring book is very cool, too—even we had fun with it.

http://www.michaels.com/online/kidsclub/
   kidsclubhomenew.htm

★ TUKIDS Art Barn

The crafts here are extraordinary! Make wind chimes out of old keys or jar lids. Mold a bracelet out of tissue paper and white glue. Construct a squishy anti-stress ball from balloons and cornstarch. The possibilities for fun are almost endless at this extensive resource! Besides craft ideas, you'll find games, downloads, and lots more from the people who run the TUCOWS software archive.

http://greenapple.tukids.tucows.com/crafts/

You Can Make Paper

Have you ever seen homemade paper? The rough, uneven edge (called a deckle) gives it that homemade look. You can recycle old newspaper or other printed materials into paper pulp. You can even throw in a bit of yucca, lawn grass, flowers, or other plants. Then make your own homemade, natural paper. Try it here.

http://www.beakman.com/paper/paper.html

BEAD CRAFTS

Margo's Beadie Critter Collection

Pony beads, wee pony beads, micro pony beads—whichever ones you choose can be crafted into the most clever critters ever. Margo has designs for everything from siamese cats to penguins, from mermaids to Mickey Mouse, and from Harry Potter to R2D2. All you need is a few supplies and a whole lot of patience.

http://beadiecritters.hosting4less.com/

Pin Directions

Learn how to make cool patterned jewelry using safety pins and seed beads. This site gives all the directions. For more patterns, try <*http://home.att.net/~mcdermand/beadies/swap/swap.html*>.

http://members.nbci.com/gstroop245/pins/
   pin-directions.html

Rings & Things' Jewelry Projects

If you have ever wanted to make some Santa earrings out of beads, or desired a beaded rose, or wanted to learn how to make a simple macramé bracelet, this is the site you need to see. The wire-wrapped people are a hoot!

http://www.rings-things.com/PROJ1.HTM

NEEDLECRAFT AND SEWING

How to X-Stitch

Type in your name (in the Celtic Alphabet area), and this site will generate a free pattern for you in Celtic-style letters. There is also a brief tutorial with animated stitches, which will show you where to put the needle in your cross-stitch canvas.

http://www.celticxstitch.ie/learnhow.html

Sharon B's Stitch Dictionary

Never again forget how to do that embroidery stitch! Everything from stem stitch to woven spider's wheel is pictured and described at this site. Note the level of difficulty rating system. One scissors icon means this one is easy. Three scissors means the stitch demands a good deal of skill.

http://www.anu.edu.au/ITA/CSA/textiles/sharonb/
   stitches/stitchfsite.html

Wonderful Stitches

Are you hooked on cross-stitch or needlepoint? If the answer is yes, then this site is guaranteed to keep you in stitches. Check out what other stitchery enthusiasts have been creating with their busy fingers, and then try out some of the decorative stitches featured in the monthly sampler. If you are in need of supplies or want to join a needlework group, put down your needle and look here!

http://www.needlework.com/

The World Wide Quilting Page

Of course you know what a quilt is, but do you know what goes into making one? Did you know that quilts can be computer designed, painted with watercolors, or tie-dyed, and they can even have pictures transferred onto them? The page has a detailed how-to section with every step of the quilting process, from basic quilt design to advanced stitch technique.

http://quilt.com/MainQuiltingPage.html

★ Young Embroiderers

This neat site offers directions to make a simple book bag, some splendid book covers (out of candy wrappers), rolled paper beads, a drawstring bag, and many more projects. The directions are clear and engaging—this site is just the thing if you've got a needle and thread and need an idea!

http://www.hiraeth.com/ytg/welcome.htm

ORIGAMI

See also PEACE; PRESCHOOLERS

★ Joseph Wu's Origami Page

If you've folded paper cranes until you can do it with your eyes closed, you're ready for some intermediate and advanced origami projects. From this page you can download incredible diagrams and instructions for a windmill, butterfly, or basket, among other things.

http://www.origami.vancouver.bc.ca/

A
B
C
D
E
F
G
H
I
J
K
L
M
N
O
P
Q
R
S
T
U
V
W
X
Y
Z

A
B
C
D
E
F
G
H
I
J
K
L
M
N
O
P
Q
R
S
T
U
V
W
X
Y
Z

Become one with the Net.

Let's Try Origami

Origami is the Japanese art of paper folding. The word literally means "to fold" (*oru*) "paper" (*kami*). Find a few sheets of square paper, and you can get started with some easy paper-folding projects. Here's an origami crane, an airplane, and a soldier's helmet. This site provides graphics and helpful instructions to show you how to fold them. At the "old" site <*http://www.jwindow.net/OLD/KIDS/ SCHOOL/ ART/*> you can make a yakko (yes, a yakko and that's not someone who talks too much!).

http://www.jinjapan.org/kidsweb/virtual/origami/ origami.html

NET FILES

You've always wondered if your brother is an alien from outer space. Now you get your photos back, and sure enough, he's got glowing red eyes!

What should you do?

Answer: Don't call NASA yet. According to Kodak, this effect sometimes occurs when you use a flash. It's actually the reflection of light from the flash off the blood vessels inside your subject's eyes. To reduce red-eye, you need to reduce the size of your subject's pupils so there won't be so much reflective surface available. There are several ways to do this: increase the light level in the room by turning on all of the lights, or have your subject look at a bright light just before you take the flash picture. Also, some cameras have a red-eye reduction feature. If you visit the Web site *http://www.kodak.com/global/en/consumer/pictureTaking/ remedies/flash1.shtml*, you'll discover answers to other frequently asked questions about film and photography.

Make an Origami Frog

Your family's at a restaurant, waiting for the meal to arrive. Everyone seems to be moving in slow motion. It's hot, your baby sister needs a nap, you see her crankiness level starting to rise to the boiling point . . . when all of a sudden, you pick up your paper placemat. A few quick moves later, your sister is smiling at the little origami frog you just made for her. And look, the food's here. Now all you need is another placemat.

http://www.seagrant.wisc.edu/madisonjason10/ origami.html

OrigamiUSA

Looking for a good pattern for an origami pterodactyl? Search through the index of patterns for all manner of birds, beasts, and flowers! There are also diagrams, videos, and puzzling things to fold for young and old alike.

http://www.origami-usa.org/

★ Pieces 'n' Creases: A Fun Guide to Origami

So, how long will it take for you to fold 1,000 cranes so you can get your wish? Is there one way to fold them that's faster? What happens if you have an origami jumping-frog contest? This outstanding site was created by students for the ThinkQuest Junior competition.

http://tqjunior.thinkquest.org/5402/

Ribbon Fish

Net-mom used to have a friend named Rick who knew how to make the most wonderful woven fish out of ribbon scraps. Here's a Web site that will show you how to make them, too. It's not really origami, but if you like that, you'll love this.

http://icandream.com/crafts/a/ribbon/fish/

PAPER AIRPLANES

Airplane Fold

Click through Shockwave directions to fold three different paper fliers, including the mysterious Vortex. Do you think something shaped like that can really fly?

http://www.sprocketworks.com/shockwave/
load.asp?SprMovie=paperairplanefoldweb

★ Just Plane Fun

Design your own plane using the interactive tools at this site, and then print out your creation and follow the folding instructions. Click on Flight School for some fun ideas to try with paper planes. Paper Airplane Golf sounds like a fun party game.

http://www.sonywonder.com/wonderland/sandbox/
justplane/

Kool Paper Airplanes

Some really unusual paper airplane designs are featured here, including a flying bat and a model of the supersonic Concorde.

http://koolpaperairplanes.hypermart.net/
Favorites.htm

★ Paper Airplanes

Ken holds the Guinness World Record for longest flight of a paper airplane: 27.6 seconds. Why not? He's an expert! He's the author of *The World Record Paper Airplane Book*, the *Kids Paper Airplane Book*, and the *Paper Airplane Calendar*. His Web site offers lots of material to help your airplanes fly faster, higher, and longer, too.

http://www.geocities.com/CapeCanaveral/1817/

PAPER CRAFTS

Learn to fold a perfect five- or six-pointed star at this site, where you can also discover how to make a German bell, a little boat, and paper snowflakes.

http://www.highhopes.com/5pointstar.html

Paper University

She'll read your fortune, but only if it's about paper. Each time you click on the Fortune Teller, you get a new fun fact about paper. Here's one: paper towels were invented by accident in 1907 when rolls of bathroom tissue came out too thick. This site also traces the amazing history of paper, answers questions about paper recycling, and more. Looking for some science experiments or crafts using paper? You'll find them here, too. And if you'd like a field trip idea, head over to the Admit One section to see if your city offers a tour of a paper factory.

http://www.tappi.org/paperu/

Every year the Worshipful Companies of the Vintners and Dyers participate in an unusual and ancient ritual on the River Thames in London. What is it?

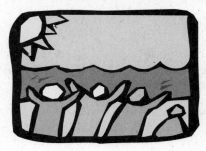

Answer: This group is charged with the royal duty of rounding up and taking a census of all the swans. For many centuries, mute swans in Britain were raised for food, like other poultry. Individual swans were marked by nicks on their webbed feet or beak, which indicated ownership. Somewhat like cattle brands in the American West, these markings were registered with the Crown. Any unmarked birds became Crown property. The swans are rounded up at a "swan-upping," and although they are no longer used for food, the Queen's Swan Marker continues the tradition to this day. For more information, check *http://www.thamesweb.co.uk/windsor/windsor1999/upping.html*

♣ Snowflake Designer - (6 Sided)

Around the holidays it's fun to fold little squares of paper (directions here) and snip them here and there to make a lacy snowflake. The trouble is, you can never visualize what all your cutting will look like before the paper is unfolded. Now you can! Try this snowflake designer, and make a whole blizzard!

http://www.explorescience.com/activities/
    Activitypage.cfm?ActivityID=13

Yamaha Motor - Paper Craft

At first, you might think it would be impossible to re-create the real-looking yellow-eyed penguin and other paper craft projects displayed on this site. But keep digging. You'll find everything you need, from assembly instructions to all those little cutouts. All you have to do is download the data and print the patterns. You supply the scissors and glue. If your creation doesn't look as good as it should, there's a section on tricks for gluing and cutting out circles. Patience is required.

http://www.yamaha-motor.co.jp/eng/papercraft/

RECIPES

Craft Recipes

Kool-Aid finger paint? Sawdust modeling clay? Soap crayons? If you ever need a craft recipe, this is the mother lode of homemade fun!

http://www.erbspalsy.org/craftrecipes.html

★ Donna's Day Activities

There's always something fun to do when Donna's around! She knows how to make play clay out of baking soda, how to make butter, and how to make soap out of oatmeal! She's shared some of her favorite "recipes" at this page, yum!

http://donnasday.com/donna/creativefun/
    activities.shtml

Ooey Gooey Recipes for the Classroom

If you want to make your own slime, gak, play dough, sparkly paint—or any other messy stuff that's too much fun, you should check the recipes here. If you try the Singing Cake, let us know how it *tunes* out.

http://www.minnetonka.k12.mn.us/science/tools/
    ooey.html

WOODWORKING

★ Sawdust Making 101

Learn about the basic components of the tool box and how each is used. You'll discover the wonders of various types of clamps, hammers, screwdrivers, and—hey, don't forget the safety glasses! You'll also find some wood projects for beginners: a napkin holder, several types of shelves, and more. There is also a primer on nails, where it's explained what a three penny nail is! Do take the link to <*http://benchnotes.com/*> and check the Tips of the Trade area for some very clever ideas!

http://www.sawdustmaking.com/

Monet at Giverny

Turn-of-the-century French artist Claude Monet is famous for his dreamy, misty garden and water lily paintings. His garden at Giverny has been reproduced online so you can stroll about and see where some of Monet's works were created. Select either the flower or water garden and begin your exploration. As you move the miniature Monet around, photographs, paintings, and facts will appear. See if you can find a painting of a Japanese bridge.
http://www.mmfa.qc.ca/visite-vr/anglais/

DANCE

Dancing for Busy People

You may have heard of square dancing, but how good is your round dance? When someone yells, "Hey, how about a Sicilian circle!" do you jump on the dance floor, ready to go? Whether your mescolanza needs a makeover or your line dance needs to be straightened, visit this site to get an encyclopedia of popular community dances and instructions.

http://www.d4bp.com/dfbp/

eHow to Do the Bunny Hop

Put your right foot forward. Put your left foot out. Do the Bunny Hop Hop, hop, hop! Further directions are at this site. For the lyrics and music, visit <*http://www.geocities.com/EnchantedForest/Glade/7438/lyrics6.html*>.

http://www.ehow.com/eHow/eHow/
0,1053,15790,00.html

eHow to Do the Hokey Pokey

You put your right foot in, You put your right foot out, You put your right foot in, And you shake it all about. You do the Hokey-Pokey, And you turn your self around, That's what it's all about! Further directions are at this site. For the lyrics and music, visit <*http://www.geocities.com/EnchantedForest/Glade/7438/Hokey.html*>.

http://www.ehow.com/eHow/eHow/
0,1053,9022,00.html

BALLET

★ American Ballet Theatre Ballet Dictionary

Any old dictionary can give you a definition of a word. But this dictionary is illustrated with QuickTime movies that show you what the word means! Watch a dancer perform the half-bend of the knee known as the *demi-plié*. Ever heard someone try to explain what a *battement sur le cou-de-pied, petit* is? See the definition's movie, and you will understand.

http://www.abt.org/library/dictionary/

★ Studio to Stage

According to this site, ballet began with a 1581 Paris performance of *Ballet Comique de la Royne*. It was a five-hour production, involving not only dance, but dramatic speech. Since then, ballet has changed quite a bit. Follow the development of dance through the years as influences from France, Russia, and other places make their pointe. Check out first steps in ballet all the way through to comments on a performance from a dancer's perspective. This site was created by students for the ThinkQuest competition.

http://library.thinkquest.org/21702/

BALLROOM

Dancetv.com: Online Ballroom Dance Tutorial

Ballroom basic tips, as well as online dance lessons, are found at this site. Whether you're a waltzing Matilda or not, you'll be able to learn the fox trot, the east coast swing, and even the waltz using the simple instructions here.

http://www.dancetv.com/tutorial/

History of Modern Ballroom Dancing

Dancesport competitors in the "Standard" division must be able to dance the Viennese Waltz, Modern Waltz, Tango, Slow Fox-trot, and Quickstep. The historical development of each dance is outlined here, with lots of graphics and interesting stories.

http://linus.socs.uts.edu.au/~don/pubs/modern.html

DANCE SHOWS

Michael Flatley's Lord of the Dance

This interesting site offers many multimedia clips from the famous production. Irish step dancing fans will love learning about the show and the stars, and there's even a behind-the-scenes look at dance theater.

http://www.lordofthedance.com/

A B C D E F G H I J K L M N O P Q R S T U V W X Y Z

A
B
C
D
E
F
G
H
I
J
K
L
M
N
O
P
Q
R
S
T
U
V
W
X
Y
Z

★ STOMP

Oh, man! Your parents are dragging you to see some stage show at the theater, and you think you'll be bored. All of a sudden, some guys come out on stage banging on trash cans and pipes, dancing a rhythm with push brooms, and in general making so much noise that no one hears you when you yell, "Hey! Who are these guys?" You've just been introduced to STOMP, the hot dance show from the British Isles. This Web page lets you hear some fantastic beats created with everyday materials; and if you go to the "Percussion for Kids" area of this site, you'll find some sound and noise experiments that you can try at home.

http://www.stomponline.com/

FOLK AND HISTORICAL DANCING
The Bassett Street Hounds Morris Dancers

As early as the 1500s, groups of dancers in the Cotswold region of western England were donning their bells and colorful ribbons, and welcoming the spring season with a ritual folk dance. Morris dancing on the Net now boasts a worldwide representation from hundreds of teams. Read more about the history of Morris dancing and its various styles, and check out the tunes and dance descriptions at this site. You can also connect to other Morris-related Web pages.

http://web.syr.edu/~htkeays/morris/hounds/

CajunZydeco Music & Dance

Cajun two-step dancing is hotter than pepper sauce! You can explore the links here to find out basic and advanced moves. There are sources of online Cajun dance lessons and music, links to sites about Louisiana culture, and more. Parental advisory: off-site links have not been viewed.

http://cajunzydeco.net/

**Nothing to do?
Check CRAFTS AND HOBBIES
for some ideas.**

California Heritage Dancers

Most "folks" in the United States don't know much about their own folk dance heritage. Dances done by the earliest settlers are all but forgotten, and the California Heritage Dancers aim to change all that. Their repertoire includes dances from the earliest Colonial times to the modern day. You'll see costumes and hear tunes from the Appalachians in the early 1800s. You'll hear some foot-stompin' calls from frontier Western dances, and you'll be amazed at some of the gowns, petticoats, and other clothing women used to wear to dress up! Did you know that automaker Henry Ford was a great square dancer?

http://www.heritagedance.com/

Clogging: What Is It?

If you've ever thought it would be fun to try clogging, read this explanation of what cloggers look like, what they wear, and what's on their feet. You'll learn about the music cloggers move to and the steps they take to complete the dance.

http://members.aol.com/mdevin/clogtext.html

International Folk Dancers of Ottawa

Folk dancing is both fun to watch and fun to do. The International Folk Dancers of Ottawa bring together the traditional social dances and authentic music of many countries and cultures. Here you can find lots of information about folk dancing in Ottawa and then link to many additional resources on the Web. The MIDI collection of folk dance tunes from around the world is fascinating to explore.

http://ifdo.pugmarks.com/

Siamsa

To get up to speed on jigs, reels, and other Irish dances, try this site. Its webmaster is a teen veteran of many an Irish dance competition. Learn all about preparing for a dance competition or feis (pronounced "fesh"). She gives lots of suggestions to young dancers, including this one: practice proper hand position by carrying a coin in each hand.

http://www.geocities.com/Broadway/Alley/9643/
   claddaghmain.html

Tabasco® PepperFest Music Stage

Fire up your Real Audio player and listen to the Cajun and zydeco musicians in the background as you take an animated dance lesson in the Cajun two-step.

http://www.TABASCO.com/html/music_stage.html

HULA AND POLYNESIAN DANCING

Hula, Hawaii's Art and Soul

The origin of hula is a mystery, but everyone agrees that it began as a sacrament, not an entertainment for tourists. You can read the legend about how goddesses brought hula to the Hawaiians and how it is performed with reverence today in many hula schools around the islands. You can also hear a chant accompanied by traditional instruments, such as the *pahu* hula drum. The drum is constructed from a partially hollowed-out tree trunk with a shark skin stretched over the top.

http://www.aloha-hawaii.com/hawaii_magazine/hula/

NATIVE AMERICAN DANCE

PowWow Dancing

The powwow drum brings the heartbeat of the Earth Mother to the gathering of Native American tribes. You can see many traditional dances at these spiritual festivals, from the colorful and exciting Fancy Dress dance to more solemn sacred dances. This site explains some of the dances and the traditions surrounding the costumes. Check the schedule to see if a powwow is planned near your home!

http://www.powwows.com/dancing/

Safeguard your privacy online! Don't give anyone your name, address, or other identifying information without reading the site's privacy policy.

★ Southern Native American PowWows

This site was created by kids for the ThinkQuest competition. In it, you'll learn where to sit (and where not to sit) to watch the dancing, and you'll know what to do if you are a dancer. Don't forget to honor the Head Man and the Head Lady and give respect to the Drum, which has probably traveled a long way to give you beautiful music. Listen to the audio files of various songs, and check out the various styles of dances for both men and women. There is even advice for the new dancer and someone wishing to get involved with this tradition.

http://library.thinkquest.org/3081/

DINOSAURS AND PREHISTORIC TIMES

★ BBC Online - Walking with Dinosaurs - Games & Quizzes

Did you know there were webcams 220 million years ago? Neither did we, but at this site you can do a little dinosaur spotting, play an extinction game, and send a dino to a friend—an e-dino postcard, that is!

http://www.bbc.co.uk/dinosaurs/games/

NET FILES

What is the fastest roller coaster in the world?

Answer: It's a tie between "Superman: the Escape" at Six Flags Magic Mountain in Valencia, California, and "Tower of Terror" at Dreamworld Parkway, Coomera, Australia. Both share top speed honors at 100 mph. For more stomach-lurching statistics on roller coasters, see http://www.rcdb.com/rcdb.dll/recordholders.htm

A
B
C
D
E
F
G
H
I
J
K
L
M
N
O
P
Q
R
S
T
U
V
W
X
Y
Z

☙ BillyBear4Kids.com Land o' Dinosaurs

You're really into dinosaurs, and your birthday is coming up. But the store was all sold out of dino invitations and party favors. Don't despair. This site will let you print invitations, name tags, party hats, and more. And for a really cool gift, make jigsaw puzzle party favors to thank your friends for coming to your party. Just download a puzzle onto a floppy disk, and you've got a super present to hand out. Oh, and if you want a little dinosaur history, this site has that, too, but it's mostly a place for online activities.

http://www.billybear4kids.com/dinosaurs/
   long-long-ago.html

Bone Yard

Funding has run out at the museum! All your reference materials have been moved to a library off-site. All the more-experienced scientists have been reassigned. It's up to you to sort through all the old fossil specimens and bones and try to put them back together again. Just pick the level of difficulty you want in this fun game, pull open a drawer, and get started. Let's see, the hip bone's connected to . . . ?

http://www.abc.net.au/science/holo/dembone.htm

BBC Knowledge - Languages

The British Broadcasting Corporation offers multimedia tutorials in French, Spanish, German, and Italian. You'll need the Real Player plug-in to see the video and hear the audio, and be sure to sharpen your listening skills as you learn to go shopping, order a meal, and lots more. There are also Welsh, Irish, and other language lessons for you to try.

http://www.bbc.co.uk/education/languages/

Did the groundhog see his shadow? Find out if it will be an early spring in HOLIDAYS.

★ Britain's Rocky Past

Enjoy a cartoon version of Earth's prehistory starting with the Big Bang theory and ending with the appearance of Man. Sit back and watch the continents slide around via plate tectonics; view ice ages as they come and go; and be amazed as the dinosaurs evolve, flourish, and then turn belly-up. When the show's over, try the interactive version. Pick any geologic period to explore. You'll learn what we know about that period from its fossil record.

http://www.bbc.co.uk/history/games/rocky/
   indexfull.html

Dino-ROAR

OK, you have seen dino bones and seen robotic dinosaurs move—but have you ever heard a dinosaur roar? Scientists took a parasaurolophus fossil and through the magic of computer modeling, managed to re-create the sound passages of its head. At this site, you can hear the eerie sound of—something. Is it the re-created voice of a dinosaur or just extreme technology?

http://www.sciam.com/explorations/121597dinosaur/

Dinorama @ Nationalgeographic.com

Are there still dinosaurs alive today? Some people would argue that birds are actually the last of the dinos. You can read about that theory, and catch up with recent news on dinosaur egg discovery in China, computer-animated dino models, and what's up with the T. rex named Sue at this site from the National Geographic Society.

http://www.nationalgeographic.com/dinorama/
   main.html

Dinosaur Eggs @ Nationalgeographic.com

According to National Geographic, dinosaur eggs and nests have been found at 199 sites around the world, mostly in China, Mongolia, Argentina, India, and the Great Plains of North America. So, unless you live in one of those places, that egg-shaped rock you found in your backyard is probably just a rock! Some of the eggs found in China and elsewhere have had tiny fossilized dino embryos inside them. See what happens when scientists "hatch" dino eggs and try to model what the dino babies would have looked like.

http://www.nationalgeographic.com/features/96/dinoeggs/

★ Dinosaur Extinction

You may have heard the theory that dinos became extinct after a giant meteor or asteroid hit Earth, creating a chain of disasters that wiped out their food supply. But that's not the only explanation. There might have been an orbital shift of Earth or possibly a supernova of a nearby star. Another theory says volcanoes made life too hot, while another guess is that disease took its toll. What's true? Visit this site and see which theory you think is correct.

http://www.cotf.edu/ete/modules/msese/dinosaur.html

The Dinosaur Interplanetary Gazette

The motto at this site is *Scientia, Sapientia, Joci Ridiculi*, which is Latin for "Science, Wisdom, Silly Jokes"! That pretty much sums it up. You can get all the latest dino news at this site, such as the fairly recent discovery of giganotosaurus (which makes T. rex look like the runt of the litter). There's also news about dino movies and details on an x-rayed fossilized dino heart. Does it prove that some dinos were warm-blooded? If you like Monty Python, you'll love this site.

http://www.dinosaur.org/

NET FILES

If you took all the salt out of the ocean and piled it up on land, how much would you have?

Answer: According to the U.S. Geologic Survey, 50 quadrillion (50 million billion) tons of dissolved salts are in the sea. If you could get them out, the resulting pile would form a layer more than 500 feet thick, or about the height of a 40-story office building! Read why the ocean is salty at *http://oceanography.palomar.edu/salty_ocean.htm*

Dinosaur Treks

Professor L. Hacker is calling on you to help him catch a thief! Dinosaur bones have been stolen from Dinosaur Treks, a virtual reality museum filled with all the clues—and passwords—you'll need to succeed. In the museum's lobby, click on the different objects to learn everything you can about dinosaurs. Find the password, and then you can take the elevator to the first floor. Each floor will broaden your knowledge about dinosaurs. On the third floor, you get a chance to catch the thief. This site was created by students for the ThinkQuest competition.

http://library.thinkquest.org/C005824/

The Dinosauria

Can we start making new live dinosaurs from DNA, as in the movie *Jurassic Park*? Probably not, at least with today's scientific knowledge! There are a lot of good scientific reasons why cloning dinosaurs is next to impossible—read about it in DinoBuzz. From this site you can get lots of interesting information about dinosaurs.

http://www.ucmp.berkeley.edu/diapsids/dinosaur.html

A B C D E F G H I J K L M N O P Q R S T U V W X Y Z

A
B
C
D
E
F
G
H
I
J
K
L
M
N
O
P
Q
R
S
T
U
V
W
X
Y
Z

Discovering Dinosaurs

Did you know that less than one percent of all the dinosaurs that ever lived have been discovered? Imagine if you were the one to find a new dinosaur. This site lets you do just that—"hatch" your own personal dinosaur. Colorful drawings let you choose your dinosaur's features, and the DinoRoots page will help you create a name for your dinosaur. It picks apart the names of dinosaurs into their real meanings so you come up with an authentic-sounding name.

http://dinosaurs.eb.com/

Ecology Past

If you visit the St. Louis Science Center, you'll want to watch where you're going. First, there's that six-foot centipede in the Pennsylvanian Period exhibit. Then you have to watch out for the spear-throwing caveman; and, finally, don't get too close to the robotic T. rex! The good news is you can visit all of these over the Internet, where you can admire everything in safety.

http://www.slsc.org/docs/galleries/mod3_2/
mod3_22/ep1000m.htm

Hocus Pocus Palace

Dare to challenge The Great Mysto in a game of mind reading and clairvoyance. Through magical and as yet unexplainable Internet protocols, The Great Mysto will astound you with his long-distance feats. Doubters may scoff and say these are simple "magic square" tricks, but we're not so sure (how did he know we were thinking of Marge Simpson?). O Great Mysto, you have a truly fun site! http://www.teleport.com/~jrolsen/

Field Museum of Natural History On-Line Exhibits

Where can you meet Sue, the largest T. rex ever found? Or see pictures of dinosaurs, hear their names pronounced, and then watch them run? You can do all of this and more by visiting the exhibit pages at the world-famous Field Museum of Natural History. In the Dinosaurs! online exhibit, you can listen to the Triassic forecast (1-900-CLIMATE) on the dinosaur weather report. Tours include the following: Life Before Dinosaurs; Dinosaurs!; Teeth, Tusks, and Tarpits: Life After Dinosaurs; and several more. Make tracks to go see it!

http://www.fmnh.org./exhibits/online_exhib.htm

Fossil Horses in Cyberspace

Scientists compare animals by looking at them very carefully and noting their similarities and differences. Not all hoofed animals are alike. Some have an even number of toes per foot (goats and pigs), while others have an odd number of toes per foot (horses, elephants). The closest living relatives of the modern horse are the rhinoceros and the tapir. Early horses had three toes on the ground, although today's horses have only one. This very interesting site explains how this happened over time. The Florida Museum of Natural History has a special interest in fossil horses, since there is a rich archaeological dig site nearby. See what's new from down under ground.

http://www.flmnh.ufl.edu/natsci/vertpaleo/fhc/
fhc.htm

Fossil Zone

We all know what dinosaurs looked like, but what did they sound like? That's the big attraction of this site—a gallery of re-created dinosaur sounds. Listen to a Triceratops bleat like a sheep, or a Tyrannosaurus rex groan (not growl). While these are imaginary sounds, they're not the figment of a wild imagination. Voice experts used the dimensions of dinosaur skulls to measure the size of their vocal chords to figure out what sounds the ancient beasts may have uttered.

http://www.discovery.com/exp/fossilzone/
fossilzone.html

Geology and Geologic Time

Just when was the Paleozoic era? Find out here as you learn about how geologic time is measured and how the science of geology began. Remember, the oldest rocks are on the bottom!

http://www.ucmp.berkeley.edu/exhibit/geology.html

Giganotosaurus

The Academy of Natural Sciences in Philadelphia exhibits a reconstruction of one of the largest meat-eating dinosaurs ever to walk the earth: giganotosaurus. Although the display is called "T. rex Meets His Match," the creatures never would have met in real life. For one thing, they lived 30 million years apart, and for another, T. rex lived in North America and giganotosaurus' turf was South America. This fossil was discovered in Argentina. One of the most fascinating parts of the story is that the bones could not leave Argentina, since the law forbids removal of such materials. The bones had to be copied in resin and then reconstructed for the museum.

http://www.acnatsci.org/gigapage/

Hadrosaurus foulkii

Where in the world was the first, nearly complete skeleton of a dinosaur found? It was found in Haddonfield, New Jersey. In the summer of 1858, vacationing fossil hobbyist William Parker Foulke led a crew of workmen digging "shin deep in gray slime." Eventually he found the bones of an animal, larger than an elephant, that once swam and played about the coastline of what is now Pennsylvania. Read about the discovery that started our fascination with dinosaurs!

http://www.levins.com/dinosaur.html

NET FILES

What are
Mancos milk-vetch, clay-loving wild buckwheat, Dudley Bluffs bladderpod, and Penland beardtongue?

Answer: Well, they are not the names of new rock groups! They are all plants on the endangered and threatened species list for Colorado. Find out more at http://www.fws.gov/r9endspp/stat1-r6.html#LnKCO and for other areas, start at http://www.fws.gov/r9endspp/endspp.html

History of the Earth

Step right up to Eternity Canyon. Not too close, there, sonny! I'll be your guide to the major geological time periods as we tour the canyon today. I'll be pointing out representative plant and animal life, describing conditions as they were then, and in general try to give you an overview of each eon, era, period, epoch, and age. Now, I must warn you that it could get a little dusty as we tour Precambrian time, but if you'll just walk this way . . . And please note the sign up ahead: "This site was created by students for the ThinkQuest competition."

http://library.thinkquest.org/20886/

★ Kinetosaurs: Putting Some Teeth into Art and Science

Don't bother looking up kinetosaur in your dino dictionary—you won't find it. These very special dinosaur re-creations are constructed to move, and their "handlers" can control them like a marionette. See how the artist accomplishes this feat, and then try moving one yourself via a cool Shockwave demonstration. In other parts of the site you can go on a virtual dig, print dino coloring pages, and learn about more than 20 different dinosaurs.

http://www.childrensmuseum.org/kinetosaur/

A
B
C
D
E
F
G
H
I
J
K
L
M
N
O
P
Q
R
S
T
U
V
W
X
Y
Z

A
B
C
D
E
F
G
H
I
J
K
L
M
N
O
P
Q
R
S
T
U
V
W
X
Y
Z

NOVA Online - Curse of T. rex

Dinosaurs roamed the earth between 250 million years ago and 65 million years ago, but they didn't have the whole place to themselves. There were other animals, insects, and plants, of course. This site gives you an overview of those other species we don't hear too much about. If you were going to look for dino fossils, where would you look? This takes you through that discovery process.

http://www.pbs.org/wgbh/nova/trex/

Ology - Paleontology

Ology simply means "the study of." When you put Paleo, which means "really old," in front of Ology, you get the study of really old things, like dinosaurs. Collect one "Ology card," or collect them all. They explain how dinosaurs are organized into a family tree. You see, dinosaurs belong to families just like humans. They're grouped together based on the characteristics that they share: a three-toed foot, or a hole in the hip socket. This site lets you sort dinosaurs into their correct groups—once you've collected enough Ology cards.

http://www.ology.amnh.org/paleontology/

Royal Tyrrell Museum - Where Palaeontology Comes Alive!

Take a virtual tour of this famous museum in Alberta, Canada. Stay on the guided tour, or use the virtual maps to go from exhibit to exhibit in any order you want. There are fantastic dinosaur displays with lots of pictures, and you'll find even more information on the second floor in Dinosaur Hall. In addition to all the dinosaurs, you can visit a paleoconservatory, which is a greenhouse full of primitive plants.

http://www.tyrrellmuseum.com/

Sue at The Field Museum

Read all about Sue the dinosaur: seems she died about 65 million years ago, and her fossilized remains were discovered in 1980, near Faith, South Dakota. There was a dispute about who really owned the skeleton, the FBI seized her, and she was held, pending an auction! The Field Museum of Chicago eventually got her and she's now on display. Over 13 feet tall at the hips, and 42 feet long, Sue would love to meet you. Why not stop in and say "Hi"?

http://www.fmnh.org/sue/

When the Dinosaurs Were Gone

Step back! Not literally, but back in time—60 million years to be exact. Your journey will take you back to a time when crocodiles, alligators, and snapping turtles ruled the Earth. The coolest part of the site is the Immersions section. Here you can immerse yourself in 360-degree virtual reality scenes of a crocodile pool, subtropical forest, and freshwater lake. The panoramas require the QuickTime Plug-in.

http://www.dinosgone.org/

NET FILES

What U.S. president once invited all of Washington, D.C., into the White House to help him eat a 1,400-pound (636-kilogram) wheel of cheese?

Answer: According to the White House at http://www.whitehouse.gov/history/presidents/aj7.html, "Anyone could come to Andrew Jackson's public parties at the White House, and just about everyone did! At his last one, a wheel of cheese weighing 1,400 lbs. was eaten in two hours. The White House smelled of cheese for weeks."

★ Zoom Dinosaurs - Enchanted Learning Software

This is a great site, and it can be enjoyed by all age groups. Everyone will love it, including your little brother and even your parents. There are lots of pictures, animations, and tons of great scientific information. There's a geologic time scale, a dino dictionary, and lots of activities and links. You'll also find some fun and really bad jokes, such as this: Why did the dinosaur cross the road? Answer: Because the chicken hadn't evolved yet!

http://www.EnchantedLearning.com/subjects/
dinosaurs/

EVOLUTION

See also BIOLOGY—GENETICS, CLONES, AND BIOTECHNOLOGY

★ Becoming Human

Step back some four million years and explore the theory of evolution and possible origins of the human race. This site features an impressive documentary. It lets you stop along the way and explore the anatomy, culture, and family tree of our ancestors. Or, you can join a dig and hear scientists explain how they use technology to find fossil sites. Each species includes an "up close and personal" profile of its diet, habitat, and age. Plan to spend some time here.

http://www.becominghuman.org/

Evolution Entrance

The University of California at Berkeley has set up a separate "exhibition area" for the subject of evolution in its online Museum of Paleontology. Here, you are greeted by Charles Darwin speaking of the course of evolution being much like a "great tree of life." From there, you can link to sections on Dinosaur Discoveries and Systematics (the classification system used in charting the families of species) and find out about the most important scientists to develop this field.

http://www.ucmp.berkeley.edu/history/evolution.html

★ NATURE: Triumph of Life

Our favorite part of this site is the section called Evolutionary Timeline. It's like a window with a view of the last 4.6 billion years or so. Use the scroll bars at the bottom of the pop-up window to navigate back and forth through time. When you see something of interest, click on it to retrieve more information. Did you know that writing has only been around in the last 6,000 years? Before that, people just relied on their memories to remember what to get at the store. ;-)

http://www.pbs.org/wnet/nature/triumphoflife/

Neandertals: A Cyber Perspective

How much do you think you know about early human evolution? This page gives a fascinating peek into the life of Neandertal, who lived 30,000 years ago in Europe and the Near East. You may know this hominid as "Neanderthal"—but according to this page, that's incorrect. Its fossilized remains were found in 1856, in Feldhofer Cave, in a German valley called Neander Tal. Included are sections on the art, language, culture, and social aspects of the lives of these cave people. It's not big dumb guys dragging clubs around, after all. There are also excellent links on human evolution, as well as a suggested reading list.

http://thunder.indstate.edu/~ramanank/

The Talk.Origins Archive

People love to argue about whether the theory of evolution is "true" or not. This newsgroup is one of the places where this discussion goes on. (Check the entries under RELIGION AND SPIRITUALITY—CREATION STUDIES in this book for more information.) Though you probably won't want to enter into this newsgroup's conversation, the FAQ section is interesting if you want to know more about these ideas. Parental advisory: please preview this site.

http://www.talkorigins.org/

A B C D E F G H I J K L M N O P Q R S T U V W X Y Z

You Be the Predator

Why are some people taller than others? Why do giraffes have longer necks than their ancestors? Why are deer and squirrels brown, while dolphins and sharks are grayish blue? If you understand the evolutionary theory of natural selection, you'll know the answers. If not, this site will tell you why. Clue: it's all about some genes surviving better than other genes. The most fun part of this site is the online game, Dot Hunter, which simulates the process of natural selection.

http://www.studyworksonline.com/cda/content/
    explorations/0,1035,NAV2-75_SEP898,00.html

DISNEY

Disney.com - Where the Magic Lives Online!

The Walt Disney Company produces movies, television shows, books, radio, and music in addition to their theme parks and cruise ships. If you want to keep up on the latest from the folks at Disney, take a look at their official home page. Besides information about the parks, you'll find online games, activities, and much, much more. If you like Disney, this is a must-see.

http://www2.disney.com/

★ LaughingPlace.com

Dreaming about visiting one of the Disney theme parks? Before you ever think of boarding the tram, your first stop should be here. It's got reviews of all the rides and attractions, including the parades, fireworks, and special shows. Best yet, click on "More Information" to rate the rides yourself, or to read comments by other users. There's lots of Disney news, a directory of links to all things Disney, and a lively discussion area.

http://laughingplace.com/

Walt Disney - His Life and Works

This fan page offers an extensive time line of Walt Disney's life and films. Did you know Disney produced many films for the U.S. Army (*Dental Health* was one) and private industry (*Prevention and Control of Distortion in Arc Welding* for the Lincoln Electrical Company)? That's only one of the interesting facts you'll learn about the man who discovered Mickey Mouse and his Toontown buddies.

http://www.intergraffix.com/walt/

DOGS AND DOG SPORTS

See also MAMMALS—WOLVES AND DOG FAMILY, and PETS

★ American Kennel Club

The American Kennel Club (AKC) is the largest registry of purebred dogs in the United States. Here, you'll find a list of the breeds they recognize, a roster of recent obedience and show winners, and information on the AKC's many educational activities. You'll also be able to search a list of breed clubs and contacts, as well as a breeder's directory. Check the Kid's Corner for Name That Breed and other quizzes.

http://www.akc.org/

Belgian Games

Stupid dog tricks—sure, this site has some really silly tricks, but you'll find some useful ones here, too. How about teaching your dog to start pawing you when your alarm clock goes off? You could teach your dog to collect your toys and put them away for you or to look for your mom's lost car keys. Or you could teach your dog to nod on command; then, when you ask your furry friend to respond to a question like "Aren't I the best, smartest, and most good-looking owner you could ever have?" the dog will always nod an enthusiastic "Yes!" The directions for how to teach these tricks are found when you click on the words "dog training page."

http://www.hut.fi/~mtt/belg_tricks.html

Canine Companions

Have you ever seen a blind person and guide dog team? Did you ever wonder how dogs for the blind are trained? How about a hearing or signal dog, who teams up with people with hearing disabilities? These animals go to their owners to "signal" when a noise is heard. They will signal on ringing doorbells and phones, smoke alarms, crying babies, and much more. There are also therapy dogs and special canine companions who know how to help people with disabilities. Find out about this very interesting class of working dogs here.

http://www.caninecompanions.org/

Dog Training and Behavior

Learn about dog obedience competition, agility tests, carting, flyball, Frisbee, and even more ways to have fun with your furry pal. Did you know that people even dance with their dogs? It's called "Freestyle." You can also find out about search and rescue dogs, the Beagle Brigade you might see at airports, clicker training, funny tricks to teach your dog, and lots more.

http://www.canine.org/training.html

Dog-Play: Fun with Your Dog

You've probably heard of dog shows and obedience trials, but there are many more activities you and your dog might enjoy. Agility tests involve encouraging your dog to run around a course of interesting obstacles (such as tunnels and huge collapsed wind socks) and climb ramps, jump jumps, and do it all in the right order. Or if your dog is less active, she might become a therapy dog and visit nursing home residents. Learn about summer camps both you and your dog can attend, too!

http://www.dog-play.com/

Doghouse Plans

Why not build Max a home of his very own? He can sit on the wide, flat roof and pretend it's a deck. He can relax in the shade while he watches you mow the lawn. You'll need some building plans first, and this site has them, plus advice on constructing your pooch palace!

http://www.hsus.org/programs/companion/dogs/
   dog_house.html

Amusement Park Physics

As your free-fall car rises to the top of the drop, you think, "I hope the designer of this ride got an 'A' in physics." As you practice your driving skills on the bumper cars, do you ever take time to thank Newton's third law of motion? Learn the physics behind many popular rides, and you'll never look at an amusement park the same way again. http://www.learner.org/exhibits/parkphysics/

Dogs: ThePoop.com

Terrific features on topics like dog health and training are only some of the things we like about this site. Another is the huge network of dog adoption and rescue organizations you can search through. Maybe you'll be able to pick out a puppy or adopt a senior dog. There are also photos of lots of dog breeds, information on famous celebrity dogs, and even recipes you can make to pamper your precious pooch. How about some cheesy garlic chunks?

http://www.thepoop.com/

Guide Dogs for the Blind, Inc.

Have you ever wondered if it's OK to pet a guide dog? According to this site, we need to remember that the dog's first responsibility is to keep his handler safe. Anything that distracts him from that duty should be avoided. However, many people like to show off their dogs, so ask first. You may be able to pet the guide dog after all. Teachers and students should download the "At a Glance" resource to find out how guide dog teams are trained. It also includes a quick guide to blindness and visual impairment, plus many lesson plans.

http://www.guidedogs.com/

A
B
C
D
E
F
G
H
I
J
K
L
M
N
O
P
Q
R
S
T
U
V
W
X
Y
Z

Fantastic Journeys: Yellowstone @ Nationalgeographic.com

Hey, what's all that mist up ahead? Wait—it's steam. Hold on, hear that gurgling and rumbling noise? RUN! Oops. This is the Net, isn't it. That's not a real geyser; that's QuickTime virtual reality. That glopping sound you hear is coming from a virtual mudpot. Still, it's pretty exciting to see and hear the various things that can happen when you mix hot water and minerals together. Don't forget to put on your virtual wet suit and dive down into the depths of the Grand Prismatic Spring to see what's below.
http://www.nationalgeographic.com/features/97/yellowstone/

★ How to Love Your Dog: A Kid's Guide to Dog Care

Wondering if dog ownership is for you? Study this site. It covers everything: what dogs cost, what various breeds of dogs are like, and how to train the new puppy. Getting a dog is a big responsibility. You will care for your pet for many years to come. Are you ready for that? If so, print out the I Love My Dog contract here, and sign it. Show the contract to your dog. He or she will be very, very impressed.

http://www.geocities.com/~kidsanddogs/

Lost your sheep? Find them in FARMING AND AGRICULTURE.

Iditarod 411

The Iditarod is a 1,150-mile dogsled race in Alaska, from Anchorage to Nome. Usually, over 60 teams compete in this annual race. Most teams have an average of 16 dogs each. If you go, you'll traverse some of the roughest, most beautiful country on Earth—behind a team of furry dogs, many of them wearing booties to protect their feet. Whoever drives the team is called a musher. This site has lots of classroom connections, musher bios, activities, and more. You should know that while no one sees anything wrong with recreational dogsledding, the Iditarod race is controversial. For an animal rights perspective, try the Sled Dog Action Coalition's site *<http://www.helpsleddogs.org/>*. Be aware it is not for the sensitive.

http://www.designperfect.com/iditarod/

Pet Name Search

Dad says you can keep that puppy who followed you home; now all you need is a name. Let's see, how about Sammy? That's one of the most popular dog names in North America, according to this Web site. Of course, if you want a really unusual name, you could pick one of the thousands of names here, like Angstrom or maybe Tsunami.

http://www.bowwow.com.au/search/index.asp

Veterinary Information for Dogs

The best health information for your pet comes from its own veterinarian—but if you need a simple question answered, try this site. You'll find answers to dog behavior questions, as well as health advice both general and specific.

http://www.vetinfo.com/doginfo.html

Woof!

Based on the popular PBS series featuring dog training expert "Uncle Matty," this site begs for recognition. Go fetch tips on how to choose a dog that fits your lifestyle. Roll on over to the information on basic obedience training, and then lie down for a good read with the dog stories section.

http://www.pbs.org/wgbh/woof/

EARTH SCIENCE

★ Geo-Mysteries @ The Children's Museum of Indianapolis

Rex, the dino detective, has a big problem on his claws. All sorts of strange things are happening. There's a rock that floats, an assortment of stone beads, and a golden cube. What on Earth is happening? Follow the clues to learn about volcanic processes, fossils, and mineral crystals.

http://www.childrensmuseum.org/geomysteries/

Sea and Sky

The ocean and the sky—sometimes known as the final frontiers. Now you can explore both at the same Web site. Take the Cousteau submersible to the ocean part of this resource, where you'll find photos and information about all sorts of sea creatures, everything from coral to marine mammals. Then stop in at the games areas to try some word searches, crossword puzzles, and Shockwave fun. There are some carefully chosen links, as well as Java applets with a sea theme, too. If you want, explore the "Sky" side of the house on the Starship Sagan!

http://www.seasky.org/

CLIMATE

Encyclopedia of the Atmospheric Environment

Sometimes reading about topics like acid rain, air quality, global warming, and ozone depletion can be a little overwhelming, especially if the material isn't written for kids. This site understands all that. For many of these subjects, you'll see a special icon next to the article. The ones with the picture of Bart Simpson are written for students, while the ones next to Mr. Burns have more technical text.

http://www.doc.mmu.ac.uk/aric/eae/

CLIMATE—GLOBAL WARMING

Global Warming: Early Warning Signs

Heat waves and days of unusually warm weather. Coastal flooding and a rise in sea level. Glaciers melting. You may think these weather events are flukes of nature, but they point to a trend—the global warming of the Earth's climate. Scientists predict that the Earth's average temperature will rise by several degrees in the next 100 years. There are already some hot spots around the world. Click on the global warming map to find them. The map also shows why global warming is bad. It makes a great educational poster, and, fortunately, you can order a copy.

http://www.climatehotmap.org/

Global Warming - Will It Affect You?

As natural and man-made "greenhouse gases" trap heat in the Earth's atmosphere, things will get warmer down here on the planet. What will happen? There may be flooding in one place or there may be drought in another. Some say it will help agriculture, while others think the opposite. This may cause a rise in medical problems, such as malaria or hanta virus outbreaks. You might not be able to play outside without slathering on some heavy-duty sunscreen, either. Find out other ways global warming will affect you, and discover ways you can help reduce greenhouse gas emission. This site was created by students for the ThinkQuest competition.

http://library.thinkquest.org/J003411/

The Greenhouse Effect

Someone in a cold climate might think the greenhouse effect is a good thing, especially for those who don't like feeling chilly. However, there are consequences connected with having more planetwide heat than usual, and this doesn't just mean less snow to play in. Find out all about the greenhouse effect from the illustrated fact sheet at the Australian Greenhouse Office.

http://www.greenhouse.gov.au/pubs/factsheets/fs_effect.html

A B C D E F G H I J K L M N O P Q R S T U V W X Y Z

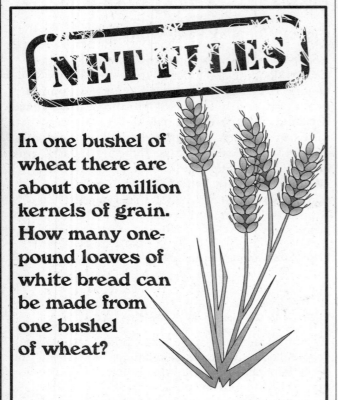

In one bushel of wheat there are about one million kernels of grain. How many one-pound loaves of white bread can be made from one bushel of wheat?

Answer: According to the Kansas Wheathearts page, "One bushel of wheat yields enough flour for 73 one-pound loaves of white bread." Find out lots more wheat trivia at *http://www.wheatmania.com/wheattrivia.html*

A Paleo Perspective on Global Warming

Winston Churchill once said, "The farther backward you can look, the farther forward you are likely to see." That's the idea behind the paleoclimatology program of the National Oceanic and Atmospheric Administration. They look at climate data from the past in order to predict future climate change. One way they do this is by studying old satellite photos of vegetation, but that takes them back only about twenty years. They also have careful weather instrument readings kept by meteorologists back into the 1800s. After that? They take core ice samples, coral reef samples, tree ring samples—and, as a result, have reconstructed data back millions of years. See how they do it at this fascinating site.

http://www.ngdc.noaa.gov/paleo/globalwarming/

ECOLOGY AND ENVIRONMENT

Backyard Wildlife Habitat - National Wildlife Federation

You don't need to go to a National park to visit a wildlife refuge. You can create an official wildlife habitat right in your backyard, front yard, or school yard. Over 26,000 other people have done it! This site has all the details on what you need to do to meet certification standards. You have to be able to show that your area meets the four basic habitat elements (food, water, cover, and places to raise young). Take a look at the sample sites to get some ideas. There is a small cost to the certification process.

http://www.nwf.org/habitats/

Baileys' Eco-Regions

Net-mom was interested to know that she lives in the Laurentian Mixed Forest region of the U.S., characterized by rolling hills, pines and maples, and squirrels everywhere. This is in contrast to the Southern Rocky Mountain Steppe, where there are rugged mountains, spruce and fir, and all kinds of large mammals like elk and bear. All of the above is really different from the Hawaiian Islands Province, with its tropical climate and ohia and koa trees. What eco-region do you live in? There are more than 50 described and pictured here.

http://www.fs.fed.us/land/ecosysmgmt/
    ecoreg1_home.html

★ Biomes of the World

A biome is the collection of creatures and plants living in a particular region. At this site you can explore six different biomes: grassland, rain forest, taiga, deciduous forest, desert, and tundra. You'll learn about the features of each area and its plants and animals. There are also special sections on both marine and freshwater ecosystems, where you can learn about everything from algae to coral.

http://mbgnet.mobot.org/

Come Along on a Nature Walk

Summer camp is a time to explore the great outdoors and make crafts you can show your parents and friends. At this site, you can do both. Come along on the nature walk to learn about life in the forest. If it's a rainy day, it's a good bet that Craft Cabin will have just the right activity for you. There are projects for making a thumb piano, bamboo chimes, shadow boxes, and more. And, when it's time to eat, go to the Dining Hall for recipes for lots of tasty treats.

http://www.worldbook.com/fun/wbla/camp/html/walk.html

Earth in the Balance

People are changing the planet, and not always for the better. There's that hole in the ozone, for example. Don't forget the extinction of plant and animal species, to say nothing of their habitat. And then there's air and water pollution. Learn all about these environmental crises at this site. Then try some classroom activities that put you in the places of those who could make a difference. Here's a sample: "Pretend you are a manager of a nature preserve that contains rare trees scientists want to cut down in order to obtain a lifesaving drug. The trees are endangered, and disturbing the area might also threaten several endangered animals. What would you do? Why?"

http://www.worldbook.com/fun/wbla/earth/html/earth.htm

Earthwatch Global Classroom

Earthwatch takes ordinary people on extraordinary research expeditions. Of course, you pay for the privilege of counting katydids or helping to save a coral reef. But when you get back, you'll have a great story to tell about how you spent your summer vacation! This page archives some of the field notes and lesson plans developed from past trips, and it's interesting to see which ecological hot spots they will attend to next. There are also a few virtual field trips online, where you don't even have to get your boots wet. High school students are encouraged to look into the Student Challenge program. Numerous scholarships are awarded each year.

http://www.earthwatch.org/ed/home.html

EEK! Environmental Education for Kids

What's in a name? Obviously, more than Shakespeare ever imagined. Play the name game (under Cool Stuff) to learn about the crazy names for animal groups. Here's one: A group of grasshoppers is called a cloud. Go figure. Once you're through, challenge yourself again with an interactive quiz on baby animal names. Is a baby ant really called an antling? Find out. Then, see if you can answer this month's riddle.

http://www.dnr.state.wi.us/org/caer/ce/eek/

The Environment: A Global Challenge

Encompassing everything from global warming to biographies of famous conservationists, this ThinkQuest award winner aims to be encyclopedic in scope. In it, you'll learn about the politics of environmental law and the economic factors influencing what happens to the environment, and even try some simulations and games. It's not just about pollution anymore.

http://library.thinkquest.org/26026/

Environmental Literacy Council

If someone asks you to name an exotic species, what do you think of? A cougar, a tiger, or an iguana, maybe? Would it surprise you that starlings, goats, and pigs are exotic species? In the United States, they are. Reason: They're not native to America. Hundreds of years ago, settlers brought these critters along with them from their home countries That's one of the things this site does best—broaden your knowledge about the environment. Learn about brownfields, urban ecology, green design, and more.

http://www.enviroliteracy.org/

Envirothon

Envirothon might sound like a race, and, in a way, it is. It's actually a competition for high school students to test their knowledge about natural resource issues in their state. The program focuses on aquatics, forestry, soils, wildlife, and current environmental issues. If your high school wants to enter this national contest, this site will tell you how. Winners receive college scholarships.

http://www.envirothon.org/

A B C D E F G H I J K L M N O P Q R S T U V W X Y Z

Math.com

In ancient Rome, what did diners do when they needed to figure out the waiter's tip? They just pulled out their Roman numeral calculators, of course! Is there such a thing? On this site, there is! But that's not all. Math.com offers a clearinghouse of everything related to mathematics. Try "math in one minute" tutorials to brush up on the basics, or inspect the fractal of the day. There are math biographies, a history of math, plus formulas and even fun games. Whether it's information on pre-algebra, geometry, or algebra, or just a handy calculator to figure out how much garden mulch to buy, we figure you'll love math.com.
http://www.math.com/

★ EPA Student Center

The Environmental Protection Agency offers a convenient collection of useful links and top-notch resources on everything from ecosystems to landfills. Be sure to look in the Air section for The Case of the Missing Ozone comic book, and don't miss the chance to Surf Your Watershed in the Water section.

http://www.epa.gov/students/

★ For Kids Only - Earth Science Enterprise

Did you know that NASA studies Earth as well as space? They use both satellites and high-altitude aircraft to check up on the weather, ozone holes, polar ice, and many other facets of our environment. Ready to test your knowledge of plate tectonics? Head for the earth science games area.

http://kids.earth.nasa.gov/

★ A Global View from Space

Would you like to see a picture of how Earth looks—right now? You can! A multinational network of satellites provides data to NASA in almost real time. These images are correlated and placed onto a spherical globe for you to view. You can manipulate the globe in any direction you want. Choose to look at cloud cover, ozone, wind, or other features. Click on any area of the map to zoom in. Click once again on the zoomed image to return to the prior view. Remember, there's no place like your home planet.

http://farside.gsfc.nasa.gov/ISTO/dro/global/

GLOBE: Global Learning and Observations to Benefit the Environment

GLOBE is an environmental education and science partnership of students, teachers, and scientists. Through collaboration, they try to increase environmental awareness throughout the world and to contribute to a better understanding of Earth. Students take measurements and make observations of the weather and the environment around their schools. Via the Internet, this data is shared with other students and scientists around the world. All the details are patched together to make a view of the world as it's seen through the student findings in 10,000 schools in more than 95 countries.

http://www.globe.gov/

Habitats/Biomes

Just like a worm couldn't live in the desert, a fish couldn't live out of water. Each creature on Earth needs a specific type of environment to thrive. These environments are complex communities of plants and animals, called biomes. This site explores the many different biomes on Earth, from the deserts to tundras to grasslands.

http://www.enchantedlearning.com/biomes/

It's hard to remember, but mnemonic memory tricks are in WORDS.

Pony up to HORSES AND EQUESTRIAN SPORTS.

★ Miss Maggie's Earth Adventures

The big red button holds the key to joining Miss Maggie as she travels around the world to protect the environment. Click it and join her on a mission, such as saving dying coral reefs in the Pacific Ocean. Each mission has lots of creative, interactive tools designed to make you environmentally smart. When you've completed a mission, watch some of the movies, or learn a fascinating fact about a wild animal. This neat site is animated like a comic book, so keep the audio turned up.

http://www.missmaggie.org/

Ranger Rick's Kid's Zone

Take a cool tour of water, wetlands, or public lands with everyone's favorite raccoon, Ranger Rick. Help the Wild Thornberrys discover endangered species, or try some of the tricky matching games or wildlife jigsaw puzzles. Find out why you should thank a tree and (if you're wise enough) search for hidden owls.

http://www.nwf.org/kids/

A Simple Guide to Small and Microscopic Pond Life

What could be simple about microscopic organisms? That they only have single cells or are green and hairy. While their structures are simple, they often lead diverse lives. Take the water flea. There are some species that prey on other tiny animals, mostly other water fleas. In contrast, Spirogyra, an algae, floats on the surface of water like green scum. To learn about other common types of pond creatures, explore the virtual pond dip. It just might make you get a real jar and collect your own microscopic pond life. The site has instructions for how to do that, too.

http://www.microscopy-uk.org.uk/pond/

NET FILES

What's a Humuhumunukunukuapua'a?

http://oldhawaii.com/lgd/keiki/games/humu.htm

Answer: Also known as the trigger fish, it's the official state fish of Hawaii, and you can see a drawing of one at

★ Wild World

Not many of us will get a chance to visit the Bering Sea to dive with humpback whales, or listen to an endangered bowhead whale. But, thanks to this site, we can travel to their habitat and listen to them croon and swoon. The sounds of other creatures that live in this part of the world are also featured. Another section to explore is a map of the Earth's ecoregions. That's an area of land with a unique climate, landscape, and plant and animal communities. Type in your ZIP code to see in which one you live. You may get a number and letter code on the screen. Click on it for your region's full picture and text screen.

http://www.nationalgeographic.com/wildworld/

★ World Wildlife Fund - Kids Stuff

Think you know a lot about biodiversity? Try the Biodiversity Performs game. After you click to start the game, a picture will be drawn on the right side of your screen. Can you guess what scientific process it is illustrating? It could be pollination, or maybe photosynthesis. Maybe you should hit the "Show me more" button to see additional parts of the animations. If you liked that game, try the challenge of the Virtual House. Normal everyday objects take on new meaning where protecting the environment is concerned. You'll love the animations and sounds, but you may need to ask for hints to find some of the items.

http://www.worldwildlife.org/fun/kids.cfm

A B C D E F G H I J K L M N O P Q R S T U V W X Y Z

GEOLOGY

★ BBC Education - The Essential Guide to Rocks

What's for lunch today? At this site, it's "Sedimentary Sandwiches"! Use layers of bread and specific foods to create your own slice of the past. For example, avocados represent the slimy rotting vegetation that eventually compressed and made coal, while chicken salad stands in for a layer when dinosaurs walked the earth (hard to get a good dinosaur salad these days, and since many people think birds descended from dinosaurs, well . . .). If that doesn't grab you, try The Geology of the Bathroom or the Graveyard Rockwalk. There's also a terrific rock primer for those who wish to rock on. This site is from the British Broadcasting Corporation, so you may run into some unusual British words and phrases.

http://www.bbc.co.uk/education/rocks/

Beauty and the Beast

The state of Hawaii is beautiful, but the islands are prone to many natural disasters: earthquakes, tsunamis, volcanic eruptions, and hurricanes. This site explains each in turn, teaches how to prepare for one, and provides warning signs so you'll know when to run for safety. Check the interviews with people who have had a personal experience with nature's dark side, and then visit suggested Web sites for more information. This site was created by students for the ThinkQuest competition.

http://library.thinkquest.org/J003007/

★ Earthforce

You won't be able to feel it, but the ground is actually moving under your feet. Tremendous forces below the surface of the Earth are constantly tugging and pushing on the planet's crust. Luckily for us, this doesn't usually affect our lives. Sometimes though, it does, as we experience earthquakes, volcanoes, floods, tsunamis, and avalanches. This site from The Franklin Institute offers an introduction to each of these topics, as well as an outstanding selection of links to further information.

http://www.fi.edu/earth/earth.html

★ Savage Earth Online

What's great about this resource from PBS are the wonderful animations! You'll gasp as lava erupts and flows. You'll be shocked as a tsunami attacks a lighthouse. You'll quake as faults happen and roads are misaligned. Besides that, there's a lot of useful information, links, and other illustrations here as well.

http://www.wnet.org/savageearth/

A Tapestry of Time and Terrain

If you painted a portrait of the surface of the United States, you'd get a tapestry of colors. That's exactly what the folks at the U.S. Geological Survey did. But, instead of using a paintbrush, they took two maps and put them on top of each other. One map shows the topography of the United States, and the other shows its underlying geology. Check out the Puzzle of Regions to see if you can reassemble the map. While it looks like a pretty picture, the different colors help scientists learn more about natural hazards and the events that shaped the Earth's history.

http://tapestry.wr.usgs.gov/

GEOLOGY—EARTHQUAKES

Earthquakes

The Tech Museum in San Jose, California, has a dynamic online exhibit on earthquakes: what they are, why they occur, and why we can't predict them (yet). It includes an interesting history of the seismograph, used to record earthquake activity. The first one may have been invented in China in A.D. 136. It involved dragon heads positioned around a copper vessel. Each dragon mouth held a ball. Below the dragons were openmouthed frogs. In the event of an earthquake, a ball would fall into a frog's mouth. By noting which balls had dropped, one could tell how the ground moved in response to the quake.

http://www.thetech.org/exhibits_events/online/quakes/

Earthquakes - The Terror from Below

The ancient Babylonians believed that the "Jupiter Effect" of planetary alignment somehow caused an increase in earthquake activity on Earth. While that theory has never been scientifically proven, no one really knows how to predict earthquakes. We think we know what causes them, though: plate tectonics. This theory says that the Earth's crust is made up of jigsaw puzzle—like plates floating on a layer of liquid magma below. The plates touch and can slide against each other. The areas where they meet are called fault zones. As plates push against each other, stresses build until suddenly they are released in an event we call an earthquake. That's the simplified version—for more detail, visit this site, created by students for the ThinkQuest competition.

http://library.thinkquest.org/21903/

Electronic Desktop Project - Virtual Earthquake

How do scientists figure out where the starting point, or epicenter, of an earthquake occurred? In this cool simulation, you pick the general region for your test earthquake (California, Japan, Mexico). Use the easy-to-follow instructions to examine seismograms, and pinpoint the epicenter and the relative strength of your quake.

http://vcourseware4.calstatela.edu/VirtualEarthquake/
    VQuakeIntro.html

★ Life Along the Faultline: Life and Science in Earthquake Country

On October 17, 1989, the first game of the World Series was being played in Candlestick Park near San Francisco, California. During the fourth inning, TV screens across the country suddenly went black as viewers heard the announcer yell, "We're having an earthquake!" You can relive that moment by watching the video clips at this site. The area had been hit by 7.1 magnitude earthquake. Freeways collapsed, buildings burned, and many people were hurt. Read eyewitness reports, see news video, and learn what modifications have been made to avoid this type of massive damage in the future. There are also some experiments to try at this excellent site.

http://www.exploratorium.edu/faultline/

Marilee's Paperdolls Page: Printable Paperdolls, Links, Books

This is the mother lode of printable paper doll pages! You can discover links to Civil War dolls, dolls featuring royalty, pets, children, and even international dolls. Parents, not every link has been checked.
http://www.ameritech.net/users/macler/paperdolls

National Earthquake Information Center: Current Earthquake Information

How many earthquakes do you think occur in the world every day? Probably a lot more than you realize. Seismic activity is monitored day and night, and any recorded activity is posted to this site not long after the real time of each event. Check here and you'll be surprised to find there's a whole lot of shakin' goin' on.

http://wwwneic.cr.usgs.gov/current_seismicity.shtml

A Science Odyssey: You Try It: Plate Tectonics

Part of a larger site explaining plate tectonics, this Shockwave game allows you to rock and roll the landscape by dragging some virtual plates around. Can you build a mountain? Can you make a volcano erupt? Keep trying!

http://www.pbs.org/wgbh/aso/tryit/tectonics/

Surf today, smart tomorrow.

A B C D E F G H I J K L M N O P Q R S T U V W X Y Z

A
B
C
D
E
F
G
H
I
J
K
L
M
N
O
P
Q
R
S
T
U
V
W
X
Y
Z

NET FILES

Pretend you have a special light switch in your bedroom and it is connected (with a really l o n g cord) to a lamp on the Moon. If you switch it on, how long will the delay be before the bulb lights?

http://209.141.118.23/jfk_fun.html

Answer: It would take only 1.26 seconds for it to light up, shining over 238,857 miles away. Find out more at

★ USGS Earthquakes for Kids

Did you feel it? Was it an earthquake? Enter your ZIP code and describe your experiences at this site. The scientists will check it out to see if you're the first one to report a disturbance in your area. If you're not hiding under a desk to protect yourself, this site will surprise you with other interesting facts about earthquakes and tell you how to prepare for one.

http://earthquake.usgs.gov/4kids/

USGS SeismoCam

Want to know what's shaking in L.A.—literally? Live shots of a seismograph as it's tracking activity in the Southern California area can be monitored here. If nothing's happening while you're watching, you can look at some archived shots from past events, including some BIG temblors.

http://www.scecdc.scec.org/seismocam/
　 SeismoCam.html

USGS - This Dynamic Earth

Have you ever seen a bumper sticker that says "Stop Plate Tectonics!"? It's something that's an impossible task. Although continental land masses look pretty stable, they are actually moving all the time. Sometimes they just drift along very, very slowly. Other times they shift or move suddenly, and that causes an earthquake. The plates don't just cruise around at random, but scientists aren't completely sure what's "driving" them, either. This nicely illustrated site explains it all.

http://pubs.usgs.gov/publications/text/dynamic.html

GEOLOGY—FOSSILS

Fossils! Behind the Scenes at the Museum

A fossil is a sort of stone souvenir from the past. When you hold a fossil in your hand, you're really looking at an animal or plant that was buried on a beach, in a mud puddle, or on a sandbar of long, long ago. If you need a quick refresher course on fossils and how they form, better start here. There are also sections on where fossils are found and how they are prepared and preserved by scientists. We liked the fossil game: see if you can match a fossil with its modern-day equivalent creature. This is harder than you'd think—how well can you do?

http://www.rom.on.ca/quiz/fossil/

Introduction to Trilobites

It lived 300 million years ago and became extinct before the first dinosaur egg hatched. What is it? A trilobite, of course. You'll learn all about these amazing little hard-shelled creatures at this site. And, if learning about trilobites makes you want to own a trilobite fossil, the author of this site trades them. Check out Trading Trilobites for the latest specimens. Parental advisory: not all links have been checked.

http://www.aloha.net/~smgon/trilobite.htm

GEOLOGY—GEMS AND MINERALS

Bob's Rock Shop

There's a real treasure to mine at this site, which is all about rockhounding around the U.S. and Canada. Consider the tale of the kid who found a 1,104-carat sapphire. Mull over Mexico's mystery mineral. Find out how all those facets get on a gemstone. And learn how to wrap a stone in wire to make a pendant—with the help of an adult.

http://www.rockhounds.com/rockshop/table.html

★ Canadian Rockhound: Junior Rockhound Magazine

If you've ever wanted to start a mineral collection, this is a good place to explore. If you've already collected boxes of rocks and would like to try to identify and organize them, you'll really like this site (almost as much as your parents will!). About 3,000 minerals have been identified, but the good news is most rock collectors will only come across about 60 of them in the field. This site offers a lot about geology in general, too, including plate tectonics, earthquakes, and the geologic time scale.

http://www.canadianrockhound.com/junior.html

Diamonds in the Rough

Wouldn't it be fun to try to find some diamonds yourself? These kids did! They visited the Crater of Diamonds State Park in Arkansas and brought along a camera so you can see what they saw. They also interviewed three successful diamond hunters about their techniques, which include looking on the soil surface, sifting through a screen, and washing soil and rocks with water. This site was created by students for the ThinkQuest Junior competition.

http://tqjunior.advanced.org/5008/

Why surf the Internet when you can sail it in BOATING AND SAILING?

A Gem of a Story

Gems and jewels: before they become treasures, they look like, well, rocks. You might be able to spot a future gemstone if you study this site. You'll see a collection of pictures and descriptions of rocks and minerals from the Smithsonian National Museum of Natural History in Washington, D.C. You can also click on each small picture to get a larger picture of that mineral. In the activities section, don't miss how to go "mining by mail."

http://www.bsu.edu/teachers/academy/gems/
  welcome.html

He Ain't Nothing but a Rock Hound, a Diggin' All the Time

Even Elvis has been spotted digging around on this page recently. If you have rocks in your head and love to collect minerals, fossils, and crystals, you will love this site and its extensive information on collecting and studying rocks. There's also a fun rock hound's crossword puzzle.

http://ur.utenn.edu/ut2kids/rocks/rocks.html

★ The Mineral and Gemstone Kingdom

Are you taking Earth Science in school? This neat resource will be a big help. Search through Minerals A–Z by name, chemical group, color, hardness, streak, and other classifications. You'll get a description of the mineral plus lots of color photos. There's also a terrific encyclopedia of gemstones, a glossary, and information on starting a mineral collection. Be sure to check out the link collection, too.

http://www.minerals.net/

★ The Nature of Diamonds

Diamonds are rare and exotic, formed deep below the ground and transported closer to the surface by volcanoes and other cataclysmic events. If you have a diamond, it is probably the oldest item you will ever own. According to this site, it's likely your diamond is three billion years old, two-thirds the age of the whole Earth! Learn all about diamonds: their physical and chemical properties, how they are mined, and what beautiful gemstones they make.

http://www.amnh.org/exhibitions/diamonds/

A B C D E F G H I J K L M N O P Q R S T U V W X Y Z

Tetra

Tetra makes fish food as well as lots of other supplies for aquarists. Even if you don't have a tank of your own, you can still experience playing with the Virtual Aquarium at this site. You don't even have to get wet! Just choose what type of tank and decorations you want, and the site will recommend some friendly fish. Then make your selections, and watch the fun. There is also information about maintaining a classroom fish tank, and links to the home pages of major public aquaria around the United States.
http://www.tetra-fish.com/va/

NOVA Online - The Diamond Deception

Scientists have figured out how to make synthetic diamonds look so much like the real thing that they are starting to fool gem experts. At this site you'll learn about the new advances, discover the optical qualities of diamonds, and puzzle over whether or not there are diamonds in space (scientists think so!). There's also a Shockwave simulation where you try to construct your own carbon atom out of quarks and other spare parts.

http://www.pbs.org/wgbh/nova/diamond/

Trick roping secrets are revealed in KNOTS.

NOVA Online - The Perfect Pearl

Pearls, known as the "Queen of Gems," are created by either salt- or freshwater shellfish such as oysters or mussels. Pearls sometimes occur naturally, or they may be "cultured" by pearl farmers. Learn about the history of pearls, pearl culture techniques, and the controversy surrounding recent culturing methods.

http://www.pbs.org/wgbh/nova/pearl/

Rock Candy

Mix two cups of water and five cups of sugar. Add one adult and boil. What you do you get? A trick, or a treat? Neither. It's a recipe for rock candy. Rock candy is just crystallized sugar, and this project will show you how sugar grows into crystals, just like some minerals. You need an adult, because the recipe involves cooking sugar at high temperatures that could easily burn small hands.

**http://www.beakman.com/rock-candy/
rock-candy.html**

Rock Identification

How do you go about identifying a rock sample? You can examine it closely, put a few drops of acid on it to see if it fizzes, and try the "scratch test." Based on the results of these examinations, you should be able to figure out what type of rock or mineral you've got. Try it with this virtual version!

**http://www.bwctc.northants.sch.uk/website/html/
projects/science/ks34/rocks/list.html**

The World of Amber

Millions of years ago, resinous sap dripped slowly down a tree. As it oozed towards the ground, it engulfed twigs, insects, and anything else in its way. As geologic time passed, the trees fell and were buried, and the sap hardened to become the gemstone we know today as amber. This site holds amber up to the light and explains where it is found, what types exist, and what legends and myths are associated with the mysterious gem.

http://www.emporia.edu/earthsci/amber/amber.htm

A B C D E F G H I J K L M N O P Q R S T U V W X Y Z

GEOLOGY—GEYSERS

★ Fantastic Journeys: Yellowstone @ Nationalgeographic.com

Hey, what's all that mist up ahead? Wait—it's steam. Hold on, hear that gurgling and rumbling noise? RUN! Oops. This is the Net, isn't it. That's not a real geyser; that's QuickTime virtual reality. That glopping sound you hear is coming from a virtual mudpot. Still, it's pretty exciting to see and hear the various things that can happen when you mix hot water and minerals together. Don't forget to put on your virtual wet suit and dive down into the depths of the Grand Prismatic Spring to see what's below.

http://www.nationalgeographic.com/features/97/yellowstone/

Old Faithful Geyser Webcam

Watch this famous geyser erupt via the magic of Yellowstone National Park's webcam. According to this site, the average interval between eruptions is about 76 minutes. You might have to wait a while to see the plume of steam and boiling water, but it's worth it! If you "visit" at night, check the archive of recent daytime pictures.

http://www.nps.gov/yell/oldfaithfulcam.htm

GEOLOGY—TSUNAMIS

Tsunami!

Tsunamis (pronounced tsoo-nahm-ee) cause severe damage to coastal areas. Learn about the Tsunami Warning System and what you can do to protect yourself if one is issued for your area. But if you are ever near the ocean and feel a deep rumble in the earth, don't wait for an official warning—get moving. It could be the first sign of a tsunami, and once the wave gets to shore, you will not be able to outrun it. Another early sign of trouble is that sometimes, just before a tsunami, the water is sucked out to sea, exposing the ocean floor. This is a warning that you should move inland quickly or to a higher area, such as the top floors of a high-rise building. You'll also find detailed information about historic tsunami events, as well as links to other tsunami sites.

http://www.geophys.washington.edu/tsunami/welcome.html

Tsunami for Kids

A tsunami is a series of big waves triggered by an undersea disturbance, such as an earthquake or a volcanic eruption. The waves may travel in the open sea as fast as 450 miles per hour and reach a height of 100 feet. When they smash into the shore, they can cause a lot of destruction. Learn the warning signs and listen to a tsunami survivor tell her story. If you think you know it all, print and take the Tsunami Trivia game.

http://www.pmel.noaa.gov/tsunami-hazard/kids.html

GEOLOGY—VOLCANOES

Mount St. Helens

Imagine that you're living near Mount St. Helens, a sleeping volcano, and suddenly it blows up! There's dust and debris everywhere, mud slides, and boulders shooting into the air. Read exciting stories from people who were there on May 18, 1980. Sponsored by Educational Service District 112 in Vancouver, Washington, this graphics-intensive site provides maps, photos, and classroom projects to help bring this devastating eruption to life. Particularly compelling is a climb to the summit with QuickTime VR at the top.

http://volcano.und.nodak.edu/vwdocs/msh/msh.html

★ Stromboli On-Line

Between Sicily and southern Italy lie the Aeolian Islands. Stromboli is the northernmost of this volcanic chain, and it has an active volcano called—Stromboli. On the main page you can find out everything from the current eruption conditions to the current weather. However, you'll be most interested in the virtual climbs to the summit. Remember, if you don't like heights, you can always click the browser's Back button. If you do get to the summit, sign the guest book. Ready for more? Other volcano-cams and information are right around the bend. This page is in English, Italian, and German.

http://educeth.ethz.ch/stromboli/

A B C D E F G H I J K L M N O P Q R S T U V W X Y Z

A
B
C
D
E
F
G
H
I
J
K
L
M
N
O
P
Q
R
S
T
U
V
W
X
Y
Z

★ Volcano Expedition

What would it be like to go on an expedition to study volcanoes? Follow along on a trip to Costa Rica, and retrace the scientists' steps through volcanic craters and acid lakes (hope you brought your virtual boots). Read their daily journals, and see what samples they collected for analysis. Be sure to watch the QuickTime movies of bubbling acid gas pools for *Volcan Arenal* (January 8 and 10) and *Volcan Miravalles* (January 11) Why shouldn't you sit on a fumarole to get warm? The answer is on January 6.

http://www.sio.ucsd.edu/volcano/

★ Volcano World

How do you become a volcanologist? Just ask Mr. Spock for lessons, of course! Well, not quite. Look at this site to find out what becoming a volcanologist is all about and what courses you'll need to take. Oh yeah, there's also the BEST information here about volcanoes, including lessons and activities for teachers and students. You can also subscribe to e-mail updates about currently erupting volcanoes.

http://volcano.und.nodak.edu/vw.html

NET FILES

What special bean was once used as money?

Answer: Cacao beans, from which chocolate is made. Cacao trees are believed to have originated in South America, and they were so valuable that the Aztecs used them as money. According to the New Mexico State University's site at http://horizon.nmsu.edu/garden/history/cacao.html, "They also roasted and ground the cacao bean and added vanilla pods, water, pepper, and other spices to make a drink, but it wasn't until after 1492 that sugar was added...to make it sweet, and it wasn't until more than 150 years later that the English people began making the drink with milk instead of water."

★ Volcanoes Online

Not all volcanic eruptions are created equal—this site identifies seven different kinds. Hawaiian eruptions flow gently, while Strombolian eruptions are characterized by explosive lava chunks raining down on the surrounding area. There's an encyclopedia of volcanoes around the world and a neat Save the Village game—but don't try it unless you have explored the site first. We warned you! This site was created by students for the ThinkQuest competition.

http://library.thinkquest.org/17457/

LAND FEATURES—CAVES AND CAVING

BLM's Resource Explorers

It's 120 degrees outside, but inside New Mexico's Endless Cave it's cool and comfortable. Here in the "twilight" section of the cave—where sunlight filters in—we'll see mice, rattlesnakes, and even a few ringtail cats. Farther into the cave, it's dark all the time, and most of the creatures we'll see are colorless and have no eyes. They don't need eyes because there is nothing to see—however, their other senses tell them what's going on nearby. Learn more about this cave and the people who explore it.

http://www.blm.gov/education/expert/3/

Borneo Caving Expedition

Get wet. Get muddy. Get tangled. Get scared. Get lost. Get down. Get up. That's what you'll experience when you explore a cave. If you don't live near one, this site will take you on a caving expedition in the rainforests of Borneo. There are lots of photos about caves and cave formations. Under Yucky Pictures, check out the disgusting picture of the dreaded Mulu Foot. If you plan to explore caves in this part of the world, you'll need to know that keeping your feet dry will help prevent this painful skin condition.

http://www.northcoast.com/~rchilds/
  borneomainpage.shtml

> ### Do you know the way to San Jose? If not, check a map in GEOGRAPHY.

Exploring Caves

Jenny and Carlos just wanted to get out of the rain. They never thought they'd be lost in a mysterious cave! Luckily, a talking bat shows up (are they lost in Disneyland?) and he agrees to lead them back to the entrance. Along the way, they meet unusual cave residents, gaze at spectacular formations, and find out why caves sometimes guard the secrets of the past.

http://www.usgs.gov/education/learnweb/caves/
intro.htm

Mammoth Cave National Park

"Captain, Spock here. According to the informative sign, I am exploring the longest recorded cave system in the world. There seem to be more than 350 miles mapped, but sensors indicate much more to this labyrinth. I chart my location as Kentucky. My Starfleet tricorder reads ambient temperature at 53 degrees Fahrenheit. Here is a sign; I will read it aloud: 'Violet City Lantern Tour, 3 hours, 3 miles (strenuous). A nostalgic tour into a section of the cave that is not electrically lit. The tour features saltpeter mining, prehistoric exploration, historic tuberculosis hospital huts, and some of the largest rooms and passage ways in the cave. The first half-mile follows the Historic Tour route. Do not bring flashlights. Restrooms not available.' No rest rooms? Illogical. Beam me up. No, wait—it says that other tours are available; some are handicapped-accessible and some are short, fun walks for kids, too. And they have rest rooms!"

http://www.nps.gov/maca/home.htm

Mount St. Helens & Other Volcanoes, Ape Cave

Ape Cave is a special geologic formation called a lava tube. Formed when Mount St. Helens (Amboy, Washington) erupted 1,900 years ago, it is 12,810 feet long—that's almost two and a half miles! It is the longest intact lava tube in the United States and the second longest in the world. You can read all about its amazing features, such as sand castles, "lava-sicles," and lava balls. Don't miss the creatures of Ape Cave, which include cockroaches, millipedes, and cave slime. There have never been any apes in Ape Cave, however. The name came from a local youth group that explored Mount St. Helens, climbing all over it like monkeys.

http://volcano.und.nodak.edu/vwdocs/msh/ov/ovb/
ovbac.html

Virtual Cave

Now you can explore the mineral wonders of the perfect cave without leaving your house or school! This site has pictures of many geologic features besides stalactites and stalagmites. For example, you'll see popcorn, bathtubs, and cave pearls. For a bat-free cave experience, try spelunking here. There's also a handy list of public "show caves" arranged by state so that you can find a real cave to visit.

http://www.goodearthgraphics.com/virtcave.html

LAND FEATURES—DESERTS

California Desert

From early black-and-white movie classics to *Jurassic Park*, more than 140 films have been made in the California desert. Specifically, at Red Rock Canyon State Park. Red Rock Canyon is just one of the many sites to see on a driving tour through the California Desert. This site maps out the others. Can rocks talk? Find out in the geology section. There's also a desert critter bingo game for you to print and try on a road trip across the desert.

http://www.californiadesert.gov/

A B C D E F G H I J K L M N O P Q R S T U V W X Y Z

A
B
C
D
E
F
G
H
I
J
K
L
M
N
O
P
Q
R
S
T
U
V
W
X
Y
Z

Desert Life in the American Southwest

Why is salty Owens Lake red? Do roadrunners really say "beep-beep"? And has anyone ever found the legendary "black gold" a prospector named Pegleg lost years ago? Find out what's hot in the desert these days.

http://www.desertusa.com/life.html

Digital Desert Library

Deserts are not always hot, barren places without water. There are deserts in Antarctica and on the ice caps of Greenland that are never hot. And some deserts, like the Sahara in Africa, have sand dunes. But that's not what makes them deserts. Explore this site to find out why. Then, visit the Chihuahuan Desert, which is the largest desert in North America. You'll discover that this desert is full of life. Just search the database to learn about the hundreds of plants, insects, fish, birds, mammals, and reptiles that live there.

http://horizon.nmsu.edu/ddl/welcome.html

Sonoran Desert Natural History Information

When you hear the word "desert," does it conjure up visions of sand dunes? There are lots of desert types, including salt flats, high mountain plateaus, and more. It doesn't mean there are no plants, either. Sloping and flat desert lands host so many plants, you can't walk without bumping into bushes! Also, flowers bloom most of the year. Learn more about the interrelationships of the plants, animals, and geology of this arid environment, as presented by the Arizona–Sonora Desert Museum.

http://www.desertmuseum.org/desertinfo/sonora.html

LAND FEATURES—GLACIERS

Frequently Asked Questions and Myths About Glaciers

If you've ever wondered why glaciers look blue, or if glacier ice is any colder than regular ice, or if glacier ice is really ancient ice—then you should check out this page. Also, are ice worms myth or fact? Find out here.

http://www-water-ak.usgs.gov/glaciology/FAQ.htm

★ Glacier Power

Ice worms can't be a myth, because they lead the tour to glaciers at this site! Find out about the different types of glaciers, like tidewater glaciers and valley glaciers. See a cross section and learn about glacier anatomy. When you think you know it all, join the glacier detectives and see if you can answer the quiz questions and solve the mystery of Miner Ed. (Note: something is broken in the quiz area, but just hit the "Back" button on your browser to go on to the next question.)

http://www.asf.alaska.edu:2222/intro1.html

Predicting the Impact of Climate Change on Glaciers and Vegetation Distribution in Glacier National Park

All over the world, glaciers are disappearing. Scientists are studying this puzzle and trying to understand what it means for the future. One of those scientists lives right up the road from Net-mom. She spent a lot of time studying the history of Glacier National Park in Montana. She's created an animation of how the glaciers have changed since 1850, and what may happen in the future. Will Glacier National Park someday need a new name? (Hint: wait for all the images to load, and then watch the animation progress through the years.)

http://www.mesc.usgs.gov/glacier/glacier_model.htm

★ Wired Antartica

The seasons may come and go in your hometown, but in Antarctica it's always cold. This southernmost continent is so cold that the snow that falls there never melts. In fact, some of the snow, which has now been turned into ice, is thousands of years old. There's a great introduction to glaciers you'll find as you explore this site. Check this out: Even though the continent holds 70 percent of the world's supply of fresh water, it's as dry as the Sahara desert. This site offers a funny and educational first-hand look at the life of a researcher in Antarctica.

http://www.geophys.washington.edu/People/
   Students/ginny/antarctica/

LAND FEATURES—MOUNTAINS

★ Destination: Himalayas - Where Earth Meets Sky

This ThinkQuest contest grand prize winner was created by a team of geographically and culturally diverse kids. It gives an overview of the Himalayan region, its flora and fauna, and its environmental problems. Himalaya is a Sanskrit word that literally means "Abode of Snow." You'll find multimedia if you choose the high-bandwidth version; otherwise, the text alone will inform and enlighten. This is an excellent site that proves what value kids bring to the Net.

http://library.thinkquest.org/10131/

★ Everest

Mount Everest is the tallest mountain in the world, at 29,028 feet. Go on a virtual expedition with an IMAX film crew. Your experience will be exhilarating, but exhausting and depressing, too. Learn about the empty oxygen canisters and other debris littering the area. Understand the human toll this journey has asked from those who dare to reach the top. Everest kills one climber for every four who reach the summit. Take the multimedia Shockwave version of the tour if you can. Otherwise, the HTML version is available.

http://www.mos.org/Everest/tour/tour.htm

Everest, Crown of the World

Most people in Nepal call it *Sagarmtha*, meaning "Forehead in the Sky." Tibetans call it *Chomolungma*, meaning "Goddess, Mother of the World." You probably know it as Everest. This site was created by students for the ThinkQuest Junior competition. See route maps, learn about great climbing successes and tragedies, and find out some very cool facts about the history of Mount Everest.

http://tqjunior.advanced.org/5069/

Lost on Everest

You don't have to leave home to climb to the top of Mount Everest, the tallest mountain in the world. Just visit this site, and go to the Climb section for some remarkable pictures of the climb up the North side of Everest. The pictures are actually panoramic virtual reality scenes. Get the QuickTime VR plug-in to view them. You can also help uncover the mysteries surrounding the disappearance of George Mallory and Sandy Irvine. To this day, no one knows for sure whether they were the first ever rock climbers to reach the summit.

http://www.pbs.org/wgbh/nova/everest/

LAND FEATURES— POLAR REGIONS
Glacier

Antarctica is the coldest and driest place on Earth—why do scientists and tourists go there? What's the attraction? How do you get there, anyway, and once you're there, what's it like? See what life is like at the major research stations, and don't forget to dress warmly when you visit this site.

http://www.glacier.rice.edu/

Iowa State Insect Zoo Live Camera

If you don't like creepy-crawlies, don't even bother connecting to this Web site! When we visited, the giant walkingsticks were on display. Eventually we gained control of the webcam (you have to wait your turn) and explored the display using the remote controlled camera. Wow! We saw two of the insects right away. Most will love this site even though it may "bug" others.
http://zoocam.ent.iastate.edu/

A B C D E F G H I J K L M N O P Q R S T U V W X Y Z

NOVA Online - Warnings from the Ice

If scientists drill down into very deep ice, they come back up with a "core sample." This cylindrical sample preserves the ice and its layers. Each layer represents a year (or sometimes a single season) of ice deposit. Along with the ice, plant material, dust, and other debris may be found. By studying this material, scientists are able to look at global climate change through time. Some of the dust might have come from a volcanic eruption, or a violent desert sandstorm. More recently, radioactive fallout from the Chernobyl nuclear disaster has turned up in ice cores. What can we learn that might help us predict the global impact of events of today? Visit the Ice Core Time Line to discover more.

http://www.pbs.org/wgbh/nova/warnings/

Secrets of the Ice from the Museum of Science, Boston

Scientists from the University of New Hampshire have been studying Antarctic ice hoping to find clues to the climate changes of the past. This site details their on-site experiences so far. Learn about how the research is conducted plus read the fascinating history of the continent's exploration.

http://www.secretsoftheice.org/

Virtual Antarctica

This is a slick resource, with audio and cool Web graphics sure to grab your attention. This site documents an expedition to Antarctica as seen through the eyes, cameras, diaries, and e-mail of the participants. You'll find lots here on geology, weather, and wildlife, as well as history.

http://www.terraquest.com/antarctica/

LAND FEATURES—PRAIRIE

★ On the Prairie: Prairie Ecology

The Great Plains region of the United States was once covered by a prairie ecosystem, but only 2 percent of native prairie remains today. This site explains why prairies are important. See how good you are at prairie restoration by playing the outstanding "Build-a-Prairie" game. Choose to restore a tallgrass or a shortgrass prairie. Then add plants and animals, but be careful! If you choose the wrong things, your prairie will not survive. Use the virtual field guide to help you decide. If you're right, you'll see an animated prairie grow right before your eyes.

http://www1.umn.edu/bellmuse/mnideals/prairie/

Terry the Prairie Dog

Follow Terry the Prairie Dog and discover facts about the plants and animals that live on the tallgrass prairie in the American Midwest. This page was created by fourth graders for the CyberFair '98 contest. You'll love the animated drawings the kids made to help you learn about this ecosystem. They do take a long time to load, but it's worth the effort. Can you guess who might want to start a prairie fire?

http://cyberfair.gsn.org/villages/

NET FILES

How do two traditional New Zealand Maoris greet each other?

Answer: They don't shake hands or wave; they rub noses. Check out proper gestures and other cultural behavior so you'll look and feel right at home when you visit another country.
http://www.webofculture.com/worldsmart/gesture_asia.html#NEW ZEALAND

LAND FEATURES—RAIN FORESTS

Amazon Life: Learning Ecology Through the Amazon Rain Forest

Learn about the biodiversity of the Amazon ecosystem, including plants, birds, and animals. Find out about deforestation, gold mining, and other forms of human impacts on this ancient area. The Brazilian government is building SIVAM (Surveillance System of Amazon) to try and monitor changes. It will be fully operational in 2002. This site was created by students for the ThinkQuest competition.

http://library.thinkquest.org/20248/

Congo Trek @ Nationalgeographic.com

Tag along with a research biologist as he treks 2,000 miles across the Republic of the Congo, documenting plants, animals, people, and landscapes he encounters along the way. You can read his diary, and see and hear lots of multimedia clips. On the left side of your screen, you'll be able to locate the position of each report on the interactive map.

http://www.nationalgeographic.com/congotrek/

A Kid Visits Costa Rica

This neat story of a fifth grader's trip to Costa Rica is filled with details about the rain forest and its inhabitants. After dodging iguanas around the hotel pool, the author moved into the jungle to sleep 85 feet in the air on a tree platform! In the morning, there were howler monkeys all around. There's more to his adventure—check it out. This site was created by students for the ThinkQuest Junior competition.

http://tqjunior.advanced.org/6066/March/costaric.htm

VIDEO AND SPY CAMS let you look in on interesting parts of the world.

From another galaxy? Learn about EARTH in the ASTRONOMY, SPACE, AND SPACE EXPLORATION area!

The Rain Forest

This site gives you a kid's-eye view of the insects, birds, and animals that inhabit the rain forests. There are more ants in the rain forest than any other creature. Learn about them as well as Goliath beetles, termites, and other things that creep and crawl. Plant life is as abundant as you'd expect. Discover pictures and facts about bromeliads, epiphytes, and liana vines, among others. It turns out that you really can't swing on them like Tarzan does in the movies. Liana vines grow from the ground up, making them unsuitable for trapeze tricks! This site was created by students for the ThinkQuest Junior competition.

http://tqjunior.advanced.org/5393/

Rainforest Action Network: Kid's Corner

You may have already heard that there are more kinds of plants and animals in tropical rain forests than anywhere else on Earth. And you probably already know that about half of all the world's species live in rain forests. But did you also know that in the rain forest you can find an antelope that's as small as a rabbit, a snake that can fly, and a spider that eats birds? The Kids' Corner is packed with just this kind of wild information about the rain forest, and it has lots of pictures of the creatures and native people living there. We all have a big problem, though: rain forests might be gone by the time you grow up. They're already disappearing at an alarming rate! Find out what you can do to help.

http://www.ran.org/kids_action/

A
B
C
D
E
F
G
H
I
J
K
L
M
N
O
P
Q
R
S
T
U
V
W
X
Y
Z

A
B
C
D
E
F
G
H
I
J
K
L
M
N
O
P
Q
R
S
T
U
V
W
X
Y
Z

Rainforest Alliance

Keep up with current news about the rain forest and those who are trying to save it at the "Rainforest Alliance" level of this site. Below is the URL for the kids' section, where you can learn about all kinds of frogs, make rain forest crafts, print coloring pages, and find out where to get more information on everything from leaf cutter ants to medicinal plants.

http://www.rainforest-alliance.org/kids&teachers/

★ What's It Like Where You Live? - Rain Forests

When you think about a rain forest, you probably think about a tropical jungle, right? Sure, this site will tell you all about those kinds of rain forests. But did you know that a temperate kind of rain forest exists in cooler parts of the world? These types are located along sea coastlines. In the U.S., you'll find one that stretches for 1,200 miles between Alaska and Oregon. In this type of forest, you will find redwoods, the world's tallest trees! Explore the features and creatures of all kinds of rain forests at this page, prepared by the Missouri Botanical Garden. Don't miss the extensive list of links to info on rain forests both tropical and temperate.

http://MBGnet.mobot.org/sets/rforest/

LAND FEATURES—SOILS

The Dirt on Soil

Yikes! There's something alive under your feet. Beetle mites, round worms, bacteria, root fungi and worms are some of the organisms and creatures that inhabit the underground world. Discover their habitat and watch them search for food and shelter. The EarthShip is waiting to take you on a Soil Safari. There's much more on the down and dirty of dirt at this site. Like, did you know there's a difference between soil and dirt?

http://school.discovery.com/schooladventures/soil/

LAND FEATURES—WETLANDS, SWAMPS, AND BOGS
Can the Everglades Survive?

It's not really a swamp and not really a bog: it's known as the River of Grass, and there is no other place like it in the world. Birds, alligators, fish, amphibians, and reptiles make it their home. You can find out about the challenges facing this important Florida watershed at this official National Park Service site.

http://www.nps.gov/ever/home.htm

Discovery Online: Everglades

The Florida Everglades are in trouble. Since the late 1800s, people have been altering nature: building a dam here, or draining a wetland there. It turns out that all of that development wasn't such a great idea. Now billions of dollars have been proposed to restore this complex ecosystem. Read all about the Everglades: past, present, and future.

http://www.discovery.com/news/features/everglades/
    everglades.html

Environmental Protection Agency - Teachers & Students

Check out these excellent handouts on the various types of wetlands, their functions, and the threats facing them today. You can find out how to adopt a nearby wetland and help protect it. To open these files you will need an Adobe® Portable Document Format (PDF) reader. The Adobe Acrobat reader can be downloaded for free at *<http://www.adobe.com/ products/acrobat/readstep.html>* if you don't already have it.

http://www.epa.gov/region01/students/teacher/
    world.html

Bring your shovel and meet us in the TREASURE AND TREASURE-HUNTING section.

★ Interactive Swamp

Here's a Web site deep in the heart of an interactive Louisiana swamp. From your vantage point on the shoreline, use your virtual magnifying glass to discover the different types of plants and animals that live in the swamp. You'll learn about their behavior and natural history, and you might even get to hear what these critters sound like. The swamp changes from daytime to nighttime with the click of a mouse. Don't forget to wave to the Cajun!

http://www.auduboninstitute.org/html/
  interswamp.html

Wet and Wild

Wetlands are important, and not just to the fish and frogs that live in them. Wetlands are nice to visit and view. They also provide flood control and help slow down spring snow melt runoff. They help filter the water and make it cleaner in the process. This ThinkQuest entry explains the various types of wetlands and then focuses on a wetland bordering a school. Lots of activities are suggested, from taking water samples to bird watching. Try the interactive animal tracks quiz to see if you can make it out of the swamp before dark!

http://library.thinkquest.org/J003192F/

🦫 Wetlands Coloring Book

Color a mallard, a moose, and many other birds and animals as you explore a wetland. You don't even need boots! You'll also find out what a "duck stamp" is—no, it's not what a water bird needs to mail a letter! Lots more wetland activities are located here <http://www.fws.gov/kids/>.

http://training.fws.gov/library/Pubs/
  Wetlands_colbk.pdf

Mr. Spock agrees it is highly logical to want to know all about STAR TREK, STAR WARS, AND SPACE EPICS.

The National Zoo

Check out the National Zoo in Washington, D.C. Admission is free. The only rule is this: Don't feed the animals—and don't smudge the computer screen with your nose! When we visited, the famous pandas, as well as the naked mole-rats, were visible on the live cams. There are loads of animal pictures and facts, and don't miss the multimedia demonstrations (we loved the annual elephant pumpkin stomp!)
http://www.si.edu/natzoo/

Why are Hawaii's Wetlands Vanishing?

Once upon a time, there was a wetland called Kaelepulu Pond in Hawaii. It was filled with fresh water and enough fish to feed the local community year-round. Sadly, this wetland is gone. Why? Take a lesson from this ThinkQuest Junior competition entry. The answer will help explain why more than 90 percent of the wetlands in Hawaii no longer exist. Colorful graphics, songs, and videos tell the story of what happened to Kaelepulu Pond.

http://library.thinkquest.org/J0110028/splash.htm

OZONE HOLE
On the Trail of the Missing Ozone

Ozone occurs naturally in our atmosphere. Near the surface of the Earth, it's considered air pollution and hazardous to health. But up in the stratosphere, ozone is necessary to protect life on the surface of the planet. That's why, in the 1970s, when an ozone hole was discovered over Antarctica, scientists took notice. What is being done to halt ozone depletion? Follow Farley the reporter as he tracks down the story.

http://www.epa.gov/ozone/science/missoz/

A B C D E F G H I J K L M N O P Q R S T U V W X Y Z

A B C D E F G H I J K L M N O P Q R S T U V W X Y Z

NET FILES

Everyone knows frogs can jump pretty far. How far? What's the longest recorded length a frog has leaped?

http://www.exploratorium.edu/frogs/mainstory/

inches in a single jump. Hop to it!

African frog holds the record for leaping 33 feet 5.5

Answer: According to the Exploratorium, a South

WATER

❧ To the Mountains and Back! The Adventures of Drippy the Raindrop

Water moves around the Earth in continuous cycles of evaporation and rain. This is called the water cycle. Follow Drippy the Raindrop, and he'll show you how he goes with the flow. Watch him evaporate from the ocean to the mountains and then fall back again as rain. Eventually he ends up back in the ocean again after a river ride. This illustrated cartoon makes learning about the water cycle fun for the littlest scientists.

http://www.kimballmedia.com/Drippy/
ToMountainsAndBack/Entry.htm

The Watershed Game

Start with the novice level of questions about watersheds and wetlands. Move quickly to the intermediate level where you'll be asked about watershed management in national parks, cities, and neighborhoods. There's a section on agriculture, too. Hint: as a small time pig farmer, you don't have enough cash to build a wastewater treatment plant.

http://www1.umn.edu/bellmuse/mnideals/watershed/
watershed2.html

Wise Use of Water - Brochures

The world is three-quarters water, isn't it? That means there is plenty to go around, right? Well, if you're talking about water that's healthy for us to drink, it's really in short supply. Consider the millions of people in the world, all of them thirsty. Now think of all the animals and birds in the world, all of them thirsty. Hmmm—better use that water wisely. Here's a list of tips and ideas to help you conserve this natural resource for future dried-out kids on hot, summer days. This site is also available in French.

http://www.ec.gc.ca/water/en/info/pubs/brochure/
e_broch.htm

WATER FEATURES—CORAL REEFS

★ Great Barrier Reef @NationalGeographic.com

The Great Barrier Reef is a carpet of coral, stretching for more than 1,250 miles off the north coast of Australia. See photographs of the reef in a stunning multimedia presentation. The Sights and Sounds slide show includes pictures of coral spawning and some of the most unusual fish you'll ever see. You can also zoom in on other pictures and find out how the photographer got these amazing shots.

http://www.nationalgeographic.com/ngm/0101/
feature2/

NOAA's Coral Reef

Corals are called sessile animals because they stay in one place and don't move around. They do build empires around themselves, using a special secretion called calcium carbonate. Eventually this builds up into a coral reef. Healthy coral reefs are characterized by lots of fish and other forms of marine life. Find out about coral reefs, as well as the problems facing them worldwide.

http://www.coralreef.noaa.gov/

How is Kwanzaa celebrated? Find out in HOLIDAYS!

Pacific Coral Reef Coloring Book

Every time you learn something new about coral reefs, you get a new picture to color. This online coloring book is brimming with facts about coral reefs and the role they play in supporting sea life. Before you print a picture to color, make sure you click on it first. That will enlarge the picture so it's big enough for little hands to color.

http://www.education.noaa.gov/books/paccoral/pacreef.htm

Reef Fish Quiz

See all the reef fish swimming by? Notice there's a clue at the top of the page. If you can click on the fish that matches the clue, you'll get a point! The fish swim pretty fast, so you'll have to be a real "Speedo demon" to catch one.

http://www.enteractive.com/store/shockfish.html

★ Venture into Hawaii's Coral Reefs

In ancient Hawaii, corals were thought of as sacred and were often used as offerings in religious ceremonies. They and the reefs they build are still precious things. This multimedia enriched site shows the diversity of life in Hawaii's reef systems, from the coral polyps themselves to invertebrates, mammals, and fish. One of the highlights is actually hearing a student pronounce "humuhumunukunukuapua'a"—the state fish of Hawaii. We loved all the colorful illustrations and animations—you will, too! This site was created by students for the ThinkQuest Junior competition.

http://library.thinkquest.org/J002237/

WATER FEATURES—OCEANS AND TIDES

A Coastal Journey

The moon is in a tug of war with the Earth's oceans. As the Earth moves, the Moon tries to keep its hold on the water. It always wins. When the bulge of the water being tugged by the Moon is near a coastline, the water creeps higher up the beach. We say the tide is "in." When the water bulge is farther away, the shoreline water level is lower. We say the tide is "out." This cycle usually occurs twice a day. Along rocky coastlines, when the tide "goes out," there are many creatures stranded in shallow pools until the tide returns. If you're careful where you walk, you can observe this sea life up close. If you don't live near the ocean, this Web site may be the next best thing. Follow along as kids explore "Who Lives in the Intertidal Zone?"

http://www.poulsbomsc.org/tutorial.htm

Dive and Discover

Exploring new places means discovering new things. So, when scientists planned a diving expedition to the far reaches of the Indian Ocean, their mission was to discover exotic species that live where hot water spews from cracks in the Earth's sea floor. After 40 days at sea, scientists did just that. See what the scientists discovered! The slide shows and movies spotlight the animals and ancient bacteria that live in this remote place. There are also classroom activities and puzzles for you to enjoy.

http://www.divediscover.whoi.edu/

Monterey Bay @ Nationalgeographic.com

Hop into your submersible submarine and explore the kelp forest of California's beautiful Monterey Bay. You'll learn about life in the kelp forest canopy, understory, and the "forest" floor. There's also an opportunity to visit the extremely deep canyon just outside of Monterey Bay via Real Video.

http://www.nationalgeographic.com/monterey/ax/primary_fs.html

A B C D E F G H I J K L M N O P Q R S T U V W X Y Z

Web Weather for Kids

Can you make a thunderstorm in your kitchen, or construct a tornado in your breakfast nook? The "recipes" are here, along with slick animations and lots of multimedia. We can't wait to try making our own lightning!
http://www.ucar.edu/40th/webweather/

National Marine Sanctuaries

When you think about protecting forests and the creatures that live in them, you probably think about national parks on land. There are also underwater "parks" set aside as refuges for marine animals and sea life. They are called marine sanctuaries. Some are home to migratory mammals like whales, while others are lush feeding grounds for many species. This site takes you on a pictorial tour of several of these special places. You'll also learn about the efforts to protect and restore them.

http://www.sanctuaries.nos.noaa.gov/welcome.html

★ Ocean AdVENTure! - Welcome Aboard!

We'll be diving to the ocean floor, over 7,000 feet below. You'll see underwater geysers, spewing mineral-rich superhot water into the surrounding cold sea. In this area, I'll point out bizarre life-forms, including a snowstorm of bacteria, tube worms, white crabs, and eyeless shrimp. Before we descend, please remove your shoes and belt buckle, as they could damage the watertight seal of our submarine. And that would be bad! And please note, your tour today was created by students for the ThinkQuest competition.

http://library.thinkquest.org/18828/

Ocean98 Victor the Vector

Victor the Vector is searching for his mother. Seems they caught different ocean currents, and he's traveling the seas to find her again. If you hitch a ride with Victor, you'll learn all about the great currents of the world and maybe a little bit about geography, too.

http://www.ocean98.org/vicin.htm

★ Oceanography: An ONR Science & Technology Focus Site

For the inside story on waves, currents, tides and more, this site from the Navy's Office of Naval Research is top class. In the resources section, you can try some experiments to learn why huge ships don't sink, how a submarine works, and our favorite—making desktop icebergs.

http://www.onr.navy.mil/focus/ocean/

Oceans Alive!

The Earth is sometimes called the "water planet." That's because 71 percent of the Earth's surface is covered by water. But, underneath lies rugged mountains, active volcanoes, vast plateaus, and almost bottomless trenches. At 36,198 feet deep, Mariana Trench in the western Pacific is the deepest point. It could easily swallow up Mount Everest, the tallest mountain on land! At this site, you can learn more about the ocean's landscape and life in the sea.

http://www.mos.org/oceans/

Oceans and Coastal Protection: Kids' Page

This page from the Environmental Protection Agency houses a whole tide pool of interesting links for you to pick up and ponder. Get out your crayons for the Louisiana Coastal Coloring Book, splash into the Center for Marine Conservation Wading Pool for some really fun games, and dive into the Non-point Source Kids' Page to help out Darby Duck and the Aquatic Crusaders. All of the above is just skimming the surface.

http://www.epa.gov/owow/oceans/kids.html

A B C D E F G H I J K L M N O P Q R S T U V W X Y Z

Savage Seas

Try the wave machine (look for it in the Crow's Nest section) and see if you can change the variables enough to create a monster wave. You'll have to choose how fast the wind is blowing, how long these conditions have kept up, and how far across open water the winds have blown. You can also view some fascinating animations about the high pressure present at extreme depths. A common Styrofoam cup would be compressed to the size of a thimble at the depth of 3,000 feet.

http://www.pbs.org/wnet/savageseas/

★ Secrets@Sea

Assume the role of a spunky detective as you investigate strange whale behavior around Alanamorris Strait. Could it have something to do with those toxic waste barrels? Where did you put your bus schedule—it's time to ace the case! This wonderful adventure game from the Vancouver Aquarium will keep you busy for a long time as you examine your field guide, collect creature cards, and examine your notes. Can you crack the code and save the whales?

http://www.secretsatsea.org/main.html

The Tide Pool Page

Exploring a tide pool can be exciting! You never know what you're going to find. There could be a green anemone, a starfish, or maybe even a hermit crab. It's important to know some safety tips first: don't turn your back on the sea because a wave could sneak up on you. Another tip is to be careful and watch where you step because rocks can be slippery. This site offers a virtual tour to the various intertidal zones and shows which creatures you might expect to find there.

http://web.mit.edu/corrina/tpool/tidepool.html

Fetch some fascinating info in DOGS AND DOG SPORTS.

NET FILES

How tall is the Oscar award, and how much does it weigh?

Answer: The Academy Awards statuette, known as "Oscar," is 13 1/2 inches tall and weighs 8 1/2 pounds. The statuettes are made from gold-plated alloy called britannium. Learn more about the awards and the winners at
http://www.oscars.org/academyawards/awards.html

★ University of Delaware Graduate College of Marine Studies

Wow! There's a lot of neat stuff here. Prowl along the interactive coastal habitat and learn how important horseshoe crabs and other species are; then hop into a submersible submarine and take a Voyage to the Deep. If you're not too water-logged after that, settle down to look at a picture book: Denizens of the Deep. Hint: don't look if you frighten easily!

http://www.ocean.udel.edu/neatstuff/neatstuff.html

Why Is the Ocean Salty?

You could describe seawater as being a very diluted soup of pretty much everything on Earth: minerals, organic matter, even synthetic chemicals. Here's the strange thing: the ocean has the same degree of saltiness everywhere. There isn't one place that is saltier than another. Where did the salt come from? If freshwater rivers and streams keep flowing into the sea, why doesn't the sea become less salty? Find out here.

http://oceanography.palomar.edu/salty_ocean.htm

A B C D E F G H I J K L M N O P Q R S T U V W X Y Z

A
B
C
D
E
F
G
H
I
J
K
L
M
N
O
P
Q
R
S
T
U
V
W
X
Y
Z

WATER FEATURES—RIVERS

American Rivers - River ABCs

Okay, you know your ABCs. But do you know your River ABCs? That would include knowing the answer to how many rivers there are in the United States. Answer: 250,000. Or, what is the longest U.S. river? If you answered the Missouri River, you're right. The Mississippi River is the largest U.S. river. But there's more than just river trivia at this site. Get the scoop on river tours, conservation efforts, water issues, and lots more. There are even fun classroom activities and games for you to try. Get muddy! Wade right in!

http://www.amrivers.org/riverabc/

Columbia River @ nationalgeographic.com

The Columbia River once ran through the Pacific Northwest, and it still does. But the once free-flowing river is now controlled by a series of reservoirs and dams. That's had both good and bad effects: good for the generation of low-cost electricity, but bad for the salmon. The taming of the Columbia River has changed the habitat of the salmon, so much so that extinction threatens some wild stocks. For a better understanding the Columbia River 's predicament, take an interactive trip down the river. Each time you click on something, another piece of the puzzle falls into place.

http://www.nationalgeographic.com/earthpulse/
   columbia/

Virtual River

A river runs through this Web site, and you can follow along its banks to learn about how geologists measure the velocity and volume of a river or stream. Animations and virtual calculators will help you understand the concepts. This is a complex lab, suitable for very motivated middle schoolers or high school kids.

http://vcourseware4.calstatela.edu/VirtualRiver/

ENDANGERED AND EXTINCT SPECIES

American Livestock Breeds Conservancy

When you think of endangered species, you imagine jungle animals, right? Usually you don't think of cows, horses, or chickens as threatened. Some very old breeds of livestock, though, are disappearing. This is important because the more genetic diversity a species has, the more able some animals may be to withstand a catastrophic disease. See what's threatened in the barnyard at this site.

http://www.albc-usa.org/

★ The American Museum of Natural History: Endangered! Exploring a World at Risk

The American Museum of Natural History is in New York City, but you can take a trip around the world of endangered species and habitats at this fascinating site. Read stop number four on the tour map, "Legend of the Meeps Island Flying Frog," for an amusing and educational look at how a creature becomes endangered. Check stop number seven on the virtual tour for "Invasion of the Lake-Snatchers." It's all about something that's not endangered: zebra mussels. See what happens if you place a VW beetle in Lake Erie for 118 days.

http://www.amnh.org/Exhibition/Expedition/
   Endangered/

The Endangered Animals of the World

Here's your chance to get involved and raise awareness of creatures on the endangered species list. Find an endangered species where you live, and submit a report on it to this site. Seventy-three schools from around the world have already done so. Prairie chickens, river otters, gray bats, and the wood frog are some of the endangered species you can read about at this site.

http://www.tenan.vuurwerk.nl/

Endangered Species Program: U.S. Fish & Wildlife Service

In the United States, 737 plants and 507 species of animals are on the threatened and endangered lists (see the Species Information section). "Extinct" means they are gone from planet Earth forever. "Endangered species" are animals and plants in danger of becoming extinct. "Threatened species" are animals and plants likely to become endangered in the future. Learn which species are listed as threatened and endangered in the United States. In the Kid's Corner there are a few games and ways kids can get involved, from helping with public awareness to species monitoring.

http://endangered.fws.gov/

★ ES2000 - Endangered Species of the Next Millennium

This award-winning ThinkQuest site was built by kids. Learn about many threatened species and how they became that way. What can be done about endangered animals? Plenty, and this ThinkQuest team will guide you into action. Their point is that by endangering wildlife, we ultimately endanger ourselves. There's also a fun interactive story you can try. Add your own chapter when you reach the end.

http://library.thinkquest.org/25014/

How Pono the Happy Face Spider Found His Smile

You know that bright yellow round "happy face" cartoon? Can you believe there's a Hawaiian spider that has similar markings? Naturally, it's known as the "happy face spider." Trouble is, it's lost its smile because it has noticed its friends are disappearing. Find out about Hawaiian endangered species and what is being done to save them and make Pono smile again. This site was created by students for the ThinkQuest Junior competition.

http://library.thinkquest.org/J002043/

The Passenger Pigeon

A hundred years ago, the passenger pigeon was the most abundant bird on the face of the Earth. Their numbers were in the billions, and their flocks often blackened the sky for miles. Unfortunately, their habitat was destroyed in the name of progress. Also, their meat tasted good, and people of the day thought it was fun to kill them. The birds could fly 60 mph. Within 50 years, humans drove this species to extinction. The last bird died in a zoo September 19, 1914. Do you think we have learned anything?

http://www.ris.net/~tony/ppigeon.html

★ U.S. Fish and Wildlife Service: Just for Kids

At this site there's a lot to enjoy. If you scroll down you'll see endangered species and wetlands coloring book pages, and the "Endangered Means There's Still Time" slide show. It's a terrific introduction to the 1973 Endangered Species Act and why it's critically important. There are 59 slides, so it will take a while to go through them all. You'll find it's a wonderful introduction to the topic of endangered species in general.

http://www.fws.gov/kids/

NET FILES

If you suffer from "Arachibutyrophobia" (pronounced I-RA-KID-BU-TI-RO-PHO-BI-A), what scares you?

Answer: This unusual phobia is the fear of getting peanut butter stuck to the roof of your mouth! Please pass the milk and find out more peanut butter facts here: http://brands.bestfoods.com/skippy/funfacts.asp.

A
B
C
D
E
F
G
H
I
J
K
L
M
N
O
P
Q
R
S
T
U
V
W
X
Y
Z

SafeKids.com

The Internet is a wonderful communications medium: you can learn a lot, make new friends, and have a whole new world opened to you. However, there may be parts of the Internet you don't want to see. As with some television programs, or books, or magazines, or parts of town, your parents decide what you can and cannot view. Make your Internet experiences great! Dr. Larry Magid, syndicated columnist and personal friend of Net-mom, is your friendly guide. *http://www.safekids.com/*

The Wild Ones

If we ate carrots all day long would we turn pink like a flamingo? Maybe not, but a substance in carrots— beta-carotene—is what gives flamingos their signature pink color. Flamingos don't eat carrots, but their diet consists of food that is high in beta-carotene. Flamingos are one of several threatened or endangered wild birds and animals profiled at this site.

http://www.thewildones.org/

World Wildlife Fund for Nature Species Programme

This organization helps animals and environments all over the globe. What's the status of the panda, black rhino, or the tiger? This part of the site will tell you. Click back a level to <http://www.panda.org> for the state of the seas or the facts on the forests. This is the site for what's news about the health of the planet.

http://www.panda.org/species/

ENERGY

See also CARS—ALTERNATIVE FUELS

Comparing Alternative Energy Forms

It's an energetic world out there, with powerful nuclear reactors, hydroelectric stations, wind turbines, and even solar collectors. This resource offers an overview of each type of system and how it works. But it doesn't run out of steam there. You'll also learn the history of each method of producing energy, as well as the geographic location of many of the world's nuclear power stations. There are also some nice charts so you can compare the various types of energy. This site was created by students for the ThinkQuest competition.

http://library.thinkquest.org/17658/

Energy Arcade

The San Diego Gas & Electric Company offers an electrifying Virtual Power Plant Tour, as well as several safety messages about working with, and around, electricity and natural gas. In the latter case, visit the world's first "scratch 'n' sniff" Web site.

http://www.sdge.com/sdge.cgi?template=Arcade/ er_f1.html&frame1=er_c1.html&frame2=er_ h0.html&frame3=er_0.html&change=yes

★ Energy Quest - Energy Education from the California Energy Commission

What was Ben Franklin's energy-saving invention? Look in Poor Richard's Energy Almanac to find out the answer. He also offers games, crafts, and even a Declaration of (Energy) Independence. This site has even more activities and games about different kinds of energy, from wind to solar and nuclear to hydroelectric. Find out who got "Devoured by the Dark," and don't miss the high-energy game "Watt's That?" This site is a must for the energy efficient.

http://www.energy.ca.gov/education/

★ Energy Sources

The Energy Information Association presents a nice site about different types of energy: nuclear, coal, oil, biomass, solar, wind, geothermal, electricity, wind, and natural gas. Each sub-page will give you answers to questions like, "What is it?," "How do we get it?," and more.

http://www.eia.doe.gov/kids/kidscorner.html

From Windmills to Whirligigs

Meet Vollis (and his dogs and ducks) and explore his magical world of spinning whirligigs, or wind toys. You can take a virtual tour to the yard and the shop and try some fun wind power activities, including making whirligigs from plastic soda bottles. If you just want an overview, take the Whirlwind Tour, but watch out for the spitting fungus!

http://www.sci.mus.mn.us/sln/vollis/top.html

Fusion: Creating a Star on Earth

Did you know that the Sun is a fusion power plant? Solar energy is produced by a "reactor" in the Sun's core that has a temperature of 15 million degrees Celsius. It would be great to be able to produce energy this way on Earth. Scientists are working on it, but they have a long way to go. Will fusion power plants be the energy source of the future? Visit this site to start your quest for the answer.

http://fusioned.gat.com/SlideShowFolder/
    SlideShowIntro.html

Guided Tour on Wind Energy

The Danish Wind Turbine Manufacturers Association wants you to breeze in and learn about how we can harness the wind's energy and put it to work for us. First though, you'll learn about the winds of the world, as well as local winds, such as sea breezes and mountain air currents. Check out the inner workings of a wind turbine and find the answers to questions like "Are wind turbines noisy?"

http://www.windpower.dk/tour/

Professor Kilowatt's Energy Heroes

Step right up to meet some energy heroes! You know about old Tom Edison, right? But you may not have heard about Nikola Tesla. He invented fluorescent lights and neon, and experimented with wireless transmission of electricity. That's right. Once he lit up 200 lamps from 25 miles away—all without power lines. Learn more about Tesla, Edison, Latimer, and Volta at this site.

http://www.edisonkids.com/sitemapexb/

Roofus' Solar Home

Look out, Snoopy! Here comes Roofus, the golden retriever with the solar-powered dog house. He's even got a solar car! Learn how he uses the sun to heat his house, and try some of the activities he suggests. Can you make a pizza box solar oven?

http://www.eren.doe.gov/roofus/roofus.html

Students' Corner

Have you ever wondered how a nuclear power plant works? The Nuclear Regulatory Commission should know! This Web site has great animations that show everything from the production of power to what happens when the plant is taken out of service ("decommissioning"). Where do they put the radioactive waste? Find out here.

http://www.nrc.gov/NRC/STUDENTS/students.html

ENGINEERING

Build It & Bust It

Engineers figure out how to build bridges that stay up, tunnels that don't collapse, and buildings that rise to the sky without tumbling down. At this site you can try building your own joint-and-beam structures and then test them for stability. If you have a hard time, just go to the Testing area and load someone else's bridge and apply forces to it. Will it stand up or go falling down, falling down? This site was created by students for the ThinkQuest competition.

http://library.thinkquest.org/11686/

A B C D E F G H I J K L M N O P Q R S T U V W X Y Z

A
B
C
D
E
F
G
H
I
J
K
L
M
N
O
P
Q
R
S
T
U
V
W
X
Y
Z

NET FILES

What animal is known as the "ship of the Andes" and why?

Answer: The cold and dry high-altitude climate of the Andes Mountains is home to a unique creature—the llama, an animal that can survive on the area's sparse grass vegetation, and is more sure-footed than a burro. Llamas are used as pack animals. They can carry as much as 125 pounds for up to twelve hours a day, up and down the rugged slopes and very high altitudes characteristic of the Andes mountains in Peru, Bolivia, Chile, and northwestern Argentina. Stop by http://www.eskimo.com/~wallama/myra/why.htm for some legends and fascinating facts about llamas.

Building Big

The next time you scratch your head in amazement, wondering about how something big was built, pay a visit to this site. There's a good chance you'll find the answer. That's because this site explains what it takes to build really big structures like skyscrapers. The neatest part of this site is the interactivity. In Challenges, you can construct big buildings for virtual cities and counties. If you want to test the strength and properties of different building materials, go to the Interactive Labs.

http://www.pbs.org/wgbh/buildingbig/

Greatest Engineering Achievements of the Twentieth Century

The top twenty greatest engineering marvels of the last century are described here. What would you say should be on the list? Yes, the Internet is there, as well as radio and TV, spacecraft, and computers, among other things.

http://www.greatachievements.org/

The New Suburb?

Today's sprawling suburban neighborhoods are so spread out, it's often too far to walk to school, or to the store. There's so much traffic, you sometimes don't feel safe walking at all. There's a new theory called "new urbanism." It seeks to design better, more user-friendly communities. Take a look at the virtual tour. What do you think? At least, we like their idea of houses with porches. There should be more porch-sitting in America.

http://www.nationalgeographic.com/earthpulse/sprawl/

★ New York Underground @ Nationalgeographic.com

Below the streets of New York City are lots of telephone and electrical cables, subway tunnels, sewers, and huge water tunnels that bring fresh water to the city from reservoirs far away. Learn all about what's underground as you explore a cross section. Do albino alligators really live in the New York sewers? The answer is here.

http://www.nationalgeographic.com/features/97/nyunderground/

A Sightseer's Guide to Engineering

If you ever need a sight-seeing guide to engineering tourism in the United States, this is it. Covering large buildings (Empire State Building), as well as offbeat landmarks (world's largest metal kazoo), there is something for everyone here. One story is about how engineers invented machines that would give chocolate its velvety texture. Use the guide to plan a trip, or browse through the site to discover other ways engineers make our lives easier and more fun. If you think a sight is missing, you can add one.

http://www.engineeringsights.org/

You never lose the pieces to the online games in GAMES AND FUN!

The Unkindest Cut: the Down and Dirty Story of the Panama Canal

It seemed like a great idea in the 1870s: cut a water passageway through Panama in order to create a shortcut to the Pacific or the Atlantic Ocean. It became a marvelous feat of engineering, but came at a staggering financial cost. It also took a toll in lives lost as well. Explore a time line of events here, and ponder why the original French construction team might have ordered 10,000 snow shovels to continue its work in the jungle.

http://www.discovery.com/stories/history/panama/panama.html

ETIQUETTE AND CUSTOMS

American Table Manners

You might have seen the movie *Titanic*—in it, the rough-and-ready Jack Dawson is invited to a formal dinner party. He is overwhelmed with all the plates and silverware and doesn't know which to use first. That will never happen to you if you study this page. It even tells you which foods are OK to pick up with your fingers. Now, you might think this is silly, but eventually you'll be at a wedding or other special occasion, or you'll even be eating lunch at a fast-food restaurant with someone you want to impress. Luckily, it is OK to eat fries with your fingers.

http://www.cuisinenet.com/glossary/tableman.html

George Washington's Rules of Civility

About 1744, 16-year-old George Washington copied down rules of proper behavior, such as "If others talk at Table be attentive but talk not with Meat in your Mouth." Then he wrote, "Cleanse not your teeth with the Table Cloth Napkin Fork or Knife but if Others do it let it be done wt. a Pick Tooth." Also he advised, "Being Set at meat Scratch not neither Spit Cough or blow your Nose except there's a Necessity for it," and, well, you get the idea. Compare table and other manners from the eighteenth century with current standards.

http://www.history.org/almanack/life/manners/rules2.htm

Learn2 Set a Table

Which side does the fork go on? Does the knife edge go towards the plate or away from it? You'll find the answers to these and other mysteries of life as you learn to set a table. This is not just a casual breakfast table, mind you, but a full-fledged formal dinner table with lots of silver and glassware! Practice the napkin-folding tricks and really show off a terrific table.

http://www.learn2.com/06/0608/0608.html

Learn2 Use Chopsticks

We used to feel ridiculous using chopsticks, but not anymore! While we once had to spear our shrimp tempura, now we deftly handle even the smallest morsels of sticky rice. And it's all because of the terrific techniques taught at this page.

http://www.learn2.com/06/0607/0607.html

Post, Emily. 1922. Etiquette in Society, in Business, in Politics and at Home

In 1922, people turned to Emily Post's book for guidance on the proper way to conduct themselves. She had an opinion and strict rules on everything, from how a gentleman greets a lady to how to behave at a funeral. Her rules, she claims may be summed up thusly, "To do nothing that can either annoy or offend the sensibilities of others." There's even a section called The Kindergarten of Etiquette, all about teaching table manners to kids. "Training a child is exactly like training a puppy," Post says. Uh, right.

http://www.bartleby.com/95/

EXPLORERS AND EXPLORING

See also HISTORY; SHIPS AND SHIPWRECKS

A
B
C
D
E
F
G
H
I
J
K
L
M
N
O
P
Q
R
S
T
U
V
W
X
Y
Z

A
B
C
D
E
F
G
H
I
J
K
L
M
N
O
P
Q
R
S
T
U
V
W
X
Y
Z

The Columbus Navigation Home Page

After all this time—more than 500 years—people can't seem to agree where Christopher Columbus first set foot upon the shores of the New World. After reading the clues, see if you can solve the mystery. Remember, it's just a theory, but the site suggests the most likely answer. And, if you doubt that Columbus discovered America, this site won't argue with you but will tell you why he gets credit.

http://www1.minn.net/~keithp/

Explorers - EnchantedLearning.com

If you just need a little bit of information about an explorer, and maybe a map of his voyage, try this site. You'll find everything arranged in alphabetical order from Afonso de Albuquerque (Spice Islands; Goa, India) to James Weddell (Antarctic).

http://www.enchantedlearning.com/explorers/

Forbidden Territory @ Nationalgeographic.com

"Dr. Livingstone, I presume?" Who said those famous words, and what were the circumstances? Between 1841 and 1873, a Scots missionary named David Livingstone made several journeys to Africa, at a time when the continent was largely unexplored. He was the first European to see many of Africa's sights, including Victoria Falls, which he named in honor of his sovereign, Queen Victoria. His writings about his exploits were always eagerly awaited back home. In 1866, Livingstone set off to discover the source of the Nile, the world's longest river. He was 53. No news came for years. Finally, in 1869, a reporter named Henry Morton Stanley was sent to look for Livingstone. According to this site, "On October 27, 1871, Stanley 'discovered' Livingstone at the village of Ujiji on Lake Tanganyika, greeting him with the now-famous words: 'Dr. Livingstone, I presume?'" What happened next? Visit this Web page to find out.

http://www.nationalgeographic.com/features/97/lantern/

The Journeys and Expeditions of Marquette, Drake, Columbus, Cortez, and DeSoto

You've heard good and bad things about Columbus, but how much do you know about these other explorers: de Soto, Cortez, Drake, and Marquette? At this site, each explorer tells of his life and exploits in his own words, sometimes with funny results. Kids illustrated the stories with crayon drawings. This site was created by students for the ThinkQuest Junior competition.

http://tqjunior.advanced.org/6297/

National Geographic.com

Take a road trip with National Geographic as they take you on a series of adventures around the world. Tour the fantastic forest, discover dinosaur eggs, and even stop at the White House. These people are exploring professionals.

http://www.nationalgeographic.com/

PBS: Conquistadors

Sail back to the sixteenth century and meet the conquistadors who set out to find gold and conquer the world. These Spanish explorers lived when Spain was a European superpower, and not even the Americas were beyond their reach. At this site you'll learn about these men and the historical legacy (for better or for worse) that they left the New World.

http://www.pbs.org/conquistadors/

★ Quia! Explorers of North America

If you need to learn your explorers and what regions they discovered, test yourself at this site. There are flash cards you can flip, a word search, Concentration, and matching games to make sure you know your de Soto from your Cartier.

http://www.quia.com/custom/48main.html

★ Vikings: The North Atlantic Saga

Long ago, Viking mariners set out from Europe. They sailed westward, over the North Atlantic. They discovered and settled Iceland, then Greenland. About 1,000 years ago they finally made their way to North America, settling in what is now Newfoundland, Canada. The American Museum of Natural History allows you to follow in their footsteps as you pilot a Viking longship of your own. You'll also see wonderful Viking artifacts in the exhibit part of this site.

http://www.mnh.si.edu/vikings/

LEWIS AND CLARK

Crossed the West: The Adventures of Lewis and Clark

In 1804, President Thomas Jefferson looked out the window and said, "Hmm, I wonder if there is a water route, maybe a river or something, that goes all the way across the continent and ends up at the Pacific Ocean? Something we could navigate with boats, so we could get supplies there, and settle, and eventually build theme parks." OK, so he didn't really say that. But he did want the West explored, and Lewis and Clark were just the guys to take on the task. Want to join their expedition and see what happens?

http://www.nationalgeographic.com/features/ 97/west/

Lewis and Clark

You're in the wild, and a bear begins lumbering toward you, growling. Do you simply observe the bear? Or shoot the bear? What would Meriwether Lewis of Lewis and Clark have done? In this game, you get to play Lewis and find out. Your answer will determine whether you get to go on and find the Northwest Passage, as Lewis did in his 1805 exploration of the Louisiana Purchase. This game really makes learning fun.

http://www.pbs.org/lewisandclark/

POLAR EXPLORATION
Antarctic Explorers

This page looks at more than 20 explorers of the Antarctic and environs, starting with Jean-Baptiste Charles Bouvet de Lozier in 1739. Soon after the North Pole was reached by Robert E. Peary in 1909, the race was on to see who could get to the South Pole first. Ernest Shackleton, Robert Scott, and Roald Amundsen attempted to reach the South Pole in the early 1900s, but only Amundsen and Scott made it. Investigate their strategies and what went wrong, or right, in each case.

http://www.south-pole.com/p0000017.htm

Shackleton's Antarctic Odyssey

It seems incredible that a team of men who sailed to Antarctica could survive six months on the frigid tundra after their ship, the *Endurance,* sank, leaving them stranded. But these men, led by Ernest Shackleton, triumphed over the odds. This site logs their epic expedition. You won't want to miss the historic film footage of some of the dramatic moments in Shackleton's journey. On the lighter side, there are some Shockwave games that will let you practice celestial navigation across a virtual sea.

http://www.pbs.org/wgbh/nova/shackleton/

2GOOD 2MISS

Yucky Worm World

Tractors and earthworms both plow the land, but you don't have to gas up worms. Just give them some garbage or organic material, and watch them go! Learn more about the different types of worms and how slimy, yet beneficial, they are. Send some worm postcards, meet Mary the worm woman, and see a video of a worm hatching. *http://yucky.kids.discovery.com/flash/worm/*

A B C D E F G H I J K L M N O P Q R S T U V W X Y Z

FAMILY FUN

Nothing to do? Want some sites the whole family—toddlers to teens to adults—can enjoy? This section's especially for broad-spectrum fun on the Net! See also CRAFTS; GAMES AND FUN—ONLINE GAMES; and PRESCHOOLERS

Alfy

Designed as a kids Web "portal," this site lets you play on other great kids' sites without making you feel like you're someplace else. Some of the more interesting and fun games, such as Infection, are about health issues. Infection lets you be the germ. Roll the germ ball, and see if you can infect someone. You might land on an open cut and enter the bloodstream. Don't say, "yecch!" until you've tried it. You just might learn something about how your body fights infection. The site is also stocked with lots of interactive stories, crafts, music, and more. All ages will find something fun to do. Note: we had trouble using this site using Internet Explorer 5 and Netscape for Macintosh.

http://www.alfy.com/

Ashley's Hand Shadows

All this amusing activity takes is a bright light and a blank wall or bed sheet. Use your own two hands to create shadows of animals and birds. This site will show you the moves!

http://www.kellys.com/ashley/shadow.html

Award Maker

Last-minute, totally cool awards and certificates can be selected and customized at this site. Just print them at home and you're good to go! Now look at this terribly long URL. We agree, it's shameful. OK, here is a shortcut that worked at press time. Go to <http://www.lightspan.com/>. See the search box at the top of the page? Leave the "Select grade" default at k-8. Type in "Award Maker" (two words) and press enter or return. If all goes well, you will then move to a results screen and the program you want will be displayed.

http://www.lightspan.com/teacher/pages/awardmaker/
   default.asp?_prod=LS

★ Berit's Best Sites for Children

Over 1,000 sites are reviewed by librarian Berit, who rates them on a five-point scale. Check out anything that got a five out of five and you'll find a real gem of a Web site. Arranged in general categories such as Holidays, Just for Fun, and Serious Stuff, you'll also discover sites to help you find a pen pal or a safe chat room.

http://www.beritsbest.com/

★ Big Top Circus Sideshow

We're not exactly sure how to describe this series of games and experiences, except to say that they are fun. The Moodalyzer is a virtual piano that plays in various types of Greek or Hindi scales. You can listen to compare them or just "mouse over" keys to make up a new tune on your own. Similar in a creepy sort of way is the Gothic Piano (great for the Halloween season!). Supported by gargoyles and lit only by flickering candles, you'll find one of its secrets as soon as you click on the sheet music. Can you figure out how to turn the singing gnomes into bells? Cool Congas involves a . . . different drummer. There is even more to explore at this rather odd site.

http://www.bigtop.com/sideshow/

Billy Bear's Fun & Games

When you do something really great, do you ever get a gold star? Next time you perform a good deed, join the online Hip-Hoppity Good Deed Club. First, choose a rabbit, and put it on your home page. Then, for every good deed you do, go back to Billy Bear pick a carrot, and put it on your site, like a gold star. Don't forget to include the membership logo, so your friends will know how to join. The Sticker Dollhouse and the storybooks you can personalize are some of the other fun activities you can play with Billy Bear. Don't miss the online games, print and play, and critter adoption areas, either!

http://www.billybear4kids.com/games/games.htm

★ Blocks: a Digital Building Toy

Is it beginning programming or is it a toy? We think it's both! See the input box over on the left? Type "new cube" into it. Now type "paint yellow." Try typing "walk 3" and see what happens. Get the idea? But that's not all. You can teach it a "function." We taught it to build a pine tree, but you'll probably have it building a metropolis in no time. You can even e-mail your construction to a friend and work on it together!

http://www.blockcorner.com/

★ Bonus.com - The SuperSite for Kids

This way to find family-safe places to visit. Head in any direction and play a game, enter a contest, find homework help, or learn about dinosaurs, the United States, or what's under the sea. For rainy-day fun, remember this site!

http://www.bonus.com/

Brain Boosters

Can you figure out how to get a coin out of a bottle? Hint: You can't pull out the cork, or break the bottle. Do you know the right answer? If you do, you won't win a million dollars, but you will boost your brainpower. This site is filled with challenging questions that will test your logic, math, and reasoning skills.

http://school.discovery.com/brainboosters/

★ CBC4kids

From the Canadian Broadcasting Corporation, this action-packed site quizzes you on rock themes that are actually from classical music compositions. Don't miss the Kids Club games. Blast into space to attack asteroids in a wild space game arcade. Think quickly (and creatively) to help save Mr. Snoozleberg—a sleepwalking diplomat. And did you ever get a tune into your head and you can't remember what it is? The "hum line" will help.

http://www.cbc4kids.ca/

Certificate Creator

It's your birthday, and your friends are coming over to play a game of baseball. You want to give the winning team a certificate of congratulations. What do you do? Go to this site, and personalize and print one. If you need a certificate for another occasion, just choose a different category. There are five of them.

http://www.CertificateCreator.com/

Cool Stuff to Try

Haven't you always wanted to learn how to juggle? This site teaches that skill, plus others you need to know: how to make the best paper airplane, how to construct a paper popper, and how to do a magical coin trick.

http://www.klutz.com/coolstuff.cfm

NET FILES

What does the Empire State Building weigh, without King Kong climbing it?

Answer: 365,000 tons, according to the official Empire State Building page. For more fascinating tower trivia, read http://www.esbnyc.com/html/body_facts.html

Sidebar: A B C D E **F** G H I J K L M N O P Q R S T U V W X Y Z

FamilyFun

A treasure chest of family activities awaits you at this gem of a Web site. Try making a clothesline fort, a balloon-powered jet boat, or a backyard miniature golf range! These are just a few of the summer activities. You'll find lots more suggestions for year-round fun at this site.

http://www.familyfun.com/

★ FunBrain

Math games can add up to "sum" fun edutainment. How about playing math baseball with your brothers and sisters? They can pick how difficult the math questions should be and decide if they want addition, subtraction, multiplication, division, or all of the above. Then the computer will ask an arithmetic question. Can they get it right? Swing—wow, it's a triple! After that, have them see how good they are at making change for a dollar. How many pennies, nickels, dimes, or quarters in change should they receive after a certain purchase is made? There are some other reading and word games, too, including a concentration matching game.

http://www.funbrain.com/

NET FILES

There's a million-gallon saltwater ocean in the middle of the Arizona desert. Why isn't it on the map?

Answer: It's inside the Biosphere 2 structure, which also houses a marsh, a savanna, and a rain forest, among other environments. It's in Oracle, Arizona, north of Tucson. Read more about this experimental research lab at *http://www.bio2.edu.*

Origami: the fold to behold! Check out CRAFTS AND HOBBIES.

Funology - The Science of Having Fun!

Did you know that when you cough, air moves through your windpipe at 1,000 feet per second? That's only one of the fun scientific facts you'll learn at this site. In the activities section, you can fashion coffee filters into butterflies or create a papier-mâché dinosaur egg. The "boredom buster" games are not the online variety. Find a few friends and try out such all-time great playground games as Sharks and Minnows, Don't Wake Daddy, and more. Still looking for fun? Ooze into the Laboratory for some kitchen chemistry experiments your mom will never forget. (Only kidding, mom!)

http://www.funology.com/

★ Funschool.com - Free Interactive, Educational Software for Kids

This site.has more fun, engaging, and educational Java games than any other site we've seen for this edition. There are separate sections for preschoolers, kindergartners, first graders, and second graders. Check the third and fourth and fifth and sixth grade sections, too. Find loads of interactive stuff—be sure to look for The Game Spot. But let's focus on the preschool activities for little kids. There are over 25 of them: matching games, concentration, ordering, opposites, even animal homes. Sometimes Java games take quite a while to load; this site even gives you something to do during the download process! Play with an online kaleidoscope while you wait. Don't miss the Stone City adventure—can you solve the puzzles and retrieve all the gemstones? Last we looked, this was in the fifth and sixth grade area.

http://www.funschool.com/

★ Golden Books Fun Factory!

If you do only one thing on this site, go to the Road to Reading Ramblin' Road trip. Make sure you take Amusement Avenue and stop at Super Sleuth. Here you'll be able to play Kid Detective. It's a detective story you make up by filling in the blanks. First, write your name on the door. Next, write in the name of four tools for your detective case. As you move through the story, there are more blanks to fill in. If you're clever enough, you'll be able to solve the mystery of the missing pooch. But don't stop there. There's so much to do at this site you may be here all day!

http://www.goldenbooks.com/fun/

★ GusTown: Fun, Games, Cartoons, and the CyberBuds!

Meet Gus, Rant, Rave, and the rest of the CyberBuds in this colorful town full of animations, articles, games, recipes, crafts, and links for kids and parents. Head over to the toy store for fun games like Ice Going. Picture a frozen lake with a lot of holes in the ice. Click on one hole—hey, a penguin pops up. Click on another hole—a whale is under that one. Too bad, they don't match. With a splash, both creatures dive back into the holes, and you can try again to make a match. (Hint: Click on the Index link—almost all the way at the bottom—to look at a quick map to all the fun on this site.)

http://www.gustown.com/home/gustownsummer.html

Hamsters! Take the 10-Minute Bedtime Tour!

Check this odd little site involving online hamster games. There are also a few crafts (like using an oatmeal box to make a hamster recreational vehicle . . .) and a recipe for a banana-rice cake-pretzel speeder for hamsters to ride.

http://www.hamstertours.com/

Go climb a rock in OUTDOOR RECREATION.

HaringKids!

Artist Keith Haring loved kids and often took his artwork to hospitals and schools. Since his death, his legacy lives on at this Web site. You will recognize his energy-filled style immediately, especially his signature "barking dog" and "radiant baby." Look at his work and try to describe what's happening in the pictures. Did you know he got his start drawing on blank pieces of paper in subway cars? This site offers coloring book pages to print, plus some entertaining morphs.

http://www.haringkids.com/

★ HBO Magnet

Nothing to do? Try this graphically engaging site and its wide variety of games and activities. Some are silly, like Ear We Are: a game of two lost ears trying to find their place in the world. Others, like Magnet Dude, are just plain fun. One of the more challenging activities is Toon Beats. This activity turns your keyboard into a musical instrument and lets you record, save, and play back songs you compose. And if you're looking for psychic predictions, visit Madame Nevinsky in the Scene section. (She just told us to get back to work!)

http://www.hbomagnet.com/hbo_family/

★ IKnowThat.com

Did you know you're in the news? The fun really begins if you upload a picture of your face to this site (read the privacy policy first). Once you do, you'll get to see a picture of yourself making news in a mock newspaper. As a scientist, you'll swim with the sharks. Choose from several different backgrounds, from a jet pilot to a surgeon to an astronaut. Each scene you select is accompanieds by some interesting facts: did you know that sharks don't have bones? They have cartilage instead, which is similar to the stiff tissue in our nose and ears. If you're concerned about using your own face, use one of the sample pictures instead. Great sticker books, games, online painting, and more round out this site.

http://www.iknowthat.com/

A B C D E F G H I J K L M N O P Q R S T U V W X Y Z

Vertical alphabet sidebar: A B C D E F G H I J K L M N O P Q R S T U V W X Y Z

Jayzee Bear

Explore the Green Forest, or play in JayZeeBear's house. Whichever you choose, you won't be disappointed. There's a lot to do. Inside JayZeeBear's house, you can pick a room and explore it. In the kitchen, open the refrigerator and get a recipe for play dough or a banana milkshake (drink one, play with the other!). Outdoors, meet some of JayZeeBear's friends, like Tito the turtle and Red the African frog, and see what activities they have in store for you.

http://www.jayzeebear.com/

JigZone: Online Jigsaw Puzzles

Does it look like it's going to rain all day? If so, choose a big puzzle of up to 247 online pieces. If the storm's going to pass over in a few minutes, better choose a short puzzle of six easy pieces. Change the shape of the pieces to triangles if you need a more difficult challenge!

http://www.jigzone.com/

Study Buddy: Your School Survival Connection

A wonderful collection of tips on everything from memorizing lines in a play to dealing with procrastination is in store for you at this site. You'll find lots of study "survival" information and a way to get a "study buddy" through a safe pen pal remailer system. It doesn't divulge your real e-mail address, so it's safe as long as you don't disclose it yourself to your pen pal. Ages 6-12, 13-17, whole classrooms, and teacher-to-teacher exchanges are encouraged.
http://studybuddy.com/

🐛 Juice Bottle Jingles

You know how you can tap a half-filled glass and make a musical note? And if you have a whole bunch of glasses, you can fill them with various amounts of water and make different tones? Well, if you don't know, this site explains the science behind it and teaches you how to re-create a juice bottle musical instrument at home. While someone else collects the supplies, go ahead and practice online. Behold a virtual six-bottle xylophone, and a tunebook for your playing (and listening) pleasure. Just follow the notes to tap out such all-time favorites as Jingle Bells and Mary Had a Little Lamb.

http://www.lhs.berkeley.edu/shockwave/jar.html

★ Kid Pix

Click on GO, see a green screen open in another window—now WAIT. Nothing? Then wait for a couple more minutes. This Java paint program takes a while to load completely. Once the tools show up on the small green screen, you're all set to go. Use colorful online rubber stamps and paints to decorate outline drawings, or click for a fresh sheet of blank paper to create your own masterpiece.

http://www.kidpix.com/kid_paint.html

★ Kid's Domain

This is a must-see site for all families. Lots of games and pictures to color, software downloads, clip art, and a list of links to similar sites. Click on Surf Safe and learn what rules you should follow when using the computer. Or go to Kids Can Program, and find software that will help you develop your computer skills. Finally, take a minute (or lots of minutes) to scroll through the What's New section to find new games, ideas, activities, and more. Our fave new feature: wizard school!

http://www.kidsdomain.com/kids.html

**Why is the sky blue?
Look in the WHY section.**

★ Kids' Space

This internationally recognized and award-winning site will become one of your favorite Internet destinations because it has something for everyone. Older kids might want to see KSC (Kids' Space Connection) to visit lots of home pages created by other kids—and they can list theirs here, too. Toddlers will love the detour to HPT (Hop Pop Town) to try out the many interactive musical experiences. But Kids' Space itself is everybody's home page. You can submit audio files of your music or digital drawings and hear and see what other children around the world have done, too. The Story Book is where kids write their own stories, using the pictures and themes provided. There is even a beanstalk that keeps growing each month in the Craft Room. Pick an artwork and create a story for it, or choose a story already written and draw a picture for it. All commands at this site include pictures with them, so even the youngest child (who may be still developing reading skills) can enjoy this creative and fun learning experience.

http://www.kids-space.org/

🦆 Knowble

This site opens in a separate browser window so you will have to use the onscreen backward and forward arrows and buttons to move around. There are a number of cool things to do here, such as Explore an Ocean (choose Stuff; then select Games). Click on some seaweed and a scary shark pops out! Don't worry—his false teeth pop out, too, and embarrassed, he slinks back into the shadows. Click on everything; there are other surprises. Look for coloring books, paper airplane directions, online and offline activities, and more.

http://www.knowble.com/

🦆 Learning Planet Kids Page

Choose a level: pre-K, grades 1–3 or grades 4–6+. Preschoolers can guess what number comes next as they load up train cars, count chickens, and explore an interactive alphabet. Older kids can play games involving geography, fractions, and more. The pop-up ads at this site are very annoying, but the games are exceptional.

http://www.learningplanet.com/kids.htm

★ MaMaMedia

This jazzy site offers lots of fun activities and games, but let's look closely. You do have to sign in (it's free, and they notify your parents), but after that, you can design your own town in the Surprise area. Just click on Presto. Netmomville has a blimp flying overhead, a cool animated GIF shop, and lots of other digital gadgets. You can change things around in your personal town until you're satisfied. Then other kids can visit and play with your stuff. Only you can change it though, which is why you need a password. Stamps and Stomps lets you make your own stamp album out of clever (and noisy) illustrations. There's a lot more to do here at MaMaMedia, so check it out!

http://www.mamamedia.com/

Mindbender Cave

The chicken may have crossed the road to get to the other side, but why didn't the parrot talk? The owner of a pet shop assured the man who bought it that the parrot would repeat any word it heard. If you go to this site to find out why, you'll see that the answer is all very logical. But, you might say it's a trick question. Well, it is. In fact, this site admits that puzzles like this one are trick questions. So, if you like puzzlers, this site's for you.

http://www.worldbook.com/fun/wbla/camp/html/mindbend.html

★ Nelvana

Feed Franklin the turtle enough flies, and he'll run and eat the pie. He's also got a memory game you can play. The Sights and Sounds section features video clips of Franklin, Babar the elephant, Little Bear, Rolie Polie Olie, and other characters created by the company that operates this site. You'll also find more games and a great online coloring book. Under no circumstances should you miss Marvin the Tap-Dancing Horse.

http://www.nelvana.com/main/kids.html

A B C D E F G H I J K L M N O P Q R S T U V W X Y Z

Postopia

Vacation in faraway Postopia, land of swaying palm trees and—frozen bowling. Huh? While weather conditions tend to vary from island to island in this odd land, the quality of fun stays the same. Join an underwater mission to find the Loch Ness monster, or sign up with the space nation pilots to smash asteroids. Some games involve Post cereals, but others are marketing-free. You can play anonymously, or register to log your high scores.

http://www.postopia.com/

★ The Prince and I

The teenage prince lives in a beautiful castle, but there's a small problem. How can he be king someday if he can't read? He needs some friends to help him learn! Become a "Friend of the Prince" (it's free), and you can submit stories to be posted at this site. Some of them are very imaginative and funny. There's even a mission you can go on to explore the village (if you can—we got lost), make your way through the forest (we got lost there, too), find the missing prince, and give him a message. (Hint: Don't play the Shockwave version; play the regular version, under "Mission." Make a map. If you get lost, click on Help and watch for the hand on the screen. It will point you in the right direction. If you lose the Forward button and the hand says to go forward, just click where the button used to be.) This royal site is produced by the National Film Board of Canada.

http://www.nfb.ca/Kids/

Prongo.com

A lot of games on the Internet test your coordination skills, but some of the games on this site will test your math skills. There's even a stock market game that uses real-time prices to show you the value of a stock. It also explains the terms you need to know to trade stocks. The companies are real, and you get to pick the ones you want to buy and sell. Young children will enjoy the matching games and other puzzles. The site also includes e-cards, jokes, and wallpaper for your computer's desktop.

http://www.prongo.com/

★ Rooney Design

This is a rather strange site with offbeat, quirky games. In Mr. Leakey's House, your job is to find all the ways that water is being wasted—and do something about it. (Hint: you'll need what's in the mailbox.) In the Mr. Veghead game, you select a vegetable and then choose eyes, mouths, hats, etc. One of the noses even has a nose ring! There's also an interactive advent calendar and an Overtime at Santa's Factory game if you happen to be in a holiday mood.

http://www.mother.com/~prdesign/
    FlashGamesFrame.html

★ Scavenger Hunt

Create a scrapbook about the special things in your community. Print the blank scrapbook pages and then go on a neighborhood scavenger hunt. Some of the things, like a map of your hometown, can be found online. But you'll have to visit different places in your community to find the others. Now, where would you go to get a crayon rubbing of an historic marker?

http://www.planning.org/kidsandcommunity/
    scavenger_hunt/instructions.htm

★ Sesame Workshop Sticker World

Everybody likes stickers—big ones, little ones, animated ones. Yes, that's right, at this site, you can collect online stickers that do things. Lions roar, flowers bloom, dragons breathe fire, test tubes boil, machines run—you get the idea. You begin with a limited number of starter stickers. Create your own free home page and decorate it with your stickers. Visit other kids' pages to "trade" stickers with them and play games. Collect points by visiting other kids' pages, and then "buy" more stickers for your collection. It's fun, free, and fabulous!

http://www.sesameworkshop.org/stickerworld/

CATS are purrfect.

Smithsonian Magazine Presents Kids' Castle

This site offers a neat mix of feature articles, message boards, and wonderful photos from the collections of the Smithsonian Institution. For example, here's a question: are fairies real? Find out how even Sherlock Holmes' author, Sir Arthur Conan Doyle, was fooled. Look in "Personalities" and then scroll through the feature articles.

http://www.kidscastle.si.edu/home.html

★ Sodaplay

Warning: this site may seriously impact your family's productivity! Create a little onscreen two-dimensional model made out of "masses and springs." They are easy to make, and may be endlessly tinkered with by adjusting various items like wave speed, amplitude, "muscles," and more. Then click on Simulate to watch your little bot cavort around the screen. If you need ideas, just load one of the models, watch its actions, and start playing with its settings. Remember to break for lunch.

http://www.sodaplay.com/

★ Spark Island

What better way to learn about English, math, and science than to play a game? At this site, you are studying these topics without even knowing it. In Find the Sun, you'll learn to identify the position of the sun by examining the shadows it casts on a make-believe town. The games (for ages 3 to 11) are straightforward and fun.

http://www.sparkisland.com/public/free_activities/
   for_home/?view=generic

Try This!

National Geographic has some cool ideas to beat the summer heat. Besides the suggested edible treats, this site teaches an easy way to make friendship bracelets, reveals some new yo-yo tricks, and describes the science behind a few weird optical illusions.

http://www.nationalgeographic.com/world/trythis/

🦆 Up to Ten

Colorful and engaging graphics, and games and songs suited to children ten and younger rate this site a perfect ten. For young children, there are mazes, guessing games, coloring books, and crafts to make. For older kids, there are puzzles, car races, and games that test your coordination skills. When you join the Boowa & Kwala club, you get extra games and a secret pass code to enter the site. Parental consent is required for club membership if you're under 13.

http://www.uptoten.com/

★ Virtual Fishtank.com

Give it big, fearful eyes, or a hungry mouth. Make it feed near the bottom, or swim near the top. Design its fins and gills. This site lets you create a fish, save it, and release it into a gigantic virtual tank. Once you do, you can watch your fish interact with other fish. If you register, you can release your fish directly into the virtual tank at the Museum of Science in Boston. If you're ever in Boston and go to the museum, you can retrieve your fish. In the virtual world, that means printing it.

http://www.virtualfishtank.com/

NET FILES

It's as long as the distance from the North pole to Miami, Florida. It's one of the few man-made structures visible from space. What is it?

Answer: The Great Wall of China. This 4,500 mile long marvel is more than 2,000 years old. Read about it here.
http://www.discovery.com/stories/history/greatwall/greatwall.html

A
B
C
D
E
F
G
H
I
J
K
L
M
N
O
P
Q
R
S
T
U
V
W
X
Y
Z

A
B
C
D
E
F
G
H
I
J
K
L
M
N
O
P
Q
R
S
T
U
V
W
X
Y
Z

Wendy's World of Crafts

There's got to be something here for your family to try! How about mashing up rose petals and making a rose bead necklace? Or maybe you'd rather try growing a sweet potato vine indoors. Or you could make your own play dough, finger paint, or everyone's favorite: ooblick! All the instructions for indoor and outdoor fun are provided.

http://ntl.sympatico.ca/~whogan/master.htm

FARMING AND AGRICULTURE

See also PLANTS, TREES, AND GARDENS; HORSES AND EQUESTRIAN SPORTS

★ 4-H Virtual Farm

You know the song "America the Beautiful"? You sing about "amber waves of grain," right? Did you know that's about a wheat field? You can learn about growing wheat, as well as farming beef cattle, dairy cows, poultry—even fish—at this multi-media–rich site. In the poultry section, you can "click and drag" to watch a movie of a chick hatching!

http://www.ext.vt.edu/resources/4h/virtualfarm/
  main.html

ARS Science 4 Kids

The Agriculture Research Service of the U.S. Department of Agriculture wants to plant some information in your brain to see if it takes root. At this site you'll learn about aquaculture and how fish farmers raise bighead carp for market. You will also discover why some farmers have radar guns under their tractors and others rely on GPS satellite systems to help them find their bees. Click around on the illustration and see what you can pull up, or choose Contents and harvest a list of all the articles.

http://www.ars.usda.gov/is/kids/

CyberSpace Farm

Tina Tractor is your shuttle guide to the Agri solar system, and although she may look a little strange, she really knows how to zoom in on the highlights. Visit Milo Moon, for example, and learn all about grain sorghum. The U.S. is the world's largest producer of this crop, used mostly for livestock feed. Or take a side trip to the Sunflower Sun and find out about the differences between oilseed sunflowers and confectionery ones. The former type is processed into cooking oils and bird seed, while the confectionery ones we eat as snacks. Be sure to check out the Pig Planet and Space Sheep before you come in for a landing at Cyberspace Farm and discover why it takes three years to make a hamburger.

http://www.cyberspaceag.com/

Farm Safety 4 Just Kids

Cawshus the crow says "no riders!" on farm equipment! It's just not safe, and you could distract the driver enough to get into an accident. But that's not all. Old Cawshus has some words to say about safety around lawnmowers, too. You'll also find crossword puzzles, "farms are fun!" coloring pages, and the answer to why you shouldn't tell secrets around a bean.

http://www.fs4jk.org/kids/

Farm School

Farmers need lots of skills to run a successful operation. They have to be good at math, for example. Want to see how well you'd do? This Web site lets you figure out how much that new combine equipment will cost, if you take out a loan from the bank. And farmers have to know quite a bit about the farm's ecosystem—how the animals relate to the water system, how the weeds relate to the soil, and other connections. Can you draw a chain of events connecting that box of cereal on your shelf to the corn crop in the field? After you visit this site you'll be able to do that and much more.

http://www2.kenyon.edu/projects/farmschool/

Crack open CODES AND CIPHERS.

John Deere Kids

Around the farm you have to be very careful, and Ready the Rooster will show you that sometimes it's OK "to be a little chicken." Don't ask for a ride on a tractor, watch out around large animals, and keep away from farm chemicals. Also, that big pile of grain looks fun to play in, but it's not—you could suffocate! See how many of the safety rules you already know and which ones are new to you. There's also a fun story called Johnny Tractor and his Pals (Dicky Disk, Henry Harrow, and Perry Plow, among others). It explains what each type of machinery does and how they must all work together to get the job done.

http://www.deere.com/deerecom/_Kids/

Kidz Korner

Farm kids in Michigan share their stories of life on the farm. You can learn about chicken and dairy farming, maple syrup production, and more. In the County Fair area, visit the link called Crops to learn about how Michigan grows those luscious blueberries and cherries. Follow the path of sugar from the sugar beet in the ground to the sugar bowl on your table. Michigan is also the largest grower of Easter lilies in the United States. Find out how they get them to bloom all at the same time. It's not magic, it's science!

http://www.mda.state.mi.us/kids/

Scarecrow

Is a garden complete without a scarecrow? We don't think so! Learn how to construct your scarecrow at this site. No garden? Why not construct a virtual scarecrow? Try the wacky one we found here <http://www.maleny.net.au/scarecrow/cre8crow.html>. It's sure to scare away virtual birds!

http://www.powen.freeserve.co.uk/kids/scarecrow/scarecrow.htm

U.S. Department of Agriculture for Kids

From this vantage point you can meet Smokey Bear, Woodsy Owl, Twig Walkingstick, Rus the Surfin' Squirrel, and S. K. Worm. You'll also learn about the History of U.S. Agriculture (1776–1990), Facts About Agriculture, and a whole bushel of information about the food pyramid. Did you know there are really two nutritional pyramids? One is for young children and one is for Everyone Else. No, Twinkies are not on either one.

http://www.usda.gov/news/usdakids/

BEEKEEPING
Honey.com for Kids

Scientists have learned that bees have been making honey for at least 150 millon years, just as they do today. Honey is stored by the bees for use as winter food; but because bees make so much more than they can use, humans harvest the excess. This site explains the whole process and offers honey history, recipes, and games.

http://www.honey.com/kids/

Popular Songs in American History

Give a listen to this unique collection of audio files, lyrics, and historical notes. Find out what songs were popular during various periods in American History. Included are interesting historical details. "Greensleeves" was popular in sixteenth-century America. "The Drinking Gourd" was from the Civil War era. "I've Been Working on the Railroad" was what the forty-niners sang as they searched for gold in California. How many do you recognize? http://www.contemplator.com/america/

A B C D E F G H I J K L M N O P Q R S T U V W X Y Z

Left margin letters: A B C D E **F** G H I J K L M N O P Q R S T U V W X Y Z

CROPS, PRODUCE, AND ORCHARDS

Corn Cam

Everyone needs a little peace and quiet now and then. Here's a good place to get it. Sit back and watch the corn grow in an Iowa field. Check the archive to see how far it's come. Be sure to keep an eye out for any famous baseball players.

http://www.iowafarmer.com/corncam/corn.html

Kingcorn.org

The corniest people in the United States bring you everything you need to know about the top crop: corn. Maybe you want to raise corn, or you need a corn recipe or a corn song. Perhaps you want to find out what products have corn in them or which ancient civilizations used corn. Well, you've *corn* to the right place. When you have had your fill of corn, you can link to the maize page and read about—more corn.

http://www.agry.purdue.edu/ext/corn/

NET FILES

The Hubble Space Telescope orbits the Earth at five miles per second. If your car went that fast, how long would it take you to drive from New York to Los Angeles?

Answer: About ten minutes! Find out more fun facts about the Hubble here.
http://hubble.stsci.edu/fun_and_games/where_a_s_hubble_now/where_is.html

Everyone's flocking to BIRDS!

Lundberg Family Partnership with Nature

The Lundbergs have been growing rice on their Northern California family farm since 1937. Follow along as they explain how they enrich the soil with cover crops and attract waterfowl and other wildlife to naturally supplement the fertility of the fields. Before they plant, they carefully put stakes around any pheasant or other nests, so they can avoid them with the big machinery. Stored rice is sometimes infused with carbon dioxide to keep bugs out. Rice is nice!

http://www.lundberg.com/partnership.html

Massachusetts Maple Producers Association

Did you know that depending on the sweetness of the sap, it can take anywhere from 25 to 75 gallons of maple sap to make 1 gallon of maple syrup? The average, though, is 40 gallons raw to 1 gallon finished. It doesn't hurt the tree to be tapped, as long as you do it the right way. This page explains how you can make your own maple syrup. If you'd rather visit a commercial "sugar bush" and see how it's done, there's a directory of maple producers, as well as lots of sticky links.

http://www.massmaple.org/

The Story of Florida Orange Juice - From the Grove to Your Glass

This page explains how citrus farmers decide when their crop is ripe. Citrus fruits do not continue to ripen after they are picked, so oranges have to be harvested at their peak of flavor. Crews pick most of the crop by hand, and then the oranges are transported to the processing plant for grading and juice extraction. The whole journey is pictured and described here.

http://members.aol.com/citrusweb/oj_story.html

Wheat Mania!

Wacky Wheat takes you on a guided tour to Kansas wheat country. Visit four farms and read the planting and harvest diaries of the families who live on them. Look inside a "prairie skyscraper" (also known as a grain elevator) and play some super wheat trivia. You'll be convinced there is such a thing as flour power.

http://www.wheatmania.com/

LIVESTOCK

See also RIGHTS AND FREEDOMS—
ANIMAL RIGHTS

4-H Farm Animal Awareness Workbook

Goats, cattle, horses, rabbits, swine, chickens, and turkeys are some of the animals you might find on a farm. This site gives you an overview of each of these animals, what they eat, how they are raised, and how we use them. Did you know baby turkeys are called poults? They eat corn, milo, soybean meal, and oats. Some of these pages include audio files and links to other sources of information.

http://www.ces.ncsu.edu/lenoir/staff/jnix/pubs/
    an.workbook/

Barnyard Palace

Welcome to the Barnyard Palace! Just to your left, we have the dairy cow building, conveniently located right next to the milking parlor. (Have you ever wondered why it's called a "parlor"? Why not a milking garage or patio or something? It's not like they serve tea and finger sandwiches in there, right? But I digress.) Now we could go in and see what's happening in the goat barn, but let's move along to the sheep since it's such a cool day. Later in our tour we'll have a look at the beef cattle, the horses, and let's not forget the pigs and the poultry!

http://www.agr.state.nc.us/cyber/kidswrld/general/
    barnyard/Barnyard.htm

Breeds of Livestock

Oklahoma State University's breed archive is extensive. You'll find pictures and info on breeds of the following animals: horses, cattle, swine, sheep, goats, and poultry. Oh, yes, did we mention the "other" category? There you'll find llamas, donkeys, and—buffalo! But let's talk cattle. Everyone's heard of the Jersey cow: "With an average weight of 900 pounds, the Jersey produces more pounds of milk per pound of body weight than any other breed." They have a nice photo here, too. Have you ever heard of the Australian Friesian Sahiwal? It's a breed being developed in Australia for use in tropical areas. How about the Florida Cracker/Pineywoods, the Florida equivalent of the Texas longhorn? Visit this site for a virtual barnyard of breeds.

http://www.ansi.okstate.edu/BREEDS/

FeatherSite - The Poultry Page

If you are more interested in what breed of chicken crossed the road rather than why it crossed the road, then strut on over to the Featherside Farm and inspect their collection of colorful chick pics and descriptions. If you say there is more to poultry than foul chickens, you're right! They've also included ducks, geese, turkeys, and peafowl guaranteed to smooth your feathers.

http://www.cyborganic.com/People/feathersite/
    Poultry/BRKPoultryPage.html

Goats and More Goats

It has some quirky habits, smells a little, and has been hanging around you all day. Do you call the police? No, all the poor goat wants is a good scratch between the shoulders! The Irvine Masa Charros 4-H Club raises dairy and pygmy goats and knows what a rewarding experience raising goats can be. With the dedication and knowledge demonstrated at this site, how can anyone not approve of these kids raising kids? Never heard of 4-H before? Check the ORGANIZATIONS section of this book. Don't miss the curiously relaxing Goat Game.

http://www.ics.uci.edu/~pazzani/4H/Goats.html

A
B
C
D
E
F
G
H
I
J
K
L
M
N
O
P
Q
R
S
T
U
V
W
X
Y
Z

Left margin: A B C D E F G H I J K L M N O P Q R S T U V W X Y Z

★ MooMilk

Cows make milk to feed their baby calves, but even after the baby is eating other food, the cow continues to make up to eight gallons of milk a day. Cows are milked in a special room called a milking parlor, and their milk is pumped to stainless steel holding tanks and immediately chilled to 38 degrees Fahrenheit. Then the milk tanker truck comes to pick it up. This happens twice a day. When it gets to the milk processing facility, the milk goes through two other steps—homogenization and pasteurization—but you'll have to read about those at the Virtual Tour. You'll find cow-related Shockwave games and other fun, too.

http://www.moomilk.com/

Pigs

Investigate the steps required to start your own pig-raising venture. Learn what breeds are available and how to care for these large but gentle swine. And don't forget the added bonus (who needs the health spa): unlimited free mud baths! Never heard of 4-H before? Check the ORGANIZATIONS section of this book.

http://www.ics.uci.edu/~pazzani/4H/Pigs.html

NET FILES

What glacier is the fastest?

Answer: The Kutiah glacier in Pakistan holds the record for the fastest glacier. In 1953, it surged more than 7.5 miles in three months, averaging about 360 feet per day. Read more fun glacier facts at http://www-nsidc.colorado.edu/glaciers/quickfacts.html

Sheep

If you are looking for a farm animal to raise, take a good look at the multipurpose sheep. Stay warm with wool sweaters made from their fleece. Feast on cheese produced from their milk. Stop mowing the lawn; instead, let sheep keep your grass closely clipped. Get your daily exercise by walking a mile a day with your lamb. Make a profit when you take them to the market. "BAAAAAA!" OK, the sheep request that you skip that last one. Here is where 4-H members show you how fun and rewarding sheep raising can be. Never heard of 4-H before? Check the ORGANIZATIONS section of this book.

http://www.ics.uci.edu/~pazzani/4H/Sheep.html

FISH

See also AQUARIUMS; OUTDOOR RECREATION—FISHING; PETS AND PET CARE; REFERENCE WORKS; and SHARKS. Are you looking for whales? Check them out in MAMMALS—CETACEANS—WHALES.

The Amazing Fish Cam

Something fishy is happening on the Net right now! See a live picture of a saltwater fish tank in Lou's office. Who is Lou? No one knows, but his fish tank is famous. Can you spot a blue surgeon fish or maybe the clown trigger?

http://www.netscape.com/fishcam/

★ Dinofish.com - Coelacanth: The Fish Out of Time

In 1938, fishermen off the coast of South Africa found the first living coelacanth in recent history, and there was another reported find in 1952, off the Comoro Islands (to the northeast, in the Mozambique Channel). This isn't just another fish story, either. The coelacanth (pronounced "see-la-kanth") is a 400-million-year-old "living fossil" fish, once thought to have become extinct long ago. This account of its amazing discovery reads like a mystery novel.

http://www.dinofish.com/

Fish and Fisheries in the Great Lakes Region

Do you know your alewife from your yellow perch? OK, how about your lamprey eel from your brook trout? If not, or if you just want information on over 25 different freshwater fish species, dive in here. There is also a special trout and salmon identification guide, if you want the angle on them.

http://www.great-lakes.net/envt/flora-fauna/wildlife/
fish.html

Fish Hatchery Tour

Sometimes fish eggs are hatched in special fish farms called hatcheries. The young fish are then used to restock streams and lakes. Visit a special hatchery for salmon, and watch QuickTime movies of the process, as seen by middle school kids in British Columbia. Don't get too close to that steelhead, though, you could get wet! (Watch the movie and you'll see what we mean.)

http://vms.sd33.bc.ca/salmon/hatchery.html

For Kids/Fish of the Great Lakes by Wisconsin Sea Grant

You can learn about Great Lakes fish species at this site, plus a lot more. Did you know there's scientific fact behind all those brightly colored fishing lures in the tackle box? Visit and find out which lures work best for which species.

http://www.seagrant.wisc.edu/greatlakesfish/kids.html

Mapping Fish Habitats at Home

You don't have to go on an expedition to a remote stream or lake to study fish habits. If you have access to an aquarium, you can learn how to map fish habitats right at home. This site explains how. You'll need some adhesive colored dots and some patience!

http://www.lhs.berkeley.edu/GEMS/mapfish.html

Marine Sportfish Identification

What's the *porpoise* of this site? Well, if you can't tell a yellowfin tuna from a chilifish or a leopard shark from a grunion, then your troubles are over! This guide to marine sport fishing in California has descriptions and photos of these creatures and many more. If you're looking for east coast marine fishes, try *<http://indian-river.fl.us/fishing/fish/ #name_index>*.

http://www.dfg.ca.gov/mrd/msfindx1.html

Northeast Fisheries Science Center Fish FAQ

Did you know that salmon generally lay from 2,500 to 7,000 eggs, depending on the species and its size, or that some lobsters hardly move more than one mile? What is the most common fish in the sea? Why do scientists classify fish? How long do fish live? How is the age of a fish determined? Visit the profusely illustrated home page, where you'll find the answers to all these questions and more. You'll discover how porcupine fish inflate themselves, too!

http://www.wh.whoi.edu/faq.html

FLAGS

Flags of the World

If you were going to design a flag for an Internet flag page, what would it look like? Fans of this site have chosen one—see what you think. We liked one of the losers (Jan Oskar Engene's, with the two crossed computer mice), but there is no accounting for taste. You'll also find pages and pages of flags of the world here. There's also a flag "coloring book," if you need an outline of a particular flag for a school assignment. An extra bonus: you'll see national symbols, anthems, and other patriotic links for many countries.

http://www.crwflags.com/fotw/flags/

A
B
C
D
E
F
G
H
I
J
K
L
M
N
O
P
Q
R
S
T
U
V
W
X
Y
Z

Heraldry and Vexillology

Discover why flags are flown at half-mast, which flags must always fly higher than others, and more flag etiquette on this neat page. There are links to pages throughout the world, including one that features heraldic clip art. There's a heraldry dictionary, a collection of flags, animated GIFs of flying flags, and so much more that you'll be waving a flag of your own for this site.

http://regiments.org/flags/flags.htm

Mooney's Flag Detective

At the Olympic Games, you saw a flag you didn't recognize. Which country does it represent? Use this site to find out. Choose from among seven colors, and see which flags use them. See any contenders? Click on a flag and learn its country and its meaning. The Coloring Book section has black-and-white line drawings of flags you can print out and color.

http://www.flags.av.org/flags/df-htri.htm

What's the recipe for air?

Answer: You mix up 79 cups of nitrogen molecules, 20 cups oxygen molecules, 1 cup argon atoms, and a dash of other gases, including water vapor and carbon dioxide. The result is colorless, odorless, and tasteless; however, as this site says, it is "especially refreshing when stirred up and served cool on a hot day." Check out

http://www.nasm.edu/galleries/gal109/NEWHTF/
HTF220.HTM

United States Power Squadron and Other Nautical Flags

Have you ever seen a tall ship "dressed"? That means it has all its colorful flags and pennants flying for a special occasion. Those flags also represent a common maritime language. Some flags stand for letters, numbers, or words. Some combinations of flags have special meanings, too. Check this site to see messages like "I am on fire!" or "I need a tow." You'll also learn a lot about nautical flag etiquette, as well as international and U.S. flag customs in general. This site is prepared by the U.S. Power Squadron.

http://www.usps.org/f_stuff/flag.html

World Flag Database

If you saw a flag with 50 stars and red and white stripes, you'd probably know that it was the flag of the United States of America. But what if the flag had one star and green and yellow stripes. Would you be able to name that flag? If not, head over to this site. You'll find pictures of all of the flags in the world and learn some interesting facts about the countries they belong to.

http://www.flags.net/

UNITED STATES

The Betsy Ross Homepage

Betsy Ross is credited with having sewn the very first U.S. flag in 1776. But did she? You can learn about the questions surrounding this cherished American figure, as well as take a virtual tour of her house in Philadelphia. Apparently, George Washington wanted six-pointed stars on the flag, as they appear on his original pencil sketch. Betsy recommended five-pointed stars instead. Everyone scoffed, saying that the stars were too hard to draw, let alone cut. Then they stood amazed as Ross folded a piece of paper, made one snip with scissors, and unfolded a perfect five-pointed star! You can learn the secret of this trick by clicking on "Cut a 5-point star in one snip" on the flag.

http://www.ushistory.org/betsy/

★ The Flag of the United States of America

For a country that is barely over 200 years old, the United States has a vast and rich accumulation of lore and tradition regarding its flag. "Old Glory" gets its due from this page in red, white, and blue embellishment. Images of every single official and unofficial U.S. flag are stored here, as well as the information you'll need if you'd like to acquire a flag that has flown over the U.S. Capitol.

http://www.usflag.org/

Folding the U.S. Flag

You're finally going to participate in a flag ceremony, maybe for school or for scouts. You've always admired how the big kids fold the flag into that neat triangle shape—but wondered how it's done. This site provides a nice animation to show you the moves. If you want to know the U.S. Air Force Academy's interpretation of what each fold symbolizes, visit <http://www.usflag.org/fold.flag.html#FFC>.

http://www.crwflags.com/folding.html

★ The Star Spangled Banner

It's 42 feet across and 30 feet high, and it was a major sewing job for Mary Pickersgill back in 1813. She was commissioned to make a huge flag to fly over Fort McHenry in Baltimore, Maryland. Little did she know her stitches created the original "star-spangled banner" that would later be sung about in the U.S. national anthem. It's on display at the National Museum of American History, and an effort is underway to clean and preserve it. Find out more here.

http://americanhistory.si.edu/ssb/

Visit the stars in ASTRONOMY, SPACE, AND SPACE EXPLORATION.

FOLKLORE AND MYTHOLOGY

★ Aesop's Fables - Online Collection

All the fables you're looking for are here—more than 665 of them—and some are in Real Audio format, so you can listen as well as read them. There are also Grimm and Andersen fairy tales, as well as a very cool scrolling time line from 1000 B.C. to A.D. 1000, showing contemporary thinkers, religious leaders, and scientists.

http://www.AesopFables.com/

Bulfinch's Mythology

This famous work, published in 1855 by author Thomas Bulfinch, is arguably one of the books most responsible for our current-day notions about Greek and Roman gods and goddesses. You may find the language somewhat quaint, but persevere and you'll discover wonderful stories that are often referred to in current literature, movies, and TV. Keep up—with the past.

http://www.bulfinch.org/

Dictionary of Phrase and Fable

Are you forever forgetting the Riddle of the Sphinx? Want to know who Apollo was? Can't wait to find out what the Seven Wonders of the ancient and medieval worlds were? The 1898 edition of this classic is online and searchable.

http://www.bartleby.com/81/

★ The Encyclopedia Mythica

This encyclopedia on mythology, folklore, and magic contains well over 5,700 definitions of gods and goddesses, supernatural beings, and legendary creatures and monsters from cultures and beliefs all over the world. You'll find Chinese, Etruscan, Greek, Haitian, Japanese, Latvian, Maya, Native American, Norse, Persian, Roman, Welsh, and other mythologies here. Check up on gnomes, unicorns, fairies, and other legendary beings in this award-winning reference source!

http://www.pantheon.org/

A B C D E F G H I J K L M N O P Q R S T U V W X Y Z

A
B
C
D
E
F
G
H
I
J
K
L
M
N
O
P
Q
R
S
T
U
V
W
X
Y
Z

The Hero's Journey

If you were told to write an original story, you could open up a blank word-processing document and begin typing. Your imagination will help you fill up the screen with your ideas. But what if you need a little help to get your creative juices flowing? A visit to this site will do just that. It creates an environment where you can create your own story using a writing method popularized by author Joseph Campbell. The technique prompts you to answer questions about the character you create, and provides the structure of the story.

http://www.mcli.dist.maricopa.edu/smc/journey/

★ Make-A-Hero

Just choose the gender of your hero, select a skin color, and background picture. Then start clicking on the picture you just made. You'll find you can change headgear, as well as upper and lower articles of clothing. Each time you change something, you'll get a little information about that item's legendary background. All done? Print your hero or heroine, and then try some of the suggested activities. It's mix-and-match heroes, and it's fun!

http://www.lucaslearning.com/myth/flash/myth.html

★ Mythology

Type in the URL below. Click Enter the Site, and then choose Myths. After that you'll be ready to explore. For example, just click on The Sun. Immediately, you'll have links to almost 20 different myths and legends about this celestial body, from cultural traditions all over the world. Maybe you're interested in myths about the sky and its constellations? There are almost 40 of those listed. If you'd rather read all the stories by geographical region, you can just click on a world map! Plus: in case you can never remember which god is related to which other god, there are convenient family trees for the Greek, Roman, and Norse mythologies.

http://www.windows.ucar.edu/

Myths and Legends

This impressive set of links contains pointers to resources from Australian Aboriginal myths to modern science fiction and fantasy. It is the single, best source for a comprehensive listing of world mythological resources. You'll find Celtic, Slavic, Greek, Roman, Norse, and many other kinds of stories here. A caution to parents: this site had too many links for us to explore individually.

http://pubpages.unh.edu/~cbsiren/myth.html

Mythweb - Greek Mythology

Legend says that twelve Greek gods and goddesses lived in a palace on Mount Olympus, overseeing the affairs of mortals below. Learn about them, as well as heroes such as Hercules and Jason. You can also read about the travels of Odysseus as told by the Greek poet Homer. The version here is much shortened, illustrated, and makes an exciting (but brief) tale.

http://www.mythweb.com/

Pegasus' Paradise

A lot of these ancient heroes and mythological beasts have really strange names: Bellerophon, Daedalus, Odysseus—how do you pronounce them? This ThinkQuest Junior site, created by kids, solves that problem. Not only can you look up animals, heroes, villains, and gods and find out all about them, but you can also hear their names pronounced! There's also a neat game that asks you to match the Greek gods with the names of their Roman counterparts.

http://tqjunior.advanced.org/4553/

Stories and Fairy Tales Theme Page

If you're seeking some stories to scare your friends as you sit around the campfire, try here. Other tales include fairy tales, Native American legends, and folklore from other countries. There are also many spiritual teaching stories, including some from the Bible as well as the Zen tradition, among others.

http://www.cln.org/themes/fairytales.html

FAIRY TALES

★ Absolutely Whootie: Stories to Grow By

Whootie's an owl whoo has collected fairy tales and stories from around the world. Select a good story by theme (honesty, friendship, etc.), age group, or even the time it will take to read. You can comment on the stories, too, or read other kids' remarks. If the story inspires you to draw an illustration, send it in for possible publication.

http://www.storiestogrowby.com/

The Cinderella Project

You may have seen Disney's animated story of Cinderella, but do you know that there are lots of other pictures and stories about her? Here is a collection of 12 different versions of the story, some with illustrations. She's really an old lady: the earliest version here is dated 1729! From here you can also explore variations on Little Red Riding Hood and Jack and the Beanstalk, too.

http://www-dept.usm.edu/~engdept/cinderella/
  cinderella.html

Tales of Wonder

This site features folk and fairy tales from around the world. Geographic areas represented include Russia, Siberia, central Asia, China, Japan, and the Middle East. Tales from Scandinavia, Scotland, England, Africa, India, and Native American nations are also included. This is an excellent site for exploring the world of folk and fairy tales.

http://members.nbci.com/darsie/tales/

TALL TALES

American Tall Tales

John Henry was a steel-drivin' man. Pecos Bill was raised by coyotes. Paul Bunyan had a blue ox named Babe. Are you familiar with these tall tales? If not, read the reports kids have written about them. They also created stamps to commemorate the stories.

http://www.inform.umd.edu/UMS+State/
  UMD-Projects/MCTP/Technology/
  School_WWW_Pages/TallTales/TitlePage.html

The Johnny Appleseed Homepage

His name was John Chapman, but you probably know him better as Johnny Appleseed. Sometime in the early nineteenth century, Chapman decided his life's mission was to travel through the wilderness on foot and plant apple seeds wherever he went. He hoarded seeds gleaned from cider mills, and soon the countryside bloomed with his efforts. No one knows very much about him, but the U.S. Postal Service has honored him with a postage stamp. You can find out more about this legendary American figure here.

http://www.msc.cornell.edu/~weeds/SchoolPages/
  Appleseed/welcome.html

The Paul Bunyan Trail

In Minnesota, there's an abandoned railroad line that's been made into a 100-mile trail for hikers and bikers. It's named after Paul Bunyan, a legendary figure closely associated with this part of America. Seems Paul and his blue ox chased each other around so much, they created the "land of 10,000 lakes" with their footprints! There's a nicely illustrated version of the story here, where you can learn about Paul's birth (it took five storks to deliver him to his parents), his first week of life (by the end of it he was wearing his father's clothes), and the rest of his amazing life in the great north woods.

http://www.paulbunyantrail.com/talltale.html

Why is ROY G. BIV important?

Answer: ROY G. BIV is the name scientists made up to help them remember the colors of the rainbow, in order from top to bottom: red, orange, yellow, green, blue, indigo, and violet. Read more about light at
http://nyelabs.kcts.org/teach/eg_print/eg16.html

A
B
C
D
E
F
G
H
I
J
K
L
M
N
O
P
Q
R
S
T
U
V
W
X
Y
Z

GAMES AND FUN

See also COMPUTERS—SOFTWARE ARCHIVES; CRAFTS AND HOBBIES; FAMILY FUN; PRESCHOOLERS; and SCIENCE. Are you looking for game codes and cheats? They are in the VIDEO AND COMPUTER GAMES section.

ACTIVITIES

Archimedes' Lab

If you're a whiz at solving crossword puzzles, you've probably got a good vocabulary. But what if you're better at numbers than your ABCs? Then, head over to this geometric puzzle site. You'll find puzzles to solve, puzzles to make, and puzzles to send—electronically, that is. Under "peculiar puzzles," check out the "vanish" puzzles. These are puzzles that when put together a certain way will make things either appear or disappear. See if you can create a banker's nightmare, and make the moneybag disappear.

http://www.archimedes-lab.org/

★ The Bubblesphere

You don't need a lot of skills to learn to blow soap bubbles, right? So what is with this guy who calls himself "Professor"? Turns out he really is an expert. At his home page, he reveals the ultimate soap solution for making the most colorful, sturdy bubbles. He explains how to make your own bubble-blowing tools from soup cans and coat hangers (ask your parents for help). You don't even need anything special—he teaches you how to blow bubbles using only your HANDS! But wait, there's more. Check the bubble FAQ, bubble games, and the other wonders of the Bubblesphere.

http://bubbles.org/

Volcanoes are an explosive subject. Find one in EARTH SCIENCE.

★ Internet Coach Puzzle Center

Make your own puzzles or try some of the ones created for you. Ever heard of a "word shape" puzzle? It looks like a line of empty boxes, but then you realize some of them go above or below the line—following the shape of the word. Can you guess the word from the clues given? If that's not hard enough, try making a crossword puzzle, secret code, word search, or other type of game. It's fun!

http://www.apte.com/puzzles/

John's Word Search Puzzles

John certainly is a creative guy. He's developed word search puzzles about many different themes, including holidays, Harry Potter, states, sports, the Bible, and other topics. Hidden words may be frontwards, backwards, on a diagonal, vertical, or horizontal. You don't solve these online, you need to print them and play with an analog word processor. What's that? A pencil, of course!

http://www.thepotters.com/puzzles.html

Puzzlemaker

You can very easily create word search puzzles, hidden message puzzles, crossword puzzles, mazes, math squares, and more. Print them out and send them to your friends and family. Everyone will wonder how you did it!

http://puzzlemaker.school.discovery.com/

CARD GAMES

Children's Card Games

You can play a lot of games with an ordinary pack of playing cards, if you know the rules. But if you don't know whether you should slap a Jack or say "go fish," this site will set you *straight*. Don't *shuffle* off! It's got all the rules for card games, such as War, Slapjack, and that timeless favorite—Go Fish. If you're ready to be challenged by a more difficult game, there are rules for Rummy, Pinochle, and Cribbage, among many others. All you need to do is supply the cards and *flush* out a few friends.

http://www.usplayingcard.com/GameRules/
    ChildrensCardGames.html

CHESS

Chess Dominion

Resistance is futile! Chess is a game, a culture, a way of life. To join the Dominion, you must learn to play this classic game of kings, knights, and pawns. But how? You could show your teacher the extensive chess lesson plans at this site and ask to add chess to the school curriculum, or you could just use the interactive tutorials on your own. Developed by ThinkQuest kids who are also chess masters, you'll learn basics; study championship games; and even meet Deep Blue, the chess champion with a power cord!

http://library.thinkquest.org/10746/

Chess for Kids

This site was created by students for the ThinkQuest Junior competition. It has the extra added attraction of preplayed and annotated games, so that you can follow every move of some games played by other kid chessmasters. And there are chess puzzles, where you decide what the next move should be.

http://tqjunior.thinkquest.org/6290/

U.S. Chess Federation: Scholastic Chess Resources

You know you love chess, and your buddies love to play chess, too. How about starting a chess club at school? The U.S. Chess Federation tells you how to do that at this site. You'll also see who's leading in the national tournament standings. If you need to improve your game, there is a list of tips plus information on how you can play "correspondence chess" with another player. If you visit the links section, you'll be busy all *knight*.

http://www.uschess.org/scholastic/

The wonderful world of worms may be admired in the section called INVERTEBRATES.

NET FILES

Eight miles long, the Confederation Bridge is the longest continuous multispan bridge over ice-covered waters in the world. It links the Canadian mainland of New Brunswick Province to Prince Edward Island. How many streetlights illuminate it at night?

Answer: 310. Read more about the building of this fascinating structure at http://www.confederationbridge.com/en/bridge/fascinating/content.htm

EDUCATIONAL GAMES

See also SCHOOLS AND EDUCATION–LEARNING GAMES; and names of the various subjects, like HISTORY, MATH AND ARITHMETIC, and more.

★ Arty the Part-Time Astronaut

Arty and Greg blast off in their little spaceship to study the solar system. You're the captain, and you can choose which planets to visit. You'll learn interesting facts like how long it would take to get to each planet—if you drove there in your family car. Engaging graphics and animation make this one a stellar package!

http://www.artyastro.com/

★ Coolmath4kids - Games - Lemonade Stand

In this easy-to-learn simulation game of high finance, you start with a fistful of dollars, a dream, and a weather forecast. Balance the cost of paper cups, lemons, ice, and sugar into your sales price per cup. Can you squeeze out a lemonade empire or will everything go sour?

http://www.coolmath4kids.com/lemonade/

A
B
C
D
E
F
G
H
I
J
K
L
M
N
O
P
Q
R
S
T
U
V
W
X
Y
Z

A
B
C
D
E
F
G
H
I
J
K
L
M
N
O
P
Q
R
S
T
U
V
W
X
Y
Z

Arthur: The World's Most Famous Aardvark

Arthur's got a terrific site going for him here. We particularly liked his boombox and its great tunes, as well as D.W.'s Art Studio, where we rubber-stamped paw prints all over Mr. Ratburn's suit. Don't miss Grandma's recipes (hope you get there before the health department does!).
http://www.pbs.org/wgbh/arthur/

Energy Quest Games

OK, these are educational games, but they really will spark your curiosity about electricity and solar, wind, and nuclear power. Don't miss playing the hilarious game called Watt's That? Be sure to use the audio version for the full comedy effect. If you run out of energy, take a nap and come back later for more fun.

http://www.energy.ca.gov/education/

Gamebrain

You'll need to register to use this site, but it's free. There are activities, games, and lots more in development. You can decide to play games like Treasure Hunt—where you are asked a question about grammar and have to dive down to the proper punctuation mark, all the while avoiding the sharks. We also tried Magic Pictures, but the directions aren't very clear. If you try it, know that you can start with any blue picture. Then you follow the directions. If it says "Move left, or down," you can move any number of spaces but you must stay in the row or column you're currently in. We liked the games and activities at this site, but thought that they should be divided by age group, as some of them had pretty hard questions.

http://www.gamebrain.com/

> What makes a good password? Something that's not your name and won't be found in a dictionary. Instead, try a combination of letters and numbers.

★ GameGoo - Learning That Sticks

There's kangaroo confusion all over the amusement park! Some of the kiddy 'roos have misplaced their parents. Luckily, each child is wearing a shirt with a letter of the alphabet on it. Click on the dad with the matching clothing, and they'll get on the Ferris wheel together. There are loads of other reading games, plus don't miss the "Fun Goo" for still more interactive monkey business.

http://www.cogcon.com/gamegoo/gooeylo.html

★ Headbone Zone

This site offers lots of fun games, and you may be able to win prizes in some of them. There is the Rags to Riches game, where you play the part of a big-time rock band promoter and try to rake in cash. Take your band, Groovy Gravy, on a ten-week concert tour. You set the venues and ticket prices, decide when to record new songs, and plan your advertising campaign. Don't miss the Headbone Derby, either. This popular and long-running series challenges you to travel the Net looking for clues to help you solve mysteries. New this year is Camp Champ, a collectable card game that's completely free. You need to sign up to collect the online cards, trade with other players, and play the game. There is a lot more on this site, including monitored chat rooms. We're sure this will be one of your favorite Internet destinations!

http://www.headbone.com/games/

IKnowThat.com

"The grumpy troll is being rather MEAN." That's one of the sentences we got when we decided to practice "long 'e'" sounds in the reading and phonics section of this site. What other words can we make that have the same sounds? If we drag over this "b" we'll hear a child's voice say "Buh. Ean. BEAN. On a towering stalk grows a giant BEAN." There are math, geography, and other games, too. In the geography states challenge, we picked the U.S. plains and Midwest region. We got a map and a series of clues to help us try to guess the right state. We knew the answer to "The Indianapolis 500 race is held in this state every year." We clicked on Indiana, and got a fun little animation showing race cars getting the checkered flag at the finish line. Some of the animations are sort of strange—they switch between contemporary and historical, from fact to fanciful. Can younger kids tell the difference? We're not so sure. Are there still wild west towns in Kansas, where people use horses for transportation? Um, we don't think so. In general, we like this site—and we really like the art section—but there's one part we ask you to ignore. After you complete a quiz, you get an award certificate. One choice is to print the award, while another is to e-mail it to one person or everyone on your buddy list. Until the site adds a privacy policy right there, we suggest ignoring this option. Anyway, who wants to be such a showoff? Just print the certificate and show it to your parents.

http://www.iknowthat.com/

K–8 Kids' Place

For some wacky word puzzles and math and logic brain teasers, visit this site hosted by publisher Houghton Mifflin. There are also author interviews and book reviews for kids, by kids. They sometimes offer summer reading contests, too, so check back often.

http://www.eduplace.com/kids/

It never rains in cyberspace.

❧ KidsPsych

Can you believe this site offers games for ages one to five and ages six to nine? The very youngest users will have fun sorting shapes, painting an online circus picture, deciding which way to go around a maze, and trying other fun activities. Older kids get to repair a space station with a secret code, sort out mixed-up faces, and play I Spy. There's also a tricky puzzle involving a fox, a chicken, and a bag of grain. You have to get them all across the river, but your boat will only hold one at a time. Don't leave the chicken alone with the grain, or the fox alone with the chicken. Can you figure it out? If you can, there's a surprise!

http://www.kidspsych.org/

★ Learning Activities

These K–8 games include a general knowledge trivia quiz, a word unscramble test, a "match the clock faces" activity, and a really challenging lunar adventure. In that one, you need to be able to plot points on a grid map of the galaxy, fly there using your hyperdrive, and blast asteroids into oblivion. Along the way, you need to look for rare crystals and gather them into your cargo hold. Trade the crystals for supplies and go at it again. Think you can make it past Outpost Alpha? We couldn't.

http://www.lightspan.com/activities/pages/portal/
    default.asp?_prod=LS&_nav=k3_lrn_learningact

❧ TutorCenter.com

There are numerous simple games at this site aimed at preschoolers through fifth grade. Third graders can visit a tropical island and sort the creatures found there. Is it a bird, a mammal, or a fish? Older kids can try a geography game that challenges them to drag famous landmarks to the right states. The youngest internauts can connect the dots to finish a picture, and then decide which animals belong in the zoo, on the farm, or home on the couch.

http://www.tutorcenter.com/

A
B
C
D
E
F
G
H
I
J
K
L
M
N
O
P
Q
R
S
T
U
V
W
X
Y
Z

A
B
C
D
E
F
G
H
I
J
K
L
M
N
O
P
Q
R
S
T
U
V
W
X
Y
Z

GAMES

★ Eldrbarry's Active Games Guide

From get acquainted games to tag, from line and circle games to indoor play, you're sure to find something fun to do with just a few friends or a whole family reunion. Here's a description of "This is a ___! A What?," one of the silliest games we know: "Equipment is an assortment of different objects. Seat everyone in a circle. Leader takes an object and passes it to his right saying: 'This is a banana.' (The hard part is, you see, it's really not a banana, it's something entirely different.) The receiver says 'A What?' and the giver repeats. Then it is passed on to the third in the same way. When asked 'A What?' each person inquires of the one who gave it to him 'A What?' before passing it on to the next. This pattern keeps on. After this has proceeded a ways the leader starts something else, 'This is an alligator,' etc. After three are in motion then objects may be started right or left. Object: to remember what each item is."

http://www.seanet.com/~eldrbarry/mous/games.htm

Footbag WorldWide Information Service

Some call it a footbag, while others know it by the trademark Hacky Sack. The object of the game is to keep the footbag in the air—with your foot—as you "hack" the "sack" around in the circle with others. There's also something called footbag net—sort of like volleyball, except played with—you guessed it. Check out this site for the full story. Patterns for making your own footbag are here, too. Find them at <http://www.footbag.org/footbags/#patterns>.

http://www.footbag.org/

GameCentralStation

Say you're having a family reunion, and mom's asked you to find some outdoor games the little kids will enjoy. "No problem," you think. But then you decide you want some games suitable for teens, too. What to do? This site holds the answers. You can search a huge archive of indoor and outdoor games by name, age group, related sport, or a combination of terms. You can also choose to see a random game, a holiday-themed one, a game that builds teamwork, and many more.

http://www.gamecentralstation.com/gcshome.asp

Games Kids Play

Remember that game you played at camp last summer? It was called Steal the Bacon, wasn't it? Or was it Red Light/Green Light? Maybe you're mixing it up with What Time Is It, Mr. Wolf? If you're a little hazy on the rules of those terrific games you had fun playing once—and then forgot— visit this site. You'll find an archive of the best kids' games EVER. There's also a handy list of jump rope rhymes and a growing list of hand-clapping games.

http://www.gameskidsplay.net/

★ Streetplay.com

From hopscotch to jacks, to stickball to double Dutch jumprope, this site has the rules (were there rules?), the moves, and the dish on what's plain fun on the playground today.

http://www.streetplay.com/thegames/

Washers - A Great American Game

Do you love to pitch horseshoes but are challenged by a lack of space? Try this all-American game— Washers! You'll learn the history of this wonderful game, the equipment needed, the rules and regulations, and a lot more. In no time at all, you'll be tossing washers and wondering why you waited so long to become a Washers champ.

http://www.washers.org/

MAZES

Logic Mazes

We thought we were pretty good at mazes until we visited this page. Just try to get out of the labyrinth in Theseus and the Minotaur. Or attempt to get the rolling ball out of a maze that tilts. Check the easy and not so easy number mazes, and then, if you don't mind extremely tricky puzzles, ponder the solution to the Sliding Door Maze.

http://www.logicmazes.com/

★ Maze Design by Adrian Fisher

Learn the history of mazes, as well as the variety of them you can visit around the world. Some are traditional hedge mazes, while others are built in cornfields and last only until the corn is harvested. Still others involve mirrors or water. The latter may seem straightforward until a door that was open a moment ago is suddenly shut behind a curtain of water. Tricky, huh?

http://www.mazemaker.com/

ONLINE GAMES

☙ AFRO-Americ@: All Fun & Games

A lot of the games listed here are just too hard for Net-mom, who gets frustrated easily! But for the rubber ducky crowd, we recommend these dress-up games: Scout at the Beach and Scout in Space. Dress up a friendly dog in scuba or astronaut gear, and create a detailed online picture of your own. We also liked Dino Design Board, where you click and drag various pieces of dinosaur around until you find a combination you like. The Make a Snow Thing activity is a little odd. Who ever heard of a snowlady wearing a pink bikini?

http://www.afroam.org/children/fun/fun.html

☙ Billy Bear's Playground

It's never raining at this playground, hosted by a friendly bear and his pals. Play weatherproof online games, or download and save some to try later. Do you love holidays? Billy Bear does too, and he's gathered his favorite holiday games, crafts, and activities to help you make your celebration the best ever! Don't forget to check out the jokes, puzzles, screen savers, stationery, and everything else in Billy Bear's wonderful world.

http://www.billybear4kids.com/

Stick to the beekeeping sites in FARMING AND AGRICULTURE, honey.

NET FILES

Who invented Silly Putty®?

Answer: James Wright, back in 1943. He was the guy who mixed silicon oil with boric acid, looking for a substitute for rubber. He worked for General Electric, which couldn't seem to find a use for this "nutty putty." Then in 1949, a man named Peter Hodgson attended a party where this item caused a sensation. He immediately saw its potential as a children's toy, and he bought the production rights from G. E. for $147. At the time of his death in 1976, his estate was worth $140 million. Read more at http://web.mit.edu/invent/www/inventorsA-H/sillyputty.html

★ Broomsticks

If you're a Harry Potter fan, you'll love this virtual quidditch game. There's no golden snitch in the free version, but the game's pretty exciting without it. Play with a friend or against the computer, and the first to score 50 points wins. Go Gryffindor!

http://brighton.ncsa.uiuc.edu/broomsticks/official.html

Build a South Florida Snowman

Do you live in a place where there is a lot of snow in the winter? Or do you live where there's never any snow? It doesn't matter, because here on the Web, you can build a snowman any day of the year. Just select the hat, clothes, facial features, and other things your snowman will need. If you successfully build one of the "thematic" snowmen, you get a surprise! On the same page there's a link to the Santa Simulator. Can you fly the sleigh and deliver packages to the right houses?

http://www.sun-sentinel.com/graphics/entertainment/snowman.htm

A
B
C
D
E
F
G
H
I
J
K
L
M
N
O
P
Q
R
S
T
U
V
W
X
Y
Z

A
B
C
D
E
F
G
H
I
J
K
L
M
N
O
P
Q
R
S
T
U
V
W
X
Y
Z

BookHive: Your Guide to Children's Literature & Books

Looking for a great book to read? Why not ask the librarians of the Public Library of Charlotte & Mecklenburg County in North Carolina? They have been as busy as bees combing their bookshelves to find just the book for you. They have found some "real honeys," too! Look for reviewed suggestions in the following topics: Fantasy; Humor; Mystery; Science Fiction; Sports; and many more. There are also a few coloring pages featuring the site's mascot, Zinger.
http://www.bookhive.org/bookhive.htm

★ Car Jam

All you need to do is get your little white car out of the parking lot and onto the main road. Sounds simple, right? That is, until you realize the car's blocked in by school buses, tractor trailers, and a host of other misaligned vehicles. How many moves will it take you to escape? Hope you have car insurance, because the puzzles get harder the longer you play.

http://www.bank-of-tidewater.com/games/carjam/

★ Castlemouse 2000

EEK! There's a mouse in the castle and the king says it's up to you to chase it out. The good news is: you're not alone. You have plenty of animals to help you. The mouse will always run away from your cat. However, the cat is afraid of your dog. The dog is frightened by the bear, and so on. Knowing all these relationships, you can construct a formidable chain reaction that forces the mouse out of the house. This game is fascinating and a wonderful family puzzle.

http://www.castlemouse.com/

Caveman Capers

You must locate, grab, and throw boulders into the volcano before it explodes. Why? Who knows? These guys are cavemen, not rocket scientists.

http://www.bbc.co.uk/gameskids/5050/caveman.html

Checkers

Here's a nice little friendly checkers game. Can you beat the computer? Click on your red game piece and move diagonally. Jump over a black piece to claim it. Watch out, the computer's good.

http://www.darkfish.com/checkers/Checkers.html

The Chiquita Challenge

Your mission? Find the motorboat key. You have to drive a little yellow sports car around a maze and hope that you don't run out of energy as you search. Wait, is that a banana up ahead? Run your car over it to get more energy, and you're on your way again. This game sounds a lot simpler than it is, and this is just the first level!

http://www.chiquitakids.com/playit/challenge.shtml

Desdemona: Interactive Othello

This site lets you play Othello, or Reversi, against the computer. Play at several different skill levels. If you're a beginner, choose to view your legal moves before you select one. You can also read about the rules and strategy.

http://www.math.hmc.edu/~dmazzoni/cgi-bin/
desmain.cgi

🐾 Etch-a-Sketch!

You know that fun drawing screen with the two knobs? If you thought that was hard, wait until you try online Etch-a-Sketch! Look through the gallery and see what other people have created. Some of them have way too much time on their hands. See how well you can do.

http://www.etch-a-sketch.com/

The Fruit Game

This is a PEACHy game. It may apPEAR simple, but LEMON tell you, it's very hard to win. It used to be set up so it was impossible to win, but people all over the Net got so MELONcholy, they finally changed the rules. Play against the computer, but be sure to be the last to take a fruit from the table! ORANGE you glad we told you?

http://www.2020tech.com/fruit/

★ Fun & Games

Youth Sports Network offers a great collection of games we loved. In Bag This, you try to catch nutritional groceries falling from above, avoiding the toxic waste barrels and the cupcakes. There's also a Soccer Shootout, a Smashball game, and more. Best yet, there's a section on Backyard Games you can play outside with your friends. Son-Of-Net-mom rates this site A+.

http://www.myteam.com/ysnim/fun/
   fun.jsp?cindex=-1

★ FunRanch.com: Games

Can you tame the wild west and fence in the prairie? Compete against a friend or the computer as you attempt to be the first to completely enclose a square. Keep at it, because every square is worth one point. The player with the most squares is the winner.

http://www.funranch.com/games.htm

A Game a Day

You know how it is when you just want to take a break? You want a little entertainment, a little fun, maybe you just want to play a little game that doesn't take very long. You want A Game a Day! You see, every day, they offer a new game. Good name for the site, huh? Naturally, we tried it out. We helped spell words before Winnie the Pooh ate all the cupcakes, and then worked out some tricky word puzzles, all containing the word "car."

http://www.agameaday.com/kidsindex.htm

Games on TUKIDS

TUKIDS has collected a nice little group of online games for your playing pleasure, including old favorites (Mastermind, Asteroids, Breakout, and more) but also some new challenges, like Canoe Clobber and Tux on the Run. We especially liked maneuvering Tux, the penguin, over the slippery ice on his way to . . . where?

http://greenapple.tukids.tucows.com/games.html

Gorilla Grab

Can you grab enough bananas for your pantry without suffering a collision of a well-aimed coconut with your unprotected noggin? Those darn chimps are ruthless!

http://www.bbc.co.uk/gameskids/5050/gorilla.html

Hunt the Wumpus

What's a Wumpus? We don't know, but there's one sneaking up behind you! In this game, your mission is to shoot the Wumpus before he takes you home for dinner—HIS dinner. Search the caves for clues, and watch out for bats and pits. Be careful, you must also dodge virtual arrows from other online players.

http://scv.bu.edu/htbin/wcl/

🦆 I Spy

Before we all wondered where Waldo was, we loved a game called I Spy. Now that game's come to the Web, and it's perfect entertainment for young children. Choose a picture, say, a screenful of colorful postage stamps. The first player looks at the picture and says, "I spy a rocket!" Player two points to the stamp with the rocket on it, if he or she can find it. Then it's player two's turn: "I spy a stamp with a dog!" And so on. See if you can find the stamp with Mt. Rushmore.

http://www.geocities.com/~spanoudi/spy/

A B C D E F G H I J K L M N O P Q R S T U V W X Y Z

A
B
C
D
E
F
G
H
I
J
K
L
M
N
O
P
Q
R
S
T
U
V
W
X
Y
Z

I Spy from Scholastic

A much more difficult set of puzzles awaits you at this site, which is based on the popular I Spy book series. A riddle contains the clues to the objects you need to find within a large picture. Click on an area of the picture to zoom in for a closer view. It's a stretch to see some of the objects even with the enlargement. It's best to just keep clicking on things when you're stuck. Hint: the second ladder is up on a roof.

http://www.scholastic.com/ispy/

★ Kaboose.com

If you like to play Hangman, you can save the pen and paper and proceed directly to this site for a new twist on an old favorite. Your goal: solve the mystery word and save Broose Kaboose from falling off a crumbling bridge. Each time you guess a wrong letter, another track falls off the bridge. Can you save him from a watery tumble? OOPS. Off the bridge he goes. You can either play again, or choose from among the other great games on this site. There's something for everyone here, and to prove it: the "Emo" cards are gross.

http://www.kaboose.com/

★ Kid's Domain

Drop in on Kid's Domain when it's a snowy, blustery day and there's no one around to play with you. The games are arranged into categories: Shockwave; Java; and more. You'll also see games written by kids in Cocoa, plus Woogle games. What's a Woogle? We're not sure either, but we loved playing Pugsley's Revenge.

http://www.kidsdomain.com/

🦆 Kid's Corner Puzzle

Here is one wing. Where is the other one? Hmm, the body goes here, and, oops, leave room for the antennae to go here. Can you guess what kind of puzzle we're doing and what picture we will have when we are done?

http://kids.ot.com/puzzle/frame.html

KidsEdge

There are sample games here that may change, so we'll just describe one. Don't swallow your chewing gum, because it means Chef D'Gest has to go search for it. Try to navigate him through the wackiest human body maze you've ever seen. Dodge the red blood cells, old apple cores, license plates, and other debris as you go where no man has gone before. Watch out for the white blood cells, and enjoy the suitable squishy and gross sound effects!

http://www.kidsedge.com/

★ LifeSavers Candystand Arcade

These games are awesome because the candy company wants you to spend a lot of time on this site. This way, you will see a lot of candy messages and maybe buy more candy in the future. That said—gee, these games are fun! The Snackwells miniature golf game is challenging, the Fruit Stripe gum hang gliding game is spectacular, and the Life Savers Intense Fruit Chews stunt bicycling is . . . intense. There are also trivia games. And many more treats are in store for you in the candy dish, oops, we mean the arcade.

http://www.candystand.com/Arcade/

★ Lycoszone

Look no further than this site for the best collection of online games and fun we've seen. All of our favorite games from Billy Bear, Alfy, Bonus.com, and other hot sites are gathered here for your playing pleasure. You'll find games for little kids, big kids, and everyone in-between. There's even a musical karaoke machine so you can sing favorites like "Alice the Camel" and "The Cat Came Back."

http://www.lycoszone.com/

**Attention everyone.
The Internet is closing.
Please go play outside.**

★ Marcia's Games

Jackson's Barn will be enjoyed by preschoolers, while the other games on this site—especially Gothic Window—will be fun for everyone. Click on Jackson's barn door to reveal a crowing rooster. Then choose another door—can you match the rooster, or will you get a neighing horse, a baaing sheep, or some other farm animal? When you make a match, those game pieces disappear from the board and part of a pretty picture will be revealed behind them. Can you guess what it is?

http://www.logicalwoman.com/games/farm/

MasterMind

This is a Web version of the popular MasterMind game. You can play this game right over the Internet. The objective is to break the "code" by finding the right combination of colors. The computer will show a black peg, which means you have the right color in the right position, or a white peg, which means you have the right color in the wrong position. There are more fun games on this level <*http://www.javaonthebrain.com/brain.html*> of this very creative site. Note: we had trouble with this with Internet Explorer 5 for the Macintosh, although Netscape worked OK.

http://www.javaonthebrain.com/java/mastermind/

Native Match

This three-dimensional matching game from the Oklahoma Tourism and Recreation Department is fun but a little tricky. Tiles can only be "matched" if their left or right edges are "free," that is, not touching another tile. There's a "Show me!" button if you get stuck, and a "Shuffle" button if there are no visible matches.

http://www.travelok.com/funstuff/arcade/match.asp

The PuzzleFactory.com

One thing that's good about online jigsaw puzzles—you can't lose the pieces. This site offers loads of puzzles, tangrams, slider puzzles, and coloring books.

http://thepuzzlefactory.com/

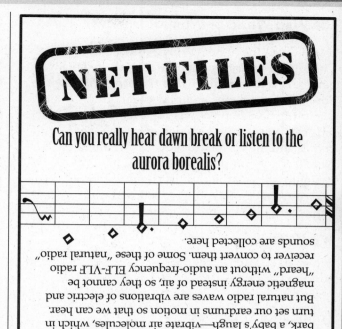

NET FILES

Can you really hear dawn break or listen to the aurora borealis?

Answer: Sure, you can. You can download these unusual .wav files at *http://www-pw.physics.uiowa.edu/mcgreevy/*

The sounds with which we are most familiar—a dog's bark, a baby's laugh—vibrate air molecules, which in turn set our eardrums in motion so that we can hear. But natural radio waves are vibrations of electric and magnetic energy instead of air, so they cannot be "heard" without an audio-frequency ELF-VLF radio receiver to convert them. Some of these "natural radio" sounds are collected here.

★ Soleau Software Shockwave Web Games

Lots of "tetris-like" games here, plus trivia games where you have to match up the first and last names of a sports player with the sport he or she plays. This is harder than it sounds. In other arcade choices, we especially like the Ant Run game. The object is to keep flipping the game pieces around so the ant continues to have a tunnel to run into. This is MUCH harder than it sounds!

http://www.soleau.com/webgames/

★ Universal Home Video Kid's Playroom

Help Beaver Cleaver find his missing bike as you maneuver through a maze, but watch out for the bully, who always scares "The Beav" back a few steps. Don't miss the Chipmunk's Great Balloon Race, where you have to fly through Egypt, avoiding pyramids while swooping low enough to grab power gems. There are a lot more games where these two came from!

http://homevideo.universalstudios.com/playroom/games/

A B C D E F G H I J K L M N O P Q R S T U V W X Y Z

A
B
C
D
E
F
G
H
I
J
K
L
M
N
O
P
Q
R
S
T
U
V
W
X
Y
Z

The Wild World of Wonka!

If you loved the movie, Willy Wonka and the Chocolate Factory, you'll love this set of Shockwave games. If you don't have that plug-in, you can still download the games and play them offline. There's a coloring book with a twist, so even the youngest kids can play. Older kids will enjoy the science games and the various arcade-type challenges. Note that the company's marketing folks are trying to sell you their candy. Remember to ask a parent before you type your name or any other personal information.

http://www.wonka.com/

Yahooligans! Games

It's easy to play online against another Internet user. Keep in mind that you may be playing with an adult, not another kid. There are no chat facilities within this playground so you won't be able to talk to your opponent. Just choose a name (from a list of those provided), and then select the game you want to play. Some of the board games are checkers, chess, go, reversi, and backgammon. There are card games, too, including everything from Go Fish to 21. If you prefer word games, you won't be disappointed.

http://games.yahoo.com/games/yahooligans.html

SCRABBLE

WorldWide Scrabble

At the official Web site, you'll be offered the choice of two sites: one for folks in North America and one for everybody else. Check out both variations, because there is much to learn and see at both sites! Learn the history of the game and get some hot tips to improve your skills. You can even find out how to get replacements for those Scrabble tiles your dog chewed up, as well as a complete set of rules for your downloading pleasure.

http://www.scrabble.com/

STRING FIGURES
Kid's Guide to Easy String Figures

You may have heard of Cat's Cradle, but what about Cup and Saucer, the Star, or Dressing a Pelt? These are all names of popular figures that you can make out of string. If you can follow instructions, this site will teach you how to make these string figures and more. You can use any kind of string, but nylon string works best.

http://personal.riverusers.com/~busybee/introkids.htm

This + That – String Figures

When you're playing with string figures, do you sometimes feel like you're "all thumbs"? Check out the animated lessons to learn some fairly easy string figures. It takes practice, but this site will help. Tired of string? This site also offers some very cool animations to show you how to juggle!

http://home.eznet.net/~stevemd/stringar.html

World-Wide Webs

Here's a collection of string figures from around the world to keep you busy all afternoon and into the evening. Try The Banana Tree or Four Boys Walking in a Row, both from Pacific islands.

http://members.xoom.com/_XMCM/darsie/string/

GARDENING

See PLANTS, TREES, AND GARDENS

From another galaxy? Learn about EARTH in the ASTRONOMY, SPACE, AND SPACE EXPLORATION area!

GENEALOGY AND FAMILY HISTORY

American Family Immigration History Center

If your ancestors immigrated to the United States, chances are they came through Ellis Island and the Port of New York. If you know their last name, you can search this site's vast archive to find them. The archive is made up of "ship manifests," which are detailed passenger lists. They contain the names of more than 22 million people who came to America between 1892 and 1924. This site should top your list if you're looking for clues to your family's history. Note: this site is extremely busy and difficult to reach. Try at different times of the day.

http://www.ellisislandrecords.org/

★ Ancestry.com

Though it offers a large selection of both free and for-fee databases, what's even more interesting about this site is its free discussion board system. There's probably someone discussing your last name right now! You can speculate with others about your common ancestors, share information to build an online family tree, and have a virtual reunion with relatives you didn't know you had. Although there's no section just for kids (yet), you might start with the beginner's area (unless you're already a pro).

http://www.ancestry.com/

★ Cyndi's List of Genealogy Sites on the Internet

This is a companion Web site to Cyndi Howell's book, *Netting Your Ancestors*, and her other books. It's a comprehensive and easy-to-use directory to thousands of Internet resources: ship passenger lists, adoption research, handy online starting points, and what to do when you've hit the wall and can't seem to get any farther in your quest to find out about your ancestors. Pay special attention to the Kids & Teens links <*http://www.CyndisList.com/ kids.htm#General*>.

http://www.CyndisList.com/

Favorite Poem Project

Do you have a favorite poem? A lot of people do, and at this site, you will see and hear them read their special poem and tell why it has made a difference in their lives. President Clinton reads "Concord Hymn," while a student recites "Casey at the Bat." The stories (and poems) are fascinating. Perhaps you could organize a "Favorite Poem" reading at your school or public library. This site, sponsored by a grant from the National Endowment for the Arts, will tell you how.
http://www.favoritepoem.org/

Deciphering Old Handwriting

Your grandma just gave you a whole trunk full of old family photos and letters. Trouble is, the handwriting is very strange. It just doesn't seem to use the same letters we do these days. The words seem to be abbreviated, too. What's going on? This Web site explains it all. There's a mystery at the end, too: what was the name of the woman who inherited the "horse named Clumse"? Based on the clues here, can you figure it out?

http://www.amberskyline.com/treasuremaps/ oldhand.html

★ Eponym

What does your first name mean? You can find out at this site! Whether you're named Abigail (father's joy) or Wayne (wagon maker), or anything else in-between, you'll find out where your name came from and how popular it is. This site features many international names as well.

http://www.eponym.org/

A B C D E F **G** H I J K L M N O P Q R S T U V W X Y Z

A
B
C
D
E
F
G
H
I
J
K
L
M
N
O
P
Q
R
S
T
U
V
W
X
Y
Z

Everton's Genealogical Helper

Here's the Web site of the world's largest genealogical magazine, *Everton's Genealogical Helper*. Some great features from the magazine and lots of help for beginning genealogists are available—for free! Some parts of the site require free registration. There are also for-fee services here for real enthusiasts.

http://www.everton.com/ols/

★ FamilySearch Internet Genealogy Service

Although this site is extremely busy, persevere until you get in. You can search through millions of records and possibly find your ancestors. The Church of Jesus Christ of Latter-Day Saints is constantly adding more and more genealogical material to this site, which searches not only census and other records but also Web sites. There are also links to the Church's beliefs, should you want to research that, as well.

http://www.familysearch.org/

★ GenealogySpot.com

Your family roots are deep. But just where do you start digging for them? Certainly not scrolling through microfiche. If you've got questions about your heritage, this site will help you find the answers using the Internet. It's got links to the best genealogy resources, how-to articles, genealogy software, and other must-see sites. It will also tell you where you can search online for old photos. Your nose had to come from someone, right? Don't miss the kid's section at *<http://www.genealogyspot.com/resources/ kids.htm>*.

http://www.genealogyspot.com/

Hamrick Software - U.S. Surname Distribution

As your ancestors married, had children, and moved to different parts of the country, their last name traveled with them. When the census was taken, these names were counted. Now you can see the names plotted against a map, and trace the spread of your last name around the country over time.

http://www.hamrick.com/names/

How to Collect Your Own Family Folklore

How well do you know the people in your family—especially your parents and grandparents? You may think you know them pretty well, but how much do you know about their childhoods and how they grew up? Are there any special family recipes? Do you have family heirlooms that have been passed down? What was a typical holiday like? Family folklore like this is not only interesting, it's fun to collect. And when you're done, you'll have a real historical document. This site will get you started.

http://educate.si.edu/migrations/seek2/family.html

Interview Questions for Family Members

"Who was your best friend?" That's just one of the questions you need to include on a family history questionnaire. What are the others? Check this site, print out the questions, and then go visit your grandma and grandpa for some amazing stories. Don't forget to bring your tape recorder or your video camera. Another interesting set of questions is available here: *<http://www.rootsweb.com/ ~genepool/ oralhist.htm>*.

http://www.rootscomputing.com/howto/intvwqus/ intvwqus.htm

★ My History Is America's History

If tracing your family's history seems like an overwhelming task, try some of these ideas. You could gather mementos about an event and create a "family history museum." Or, follow the instructions and make a family history quilt. As long as you're feeling crafty, buy some long-lasting acid-free paper and markers and have everyone in your family draw a self-portrait, including objects important to them. Will you draw a book, a computer, or an ice cream cone next to yours?

http://www.myhistory.org/kids/

AMPHIBIANS! Visit them before you croak.

★ Our Timelines

You usually only see historical time lines about very important people. But what about your very own time line? Are you important enough? At this site you are. Create a custom time line of your own important personal history, even if you're only a few years old! Want to know the names of notable individuals who share the same birth year as you? The My Peers section will generate a list. This site is a great genealogy tool for letting you see how you, or an ancestor, fit into history.

http://www.ourtimelines.com/

ROOTS-L Resources: Info and Tips for Beginning Genealogy

Ever thought about drawing your family tree? No, not the one in your front yard! We're talking about your relatives. Picture a tree with you at the bottom. On the first two branches are your parents. On the next highest branches are their parents, who are your grandparents. Farther up the tree are their parents, or your great-grandparents. Guess what—that tree reaches up higher than you can see! Get started here. This site offers checklists, family interview questions, and tips for reading microfilm.

http://www.rootsweb.com/roots-l/starting.html

Tombstone Rubbings

Old cemeteries are extremely interesting if you take the time to really look at the information on the gravestones. You can often find historical notes, snippets of poetry, and artworks, along with the name and dates of birth and death. Trouble is, a lot of old tombstones are deteriorating. Their surfaces become corroded and, eventually, the writing become illegible. You can make a rubbing of the tombstone in order to preserve its image on paper. Learn how with this step-by-step tutorial. For even more information on this art, try <http://www.savinggraves.com/rubbings.htm>. It notes that gravestone rubbings may require permission from the cemetery, so ask before you rub!

http://www.amberskyline.com/treasuremaps/t_stone.html

★ The Unwritten: Saving Your Photo Stories for the Future

They say every picture tells a story. But if no one writes down the stories, they are lost to future generations. Three girls decided to do something about that. They created a Web site to showcase some of their own family photos and folklore. The result is a moving and empowering experience—don't miss this site! Included are tips and suggestions so that you can do that same thing with that box of old pictures up in the closet. This site was created by students for the ThinkQuest competition.

http://library.thinkquest.org/C001313/

What Is a First Cousin, Twice Removed?

You're pretty clear on your parents, your brother and sister, and maybe even your aunts and uncles. But where do your first cousins come in—and what's this "twice removed" stuff? If you're a little fuzzy on relationships and the terms that describe them in our Western culture, check here. Can you really be your own grandpa?

http://www.genealogy.com/genealogy/16_cousn.html

NET FILES

The first U.S. patent was issued in 1790. What product or process was patented?

Answer: It was granted to Samuel Hopkins of Philadelphia, Pennsylvania, for a cleaning product called "pot and pearl ashes." You can learn more about the U.S. patent office at http://www.uspto.gov/go/kids/kidprimer.html

A B C D E F G H I J K L M N O P Q R S T U V W X Y Z

Math Games

Math games can add up to "sum" fun edutainment. How about playing math baseball with your brothers and sisters? They can pick how difficult the math questions should be and decide if they want addition, subtraction, multiplication, division, or all of the above. Then the computer will ask an arithmetic question. Can they get it right? Swing—wow, it's a triple! After that, have them see how good they are at making change for a dollar. How many pennies, nickels, dimes, or quarters in change should they receive after a certain purchase is made? There are some other reading and word games, too, including a concentration matching game. *http://www.funbrain.com/*

GEOGRAPHY

See also EARTH SCIENCE; TREASURE AND TREASURE HUNTING

★ About.com - Geography

Everything you could ever want to know about geography is probably linked here. (Unfortunately every ad seems to be linked here, too.) Outline maps, population, games, historic maps, even an interesting collection of frequently asked questions. In the latter section, you'll discover which country has the longest coastline, what the highest temperature ever recorded was, and where you'd be if you were in the world's smallest country.

http://geography.about.com/science/geography/

America's Roof

The highest points in the United States are listed here, and some avid hikers are trying to reach all of them. Other people make it their goal to reach the highest point in every county of their state. If it all sounds like fun, you can read the trip reports here. If you're looking for lists of the world's highest points, lowest points, and more extremes, check *<http://www.americasroof.com/world.html>*.

http://www.americasroof.com/

Geo-Globe: Interactive Geography!

This ThinkQuest contest finalist site, built by kids, will rock your world! How much do you know about geography? In Geo-Find, you can play at the beginner, intermediate, or advanced levels. Is Santiago the capital of Chile? What countries contain part of the Sahara Desert? Is Egypt south or north of the equator? Right or wrong, you'll get more links for you to explore on that topic. Geo-Quest involves ten questions: try to guess the right animal or bird, based on the answers to the questions you pose. Don't stop there—you'll find several more games that will test your knowledge of the seas, lands, and skies of Planet Earth.

http://library.thinkquest.org/10157/

GeoBee Challenge @ Nationalgeographic.com

Each year, thousands of schools participate in the Geography Bee, using materials and questions prepared by the National Geographic Society. Millions of kids compete for a chance at winning a $25,000 scholarship and other prizes. Some of the questions are easy, and some are real stumpers! How many of these practice questions can you get right? They change them every day, so play often. For information on entering next year's bee, visit *<http://www.nationalgeographic.com/geographybee/>*.

http://www.nationalgeographic.com/features/97/ geobee/

Geogame - Discovery Channel School

Are you up to the challenge? Click on any photo to start the game. You'll get a general question and be asked to click on the correct continent. Then the questions get more specific, You'll have to know the country, and then the city referred to in the clues. If you answer correctly, you get more information about the country in question, including a map and links to other scenic spots on the Web.

http://school.discovery.com/schooladventures/
geogame/

★ KODAK: Taken On The Road - American Mile Markers

Now here's an interesting site. The premise is this: drive coast to coast, from the Statue of Liberty in New York to the Golden Gate Bridge in San Francisco. Every mile, point your camera out the window and take a photograph. Put the whole thing up on the Web. Users will be able to retrace your trip and see the city morph into corn fields, the mountains rise up out of the plains, and the Pacific come into view.

http://www.kodak.com/US/en/corp/features/
onTheRoad/home/

The License Plate Game

Try to guess the name of the U.S. state or Canadian province before you click on it on the colorful outline map. See a picture of that area's license plate, at least the way it looked a few years ago.

http://www.klutz.com/licenseplategame/intro.html

"Pole to Pole" Projects

What would happen if you started at the North Pole, picked any line of longitude, and walked along it until you came to the South Pole? You'd travel through many different countries, need lots of different types of clothing, eat quantities of unusual foods, and carry numerous types of strange bills and coins. A class of fifth and sixth graders in the Netherlands pretended to do just that, and they wrote reports about their virtual travels. See how it's done at this interesting page.

http://www.best.com/~swanson/pole/pole_menu.html

NET FILES

The Statue of Liberty has 25 windows and seven rays in her crown. What do they represent?

Answer: Lady Liberty's crown has 25 windows, representing 25 types of precious gemstones found on Earth. The seven rays of the statue's crown stand for the seven seas and continents of the world. Find out more at http://www.nps.gov/stli/prod02.htm

★ The Professor's Postcards

The Professor takes trips to UNESCO World Heritage sites all over the world, and she's great about sending postcards back to her friends. Unfortunately, she always seems to leave out the most important words—like where she is! Can you figure it out from the clues on the postcards?

http://www.un.org/Pubs/CyberSchoolBus/special/
profesr/

★ Traveling Buddies

It's always more interesting to learn about a far-off place from someone who has actually been there. How would you like to learn about geography from a stuffed animal? Lots of toys are now traveling the world and sending back reports. Classes take the animals on local field trips, write in journals about the animal's experiences, and send pictures and postcards back to the animal's home school. Then the toy is packed up and sent on to the next destination. Maybe your school or family can host one of them in the future. This page explains how you can get started.

http://www.siec.k12.in.us/~west/article/travbud.htm

A B C D E F G H I J K L M N O P Q R S T U V W X Y Z

A
B
C
D
E
F
G
H
I
J
K
L
M
N
O
P
Q
R
S
T
U
V
W
X
Y
Z

NET FILES

What do Julius Caesar, Annie Oakley, Betsy Ross, and Leonardo da Vinci have in common?

Answer: According to the Chinese Zodiac's twelve-year cycle, these famous people were all born in years of the Monkey. The Chinese belief is that people born in the year of the Monkey are very intelligent and always well liked. Find out more at http://www.lausd.k12.ca.us/Haskell_EL/calendar%20past%20events/chinese new%20year%20gifts/chinesenewye ar.htm

★ Traveling Stuffies - CanOz Connection

In the spring of 2001, Net-mom participated in a traveling stuffie project with Nora Boekhout's second grade class in Coquitlam, British Columbia. You can read all about Monty Moose in New York, and see loads of photos, at this warm and fuzzy Web site.

http://www.teacherwebshelf.com/canozconnection/
travellogs/travelcontents.htm

Xpeditions @ Nationalgeographic.com

Quick—you need an emergency map of Idaho to complete your homework! Relax, this site offers a fast way to get one onto your screen, and then you can save it or print it. The atlas at this site offers hundreds of maps from around the world, all optimized for printing to paper or screen. (Note: The Xpeditions atlas is fast, but you'll just get black-and-white maps. National Geographic's Map Machine, described on the following page, will get you a color map plus information on each state.) In the Xpeditions Hall galleries, explore physical, natural, and cultural aspects of geography, using multimedia and QuickTime virtual reality. There is also a forum to ask and answer geography questions.

http://www.nationalgeographic.com/resources/ngo/
education/xpeditions/

GAMES

Online Detective Games - Carmen Sandiego

You need to know a little about geography—and outer space—to catch Carmen Sandiego. She's the Duchess of Dastardly Deeds, and she's about to steal the polar ice caps, lift the stripes off zebras, and burglarize the constellation Orion's belt. As an agent for the ACME Virtual Detective Agency, you can stop her, if you answer the questions correctly. When you catch Carmen, you'll feel like you're on top of the world. Now, where would that be? The North Pole, Iceland, or Antarctica?

http://www.carmensandiego.com/

MAPS

Central Europe Jigsaw Puzzle

How is your knowledge of European geography? Can you place the twelve sections of the map back together? Hint: almost in the center of the map is Geneva, Switzerland, where the World Wide Web was invented.

http://highschoolhub.org/hub/f-europe.cfm

Color Landform Atlas of the United States

What state are you interested in? They are all here, but let's use New York as an example. At this site, you can see a color physical map of the state, or a black-and-white map, or an 1895 map, or a counties map. There is also a satellite photo of the state, with its outlines marked. Here's the fun part. You'll find links to other specific types of information. See New York watershed maps, find out where the toxic waste dumps are, explore national parks and historic sites in New York, and find out about roadside attractions such as the Cardiff Giant hoax. Parental advisory: be sure to explore the Roadside America part of the site with your kids.

http://fermi.jhuapl.edu/states/states.html

The Degree Confluence Project

You know that there are imaginary lines of latitude and longitude encircling the globe, right? The most famous latitude is the equator, dividing the northern and southern hemispheres. The equator is at zero degrees latitude. If you want to talk longitude, the most famous line (at zero degrees longitude) is the Prime Meridian. Where a line of longitude meets and crosses a line of latitude—well, there, my friends, you have a "Degree Confluence." Now what if someone were to go out and take photographs at every latitude/longitude intersection on the planet? That's the idea behind this site. According to the introduction, "There is one within 49 miles (79 km) of you if you're on the surface of Earth." There are still plenty of them left to photograph.

http://www.confluence.org/

GIS for Everyone

GIS stands for Graphical Information System. It's a special kind of mapping software that allows the user to overlay all sorts of databases onto a map. That way, you can see patterns, like crime areas in a city, or where people buy a lot of office supplies. This way of looking at information helps city planners, marketers, scientists, and students. You can get an overview of GIS mapping here.

http://www.esri.com/gisforeveryone/

Map Machine @ Nationalgeographic.com

Everyone knows how wonderful the National Geographic Society's maps are. Now many of them are online. Need a quick color map; facts about a country, state, or province; and a picture of its flag? You'll find it right here at the Map Machine Atlas. You can also get political and physical maps (useful for school reports).

http://www.nationalgeographic.com/resources/ngo/maps/

You are your own network.

MapQuest!

Get customized maps for places all over the world, using the interactive atlas. You can get street-level information and door-to-door directions for many places. It's outstanding, it's fun, and it's free! There's also a TripQuest driving planner. How long have you been begging Mom and Dad to drive you to Disneyland? Maybe they say, "Oh, it's so far, and we'd get lost on the way." No problem. Just go to this site, type in the name of your town, and type in the nearest city to Disneyland (Anaheim, California, is close enough). Magically, you'll get back not only a map but also detailed driving directions, complete with the mileage of each segment! It works for the United States and Canada only (driving to Disneyland from Halifax, Nova Scotia, is 3,618.7 miles). Unfortunately, you can't drive from Hawaii, but you get the idea.

http://www.mapquest.com/

NET FILES

What lighthouse is also one of the Seven Wonders of the ancient world?

Answer: The Lighthouse of Alexandria, on the island of Pharos, off Egypt, is one of the Seven Wonders of the ancient world. Built around 300 to 220 B.C., it was as tall as a modern-day 40-story building, making it the tallest structure in the world at that time. It had a miraculous mirror lit by the sun during the day and by fires at night. The light could be seen 35 miles away. By the mid-1300s it was in ruins, and for a long time its exact location was not known. Have pieces of the ancient lighthouse now been found? Discover more at http://unmuseum.mus.pa.us/pharos.htm

A
B
C
D
E
F
G
H
I
J
K
L
M
N
O
P
Q
R
S
T
U
V
W
X
Y
Z

GEOGRAPHY—MAPS
★ MapTech

Going on a hike? Download a free topographic map first. Or maybe you're going sailing, or on vacation near a beach or a body of water. You can get a free nautical chart at this site too. Find out the water depth, water hazards, channel markings, and lots more. Start by clicking on "Online Maps, Charts, and Photos." You'll soon be on your way!

http://www.maptech.com

The National Atlas of the United States of America

You're familiar with physical and political maps, and now you can explore the United States as you have never seen them before. Click on the "layers" you want to see: forest fragmentation; butterfly distribution, toxic waste areas; population; per capita income; and lots more. You may find relationships between these layers that no one has ever thought of before. Find the airports in earthquake zones, see if there's any correlation between moths and nuclear power plants, and have fun manipulating the data.

http://www.nationalatlas.gov/

Perry-Castañeda Library Map Collection

Available from the University of Texas Library, this collection includes maps from around the world and links to some of the best map collections on the Internet. Check out the historical maps and the current events maps of Nepal or whatever world hotspot is in the news. If you need a map, check here!

http://www.lib.utexas.edu/maps/

Round Earth, Flat Maps

How do mapmakers manage to portray a round planet on a flat paper surface? It all starts with a projection, and there are several types, each having pros and cons. Find out why you might choose to use the conic projection over a planar or cylindrical one if you were drawing a map of the United States. On the other hand, a planar projection would be a great idea for a map of Antarctica. Depending on the point of view of the map on your wall, your view of the world may be true or distorted. Clear things up at this site.

http://tectonic.nationalgeographic.com/2000/
    exploration/projections/

TopoZone

Wow! You might be here exploring topographic maps all day. According to this page, "We've got every USGS 1:100,000, 1:25,000, and 1:24,000 scale map for the entire United States; Alaska (1:63,360) and Puerto Rico (1:20,000) will be coming soon." The scales mean that, for example, one inch on the map is equivalent to 100,000 inches on the Earth. Try typing in something interesting like "volcano" or the name of a city or town.

Http://www.topozone.com/

USGS: What Do Maps Show

This site has comprehensive lesson plans and hands-on activity sheets for students—all related to understanding maps. You can also download student map packets, which you can print for use with the lessons. This is a great geography teaching and learning tool.

http://info.er.usgs.gov/education/teacher/
    what-do-maps-show/WDMSTGuide.html

NET FILES

What's a
Labradoodle?

Answer: It's a breed based on a Labrador-standard poodle cross, often used in Australia and Great Britain as a guide dog for the blind. Discover more about this unusual breed at http://www.labradoodle.com/

GOVERNMENT

See CANADA; COUNTRIES OF THE WORLD; UNITED STATES

Whooooooo will you
find in BIRDS?

HEALTH AND SAFETY

See also HELP

DENTAL CARE

American Dental Association Kids' Corner

Kids visiting the Kids area can watch cartoons about proper tooth care and download some coloring book pages. And don't miss the interactive game "To Tell the Tooth," starring your game show host Al Smiles. Teens might want to check out the topics section and then click on "Teen" for information on dental sealants, root canal therapy, and the answer to the question "Who needs wisdom teeth?"

http://www.ada.org/public/topics/kids/

★ Yo! It's Time for Braces!

It makes you wonder why no one has come up with this idea before: explain braces and other orthodontia from the perspective of a kid. The class members who created this site were finalists in the ThinkQuest Junior competition, and they do have a wonderful Web page. The American Association of Orthodontists recommends that kids get their "bite" checked when they are about seven or eight. No, that doesn't mean you bite the dentist! The dentist will look at the way your teeth interact with each other. It's possible that you might need to wear braces on your teeth in order to straighten them and improve your bite—millions of kids do. This site explains it all and follows one girl through her first few months of living with braces.

http://tqjunior.thinkquest.org/5029/

DRUGS, TOBACCO, AND ALCOHOL

Campaign for Tobacco-Free Kids

This site reports that "nearly every adult who smokes (almost 90 percent) took his or her first puff at or before the age of 18." One of the problems is that tobacco companies target ads at kids, advertising in magazines with high teen readership. Another problem is that nicotine in cigarettes and smokeless tobacco is addictive, so once someone starts smoking, it may be difficult to quit. Keep up with the latest news, and join the tobacco-free kids campaign, which says "Send the camels back to the desert and the cowboys back to the ranch."

http://tobaccofreekids.org/

For Kids Only

Go to Be Smart, Don't Start, then Pick a Brain, any brain. You'll find out what effects marijuana, alcohol, inhalants, and tobacco have on brains. Does someone you know abuse drugs or alcohol? There's a section called How to Help Someone that will tell you what you can do. Wally Bear and the Know Gang offer word search puzzles, coloring books, and even information on Internet safety. Just say yes and visit this site.

http://www.health.org/kidsarea/

Freevibe

Because this site is directed at teens, parents should steer young children away. It offers explicit talk about drugs, and the bulletin board discussions feature teens talking about their drug experiences. The language is nothing worse than you'd hear on MTV, and you won't see any messages promoting illegal substances. You will see a lot of kids telling their real stories, in the hope that their peers will listen. This site is a collaborative effort of the National Clearinghouse for Alcohol and Drug Information of the United States Public Health Service. They are helping to manage Freevibe for the White House Office of National Drug Control Policy.

http://www.freevibe.com/

A
B
C
D
E
F
G
H
I
J
K
L
M
N
O
P
Q
R
S
T
U
V
W
X
Y
Z

A
B
C
D
E
F
G
H
I
J
K
L
M
N
O
P
Q
R
S
T
U
V
W
X
Y
Z

Gotta Quit

If you know someone who is trying to quit smoking, this site may help. Quitting 101 offers a four-step attack plan, "recovery symptoms" to watch out for, and specific suggestions on how to stay smoke-free.

http://gottaquit.com/

Just One Night

Just one night. That's all it took for Tom Boyle of Concorde, New Hampshire, to drink, drive, and destroy a life. In his own words, Boyle will tell you about the events that culminated in a car crash that took the life of a stranger. If his story isn't sobering enough, read the facts about the dangers of drinking and driving. There's also a chart showing blood alcohol limits under DWI (driving while intoxicated) and DUI (driving under the influence) laws across the country.

http://www.pbs.org/justone/

NET FILES

Why do bees buzz?

Answer: Bees buzz because their wings are moving up and down more than 11,400 times per minute. This motion produces that distinctive drone.
http://www.honey.com/kids/facts.html

Mind Over Matter

Produced by the National Institute on Drug Abuse, National Institutes of Health, this site lets you follow research scientist Sara Bellum as she investigates the effect of drugs on the human body. Marijuana, opiates, inhalants, hallucinogens, nicotine, steroids, and stimulants are covered. Find out where the drug comes from, what it does to your brain and other parts of your body, and where you can find more info on the Net and in the library. The site says it is aimed at grades five through nine.

http://www.nida.nih.gov/MOM/MOMIndex.html

Parents. The Anti-drug

Although this site is focused on the needs of parents, we're listing it because of the detailed information on drug abuse and its effects. The site includes frank talk from teens who have taken drugs, and a drug quiz if you think you know it all (we only got 50 percent right!). There's also some great advice on how to practice dealing with peer pressure by using role-playing scenarios first. And check this out: if your parents are having trouble talking to you about this subject, send them an e-vite to set aside a particular day to talk about about it. You might want to set up a special appointment once a week to talk about anything that's on your mind. But parents aren't the only anti-drug, you know. Your anti-drug might be soccer, or music, or friends. For the phat site of choice, you want <http://www.whatsyourantidrug.com/>, also reachable as Freevibe.com (see review on previous page).

http://www.theantidrug.com/

The Reconstructors

When you play this game, you travel to Neuropolis, a futurist world. There you're called on to help solve medical mysteries about drugs. As a member of an elite group known as the Recontructors, you'll follow clues all over the globe to solve the mystery. Along the way, you'll learn about the helpful and harmful qualities of pain-relieving drugs like opium and aspirin. You'll also learn more about chemistry, neuroscience, public policy, history, and more. But remember: Once you start a game, there's no turning back.

http://reconstructors.rice.edu/

The Whole Truth

They're not the "prize patrol" but the "truth crew," and they drive around in a truck letting people know all about what the tobacco industry is up to. If you don't see them in your neighborhood, you can still hear their message. Just visit this site to read all about the tobacco industry and its efforts to conceal the real truth about the effects of nicotine. Once-secret documents, inside information, propaganda, the names of tobacco industry chairmen and their salaries: it's all here.

http://www.wholetruth.com/

HEALTH

All About Enuresis

It's estimated that between five and seven million kids in the U.S. wet the bed at night. Fortunately, most kids will grow out of it—no kid likes to wake up in a wet bed! This page offers some advice on enuresis (en yer REE sis) and its treatments.

http://kidshealth.org/kid/health_problems/bladder/
    enuresis.html

BrainPOP - Health

The only stars in these movies are your body parts. Pick one, and you'll learn all about it in a short movie hosted by Tim and Moby the robot. From muscles to puberty to acne, there are dozens of movies from which to choose. After each movie, take the quiz and see how much you learned. Bet you thought that eating chocolate will cause zits. Tim and Moby say it isn't so. But rubbing chocolate on your face might. Watch the acne movie to learn more.

http://www.brainpop.com/health/seeall.weml

FDA Kids

The Food and Drug Administration is the government authority that makes sure our food supply is safe, and drugs and medicines actually do what they claim to do. Learn about vaccines and how they work to protect us from disease. Check out articles on protecting your hearing at rock concerts, on eating disorders, and lots of other teen topics. Younger kids will enjoy the food safety coloring book.

http://www.fda.gov/oc/opacom/kids/

★ Harcourt Health

Do you know how to dress for safety when you play football or speed down the street on your inline skates? If not, you can practice by dressing up an otter in the Grade 2 selection area. Just click and drag on the various pads and mouth guards and boxer shorts and sandals, and see if you can make the right choices. You can also look for the 13 hazards in the Disaster Kitchen, waiting for you in the Grade 3 section. Check Grade 5's Skeleton Shakedown to see how good you are at putting a skeleton back together, and in Grade 6 there's even more, including a tobacco and alcohol quiz.

http://www.harcourtschool.com/menus/
    your_health.html

★ KidsHealth

This is the best kids' health resource out on the Net. Now, you might be thinking, "Diseases, ick! Why would I want to visit a Web page about health?" Well, haven't you always wanted to know what causes hiccups? Or what happens when you have to get stitches? Or what to expect when puberty creeps up on you? The answers are here! Enter via the Kids door. Choose My Body to try the animations about how your lungs breathe, your brain thinks, and your tummy rumbles. There is a LOT more here; we recommend the whole site for learning about nutrition, feelings, and lots of ways to stay healthy.

http://kidshealth.org/

Sometimes I Just Stutter

Did you ever start talking and then stumble over your words? They seem to get stuck somewhere south of your brain but north of your tongue. This is called stuttering, and it's common in children. Many adults also stutter from time to time. It's embarrassing, and sometimes other people make fun of you. This online book explains what causes stuttering and gives some suggestions for coping with it. The main thing to remember is that "it's OK to stutter, just don't splutter!"

http://www.stutteringhelp.org/sijs/sijs.htm

A
B
C
D
E
F
G
H
I
J
K
L
M
N
O
P
Q
R
S
T
U
V
W
X
Y
Z

HEALTH CARE AND HOSPITALS

★ BioInteractive

Trying to diagnose an illness involves a lot of detective work. How well do you think you could do if you were a physician? These interactive labs allow you to "become" a cardiologist, a DNA sequencing technician, and a research scientist working with (yeech!) a leech.

http://www.biointeractive.org/

Medicine Through Time

In the ancient world, the remedy for curing a fever was to cook the flesh of frogs in olive oil. Thankfully, times have changed, and so has the treatment of fever. Anyway, you can't get frogs at the pharmacy. At this site, you'll travel through time to discover how medicine has developed through the ages.

http://www.bbc.co.uk/education/medicine/

★ A Science Odyssey—You Try It: Doctor Over Time

Not feeling well? What seems to be the trouble? You'll find our clinic is a little unusual. Step into the doctors' waiting room. Now which health care professional would you like to see? A doctor whose technology is right up-to-date—for 1900? Or would you prefer to speak to a physician from the fabulous 1950s? Or perhaps you think you'll get better care with our M.D. from late great 1998? You know, they all have appointments open right now, why not consult them all and compare treatments?

http://www.pbs.org/wgbh/aso/tryit/doctor/

Stay skeptical—people in chat rooms aren't always who they say they are.

HUMAN BODY

See also SCIENCE

Brain Connection

What weighs about three pounds and has mystified and intrigued scientists for centuries? The answer is the human brain. How does it work? How are thoughts formed? How are memories recalled? How does language develop? The answers lie within this site. You just need to explore it to learn some of these and other mysteries of the living brain.

http://www.brainconnection.com/library/
  ?main=explorehome/main

Can You Put a Skeleton Back Together?

OK, you know the skull goes at the top and the feet go at the bottom—but can you put the rest of Mr. Bones' skeleton back together? If you get the piece in the right area, you'll hear a click, and it will lock in place and stick. If you get everything correct, you'll get a surprise. Otherwise, the skeleton will collapse, and you can try again.

http://www.lhs.berkeley.edu/shockwave/bones.html

★ Come to Your Senses

This site makes a lot of sense. You can see what we mean if you touch base here. In fact, we hear that there are really nine senses: taste, sight, hearing, touch, smell, hunger, thirst, pain, and balance. This page was created by kids as an entry in the ThinkQuest Junior contest. In it, you'll get a taste of all the senses; the research here smells OK to us.

http://tqjunior.thinkquest.org/3750/

Habits of the Heart

If you saw how your heart works, what would you compare it to? After exploring the pictures and diagrams on this site, you might say it looks like an intricate indoor plumbing system. That might be an oversimplification. But arteries and veins do carry fluid through a series of pipes and valves in the heart, so it's not that far-fetched. There are lots of pictures showing how the heart functions, and, if you can stomach it, there's a video of a heart transplant.

http://www.smm.org/heart/

The Heart: An Online Exploration

Probably the only time you think about your heart is when you run fast and you feel it beating in your chest. Or maybe you think about your heart when you put your hand over it and you feel it go thump, thump. Even if you don't think much about your heart, everybody knows the heart is important. After all, without hearts, what shape would valentines be? To learn all kinds of cool things about the heart, check out the Franklin Institute's info. You'll never take your heart for granted again!

http://sln.fi.edu/biosci/

★ Human Body "Blending in but Staying Special"

This wonderful site covers an unusual topic for children: human organ donation. Find out about body systems: skeletal, muscular, nervous, digestive, circulatory, respiratory, and urinary. Sometimes the organs supporting these systems aren't quite right. They may have failed due to injury, disease, or other causes. Sometimes the only thing that will help is a transplant of another organ. These donated hearts, lungs, and other organs come from people who have recently died. It is sometimes very hard for families to decide to donate the organs of their loved ones, but they are often comforted by the fact that their generosity may help save another person's life. Learn about the new kidney for a third-grade teacher and the gift of life bestowed on others by the school's speech therapist after the tragic death of her step-son. This site was created by students for the ThinkQuest Junior competition.

http://tqjunior.thinkquest.org/5777/

Modern Miracles: Organ Transplants

This award-winning site was created by students for the ThinkQuest competition. It further explores organ donation, including which organs are most commonly transplanted, and why. Look over the horizon at medical technology and recent advances in cloning, genetic engineering, and artificial organs. What are some concerns surrounding this topic? Some are religious or ethical, while others are only misinformed myth.

http://library.thinkquest.org/28000/

Neuroscience for Kids - Explore the Nervous System

When you bite into a chocolate bar, how do you know it's delicious? How do you know to say "Ouch!" when you get stung by a mosquito? Little sensors, called neurons, are all over your body, and they carry messages to your brain through a system of nerves. Your brain then sorts everything out. This resource is crammed with great info about brains, your senses, spinal cords, and careers in neuroscience. Be aware, though, that many of these folks go to school for 20 years before they become neuroscientists!

http://faculty.washington.edu/chudler/introb.html

★ Seeing, Hearing, and Smelling the World

Trying to make sense out of your senses? Visit this site from the Howard Hughes Medical Center. Discover how we see color, why we have two ears, and the differences in brain scans as we see a word or hear it. Amazing!

http://www.hhmi.org/senses/start.htm

The Monterey Bay Aquarium

Visit the Monterey Bay Aquarium page and get a diver's-eye view of the fish in the kelp forest tank. Maybe you'll see sharks, rockfish, and eels that inhabit the underwater seaweed forests. Don't miss the interactive exhibit called Splash Zone. It offers lots of online fun, and you'll learn about rock and reef homes for sea creatures, too. The Learning Center features the kids' E-Quarium where you can just choose a habitat and explore. Will you select the sandy sea floor, the deep sea, or the rocky shore? *http://www.mbayaq.org/*

A B C D E F G H I J K L M N O P Q R S T U V W X Y Z

★ Sighting the First Sense

"Turn on more light, or you'll hurt your eyes." How many times have you heard that! If you read in poor lighting, you'll be glad to know that it won't damage your eyes. But it may cause headaches or eyestrain. That myth is among ten common eye myths found on this site. It's also just a sampling of the wide variety of information about the eye you'll find here. You'll also learn about eye disorders, how the eye functions, and ways to improve vision, including eye exercises. This site was created by students for the ThinkQuest competition.

http://library.thinkquest.org/C001464/

Smartplay

Learn to prevent sports injuries to various parts of your anatomy by stretching and warming up first. If you are hurt, remember to use the "RICER" technique: Rest the injury, Ice it, Compress it, Elevate it, and Refer it to a health care practitioner. At this site you'll learn about the intricate wonder called your knee, as well as other parts of your body. If you're squeamish, avoid the Ouch! movies, which show sports injuries as they occurred.

http://www.smartplay.net/

NET FILES

What extremely well-known science fiction movie was partially filmed in a place where it is so hot that people live underground?

Answer: The movie saw *Star Wars*, and Tunisia was the site of Luke Skywalker's uncle's moisture farm on Tatooine. Find out more at http://imdb. com/Trivia?0076759

Test Your Reflexes

Do you think you would react faster if you saw a warning sign, or if you heard a warning sound? At this Web site you can test your guess.

http://www.explorescience.com/activities/
    Activity_page.cfm?ActivityID=38

★ Yucky Gross and Cool Body

Everything you've ever wondered about the science of sweat, pimples, burps, ear wax, and unseemly bodily noises is here. There are even audio recordings of stuff like a stomach growling—but it's not the real thing, and you get to guess what they used to make the sounds. It's not really disgusting, but it is gross, so if you're over 13 or so, don't even think of visiting this site! Those that do will learn a lot about digestion, the circulatory system, and other things about the human body and its mysteries.

http://www.yucky.com/body/

ILLNESS AND DISEASE

Asthma Tutorial

Asthma is no fun: wheezing, coughing, struggling to breathe; anyone with asthma knows what problems this illness causes. To learn about asthma, take a look at this site, provided by the Children's Medical Center of the University of Virginia. You'll see cool graphics and hear some great audio files, including what the doctor hears when listening through the stethoscope.

http://hsc.virginia.edu/cmc/tutorials/asthma/
    asthma1.html

★ Band-Aides and Blackboards

Subtitled "When Chronic Illness . . . or Some Other Medical Problem . . . Goes to School," this site is about growing up with a medical problem. Just because kids and teens have an illness doesn't mean they aren't interested in pets, TV, music, video games, and other stuff. Meet kids with cancer, kids with cerebral palsy, kids with ADD, and many more. You'll also find poems written by kids with chronic illnesses, go on virtual hospital tours, and find out once and for all what to do about teasing.

http://www.faculty.fairfield.edu/fleitas/contents.html

★ CELLS Alive!

You get a bad case of the sniffles, and your doctor gives you a shot of penicillin. Ouch! That hurt, but in a few days you feel better. What happened? To see how penicillin works and to learn plenty of information about cells, take a look at this site. If you're really sharp, you'll also find the "anatomy of a splinter" section. Don't miss the "cell cams." See how cells have divided over the last 24 hours. Amazing!

http://www.cellsalive.com/

Dying to Be Thin

Accounts of anorexia date back hundreds of years. In the fourteenth century, St. Catherine of Siena starved herself to death at the age of 33. Unlike young women today, St. Catherine's pathway to anorexia was motivated by her faith. This site takes a stark look at eating disorders affecting mostly women. The main attraction is the *Dying to Be Thin* television program. If you missed it on PBS, you can watch it in its entirety on this site. There is also an extensive list of resources and sites specializing in eating disorders.

http://www.pbs.org/wgbh/nova/thin/

Eating Disorders Awareness and Prevention

Anorexia nervosa. Bulimia nervosa. We know the words, but do we know the warning signs? The ED-Info section of this site offers tips on how to help a friend you suspect has an eating disorder. It gives information and resources on self-esteem. One thing everyone can do is educate others about the seriousness of eating disorders. It is not "just a girl's problem." Find out more here.

http://www.edap.org/

Growing Up with Epilepsy

Find out what causes epilepsy, take a virtual trip to a neurologist, and learn what to do if someone around you has a seizure. Discover what it's like to be a kid with epilepsy: Alyssa lets you read her diary. This site was created by students for the ThinkQuest Junior competition.

http://library.thinkquest.org/J001619/

The Hidden Killers: Deadly Viruses

The opening screen to this site is pretty gross, but click on ENTER and you'll discover information on virus basics. There are also profiles of the best-known viruses and some reassuring words about the defenses we have against some of them. On the other hand, there is also some frightening commentary about those that we don't know how to kill. There's also an interesting section on the military uses of viruses in biological warfare. You'll want to wash your hands well after leaving this site. This site was created by students for the ThinkQuest competition.

http://library.thinkquest.org/23054/

★ Infection, Detection, Protection

Meet the microbes! They are everywhere, and they are among the oldest life-forms on Earth. At this site you'll learn about bacteria, viruses, and protozoa. Some of these can cause diseases, but over 95 percent of them are harmless. Use the Size-o-Meter to get a sense of how small these critters actually are, and then go on a microbe quest in the school cafeteria and try to solve the microbe riddle. Learn how Lou got the flu, and try playing detective in the Case of the Mixed-Up Microbes.

http://www.amnh.org/nationalcenter/infection/

The Minifig Generator

This neat interactive site uses Lego body parts and JavaScript so you can have fun choosing heads, torsos, and legs to create your own mini-figure. How about a pirate's head on a doctor's lab coat, with skeleton legs? You can make your own selections or let the computer randomly pick its own. Name your creation and print out a copy. Cool, huh? *http://www.baseplate.com/toys/minifig/*

A
B
C
D
E
F
G
H
I
J
K
L
M
N
O
P
Q
R
S
T
U
V
W
X
Y
Z

NET FILES

What is the Stone of Scone?

Answer: For at least a thousand years, all the Scots kings were crowned upon a stone whose legendary ancestry went back to Biblical times. England's King Edward I defeated the Scots in 1296, and took the Stone back to England with him. It was placed in the base of Westminster Abbey's Coronation Chair, last used in 1953 at the coronation of Queen Elizabeth II. The Stone (or the object currently claimed to be the Stone) was returned to Scotland in 1996. It is on display in Edinburgh Castle. Read about the fascinating lore and legend of this 336-pound sandstone block. *http://www.tartans.com/articles/stoneofscone.html*

Locks of Love

There's a disease called alopecia areata and its main symptom is hair loss. Some other medical conditions, or their treatments, also cause this. Some kids don't like how they look this way, so they wear custom-fitted wigs made out of human hair. These are generally very expensive, and many children can't afford it. Then someone got an idea. What if people donated hair so these wigs could be made at less cost? What if an organization arranged for disadvantaged kids to get these wigs for free or at low cost? Locks of Love is that organization. Do you want to cut off your at least ten-inch long ponytail and try shorter hair for a while? Think about donating your hair to kids who don't have any. There's a special way your stylist needs to prepare your hair, but all the instructions are at this site. Remember though, hair swept up from the floor won't work. It takes 12 donated ponytails to make one hairpiece.

http://www.locksoflove.org/

New York State Department of Health - Communicable Disease Fact Sheets

Ahh-chooo! Nobody likes getting sick. Chicken pox, mumps, influenza (that's the long way to say the flu) are among the many illnesses you can catch, called communicable diseases. Learn about lots of these from info provided by the New York State Department of Health. So, remember always to cover your face when you sneeze, wash your hands before you eat, and be health-smart!

http://www.health.state.ny.us/nysdoh/consumer/
commun.htm

MENTAL HEALTH AND PSYCHOLOGY

See also HELP

American Foundation for Suicide Prevention

This site offers advice, statistics, and more on the problem of teen suicide. Is someone you love so depressed he is talking about taking his own life? There are things you can do to help. Take your friend seriously. Also, encourage him to go for counseling and go with him yourself if necessary. Talk to an adult you trust, don't be the only one trying to help your friend. Danger signals may be found here *<http://www.afsp.org/about/whattodo.htm>*.

http://www.afsp.org/education/press.htm

Dreams: An Exploration into the Subconscious

In this corner Sigmund Freud, reigning psychoanalyst. And in this corner, the challenger, Carl Jung. Whose theory of dreams do you support? Learn what we know about the science of dreams and sleep. Visit the gallery to look at some dream-inspired and surrealistic artworks; then wander into the Interpretation area and have a go at figuring out what your own dreams mean. Maybe they just mean you should make your restless dog sleep on the floor. This site was created by students for the ThinkQuest competition.

http://library.thinkquest.org/17039/

A
B
C
D
E
F
G
H
I
J
K
L
M
N
O
P
Q
R
S
T
U
V
W
X
Y
Z

Exploratorium: The Memory Exhibition

What are your earliest memories? Drawing with a green crayon? Holding a white bunny? Getting sick all over your sister? What is memory, anyway? Try some online experiments and learn more. There's also a fascinating exhibit of an artist's paintings, created from his childhood memories, juxtaposed with photos of the same areas today. How closely do they match?

http://www.exploratorium.edu/memory/

PERSONS WITH DISABILITIES

★ Ability Online Support Network

Ability OnLine connects kids with disabilities or chronic illnesses to other kids facing the same challenges. Family members and caregivers are welcome, too. You'll make new friends; share experiences; and most of all, discover that you're not alone.

http://www.abilityonline.org/

Cerebral Palsy: A Multimedia Tutorial for Children and Parents

Cerebral palsy, also known as CP, is a medical condition causing uncontrolled muscle movements. It's not a disease, and you can't "catch" it from someone who has it. People with CP have it all of their lives. Many times kids who have CP use wheelchairs around school, and sometimes they can't speak clearly. To learn more about CP, take a look at this site.

http://hsc.virginia.edu/cmc/tutorials/cp/cp.htm

Children with Disabilities

If you suffer from a disability or have a child in your family who does, you might feel alone or helpless at times. This resource is likely to ease some of your anxieties. Here you'll find all sorts of links just for families of children with disabilities. There are links to local, state, and federal programs to help with reading, learning, and recreation. There is also a section directed towards children. It contains links to camps, puzzles, games, bulletin boards, and books.

http://www.childrenwithdisabilities.ncjrs.org/

The Disability Rights Movement

When you visit a museum, there are often kiosks that provide more information about an exhibition. You touch the screen, a menu appears, and you make a selection to learn more about a particular topic. This site is a Web-based version of a kiosk in a real museum. But instead of touching a screen to move through the menu, you click your mouse. When you do, you'll learn about the efforts to secure civil rights for people with disabilities in the United States.

http://www.americanhistory.si.edu/disabilityrights/

Down Syndrome

This site was created by kids to explain Down syndrome to other kids. One of the kids on the Web team has Down syndrome. You can read all about him at this page and also see a video of him in a wrestling competition. This resource explains that kids with Down syndrome are not so different after all. You'll also find out about the history of the syndrome, as well as other facts. This resource does its job so well, it won the 1998 ThinkQuest Junior competition!

http://tqjunior.thinkquest.org/3880/

IBM Accessibility Center

Want to know how IBM computers can be adapted for use by persons with disabilities? This resource offers information on products, software to download, and lots of advice on making Web pages and Java applications accessible to all. See also the listings for Microsoft Accessibility, and Macintosh Assistive Technologies sites, also in this section.

http://www-3.ibm.com/able/overview.html

★ Internet Resources for Special Children (IRSC)

Whether you need some adaptive clothing, a newsgroup on diabetes, or some therapeutic humor, you'll be sure to find what you want at this site. There are hundreds of links about kids with disabilities and the families who love them.

http://www.irsc.org/

A B C D E F G H I J K L M N O P Q R S T U V W X Y Z

A
B
C
D
E
F
G
H
I
J
K
L
M
N
O
P
Q
R
S
T
U
V
W
X
Y
Z

Just Because We Have a Disability Doesn't Mean We Byte!

Sometimes you can see a disability, like a broken arm. But others are invisible—such as bulimia or ADD (attention deficit disorder). What's it like to be "different"? Try some of the simulations to find out how your life would be if you were differently abled. This site was created by students for the ThinkQuest competition.

http://library.thinkquest.org/11799/

LD OnLine: Learning Disabilities Information and Resources

Did you know that Walt Disney, Winston Churchill, and Albert Einstein all had learning disabilities of some kind? According to this site, actor Tom Cruise is dyslexic and learns his lines by listening to them on tape. This site is a real encyclopedia of information on learning disabilities and disorders (LD). You'll find lots of info on Developmental Speech and Language Disorders, Academic Skills Disorders, and Other Learning Differences. One of the treasures this site offers is the First Person stories. Discover how kids and adults deal with and overcome their disabilities to celebrate their abilities.

http://www.ldonline.org/kidzone/kidzone.html

Macintosh Assistive Technologies

Now we're talking MICE! Mice of different sizes and speeds, remote-controlled mice, and head-controlled mice. But don't look here for information about cute, little, furry rodents—this site is for you and your family if you're looking for adaptive technology solutions for your computer! The Mac Access Passport (under Learning and Speaking Solutions) is a comprehensive database of access products. You'll find expanded keyboards and other neat gadgets for the physically challenged, innovative software for the visually impaired, and lots of special education software. There is a list with links to popular shareware for you to download and a list of organizations that provide other adaptive technology resources. See also the listings for IBM and Microsoft Accessibility, also in this section.

http://www.apple.com/disability/

Microsoft Accessibility: Technology for Everyone

There are many ways computers can be adapted for people with varying physical disabilities. Microsoft offers a free video illustrating how some of them may be used. There are also online training manuals with step-by-step instructions for adjusting the accessibility features of Microsoft products. Don't miss the selection of accessibility products, including voice input, keyboard, and screen utilities, among others. See also the listings for IBM and Macintosh Assistive Technologies, also in this section.

http://www.microsoft.com/enable/

National Sports Center for the Disabled

If you love outdoor recreation, adventure, and freedom, then read about all of the fun programs sponsored by the National Sports Center for the Disabled. The NSCD, a nonprofit organization located in Winter Park, Colorado, celebrated its 30th year of "enabling the spirit through sports" in 2000. If you're a winter sports fan, you can join their Ski Pals Program, where disabled and able-bodied kids of ages 8 to 14 hit the slopes. If skiing, snowboarding, or snowshoeing aren't for you, then how about the Family Camp? You and your family can enjoy white-water rafting or hiking on nature trails designed to accommodate any special needs. There's even a rock-climbing course for the blind and visually impaired.

http://www.nscd.org/

Seeing Disabilities from a Different Perspective

This site focuses on several different disabilities: autism, blindness, cerebral palsy, and deafness. In each section you'll find information about the topic plus personal narratives, such as "Jessica's Perspective on Having a Brother Who Has Autism." There's a wonderful list of links, as well as suggested simulation activities and book reviews. This site was created by students for the ThinkQuest Junior competition.

http://tqjunior.thinkquest.org/5852/

Sounds of Silence

What is it like to be deaf in a world of hearing people? Find out at this Web page, which tries to give insight into the world of the deaf and the deaf community. How do deaf kids watch TV? How do deaf adults drive cars? Don't miss the poem in which you may find out "What it's like to 'hear' a hand." This site was created by students for the ThinkQuest competition.

http://library.thinkquest.org/15390/

What the Blind Can See

Follow along with a sighted class as they visit a school for the blind to learn about guide dogs, white canes, and special adaptive equipment used by blind people every day. The kids tried on special goggles to simulate blindness of various types. They learned a lot from their experience, which they share with their Web readers. This site was created by students for the ThinkQuest Junior competition.

http://library.thinkquest.org/J001326/

PUBERTY

An Educator's Online Resource for Teaching Puberty and Menstruation

Aimed at teachers and school nurses, this resource provides lots of information about puberty for both girls and boys. You'll find out about the major events of puberty for both sexes, and there are drawings to make sure you have all the right names for your own anatomy. In Ask the Doctor you'll find all sorts of questions, answered by health care professionals. Make sure you have all the right answers when your friends ask you what's up with growing up!

http://www.teachingteens.com/

Kotex Information

Girls—get to know your body and your emotions as you enter the exciting world of womanhood. This site, from a manufacturer of women's products, offers much more than marketing hype. Find out about your anatomy, the mysteries of menstruation, and even what happens during a gynecological medical exam.

http://www.kotex.com/info/

A Global View from Space

Would you like to see a picture of how Earth looks—right now? You can! A multinational network of satellites provides data to NASA in almost real time. These images are correlated and placed onto a spherical globe for you to view. You can manipulate the globe in any direction you want. Choose to look at cloud cover, ozone, wind, or other features. Click on any area of the map to zoom in. Click once again on the zoomed image to return to the prior view. Remember, there's no place like your home planet.
http://farside.gsfc.nasa.gov/ISTO/dro/global/

Sexual Health

It happens to every boy. All of a sudden, his voice starts croaking, his Adam's apple starts growing, and peach fuzz turns into whiskers. As a girl grows into a woman, her body changes in many ways. These changes signal puberty, and sometimes it can be scary and confusing. Find out more here.

http://kidshealth.org/teen/sexual_health/

TeenGrowth

Parental advisory: please preview this site. Developed by a medical board of well-known physicians, this site focuses on the health needs of adolescents. Its mission is to provide authoritative answers to questions teens have, whether it's a question about body development, depression, gangs, or sexuality. The information given at this site should not replace the advice of your own doctor, your parents, or your religious authority.

http://www.teengrowth.com/

A B C D E F G H I J K L M N O P Q R S T U V W X Y Z

A
B
C
D
E
F
G
H
I
J
K
L
M
N
O
P
Q
R
S
T
U
V
W
X
Y
Z

Why Do I Get Acne?

It seems that you always get a pimple right before a school dance, or party, or some event where you want to look and feel your best. What's to blame? Was it that chocolate you ate? All that dark cola you drank? That greasy cream you put on your face? The truth is, acne in teens is normal, and it's caused by all the hormones you have pumping around in your body during puberty. What can you do about it? Visit this site to clear things up.

http://kidshealth.org/teen/body_basics/acne.html

SAFETY

See also INTERNET—SAFETY

Food Safety Music

Don't just read about food safety. Sing about it. If you're stuck for words, you won't be after visiting this site. The music from old rock songs is paired with new lyrics covering a variety of food-safety issues. Stayin' Alive, a song made famous by the Bee Gees, becomes an anthem to battling E. coli. This is a fun site with a serious message.

http://foodsafe.ucdavis.edu/music.html

NET FILES

Where might you be able to see "balloons," "moonmilk," "popcorn," and "soda straws"?

Answer: These are some of the wacky names scientists have given to various features and formations found in caves. Learn more about them at The Virtual Cave at http://www.goodearthgraphics.com/virtcave.html

★ Kidd Safety

The Consumer Product Safety Commission wants you to try all of "Kidd" Safety's games. (He's a little cartoon goat. His name is Kidd. Get it?) Look for the dangerous situations around the house. Do you see one? Good—now click on it and play a concentration-style matching game. After that, you can try a word search puzzle, or try to skateboard to the park while picking up safety equipment and avoiding branches and squirrels. You have 90 seconds—GO!

http://www.cpsc.gov/kids/kidsafety/

My 8 Rules for Safety

What are "Checking first," "Using the buddy system," and "Trusting your feelings"? These are three of the eight rules for safety developed by the National Center for Missing and Exploited Children. To stay safe, it's important to stay with friends when you are outside, to always tell your parents or caregiver where you are going, and to trust your feelings if you think something is wrong. This site is presented by the National Center for Missing and Exploited Children, see the main description next.

http://www.missingkids.com/html/
    ncmec_default_8_rules.html

★ National Center for Missing and Exploited Children

Some families are looking for their missing children. Check their photos. Have you seen any of these kids? Maybe you can help! This site lets you search by state, physical description, and other characteristics. If you have a Web page of your own, check the How You Can Help area. It will tell you how to put a link at your page that will show photos of recently missing kids to your Web site visitors, like the pictures on milk cartons. Another way you can help is to join the Poster Partners program. As soon as a child from your area is reported missing, you will receive an e-mail and a link to that child's photo poster information. You print it and ask permission to put the poster up in a public place. You must also agree to retrieve the poster when the child is found.

http://www.missingkids.org/

♣ The Otto Club

The California State Automobile Association has a terrific site to help very young kids learn about traffic safety. Visit Otto the car and his interactive town. Talk about street smarts—Otto is a real know-it-all! There is a full-featured animation and sound version or a lighter version for those who believe less is more. Sing along with the Seat Belt Song by pressing the radio buttons on Otto's dashboard. Play the traffic light game, and see if you can compare the two pictures and decide who's stopped for red, based on the signals YOU can see. There are little games on helmet safety and playground safety, too. Be sure to click on the question mark in each area, though, to find out what you can do in each section.

http://www.ottoclub.org/

Poisonous Plants and Animals

When you walk through the woods, it's a good idea to wear long pants, and don't touch any plant unless you know that it won't hurt you. You've heard of poison ivy, haven't you? It will make you itch and scratch if some of its sap rubs off on your skin. Besides poison ivy, there are many other plants that are irritating or poisonous to touch or eat. You'll learn their names and the toxins they contain at this site. Also covered are poisonous insects, reptiles, and marine animals. This site was created by students sfor the ThinkQuest competition.

http://library.thinkquest.org/C007974/

SAFETY—FIRE SAFETY

Fire Administration Kids Page

The U.S. Fire Administration wants everyone to be safe from fire, including you. Every year, kids start over 100,000 fires—don't be one of them! This site explains smoke alarms, home fire safety, and escape plans. Visit Hydro's Hazard House and see if you can spot the dangers in each room. There is also a Parent-Teacher Lounge with lesson plans and more resources to help clear the smoke on fire safety.

http://www.usfa.fema.gov/kids/

★ Kidde Home Safety Education Center

Take a look at the Java games at this resource promoting fire safety. It's presented by a company that makes extinguishers and alarms of various types. Captain Kidde, a colorful superhero, teaches children about fire protection equipment, how to conduct fire safety checks and fire drills, and ways to save themselves and others in the event of a fire. We had fun creating blueprints of imaginary houses and dragging around various appliances, smoke alarms, and fire extinguishers until we figured we'd done a pretty good job. Captain Kidde evaluated our work, and luckily he agreed. There are various games for ages 5 to 13 and lots of information for parents, too. Teachers will find lesson plans designed for grades K–8 and safety tips on preventing fires and carbon monoxide poisoning. There are also home safety education tools for firefighters to use during community open houses, in-school visits, and similar outreach activities. You'll find loads of links, too.

http://www.kiddesafety.com/kiddesafety/

★ Preventing and Fighting Fires

Different types of materials produce different types of fires. Charcoal burns slowly, with an even glow. Other materials, such as coal and wood, produce a flame. A very rapid burning fire is created by gunpowder or dynamite, and the large amount of gases produced makes a violent explosion. Find out about fires and the various techniques used in fighting them at this site from *World Book Encyclopedia*. There is also an interesting section on great fires throughout history.

http://www.worldbook.com/fun/fire/html/intro.htm

★ Smokey Says

Who can prevent forest fires? Only you, of course! You need to know how to safely handle matches and fire, and Smokey Bear and his friends can help you learn how. Try the interactive games, or the coloring pages, and you won't get burned, even though this site is hot!

http://www.smokeybear.com/

A
B
C
D
E
F
G
H
I
J
K
L
M
N
O
P
Q
R
S
T
U
V
W
X
Y
Z

NET FILES

If you were to go fishing for a glacier, what kind of bait would you use?

Answer: Ice worms, of course! These little critters are the only animals that live inside glacial ice. You can read a bit more about them and see a picture of one at http://www.execpc.com/~washman/iceworms.htm

HELP

Befrienders International

If you are feeling depressed or suicidal, or you know someone who is, please visit this Web page now. You will not only learn about suicidal feelings but also find out what you can do to cope with them. This site offers free and confidential e-mail support and will also direct you to a crisis hotline. This page is offered in nine languages, and e-mail support is available in eight.

http://www.befrienders.org/talk.htm

National Runaway Switchboard

According to this site, America has over 1.3 million runaway or homeless kids on the street. This site can help them. It can also help kids in crisis at home, who are thinking of running away. Every Tuesday night, there's an open chat for two hours. You can also call a free phone number for counseling: it's confidential and there's no charge. They help you sort through your options and decide for yourself what to do. If you are a runaway, you can use this service to get a message to your parents. It is also possible to get a free bus ticket home. Call them.

http://www.nrscrisisline.org/

Project Safe Place

Over 9,000 businesses in 32 states have banded together to get teens the help they need—fast! They display a yellow and black diamond-shaped "Safe Place" sign. All you have to do is go in and tell the first employee you see that you need help. You will be given a place to sit and relax while they arrange transportation to the local youth crisis shelter. Many fast food restaurants and grocery stores are part of this program.

http://www.safeplaceservices.org/

Sourcebook Online: Toll-Free Help Numbers

Find other kids with the same disease you have. Hook up your friend with an AIDS counselor. Learn about organizations that help children of alcoholics and drug abusers. This site offers hundreds of ways to get help, backed up with phone numbers and Web addresses.

http://mentalhelp.net/selfhelp/fonenums/helpline.htm

★ Suicide—Read This First

Here's how this site starts: "If you are feeling suicidal now, please stop long enough to read this. It will only take about five minutes. I do not want to talk you out of your bad feelings. I am not a therapist or other mental health professional—only someone who knows what it is like to be in pain . . . I have known a lot of people who have wanted to kill themselves, so I have some small idea of what you might be feeling. I know that you might not be up to reading a long book, so I am going to keep this short. While we are together here for the next five minutes, I have five simple, practical things I would like to share with you. I won't argue with you about whether you should kill yourself. But I assume that if you are thinking about it, you feel pretty bad. . . . Start by considering this statement: 'Suicide is not chosen; it happens when pain exceeds resources for coping with pain.'" There are excellent resources available on this site. You aren't alone.

http://www.metanoia.org/suicide/

HISTORY

★ EyeWitness - History Through the Eyes of Those Who Lived It

Read accounts of historical events written by those who experienced them, or witnessed them. What happened on Scott's doomed 1912 South Pole expedition? How did people cope with the horrendous conditions on a slave ship in 1829? What was the Battle of Gettysburg really like? These are just a few of the first-person stories at this site, stories that span from the ancient world through the twentieth century. There are also audio files so you can hear history as it happened.

http://www.ibiscom.com/

★ The History Channel

Who says history's boring? If you get this cable channel, you know the truth is out there! Even if you don't have cable, you can visit this Web site. Try This Day in History (little menu bar box at the top of the page—click, and on the next screen, type the date you want), and get historical facts, plus the top ten in music for past years (select What Else Happened Today). Even if you think you have no interest in history, stop in—we think you'll be pleasantly surprised.

http://www.historychannel.com/

★ HyperHistory Online

Hey, your mom says you can have some friends over for lunch! She says to invite three people you admire from history—which heroes would you choose? You might get some ideas here. This site will teach you about important people from 1000 B.C. to the present. You'll find scientists, artists, musicians, authors, politicians, explorers, and many others. But that is not all: you can also trace events through history, as well as look at important maps of time periods and the spread of civilizations.

http://www.hyperhistory.com/online_n2/History_n2/a.html

Modern World History

Take a tour through the political and other events that shaped world history during the twentieth century. Follow the time line stretching from World War I in 1914 through the Wall Street crash in 1929, to the rise of Hitler and the end of World War II. This site, created by the BBC, is illustrated with many photos and activities to help you understand each period in time. Hint: once you've selected a section, click on the spinning globe to access a drop-down menu. The essays, pictures, and further information may be found there.

http://www.bbc.co.uk/education/modern/mainmenu/mainfla.htm

National History Day

Don't go looking for dates and facts about what happened 200 years ago. You won't find any here. What you will find are the contest rules for a national history competition for junior high and high school students. The contest is sponsored by National History Day, which, by the way, is not a single day but a year-long campaign to change the way history is taught in schools across the United States. Winners earn $1,000.

http://www.thehistorynet.com/NationalHistoryDay/

On This Day

What was in the news today? You could pick up the newspaper, or turn on the television, and find out the day's current events. But that won't do you much good if you want to know what happened in history today. For that, turn to this site. It highlights news events of the past and links them to newspaper articles. Also included are birthdays and obituaries of notable individuals.

http://www.nytimes.com/learning/general/onthisday/

ANCIENT HISTORY
See ANCIENT CIVILIZATIONS AND ARCHAEOLOGY

Read any good Web sites lately?

A B C D E F G H I J K L M N O P Q R S T U V W X Y Z

HISTORIC DOCUMENTS
★ The History Channel - Great Speeches

Hear some of the words that changed the world. You'll be able to hear speeches made by Mahatma Gandhi, Malcolm X, and Douglas MacArthur, as well as historic words like those from *Apollo 13*: "Houston, we've had a problem." (Hint: For this one, look under John L. Swigert, Jr.)

http://www.historychannel.com/speeches/

Magna Carta

In 1215, the English barons were fed up. They thought their king had gone too far, on more than one occasion. They wanted a line drawn that would explain the difference between a king and a tyrant. They defined laws and customs that the king himself had to respect when dealing with free subjects. That charter is called the Magna Carta. It's made it all the way from 1215 to the Net, as part of the Treasures Digitisation Project at the British Library. You can view the whole manuscript and read a translation of it. A brief history and further reading suggestions are included.

http://minos.bl.uk/diglib/magna-carta/overview.html

NET FILES

The official folk dance of the state of South Carolina is the square dance. The official waltz is the Richardson Waltz. There's an official dance, too. What is it?

(Hint: It's not the Macarena!)

http://www.lpitr.state.sc.us/shag.htm

Answer: It's the Shag! "The Shag," one of the great developments of terpsichorean culture and native to this State, is performed to music known as rhythm and blues. Both the music and dance are structured on time signature and can be performed to almost any tempo, as long as the basic step is maintained and kept in time to the music." See

HISTORIC DOCUMENTS—U.S.
★ The Declaration of Independence

The History Channel offers this special online exhibit about the creation and signing of one of America's most treasured documents. Find out about the history leading up to all those famous signatures at the bottom of the page. Preserved today at the National Archives, the treasure has not been opened for 50 years. It is sealed in a bronze and bulletproof glass container, pumped full of humidified helium. A new encasement strategy is being planned, involving a new titanium case and argon gas. The documents are currently off exhibit while the National Archives building is renovated. The project's expected completion date is 2003.

http://www.historychannel.com/exhibits/declaration/

Declaring Independence: Drafting the Documents

You know the Declaration of Independence was first signed on July 4, 1776. It begins this way: "When in the course of human Events, it becomes necessary for one People to dissolve the Political Bands which have connected them with another . . . ." The colonists didn't one day just wake up and decide to send this letter to King George III of England. This Library of Congress exhibit presents a chronology of events. You'll find fascinating information about how the documents were drafted, plus photos of important objects. Some of these include fragments of the earliest known draft, the original draft, and various prints relevant to the exhibit, as well as correspondence from Thomas Jefferson. Did you know he was the one who wrote the original?

http://lcweb.loc.gov/exhibits/declara/declara1.html

You know something the Net doesn't——create your own home page! Look in the INTERNET- WEB BUILDING AND HTML section to find out how!

The Gettysburg Address

The Library of Congress has devoted this page to President Abraham Lincoln's Gettysburg Address. Lincoln was invited to dedicate the Union cemetery only three weeks before the ceremony, so he did not have much time to write the speech. View the working drafts of the eloquent words Lincoln eventually delivered. You'll also see the only known photo of Lincoln taken at Gettysburg, Pennsylvania. These precious original documents have been preserved for future generations. Find out how.

http://lcweb.loc.gov/exhibits/gadd/

National Archives Online Exhibit Hall

The National Archives and Records Administration (NARA) is a nationwide system that preserves U.S. government records of permanent value. The online exhibits help to bring some of the rich and varied holdings of the National Archives to the public. In the Exhibit Hall, you will find some cool special exhibits; for example, "The Charters of Freedom" features the Declaration of Independence, the Constitution of the United States, and the Bill of Rights. You'll also find a special exhibit on the Emancipation Proclamation, issued by President Abraham Lincoln, which ended slavery. Other featured documents include the Nineteenth Amendment and Japanese surrender documents. Visit this site for firsthand looks at the historic documents of the United States, several of them written in longhand!

http://www.nara.gov/exhall/exhibits.html

★ Sign the Declaration of Independence

Would you have signed the Declaration of Independence? It meant you were a traitor to the King. Find out what else it meant, and (if you still want to), select a quill and "sign" the document yourself. If you have a printer handy you can keep a copy for your wall.

http://www.archives.gov/join_the_signers/
    sign_the_declaration/sign_the_declaration.html

The Signers of the Constitution

Can you match the line drawings of the men who signed the U.S. Constitution? At this site, you'll get plenty of help. Just scroll past the picture, and see the names of all 40 men and the number that they correspond to in the drawing. While you should know who George Washington was, you might not know many of the others. The site also provides a brief biography of each signer.

http://www.nara.gov/education/teaching/
    constitution/signers.html

U.S. Founding Documents

If you want a transcription of the Declaration of Independence with the original "Dunlap Broadside" capitalizations preserved, visit this site. There are also scanned originals of Thomas Jefferson's drafts of that document. The site also presents other U.S. founding documents such as the Constitution and the Federalist Papers. You can search the Constitution by keyword, too. How many items mentioned in the Bill of Rights (those are the first ten amendments) can you name?

http://www.law.emory.edu/FEDERAL/

Inventions! @ Nationalgeographic.com

Guess the purpose of a wacky patent drawing. Hmmm, is it an automatic baby-patting machine or a mitten stretcher? If you guess right enough times, you'll get a token. Play five games about inventions and inventors. If you get five tokens, you can operate the coolest invention of them all: the Action Contraption!
http://www.nationalgeographic.com/features/96/
inventions/

A B C D E F G H I J K L M N O P Q R S T U V W X Y Z

U.S. Historical Documents

The University of Oklahoma Law Center hosts "A Chronology of United States Historical Documents." The chronology begins in the precolonial era, with the Magna Carta and the Iroquois Constitution, and concludes with the Inaugural Address given by President George W. Bush in 2001. Along the way, you'll find the Mayflower Compact, the famous "Give Me Liberty or Give Me Death" speech by Patrick Henry, the Monroe Doctrine, the Emancipation Proclamation, and Martin Luther King, Jr.'s "I Have a Dream" speech. Take a peek at the "other" verses of the U.S. national anthem, too (1814): *Oh! thus be it ever, when freemen shall stand Between their loved homes and the war's desolation! Blest with victory and peace, may the heaven- rescued land Praise the Power that hath made and preserved us a nation. Then conquer we must, for our cause it is just, And this be our motto: "In God is our trust." And the star-spangled banner forever shall wave O'er the land of the free and the home of the brave!*

http://www.law.ou.edu/hist/

NET FILES

Why is speed at sea measured in "knots" rather than miles per hour?

Answer: A nautical mile (6,080 feet) is not the same length as a land mile (5,280 feet). Visit this site to find why this is so. According to BoatSafeKids.com, a crude shipboard speedometer was invented in the 1500s. Called a "chip log," it involved a line with knots tied at intervals of 47 feet, 3 inches. This odd length relates to a specific fraction of a nautical mile. The weighted end of the line would be tossed overboard at the rear of the boat and allowed to play out. In the days before watches, the sailor used an hourglass to keep track of time. The special one used for this particular purpose counted only 28 seconds of sand. The sailor would count the number of knots that fed overboard within this short time period. This would give the ship's speed in nautical miles per hour. *http://boatsafe.com/kids/roger1099.htm*

HISTORIC SITES

See also AFRICAN AMERICANS—HISTORY; ARCHITECTURE—GOVERNMENT AND PUBLIC BUILDINGS

Find a Grave

Want to know where Ben Franklin is buried and see a photo of his grave? Or how about the grave of Walt Disney, or maybe that of a baseball great like Ty Cobb. Or say you're going to Concord, Massachusetts, and want to know if anyone famous is buried there. Wow—Louisa May Alcott, Henry David Thoreau, and Nathaniel Hawthorne are in the Sleepy Hollow Cemetery among lots of others! Find graves all over the world at this unique site.

http://www.findagrave.com/

Great American Landmarks Adventure

At this page you can download pages of historic landmarks to color. But it's not the usual type of famous landmark. Here you'll find some really weird stuff, such as Independence Rock (Casper, Wyoming), where folks traveling along the Oregon Trail got out of their covered wagons long enough to scratch their names. You'll find the U.S. Capitol here, too, or you can also choose to color the Taos pueblo.

http://www2.cr.nps.gov/pad/adventure/landmark.htm

National Park Service

The U.S. National Park Service administers everything from Abraham Lincoln's birthplace national historic site (Kentucky) to Zion National Park (Utah). Between those two sites in the alphabet are hundreds of other monuments, parks, battlefields, trails, seashores, and other places of special importance to Americans. Search the Visit Your Parks area by name, location, or theme.

http://www.nps.gov/

National Trust for Historic Preservation

Many historic sites are old—so how come they look so nice? Because people like you care enough to save them from deterioration. This is called historic preservation. This resource will help you find out how to save historic sites in your area.

http://www.nthp.org/

Teaching with Historic Places

There's much to be learned about the past by looking at today's historic landmarks. This page suggests lesson plans, activities, and readings to expand your knowledge of Civil War history, African American history, American Indian history, Asian American history, Hispanic American history, and much more. You can search for lesson plans by location of site, time period, or theme.

http://www.cr.nps.gov/nr/twhp/

HISTORIC SITES—BOSTON, MA

The Boston Freedom Trail and Black Heritage Trail

It's only 2.5 miles long, but if you visit it, you'll be walking through years of Boston's history. Check out the Paul Revere House and the Old North Church ("one if by land, two if by sea . . ."). Don't miss the Boston Massacre site or the Bunker Hill Monument. Bring a cup of tea and take the virtual tour to the Black Heritage Trail as well.

Http://www.vboston.com/VBoston/
    index.cfm?profile=historians

The Old North Church (Christ Church Boston)

On April 18, 1775, church sexton Robert Newman climbed into the belfry of the Old North Church and hung up two signal lanterns. To Paul Revere, watching from a boat, that meant the British were coming—by sea—up the Charles River towards Lexington. Revere's famous "midnight ride" was immortalized by poet Longfellow. This page tells the history of the church, as well as what's going on there today. It's still an active Episcopal church. Find out who more recently hung the third lantern, and why.

http://www.oldnorth.com/

HISTORIC SITES—CALIFORNIA
Angel Island

What today is a grassy, sunny island in San Francisco Bay was once a U.S. quarantine and detention center, largely for Asian immigrants. The story of their entry and detention in the United States during the 1890s and early part of the twentieth century is not a pretty one. While immigrants could be processed through the East Coast's customs center on Ellis Island in a matter of hours or days, travelers through Angel Island were often detained for weeks or months. More than 70 percent were Chinese. Read about it at this site and its related links.

http://www.aiisf.org/

California Missions

Parental advisory: please preview this site and avoid the message board. Take a virtual tour to 21 famous California missions, founded in the 1700s and 1800s. Listen to music that would have been sung by the Franciscan Friars of that time period. View numerous annotated links to other sources of information for students and teachers. One of our favorites is The Spanish Missions of California at <http://library.advanced.org/3615/>. That site was created by students for the ThinkQuest competition.

http://www.californiamissions.com/

HISTORIC SITES—NEW YORK HARBOR, NY

★ Ellis Island - Through America's Gateway

Between 1892 and 1954, Ellis Island was the gateway to America for over 12 million immigrants. Before they could set foot in America, they had to be "processed" on this island in the New York harbor. This meant a three- to five-hour wait, medical and legal questions, and inspections. Some were eventually turned away. Learn about the journey, the processing center, and life in the new land at this excellent example of multimedia education. You will hear audio recollections of some of the immigrants themselves. There is also an "Ellis Island cookbook" with recipes such as cabbage rolls and gingersnaps.

http://www.internationalchannel.com/education/ellis/

A
B
C
D
E
F
G
H
I
J
K
L
M
N
O
P
Q
R
S
T
U
V
W
X
Y
Z

NET FILES

If you could take out all your cell chromosomes, unravel the DNA, and lay it all end to end, how far do you think it would stretch? (Hint: The answer is out of this world.)

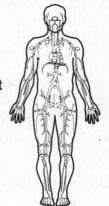

Answer: According to The Tech, "the strands would stretch from the Earth to the Moon about 6,000 times." Find more amazing facts at http://www.thetech.org/exhibits_events/online/genome/DNA4.html

★ History Channel Exhibits: Ellis Island

For further detail on the Ellis Island immigrant experience, check this site. Some famous immigrants include actor Bob Hope, author Isaac Asimov, and musicians Baron von Trapp and his family. How many more names do you recognize from the list at this site?

http://www.historychannel.com/exhibits/ellisisle/

The Light of Liberty

On July 4, 1884, the United States received a monumental birthday gift from France. The 15-story-tall Statue of Liberty was designed by sculptor Frédéric-Auguste Bartholdi. He used his mother as the model! Learn more at this illuminating site.

http://www.nationalgeographic.com/world/9907/liberty/

Curl up with a good Internet site.

The Statue of Liberty

Give me your tired, your poor, Your huddled masses yearning to breathe free, The wretched refuse of your teeming shore. Send these, the homeless, tempest-tost to me, I lift my lamp beside the golden door! This is part of the poem inscribed on the Statue of Liberty. It was written by Emma Lazarus, and you can learn more about the statue's history at the official National Park Service site.

http://www.nps.gov/stli/

HISTORIC SITES— PHILADELPHIA, PA

Historic Philadelphia

Take a tour of over 50 famous landmarks in Philadelphia, Pennsylvania. You'll visit Independence Hall, where the Declaration of Independence was signed, and see Betsy Ross' House, where some say she sewed the very first American flag. Along the way, stop in at the Pretzel Museum for a quick snack.

http://www.ushistory.org/tour/

HISTORIC SITES— WASHINGTON, D.C.

Ford's Theater National Historic Site

The theater where President Lincoln was shot is now a national historic site. If you click on Expanded Home Page, you will learn some fascinating facts about the assassination. Why was there no guard—or was there? Where is the chair in which Lincoln sat? And where is the bullet that killed him? The surprising answers are all here.

http://www.nps.gov/foth/

Mount Vernon - The Home of Our First President, George Washington

We know this isn't really in Washington, but it is nearby. And many of Washington's visitors make the short trip to Mount Vernon. Seeing where our first president lived makes him more real to us. Walking up his front steps, lounging on his lawn—these things connect us to a real person instead of a historical figure. Maybe you can't visit Mount Vernon, Virginia, in person, but you can stop in via the Net. At Mount Vernon, you can take a tour, read some astounding facts, and even check out the Washington "trading cards." You can also learn about archaeology at Mount Vernon and explore related links. The Mount Vernon virtual tour includes the East Front, the large dining room, study, master bedroom, gardens, the Washingtons' tomb, and a slave memorial. Washington was the only one of the Founding Fathers to free his slaves; in his will he gave them their freedom upon his death.

Http://www.mountvernon.org/

Vietnam Veteran's Memorial

The U.S. National Park Service administers this memorial site, which is in Washington, D.C. Over 58,000 American men and women died in the Vietnam War, a conflict so controversial it divided the generations as well as the country. All their names are engraved on a mirrorlike granite wall. People leave flowers, poems, military gear, and other objects around the wall. It is a very moving place to visit, and we guarantee you will never forget your experience there. Be sure to take the link to the expanded home page.

Http://www.nps.gov/vive/

> **Want a snack? Learn to make one in COOKING, FOOD, AND DRINK.**

White House for Kids

Now that there's a new administration in the White House, the White House for Kids site has undergone some changes. The information is still there, but the presentation just isn't the same (see what we mean for yourself, here's the old one: <http://clinton4.nara.gov/WH/kids/html/home.html>). At this site you'll learn how the White House was built (bricks were made on the front lawn), tour the rooms, and find out about the First Family pets that have lived there (don't miss President Harrison's goat or Caroline Kennedy's pony). Did you know the president's desk was once part of a ship, abandoned north of the Arctic circle in 1854? The HMS Resolute was later found by the crew of an American whaling ship. It was repaired and refitted, then sent to Queen Victoria as a gesture of goodwill. Later, when the ship was taken out of service and dismantled, a desk was made from some of its timbers. Queen Victoria presented the desk to President Hayes in 1880. The desk has been used by most presidents since then.

http://www.whitehouse.gov/kids/

★ White House Historical Association

The year 2000 marked the bicentennial year of the White House. This wonderful Web site will tell you the origin of the Oval Office, what White House china looks like, what sorts of souvenirs Lewis and Clark sent to President Jefferson from their expedition, and where you can order White House Christmas decorations. There are games and activities for many age groups; all contain fascinating facts. Don't miss the Learning Center for K–12 with lesson plans, activities, and other resources to help everyone learn more about the world's most famous house.

http://www.whitehousehistory.org/

MIDDLE AGES
A Boke of Gode Cookery

Are you hungry for a trencher of *Bruet Sarcenes*? Well, the recipe's here, so messe it forth. You'll find loads of historical fare to bring to the Medieval (or Renaissance) Faire, including a gingerbread recipe where ginger is optional! Further links from this page explore the Black Death and other timely topics.

http://www.godecookery.com/godeboke/godeboke.htm

A B C D E F G H I J K L M N O P Q R S T U V W X Y Z

A B C D E F G **H** I J K L M N O P Q R S T U V W X Y Z

Castle Learning Center

Learn about types of castles and the people who lived in them. Life was very hard and, well, damp, even in the summer. This site really gives you the feel of the Middle Ages (minus the smell). By the way, is there any truth to the rumor that the moats were filled with alligators? Visit this site to find out!

http://www.castles-of-britain.com/castle6.htm

Discovery Online - Black Death

Just follow the onscreen rat to explore the spread of plague, the "Black Death," in fourteenth-century Europe. Its source was plague-infested rats and fleas. Or, was it? Why did this disease spread so fast, and with such fury, during this time period? Both these pests had been common for centuries. Was this deadly disaster ultimately caused by ecological changes?

http://www.discovery.com/stories/history/blackdeath/
    blackdeath.html

Exploring Space

The NASA Ames Research Center says this site is "As close as you can get without being a rocket scientist!" Click on Pressure Girl to explore air pressure in different earthly environments plus several that are out of this world! Not to be outdone, Gravity Boy shows off his jumping skills on Earth, the Moon, and Mars. Speaking of Mars, don't miss the Mars Virtual Landing Site's virtual reality panoramas. (Spot any Martians? Call NASA!) You can also try the Lunar prospector simulation and maneuver the craft into orbit around the Moon. (Hint: attend the "Mission Briefing" session before launch (or dinner).

http://www.exploringspace.arc.nasa.gov/

Expect a miracle in RELIGION AND SPIRITUALITY!

End of Europe's Middle Ages

If you need something for your homework paper that's a little more complex than knights and castles, try this site. It traces the development of medieval language, literature, and music, among other topics. You'll also learn about the changes in the feudal system, marvel at the reach of the Holy Roman Empire, and discover why people were so afraid of the Ottoman Turks.

http://www.ucalgary.ca/HIST/tutor/endmiddle/

★ Ghosts in the Castle!

Wouldn't it be neat to live in a castle? Here's your chance to explore one built in Britain in the 1300s! We took the virtual tour and met a lot of really neat people who were there to protect us, the castle owners. James, the archer, was one. He claims to be able to shoot a steel-tipped arrow more than 100 yards! With a few carefully placed clicks of your mouse, you will be transported through this marvelous place. Watch for the ghosts, though.

http://www.nationalgeographic.com/features/97/
    castles/enter.html

Journey Through the Middle Ages

On your quest to rise from a squire to a knight you'll have to solve puzzles and answer questions relating to medieval history and castle life. The answers are all within these Web pages, and never fear, because you'll have James the Jingling Jester to help you out with some clues. This site, created by kids, was a finalist in the 1998 ThinkQuest Junior contest.

http://tqjunior.thinkquest.org/4051/

Leaves of Gold

Creating a manuscript during the Middle Ages involved much more than drawing fancy letters on paper. Back then, manuscripts were written on vellum, a special paper made from animal hides. To make the ink, rocks, flowers, insects, and even animal bones were ground up and mixed with liquid. The finished product looks like the manuscripts on this site. Five major types of medieval manuscripts are shown. You can also create your own manuscript. But you don't need to buy vellum or have good penwork—just Shockwave and the ability to click a mouse button.

http://www.leavesofgold.org/

Medieval and Renaissance Instruments

Can you actually play a lizard? You can if it's a wind instrument from the Renaissance. Listen to its odd sound and learn about its history at this site. Check out more than 30 other medieval and later musical instruments and imagine yourself back in time.

http://www.s-hamilton.k12.ia.us/antiqua/instrumt.html

★ Medieval Women - An Interactive Exploration

For a woman, life in the Middle Ages was anything but the usual image of a damsel in distress being rescued by a knight in shining armor. A woman during these times was more likely to be a nun, or someone who cared for the sick and poor, or a mom, raising a family. At this site, you can explore the life and times of a young woman during the fifteenth century. The journey she will take you on is filled with colorful graphics, music, and video. There is a lot to explore. If you get lost, the Timeline section will set you straight.

http://mw.mcmaster.ca/intro.html

OPTICAL ILLUSIONS: now you see them, now you don't!

NET FILES

What famous event occurred in 1989, marking the end of the Cold War?

(Hint: it attracted a huge flock of "wall woodpeckers.")

Answer: The demolition of the Berlin Wall, dividing East and West Germany. Many people chiseled off pieces as souvenirs. With all their tapping, they were called "wall woodpeckers"! Learn more here:
http://www.coldwar.org/articles/80s/fall_berlin_wall.html

The Middle Ages

We think of Camelot and King Arthur, brave knights and beautiful ladies, wily wizards and comical jesters—but what were the Middle Ages really like? This site aims to give you a complete look at the age of feudalism, with both its diamonds and fleas. Check out sections on clothing, housing, town life, arts, health, and religion. This is a resource from the Annenberg/CPB Projects Exhibits Collection.

http://www.learner.org/exhibits/middleages/

NOVA Online - Secrets of Lost Empires - Medieval Siege

Get a glimpse of life inside a medieval castle, and discover who had the most important job (it's not who you'd think). How were castles defended in battle and what weapons and siege methods were in common use? Ever heard of a trebuchet? That's a big catapult used to try and destroy a castle's fortifications. Can one be built today? You'll find out at this site, which also challenges you to try a game called Destroy the Castle. See if you can aim the catapult just right.

http://www.pbs.org/wgbh/nova/lostempires/trebuchet/

A B C D E F G H I J K L M N O P Q R S T U V W X Y Z

Regia Anglorum - Anglo-Saxon, Viking, Norman and British Living

Visit the tenth century in the village of Wichamstow, where the Vikings and Anglo-Saxons are still fighting it out. Hear a story or two from the local bard, then play a game of Nine Men's Morris at the tavern. Riddling was also a form of entertainment in those times before TV. Can you guess the answers to the riddles posed at this site?

http://www.regia.org/

RENAISSANCE

Elizabethan Costuming Page

Don't be caught by the Elizabethan fashion police! If you don't know your kirtle from your farthingale, better bone up here. There are pattern generators, pictures, reviews of commercially available patterns, and advice for everyone from theater costumers to those who just want to fit in at a Renaissance Faire.

http://www.dnaco.net/~aleed/corsets/

Life in Elizabethan England: A Compendium of Common Knowledge

What's "common knowledge" today? That's easy. Things we all know about without even thinking, such as how many pennies are in a dollar, what bread looks (and tastes) like, and what subjects are usually taught in school. But it wasn't always like this. Common knowledge now wouldn't serve us at all if we were suddenly transported back to Elizabethan times. See what's alike, and what's different, at this most interesting site.

http://renaissance.dm.net/compendium/home.html

The Renaissance

When you think about the Renaissance, you might think of famous painters, or gothic cathedrals, or maybe well-known composers. But beyond that, we have a flat picture of that period of history. This site adds new dimensions to our view with information on exploration and trade, printing and thinking, art, architecture, and music. There is also a special feature on Florence, Italy. This is a resource from the Annenberg/CPB Projects Exhibits Collection.

http://www.learner.org/exhibits/renaissance/

Shrewsbury Renaissance Faire

Art thou off to the faire? Don't forget your Renaissance-era costume and your muffin hat (you can learn to make one here). Yum, those gingerbread cookies look good! Care for some fried "dragon scales"? Look in the Historical References section to find out what your U.S. currency is worth in Elizabethan English pounds. See what goes into a reenactment of a sixteenth-century Welsh village—this one is located near Corvallis, Oregon. You can check *<http://www.faire.net/SCRIBE/>* to find a Renfest near you. Remember to learn history by playing faire, anon!

http://www.shrewfaire.com/

Virtual Renaissance

Built by a class in Buffalo Grove, Illinois, for the ThinkQuest competition, this site allows you to visit such historic locales as the Globe Theater, the Sistine Chapel, and the Tower of London, among others. You'll learn about the sites from people of the Renaissance as they tell of medical knowledge, art techniques, and even games of the times. There are also links to more Renaissance materials around the Web.

http://www.twingroves.district96.k12.il.us/
Renaissance/VirtualRen.html

U.S. HISTORY

See also AFRICAN AMERICANS—HISTORY; PEOPLE AND BIOGRAPHIES; U.S. PRESIDENTS AND FIRST LADIES

★ America's Library

Pick any American time period between 1492 and the present and find out who was hot, what events people talked about, and what they did for fun. You can "meet" some fascinating famous Americans, too: real characters like magician Harry Houdini as well as scientists like Thomas Alva Edison. Don't miss the scavenger hunt game. There are also multimedia animations and sound files, plus interactive quizzes around every bend of this wonderful site from the Library of Congress.

http://www.americaslibrary.gov/

Earthquakes are only part of what's shakin' in EARTH SCIENCE.

American Memory from the Library of Congress

You have memories of your own life. Your parents have memories of their lives, and your grandparents have memories of theirs. Wouldn't it be great to find a place to archive all those memories, so they wouldn't be lost when someone died? You could call it the American Memory Project! Look no further. Browse through 25,000 turn-of-the-century postcards; maybe some are from your hometown. Go to the Collection Finder and look in the Photos and Prints Division under "Turn-of-the-Century-America—Detroit Publishing Company" (show this to your parents—they will love it). Check old movies of New York City made by Edison himself in 1903. Look into the eyes of the immigrants coming to America—so much hope is expressed there. The historical periods covered are from the Civil War to the present. Each collection is annotated, and broad topics are listed. This is an excellent source for students looking for sound recordings, movies, and other nonprint sources to accompany an American history report. Don't forget to remember American Memory.

http://rs6.loc.gov/amhome.html

★ A Biography of America

The biography of this country stretches back 30,000 years, to when Stone Age hunters migrated from Siberia to Alaska. Can you name the country? Hint: the Mississippi River runs through it. If you didn't say America, then visit this site. It is the Web version of a PBS television series that traces the history of America through 26 major time periods. Loaded with facts, dates, pictures, maps, and narratives, this site has it all.

http://www.learner.org/biographyofamerica/

Going, Going, Gone - The Way Things Used to Be

Have you ever had to make your own soap? In the old days, that's what they did. People saved scraps of fat until they had enough, and then cooked the fat until it was melted and smooth. Folks saved ashes too, and they poured water over them to release the lye. Then they added the lye water to the rendered fat. They cooked and stirred for several more hours, and the soap was then poured out into molds and left to harden. Those days are gone, because now we all buy scented soap in the store. What other things are different now than they used to be? Check out a fascinating list of them here.

http://library.thinkquest.org/3205/

NET FILES

Did you know that sunspots rotate around the Sun? How long does a sunspot take to go completely around and get back to where it started?

Answer:
A sunspot takes about 27 days to rotate around the Sun's surface. Read all about sunspots at http://www.sel.noaa.gov/primer/primer.html

A B C D E F G H I J K L M N O P Q R S T U V W X Y Z

A
B
C
D
E
F
G
H
I
J
K
L
M
N
O
P
Q
R
S
T
U
V
W
X
Y
Z

The History of the United States Postal Service 1775–1993

The Continental Congress named Benjamin Franklin the first postmaster general in 1775. The mail was critical to government matters, as well as to the growth of commerce. It was also fun to get a letter that would offer a new job, pledge a betrothal, or just say hi. The history of the U.S. postal service mirrors the development of the nation. Learn about the Pony Express, the rural free delivery program, and lots more at this site that leaves its own stamp on history.

http://www.usps.gov/history/his1.htm

Learning Adventures in Citizenship

A lot has been written about the history of New York City, and this site will tell you about it. But what about your city? Maybe you don't know much about its past. If you want to learn more, the online resources listed here will help you piece together your hometown's history. They're indexed by state, making them easy to find. You can also learn how to become a more active citizen in your community. The site shows you how to identify a problem and create a solution. Submit it, and you just might see it featured on the site.

http://www.pbs.org/wnet/newyork/laic/

★ Tenement Museum

What do you think an "urban log cabin" would be like? The Lower East Side Tenement Museum thinks it has a pretty good idea. They say that between the years 1870 and 1915, over 10,000 people moved in and out of the apartments at 97 Orchard Street in New York City. This building was abandoned in 1935 and boarded up until 1987. When it was reopened, it was like stepping into a time machine. Everything was as it had been left in 1935. See what was found in the rooms and what has been excavated in the courtyard. Click on the windows in the virtual tenement house to meet some of the residents and learn their stories. Touch the wall and click through 13 layers of wallpaper!

http://www.wnet.org/archive/tenement/

Today in History

Going far beyond other "Today in History" sites, the Library of Congress illustrates today's historical happenings with posters, photos, and other memorabilia from their collections. What happened on your birthday? Type in the date to find out.

http://lcweb2.loc.gov/ammem/today/archive.html

Within These Walls

If the walls in your house could talk, what would they reveal about its history? Who were its owners? This site will show you how to become a house detective and discover the names of your home's former owners, the year it was built, and how it was changed. If you don't think your house has much to say, explore the stories of five families who lived in a house from Ispwich, Massachusetts, over the course of 200 years. It may change your mind.

http://www.americanhistory.si.edu/house/

U.S. HISTORY—1500S

Roanoke: A Mystery in History

This 1998 ThinkQuest Junior finalist explores the lost colony of Roanoke Island, in what is now North Carolina. In 1586 it was a tiny garrison of 15 men, but it was later found abandoned in July of 1587. One mysterious human skeleton was found on the beach, but no other trace was found. Ninety-one men, women, and children arrived from England and started fixing up the fort so they could live in it. They had the beginnings of a thriving settlement and had begun to make friends with the Native Americans. In August, some of the colonists went back to England for more supplies. Because England was at war with Spain, no ships could be spared to resupply Roanoke until three years later. When the search party arrived in 1590, no one could be found, although a large fire blazed on the north end of the island. Where did the colonists go? Examine some of the theories at this site, and see what seems believable to you.

http://tqjunior.thinkquest.org/3826/

Be swampwise in EARTH SCIENCE.

U.S. HISTORY—1600S

Discovery Online - A Village Possessed: A True Story of Witchcraft

In 1692, the Massachusetts community of Salem was torn apart by accusations of witchcraft. Hysterical girls had uncontrollable "fitts," and they and their families pointed fingers of blame at innocent citizens, charging them with spellcraft and laying curses on the girls. Read about the history of these events at this site. The witchcraft trials eventually took 25 lives.

http://www.discovery.com/stories/history/witches/witches.html

Mayflower Web Pages

In 1620, the *Mayflower* set off on a 66-day voyage from England to the New World. At least 30 of the passengers were under age 17. The kids on board got into all sorts of trouble, which was recounted in journals of the time. Read about it at this site: one of the boys shot off a gun and set part of the ship on fire! By the way, boys and girls wore almost the same type of clothes—long dresslike garments! At this well-researched page, you'll also find historical information, books and journals by the Pilgrims, myths about the *Mayflower*, and all sorts of details about the voyage.

http://members.aol.com/calebj/mayflower.html

Plimoth-on-Web

Take a virtual tour of "Plimoth Plantation." In this living history museum, all the employees dress and act as Pilgrims would have in 1627. Visit the re-created village and farm site, learn about the voyage of the Mayflower, find out about seventeenth-century shoemaking, Thanksgiving, and lots more.

http://www.plimoth.org/

Salem Witchcraft Hysteria

Parental advisory: Please preview this site. It allows you to experience a simulated yet frightening witchcraft trial. The way to survive it is chilling. This National Geographic site is realistic and not for the sensitive.

http://www.nationalgeographic.com/salem/

U.S. HISTORY—1700S

The Birth of a Nation

This site won the social science division in the 1998 ThinkQuest Junior contest. You can learn all about the events of April 18–19, 1775. You remember, that's when Paul Revere rode to warn the countryside that "the British are coming!" If you're not up to speed on the Minutemen, this site will give you an overview of the important names, places, and deeds. There's also a neat game on daily eighteenth-century wear for men, women, and kids. You can mix and match parts of the photos and try to come up with a complete historical costume.

http://tqjunior.thinkquest.org/3803/

How to Love Your Dog: A Kid's Guide to Dog Care

Wondering if dog ownership is for you? Study this site. It covers everything: what dogs cost, what various breeds of dogs are like, and how to train the new puppy. Getting a dog is a big responsibility. You will care for your pet for many years to come. Are you ready for that? If so, print out the I Love My Dog contract here, and sign it. Show the contract to your dog. He or she will be very, very impressed.
http://www.geocities.com/~kidsanddogs/

A
B
C
D
E
F
G
H
I
J
K
L
M
N
O
P
Q
R
S
T
U
V
W
X
Y
Z

A
B
C
D
E
F
G
H
I
J
K
L
M
N
O
P
Q
R
S
T
U
V
W
X
Y
Z

★ A Colonial Family and Community

Meet the Daggetts, your typical colonial family living on a farm in eighteenth-century Connecticut. But Sam Daggett did other things besides farm. Look through his account book to see what other jobs he did. View QuickTime movies of family life in the household and on the farm. You'll learn about making maple sugar, socializing at spinning sessions, colonial church services, and militia musters. Visit all the places on the map and find the clues to answer all the questions; then try the "what's wrong with this picture" puzzles. (Hint: There were no Pop-tarts in the eighteenth century!)

http://www.hfmgv.org/smartfun/colonial/intro/

Colonial Kids

What did colonial-era kids do once their chores were finished? They wrote Web pages! Wait, no, that's not right. This site was created by students for the ThinkQuest Junior competition. And they played colonial kids on the Web. We get it now. Scroll through Aunt Abigail's cookbook (the pumpkin soup looks yummy), then stop by Ye Olde Colonial Crafts to learn how to dip a candle and how to make a sweetly scented pomander ball. Don't miss the barn tour. The place may look old, but as the kids say, "it's very stable."

http://library.thinkquest.org/J002611F/

Colonial Williamsburg Foundation

What would it be like to be suddenly transported back in time to the 1700s? For fun, you would play cards and board games, or you'd work at puzzles; outside, you would roll hoops, walk on stilts, and play a rousing game of ninepins bowling. What kinds of foods would you eat? How would people behave—are manners the same now as they were back then? What kind of job would you have? Experience the eighteenth century by visiting this site. Colonial Williamsburg is a living history museum in Virginia, where the people dress and act as if they were living in colonial times. They have to know a lot about history to do that, and some kids work at the museum, playing the roles of kids back in the 1700s. This is a great site to learn how people lived in early times in America.

http://www.history.org/

★ You Be the Historian

This site invites you to find out all you can about an American family's life in the 1700s. By examining artifacts and documents at this site you may be able to get a fairly good picture of what life was like for Thomas and Elizabeth Springer's family in New Castle, Delaware, 200 years ago. Compare your guesses to what historians have concluded. What could future archaeologists and historians learn about your family from what's on the floor of your closet, under your bed, or in your trash?

http://americanhistory.si.edu/hohr/springer/

U.S. HISTORY—1700S—REVOLUTIONARY WAR
The American Revolution Home Page

Explore a time line of the events leading up to the American Revolution, the War itself, and the aftermath. Learn about famous Americans such as Samuel Adams, Molly Pitcher, and James Lafayette. In the interest of equal time, you can also read about well-known British as well as American generals.

http://www.dell.homestead.com/revwar/files/INDEX.HTM

Liberty! The American Revolution

Visit this PBS site for a time line of the Revolution from 1760—when King George ascended the throne in England—to 1791, when the Bill of Rights was passed by the first American Congress. Read The Chronicle of the Revolution, with its "newspaper" accounts of the events of the times. There is information on a colonist's daily life, as well as that of both a British and a colonial soldier. There's also a quiz game called The Road to Revolution you can try, but make sure you do some reading at this site first.

http://www.pbs.org/ktca/liberty/

Watch your steps in DANCE.

The Revolutionary War: A Journey Towards Freedom

The Infopedia has it all. Take a virtual tour of Washington's headquarters at Valley Forge. Check a history of the American flag. There are even some colonial recipes: Yankee pot roast—yum! There are some neat games, too. Answer the questions quickly in order to move Paul Revere forward to warn the colonists. Otherwise, the British will win! This site was created by students for the ThinkQuest competition.

http://library.thinkquest.org/10966/

U.S. HISTORY—1800S

Erie Canal Online

As this site says, "The Erie Canal was the superhighway of pre-Civil War America." It allowed boats to go from the New York City harbor quite a way west, as far as the Great Lakes. This helped open up western development, and it spawned a great hit song, too. Hear it at this site, where you can also follow the story of a young girl as she travels the canal and learns about life on it and along its banks.

http://www.syracuse.com/features/eriecanal/

Old Sturbridge Village

Do you think it would be fun to live in the past? Why not visit the nineteenth century and see how you like it? You can experience the sights and sounds of this re-created New England village by taking a virtual visit. Let's visit the blacksmith shop—can you hear the clang of the hammer on the anvil? Listen for the team of horses pulling a sleigh. Why not stroll over to the confectionery shop for some horehound drops or rock candy? Got a question? Ask Jack in the Kids area. There are puzzles in that section, too. If you visit the real Sturbridge Village in Massachusetts, you'll find a fascinating living history museum, where all the kids and other villagers dress, talk, and act like they are living in 1830.

http://www.osv.org/

World's Columbian Exposition: Idea, Experience, Aftermath

Back in 1893, a wonderful fair took place in Chicago, Illinois, and it was called the Columbian Exposition. It introduced the American public to the wonders of the day: electric lights, the cotton gin, typewriters, and all manner of nineteenth-century technology. It was also the first appearance of food products we know so well today: carbonated soda, hamburgers, Juicy Fruit gum, Cracker Jack, and Aunt Jemima syrup, among many others. There were strange displays, too, such as a map of the United States "made entirely of pickles" and "not one, but two Liberty Bell models—one in wheat, oats, and rye, and one entirely in oranges." Take a virtual visit to the past here! Click on Legacy and learn how it has influenced places such as Disney World. Find out which famous composer wrote a piece in honor of the Exposition and learn even more as you explore this site.

http://xroads.virginia.edu/~MA96/WCE/title.html

Why is the left side of a boat called the "port" side?

Answer: According to BoatsafeKids.com, no one really knows. However, the other side of a boat—the right side—is called the "starboard" side. Before the invention of rudders, boats were steered by use of a steering board that hung over the right side of the ship. Only the left side remained free of obstruction with the ability to tie up to the dock when coming into the seaport, or "port." http://boatsafe.com/kids/portkidsques.htm

U.S. HISTORY—1800S—CIVIL WAR

Army Hardtack Recipe

Also known as "sheet iron" and "teeth dullers," hardtack was the staple food of Civil War soldiers. Want to try some? You can't get it at the store, you'll have to make it yourself. If you have a taste for history, here's the recipe.

http://www.hevanet.com/1860colt/hardtack.html

The Battle of Gettysburg

How did the war begin? Who were the participants and what were the most important battles? This heavily illustrated site will help further your understanding of the Civil War as you follow along day by day. Numerous quotes from primary sources help give you a clear picture of the events. In the Aftermath section there are photographs of war casualties, and this section is not for the sensitive. This site was created by students for the ThinkQuest competition.

http://library.thinkquest.org/17525/

The Battle of Gettysburg: The Turning Point of the Civil War

It was the turning point of the Civil War: on July 1, 2, and 3, 1863, at Gettysburg, Pennsylvania, more men fought and died than in any other battle on North American soil. A total of 51,000 were killed or wounded. Today, the battlefield is a national military park, with over 1,000 monuments. Follow the maps of the battles and explore other Civil War links from this site.

http://www.800padutch.com/gbgbattle.html

★ Behind the Stonewall - 360 Degree Panoramic Images from Civil War Battlefields

If you're having trouble visualizing the battlefields and the strategic advantages gained or lost, visit this site. You'll be treated to a 360-degree panoramic image of each location. More than 100 Civil War sites have been mapped in this way. Some of them contain detailed descriptions to put the view into historical perspective.

http://www.jatruck.com/stonewall/

★ Camp Life: Begin Your Tour

Between the excitement of battle, there was a lot of waiting around back in camp to do. What was it like? How did soldiers pass the time? Find out in this heavily illustrated National Park Service site. Try not to miss the authentic lice comb.

http://www.cr.nps.gov/csd/gettex/

Early Victrola Recordings of Civil War Music

Listen to some of the tunes Civil War troops probably sang around the campfires as they dipped their hardtack in their coffee mugs and prayed for the war to end.

http://www.earlyrecordings.com/civilwar.html

U.S. HISTORY—1800S—WESTWARD EXPANSION

See also BOOKS AND LITERATURE—CLASSICS

Adventures of Wells Fargo - Original Information Superhighway

These days, you can hop on a jet plane and travel the width of the U.S. from coast to coast in five or six hours. In the 1800s, however, there were no planes, so people traveled as far as they could by rail, ship, and other transportation, and then made the rest of the trip by a bouncy overland stagecoach pulled by a team of horses. They often began their stagecoach journey from places halfway across the country, such as St. Louis, Missouri. The trip from St. Louis to San Francisco, California, generally took about 24 days! Wells Fargo was one of the companies to offer this form of travel, and they present some maps, stories, and tall tales about it all here.

http://www.wellsfargo.com/about/stories/ch11.jhtml

Be an angel and check what we've found in RELIGION AND SPIRITUALITY.

America's West - Development and History

Return with us now to the days of yesteryear—of gold rush and ghost town, the heyday of cowboy and gunslinger. At this site, you'll discover links to information on America's westward expansion, famous Western trails, pioneers, and trappers, and biographies of Kit Carson, Davy Crockett, Daniel Boone, Billy the Kid, Sitting Bull, Roy Rogers, and lots of famous folks in between. There are links to movies about the West, as well as to Western theme parks and dude ranches. A caution to parents: not all the outbound links have been reviewed.

http://www.americanwest.com/index2.htm

The American Experience - WayBack - Gold Rush

After gold was discovered in 1848 in California's American River, the news traveled slowly. The great influx of people didn't get there until 1849—another name for the gold-seekers was the forty-niners. Find out about the "affliction" known as gold fever, the various routes to the gold fields (getting there was no picnic), and what happened when the would-be miners finally arrived. Meet famous people from the gold rush era, and (in the Joke Space) discover how hard it is to make up humor about this period of history.

http://www.pbs.org/wgbh/amex/kids/goldrush/

Bannock Recipe

Bannock, cooked over an open campfire, was a staple food of settlers and those on the move. It's also good eating for scouts and family campfire cooking. This site also explains how to bake it in your oven.

Http://www.melborponsti.com/speirs/cooking/
  bannock.htm

By the Great Horn Spoon! A Gold Rush Adventure

Based on the Sid Fleischman book, this site was created for the ThinkQuest Tomorrow's Teacher's contest. Tag along with a young boy and his butler on their sea voyage around the tip of South America. They are enroute to the gold fields of California! Along the way you'll find quizzes, facts, trivia, and even some music to listen to while you explore various aspects of the journey, the city of San Francisco, and "the diggin's."

http://library.thinkquest.org/50048/

A Science Odyssey

Just visit this site. You will not be disappointed. Check out the Shockwave simulations in the You Try It section. In the Technology at Home area, scroll through the decades of the twentieth century and see what changes in the living room and kitchen. Old iceboxes disappear, to be replaced by modern refrigerators. Telephone equipment improves—what else will you notice? You can mouse over each item and see some facts about it: what it is, who invented it, and when it came into vogue or went out of style. Now try the other explorations: human evolution, radio transmission, probe the brain, atomic structure, and several more. When you get done with those, read the On the Edge comic books about various scientists and their discoveries. Did radio astronomer Jocelyn Bell really think she received a message from little green men in outer space? Find out here. Don't miss the hit game show That's My Theory! You can question the three contestants to see which one is the real Einstein, the real Freud, and the real ENIAC. http://www.pbs.org/wgbh/aso/

A B C D E F G H I J K L M N O P Q R S T U V W X Y Z

A B C D E F G H I J K L M N O P Q R S T U V W X Y Z

California Gold Rush at Oakland Museum of California

The California Gold Rush of 1849 was one of the most dramatic quests for gold. At this site, you can either read about the history of the Gold Rush, or take a virtual reality tour of it. Just get the QuickTime Virtual Reality plug-in, and get ready to view panoramic pictures of mines, mining towns, and objects used to find gold. You can also zoom in (or out) to take a closer look. For an audio and pictorial narrative, click on Stories of the Lure and the Legacy.

http://www.museumca.org/goldrush.html

Central Pacific Railroad Photographic History Museum

You can almost hear the ring of tools on the rails at this unique site. Stunning photos offer a rare glimpse into the effort that went into building the first U.S. railroad to link the East with the West. They are also all that remain of the United States' first transcontinental railroad. In 1942, the rails were taken up to support the war effort.

http://www.cprr.org/

NET FILES

What "carnivorous bear" isn't really a "bear" after all, and doesn't even eat meat?

Answer: The giant black-and-white pandas in China. Pandas actually belong to a subfamily of their own, closely related to raccoons. The panda has the digestive system of a carnivore, but long ago adapted to a vegetarian diet and now feeds almost entirely on the stems and leaves of bamboo in the forests of southwestern China.

http://www.panda.org/kids/wildlife/mnpanda.htm

Crossed the West: The Adventures of Lewis and Clark

In 1804, President Thomas Jefferson looked out the window and said, "Hmm, I wonder if there is a water route, maybe a river or something, that goes all the way across the continent and ends up at the Pacific Ocean? Something we could navigate with boats, so we could get supplies there, and settle, and eventually build theme parks." OK, so he didn't really say that. But he did want the West explored, and Lewis and Clark were just the guys to take on the task. Want to join their expedition and see what happens?

http://www.nationalgeographic.com/features/97/west/

Deer Creek School: Our Gold Country Community

This award-winning Web site commemorating the the discovery of gold in Nevada County, California, was produced by students who did extensive research, conducted interviews, and even visited a mine. Learn about placer, hydraulic, and hardrock mining. Read the exciting story of the Whopper, an 18-pound nugget found at a local mine. It made a class visit, and the kids photographed it. Using QuickTime VR, you can rotate it and examine it from all sides. See artwork and photos from the gold rush era. This site is a real gem!

http://www.ncgold.com/goldrushtown/

The Frontier House

Do you think you and your family would be able to survive 1880s life in the rugged West? Several families tried it during the summer of 2001 as part of a PBS documentary. They agreed to surrender their cell phones and modern clothes and wear only clothing from that period. They agreed to grow or find historically correct food, and contact the outside world only by mail or telegraph. Each family did have a sealed "emergency box" with a mobile radio for communications, a fire extinguisher, and bear pepper spray, among other things. How did they do? Visit this Web site to see!

http://www.pbs.org/wnet/frontierhouse/

If you feel funny,
think what we went through
when we wrote the JOKES
AND RIDDLES section!

The Gold Rush

The chances of striking it rich in California during the Gold Rush of 1849 were greatly improved if you could get there faster than your neighbor. That led to some weird contraptions. One was a "wind wagon." It was sort of a cross between a wagon and a sailboat that could barrel across the plains at 15 m.p.h. The prototype actually worked, but then it went out of control and crashed. That's some of the lesser-known history about the Gold Rush you can find at this site.

http://www.pbs.org/goldrush/

Gold Rush Sesquicentennial

The California gold rush began after gold was discovered at Sutter's Mill in January, 1848. It took over six months for the news to reach the east coast, and by then it was too late in the year to set out via wagon. Some took ships and went around the tip of South America. Others took a dugout canoe shortcut through the jungles and wetlands where the Panama Canal is today, but this route was dangerous and travelers often caught malaria and other diseases. Many waited until the following spring of 1849 and set off in overloaded wagons, heading for the gold fields. The sesquicentennial anniversary of the gold rush was celebrated in 1998, and the Sacramento paper provides a thorough Web site about it. Check out the travel section for information about where you just might find gold today!

http://www.sacbee.com/goldrush/

GORP - National Scenic Trails - National Historic Trails

Ever wondered if you could find any of the old pioneer routes, like the Oregon Trail? You can! To this day, some of the old wagon ruts are still visible, and you can walk in the footsteps of early settlers during the westward expansion of the United States. You'll find maps and detailed descriptions of the Oregon Trail, plus the following: Santa Fe Trail; Trail of Tears; Iditarod National Historic Trail; Juan Bautista de Anza National Historic Trail; Lewis and Clark National Historic Trail; Mormon Pioneer National Historic Trail; Nez Perce National Historic Trail; and the Overmountain Victory National Historic Trail.

http://www.gorp.com/gorp/resource/us_trail/
historic.htm

New Perspectives on the West

This is a companion site to the eight-part PBS television series *The West*. It is a history of the expansion of the American West, and we are including it because of the richness of its information about people, places, and events during the westward expansion. Whether you need information about Great Salt Lake or a photo of George Armstrong Custer, this is the right place.

http://www.pbs.org/weta/thewest/

★ Pioneers

This beautifully illustrated site was a finalist in the 1999 ThinkQuest Junior competition. It answers the questions you may have about who the pioneers were, why they went west, where they traveled to, and what trails they used to get there. You'll be interested to find out what they took with them and what life was like along the route of the wagon trains. Look for the directions for making a "whimmydiddle"—a popular trail toy. They are in the Pioneer Pastimes section.

http://tqjunior.thinkquest.org/6400/

A
B
C
D
E
F
G
H
I
J
K
L
M
N
O
P
Q
R
S
T
U
V
W
X
Y
Z

2GOOD
2MISS

The British Monarchy

This is the official Web site of the British monarchy. Here you will learn about the monarchy as it exists today, as well as its historic past. You'll visit the palaces and the Crown Jewels, and follow along on a typical day in the life of Her Royal Highness. You'll even find out why Elizabeth II keeps corgis as pets! There is also a special section on the life of Diana, Princess of Wales.
http://www.royal.gov.uk/

Women of the West Museum

Be sure to visit the online exhibit "There are no Renters Here" and follow the story of one Nebraska farm family and their lives in a prairie sod house. Read letters and diary entries to learn about one year's incredible crop of watermelons and find out what families used for fuel. (Hint: Buffalo chips aren't something you eat.)

http://www.wowmuseum.org/gallery/sod/

U.S. HISTORY—1900S

Alameda County Library - Doing the Decades Report

Did your teacher assign you "The Decades Report"? You know the one. You need to find out everything you can about, say, the '50s. Don't despair. A California librarian has put together a series of Web sites to help. He's got six sites on the '50s alone! You'll find what you need arranged by decade, and don't forget to take a look at the sites covering more than one time period.

http://www.aclibrary.org/teenroom/1900s.asp

★ American Cultural History - The Twentieth Century

Parental advisory: Please preview this site. Try this excellent resource when you have an assignment about a particular decade and don't know where to turn to find information on "the music of the 1920s" or "the fads of the 1960s." There are also many links and recommended books should you need further information. (Note: each decade takes a while to load, so be patient.)

http://www.nhmccd.edu/contracts/lrc/kc/ decades.html

Dynamo's History

One hundred years ago, people lived a lot differently than they do now. For one thing, there was no electricity, only gas or oil lamps. For another, well, you'll have to visit this site to find out. Come along with Gleep the alien and his friend Josie the Earthling as they step back in time to discover how people lived. This interactive adventure shows what Josie's house would have looked like in 1900. You can be sure that there weren't any CDs, computers, or microwave ovens.

http://www.bbc.co.uk/education/dynamo/history/

The Learning Channel - Countdown 100

Prominent historians were asked what 100 achievements were the most important of the twentieth century. Their answers are presented by decade. In the 1900s, the consumer-oriented Brownie camera was a big deal, as were the development of motion pictures and the Wright Brothers' airplane. By the 1930s, synthetic fibers like nylon were all the rage, and labor unions began to exert their collective bargaining powers. What other achievements are on the list? Stop in and see.

http://tlc.discovery.com/tlcpages/countdown100/ countdown100.html

Wolves are a howl in MAMMALS.

★ A Science Odyssey: You Try It: Technology at Home

This Shockwave application isn't really a game, although it is a lot of fun. Scroll through the decades of the twentieth century and watch how technology changes in the kitchen and living room. Oops! There goes the refrigerator. Hey, look at that goofy phone. Roll your cursor over each item to get more information about what it is. Ever seen a superheterodyne radio?

http://www.pbs.org/wgbh/aso/tryit/tech/

★ TIME 100: 1900 vs. Now

It's hard to imagine what the year 1900 was like, so this site offers a way to compare the then of yesteryear to the now of today. Back in 1900, 1 in 7 homes had a bathtub, 1 in 13 had a telephone, and a pound of sugar cost 4 cents. Now a pound of sugar is 43 cents, 20 percent of the U.S. is connected to the Internet, and a lot more of us are able to take a bath any time we want. The average weekly wage was $9.70 and now that figure is $435.00. Compare statistics in the U.S. and around the world at this thought-provoking site. Don't forget to visit other parts of this resource, such as The Most Important People of the 20th Century (click on Time 100 Poll).

http://www.pathfinder.com/time/time100/timewarp/timewarp.html

U.S. HISTORY—1900–1909

The 1900 House

What happens when a modern family moves into a house outfitted with state-of-the-art conveniences—for the year 1900? No TV, no microwave—no Internet! Find out at this companion site for the PBS series.

http://www.pbs.org/wnet/1900house/

The Old Timer's Page

Making butter, soap, or bread—how was it done in the "old days"? Find out at this site, which is a collection of memories and reminiscences of everything from the ice house to the outhouse.

http://www.waltonfeed.com/old/

★ Technology in 1900

You know how much technology affects your life now, what with telephones, television, computers, and other things you take for granted. What about kids living 100 years ago? What was considered high tech back then? According to this site, kids would have been drooling to get their hands on a phonograph record! And electricity really hadn't even made its way to many places yet. What predictions did people make for the future? How many of them have come true? Why did phone companies stop using boys as operators and start hiring girls instead? The answer may surprise you.

http://www.pbs.org/wgbh/amex/kids/tech1900/

U.S. HISTORY—1910–1919

★ Old Time Victrola Music on Cassette Early 1900s Recordings

These old recordings give you an idea what turn-of-the-century teens tapped their feet to. Besides popular tunes, you'll hear recordings of Sousa marches, W.W.I songs, early bluegrass, and even an old-time musical exercise program. Watch out, Richard Simmons! This is sweating to the real oldies.

http://www.earlyrecordings.com/

World War I - Trenches on the Web

Anyone who can view all the material on this site deserves at least three college history credits. This "work in progress" is packed with articles, pictures, artwork, music, time lines, and more. Follow a trail of links to discover something—or someone—new about the what, who, when, and where of W.W.I. A good starting point is the Special Features section at <http://www.worldwar1.com/sfguide.htm>. It offers several guided tours of this site.

http://www.worldwar1.com/

Have you written to your PEN PALS lately?

A
B
C
D
E
F
G
H
I
J
K
L
M
N
O
P
Q
R
S
T
U
V
W
X
Y
Z

World War Web: A World War I History Site

World War I (1914–1918) had far-reaching social, political, and economic effects. Click on Biographies and read about 12 major figures in World War I, from the principal world leaders to fighter pilots Eddie Rickenbacker (U.S.) and Raoul Lufbery (France). Check the Armory to see the weapons, aircraft, land units, and naval units on both sides. Find out how the war started and what were its outcomes. There's also a Shockwave game and links for further exploration. This site was created by students for the ThinkQuest competition.

http://library.thinkquest.org/12367/

U.S. HISTORY—1920–1929

Edison Recordings

Lend your ear to this site, and you're in for a treat. You'll get to hear the earliest phonograph recordings of tunes and spoken words, as well as some popular musical hits of the '20s. A sampling of the sound files includes an 1888 recording of Thomas Edison's voice and a 1927 sound recording of "Mary Had a Little Lamb," as well as the "Jazz de Luxe-fox trot."

http://www.pbs.org/wgbh/amex/edison/sfeature/
   songs.html

Flapper Station

Parental advisory: Please preview this site. It is the bee's knees. Now we're not thinking you're a pushover or giving you a line; everything is Jake. If you have no idea what we mean, you need to visit the 1920s slang area of this fun historical site. You'll also find info on Prohibition, trends, trains, cars, music, and much more.

http://home.earthlink.net/~rbotti/

Roaring 1920s Concert Extravaganza

Before television, people gathered around the radio to listen to live concerts from distant places. This popular form of entertainment is re-created here, as you listen to minute-long sound files from such 1920s artists as Al Jolson, Maurice Chevalier, Fanny Brice, and Helen Kane, "the Boop Boop A Doop Girl."

http://bestwebs.com/roaring1920/

Let balloonists take you to new heights in AVIATION AND AIRPLANES.

U.S. HISTORY—1930–1939

★ 1930s Front Page

Created for the American Studies Program at the University of Virginia, this site offers a window to the complexities of the 1930s. It was a decade of crushing economic depression set against the hope of the modern age's dawn. Visit sections on film, print media, and art. Don't miss the audio archive of vintage radio programs.

http://xroads.virginia.edu/~1930s/front.html

The 1939-40 New York World's Fair

Come on, let's visit the 1939 World's Fair, in Flushing Meadows, New York. Look, it's the big ball and tower known as the Trylon and Perisphere. That's supposed to symbolize purity of form in the world of tomorrow. Hey, it says here you can go inside and see the future! There are loads of illustrations and lots of information. Sounds good—let's get a lemonade first though; it sure is hot!

http://xroads.virginia.edu/~1930s/DISPLAY/39wf/
   front.htm

The American Experience - Riding the Rails

It was a hard time to be a teenager in the 1930s. There was widespread poverty and many troubled families. Over 250,000 teens ran away from home, looking for better lives. Unfortunately, life on the road was often more desperate and lonely than the lives they left. Although it was dangerous and illegal, many crisscrossed the country by hopping the freight trains of the time. These "kids" are now senior citizens, and they told their stories for a PBS television program. You can read them at this site.

http://www.pbs.org/wgbh/amex/rails/

A B C D E F G H I J K L M N O P Q R S T U V W X Y Z

The American Experience - Surviving the Dust Bowl

The dust storms during the 1930s were horrendous. People thought the world was at an end. Being inside was the safest, but dust sifted in behind closed doors, getting into the dishes, glassware, food, and water. The people of Kansas were being pelted with the landscape of Oklahoma and even Texas. When the dust storm was over, people found their homes and farms buried. A reporter called it the "Dust Bowl." Although some left for better lives elsewhere, others stayed on waiting for the rains to come. They would wait five years. Why was there so much dust? Blame it on the wheat production for World War I. Farmers plowed under the intricate weave of prairie grasses in their zeal to increase food production to help win the war. After the harvest, and without the roots of those grasses, nothing could hold the dry soil in place. Could it happen again?

Http://www.pbs.org/wgbh/amex/dustbowl/

The Day of the Black Blizzard

"To talk about April the 14th, 1935 . . . it was a beautiful clear Sunday afternoon, and I was out skipping rocks on the horse pond," recalls Harley "Doc" Holladay. Although the temperature was 90 degrees that Palm Sunday, over a few hours it dropped more than 50 degrees. Suddenly, a "black as coal" cloud of dust rolled into town. People couldn't see to cross the street. You couldn't walk anywhere because the flying sand and dirt would sting your face and legs. Be sure to listen to the audio files of people who lived through this event.

http://www.discovery.com/area/history/dustbowl/ dustbowl1.1.html

What did grandma do when she was a kid? There is a list of questions to ask in GENEALOGY AND FAMILY HISTORY.

New Deal Network

As America struggled to get back on its economic feet after the Great Depression, President Franklin Delano Roosevelt announced the New Deal during the presidential race of 1932. It pledged many new government projects to increase financial stability and help along social reform. Remember, one out of four people was unemployed at this time, and many schools had to close because they didn't have the funds to stay open. Poor children wrote to the president's wife, Eleanor Roosevelt, and begged her for cast-off clothing for themselves and their parents. Read some of the children's letters, and Mrs. Roosevelt's responses, at this site. You'll also learn about the CCC (Civilian Conservation Corps) camps and the TVA (Tennessee Valley Authority) water projects, which brought affordable electricity to many Americans for the first time.

http://newdeal.feri.org/

NET FILES

What do Gerald Ford, Ronald Reagan, George Bush, and Bill Clinton all have in common (besides the fact that they have all been U.S. presidents)?

Answer: They are all left-handed! Find out more about famous lefties at http://www.indiana.edu/~primate/left.html

A
B
C
D
E
F
G
H
I
J
K
L
M
N
O
P
Q
R
S
T
U
V
W
X
Y
Z

NET FILES

What country "spans 11 time zones, 2 continents, and comes within 50 miles of North America"?

Answer: Russia, of course! The Official Guide to Russia ought to know, and it will show you more at http://www.interknowledge.com/russia/

WPA Life Histories

In the late 1930s, Federal Work Project Administration writers were employed to go around and collect "life histories" of Americans in order to preserve folklore and memories of the past. Reports from over 20 states are online for your reading pleasure. You'll find out about life in the '30s, but it's also fun to search for "tall tales" and read some of the amazing stories that have been passed down through the generations—now to you!

http://lcweb2.loc.gov/ammem/wpaintro/
wpahome.html

U.S. HISTORY—1940–1949

What Did You Do in the War, Grandma?

During World War II, food, shoes, sugar, and gasoline were rationed. You could only get so much for your coupon; and if you ran out, too bad, until the date you could use your next coupon—because you couldn't hoard supplies, either. Find out what life was like during the war years by listening to these women who made important contributions as teachers, news reporters, nurses, and in other professions. There is also a time line and glossary so you will be able to understand some of the references. Parents: not all oral histories at this site have been checked.

http://www.stg.brown.edu/projects/WWII_Women/
tocCS.html

U.S. HISTORY—1940–1949—WORLD WAR II

★ America @ War!

Motivated by the propaganda posters in the Gallery, you decide either to join up as a virtual soldier or help the war effort on the home front. Gone for a soldier? You'll experience boot camp training, several main battles, and all the horror that is war. Along the way you'll hear how the soldiers felt about the war via audio interviews and see what happened by viewing the many historic photos. Don't forget to look at the list of links for further study. This site was created by students for the ThinkQuest competition.

http://library.thinkquest.org/17573/

Atomic Archive

Parental advisory: please preview this site. This fascinating resource explores both the science and the history of the atomic bomb's development, deployment, and aftermath. Read biographical information about the scientists involved, and then pore over their accounts of the actual test blast at the Trinity site in New Mexico. There's also a chilling scenario of what would happen if a nuclear device exploded one spring day in Manhattan.

http://www.atomicarchive.com/

A Day That Will Live in Infamy

Pssst! This site has some top-secret documents! Luckily, they've been declassified. You're free to explore them in the Mission Impossible game. As soon as you figure out how to enter the Ninja headquarters, you can start finding those documents to see how much you know about the events surrounding and leading up to the Japanese attack on Pearl Harbor. See if you can answer all 15 questions correctly. This site was created by students for the ThinkQuest Junior competition

http://library.thinkquest.org/J0112601/

What do you want to be when you grow up? JOBS AND CAREERS has some ideas!

The History and Making of the Atomic Bomb

Is the atomic bomb an instrument of destruction or a maintainer of world peace? Was its creation a giant achievement for the scientific minds of the day or a huge step backward for humanity? This site examines the creation of the atomic bomb, its scientific principles, and its subsequent testing and use during World War II. This site was created by students for the ThinkQuest competition.

http://library.thinkquest.org/20920/

The Holocaust: A Tragic Legacy

This award-winning site was created by high school students as part of the ThinkQuest competition. It traces the roots, events, and legacy of the worst of times, when many European civilians, especially Jews, were killed by the Nazis during World War II. You can visit a VRML concentration camp; and while you're in that area, see how you would react when faced with making a terrible decision. Parents: this site is not for young children.

http://library.thinkquest.org/12663/

Remembering Pearl Harbor @ nationalgeographic.com

Learning key facts and dates is one way to learn about history. Another is to listen to eyewitness accounts of an event. At this site, the story of Pearl Harbor is told through the eyes of its survivors and eyewitnesses. Each firsthand account is depicted with audio and video.

http://www.nationalgeographic.com/pearlharbor/

The Second World War: The Pacific Theatre

Although much attention is given to the European theater of war, this site is focused on the war in the Pacific. There's a quick summary of events, as well as a time line; in-depth articles about major battles; and pages about weapons, aircraft, and aircraft carriers. Hear interesting audio interviews with war veterans. One was only 16 when he joined up. A library of photos and a memorial page rounds out the offerings at this very special site. This Web resource was created by students for the ThinkQuest competition.

http://library.thinkquest.org/18106/

Through Our Eyes and Hearts and Minds—World War II

Why do countries go to war? If that question could be answered, would it be enough to preserve peace throughout the world? The ThinkQuest Junior competitors who created this site hope so. By using World War II as an example, they want you to understand the emotional side of war and how it affected survivors. Interviews, video, and photos help bring a fresh perspective to what it means to go to war.

http://library.thinkquest.org/J0110055/

★ World War II, An American Scrapbook

World War II has been in the news in recent years since it has reached its 50th anniversary. One school's assignment was to develop a Web site on World War II and to get the information for it by talking to family members who had been involved in the war. They shared their memories, and here they are! You can also explore links to a number of other World War II Web sites. This site was a finalist in the ThinkQuest Junior competition. The students are from McRoberts School in Katy, Texas.

http://tqjunior.thinkquest.org/4616/

Visit the CHEMISTRY section periodically.

A B C D E F G H I J K L M N O P Q R S T U V W X Y Z

Star Wars Kids

Themed and written expressly for the youngest Star Wars fans, this site offers games, trivia, and news about the much-anticipated Episode II and other Star Wars movies. There are also some interesting polls, like "Who would you rather hang out with: Princess Leia or Queen Amidala?" The results showed a distinct preference for Queen Amidala. *http://www.starwarskids.com/*

U.S. HISTORY—1950–1959

The Fifties

Parental advisory: please preview this site. Take a spin through this Web site and you'll find out about lots of music from the '50s, including that of Elvis, Patsy Cline, and even old TV theme music. Discover what things cost in the 1950s—how does 20 cents for a gallon of gas sound? This site is a little gem of popular culture, but parents should be forewarned that there are occurrences of PG-13 language and behavior.

http://www.fiftiesweb.com/

History Channel Exhibits: The Fifties

The History Channel has a lot of really good facts about the squeaky-clean era some call "vibrant and wholesome." You will learn a lot and might even find an idea for a school term paper right here. After all, in the '50s, a general was the president, and television came in two colors only: black and white!

http://www.historychannel.com/exhibits/fifties/

U.S. HISTORY—1960–1969

The Berlin Wall

The year was 1961, and people in East Berlin, Germany, were fleeing the city to escape the clutches of communism. The government wanted to stop people from getting out, so they built a huge wall out of concrete, barbed wire, and stone. It was called the Berlin Wall and stretched for 7.5 miles, splitting Berlin in two. When the wall was torn down 28 years later, it marked the end of communism. There is a lot more to the story, and this site will tell you all about it.

http://www.wall-berlin.org/

Radical Times: The Antiwar Movement of the 1960s

No discussion of the tumultuous 1960s would be complete without a look at the antiwar movement. Although teens of this period hardly knew where Southeast Asia was, let alone Vietnam, the fact that their buddies were being drafted to go off and fight in a controversial war did catch their attention. Some decided to exercise their civil rights and protest against the war. This led to riots, massive civil unrest, and—hippies. This site was created by students for the ThinkQuest competition.

http://library.thinkquest.org/27942/

What Happened in the Sixties?

Parental advisory: please preview this site. Meanwhile, in 1964: a gallon of gasoline costs 30 cents; Hasbro introduces the GI Joe doll; the Beatles appear on *The Ed Sullivan Show*; and President Johnson announces a substantial increase in U.S. aid to South Vietnam "to restrain the mounting infiltration of men and equipment by the Hanoi regime in support of the Vietcong." Read about the swinging '60s at this site, but parents should be advised that this is part of a larger site on baby boomers and not all links have been checked. Kids: See how well Mom and Dad can do with Name That Tune! It's in the Boomer Music section.

http://www.bbhq.com/sixties.htm

A B C D E F G H I J K L M N O P Q R S T U V W X Y Z

> DINOSAURS AND PREHISTORIC TIMES are in the past, but they are under "D."

The Whole World was Watching

Parental advisory: please preview this site. To really understand the '60s, you should talk to someone who lived through it. That's exactly what these teens did. Interviews with more than 30 people may give you insight on the civil rights issues, antiwar protests, and other political movements of the times.

http://www.stg.brown.edu/projects/1968/

U.S. HISTORY—1970–1979
DeeT's 70s Page

Parental advisory: please preview this site. Take a ride on the time machine and step back into the 1970s. Some things haven't changed much. Kids watched *Sesame Street* and *The Electric Company* on television, and back then *Gilligan's Island* was being shown for the first time. If you'd like to see these and lots of other '70s stuff, Dee T's is the place to be.

http://www.rt66.com/dthomas/70s/70s.html

U.S. HISTORY—1980–1989
The Good, the Bad, the Cheezy of the '80s

If you remember Crispy Critters cereal, deelybopper antennae headgear, and "Don't have a cow, man!," you might be a child of the '80s. See how much of the foods, fads, and fun you remember from those great times when we thought the Nintendo Entertainment System was about as good as it could get.

http://www.hardtech.com/80s/

U.S. HISTORY—1990–1999

We continue to look for a site about the '90s that meets our selection policy.

WORLD HISTORY
Baxter's EduNET - Time Machine

What happened 50 years ago in India? What about 25 years ago in Australia? Or can you guess what happened 5,000 years ago in the Mediterranean? You can learn so much traveling back and forth on the time line at this site that all your friends and family members will think you are a genius! You probably are if you take our advice and give this site a try.

http://www.edunetconnect.com/cat/timemachine/

Discovery School History

Click on any letter of the alphabet to discover information about world history, and who helped make it. Read a bio of Julius Caesar, Louis XIV, Sacagawea, and hundreds of others. Find out about events, too, like the Hundred Years' War (it was really longer than that, but who's counting?) and the Boston Tea Party (nobody asked for refills).

http://school.discovery.com/homeworkhelp/
    worldbook/atozhistory/

History of the World Timeline

Choose a decade and go! For example, let's pick 1900–1909. From there, click on "1900" to find out about the Boxer Rebellion in China, the first auto show in New York, the invention of the hamburger in Connecticut, and the Carry Nation anti-alcohol bar-smashing tour of Kansas. Everything has hyperlinks to other parts of the History Channel site if you need more in-depth information.

http://www.historychannel.com/Centurytime/

HistoryWiz

This site is like a time machine offering trips between now and the ancient past. Click on one of the pictures, and transport yourself back in time to explore different historical topics. You can discover more about the French and American Revolutions. Or, learn about some of the most tragic episodes in modern world history, such as the Holocaust and the Cambodian genocide. This site loads better with Internet Explorer.

http://www.historywiz.com/

A B C D E F G H I J K L M N O P Q R S T U V W X Y Z

Sidebar: A B C D E F G H I J K L M N O P Q R S T U V W X Y Z

★ Walk Through Time - BBC Education History - Age 7–9

Let's try "Odd One Out." Hmm, seems to be a street scene from Victorian times. Wait—something's not quite right. The gentleman is dressed rather strangely for this time period, isn't he? And doesn't the fire-fighting apparatus look positively medieval? Click what doesn't belong, and try to drop it in the time tunnel. If you're right, the item will disappear, to be replaced by its timely equivalent. If you drag the wrong thing, it will come back, along with a short explanation. Try scenes from many different time periods.

http://www.bbc.co.uk/history/walk/

World History Lesson Plans

There's enough information at this site for every term paper you will ever have to write! Well, almost every one. Middle Ages, Age of Exploration, Renaissance and Reformation, World History, Pirates . . . we'll never finish reading it all. Mr. Donn definitely gets an A+ on this great resource.

http://members.aol.com/MrDonnHistory/World.html

WORLD HISTORY—1940–1949— WORLD WAR II

Anne Frank Online

She was a kid just like you. Her diary helps us remember that she lived and then died in a German concentration camp. Who is she? Anne Frank. Here is her history, along with photos of Anne and her family. Read some of the things she wrote in her small red-and-white plaid diary. Maybe you would like to start keeping a journal about your life. Also see another Anne Frank site in the PEOPLE AND BIOGRAPHIES section of this book.

http://www.annefrank.com/

"Use the source, Luke!" and look it up in REFERENCE WORKS.

Children of World War II

There was no pizza. If you lived in the city, you might have been evacuated to the countryside for safety. If you still lived at home, you had "blackout" curtains in your bedroom. This is some of what life was like if you were a child during World War II. For more, take a virtual reality tour of a wartime home, go on an interactive grocery shopping adventure, or read some of the letters that children wrote their parents when they were evacuated from the city of London. In the shopping activity, don't be surprised if the grocer tells you to make something tasty out of fried bread.

http://www.bbc.co.uk/history/ww2children/

United States Holocaust Memorial Museum

Parents: descriptions at this site may be too graphic for youngsters. The United States Holocaust Memorial Museum in Washington, D.C., offers general information on this painful chapter of world history. The education page offers a guide to teaching about the Holocaust, a brief history, FAQ, a heartbreaking article about children in the Holocaust, and a videography. An online reservation form for groups is available.

http://www.ushmm.org/

HOLIDAYS

🦆 Billy Bear's on Holiday

Billy Bear offers special sites for more than ten fun holidays. Each one has games, activities, and facts about the holiday that may be new to you. If we don't have a separate listing for a holiday in this book, check with Billy Bear. Net-mom loves Billy Bear because he gives such great bear hugs!

http://www.billybear4kids.com/holidays/fun.htm

BlackDog Loves Holidays!

Whether it's Father's Day, Christmas, or any one of eight other holidays, you'll discover it's great fun playing with a kid's best friend, BlackDog. Lots of games, puzzles, and crafts are available, and be sure to look for the weird things that magically appear and follow your cursor around. Warning: if you click on the Summer Camp section, you'll have virtual ants crawling all over your screen!

http://www.blackdog.net/holiday.html

Kid's Domain Holidays

More than 30 cool holidays to celebrate (or observe, in the case of Memorial Day) may be found at this section of the Kid's Domain site. You'll also read suggestions for each season plus information on a handful of international holidays. Choose any of them to find online and downloadable games, crafts, activities, and links to pages for more fun.

http://www.kidsdomain.com/holiday/

100TH DAY
The 100th Day of School

Lots of kids are counting the days they go to school—it's because they want to be sure not to miss the 100th day! Teachers and kids are celebrating the 100th day of school in lots of special ways; read about them at this site and its links. For example, each child might bring in 100 pennies to donate to charity. The school nurse might collect 100 healthy hand prints, finger painted on a big sheet of paper outside the office. Kids could try to dance for 100 seconds, or (even harder) be quiet for 100 seconds. Some kids like to draw pictures of what they will look like when they are 100 years old! The possibilities are endless—get started at this site.

http://users.aol.com/a100thday/

Fetch some fascinating info in DOGS AND DOG SPORTS.

NET FILES

Your buddies (who like math as much as you do) invite you to the Pi Day celebration at the Exploratorium—but they've forgotten to tell you when it is and what time to show up!

Mathematically speaking, what's your best guess?

Answer: Pi Day is celebrated every year on March 14, at 1:59 in the afternoon. Third month? Fourteenth day? The value of pi to a few decimal places is 3.14159! This irrational celebration happens to coincide with Albert Einstein's birthday. Read about it at http://www.exploratorium.edu/pi/pi97/pi_one.html

BIRTHDAYS

🐾 Billy Bear's Birthday Party

Happy Birthday to YOU! Happy Birthday to YOU! This site is a present from Net-mom to you. You can play virtual pin the tail on the donkey, bake a virtual cake, pick out some virtual party favors, color some pictures, and more. This site also suggests you make your own Web page with the party icons supplied here.

http://www.billybear4kids.com/holidays/birthday/party.htm

Birthday Crafts, Cards, Banners, and Activities

Having a birthday party? This site offers free color birthday banners, printable cards and invitations, and even ideas for unusual birthday cakes. Don't stop there: check the suggested party games, directions for making hats and goodie bags, and lots more.

http://www.dltk-kids.com/crafts/birthday/

A
B
C
D
E
F
G
H
I
J
K
L
M
N
O
P
Q
R
S
T
U
V
W
X
Y
Z

Today in History

Want to know who shares your birthday or what famous events throughout history happened the day you were born? Just visit this site and type in the month and year you want. For example, famous people born on February 8 include author Jules Verne, actor James Dean, and actress Audrey Meadows, who played Alice in The Honeymooners. Find out when and where these folks were born, too; Meadows, for example, was born in China. You can also find out who died on this day (Mary, Queen of Scots) and find out what important historical events took place. On February 8, the Boy Scouts organization was incorporated (1910), radio first came to the White House (1922), and Walt Disney Studios was formed (1926). Know anyone with a brand-new baby? Give the proud parents a printout of their baby's birth date.

http://www.scopesys.com/anyday/

CHRISTMAS

Castle Arcana Christmas

Did you know that there's a special calendar that is used to mark the days until Christmas? It's called an Advent Calendar, and this site will show you one. When you click on the date, you'll get an interesting tidbit about a Christmas custom or seasonal pagan celebration. If you try to open a window before the proper day, you'll be thwarted.

http://www.castlearcana.com/christmas/

★ Delight in the Magic

Yes, this is a commercial site, designed to make you feel thirsty so you'll drink gallons of Coca-Cola— but—it's also a heck of a lot of fun! Mouse over the Christmas tree to turn on the twinkling lights. Can you find (and mouse over) the toy horse? See the little mouse hole? Don't forget to light the candles on the mantelpiece! Hey—who's that at the window? And the fun really starts when you click on one of the special stockings.

http://holidays.coca-cola.com/

Ginger Lane Kitchens

Several years back, Net-mom and family made a totally cool gingerbread house. Every year we display it during the holidays, and it looks as good as new! Just put the whole thing into a plastic trash bag and keep it in a cool place. If ours ever breaks, though, we're going to use the recipe at this site to make another one.

http://www.gingerbreadlane.com/

Golden Books e-Magic Pages

The pages on this site turn like the pages in a book. But, best of all, this site will actually read itself to you. So, the only lap you have to sit on is your chair's. Choose A Frosty Day or Rudolph the Red-Nosed Reindeer. Then, flip through the colorful graphics, and listen to the story.

http://www.goldenbooks.com/fun/emagic/

★ A Holy Christmas

Visit this wonderful site for a family-centered emphasis on the true meaning of Christmas, the Advent season, and the Epiphany. This site also has Christmas clip art, audio files, and recipes. You'll also find info on Christmas around the world among the many treasures here.

http://www.rockies.net/~spirit/sermons/
  christmaspage.html

Kid's Domain Christmas

Lots of little holiday games are collected here from all over the Net. Decorate a virtual tree, snowman, or gingerbread house. Try the animated toy maker machine. And don't miss the jokes. Sample: "What does an elf study in school?" Answer: "The ELF-a-bet!"

http://www.kidsdomain.com/games/xmas.html

A
B
C
D
E
F
G
H
I
J
K
L
M
N
O
P
Q
R
S
T
U
V
W
X
Y
Z

Have an order of pi in MATH AND ARITHMETIC.

Li'l Fingers Christmas

Parental advisory: please preview this site; the ads are very annoying. One- and two-year-olds can put their mouse skills to work at this site. The games require a lot of clicking, and some guesswork. Somewhere there's an angel hiding in one of the stockings. But where should you look? Another game lets you guess what's under the wrapping paper. The covered object with the wagging tail sure looks like a dog. The answer is just a click away.

http://www.lil-fingers.com/holidays/christmas/
content.html

National Christmas Tree Association

Too bad they don't have "smell attribute" plug-ins (yet). If they did, this site would smell terrific! The National Christmas Tree Growers page provides a dictionary of 16 evergreen types, from the Arizona cypress to the white spruce. You'll also find a directory of tree farms close to you (if you want to cut your own), selection tips, and interesting facts and figures.

http://www.christree.org/

Noel Noel Noel

Fill your ears with Christmas music—many of your favorite carols and songs may be heard here. You'll also find sheet music to print (even big-note music for beginners), as well as musical scores. The site also offers links to online shopping sites that sell some of the CDs you'll hear playing. If you buy a CD, make sure you come back to this site. It has gift tags to print, but you'll have to supply your own wrapping paper. There is a whole sleigh-full of information about Christmas traditions, recipes, crafts, and activities, too.

http://www.noelnoelnoel.com/

★ NORAD Tracks Santa

Every Christmas eve, the good folks at the North American Aerospace Defense Command track Santa on their radar systems. At their Web site, you can find out the technical details of how they accomplish this feat (it involves the infrared signal given off by Rudolph's nose). There are also scientific explanations for how Santa manages to fly around the world so quickly, and how he manages to consume all those cookies. There are also specifications for both the Canadian CF 18 Hornet and Santa's sleigh. The former is 56 feet long, while the latter is 75 cc (candy canes)/ 150 lp (lollipops) long.

http://www.noradsanta.org/

A Religious Christmas

Choose the carol you want to hear, and then explore the many links to Christmas as celebrated in scripture, essays, art, drama, prose, and more music. Click on the Bethlehem section to see pictures of the traditional place of Christ's birth.

http://www.execpc.com/~tmuth/st_john/xmas/
main.htm

Nurit Reshef: Funland

This site is chock-full of fun little Java games to help you practice Hebrew. For example, check out Word Match. There are four pictures of common objects. Click on English and match the words with the pictures. Now click on Hebrew and see if you can do as well! (Hint: Play the audio of each word, listen to how it sounds, and match the picture to the word that looks like what you heard.) Press Score to see how well you did; then click on New to get four new words to try.
http://www.bus.ualberta.ca/yreshef/funland/funland.html

A
B
C
D
E
F
G
H
I
J
K
L
M
N
O
P
Q
R
S
T
U
V
W
X
Y
Z

Santa Simulator

It's a bird. It's a plane. No, it's a hydrogen-cooled rocket sleigh, and you get to fly it. In this game, you play Santa Claus. Your mission is simple: drop your presents into the lighted Christmas houses before you run out of fuel. Remember, timing is everything, and watch out! If it's not a cloud, it will crash your sleigh. Or, play the kid-friendly version with no crashes.

http://www.sun-sentinel.com/graphics/entertainment/ santasim.htm

A Search for the Meaning of Christmas

Are you searching for the true meaning of Christmas? Here's a don't-miss noncommercial site with religious traditions, family traditions, customs, songs, thoughtful links, and more. This is part of a larger site with information on Hanukkah as well.

http://techdirect.com/christmas/

The Adventure of Echo the Bat

Follow the story of Echo, the baby bat, as he learns to fly, catch insects, and "see" with his ears. How is that possible? It's called echolocation, and you'll learn all about it right along with furry Echo. A sudden storm separates Echo from his mom, but he remembers she told him something about a big cave down south, where bats meet up to spend the winter. Can he find his way there? Turns out he also has a special tag that allows his route to be tracked by satellite. If you have a 4.0 or better browser, you can become a scientist and track Echo on his journey to find Mom.
http://imagers.gsfc.nasa.gov/

Songs of the Season

Here's a nice songbook of seasonal carols. Listen to the music and sing along, because the words are right on the screen for you. You'll also find the lyrics to the exploding cigar parody version of "We Three Kings."

http://www.night.net/christmas/songs12.html-ssi

★ The Very First Story of Christmas

Do you know that Christmas really celebrates the birth of the baby Jesus? To read the traditional Bible story about Mary and Joseph and the birth of Jesus in Bethlehem, try this beautifully done site. Listen to holiday background music while you read the familiar story, illustrated with Renaissance and contemporary artwork.

http://www.geocities.com/Heartland/8833/xmas.html

★ World Book Christmas

Enjoy this fascinating overview to the holiday season, beginning with Advent and continuing through New Year's. You can learn about the origins of Christmas trees, use the recipes to make some delectable holiday treats, and even try a few international craft suggestions.

http://www.worldbook.com/fun/holidays/html/ christ.htm

A World Wide Christmas Calendar

This worldwide Advent calendar has a tree with gift-wrapped packages below it. Open a package and discover how a youngster in another country might celebrate this holiday. In Denmark, according to one nine-year-old writer, they make oatmeal balls, decorate their homes with elves, and eat duck and pig for dinner on Christmas Eve.

http://www.algonet.se/~bernadot/christmas/ calendar.html

CINCO DE MAYO

Cinco de Mayo

Do you like a really good party? Well, every May 5, many Latino Americans and citizens of Mexico celebrate a grand event, and they have a party in the process. In 1862, on Cinco de Mayo (that's Spanish for May 5), a handful of Mexican troops defeated a much larger and better-armed force of soldiers from France. This victory showed that a small group, strengthened by unity, can overcome overwhelming odds. Ever since, Cinco de Mayo is celebrated with music, tasty food, parades, and a party.

http://latino.sscnet.ucla.edu/cinco.html

DAY OF THE DEAD

★ The Calaca Feast

In November, Mexicans celebrate the annual Day of the Dead. It's not a sad occasion. They make special foods and prepare a feast to honor their ancestors. They have picnics on their relatives' graves so the dead can join in the festivities, too. Learn more about this holiday, its origins, and death rituals in other cultures.

http://www.calacafeast.com/

Day of the Dead

One of the special foods eaten on this day is called "Bread of the Dead" (*pan de muerto*). The baker hides a plastic skeleton in each rounded loaf, and it's good luck to bite into the piece with the skeleton! People also give each other candy skeletons, skulls, and other treats with a death design. Check the recipes section for more.

http://www.public.iastate.edu/~rjsalvad/scmfaq/muertos.html

Day of the Dead - Dia de los Muertos

Discover many of the traditions and rituals surrounding this Mexican holiday, derived from Aztec culture. There is a rich section with links to explore, but parents should note that we didn't get to look at all of them.

http://www.mexconnect.com/mex_/feature/daydeadindex.html

EARTH DAY

Earth Day Online Games

Try loads of fun games, including "Protect the Environment." Spot hidden litter in a woodland stream, and then see if you can sort it all into the right bins. Prefer arcade-style recycling? "Muck Cleans Up" is your destination. The "Dumptown Game" and "Shrink the Landfill" challenge more experienced sanitation engineers.

http://www.kidsdomain.com/games/earthday.html

Happy Earth Day Activity Book

Earth Day is April 22, and many kids make plans to help clean up the environment that day. Start with collecting trash in your neighborhood (or maybe—gasp!—in your room), and then download this 12-page booklet to learn about all the other ways you can live "green." Whimsical drawings show you how to save water, recycle paper, and conserve energy.

http://www.epa.gov/docs/Region5/happy.htm

Virtual House

Paper or plastic? That is the question when you check out at a grocery store. But what is the answer? Come to this site and find out. When you do, you'll enter a virtual house. Move from room to room and click on different objects until you get the right answer. Even if you get the wrong answer, you'll learn something new about conservation. If you get stuck, ask for a clue. So, what IS the right answer? Go to the closet and find out. When you start over, you get a new question. It all helps you celebrate Earth Day.

http://www.virtualhouse.org/

Watching Over the World

Can one person help save the environment? Sure! Read how kids like you are making a difference in their own hometowns. On a more global scale, salute real-life heroes working to save endangered animals and habitats all over the world. Print the special passport and "visit" each location.

http://www.timeforkids.com/TFK/explore/story/0,6079,56763,00.html

A B C D E F G H I J K L M N O P Q R S T U V W X Y Z

A
B
C
D
E
F
G
H
I
J
K
L
M
N
O
P
Q
R
S
T
U
V
W
X
Y
Z

Art Tales: Telling Stories with Wildlife Art

Pretend you're a frontier explorer with a story to tell. Select wildlife artworks to illustrate your tale, and add a soundtrack of animal sounds or music. You might also choose to be a field guide writer or a museum curator. When you've produced your story, or book, or your gallery guide, you can send it in for possible publication on the Net.
http://www.wildlifeart.org/arttales

EASTER

Absolutely Easter

After you've colored all your Easter eggs, what do you do with them? Do you put them in a bowl on the table? That looks pretty, but try something new—check the Easter Village. Just print the pictures and color them. In fact, some of them are already in color. Then wrap the pictures around the eggs, set them up, and play with your beautiful creation. This is part of a larger site about many holidays.

http://www.geocities.com/Heartland/7134/Easter/

Billy Bear's Happy Easter

Why not build a virtual Easter basket and e-mail it to a friend or relative? Billy Bear has all the colored eggs, chicks, Bibles, and other components you'll need! There are Easter puzzles, games, and crafts galore, but don't forget the most important part of this site: the Interactive Easter Story.

http://www.billybear4kids.com/holidays/easter/fun.htm

BlackDog's Easter Celebration

Retrieve plenty of Easter fun at this site, including an egg hunt, matching games, Java mazes, and crossword puzzles. Don't miss the links section for crafts, recipes, and lots more!

http://blackdog4kids.com/holiday/easter/

Easter Egg Factory

There's nothing like decorating Easter eggs the old-fashioned way, even if it is a bit messy. But if you don't have the time or run out of dye, hop over to this site. It's got an egg-painting machine that will let you color as many eggs as you like. While you can't eat them, you can save your creations and view them in your own personal Egg Gallery.

http://www.sun-sentinel.com/graphics/entertainment/easter.htm

Ecclesiastical Calendar: Enter a Year

Easter is a movable feast. That means it's on a different day each year. Why? The answer is a long one, but here goes: Easter is observed on the first Sunday following the first full moon after the first day of spring (vernal equinox) in the Northern Hemisphere. This can occur any time between March 22 and April 25. This site lists the dates for both the Western Easter and the Orthodox Easter, through the year 2024. It also calculates the dates of many Christian holy days for any year you please.

http://www.smart.net/~mmontes/ec-cal.html

★ The Great American Egg Hunt

If it's around Easter when you're reading this, Net-mom's friend, Hazel Jobe, is no doubt running another virtual egg hunt. It's aimed at K–6 students, but anyone can play. Students have designed colorful eggs that have been hidden on school sites around the World Wide Web. Hazel says, "Participants will visit the school sites to hunt for the egg and then follow the link to answer the questions. It will give these young students practice navigating the Web for a purpose. Participants will receive a certificate when they have found all the eggs and answered all the questions." You can also win great prizes!

http://www.marshall-es.marshall.k12.tn.us/jobe/egghunt/info.html

History of the White House Easter Egg Roll

Sometime during the presidency of Andrew Johnson, the beloved Washington tradition of the Easter Egg Roll was initiated. Its original site was the U.S. Capitol grounds. By 1877, some members of Congress got tired of complaining about the leftover hard-boiled eggs (they kept slipping on ones the kids hadn't found), debris, and general disorder of the whole event. Policemen shooed that year's Easter crowds away. Tearful children converged on the White House lawn to petition President Hayes to hold an impromptu egg roll there. He did. The idea caught on. In 1878, President Hayes and his wife, Lucy, officially opened the White House grounds to the children. It's been held there ever since, except for brief breaks during the war years. Visit this site to learn a basketful of facts and trivia about this colorful event, which includes games, as well as an egg hunt. The most precious eggs are those with the signatures of famous sports players and other celebrities, who are asked to sign the wooden eggs when they visit the White House throughout the year. You can buy a souvenir egg from the White House link you will find at this site.

http://www.nara.gov/publications/prologue/
    eggroll1.html

A Holy Easter

Although this extensive site collects links about bunnies, eggs, clip art, and audio files, its main emphasis is on the religious observances of Easter and the Passover season.

http://www.rockies.net/~spirit/sermons/easter.html

Safeguard your privacy online! Don't give anyone your name, address, or other identifying information without reading the site's privacy policy.

How to Make Ukrainian Easter Eggs

This page explains everything you need to know about the art of *pysanky*, the Ukrainian Easter egg. You need an adult to help, because this process involves a candle and hot wax. First, you must decide on the designs you're going to use. Many geometric patterns have traditional meanings—for example, curlicues mean protection and diamonds signify knowledge. You'll find suggested beginner designs here, so get your equipment and get started (the page lists several sources for materials). Using a special stylus, called a *kistka*, apply wax to the egg wherever you want the shell to remain white. Then dip the egg in colored dyes. When completed, you melt the wax off. It takes a long time to make one of these, but in the end you'll have a true work of art. If handled carefully, you'll be able to give these eggs to your children and maybe even your grandchildren. This may be *eggs-actly* the hobby you've been looking for!

http://www.3.ns.sympatico.ca/amorash/ukregg.html

Rosie's Easter Basket

Rosie offers some yummy Easter recipes, activities, and hints for coloring eggs using natural materials. Did you know that if you want red eggs, you boil them with red onion skins? Grape juice gives you lavender eggs, while turmeric will dye eggs yellow. There is a whole rainbow of ideas here!

http://www.night.net/easter/

FATHER'S DAY

🦆 Billy Bear's Happy Father's Day

What should you give your dad this year? He has enough ties. You know he can never have enough hugs! You can give him a Promise Card, too. Look at the example on this page, and then make one yourself. You can promise to rake the leaves, walk the dog, or help Dad clean out the garage. There is also Father's Day clip art, a fun little fishing game, and lots more.

http://www.billybear4kids.com/holidays/father/
    dad.htm

A B C D E F G H I J K L M N O P Q R S T U V W X Y Z

A
B
C
D
E
F
G
H
I
J
K
L
M
N
O
P
Q
R
S
T
U
V
W
X
Y
Z

★ Kid's Domain Father's Day

Mazes, coloring pages, cards, and crafts you can make—all for your dad on Father's Day. Don't miss the paper car craft—Dad would love his own Ferrari. There are also some fun games for little kids and medium kids—and all kids!

http://www.kidsdomain.com/holiday/dad/

GROUNDHOG DAY

CNN - Groundhog Quartet Agrees on Early Spring

Punxsutawney Phil, the granddad of all weather-predicting groundhogs, was the lead rodent in this CNN report on weather-predicting animals. A cult hero of sorts, Phil has been making news with his February 2 shadows for many years. There are others in the field—and you can "read all about them" right here.

http://www.cnn.com/US/9702/02/
    groundhog.conspiracy/

The Official Site of the Punxsutawney Groundhog Club

Long before we had weather satellites, Doppler radar, and the Weather Channel, we got our winter weather forecasts from a rodent. Yes, it's part of what has made America great, and the tradition continues in Punxsutawney, Pennsylvania. Now you can get up close and personal with Punxsutawney Phil, groundhog extraordinaire. Some may call him a woodchuck, and some may call him a gopher. We call him a great publicity stunt, but we always pay attention to his predictions for an early or late spring. As the legend goes, if Phil comes up out of his hole on February 2 and sees his shadow, he'll be frightened back for six more weeks of winter; if, on the other hand, it's cloudy, we'll get an early spring. Will he see his shadow? Film at 11!

http://www.groundhog.org/

Wiarton Willie

Lest you think Canadians don't have a weather rodent (*en Français, météo marmotte*) of their own, meet Wee Willie, an albino marmot. Son of the lately departed Wiarton Willie, Wee Willie stands poised to pick up the weather forecasting duties where his dad left off: "Born on the 45th parallel, exactly midway between the Equator and the North Pole, this white groundhog has the uncanny ability to signal the end of winter. Weather watchers around the world look to Willie's shadow and its 90 percent accuracy rate to see just how long winter is going to continue!" You can even send him e-mail (he must have a modem in his burrow). Come join the fun in southwestern Ontario on Lake Huron.

http://www.wiarton-willie.org/

GUY FAWKES DAY

Guy Fawkes Day

On November 5, people in the United Kingdom gather around roaring bonfires and burn a "guy" in effigy. What's it all about? You can find out at this nicely designed page, but the short form is that Guy Fawkes and others tried to blow up the Houses of Parliament back in 1601. It was because they were really mad at the king. The plot was discovered in time—or were Fawkes and the others framed?

http://www.bonefire.org/guy/

HALLOWEEN

See also MONSTERS

☙ Billy Bear's Halloween

This site has great ideas for holiday parties. Also, you'll find lots of online Halloween-related games, for example, Halloween Dress-up and Carve a Virtual Pumpkin. The Haunted House is pretty spooky, too. Check the free downloads to make your holiday the creepiest ever.

http://www.billybear4kids.com/holidays/halowen/
    halowen.htm

Cool Ghouls

How do you tell if someone is a werewolf? This site will give you the folk wisdom on that (personally, we don't believe in werewolves), as well as other scary tidbits. There are also some ghoulish activities to play at this site. Have you ever heard of Zombies (we don't believe in them either)? Help Josh dodge them. He needs to get to the Dead House alive! See what we mean? Isn't that a contradiction in terms?

http://www.tcfhe.com/goosebumps/bump.html

Create Your Own Costume at Goodwill

Costumes galore are available for not too much cash at your local Goodwill store. Follow the directions here to be Judge Judy, a Post-it note, Dilbert, a bag of jelly beans, and loads of other great characters.

http://www.goodwillnj.org/halloween/
    make-costume.html

Ghoulish Recipes

From "Roasty Toasty Pumpkin Seeds" to "Nuclear Punch" this collection of spooky recipes is sure to give you a fright, if not indigestion. No, really, the raisins only look like bugs.

http://www.gustown.com//Cafe/Recipes/
    GhoulishRecipes.html

Golden Books e-Magic Pages

Who's that flying through the sky, cackling as she passes by? And, who's in the kitchen rattling around? Why they're ghosts—here and there and up and down. Can you find them all? This game is no trick; just one of many treats you'll find on this site. The Slightly Scary Halloween Flap Book has especially good graphics, but you'll have to decide if the house is really haunted.

http://www.goldenbooks.com/fun/emagic/

NET FILES

The world's largest waterfall is sixteen times the height of Niagara Falls! Where can it be found?

Answer: Angel Falls, in Venezuela, is one of that country's numerous natural wonders. It has a total height of 3,212 feet (979 meters) and an uninterrupted drop of 2,648 ft. (807 meters). To find out more, visit http://school.discovery.com/homeworkhelp/worldbook/atozpictures/lr002089.html

Halloween Magazine

Tricks and treats abound at this enormous Halloween site. (That reminds us of a seasonal joke: Why does a witch ride on a broom? Because vacuum cleaners have to be plugged into the wall!) Stroll through the site (keep your eyes closed if you're scared), and get some tips on easy-to-make costumes, decorations, and party food. There's also a great Halloween safety game. You'll find lots of links to other haunted Web sites, none of *witch* we have checked, so parents, please preview this site, because it may be too scary for little ones.

http://www.halloweenmagazine.com/

HalloweenKids.com

Have you got a friend or relative you won't be seeing on Halloween? Well, why not send them a ghostly e-card? It won't really scare anyone, but it will show that you're thinking of them. Choose from several different designs, from Casper the friendly ghost to Alvin and the Chipmunks. Now, isn't that a boo-tiful idea? Other parts of the site feature costume ideas, other celebrations around the world, and safety tips.

http://www.halloweenkids.com/

A
B
C
D
E
F
G
H
I
J
K
L
M
N
O
P
Q
R
S
T
U
V
W
X
Y
Z

A
B
C
D
E
F
G
H
I
J
K
L
M
N
O
P
Q
R
S
T
U
V
W
X
Y
Z

NET FILES

The Iditarod is a 1,150-mile dogsled race in Alaska, from Anchorage to Nome. It traverses some of the roughest, most beautiful country on Earth, and often the dogs wear booties to protect their feet. According to race rules, how many booties per dog are mushers required to bring?

Answer: Eight per dog, according to the rule book. As the site at http://www.iditarod.com/00-rules/00-rules.htm explains: "In fact most competent mushers keep their dogs bootied from Anchorage to Nome and use about 2,000 booties all together. Booties are usually made of polar fleece and one bootie will last several hours and up to 100 miles."

Kid's Domain Halloween Games

Play over 40 seasonal online challenges, including a matching game from Hershey's in which you will compete against . . . a peanut butter cup. Other treats include costume dress-up games, and another where the trick is to help Clicky photograph the phantom ghosts of Badd Manor. Click on Halloween Home for crafts, jokes, and more.

http://www.kidsdomain.com/games/hall.html

Lil' Fingers Games

It's not quite Mr. Potato Head, but it's just as fun, and you won't lose any of the little pieces. At this site, you get a virtual pumpkin, and lots of eyes, noses, lips, and hair to help you make a funny pumpkin face. If that doesn't amuse your baby brother, try one of the other games. The Pumpkin Storybook is sure to put on a funny (or sad) face, and may even teach tots something about using the mouse.

http://www.lil-fingers.com/holidays/halloween/
    content.html

Haunted Carnival Shockwave Game

Step right up and try your luck aiming and throwing poisoned apples at the moving ghosts, pumpkins, and monsters. The arcade targets go alarmingly fast, and the monsters have a nasty habit of changing direction at the last minute! Be sure to practice first: the apples have a wicked spin.

http://www.adveract.com/games/haunt/haunt.htm

Pumpkin Carving 101

Whether you're a pumpkin purist and want to carve them the old-fashioned way, or prefer to use a stencil pattern or other modern pumpkincraft tool, this site has something for you. View step-by-step illustrated instructions, learn pumpkin-carving history, and ponder a suggested pumpkin burial ritual after Halloween is over. Did you know that coating cut pumpkin surfaces with petroleum jelly will help preserve them and prevent mold?

http://www.pumpkin-carving.com/

Jack-o-Lantern.Com

If you'd like to try to carve some of those fancy but finicky pumpkins you see on TV, download free stencils at this site. Some of the patterns include aliens, witches, spiders, and more. There are also patriotic watermelon patterns for Independence Day picnics.

http://Jack-o-Lantern.Com

A Slimy Halloween Party

Your Halloween party is sure to be ghoulish if you follow some of the ideas here. There are Halloween games and activities that any witch, wizard, or goblin will love. Just add some bloodcurdling menu items and you're all set!

http://family2.go.com/features/family_2000_09/famf/
    famf0900slimeparty/famf0900slimeparty.html

Universal Studios Halloween Kids.com

It's nighttime as you enter the castle of that scary monster Dracula. Beware! Dracula is also roaming around and looking for a tasty tiny morsel, and you're looking quite delicious. If you lose, don't despair. There are other games. You can play with Alvin and the Chipmunks, meet Frankenstein, or create your own monster. These games are so much fun, they're spook-tacular!

http://www.halloween99.com/halloweenkids/
k_games.htm

Virtual Haunted House

This was created by middle-grade kids for other middle-grade kids, so be prepared for a lot of horror-ible stuff!

http://www2.ncsu.edu/ncsu/cep/ligon/haunted96/
haunted96.menu.html

INDEPENDENCE DAY

★ Create Your Own Fireworks Show

Choose a background: San Francisco, New York, or another city. Then select the color starburst you want and the type of shell you want to launch. Keep clicking and enjoy the show (and the sound effects). This is part of a larger site with trivia games, music, and lots of patriotic fun.

http://www.aristotle.net/july4th/fireworks/

NOVA Online - Kaboom!

This resource is explosive! Learn all about the science of BOOM, the chemistry of WOW, and the precision ballet of controlled demolition. Dare we say this site is DYNAMITE?

http://www.pbs.org/wgbh/nova/kaboom/

The Worldwide Holiday & Festival Site

The United States celebrates its birthday on July 4. There are parades, picnics, and at night—fireworks. Most countries celebrate national holidays that are their equivalents of the American Independence Day. You'll find a searchable list of many national and religious holidays here.

http://www.holidayfestival.com/

> ## Know your alphabet?
> ## Now try someone else's in
> ## LANGUAGES AND ALPHABETS.

JEWISH HOLIDAYS

See also RELIGION AND
SPIRITUALITY—JUDAISM

Calendar of Jewish Holidays

This resource, offered by B'nai B'rith, gives the dates for all important Jewish holidays through the year 2006. Mark your calendars in advance.

http://bnaibrith.org/caln.html

Jewish Outreach Institute Celebrates the Holidays

You might know that during Hanukkah, Jews light candles on a menorah, which looks like a candelabra. But do you know which Jewish holiday is celebrated by making a tent? That would be Sukkot, which comes on the fifth day after Yom Kippur. At this site, you'll learn about the major Jewish holidays and how to celebrate them. There are even some traditional Jewish recipes if you get hungry.

http://www.joi.org/consumer/celebrate.html

Uncle Eli's Rosh Hashanah and Yom Kippur Prayer Book

Uncle Eli has a way of making religious themes understandable for kids. It's as if Dr. Seuss wrote scripture. Here's a sample from the Yom Kippur Prayer Book: *I did it! I'm Sorry! Next year I'll be good. I'll try to be better, and do what I should.* Those who prefer prose explanations will not be disappointed. There's an excellent glossary, and even audio of the sound of the ram's horn, the shofar, being blown.

http://www.acs.ucalgary.ca/~elsegal/EliMahzor/

A
B
C
D
E
F
G
H
I
J
K
L
M
N
O
P
Q
R
S
T
U
V
W
X
Y
Z

JEWISH HOLIDAYS—HANUKKAH

Aish HaTorah - Chanukah Site

Can you sing the dreidel song? It goes like this: *My Dreidel/I made you out of clay/And, when you're dry and ready, oh Dreidel I will play*. If that's all you know and want to learn more, you can find the rest of the words on this site. It also has the words (and audio recordings) to other popular Hanukkah (also called Chanukah) songs. For an art project, go to the Coloring Pages and print the pages of the coloring book. While these are some of the fun things to do, this site also contains short articles and true stories reflecting the deeper meaning of Hanukkah.

http://aish.com/holidays/Chanukah/

A Search for the Meaning of Chanukah or Hanukkah

Searching for the true meaning of Hanukkah? Here's a don't-miss noncommercial site with religious traditions, family traditions, customs, songs, thoughtful links, and more. This is part of a larger site with the search for the true meaning of Christmas.

http://techdirect.com/christmas/chanukah.html

Questacon

Australia's National Science and Technology Centre has a fabulous online museum. Explore virtual galleries of interactive exhibits, head-scratching puzzles, challenging games, and more. Dinosaurs, meteors, optical illusions, and clever science activities abound here. It's one of the best sites on the Net for kids interested in science. *http://www.questacon.edu.au/*

Temple Israel Celebrates Chanukah

At this site you'll find history, games, directions on how to make latkes (potato pancakes), and more. Also included (under Blessings) is the correct procedure for lighting the menorah candles and audio of the traditional Hebrew blessings associated with their kindling.

http://tiwestport.org/chanukah/chanukah.html

Torah Tots Chanukah Fun & Games

A long time ago, in 165 B.C., the Maccabees (after a lengthy struggle) successfully defeated a Judean tyrant. Ready to celebrate the reclaiming of their Temple, they worried because only a very small container of holy oil was left with which to light all the holy lamps. Miraculously, this limited amount of oil lasted for eight days! Every year, Jewish families recall this wonder by lighting candles in a special way each night for eight days. Learn more at this site, and take a moment to spin the virtual dreidel, a traditional children's game.

http://www.torahtots.com/holidays/chanuka/ chanstr.htm

JEWISH HOLIDAYS—PASSOVER

❧ Billy Bear's Pesach Holiday

Billy Bear has really outdone himself this time! Get ready for lots of print and play mazes: help people cross the Red Sea, help Moses find the Ten Commandments, and more. Then get ready for the Java Chametz game, in which you try to find and remove all the pieces of bread and cake in the house before Passover begins. Note that it works very slowly on Macs running Netscape; see the instructions. There are also links to other Pesach (Hebrew for Passover) sites for kids.

http://www.billybear4kids.com/holidays/pesach/ pesach.htm

A B C D E F G H I J K L M N O P Q R S T U V W X Y Z

Haggadah for Passover

The Seder meal is a retelling of the Exodus story. It involves history, but it is very much like a play, because it involves the participation of all at the table. This site offers the "script" to lead your family's ritual Passover meal.

http://www.vbs.org/religious/hagadah/

★ Uncle Eli's Special-for-Kids Most Fun Ever Under-the-Table Passover Haggadah

During the Passover meal, everyone reads a special story, called a Haggadah. Uncle Eli and Dr. Seuss have a lot in common; Haggadah was never like this! A sample from this site: *We were slaves to King Pharaoh, that terrible king, and he made us do all kinds of difficult things. Like building a pyramid of chocolate ice cream when the sun was so hot that the Nile turned to steam, and digging a ditch with a spade of soft cotton. That Pharaoh was wicked and nasty and rotten!*

http://www.acs.ucalgary.ca/~elsegal/Uncle_Eli/ Eli.html

Virtual Seder Plate

The Passover Seder meal is very symbolic. This site features a special Seder plate; click on it to learn about the various foods eaten during this ritual meal. For example, bitter herbs (usually horseradish) symbolize the bitterness of slavery. This plate has room for six foods; others have five—the page explains why this is so.

http://www.shamash.org/reform/uahc/congs/nj/ nj006/seder/plate.html

KWANZAA

Kwanzaa at the History Channel

Roll your cursor over the objects on the festive Kwanzaa table to discover their symbolic meanings. See a video clip of Dr. Maulana Ron Karenga discussing his creation of this African-American cultural holiday back in 1966.

http://www.historychannel.com/exhibits/holidays/ kwanzaa/

Kwanzaa Fun from Billy Bear

Billy Bear's celebrating by making Kwanzaa crafts, coloring pictures, and playing some holiday-centered online games. You'll also find lots of icons, screen savers, and wallpaper to decorate your computer for the season.

http://www.billybear4kids.com/holidays/kwanzaa/ kwanzaa.htm

Kwanzaa Time at Kid's Domain

You'll not only find Kwanzaa crafts, downloads, and activities, but also links to celebrate Black History month (remember these in February!) Make a family history book, candle favors, or a woven mat. Can you beat dad at the downloadable African stone games?

http://www.kidsdomain.com/holiday/kwanzaa/

Official Kwanzaa Web Site

In 1966, a man named Maulana Ron Karenga and the U.S. Organization invented a new American holiday based on harvest celebrations in Africa. They called this celebration *Kwanzaa*, a Swahili word meaning "first," signifying the first fruits of the harvest. Many Americans of African heritage celebrate this holiday each December. Find out how at the official Web site.

http://www.OfficialKwanzaaWebsite.org/

What Is Kwanzaa?

The symbolic lighting of candles is associated with many holidays. And so it is with Kwanzaa, an African American spiritual holiday emphasizing the unity of the family and encouraging a festive celebration of the oneness and goodness of life. Learn how the seven candles, the *Mshumaa*, represent the seven principles of *Nguzo Saba*. Read about the history and meaning of the other symbols used in the celebration of this holiday. A list of children's books about Kwanzaa is also provided here.

http://www.melanet.com/kwanzaa/whatis.html

A B C D E F G H I J K L M N O P Q R S T U V W X Y Z

A B C D E F G H I J K L M N O P Q R S T U V W X Y Z

NET FILES

SOUTH POLE

Is there really a striped pole stuck in the ice at the South Pole?

Answer: Can you believe there are really three "South Poles"? You can see photos of two of them at the following site. There is a red and white striped ceremonial pole, which is several yards away from the actual geographic South Pole. The "real" pole is marked by a metal rod with a U.S. Geological surveyor marker on top. It has to be re-staked in a different spot every year because the ice above it is sliding! The magnetic South Pole isn't marked by anything because it's in the Antarctic Ocean. There's also a geomagnetic pole you can read about it (and the others) at http://astro.uchicago.edu/cara/vtour/pole/poles/

MOTHER'S DAY

Billy Bear's Happy Mother's Day

Mom might love a hug, but if you want to give her more, how about a Promise Card? There's one at this site that you can use as a sample. You might promise to walk the dog, do the dishes, or clean your room. You'll also find some fun mazes (Help Mom Find All the Dirty Socks) and other games. As usual, Billy Bear offers other links for further exploration.

http://www.billybear4kids.com/holidays/mother/mom.htm

Mom's Day Fun at Kid's Domain

You know you want to make something to give your mom on Mother's Day—but what? This site gives you lots of ideas: you could make her breakfast in bed (if you had a little help from an adult), or you could make her a nice card, or a picture frame. There's even an easy recipe for making soap using your microwave, but get more help from that friendly adult, OK?

http://www.kidsdomain.com/holiday/mom/

NEW YEAR'S DAY

Billy Bear's Happy New Year's

Billy offers coloring book pages, recipes for tasty beverages, online games, and a real calendar to print out and color. There are also links to January holidays pages around the Net.

http://www.billybear4kids.com/holidays/newyears/fun.htm

Chinese New Year

Around the Chinese New Year, you'll see many red and gold decorations. The red is for luck, while the gold is for wealth. This page explains how Chinese New Year is celebrated. It includes audio of how to say "Happy New Year!" in Chinese, plus music, a recipe for festive rice cakes, and much more.

http://www.brokersys.com/~kcyong/cny.html

New Year's Eve in Times Square

On New Year's Eve in December, 1998, Net-mom and Family of Net-mom were trying to get back home after a trip to India, but we missed our connections and found ourselves far from home on a holiday layover in an airport hotel in Frankfurt, Germany. We watched TV until the early hours of the day. Amazingly, CNN-Europe was showing the events back home in New York! We all got a kick out of watching the big mirrored ball drop down in Times Square, designating the beginning of the new year. Find out all about what's going on there this year.

http://www.timessquarebid.org/new_year/

PAGAN HOLIDAYS

See also RELIGION AND SPIRITUALITY—PAGANISM

Candlegrove's Ancient Origins of the Holidays

Celebrate Winter Solstice, Saturnalia, and the Yule season as the ancients did, but with a new twist. Although we have listed this site under Pagan Holidays, you will find many parallels to Christmas, Hanukkah, and even Kwanzaa celebrations.

http://www.candlegrove.com/home.html

Circle Sanctuary

According to this site, the myth that witches worship the devil is "wrong, wrong, wrong." Learn more about this "earth religion" and its holidays: Samhain, Beltane, Lammas, and many more. This site will answer many of your questions about this religion.

http://www.circlesanctuary.org/

PI DAY

★ The Ridiculously Enhanced Pi Page

Every March 14, at 1:59 P.M., the Exploratorium museum celebrates Pi Day. Get it? The value of pi to a few decimal places is 3.14159! This irrational celebration happens to coincide with Albert Einstein's birthday. Read about the ceremonial addition of a pi bead to the strand (they are up to 1,600 decimal places) and other events that make San Francisco a unique place to live. There are also plenty of links to places where pi is elevated to new heights of acclaim by its many fans around the world. See the MATH AND ARITHMETIC—FORMULAS AND CONSTANTS section for more on Pi.

http://www.exploratorium.edu/learning_studio/pi/

ST. PATRICK'S DAY

🦆 Billy Bear's Happy St. Patrick's Day

They say that on St. Patrick's Day everyone is Irish! Come join the parade as you March through this site. Try the Pot o' Gold Money Math game, print out some coloring book pages, or dress up the leprechaun. If you don't get upset playing tricky games, try the Catch the Leprechaun game. Every time you move the mouse to where he is, he moves away! Is it possible to catch him? Yes, but you may go nuts trying! By the way, if you think the shamrock is the official emblem of Ireland, guess again—it's the harp, a favorite musical instrument in Ireland, dating back hundreds of years.

http://www.billybear4kids.com/holidays/stpatty/fun.htm

BlackDog's St. Patrick's Day Fun and Games

Can you find the hidden Pot-o'-Gold? It's somewhere in the picture, just keep clicking until you find it. This makes the resident leprechauns very cranky though, but keep clicking until you succeed. You'll also find match games, slider puzzles, coloring books, and word searches, all with a holiday theme.

http://www.blackdog.net/holiday/pat/

The Leprechaun Watch

Sshhh . . . quietly visit this webcam hidden in the misty Glen of Cloongallon. Perhaps you'll see a leprechaun! There's a handy field book to help you identify any wee folk, fairies, or other supernatural beings you might see. After you have searched, download an official certificate signed by the Secretary of the Irish Leprechaun Society!

http://www.irelandseye.com/leprechaun/leprechaun.htm

St. Patrick's Fun at Kid's Domain

You've found the pot of gold at Kid's Domain! There are lots of seasonal online games collected here, as well as holiday PC and Mac downloads (some of these are free, while others have shareware fees). This rollicking site offers craft ideas, recipes, even animated cursors and decorative pictures to color, and that's no blarney.

http://www.kidsdomain.com/holiday/patrick/

A Wee Bit o' Fun

Have you ever wondered who St. Patrick really was and why we celebrate St. Patrick's Day? Is there really such a thing as a leprechaun? Americans have been celebrating this holiday for over 200 years. Read all about the history of St. Patrick's Day at this site.

http://archive.nandotimes.com/toys/stpaddy/stpaddy.html

A B C D E F G H I J K L M N O P Q R S T U V W X Y Z

A B C D E F G H I J K L M N O P Q R S T U V W X Y Z

THANKSGIVING

The American Thanksgiving Tradition

Would you like to fix the perfect Pilgrim-style Thanksgiving dinner? Check out this site to learn about the Pilgrims and the first Thanksgiving in 1621. Great recipe ideas will help you re-create that seventeenth-century harvest feast. There is also information about Pilgrim clothing, religious practices, and lots more in this site from Plimoth Plantation.

http://www.plimoth.org/Library/Thanksgiving/ thanksgi.htm

The First Thanksgiving

What was life like on the voyage of the Mayflower? Take a virtual tour, and then find out what happened during the first year of the Plimoth settlement. Can you beat the Cyberchallenge quiz? Hint: there was no cranberry sauce at the first Thanksgiving!

http://teacher.scholastic.com/thanksgiving/

2GOOD 2MISS

Harcourt School Publishers - The Learning Site

Enter this site for a spectacular collection of entertaining and educational games for all age levels. In Science, for example, go to the Activities and Resources student area. Scroll to the third-grade section and take a walk on The Resource Trail. Move the ant from start to finish based on your answers to questions like "What resource is used to produce forests?" Is it mineral, plant, animal, air, water, or some other resource? There are spelling, reading, math, social studies, art, health, and other games and activities that you can use for free. http://www.harcourtschool.com/

> **VIDEO AND SPY CAMS let you look in on interesting parts of the world.**

Kid's Domain Thanksgiving

The riddles and jokes at this site are real "groaners," but don't let that stop you from playing the online games, trying out the Mac and PC Thanksgiving downloads, and printing out the coloring pages and mazes to play with while dinner's cooking. Decorate your table with the creative (and easy!) autumn crafts offered at this cornucopia of holiday fun.

http://www.kidsdomain.com/holiday/thanks/

Not Just for Kids! An American Thanksgiving for Kids and Families

This site has tasty recipes, turkey hotlines, and even Thanksgiving games and fun. Historical information on the first Thanksgiving and additional links to other sites are included.

http://www.night.net/thanksgiving/

Thanks-Giving Square

Giving thanks and showing reverence to a higher power is a practice followed by many cultures around the world. Sometimes "thanks-giving" is centered around a harvest celebration, as is the holiday celebrated each November in the United States. Find out about other traditions at this site from Thanks-Giving Square in Dallas, Texas. You can also read famous Thanksgiving quotations, such as this one from John Templeton: "How wonderful it would be if we could help our children and grandchildren to learn thanksgiving at an early age. Thanksgiving opens the doors. It changes a child's personality. A child is resentful, negative—or thankful. Thankful children want to give, they radiate happiness, they draw people."

http://www.thanksgiving.org/

VALENTINE'S DAY

🐾 Billy Bear's Be My Valentine

Net-mom loves a good holiday, and Valentine's Day really fits the bill! At this site you'll find cute online games, electronic greeting cards, screen savers, and wallpaper for your desktop backgrounds. Even the smallest cherubs will love the Mix and Match 'Em Up Game where you can select various hats and other articles of clothing—plus valentine messages—for Sarah Bear to carry. Can you make her look like a Valentine angel? There's also a kissing booth (pucker up for your favorite stuffed Teddy Bear) and a selection of crafts for beginners and advanced crafters alike. E-mail good enough to eat? Well, not quite, but you can select a piece of virtual valentine candy and e-mail it to your friends. Send one with nuts to that joker in math class, or a yummy fudge-coated strawberry to your crush. Can't decide? Send the whole box!

http://www.billybear4kids.com/holidays/valentin/ fun.htm

Blackdog's Valentine Kissing Test

Once there was a princess who kissed a frog. EEEUUWWW! But wait. It turns out the frog was enchanted. Kissing it broke the spell, and the frog turned out to be a dreamy prince! Try your skill at kissing frogs. Will you end up with slimy lips, or a trendy castle address?

http://blackdog4kids.com/holiday/valentine/kiss/

Bonnie's Valentine Page

This site features links to lots of holiday games and activities from all over the Web. Net-mom hasn't looked at every one Bonnie suggests, though, so parents, please preview them for your kids!

http://www2.arkansas.net/~mom/hol2.html

Brother reading your diary again? Learn to encrypt in CODES AND CIPHERS.

Crack open CODES AND CIPHERS.

Heart Basket

Deliver your real valentine candies in this pretty paper basket! Although the woven hearts look tricky, you will be surprised at how easy these are to make. Just print the pattern and follow the illustrated directions. More baskets than sweethearts? No problem—these will also look great on next year's Christmas tree.

http://piggy.wilsons.org/val/val.html

The History of Valentine's Day

Big red hearts, chocolate candy, and cards—all symbols of February 14. But the original Valentine's Day was not a bed of roses for the saint for whom this holiday is named. According to one legend, Valentine was a priest who was imprisoned and later killed for defying the emperor. While in jail, he fell in love with a young woman and wrote her a note, signing it "From your Valentine." But that's just one legend. This site will clue you in on the others.

http://www.historychannel.com/exhibits/valentine/

Valentine Fun at Kids Domain

A recipe for stained glass cookies, a "count the hearts" game, and easy crafts for little hands are only some of the features at this delightful site. Links to many Valentine-themed Shockwave and Java games, coloring book pages, and even downloadable software will make your family fall in love with Kid's Domain.

http://www.kidsdomain.com/holiday/val/

A B C D E F G H I J K L M N O P Q R S T U V W X Y Z

A
B
C
D
E
F
G
H
I
J
K
L
M
N
O
P
Q
R
S
T
U
V
W
X
Y
Z

HORSES AND EQUESTRIAN SPORTS

See also DINOSAURS AND PREHISTORIC TIMES; MAMMALS—HORSE FAMILY

The BLM National Wild Horse and Burro Program

Ever thought of adopting a wild horse? This site tells you all about what you have to do to adopt one from the U.S. Bureau of Land Management. There are requirements, though; and remember, these are wild animals that have never been around people before, so folks sometimes have difficulty getting the horses tamed. This site has a schedule of adoption locations and dates and plenty of information for the potential adoptive family. You should know that this program is controversial and not without its critics. One such site is at <*http://www.api4animals.org/default.asp?ID=89*>.

http://www.wildhorseandburro.blm.gov/

Breeds of Livestock - Horse Breeds

Sure, you've heard of Thoroughbreds, and Morgans, and maybe even Dutch Warmbloods and Trakehners, but you haven't heard of all of the breeds mentioned here! Some of them are quite rare and you don't see them very often. Check out the Zhemaichu—a Lithuanian forest breed—or the Ukrainian Saddle Horse, or Guangxi pony. Most breed descriptions include a photo, too. Don't miss HorseSmarts, the downloadable interactive quiz (PC only). But you'd better know your billets from your bog spavins first.

http://www.ansi.okstate.edu/breeds/horses/

Breyer Animal Creations

If you love horses—we mean really love horses—then chances are you have a model horse or two. Did you know there are horse shows for model horses, too? At this site you can find out how they work and what classes you and your model horse can enter. You'll also get tips about painting and otherwise reworking your Breyer or other collectible horse models.

http://www.breyermodelhorses.com/

RAILROADS AND TRAINS are on track.

★ Halt@X: An Animated Guide to Dressage

Do you get leg-yield mixed up with half-pass? You won't anymore after you visit this fascinating Web site. It uses animated GIF images of famous riders and famous horses to illustrate dressage moves like those named above in addition to piaffe, extended trot, passage, 1-tempo and 2-tempi changes, and canter pirouette. Now if you can just drag your horse into the computer room to see these movies!

http://www.ridinghabit.com/guide/animation/

The HayNet

This site is the Internet equivalent of sweet feed for horse owners: all sorts of delicious grains, dripping with molasses, each crunchier than the last. Let's move into the barn and see all the home pages for different breeds: Arabians, quarter horses, Thoroughbreds, sure; you'll also find Icelandic ponies, Halflingers, and all kinds of drafts. What's this little one here, not moving at all? Oh, it's a model horse—you'll find lots here on them, too. Check the Olympic events, the Denver Stock Show, and lots of racing and driving information. Don't miss the kids' sites, including many simulated stables and horse shows for you to join. Pull up a hay bale and make yourself comfortable.

http://www.haynet.net/

Horse Colors

You'll love this interactive horse of a different color. Click—he's an Appaloosa. Click—he's a buckskin. Click—he's a gray at age four or age ten (they start out dark gray and lighten up over time). Which color do you like best?

http://www.sprocketworks.com/shockwave/load.asp?SprMovie=horsecolorsweb

The Horse Interactive: Your Online Guide to Equine Health Care

How do you tell the age of a horse by looking at his teeth? Is it really necessary to get your horse vaccinated for rabies? What's the deal with so-called "Spring syndromes"? How can you tell if your saddle really fits your horse? All this and much, much more is available at this great site.

http://www.thehorse.com/

★ Horse-country.com

This is the ultimate horse site for juniors. Horse history, care, stories, sounds, images, and associations are all here. There's a Junior Riders Mailing Digest and an International Pen Pal List for horse lovers. "Call a check" at the simulation games—why not open your own virtual stable? Don't miss the online gymkhana or the equestrian paper dolls. This site is the best thing to happen to junior riders since Misty of Chincoteague.

http://www.horse-country.com/

Kentucky Horse Park & International Museum of the Horse

"Our history was written on his back," says this site, dedicated to the history of horses and horsemanship. Learn about horses in war, in sport, in work, and in recreation. There are also some fascinating online special exhibits: "The Draft Horse in America: Power for an Emerging Nation"; "The Buffalo Soldiers on the Western Frontier"; and the famous Thoroughbreds at "Calumet Farm: Five Decades of Champions." Don't miss the fabulous online equine art gallery, as well as a comprehensive selection of links to horse farms, racetracks, breed clubs, and commercial sites all over the Web.

http://www.imh.org/

New Rider

You really want to start riding lessons, but—how do you start? What should you wear? All these questions and more are answered at this site aimed at the very new British rider. There's also a very active message board for everyone.

http://www.newrider.com/

NET FILES

Where would you look for a tiger's pug mark?

Answer: On the ground. It's another word for a footprint or track. Its actual size is 5.5 inches by 4.5 inches (10.8 cm by 8.75 cm)! You can see a tiger's pug mark at
http://www.5tigers.org/pug.htm

North American Riding for the Handicapped Association

Many, many kids and adults with disabilities find that with some help, they can ride a horse. Net-mom herself used to volunteer at a therapeutic riding facility, so she's speaking from experience! Everything is done with the greatest safety in mind. Depending on the rider's abilities, the instructor usually has a side walker on each side of the horse, watching and spotting the rider and helping with a leg position if needed. There is also a person leading the horse (that was Net-mom's job) who just pays attention to the horse's gait and also takes care of most of the steering. It's amazing what the warmth of a horse can do to ease a muscle spasm or what the horse's rhythmic gait can do for confidence. You can read about specific therapies on this site and perhaps find a facility near you. If you don't need their services yourself, consider volunteering to help as a side walker or groom. You can even help by cleaning tack.

http://www.narha.org/

A B C D E F G H I J K L M N O P Q R S T U V W X Y Z

NET FILES

Where is the world's largest bell?

Answer: The Tsar Bell, weighing 210 tons, is in Moscow, Russia. It stands 20 feet high and has a diameter of 22 feet at the base. A fire swept Moscow in 1737, including the bell's location in the Kremlin. When water was poured on the hot bell, it cracked, and a huge piece broke off. The bell now rests on a special granite stand at the foot of the Ivan the Great bell tower. See a picture of it at *http://www. online.ru/sp/comit/kremlin/english/3l.html#*

Inside the White House @ Nationalgeographic.com

Imagine you've just been elected president of the United States! What would your first decision be? What can people expect of your presidency? You can let your imagination soar and get an idea of what it's like to sit in the president's Oval Office right here at this Web page. Best yet, you'll learn loads about presidents and U.S. history while having fun. Be careful of those pesky newspaper reporters and radio talk show hosts! *http://www.nationalgeographic.com/features/96/whitehouse/whhome.html*

The Royal Canadian Mounted Police Musical Ride

The Musical Ride of the Royal Canadian Mounted Police developed from a desire by early members to display their riding ability and entertain the local community. The series of figures that form the basis of the Musical Ride were developed from traditional cavalry drill movements. The Ride is performed by 32 regular member volunteers (male and female) who have had at least two years of police experience. The Ride contingent consists of 36 horses. It travels throughout Canada and sometimes all over the world. Visit this site to learn more about the Ride and to check their tour schedule.

http://www.rcmp-grc.gc.ca/musicalride/

The United States Equestrian Team Online

Who's on the USET (United States Equestrian Team) this year, and where are they riding next? What were the results of the Devon Horse Show? How tall is Leslie Webb's horse, Hannabal? At this site you can learn about the team, find out little-known facts, and see what's next on the schedule. See wonderful photos of medal-winners in the About USET area. How can you get on the team? You've got to be at least 16 to be considered, so you'd better go practice that sitting trot some more.

http://www.uset.com/

HOWLAND ISLAND

See UNITED STATES—TERRITORIES

Something fishy going on? Visit AQUARIUMS.

Curl up with a good URL in BOOKS AND LITERATURE!

INSECTS AND SPIDERS

See also INVERTEBRATES

★ Alien Empire

From the "Voyagers" known as monarch butterflies to the prolific "Replicators," also called mayflies, at this site you'll learn a great deal about the alien world of insects. Check the Battlezone to find out who's eating whom, visit the Metropolis to learn about termites, and explore the rest of the site on your own—if you dare. Along the way be treated to short but informative video presentations and fun puzzles.

http://www.thirteen.org/nature/alienempire/

★ AntCast at the NHM

Here's your chance to watch a live webcam as leafcutter ants go marching right across your screen. Ponder why there are few head-on collisions as the ants careen over the twig. Read the scrolling facts to learn more about leafcutter ants and their mission. An infrared camera at London's Natural History Museum lets you view them close-up.

http://www.nhm.ac.uk/museum/creepy/ antcastintro.html

Citybugs

You don't need to go to some exotic locale to study insects. They can be located everywhere! Take a look in your backyard, or your kitchen, or underneath a bright light at night. This site explains how to identify bugs and how to collect them if you're not squeamish.

http://www.cnr.berkeley.edu/citybugs/

Entomology for Beginners

This very basic page gives an introduction to insect anatomy and metamorphosis. Click on a part of the insect to find out its name and what it's for. Notice that butterflies and moths have coiled tongues for feeding on nectar inside flowers, while other insects have mouths shaped for chewing or sucking instead. In the metamorphosis section, you can see how a caterpillar changes from a crawler to a flier as it morphs into a moth. The same author has a little page of insect-related sayings, such as "ants in his pants." Read it here <http://www1.bos.nl/homes/ bijlmakers/entomology/citaten_engels.htm>.

http://www1.bos.nl/homes/bijlmakers/entomology/ begin.htm

The Firefly Files

Hey, did you see that? *FLASH!* There it is again! Must be summer, because that's a firefly for sure. You may know them better as lightning bugs. If you've ever wondered what makes a firefly glow, check here. To attract more fireflies to your yard, stop using lawn chemicals, cut down on outside lights, and let the grass grow a little longer than normal.

http://IRIS.biosci.ohio-state.edu/projects/FFiles/

Insect Recipes

They say insects can be tasty. Check this site and you will learn how to make Banana Worm Bread, Chocolate Chirpie Cookies, and more. "As seen on the Jay Leno Show," according to this page. Note their disclaimer: "The Department of Entomology at Iowa State University is not responsible for gastric distress, allergic reactions, feelings of repulsion, or other problems resulting from the ingestion of foods represented on these pages."

http://www.ent.iastate.edu/misc/insectsasfood.html

Do you know the way to San Jose? If not, check a map in GEOGRAPHY.

A B C D E F G H I J K L M N O P Q R S T U V W X Y Z

A
B
C
D
E
F
G
H
I
J
K
L
M
N
O
P
Q
R
S
T
U
V
W
X
Y
Z

Insecta Inspecta World

The world is crawling with insects. Isn't it time you knew something about them? This terrific page built by seventh graders will give you a basic overview on everything from malaria-carrying mosquitoes (don't let the audio file bug you) to beautiful monarch butterflies. There's a fascinating section on insects that appear on coins, and another on fear of spiders (arachnophobia) and what can be done about it.

http://www.insecta-inspecta.com/

Insects and Other Arthropods

Hey, check the cool dude in the fly shades. Wait— that's . . . a REAL FLY. You'd never know about his radical attire unless you were able to look at him really close-up, under a special kind of microscope. Frankly, this level of inspection makes our skin crawl. On the other hand, did you know some spiders' eyes will reflect a flashlight beam, much like a cat's?

http://www.microscopy-uk.org.uk/intro/insect.html

★ Insects on the Web

In "shameless promotion of insect appreciation," this site offers a close-up look at butterfly wing patterns, an insect encyclopedia (look under "entophiles"), and something called CE Digest (for "Cultural Entomology"). The latter features intriguing articles on such things as butterfly designs used in Japanese family crests, Cicely Mary Barker's Flower Fairies, and beetles as religious symbols. There's also a set of annotated links for your further enjoyment.

http://www.insects.org/

★ InsectSafari.com

There's no freight inside this truck. Just lots of insects. The Insect Safari truck is making its way around the country, stopping at cities along the way. And, you might be able to actually go inside the truck to see its insect exhibit. To see if the truck will be in your city, check out the tour schedule. There are also some fun games to play, including Name That Bug and Fred's Bugalizer coloring studio.

http://www.insectsafari.com/

A Look Through Insect's Eyes

Have you ever wondered how other creatures see the world? Here you can find out. Well, at least you can find out how a fruit fly and a small parasitic wasp see the world, or at least what scientists think they see.

http://www.sun-sentinel.com/graphics/news/
   insecteyes.htm

The Minibeast World of Insects & Spiders

Question: Why was the inchworm angry? Answer: He had to convert to the metric system! For more insect jokes sure to bug you, try this site. You'll also find educational resources here, so you can learn fascinating bug trivia, bug care, and bug facts.

http://members.aol.com/YESedu/welcome.html

Most Wanted Bugs

The FBIA (Federal Bug Intelligence Agency) is looking for 24 "most wanted" bugs, and they need your help. Study these fascinating mug shots—have you seen any of them? That's unlikely, at least at this close range. The photos were made with powerful microscopes. Each bug has a "rap sheet" listing its name, habitat, and why it's "wanted." Is it a coincidence that they look like space aliens? "Hello, Fox Mulder, please."

http://www.pbrc.hawaii.edu/~kunkel/wanted/

★ The O. Orkin Insect Zoo

Ugh, it's a bug! Bugs aren't really so bad. Butterflies are pretty, ladybugs are cute, and praying mantises are helpful in a garden. Insects produce valuable items too, such as honey, silk, wax, and dyes. Some insects are used for human food, and others have proven to be very useful in scientific and medical research. Explore the world of insects here—they are the most successful life-form on the planet! This site takes you on a virtual tour of the O. Orkin Insect Zoo at the Smithsonian Institution.

http://www.orkin.com/Pages/educational_info.html

PetBugs.com

You don't have to brush it or give it a bath, but you do have to know how to take care of your tarantula, walking stick, millipede, or other pet bug. This is the place to find out. By the way, contrary to popular belief, millipedes don't have a thousand legs. Here's a handy method to know how many legs your millipede has: "To find the number of legs on your millipede, count the body segments, multiply by two, and subtract six." It just goes to show that you can find anything on the Internet.

http://www.petbugs.com/

Phasmids in Cyberspace

You may not know them by their scientific names, but perhaps you have heard of a "walking stick" or "praying mantis." Some of these critters look so much like twigs and leaves that it's hard to see them in the terrarium. Apparently, they make interesting and friendly pets. Care sheets and info are available here.

http://www.ixpres.com/phasmids/

StevesAntFarm.com

This is a happenin' place. In fact, it's a crawlin' place. Steve's got an ant farm, and he's got a camera pointed at it. Every five minutes, the camera posts a new picture to this Web site. You can watch ants build tunnels, construct bridges, and make molehills out of mountains.

http://www.stevesantfarm.com/

★ University of Kentucky Department of Entomology

Is your class looking for a mascot? How about an insect? Here you'll find some guidelines to help pick the best choice for your classroom. Interested in an insect treat? How about ants on a log? Come on, it's just a stalk of celery spread with peanut butter and sprinkled with raisins! Find out which insects are harmless, like daddy long-legs and millipedes (in the Insect Stories section). Don't go buggy looking at all the creepy stuff here.

http://www.uky.edu/Agriculture/Entomology/ythfacts/
    entyouth.htm

NET FILES

What makes a rose smell like a rose?

Answer: According to the Timeless Roses site, "Fragrance is determined by the concentration of chemicals in the petals of the flower, and how these chemicals interact with each other and the atmosphere. Oils, resins, alcohols, fatty acids, and phenols all contribute to the character of scent. As a general rule, darker colored roses are more fragrant than white or yellow roses. Environmental factors which determine how a rose smells on a specific day include climatic conditions such as temperature, humidity, and time of day. Warm, sunny days with low humidity will bring out the best rose fragrance in the garden." Find out more at http://www.timelessroses.com/fragrant.htm

★ Yucky Roach World

Visit the yuckiest site on the Internet, where you can find out all about cockroaches and other bug stuff. Check out roach anatomy. Learn what they do for fun. You'll also discover that cockroaches spend 75 percent of their time resting up for those late-night snack runs. There are links to Worm World, too, if you haven't gotten your fill of yucky yet.

http://www.yucky.com/flash/roaches/

BEES

B-EYE: The World Through the Eyes of a Bee

When a bee's approaching a flower, exactly what does it see? Now you can visualize the world through simulated bee-vision. Choose a preprocessed image or interact with the images to create your own view. Check the explanation of how this works in the Description area of the site.

http://cvs.anu.edu.au/andy/beye/beyehome.html

A
B
C
D
E
F
G
H
I
J
K
L
M
N
O
P
Q
R
S
T
U
V
W
X
Y
Z

A
B
C
D
E
F
G
H
I
J
K
L
M
N
O
P
Q
R
S
T
U
V
W
X
Y
Z

Carl Hayden Bee Research Laboratory

You'll have a great time buzzin' through these pages, honey! Learn lots about bees and how they make our lives a lot sweeter. Then when you're sure you know everything, click on the *Tribeeal* Pursuits site and learn a lot more.

http://gears.tucson.ars.ag.gov/ic/

★ NOVA Online - Tales from the Hive

If you've ever wondered about the inner structure of a bee hive, here is your chance to take a safe virtual look. Learn about the queen bee and her army of workers, the mysteries of the honeycomb, and the agony and the ecstasy experienced by the hapless male drones. Find out how to interpret the "waggle dance," and see if you can guess the location of the nearest nectar.

http://www.pbs.org/wgbh/nova/bees/

BUTTERFLIES AND MOTHS

BillyBear4Kids.com Butterfly and Bugs

You won't need to test your knowledge about butterflies here. This site is all fun and games. You'll find lots of butterfly jigsaw puzzles that you can play online or download. The bigger ones have as many as 88 pieces. For a different kind of puzzle, try one of the butterfly crossword puzzles. Or, make a butterfly craft—we loved the butterfly mobile!

http://www.billybear4kids.com/butterfly/
    flutter-fun.html

Butterflies of North America

If you can't find your favorite butterfly here, it's possible you really want the Moths of North America page (see separate entry). Pick your state and see a checklist of the butterflies to be found there. Most entries offer at least one color photo, as well as lots of information, like what types of plants you might find that species' caterpillars eating. This is good information to have if you want to make a garden with host plants for butterfly eggs and caterpillars.

http://www.npwrc.usgs.gov/resource/distr/lepid/
    bflyusa/bflyusa.htm

Butterflies: On the Wings of Freedom

Start your study of butterflies at this beautiful award-winning and internationally recognized site. It has educational information, crafts, interactive sharing, multimedia, and lots more. These ThinkQuest participants weren't satisfied with the pictures of butterflies they could find, so they decided to make their own. They used everything from a camera to an electron microscope in the process! They also built models of caterpillars and butterflies, and made a movie to illustrate metamorphosis. Net-mom was pleased to meet one of the "actors" along with the site authors.

http://library.thinkquest.org/C002251/

★ The Butterfly Collection at the Field Museum

Although there are about 20,000 butterfly species in the world, they are found only in specialized habitats. That's because at their caterpillar stage of development, they have a very limited taste for food. According to this site, some of them eat only one species of plant! Compare alpine butterflies to rain forest varieties, learn the difference between butterflies and moths, and explore other basics at this page presented by Chicago's Field Museum.

http://www.fmnh.org/butterfly/

The Butterfly Web Site

Do you know what the first butterflies of spring are? Here's a hint: they have a blue sparkle about them. Give up? The azure butterflies are the first, followed by the sulphurs, then the whites. But you don't have to wait for spring to see butterflies. There are hundreds of butterflies and moths waiting for your discovery year-round. Find out how to locate moths and butterflies any time of the year. Learn about butterfly gardening and which flowers and plants attract butterflies and encourage them to lay eggs.

http://www.mgfx.com/butterflies/

Children's Butterfly Site

This great little page has a coloring book featuring the metamorphosis of a caterpillar to a butterfly. There's also a terrific frequently asked questions file. What's the difference between a butterfly and a moth? How do butterflies go to the bathroom? Where do butterflies go in the rain? Can butterflies communicate with each other? The answers are surprising!

http://www.mesc.nbs.gov/butterfly/Butterfly.html

Flying Tigers

Lots of people know about "wooly bear" caterpillars. This site explains how you can collect wooly bears and keep them over the winter. In the spring, they will pupate and turn into flying tiger moths. Some people think you can predict the severity of the oncoming winter by looking at wooly bears in the Fall. See <*http://www.almanac.com//preview2000/woollybears.html*> for more on that.

http://insects.ummz.lsa.umich.edu/MES/notes/
    entnote19.html

★ Journey North

Journey North is a project where the Internet really shines. Each year, monarch butterflies migrate from Canada and the U.S. to their wintering grounds in Mexico and California. In the spring, they start their journey north again. Where are they now? Go outside—see any monarch butterflies? OK, now go back inside, and log on to this site to report your findings. Click on Help Track Spring's Journey North. Your results will be combined with other reports from all over the U.S., and a map will be created to show where the migratory monarchs have landed. Butterflies aren't the only things monitored here. Besides tracking various animals and birds, this site tracks when the ice goes out of various lakes and rivers, where the tulips are blooming, and where the spring frogs are peeping.

http://www.learner.org/jnorth/

Vocabulary University

Sam Mantics, Dean of Admissions and Directions at Vocabulary University®, guides you through several levels of puzzles as you search for the meaning of words in the limitless quest for vocabulary acquisition. Don't get the idea this is very easy—start with the lowest level first and work up. Cinny Nym and Auntie Nym are available to give you hints, and there are clues everywhere. After you do a few of these, you'll catch on quickly! *http://www.vocabulary.com/*

Monarch Watch

Scientists know that the monarch butterflies of North America travel to warmer climates when winter comes. But they don't know how they move across the continent, or how weather influences the path they take. To answer these questions, scientists have come up with a program to tag these lovely black and orange creatures. Want to help? At this site you can learn how to become a volunteer. You'll need to learn the methods for capturing and tagging monarchs, keeping a monarch journal, and making a butterfly net.

http://www.MonarchWatch.org/

Moths of North America

If you can't find your favorite moth here, it's possible you really want the Butterflies of North America page (see separate entry). While you're here, check out the delicate beauty of the luna moth (*Actias luna*).

http://www.npwrc.usgs.gov/resource/distr/lepid/
    moths/mothsusa.htm

A
B
C
D
E
F
G
H
I
J
K
L
M
N
O
P
Q
R
S
T
U
V
W
X
Y
Z

A
B
C
D
E
F
G
H
I
J
K
L
M
N
O
P
Q
R
S
T
U
V
W
X
Y
Z

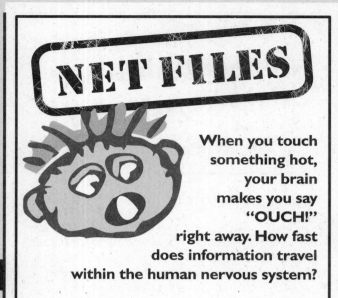

NET FILES

When you touch something hot, your brain makes you say "OUCH!" right away. How fast does information travel within the human nervous system?

Answer: It depends on which type of neuron is sending the message. According to the Neuroscience for Kids - Explore the NS page, "Transmission can be as slow as 0.5 meters per second or as fast as 120 meters per second. That's the same as going 268 miles per hour! Check the math out yourself." Speed over to

http://faculty.washington.edu/chudler/what.html
for more fun facts from the world of neuroscience.

🦆 Where do Butterflies Come From?

Where do butterflies come from? You'll know the answer to that question if you visit this Web page and create your very own chrysalis with a surprise inside!

http://www.hhmi.org/coolscience/butterfly/

SPIDERS AND ARACHNIDS

Arachnology for Kids

Why do you think they call it the Web, anyway? It's to honor that famous arachnid—the spider! But this site doesn't stop with spiders. It moves right on into scorpions and other creatures with lots of legs and bitey parts. You'll love it. Check the links to origami spiders and scorpions and lots of other fun stuff.

http://www.ufsia.ac.be/Arachnology/Pages/Kids.html

Construction of a Web

If you've ever wondered how spiders make those beautiful wheeled webs, this very simple site will show you the ropes. Do you think you could duplicate this feat with a ball of yarn?

http://www.xs4all.nl/~ednieuw/Spiders/Info/ Construction_of_a_web.html

INTERNET

★ An Atlas of Cyberspaces

You're not likely to take this atlas with you on your next road trip. But you may find it fascinating if you do much traveling on the Web. It's a funky collection of maps that visually depict various digital territories. Some look like a traditional real-world map, while others are much more abstract, like the one showing the structure of Web sites connected by their hypertext links. A must-see!

http://www.cybergeography.org/atlas/atlas.html

Glossary of Internet Terms

Use this glossary to attach some meaning to the unfamiliar words you will no doubt run across while wandering through the Web. Some descriptions will enlighten and some will confuse, while others may be so technical they make no sense at all. Whether you're interested or just curious, you will definitely increase your "Net" knowledge if you stop by this site.

http://www0.delphi.com/navnet/glossary/

★ Matisse's Glossary of Internet Terms

Confused by all those Internet terms? Can't tell an IMHO from a TTFN? Don't SLIP in the MUD—come on over to this terrific glossary, and all will be revealed.

http://www.matisse.net/files/glossary.html

The Net: User Guidelines and Netiquette

Everybody knows that politeness and good etiquette make life easier. Waiting your turn in line, keeping your locker in order, or being nice to your friends—all this helps you as much as the people around you. The same is true on the Internet. There are some basic rules of etiquette (on the Internet it's called netiquette) that help keep things running smoothly. Check out some of these basic rules of Internet good behavior. To find this document in other languages, just click on the words "TRANSLATED VERSION OF THE GUIDE" at the top of the home page.

http://www.fau.edu/netiquette/net/

BEGINNER'S GUIDES

Beginners' Central, a User's Guide to the Internet

We consider this an advanced beginner's site. While it covers all the basics on the Internet and Web, you'll find enough in-depth information to keep you reading (and rereading) for a while. Want to know how to make your own name and address "signature file" for your e-mail? Need to know just a little about Telnet and FTP? Want to print out the contents of a Web frame? What are e-mail attachments, and how do you send one? These are examples of some of the questions answered by this very nice site.

http://www.northernwebs.com/bc/

★ CNET Help.com Internet

Browsers, chat, AOL, cable modems, e-mail, downloading—would you like to know more than you do now about these and other topics? CNET offers a terrific guide to all of them. There's a very complete tutorial on how to use Internet Explorer (there's one on Netscape, too!) plus links to free or fee lessons on everything from ICQ to (yikes) Unix Sendmail.

http://www.help.com/cat/3/

The Cyberpilot's License

What should you do if you receive an unpleasant e-mail? Do you "flame" the sender right back? That's not the best idea. Learn how to cope with problems like this by trying out various scenario exercises and solutions. This site's not just about e-mail. You'll also find out about cyberpilot rights as well as responsibilities, including ethics.

http://www.cwrl.utexas.edu/~burniske/cpl/

★ Get CyberSavvy

Get cyber savvy! There are two paths you may choose at this site. One is just for new users of the Net, and the other is specifically for families concerned about Net dangers. In the beginner's section, you can get an overview of what you can do on the Internet. The Family Guide includes "What should I do if . . ." situations to help parents begin a dialog with their kids about specific Net hazards. This very interesting site is from The Direct Marketing Association at <http:// www.the-dma.org/>.

http://www.cybersavvy.org/

Getting Started on the Internet

This great little guide gives you a bird's-eye view of e-mail, how to find something on the Web, and how to distinguish between newsgroups and mailing list discussion groups. Check the section on Internet Concerns, which includes Internet safety, Internet fraud, viruses, and advice on what to do about unsolicited commercial e-mail, or spam.

http://www.imaginarylandscape.com/helpweb/welcome.html

Internet for Kids

You need to crawl before you can walk. On the Internet, you need to click and scroll before you can surf—the Web, that is. If clicking and scrolling is something new to you, head over to this site for a few lessons. Once you can maneuver your mouse, you'll move on to identifying links that let you navigate a Web site or jump from one site to another. In a kid-friendly way, the site also answers that big question: What is the Internet?

http://www.burlco.lib.nj.us/Classes/Intforkids/

A B C D E F G H I J K L M N O P Q R S T U V W X Y Z

★ Learn the Net

Parental advisory: please preview this site, there are loads of ads. Besides English, this beginner's guide is offered in German, Spanish, French, and Italian. There's a wonderful tutorial on connecting to the Internet, getting started with your Web browser, and making sure you have a safe experience on the Net. Find sections on protecting your privacy, buying things online (see Protect Yourself), and safety tips. Check out the Netiquette section for tips on finding your place in cyberspace.

http://www.learnthenet.com/

★ PBS Online Presents . . . Life on the Internet

Want to get up to speed on the information superhighway? Check the map here at the PBS Online Beginner's Guide. Learn about Internet search tools, netiquette, and applications such as e-mail and Web browsers. Take a detour to the Stories and Links area to find out how people around the world actually use the Internet. You may be surprised to learn that the list ranges from rock stars to the Vatican's religious leaders! Don't forget to visit the Timeline of Internet history (alas, only through 1997) and the section Young, Smart, and Online. Maybe you'll get some ideas that will let you create your own spot in the Net's future history.

http://www.pbs.org/internet/

Tek Camp

There are camps for playing baseball, camps for riding horses, and camps for pretty much every pastime. So, it should come as no surprise that there are camps for learning about the World Wide Web. This particular Web camp, of course, is a virtual one, and so are the adventures you'll take on Paw Island, a magical island of dogs and cats. Your Web-learning skills begin when you pick up Butch, an orphan puppy who's coming to live on the island. Complete all seven adventures, and you'll become an "official Web guide."

http://www.pawisland.com/mainmenu.html

BROWSERS

BrowserWatch

Who is winning the Web browser wars these days? What's the best browser for you to use? BrowserWatch has news almost every day. You'll find rumors, product announcements, and plug-ins galore. Notice this site even keeps up with exotic stuff, like browsers for the Amiga.

http://browserwatch.internet.com/browsers.html

CNET.com - Internet - Browsers

Want to know if you're using the latest version of your browser, or want to test-drive a different one? All the tools you need are right here: browsers, specialized plug-in applications like Shockwave Flash and Alexa, and more. Remember, if you don't have the newest stuff in your toolkit, everything looks like a This Old Net rerun. This site also offers beginner's guides to the major browsers.

http://home.cnet.com/category/0-3773.html

Surf Monkey

Is it a browser? Is it a filter? Is it a kid-safe Web site? Is it a safe place to chat? It's all of these things and more. You need parental permission to join the club (there's a monthly fee), but once you do, you can set up private chat rooms with your cyberfriends. Your parents get to pick who's on your cyberfriends list, and only those kids and the kids on their cyberfriends list can be involved in your chat room. To say it a different way, the only people you can have in your private chat room with you are friends and friends of friends.

http://www.surfmonkey.com/

CHAT, MUDS, MOOS, AND IRC

See also INTERNET—SAFETY.

MUDs and MOOs (you'll also hear of similar MUSHs and MUSEs) are programs that let you explore, and sometimes create, computer-generated, text-based worlds. For example, you can build a stream next to a mountain and maybe put a magical fish in it. You can talk live, via your computer keyboard, to kids from all over the world and learn about science, history, and computers. Best of all, these are a ton of fun! You'll also see one recommended IRC (Internet relay chat) channel in this section. It involves a multichannel real-time chat with kids all over. There's a nice tutorial for IRC here <http://www.irchelp.org/>.

Chat Rooms and Instant Messaging

Net-mom lists only chat rooms that are monitored and safe for kids. You may also want to try some of the free "instant message" or "pager" services that let you chat with your online buddies. Be sure to ask your parents first, and then you may want to check out ICQ at <http://web.icq.com/> and the nice user's guide at <http://www.icq.com/products/ webguide.html>. Yahoo Messenger (formerly called Yahoo Pager) at <http://pager.yahoo.com/ pager/> and AOL Instant Messenger (AIM) at <http://www.aol.com/aim/> offer other choices. Note that you do not have to be an AOL member to use AIM.

Chatdanger

Although chat rooms are fun, you have to remember that it's possible you're not talking to another kid. This site outlines this and other dangers (the true stories are chilling), and suggests ways to help keep yourself safe. Learn how to evaluate a chat room and its procedures. Parents should also check the special section for them if they don't know much about IRC and other types of chat.

http://www.chatdanger.com/

Trick roping secrets are revealed in KNOTS.

Headbone Zone

There are several chat rooms here, including some for teens and some for younger kids. Before you sign on, remember to read their rules: don't give out personal information in chat (addresses, last names, school names, ICQ#s, phone numbers). Once someone has this kind of info, it takes only about five seconds to track you down. Besides, if you do give out this info in chat, you'll be booted. Bummer.

http://www.headbone.com/

Internet Relay Chat (IRC) Help

There's a nice overview of what IRC is, how you use it, where to find a server and log on to a channel, and other insider tips. Son-of-Net-Mom highly recommends the information here as being a good beginner's guide.

http://www.irchelp.org/

NET FILES

In London's Westminster Abbey, who is buried standing up?

Answer: According to the official Westminster Abbey Web site, "The Elizabethan poet Ben Jonson, who died in 1637, was buried standing up. One story says that, dying in great poverty, he begged 18 inches of ground in the Abbey from Charles I. Another story relates that the poet told the Dean of Westminster that he was too poor to be buried in Poets' Corner and that 2 feet by 2 feet would be sufficient for him. The story is thought to be true."
http://www.westminster-abbey.org/library/burial/jonson.htm

A
B
C
D
E
F
G
H
I
J
K
L
M
N
O
P
Q
R
S
T
U
V
W
X
Y
Z

A
B
C
D
E
F
G
H
I
J
K
L
M
N
O
P
Q
R
S
T
U
V
W
X
Y
Z

KIDLINK IRC

KIDLINK is one of the oldest kid-friendly sites on the Net. Internet relay chat (IRC) is a way for you to talk to kids all over the globe in real time. With IRC, when you type something, other kids can type right back! Some IRC channels are open to everyone, and they are pretty wild. This one is just for kids, and you have to register before they will let you use it. It is carefully monitored. Don't pass by, give IRC a try.

http://www.kidlink.org/rti/irc/

MOOSECrossing

Would you like to build your own world with other kids from around the planet? Would you like to work on special projects with kids age 13 and under? (People older than that are welcome, too; they are given the title of "Ranger" and act as role models.) Would you like to create your own virtual Hogwarts or other world of fantasy? If you answered "Yes" to these questions, then MOOSE Crossing is the place for you. Teachers are also welcome to use MooseCrossing with their classes.

http://www.cc.gatech.edu/elc/moose-crossing/

Britain's Rocky Past

Enjoy a cartoon version of Earth's prehistory starting with the Big Bang theory and ending with the appearance of Man. Sit back and watch the continents slide around via plate tectonics, view ice ages as they come and go, and then be amazed as the dinosaurs evolve, flourish, and then turn belly-up. When the show's over, try the interactive version. Pick any geologic period to explore. You'll learn what we know about that period from its fossil record.
http://www.bbc.co.uk/history/games/rocky/indexfull.html

> **Try actual reality.**

DEVICES ON THE NET

See VIDEO AND SPY CAMS

E-MAIL

Accessing the Internet by E-Mail FAQ

A lot of people don't know it, but you can use e-mail to surf the Web and retrieve files. Yes, you read that right. It's possible to read the information on Web pages even if all you have is e-mail access to the Net. This site reveals this secret. OK, so it's not that easy, but it is possible.

http://www.faqs.org/faqs/internet-services/
    access-via-email/

Free E-mail Address Directory

This resource lists more than 1,000 places to get free e-mail accounts and more. What more could you want? Well, how about free online calendars and pagers? Free disk drive space? Or maybe you'd prefer free Internet access? Check it out, but be sure to ask your parents before you sign up for anything.

http://www.emailaddresses.com/

Gaggle.Net Free Filtered E-mail for Schools

Does your school offer e-mail for students? If not, ask your administrators to check into this free product. Advertiser supported, it offers unlimited student accounts, filtered e-mail, and teacher control. If your school has a no-ads policy, there is also an option to pay a nominal per-account fee. Take a look at the online tour and the screen shots.

http://www.gaggle.net/

Take Back the Net - CNET Teaches Self-defense Against Spam

You won't be learning Kung Fu in this self-defense class. But you will learn how to defend yourself against unwanted e-mail, commonly referred to as spam. The first line of defense is to avoid spammers, and the tips on this site will show you how to do that. If you're already a victim of spam, there are reviews of products and services that will help rid your inbox of spam.

http://www.cnet.com/internet/
0-3793-8-5181225-1.html

What Can Be Done About Spam?

Spam, or unsolicited commercial e-mail, is an annoyance for everyone. From the "make money fast" variety to ones containing subjects that can't even be printed in this book, junk mail clogging your e-mail inbox can be a real problem. Other sites with useful information about how to deal with spam include Junkbusters <http://www.junkbusters.com/> and E-mail Abuse <http://www.emailabuse.org/>.

FILE STORAGE
Virtual Hard Drive Space

A convenient way to swap files with friends, or store your backups remotely, exists for anyone with a net connection. Remote hard disk space, or "virtual floppy drives," is available at NetFloppy <http://www.netfloppy.com/> and it is free. Apple Computer also provides this and other free services for Mac owners. Find it at <http://itools.mac.com/>.

HISTORY
Hobbes' Internet Timeline - The Definitive Internet History

How did all this Internet stuff get started, anyway? The unofficial history of the Internet is here. You'll find lots of facts and lots of definitions that you'll probably need help defining from Matisse's Glossary of Internet Terms (see separate entry).

http://www.isoc.org/guest/zakon/Internet/History/
HIT.html

Nerds 2.0.1

If you've ever wondered about the history of the Internet, this is a good site to visit. Just click on the Timeline section. You'll find out how the Internet went from "Networking the Nerds" to "Serving the Suits" to "Wiring the World." It's easy to read an entire multipage section once you figure out that the Next Page button is at the top of the text. The Next Section button is at the bottom. There's also a nice glossary, as well as a Cast of Characters.

http://www.pbs.org/opb/nerds2.0.1/

MEDIA LITERACY
Awesome Web Sites

How do you tell a bad Web site from an awesome one? Enter MAC's School for Website Investigators and find out. When you learn the difference, you could become one of MAC's Junior Website Investigators and help him identify awesome sites. If MAC picks the site you reviewed, he'll post it. But don't expect to find an extensive list of awesome sites here. You'll only get to see the recent winners of the Awesome Website Award.

http://istweb.syr.edu/AWArds/

★ Parenting WebSmart Kids

How do you know if the information you find on the Internet is true? There are many ways to evaluate resources, and this Web site shows you how. Get your parents up to speed, too, by exploring these activities together.

http://www.websmartkids.org/

The Quality Information Checklist

This page offers eight ways of evaluating Web pages. Click through these tips, and you'll know a lot about who's saying what and whether or not to believe it!

http://www.quick.org.uk/menu.htm

A B C D E F G H I J K L M N O P Q R S T U V W X Y Z

A B C D E F G H **I** J K L M N O P Q R S T U V W X Y Z

> ## Mr. Spock agrees it is highly logical to want to know all about STAR TREK, STAR WARS, AND SPACE EPICS.

★ Web Awareness

Check out the Parent's section to learn how to keep safe on the Net, as well as explore the "5 'W's and 1 'H' of Cyberspace." These great rules to remember include Who created the information? Where are you on the Web? When was the site created? and lots more. There are also special sections for teachers and librarians.

http://www.webawareness.org/

SAFETY

See also INTERNET—CHAT, MUDS, MOOS, AND IRC

BrainPOP - Online Safety

You might be safe in your own home, but when you connect to the Internet you're entering an unsafe world. While the Internet is a great tool for learning and talking to family and friends, you're also likely to run into creeps and strangers. When that happens, what do you do? At this site, you'll learn the rules to protect yourself online.

http://www.brainpop.com/specials/onlinesafety/

Center for Media Education

Find out how online marketeers are targeting kids like you, and discover what you can do about it. While you're visiting this site, be sure to read the information about violence in TV programming, local TV station educational programming requirements, and how you can become media literate.

http://www.cme.org/

★ Childnet International

In the crowded arena of Internet safety sites, it is refreshing to find a person and an organization that not only means well but does well. Childnet International, founded by Nigel Williams, works against child porn and for media-savvy kids everywhere. Childnet International (in association with Cable and Wireless) runs a prestigious annual contest to reward innovation in kids' Web sites, and hard work by individuals and organizations worthy of particular recognition. Find out how you can enter here. Additionally, read the great safety tips and other suggestions to help you make the most of your Internet excursions.

http://www.childnet-int.org/

★ CyberNetiquette

You want to help your little sister learn about Internet safety rules? If she likes Disney characters, just take her to this site, pull up a chair, and settle back for a story. The stories do take a while to download, but they teach you what you need to know to stay safe. There are several stories currently available: "Who's Afraid of Little Sweet Sheep," about chat room safety, "The Bad Apple," concerning computer viruses, and "Web Mania," which will educate you about e-mail netiquette and polite Netsurfing behavior. There's also a nice list of Internet safety tips.

http://disney.go.com/cybersafety/

★ GetNetWise - You're One Click Away

There's been a lot of talk in the news about the Internet having stuff on it that is inappropriate for kids. The overwhelming majority of information is OK, but those news stories can make you nervous. Some people are even talking about keeping kids off the Net entirely, which would be terrible! We think that access to information is a good thing. But we also recognize that parents may want to use filtering software and other tools in the digital toolbox. This page, from a coalition of Internet Service Providers and content providers, will tell you what's available. There are also safety tips written by Dr. Larry Magid and additional great content for kids.

http://www.getnetwise.org/

Kids Online

Parents should be sure to look through the resources on this site, which include statistics on Internet dangers, a sample chapter from Donna Rice Hughes' popular book, and links to useful sites on Internet safety. There are also links to various self-help groups dealing with overcoming online addictions.

http://protectkids.com/

★ Media Awareness Network - the Three Little CyberPigs

The Three Little Cyberpigs have different adventures every time we visit this page, so there is no telling which adventure you'll see. Today though, we are enjoying the Second Adventure, called "Cybersense and Nonsense." It's all about chat room safety, and how you can't trust everything you read on the Internet. You can download it to your Win or Macintosh computer and play it as many times as you want to.

http://www.media-awareness.ca/eng/cpigs/cpigs2.htm

Net Family News

What's news? Subscribe to this weekly newsletter and find out. It will alert you to the latest Internet safety and privacy tools, Web resources, Net-use policies at schools and libraries, and more. Although the newsletter is aimed at parents and teachers, children will enjoy visiting many of the sites it reviews. Get the newsletter via e-mail, or visit the site to read the archives.

http://NetFamilyNews.org/

★ The NetSmartz Workshop

For some online safety games that take a fresh approach, click over this site. You'll meet Nettie, who will help you improve your safe-surfing habits. Nettie knows how to avoid "WizzyWigs" like "Follow-Me Fiona," a scary cyberstalker and sexual predator. She'll also introduce you to "Spamozoid," who sends e-mail to people she doesn't know, and "Oogle," who spies on what you do on the Internet. If you come across "Clicky," he's a good guy, so listen to what he says.

http://www.netsmartz.org/

★ PBS Kids: Techknow

"Get Your Web License Here" is a ten-question quiz. It asks you what information is safe to give out online. You may know those answers by now, but how good are you at answering more technical questions, say, on the fine points of domain names? You can print a certificate once you have passed the test.

http://pbskids.org/did_you_know/techknow/

★ SafeKids.com

The Internet is a wonderful communications medium: you can learn a lot, make new friends, and have a whole new world opened to you. However, there may be parts of the Internet you don't want to see. As with some television programs, or books, or magazines, or parts of town, your parents decide what you can and cannot view. Make your Internet experiences great! Dr. Larry Magid, syndicated columnist and personal friend of Net-mom, is your friendly guide.

http://www.safekids.com/

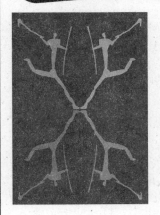

Some early scientists thought they grew from seeds dropped by stars. Others were sure these objects were carved from stone by ancient, forgotten artists. What are they?

http://www.fmnh.org/exhibits/exhibit_sites/tt/TTTb.htm

Answer: Fossils. You can even make your own fossils using the handy recipe at this site. First you take a dead insect, follow the simple instructions, and wait about 400 million years. For an explanation, check

A
B
C
D
E
F
G
H
I
J
K
L
M
N
O
P
Q
R
S
T
U
V
W
X
Y
Z

The Geometry Center

If you're looking for interactive geometry, you've come to the right place. Manipulate Java or other Web-based geometric drawing programs. You can also download many of them to play on your own computer. One of our favorites is KaleidoTile for the Mac, which lets you create geometric figures you've never heard of before and can't pronounce (fortunately, a voice tells you what they are). The interactive "math you can manipulate" programs have big names, but don't let that put you off. Check out the directions for building the world's largest 20-sided icosahedron. You probably need one for your room. Find the construction plans at *http://www.geom.umn.edu/docs/education/build-icos/*

Safeshopping.org

Is it safe to buy something online? How much do you know about the seller? What happens when good deals go bad? This site offers answers from the legal staff of the American Bar Association.

http://www.safeshopping.org/

SafetyEd International

Teaching kids about Internet safety since 1998, Colin Gabriel Hatcher's renowned cyberwatchdog organization offers loads of useful information for kids, parents, and teachers! There is also an opportunity for those 21 and over to help track down pedophiles and scout out instances of online child pornography. Specialized training is necessary, of course. Find out how you can help, and perhaps participate, with the work of this worthy organization.

http://www.safetyed.org/mainclouds.html

Stay Safe Online

What does Shaquille O'Neal know about Internet safety? As it turns out, quite a bit! Watch the presentation to learn how to protect your privacy and stay safe online. At the end, you can take a quiz to earn your Internet license. There's also a closed captioned version if you'd like to read along with the animation. This site was developed by Shaquille O'Neal, Microsoft, and the Boys and Girls Clubs of America.

http://www.msn.staysafeonline.com/

★ Surf Swell Island

The surf's up at Surf Swell Island, and you're just in time to help Mickey and his friends go on a treasure hunt to learn about online safety. One adventure lets you help Mickey and Minnie decide what's OK to share with your online pals and what should be kept private. Your good manners and knowledge of Internet symbols will help Goofy open the doors of the Temple of Tact and collect another jewel. Collect all of the jewels, and you'll enter the Treasure Palace. If you make it that far, you'll get something neat that you can print and keep.

http://www.surfswellisland.com/

★ Teen Safety on the Information Highway

If you cross a road unsafely you could be hurt. But that doesn't mean you should never cross a road. Once you learn to "look both ways" and stay aware, it becomes a safe, instinctive task. The same rules apply to using the Internet. Learn the turf, follow the rules, and know the dangers, and it, too, can become a safe, instinctive journey. This lively site shows the dangers and explains the rules to keep your Internet travels safe.

http://www.safeteens.com/

Bring your shovel and meet us in the TREASURE AND TREASURE-HUNTING section.

SAFETY—HATE SPEECH

Hate on the Internet

Parental advisory: please preview this site. If you need to do a report on "hate speech on the Internet," or if you just want to see what all the controversy is about, this site will give you an overview. See sample pages from several sites that will never be "Net-mom Approved."

http://www.tolerance.org/hate_internet/

A Parent's Guide to Hate on the Internet

Parental advisory: please preview this site from the Anti-Defamation League. When kids say they hate somebody, they usually mean they don't like the person. But on the Internet, "hate" extends to sites that promote violence, racism, bigotry, and the like. If you encounter one of those sites, you may not fully understand what you're seeing and reading. Ask a parent to visit this site with you. Together, it will help you talk about hatred and prejudice on the Internet.

http://www.adl.org/issue_education/
    parents_guide_hate_net.html

SAFETY—PREDATORS

★ CyberTipline

Parental advisory: please preview this site. CyberTipline, sponsored by the National Center for Missing and Exploited Children (NCMEC), is a national clearinghouse for tips and leads regarding the sexual exploitation of children in cyberspace. Anyone may use the report form on this site to report incidents of suspicious or illegal Internet activity, including the distribution of child pornography online or situations involving the online enticement of children for sexual exploitation. You can also call your report in to the Center's toll-free, 24-hour tipline at 800-843-5678. Net-mom salutes the supporters and sponsors that make this service possible.

http://www.missingkids.com/cybertip/

NET FILES

What are "Moki Steps" and where can you find them?

Answer: In the 1200s there was a flourishing culture of cliff dwellers in Southwestern Colorado, in a beautiful place called Mesa Verde, now a National Park. How did they climb from their cliffside homes to the top of the mesa to get water and harvest crops? The "Moki Steps" are hand- and footholds built right into the vertical cliff faces—hundreds of feet above the canyon floor. The Anasazi carved these into the rock spaced in such a way that if an enemy (who didn't know the secret) started climbing down with the wrong foot he would get stuck halfway! Travel back in history to http://www.ausbcomp.com/RedMan/mesa_verde.htm and read more about the Anasazi cliff dwellings and other mysterious places.

Kid Tips 101: The Bad Guy's Toolbox

Parental advisory: please preview this site, which contains frank language. On the Internet, it's hard to tell the good guys from the bad guys. Sometimes, you can decide who should be avoided by looking at the way they behave online. This site gives you a peek inside this not-so-nice toolbox. Hint: people don't offer you modeling jobs over the Internet.

http://www.kidprints.org/toolbox.html

SAFETY—PRIVACY

Kids Privacy

Did you know that if you're under the age of 13, there are special rules Web sites must follow when they ask you for information? It's due to the provisions of the Children's Online Privacy Protection Act (COPPA). This particular site focuses on what parents should know about COPPA.

http://www.kidsprivacy.org/

A
B
C
D
E
F
G
H
I
J
K
L
M
N
O
P
Q
R
S
T
U
V
W
X
Y
Z

A
B
C
D
E
F
G
H
I
J
K
L
M
N
O
P
Q
R
S
T
U
V
W
X
Y
Z

Catch a ride on a Carousel in AMUSEMENT PARKS.

Kidz Privacy

This is the official Federal Trade Commission kids' site outlining the safeguards protecting the privacy of kids under 13. Read why some sites are required to get your parents' permission before you join chat rooms, enter contests, and participate in activities. Check out the safety rules. Your best protection against loss of privacy is your own determination to avoid it.

http://www.ftc.gov/bcp/conline/edcams/kidzprivacy/

Who hit baseball's first recorded home run, and when?

Answer: Ross Barnes on May 2, 1876. For more baseball stats than you can shake your bat at, go to *http://baseball-almanac.com/first1.shtml*

SEARCH ENGINES AND DIRECTORIES

AltaVista

Ask AltaVista a question in "natural language." That means you can ask, "What breed of dog should I get?" rather than having to create some weird search strategy with lots of plusses and parentheses (although Alta Vista lets you do that, too, in Advanced Search). And if you want a picture of a dog, just click on Image. You could also click on Video or Audio if you wanted to search for multimedia, including MP3 files (read about them in the MUSIC AND MUSICIANS chapter of this book). AltaVista allows special searches on URLs and host names, too. Do you have a cool home page? Do you want to know if other pages around the Web have linked theirs to yours? Then type this into the AltaVista Simple Search form: link: *your page name here*. Find more of these tips in The Help Section at *<http://doc.altavista.com/help/search/ introduction.shtml>*. There's also a Family Filter offered by AltaVista. Try it out and see what you think. And don't forget AltaVista's translation service called Babel fish. It provides pretty good translation of a Web page from one language to another, for free. If you'd rather browse a directory rather than search the Web, they offer that option, too.

http://www.altavista.com/

★ Ask Jeeves for Kids!

Why doesn't someone invent a kid-safe search engine that lets you type in a real question rather than all those plusses and minuses and quotes and other weird terms? So, you could just type in "I want information on the SuperSoaker 3000," and you'd get back just a few targeted sites, not 23,000 choices! And if you weren't the World's Greatest Speller, the search engine would check the spelling of your question, too. You could type in "I need a map of Arizionia (sic)," and it would ask you if you really wanted "Arizona." Why doesn't someone invent a search tool like that? Guess what, someone did. Why not go and Ask Jeeves?

http://www.ajkids.com/

Coachfind.com

Don't scratch your head if you can't find what you're looking for online. Head over to this site for some tips and techniques for searching the Internet. The site reviews search engines and offers the latest news about them. You'll also find a roundup of the best search engines and Internet directories. If you can't find the answer to your search question on this site, ask the Internet Coach.

http://searchtips.apte.com/

★ FindSounds.com

If for some reason you need to find the song of a bluebird, the roar of a lion, the scream of a jet, or the gurgle of a brook, try this site. It offers a search engine index to the Web's sounds and audio samples. You can search by the name of the sound, by file format, size, or other choice. What's cool is that for each "hit," you'll see a colorful graphic waveform representation of what the sound "looks" like. Even with no audio expertise, you'll be able to compare the hits and decide which ones might be best.

http://www.findsounds.com/

★ Google

One of the best-kept secrets of Web searching is the search engine known as Google. When you ask a question, it tries to put the "right" sites at the top of your hit list. It's usually very accurate. You'll note the button labeled "I'm Feeling Lucky." That means you're so sure about the way you phrased your question that there's little chance the first hit won't be the right one. For example, if you typed "Harry Potter" you might think the first hit would take you directly to the official page. Will it?

http://www.google.com/

Get on board, little children, in RAILROADS AND TRAINS.

★ KidsClick! Web Search

Browse thousands of educational and fun Web sites in 15 different categories. All of them have been selected, categorized, and described by a team of librarians who know what kids want. How do they know? Because kids come into their libraries and ask for these types of things! There is a neat and fast search engine to get you where you want to go. You can search for sites by your reading level, as well as the amount of graphics you care to load.

http://sunsite.berkeley.edu/KidsClick!/

★ KidsClick! Worlds of Web Searching

Learn the secrets of searching the Web from the Web-savvy librarians of Kidsclick. This site is a must-see!

http://www.worldsofsearching.org/

★ Lycos Zone

The Lycos FunZone selections for kids are arranged in several big areas: Fun, Games, Alfy's Playground, Homework, and Sing Along. There are also sections especially for Parents and Teachers. Parents will want to know about Lycos' easy-to-use SearchGuard. It screens both searches and Web sites for adult content. It's free, and it can also be set up to disallow chat, discussion boards, and Web-based e-mail. More information about SearchGuard may be found at <http://searchguard.lycos.com/>.

http://lycoszone.lycos.com/

Search Engine Showdown: The Users' Guide to Web Searching

Read the latest news and reviews on search engines and directories. Find out which ones have family filters, which ones give the most relevant results, and which are the biggest and best. We also suggest a similar site, Search Engine Watch, for news about searching, new features, legislation, search tips, and more <http://searchenginewatch.com/>.

http://searchenginesshowdown.com/

A
B
C
D
E
F
G
H
I
J
K
L
M
N
O
P
Q
R
S
T
U
V
W
X
Y
Z

Seven Steps Toward Better Searching

"My plump starfish quickly lowered Lincoln's tie." Huh? What's that mean? According to this site, it's a secret code to help you remember how to refine your search strategies and get better results that will give you the answer you're looking for.

http://edweb.sdsu.edu/WebQuest/searching/
    sevensteps.html

★ Yahoo!

Yahoo! is a directory. In other words, Yahoo! does not index the whole Internet, but a selected view of it. This directory is fun and easy to use. Browse general categories, such as science or education. Under those are smaller subdivisions, which branch into still smaller sub-subtopics, and on and on. Don't worry, it's simpler than it sounds. We particularly like their My Yahoo! service. It creates a home page for you, based on your preferences. Want to follow the scores for just your favorite teams? Want to see the weather for your city and for someone you know in another state? Want to read news about computers but not news about entertainers? Set your news up your way by clicking the My button (or Personalize link) at the top of the page.

http://www.yahoo.com/

★ Yahooligans!

This directory is just for kids. Want a quick pointer to a valuable site to help with your homework? Got a few minutes to play an online game, but need to find one fast? The Yahooligans! directory can save your day. It arranges terrific Internet sites into six subject categories, and it's easy to use. Even if you don't know what you want to find, you can try the Cool Sites section, which suggests five of the Internet's greatest hits. There are also tons of downloadable pictures, sounds, and video clips. Now there are new international Yahooligans! for Japan and Korea, too.

http://www.yahooligans.com/

VIRUSES, MYTHS, AND HOAXES

CERT Coordination Center

The most current information on viruses and hoaxes comes from the Computer Emergency Response Team (CERT). When someone forwards e-mail to you about a dire new virus warning, please take a minute and check it out before you pass it on. It's possible the virus alert is bogus. Stopping hoax junk mail is also part of good Internet citizenship. It conserves Internet bandwidth and makes for a faster Internet for us all. :-)

http://www.cert.org/

HoaxBusters

How do you spot a hoax? These folks know. The U.S. Department of Energy's Computer Incident Advisory Capability wants you to know, too. Check their Web page for tips on hoax busting! (Hint: Bill Gates does not want to give you $1,000.)

http://HoaxBusters.ciac.org/

Symantec AntiVirus Research Center

Is it a hoax or a real virus? If it's the latter, what do you do about it? This site is a great clearing house on virus information. Find out which viruses are considered "Top Threats" and which are completely bogus.

http://www.symantec.com/avcenter/

WEB BUILDING AND HTML

★ Bobby

You think you've got a pretty good Web page, but how accessible is it to people with disabilities? Some of these folks use text-to-speech readers and other technologies. Do your pages pass the Bobby test? Try it and see! It's free and only takes a few seconds.

http://www.cast.org/bobby/

★ Builder.com - Web Authoring

If you're trying to advance your Web site building skills, this site is a good place to start. Find reviews for Web authoring software; tips from experts; and advanced tips on subjects such as frames, Dynamic Hypertext Markup Language (DHTML), and cross-platform compatibility. There is also beginner's stuff, but if the material here sounds too complicated, check out some of the other sites in this subject listing first. If you decide to take the plunge into Web authorship and need to learn more, remember this site.

http://builder.cnet.com/

★ Building a School Web Site

This site's teacher, Wanda Wigglebits, proclaims: "If you can follow a recipe, you can build a Web site!" Although the title mentions school Web sites, this tutorial works for any kind of Web page. Go from rank beginner to a creator of animated GIFs in just a few short, free lessons! Wanda, you go, girlfriend!

http://www.wigglebits.com/

Copyright with Cyberbee

It's OK to copy anything that's on the Internet and use it on your own Web site, right? WRONG. Learn all about the Ten Big Myths About Copyright, and how you can avoid breaking the law.

http://www.cyberbee.com/copyrt.html

★ eBoard

Maybe you don't really need a Web page. Maybe you just need a virtual corkboard. You can get a free one here, along with the simple tools needed to use it with your class or your family.

http://www.eboard.com/

Miami Museum of Science - The Atoms Family

How many times can you cut a 28-centimeter piece of paper in half? If you could do it 31 times, that would be the size of one atom! Most people can't get beyond cutting 10 times, but go ahead, give it a shot. The directions are here. This wonderful site leads you through the rather odd world of the Atoms Family: Frankenstein's Lightning Lab, Dracula's Library (he wants to read all he can about light, so he can avoid it, we guess), and the Phantom's Portrait Parlor (matter, atoms, that paper cutting activity, and molecules).
http://www.miamisci.org/af/sln/

From Pokémon® to Picasso: Art Rights and Wrongs

Is it OK to take a graphic, music, or text from someone else's Web site without permission? No, and this page explains why. You'll read fascinating interviews with webmasters, advice from the Library of Congress, and lots more. There are also permission letters you can use to write and ask for clearance to use other people's material. This site was created by students for the ThinkQuest Junior competition.

http://library.thinkquest.org/J001570/

★ Learning HTML for Kids - A Step-by-Step Tutorial

You might want to start with this tutorial to learn the basics of HTML and what you need to learn to make your Web pages look like you want them to look. The lessons here are clear, nicely presented, and fun to try.

http://www.teleport.com/~jgoodell/tutorial/

A
B
C
D
E
F
G
H
I
J
K
L
M
N
O
P
Q
R
S
T
U
V
W
X
Y
Z

A
B
C
D
E
F
G
H
I
J
K
L
M
N
O
P
Q
R
S
T
U
V
W
X
Y
Z

★ Lissa Explains It All - HTML Help for Kids

Lissa's a teen who was born to code HTML. She's gotten so many questions about her Web pages that she decided to put up some brief tutorials. Learn everything from basic tags to more advanced tricks like how you get that cool rippling lake effect on your graphics. You'll also see how changing color or graphics on mouse overs is done, and you can check out lots of resources for finding free graphics.

http://www.lissaexplains.com/

Online Graphics Generator

Ever wanted to make a fancy logo or letters that look like they are burning, or carved out of wood, or something else? Now you can. Just select the effect you want, type in your text, and it will be rendered to your computer screen. To save the image to your hard drive, follow the directions.

http://www.cooltext.com/

Who are "the four most famous guys in rock"? (Hint: It's not the Beatles.)

Answer: They are the four American presidents carved into the granite of Mount Rushmore, South Dakota. At http://www.travelsd.com/parks/rushmore/ you can find out why the faces of George Washington, Thomas Jefferson, Teddy Roosevelt, and Abraham Lincoln are sculpted there, and how the feat was accomplished.

Palette Man

This is basically a tool for Web designers who want to set a particular mood at the sites they create. They may want an active mood or a tranquil one. They may want to shake people up or calm them down. They set these moods with color, and you can experiment with the preset color palettes at this site or create your own. Doesn't your home page need a fresh coat of paint?

http://www.paletteman.com/

Web Site Garage - Improve Your Web Site

You've created this wonderful Web page that you're really proud of, but you're getting complaints from some users that the page looks awful. After your first reaction that they must be using some text-based browser on an old DOS system, you realize you're getting so many complaints that something must be wrong. The Web Site Garage offers some free services that could help you through this mess. Try the free tune-up, and run various diagnostics on your URL. It will report bad links, questionable HTML tags, cross-platform browser compatibility, spelling, load times, and more. Other services include Web site registration and a GIF tune-up.

http://websitegarage.netscape.com/

WebDeveloper.com

The HTML tutorials here are great, but the tools, animated GIF libraries, and other resources offered are even better. Check Dr. Website's Top Questions for really interesting, hard-to-find tips.

http://www.webdeveloper.com/

Webmonkey For Kids

Aimed at kids creating their first Web page, you'll find an easy-to-use tutorial, including complete instructions on how to upload your creation to one of the free home page services. Tripod is used as an example, but they are all similar. There's also a toolbox of downloadable software and plenty of suggested projects.

http://hotwired.lycos.com/webmonkey/kids/

WEB RINGS

Family Connection Webring

Parental advisory: we believe this site is OK but can't vouch for the more than 1,000 links in this ring. Did you know there's now a way to surf the Web "sideways"? Web rings are user-built and-maintained directories that focus on a particular subject or idea. Anyone can start a Web ring and invite other similar sites to join the collection, or ring. You navigate a ring by selecting links to the previous and next sites on the ring. A link to the ring's index and home page is also available at each site. Here's an example we chose because it has family content. At this site, you can either search the collection of sites or browse through them yourself. Parents should know that many Web rings are adult oriented; but as mentioned, we believe this one is OK.

http://www.geocities.com/Heartland/Hills/6365/

INVENTIONS AND INVENTORS

See also PEOPLE AND BIOGRAPHIES; SCIENCE; and WHY

★ 3M Collaborative Invention Unit

Could you be an inventor? Before you answer, how do you think a product is invented? Many times, it's not just one person dreaming up a new product. It's a collaboration of several people, or even teams of people, who bring a new item to the market. First, a Scout identifies a problem that needs a solution. Next, a Wizard takes a look at the problem and brainstorms possible solutions. After that, a Critic examines what the Wizard suggests and weighs factors like how much the product will cost to make, how much demand for the product there is, and other factors. Whatever survives this process is given to the Trailblazer, who balances the Five Ps: product, price, promotions, publicity, and place (where the product will be available). This site spells it all out!

http://mustang.coled.umn.edu/inventing/
    inventing.html

Argonne National Laboratory - Rube Goldberg Machine Contest

Reuben Lucius Goldberg, better known as Rube Goldberg, was a cartoonist with a wacky sense of humor. He loved to draw machines that would perform simple tasks, like pouring a glass of milk. First, he would draw a way to open the refrigerator, then a way to get the bottle, then a way to open it—before he would ever get the milk into the glass! He accomplished this easy job by using the most complex, roundabout methods possible, often using common household objects in uncommon ways. You can see some examples of this here. A contest is held every year to see which team of students can perform a simple assignment using the weirdest, wackiest, and most complex machine. Visit here to discover what they invent. You can also find out how to get your school involved in the fun!

http://www.anl.gov/OPA/rube/

★ Bad Human Factors Designs

Ambiguous signs, doors that you think should push open (but they really require a pull), light switches that don't do what you'd expect—guess what, you're not stupid, these are all examples of bad design! This fascinating look at the wacky world of poor design can only make you a better inventor.

http://www.baddesigns.com/

BrainPOP - Technology

Turn to this site for short, animated movies that cover dozens of innovations, discoveries, and inventions. You'll learn how fireworks work, who invented braces, and how the click of a computer mouse activates computer programs. After you watch a movie, take the quiz. It will help to reinforce what you just learned.

http://www.brainpop.com/tech/seeall.weml

Nothing to do? Check
CRAFTS AND HOBBIES for
some ideas.

A
B
C
D
E
F
G
H
I
J
K
L
M
N
O
P
Q
R
S
T
U
V
W
X
Y
Z

A
B
C
D
E
F
G
H
I
J
K
L
M
N
O
P
Q
R
S
T
U
V
W
X
Y
Z

CBC4Kids: History of Inventions, a Time Line

In the sixteenth century, Sir John Harington of England invented the very first flush toilet. Back then, it was called a "water closet." To this day, the toilet continues to be reinvented, though the basic concept remains the same. You might say that the toilet has changed the way we live. You could say that about a lot of other inventions, such as the printing press, the wheel, paper, eyeglasses, and so on. This site describes, century by century, some of the most important inventions. If you think one's missing, let the site know. You might see it featured.

http://www.cbc4kids.ca/general/the-lab/
   history-of-invention/

Club Girl Tech - Invention

Girl Tech will introduce you to some cool inventions by women throughout history. The first U.S. patent granted to a woman went to Mary Dixon Kies. In 1809, Kies got a patent for inventing a new way to process and weave straw with thread. But you may want to read about more recent inventions, such as the one by preteen Becky Schroeder. She thought up a way to write in the dark, using a phosphorescent clipboard! She got a patent on her invention and became famous. Have you got a brilliant idea like that? There are lots of links to other sites featuring women inventors, too.

http://www.girltech.com/Invention/
   IN_menu_frame.html

Discovery Online - Toys Were Us

Ever wonder who invented the Slinky? Who thought up the Frisbee? How the skateboard got started? And who the heck programmed the first computer to play the game Pong? Find out at this neat site from the Discovery Channel.

http://www.discovery.com/stories/history/toys/
   toys.html

Friends don't ask friends for their passwords.

Exploravision Awards

Sometimes ideas don't go anywhere. But other times, they lead to inventions that pay off. At this site, your classroom could learn how to turn an idea into a savings bond worth $10,000. The students at French Road Elementary School in Rochester, New York, did just that. They came up with the idea for an alarm to remind you to return your library books before they're overdue! They won first place in this technology contest, sponsored by Toshiba and the National Science Teachers Association. At this site, you can request an entry kit and view past winners.

http://www.toshiba.com/tai/exploravision/

★ Explore Invention at the Lemelson Center

Visit the Centerpieces area to find in-depth looks at inventions like the quartz watch and the electric guitar. In the same section, read about Edison and find out how you can make your own light bulb (the first "ingredient" is a helpful parent!). The Innovative Lives part of the site spotlights both famous inventors and those not quite so famous—yet. You may be familiar with their products, though! There's also a nice section called Women Inventors, where you can find out about lots of smart women, including actress Hedy Lamarr and her patented encryption device, which might have made torpedoes undetectable during World War II.

http://www.si.edu/lemelson/

Exploring Leonardo

If you think this site is about the hero of *Titanic*, sorry. This Leonardo is famous for painting the *Mona Lisa*. But did you know Leonardo da Vinci also designed a helicopter, a hang glider, a parachute, and several other contraptions that didn't actually get built until hundreds of years later? Which ones can you recognize from their original drawings? This special exhibit comes from Boston's Museum of Science.

http://www.mos.org/sln/Leonardo/

The History of Eating Utensils

What came first? The spoon or the fork? This is not a trick question. The answer, if you know your history of eating utensils, is the spoon. They've been around since prehistoric times, while forks can be traced back to the time of the Greeks. So, the next time you sit at the dinner table, don't take your eating utensils for granted. They've got a rich history, and you can get a taste of it at this site.

http://www.calacademy.org/research/anthropology/ utensil/

★ The Invention Dimension

Would you like to win half a million dollars? All you have to do is invent something so cool, so unique, and so compelling that everyone says, "Wow!" That's the idea behind the Lemelson-MIT Prize, which is presented every year to an American inventor-innovator for outstanding creativity. You can find out about the prize and its past winners here, and you'll also find a collection of material about other great inventors and inventions. Check the Inventor of the Week archives, and don't miss the Links area for more inventions and resources.

http://web.mit.edu/afs/athena.mit.edu/org/i/invent/

★ Inventions! @ Nationalgeographic.com

Guess the purpose of a wacky patent drawing. Hmmm, is it an automatic baby-patting machine or a mitten stretcher? If you guess right enough times, you'll get a token. Play five games about inventions and inventors. If you get five tokens, you can operate the coolest invention of them all: the Action Contraption!

http://www.nationalgeographic.com/features/96/ inventions/

The Official Rube Goldberg Web Site

Visit the gallery to see wacky inventions for a new type of pencil sharpener, a safer (?) way to walk on icy sidewalks, and a new way to remember to mail a letter. You can also find out about the various Rube Goldberg invention contests, as well as read Goldberg's life story.

http://www.rube-goldberg.com/

Try Science

The content at this site changes from time to time as it is all contributed by science museums around the Web. You might try to build and test a paper bridge, investigate the best way to clean up an oil slick, or measure your own lung capacity. If you click on Field Trips you can check out live cams at science centers all over the world. Don't miss the Adventures section with the Star Trek Starfleet Academy simulation. If you explore all the activities, you can graduate as an ensign!
http://www.tryscience.com/

Out of This World Design

The aliens have landed and it's your job to make them feel right at home. Trouble is, they have three legs, four mouths, and claw-like fingers. You need to redesign their hotel room chairs—fast! While you're at it, better rig up a special phone, a pen, and a vehicle as well. Can you learn enough about industrial design in time, or will you create an interplanetary crisis?

http://www.sanford-artedventures.com/play/id2/

Pencil Inventions

Look at your pencil. How would you improve it? Make it longer, shorter, fatter, or thinner? Maybe put a light on it, or a pretzel on it, or maybe even add a calculator? Getting your brain going on a problem like this is the first step towards being a real inventor. See what this class of kids came up with to improve their pencils.

http://www.noogenesis.com/inventing/pencil/ pencil_page.html

A
B
C
D
E
F
G
H
I
J
K
L
M
N
O
P
Q
R
S
T
U
V
W
X
Y
Z

A
B
C
D
E
F
G
H
I
J
K
L
M
N
O
P
Q
R
S
T
U
V
W
X
Y
Z

The Race for the Superbomb

Parental advisory: please preview this site. Since 1945 there have been over 2,000 known nuclear tests worldwide. Read about the research and testing that led up to the development of the atomic bomb in the 1940s and, later, the hydrogen bomb in the '50s. There's a chilling nuclear blast scenario, a panic quotient quiz, and a virtual tour of a secret government bunker. This site is not for young kids.

http://www.pbs.org/wgbh/amex/bomb/

The Robert C. Williams American Museum of Papermaking

This book is made of paper, and so is your milk carton, your cereal box, and your report card! How was paper invented? It started in China long ago, but there have been many improvements since then. You'll also discover how modern paper is made, used, and recycled.

http://www.ipst.edu/amp/

By the time the average person reaches the age of 70, he has watched a lot of TV. If you added up all those sitcoms, game shows, cartoons, and commercials, how many years would you have?

http://www.cme.org/children/kids_tv/c_and_t.html

Find out more at day. Kids watch an average of three to four hours of TV every have spent 10 years of their lives watching TV. Education, by the age of 70 most Americans will **Answer:** According to the Center for Media

Technocopia

What types of technology would you like to include in your lifestyle? Do you think a robotic dog can ever replace sweet old Rover? Would you drive a flying car? Described as " . . . a kind of *Consumer Reports* with an eye to the future," this site helps you sort the fad products from the truly useful ones.

http://www.technocopia.com/

The Telephone

The telephone is one invention that looks much different than when it was first invented 150 years ago. Over time it has evolved from a big wooden box with wires to a small, pocket-sized device. This site invites you to take a visual tour of phone design history. You'll also learn about its inventor, Alexander Graham Bell.

http://www.pbs.org/wgbh/amex/telephone/

Tesla : Master of Lightning

Nikola Tesla was an inventor and electrical engineer. He invented the AC (alternating current) motor, high-voltage lighting, and many other electrical devices. He also invented the radio, even though Marconi first got credit for it. At this site, you can learn more about this brilliant man and his key inventions. You'll also learn that he led a strange life. Turns out he had some phobias, including pearl earrings worn by women!

http://www.pbs.org/tesla/

MICROMACHINES

MEMS (MicroElectroMechanical Systems)

A teeny lock, smaller than a dust mite! Another mite, straddling a set of microgears! See machines more miniaturized than you have ever seen before, and imagine their uses, via the material at this fascinating site.

http://mems.sandia.gov/scripts/

Nanotechnology

Imagine little robotic machines, snapping parts together on the atomic level. Scientists think that vision will be the wave of the future. Learn about nanotechnology at this site, which includes articles and videos, among other things. You should also take a look at the Foresight Institute, which tries to look ahead to social impacts of this brave new world <http://www.foresight.org/>.

http://www.zyvex.com/nano/

INVERTEBRATES

See also INSECTS AND SPIDERS; WORMS

All About Lobsters

A newly hatched baby lobster looks something like a water flea to us, which is perhaps why lobstermen call it a "bug." Read all about the life cycle of the lobster, follow a clam through the lobster's digestive system, and check out the history of lobstering. There are also a few activities, crustacean poems, and trivia pages for your amusement. In a pinch, you can ponder the directions for how to hypnotize a lobster.

http://octopus.gma.org/lobsters/

The Cephalopod Page: Octopuses, Squid, Cuttlefish, and Nautilus

An octopus is more than just a tentacled cephalopod that squirts ink and runs. It is the smartest of the invertebrates, with both a long- and a short-term memory. It learns through experience and solves problems using trial and error. Check out this site about the octopus and its relatives, and you'll soon realize that these octopi are not just a bunch of suckers.

http://is.dal.ca/~ceph/TCP/

Crustaceans

There's a lot of neat stuff to know about crustaceans like lobsters, crayfish, barnacles, and shrimp. Some crustaceans lay eggs in the mud. These can experience drying out over and over—yet even hundreds of years later some of these eggs will still hatch. Here's another odd fact. In some crustacean species, there are no males at all! Learn about the biology of the crustacean family at this site.

http://www.uoguelph.ca/zoology/great_lakes/crust/crust.htm

Discovery Online, Jellyfish: My Life as a Blob

How do jellyfish eat? No heading to the freezer for something delicious! Some of them troll through the water, others "open their enormous lips and engulf their hapless victims." But eating isn't the only interesting thing about jellyfish. They're cool to look at, and there are some great photos at this site. It also links to other resources about these fascinating underwater creatures.

http://izzy.online.discovery.com/area/nature/jellyfish/jellyfish2.html

Horseshoe Crabs - Living Fossil

Learn about this "living fossil" and its natural history. They are not really crabs but are more closely related to spiders and scorpions. Did you know that this creature has blue blood? It has a special substance in it that makes it important to human medicine. Every year thousands of horseshoe crabs "donate" blood and then they are released.

http://www.aqua.org/animals/species/prhcrab.html

Jellies

Graceful, delicate-looking—and ferocious! That describes the mysterious jellyfish, the "passive but efficient predator" of the sea. Learn about the life cycle of the moon jelly, how a jellyfish's stingers work, and who likes to eat these unusual creatures. This site also details the jellyfish exhibit at the Tennessee Aquarium.

http://www.tennis.org/Special/jellyspecial.html

A B C D E F G H I J K L M N O P Q R S T U V W X Y Z

A
B
C
D
E
F
G
H
I
J
K
L
M
N
O
P
Q
R
S
T
U
V
W
X
Y
Z

Kaikoura @ Nationalgeographic.com

Let's travel to New Zealand and the Kaikoura Canyon in search of a giant squid. Join researchers, writers, and photographers from *National Geographic* as they begin a search for the elusive squid. Dr. Clyde Roper, teacher-scientist, is known as "Dr. Squid," who seemingly knows all there is to know about the giant squid. Yet neither he nor any other scientist had ever seen an intact giant squid alive in the sea. Dr. Roper often compares giant squids with dinosaurs. But, unlike the dinosaur, the giant squid exists today and is swimming in the depths of Kaikoura Canyon. Somewhere. Join the hunt!

http://www.nationalgeographic.com/features/97/
    kaikoura/

NOVA Online - Kingdom of the Seahorse

They aren't horses, but these fascinating creatures do live in the sea. Find out about seahorse basic anatomy, seahorse research, and just what makes sea horses superdads!

http://www.pbs.org/wgbh/nova/seahorse/

Underground Adventure

What would the world look like if you were one-half inch tall? Transmogrify yourself at this site and then get an invertebrate's eye view of life underground. Explore the QuickTime VR image until you see your green-clad tour guide. Click on her to begin.

http://www.fmnh.org/ua/

WORMS

The Adventures of Herman

Question: What has no arms, legs, or eyes? Hint: It's squishy and likes mud. Did you guess the earthworm? You're right. The earthworm just has a head and a tail. Luckily, it can grow a new tail if it gets cut off. But if it loses its head, well, it's a goner. At this site you can read the autobiography of Herman the earthworm. He'll tell you about where he came from and what he likes to eat. He's also got some wormy games you can play.

http://www.urbanext.uiuc.edu/worms/

Loveable Leeches

This site sticks to the subject of how to collect, raise, and study leeches. The question is why you'd want to do that. Visit this resource to learn all you can about leech habitat and lore, but try not to get sucked in.

http://www.accessexcellence.com/LC/SS/
    leechlove.html

♣ Vermicomposting

Learn how to make a "worm wigwam" to help compost your kitchen scraps. While you're digesting that information, try playing a little game. Click your mouse to feed the "worms" on the screen. There doesn't seem to be any way to "win," although you could see how big you can get the virtual worms to grow.

http://www.niehs.nih.gov/kids/worms.htm

Worms

These first graders made chocolate-covered worms, and then they ate them. As it turned out, they were delicious (made of butter, corn syrup, chocolate, and other yummy stuff). Then they did some gummi worm math experiments, followed up with some worm poetry and songs; and finally, they drew some worm pictures. It makes you wonder what's left to do in second grade.

http://www.sci.mus.mn.us/sln/tf/w/worms/worms/
    worms.html

★ Yucky Worm World

Tractors and earthworms both plow the land, but you don't have to gas up worms. Just give them some garbage or organic material, and watch them go! Learn more about the different types of worms and how slimy, yet beneficial, they are. Send some worm postcards, meet Mary the worm woman, and see a video of a worm hatching.

http://yucky.kids.discovery.com/flash/worm/

JARVIS ISLAND

See UNITED STATES—TERRITORIES

JOBS AND CAREERS

The Career Key

Make up a name (and don't put in your e-mail address) and take the test to see what careers might match your personality. The entire test takes about 15 to 20 minutes. Try it, it's fun, and there are no wrong answers! You can also learn which college courses to take to match your career goals.

http://www.ncsu.edu/careerkey/

Careers in Botany

Who knows—you might grow up to be a botanist! There are lots of interesting careers for kids who want to branch out into the world of plants. Be an ecologist, or forester. Or a horticulturist or agronomist (field crops). This site covers it all, including typical salaries, training needed, and more.

http://www.botany.org/bsa/careers/

Department of Labor Educational Resources

If you're thinking about dropping out of school, DON'T. This site explains what you will be facing in the world of work without a high school diploma. Did you know that dropouts earn an average of 27 percent less than teens with a diploma? You will also find out about child labor laws and youth employment laws, and be able to explore many careers at this site.

http://www.dol.gov/dol/asp/public/fibre/main.htm

Engineering: Your Future

What's up with engineering? Do you have to look like Dilbert? Will you be forced to work in a cubicle and have a pointy-haired boss? Not always! Check the Alphabet of Engineering and discover that you can be an aerospace engineer, a transportation engineer, or someone in many other fields in between. Which ones interest you? There are also additional links to find more.

http://www.asee.org/precollege/html/engineering.htm

Healthcare Career Resource Center

How much do you know about careers in the health sciences? Take a quiz and see. Then learn about how to prepare for your chosen profession. This site was created by students for the ThinkQuest competition.

http://library.thinkquest.org/15569/

NET FILES

Who invented the first pretzel?

Answer: Legend has it that a sixth-century Italian monk used to give out these doughy treats to children who were good during Mass. The pretzel shape is supposed to represent arms crossed in prayer, and the three holes represent the Father, Son, and Holy Spirit. It may be the world's oldest snack food! Read more about the pretzel and its fascinating history at
http://www.ushistory.org/tour/tour_pretzel.htm

IPL Teen Division: Career Pathways

The Internet Public Library offers this useful section on career planning for teens. You'll find facts about each field, a personal interview with someone in that profession, and additional links. Don't miss the Career Preparation section, which guides you through crafting a snazzy cover letter and resume, gives hints on how to nail your job interview, and suggests ways to evaluate a job offer.

http://www.ipl.org/teen/pathways/

JobQuest

This site contains valuable information on how to prepare for a job interview, the best way to detail your accomplishments and skills in a resume, and tips on finding an internship program. You can also learn what types of jobs kids think will be most popular in the future. This site was created by students for the ThinkQuest competition.

http://library.thinkquest.org/15111/

NET FILES

What is the most easterly point in North America?

Answer: Cape Spear in Newfoundland, Canada. It is the site of Newfoundland's second lighthouse, built in 1835 to help transatlantic mariners and local fishermen navigate the treacherous coastline. The keeper's house at Cape Spear was constructed on top of a 300-foot sandstone cliff with a stone light tower built at its center, which anchored the house to the rock. Come visit this and other historic Newfoundland lighthouses at *http://www.ucs.mun.ca/~dmolloy/lighthouse.html*

My Successful Business

Find out how a sixth-grade girl took an idea and turned it into cash. She came up with a design for Beanie Baby leashes, suggested it as a 4-H project, secured a loan from the bank, and went into the manufacturing and marketing business. Read how she made a $500 profit!

http://tqjunior.thinkquest.org/6066/March/
   business.htm

Occupational Outlook Handbook

What are the fastest growing industries? What occupations are adding the most jobs? What do firefighters make as a salary? These are the types of questions you'll find answered in this government publication. Be sure to take the link to the Student Resources section <*http://stats.bls.gov/k12/html/edu_over.htm*> to discover what careers might interest you if you like particular subjects in school. For example, if you enjoy gym class, you might be a professional athlete, a recreational therapist, a carpenter, or a surveyor.

http://stats.bls.gov/ocohome.htm

★ Peterson's

Your family may be familiar with this resource. Have your parents and older brothers and sisters been investigating colleges, distance learning, or semester abroad programs? Peterson's is a wonderful site for that, but did you know it can also be used to find a summer job (maybe at a summer camp) and to explore the world of work?

http://www.petersons.com/

Planet Ag

Agricultural science may be the path for you if you're into plants, animals, biochemistry, engineering, or health. This site explains 40 such careers and offers many links to other agricultural information, as well as science fair ideas.

http://www.fl-ag.com/PlanetAg/menu.htm

Preparing for a Career in Veterinary Medicine

Wouldn't it be great to help care for companion animals like dogs and cats? Or perhaps you're more interested in large animals, like horses and cows. There are other specialties too: maybe you'd like to be a bird or reptile doctor, or be the primary physician for zoo animals. This site will teach you what you need to know to prepare for one of these exciting careers.

http://aavmc.org/prevet/prevet.htm

★ Real Science!

Learn about lots of careers—from acoustical research engineer to wildlife psychologist. For each entry you will meet a person who actually is a park ranger or a plastic surgeon, among others. Find out what their days are like, and see if you'd be interested in becoming, say, a paleobotanist or maybe a cartographer.

http://www.realscience.org/

So You Want a Career in Sports?

According to this site, "Only one in 10,000 junior and senior high school athletes ever makes the pros. Over the last three years, of roughly 320,000 college student-athletes, only 3.3 percent of football players have made it to the NFL and only 1.9 percent of basketball players to the NBA." If you become a professional athlete against those odds, your career may not last long due to injury or other reasons. Then it's back to the real world. If you think you've got what it takes, by all means, go for it—otherwise, listen to what some professionals have to say, and explore sports-related careers.

http://www.lifesplaybook.com/career_intro.html

Starting and Running a Business

Penny, Bill, and Buck give you quick tips on starting your own business, including the creation of a business plan. There is not a lot of information here, but there is enough to give you an overview. This site was created by students for the ThinkQuest Junior competition.

http://tqjunior.advanced.org/5996/

What makes a good password? Something that's not your name and won't be found in a dictionary. Instead, try a combination of letters and numbers.

Welcome to My World! Careers in Science and Technology

What do you want to be when you grow up? Your answer might change from year to year, and that's OK. But if you're leaning toward a career in science and technology, this site will help you sort out which profession is right for you. Here you can spend a day in the life of a science teacher, chemist, meteorologist, computer administrator, and geologist. Each profile tells you the subjects you need to be especially good in and includes a list of other sites if you want to know more.

http://sln.fi.edu/careers/careers_flash.html

The World of Experience

Getting a job and earning money is important, but so is getting experience. Sometimes it will be experience with a hands-on skill; other times, it will be a people skill, such as learning how to be a productive member of a team. This site offers suggestions on gaining experience through volunteer work, internships, extracurricular activities, and more.

http://www.futurescan.com/realworld.html

JOHNSTON ATOLL

See UNITED STATES—TERRITORIES

A
B
C
D
E
F
G
H
I
J
K
L
M
N
O
P
Q
R
S
T
U
V
W
X
Y
Z

Billy Bear's Playground

It's never raining at this playground, hosted by a friendly bear and his pals. Play weatherproof online games, or download and save some to try later. Do you love holidays? Billy Bear does, too, and he's gathered his favorite holiday games, crafts, and activities to help you make your celebration the best ever! Don't forget to check out the jokes, puzzles, screen savers, stationery, and everything else in Billy Bear's wonderful world.
http://www.billybear4kids.com/

JOKES AND RIDDLES

Charles Landers Kids Pages

Q: If you drop a white hat into the Red Sea, what does it become? A: Wet! There are 20 more pages of jokes like this. Enter, if you dare.

http://www.users.bigpond.com/lander/

The Droodles

What's a droodle? Well, it's a little drawing, called a doodle, crossed with a riddle—droodle, get it? In other words, it's a drawing with a puzzle in it. You can puzzle over lots of droodles here and submit your guesses as to their meaning. For even more, try the Exploratorium exhibit <*http://www.exploratorium.edu/exhibits/droodles/*>.

http://www.droodles.com/

★ Joke Shop!

Laugh at jokes, or submit your own. It just might be chosen for the weekly Top 10 Joke Shop Poll. If it is, it will be posted on the site. Vote on what you think is the best joke, because the winner gets a prize. By the way, did you hear what happened to the cat who ate a ball of yarn? She had mittens!

http://www.cbc4kids.ca/general/kids-club/joke-page/

Knock Knock Jokes

There were more than 100 knock-knock jokes at this site when we visited. But if knock-knocks make you nuts, try the riddles, elephant jokes, or brain teasers. Here's one sample: "Johnny's mother had three children. The first was April, the second was May. What was the name of her third child? Answer: Johnny!"

http://www.azkidsnet.com/JSknockjoke.htm

Patty Parrot's Bird Brain Jokes

Why did the doughnut man stop making doughnuts? Because he was tired of the hole business! For more corny jokes, visit Patty Parrot's perch.

http://www.blackdog.net/pattyparrot.html

Tree and Forest Jokes - Hands On Children's Museum

The jokes here change all the time; you can even submit your own, and maybe the museum will use them. These are some of the jokes we liked when we visited: Q: What time is it when an elephant sits on your bed? A. It is time to get a new bed! Q: Why does a glow worm glow? A. Because they only eat light meals!

http://www.hocm.org/treejokes.html

How is Kwanzaa celebrated?
Find out in HOLIDAYS!

JUGGLING

See also CIRCUSES AND CLOWNS

How to Devil Stick

The first time we tried these juggling sticks, the cats went running for cover. With a little practice, we got so we could do some simple flips, but what we really needed were the pictures and explanations at this Web page. You'll learn how to start the sticks into motion, plus how to do tricks we haven't mastered yet: the helicopter and the propeller spin.

http://www.yoyoguy.com/info/devilstick/

International Jugglers Association

One of the things the International Juggler's Association does is work with the Special Olympics to help kids learn to juggle. You can read about that worthy activity on this page, along with other association news. Want some juggling merchandise, such as postcards or posters? Buy them here. There's also a great selection of annotated links, including sites about boomerangs, Ethiopian jugglers, jugglers in New Zealand, and another organization called Clowns Without Borders.

http://www.juggle.org/

JuggleAnim

Need some fresh ideas for juggling patterns? Try this ultra-cool Java applet. Browse through the pattern library and watch the animation. They even have that pattern where one "ball" is really an apple and you keep taking bites out of it! If you can figure it out, you can program the applet to create new patterns, too.

http://www.juggling.org/programs/java/JuggleAnim/ja.html

NET FILES

If you had ten billion $1 notes and spent one every second of every day, how many years would it take to go broke?

http://www.bep.treas.gov/fact9.htm

Answer: According to the U.S. Bureau of Engraving and Printing, it would require 317 years!

Learn to Juggle

With the help of the cool animations at this site, you can learn to juggle three balls in just six steps. If you can accomplish that, go on to the advanced class in juggling four balls at a time. You can also learn to manipulate string figures (like "cat's cradle") here if you have to give up on juggling <http://home.eznet.net/~stevemd/stringar.html>.

http://home.eznet.net/~stevemd/juggle.html

Learn2 Juggle

Forget starting out with watermelons; learn to juggle three items with this easy-to-use tutorial. Don't expect to be able to do this right away! This site suggests that you should try three half-hour practice sessions to get the hang of it, and then practice about 90 more minutes before you're ready to perform in public. All you need to know is here—just provide three handkerchiefs or beanbags.

http://www.learn2.com/04/0418/0418.html

A
B
C
D
E
F
G
H
I
J
K
L
M
N
O
P
Q
R
S
T
U
V
W
X
Y
Z

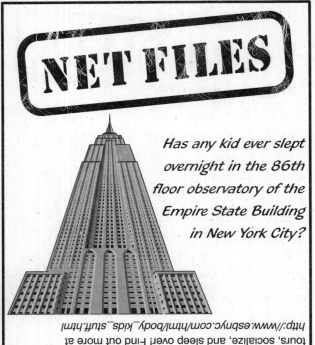

NET FILES

Has any kid ever slept overnight in the 86th floor observatory of the Empire State Building in New York City?

Answer: Plenty of scouts do just that every year in "urban camp outs"; there's one in November for Boy Scouts and one in March for Girl Scouts. Three troops at a time can take tours, socialize, and sleep over! Find out more at http://www.esbnyc.com/html/body_kids_stuff.html

KINGMAN REEF

See UNITED STATES—TERRITORIES

KITES

20 Kids * 20 Kites * 20 Minutes

What if the kite-flying conditions are perfect, but you left your kite in the back of your mom's car and she just drove to work? Make a kite in just 20 minutes! Do you have a piece of typing paper? Ask dad. You'll also need some bamboo shish kebab sticks and some long, plastic nonsticky tape (surveyor's tape or equivalent). The directions at this site have been time-tested in many Hawaiian classrooms.

http://www.molokai.com/kites/20kidskites.html

Bob's Java Kite

Sometimes there's just not enough wind to fly a kite. Or it's raining. Or it's snowing. Or it's too dark, or . . . it doesn't matter anymore. Here on a beach beside the Golden Gate Bridge, the conditions are always perfect. You need a Java-enabled browser, and be sure to read the instructions carefully. Otherwise, your virtual kite will spend more time in the sand than in the sky.

http://www.bsteele.com/kite.html

Clem's Homemade Kites

You don't need to spend hundreds of dollars on a fancy stunt kite—just try Clem's homemade pattern, made of newspaper and adhesive tape. The directions for making one are all at this site, including some important safety rules for flying your creation.

http://www.clem.freeserve.co.uk/

Kel's MicroKite Site

"Any day is a good day to fly a kite," says Kel, "if you remember to put one in your pocket!" At this site you'll see the world's smallest kite (1/16 square inch) and learn how to make microkites of your own. You can fly these sub-one-inch kites indoors, or fly them outside on windless days. Or tie one to your wheelchair, and take off!

http://home.rconnect.com/~kitenut/

★ Kite Aerial Photography

Ever wonder what the view is like from your kite as it soars high above your head? Now there's a way for you to see it. Check the tools and techniques at this site (it can be expensive); then go fly a kite!

http://www-archfp.ced.berkeley.edu/kap/

★ Kitecast: Specialized Weather for Kite Flying

There's some terrific kite-flying information here, from "Kite Flying 101" to today's kite-flying forecast for major U.S. cities. Click on "National Kite Month" to discover some high-flying March events—are there any near you?

http://www.intellicast.com/KITEcast/

Kites for Kids Only

You'll find links to lots of kite plans for kids, although some are easier to put together than others. At this site, you can go around the world on a kite: learn to make a box kite from Australia, a sled kite from England, or a Bermuda kite from—that's right—Bermuda! There is also a link to software that will help you design your kite.

http://www.sound.net/~kiteguy/kidspage/
kidspage.htm

National Kite Month: Kite History

Can you name "Five People Who Flew Kites and Changed History"? Well, let's see, there was Ben Franklin, right? And, uh, OK, we mentioned Ben Franklin, and, of course, there was that other guy. What's his name, you know who we mean. We'd better go back and look at the surprising stories collected at this Web site. You won't believe the one about the ten-year-old kid and how his kite helped span Niagara Falls.

http://www.kitetrade.org/history.shtml

★ Prism Kites' Flight Training and Safety

If you're using a fairly new browser, you'll love the flight training area. Enjoy slick animations of both basic and advanced kite-flying skills. There's also a section on where to fly kites, how to adjust your kite, and lots more.

http://www.prismkites.com/new-site/
flight-training.htm

★ The Virtual Kite Zoo

Start here for a tour to the various types of kites and their fascinating histories. Did you know that some people use kites for fishing? Or that you can make a tetrahedral kite from drinking straws? Maybe you want to attend a kite festival, or you just want to get some online tips for flying technique. This is the site you'll want to visit! Be sure to click on Kites in the Classroom for many easy-to-make kite plans.

http://www.kites.org/zoo/

KNOTS

See also CRAFTS AND HOBBIES

BoatSafe Kids! Learn to tie Knots

Check out a few handy knots so that the next time you tie your freighter to the dock, it won't drift away. Cool animations show you the moves for the cleat hitch, the bowline, and several others.

http://boatsafe.com/kids/knots.htm

Essential Scout Skills

If you ever become a contestant on that TV show *Survivor*, you'll need to know how to fashion branches into some kind of shelter. If you've got rope, you're all set. You can lash the materials together. Find out how at this site. There is also a nice knot tutorial.

http://www.4thtyldesleyscouts.co.uk/skills/

A Science Odyssey—You Try It: Doctor Over Time

Not feeling well? What seems to be the trouble? You'll find our clinic is a little unusual. Step into the doctors' waiting room. Now which health care professional would you like to see? A doctor whose technology is right up-to-date—for 1900? Or would you prefer to speak to a physician from the fabulous 1950s? Or perhaps you think you'll get better care with our M.D. from late great 1998? You know, they all have appointments open right now, so why not consult them all and compare treatments?
http://www.pbs.org/wgbh/aso/tryit/doctor/

A B C D E F G H I J K L M N O P Q R S T U V W X Y Z

A
B
C
D
E
F
G
H
I
J
K
L
M
N
O
P
Q
R
S
T
U
V
W
X
Y
Z

NET FILES

If you were to place every Oreo cookie ever made in a tall stack, one on top of the other, how high would the pile reach?

Answer: Since the beginning of time (1912), more than 362 billion Oreos have been made. The pile would reach all the way to the moon and back more than five times. Placed side by side, they would encircle Earth's equator 381 times! Find out more fun facts about the Oreo, America's favorite sandwich cookie, at http://www.oreo.com/Oreo/or_info.htm

The Freedom Knot

Are your shoelaces always coming untied? Are you tired of tripping over your laces when you try to run? Behold the Freedom Knot. Follow along with the animated directions until you learn the moves. It took us a couple tries but we figured it out. You can too.

Get Knotted! - Animated Knots for Scouts

Have you ever tried to learn to tie a knot that's new to you? Sometimes just reading a description and trying to figure it out from a text description doesn't work. The animated knots at this site pay an excellent tribute to the phrase "a picture is worth a thousand words." Watch as these 15 knots show you the ropes.

http://www.mistral.co.uk/42brghtn/knots/42ktmenu.html

HAY!
Gallop over to HORSES AND EQUESTRIAN SPORTS.

How to Tie a Tie

Say good-bye to clip-on ties and hello to the knots for the windsor, the half-windsor, the four-in-hand, and even a bowtie!

http://www.thetie.com/knots.htm

★ Knotting - Resources, How to, and More

This terrific collection of tips and tricks includes directions for tying a friendship knot, among others. You can also learn how to tie a knot that looks like a dragonfly, and another one that makes a perfectly wonderful zipper pull. Don't forget the "trucker's hitch," which comes in handy for securing your kayak/Christmas tree/surfboard to the top of the family car.

http://www.dfw.net/~jazzman/knotter/knot.htm

Mathmania Knot Menu

Boy Scouts, sailors, ladies, and gentlemen. Step right up and join the fun. Here's a site that will have you literally tied up in knots. Mathematical knots, that is! Stop by and read all about the theories behind these special knots, which have no loose ends. The ends are joined to form one single, twisted loop, like an electrical extension cord plugged into itself. Activities and experiments exploring this very knotty problem are included in the discussions.

http://www.theory.csc.uvic.ca/~mmania/knots/menu.htm

LANGUAGES AND ALPHABETS

AltaVista Translations

This great Web page is also known as Babelfish. You may not need it right now, but it's a good one to remember, just in case. Say you're exploring the Web and your search engine turns up a resource that looks useful for your school report—at least it looks that way because of the pictures. If you could only understand the language the page is written in! But you don't speak German, or French, or Spanish, or Italian, or Russian, or even Portuguese. Ask Babelfish. He speaks those languages, and if you give him a Web page address, he will do his best to return a translated page to you. You can also type in anything you want and have it translated. This is fun to try—check it out.

http://babelfish.altavista.com/translate.dyn

★ BBC Knowledge - Languages

The British Broadcasting Corporation offers multimedia tutorials in French, Spanish, German, and Italian. You'll need the Real Player plug-in to see the video and hear the audio, and be sure to sharpen your listening skills as you learn to go shopping, order a meal, and lots more. There are also Welsh, Irish, and other language lessons for you to try.

http://www.bbc.co.uk/education/languages/

Ethnologue - Languages of the World

What languages do they speak in Croatia? Did you know that in Kenya, more than 60 languages are spoken, including Kenyan Sign Language? You can select any of the 228 countries on this page and then discover which languages are spoken there. Also find out how different languages are related, using the language family tree. The Inuit language, Aleut, is related to the Russian Siberian language, Yupik. Do you know why that could be?

http://www.sil.org/ethnologue/

Evolution of Alphabets

Although you might be interested in the animated history of cuneiform or modern Cyrillic from Greek letters, you'll probably be most intrigued by the last item on the menu, the evolution of the Latin alphabet, with which American kids are probably most familiar. See how "z" used to be in the middle of the alphabet and not at the end. Can you tell from the animation when that happened? And when did "j" show up? (Hint: Under some conditions, the animation has to redraw itself in order to get all the way to the end, which you'll recognize because it says "Some European Additions." You may need to wait a bit.)

http://www.wam.umd.edu/~rfradkin/alphapage.html

Exploratorium Magazine Online: "The Evolution of Languages"

Where does language come from? How do you account for regional variations and dialects? See if you can tell which languages are related and see how much potential you have at being a word historian. There are also plentiful audio files should you prefer to learn about language by hearing it, rather than reading.

http://www.exploratorium.edu/exploring/language/

Hindi/Urdu Conversation Lessons

Hindi is written from left to right in the Devanagari script, which may look very unusual to you at first. This easy-to-use resource puts the basics of the alphabet, numbers, and color names up front in the first lessons. On the alphabet page, sound files let you hear the names of the letters, and you can see an animation of the intricate strokes used to write each letter. When you get into lessons with longer phrases and dialogue, you can hear the audio files at two different speeds: "normal" is how two native speakers would talk, while "slow" allows you to really hear each word separately.

http://faculty.maxwell.syr.edu/jishnu/101/

A
B
C
D
E
F
G
H
I
J
K
L
M
N
O
P
Q
R
S
T
U
V
W
X
Y
Z

America's Library

Pick any American time period between 1492 and the present and find out who was hot, what events people talked about, and what they did for fun. You can "meet" some fascinating famous Americans, too: real characters like magician Harry Houdini, as well as scientists like Thomas Alva Edison. Don't miss the scavenger hunt game. There are also multimedia animations and sound files, plus interactive quizzes around every bend of this wonderful site from the Library of Congress.
http://www.americaslibrary.gov/

HotBraille.com

Imagine if you could read words by touching them. That's one of the ways blind people read, by feeling little bumps on the page, which represent letters. This method of printing is called Braille, and you can learn about it at this page. What's cool is that you can also use this site to send e-mail to someone who reads Braille. Your letter will be translated into Braille and mailed anywhere in the world for free.

http://www.hotbraille.com/l_braille.asp

iLoveLanguages

Do you like to amaze people by saying things in a different language? Here's the place to get more vocabulary words in your favorite language. There are tons of links to over 100 different tongues. You'll also find lots of translating dictionaries, tutorials, organizations, internships, and much more.

http://www.ilovelanguages.com/

Native Tongue - Discover the Hawaiian Language

Learn about petroglyphs: ancient pictographs found on rocks all over the Hawaiian Islands. What do they mean? Who left them there for us to discover? Listen to audio clips of Hawaiian vowels and (on the separate glossary page) many common words and phrases. Check out this site *wiki-wiki* (fast)!

http://www.aloha-hawaii.com/0common/
    speaking.shtml

Say Hello to the World Project

If you wanted to say "Hello!" to the world, you'd have to speak 2,796 languages, according to the Internet Public Library. Learn to greet others in quite a few languages here, including Tagalog, Swahili, and Mayan. Hear Real Audio files of the words and then practice on your own.

http://www.ipl.org/youth/hello/

Yamada Language Guides

This is a neatly organized set of guides to 115 languages. Let's say you wanted to learn some Italian because you're going to Italy on vacation. You could look up phrases that you'd need to know, find information about Italian culture and history, and even get the daily news in Italian. Besides languages, this gives links to cultural and historical information about the people who speak these languages. Check the Lakota or the Inuit home pages, for example; there are even pages for Klingon and the languages from J. R. R. Tolkien's books!

http://babel.uoregon.edu/yamada/guides.html

YourDictionary.com—Grammars

Browse through links to grammars, tutorials, and other resources on learning languages from Abenaki to Wolof. If you need a special language font for Chinese or Urdu, there are links to those as well.

http://www.yourdictionary.com/grammars.html

> ## You won't believe how the PLANTS, TREES, AND GARDENS section grew!

CHINESE

Learn Chinese

What we loved about this site is the section on Chinese for adoptive parents of Chinese children. Now we know how to say "Put away your toys" in Chinese. If you'd rather learn vocabulary to help you in a restaurant or in a shop, those audio files are here, too.

http://www.wku.edu/~yuanh/AudioChinese/

Learning Chinese Online

From the Chinese Language: Questions & Answers FAQ file, you can discover all sorts of things about learning Chinese. You can also hear how "Beijing"— the city—is supposed to sound. Most news anchors on TV are pronouncing it wrong! Other sections of the site guide you to online tutorials, live practice chat sessions, and lots more.

http://www.csulb.edu/~txie/online.html

On-line Chinese Tools

At this site, there are many tools to help you learn Chinese. One of them is a flash cards applet. You choose the level of difficulty and the number of strokes in the Chinese character you want in your challenge set. Then see if you can match the characters to their English equivalents.

http://cgibin.erols.com/mandarintools/

ENGLISH

Dave's ESL Cafe

If your first language isn't English, you'll find a lot of company at Dave's ESL Cafe. ESL is shorthand for English as a Second Language. Check out the hints for both learning and teaching. Ever heard of an idiom? That's a word or phrase used in a somewhat unusual way, and there is a dictionary of English idioms at this site. For example, sometimes moms say, "There, there" to comfort their crying kids. That may make a new learner of English say, "Huh? There—where, where?" Or how about this one: you ask for a cookie and you get a really small one. You say, "That's a pretty small cookie." A new learner of English would wonder if you meant the cookie was beautiful. Even if you're not a new learner, you'll enjoy Dave's site, since he puts so much energy and fun into everything he does.

http://www.pacificnet.net/~sperling/eslcafe.html

How Does a Word Get in the Dictionary?

Have you ever wondered how editors of dictionaries choose which words to list and which definitions to use to describe words? This page explains how Merriam-Webster does it, and they should know the best way, because they have been doing it since the 1880s. There are almost 15 million citations for word uses in their database today.

http://www.m-w.com/about/wordin.htm

Interesting Things for ESL Students

We think this one would be good for anyone learning to speak or read English. In the Listening Room, pay close attention to the audio sound file and then try to answer questions about it. There are also other audio quizzes in pronunciation using Flash animation. Reading games include hangman, drag and drop puzzles, slider puzzles, and lots more.

http://www.manythings.org/

A B C D E F G H I J K L M N O P Q R S T U V W X Y Z

A
B
C
D
E
F
G
H
I
J
K
L
M
N
O
P
Q
R
S
T
U
V
W
X
Y
Z

ESPERANTO

Esperanto League for North America

Esperanto is a fairly new language as these things go: it's been around about 100 years or so. It is no one's native language. Rather, it's an attempt to have a common world language many people can easily learn to speak. In Esperanto, every word is pronounced exactly as it is spelled. There are no "silent" letters or exceptions. This makes Esperanto one of the easiest languages to learn quickly, according to experts. There's a free ten-lesson course you can take via e-mail. Here is how to say "I love you" in Esperanto: *Mi amas vin.* Try it on your mom.

http://www.esperanto-usa.org/lessons.html

FRENCH

★ BBC Languages - French

Maybe you have taken a little bit of French in school but you'd like to know more. Or maybe you're a French whiz and you'd just like to learn some cool French student slang to jazz up your street credibility. Or perhaps you're a complete beginner and just want to try this language on for size. It doesn't matter what your level of skill is, this multimedia-rich site has something for you.

http://www.bbc.co.uk/education/languages/french/

Cultural Explorer - Say It in French

Traveling to France and need to brush up on your language skills? Go to this site and click on "Fasten your seatbelt!" When you do, you will begin playing a game to help you improve your French. You'll land, virtually, of course, at Roissy-Charles-De-Gaulle airport just north of Paris. From there, use your knowledge of French to reach the Eiffel Tower and meet Mr. Langlois for dinner. You have six hours. Watch the hourglass. It will tell you how well you're doing.

http://culturel.org/ALF/

Quia - French - Top 20 Activities

Is it "*avoir*" or "*être*" when it comes to constructing a verb's past tense form? You'll know the answers if you check the fun drill and skill games at this site. Learn basic food, number, and conversational vocabulary in this entertaining way.

http://www.quia.com/dir/french/

GERMAN

★ BBC Languages - German

Put down the wurst, it's time to learn a little German. Whether you're a beginner or an advanced student, there's something here for you at this extensive site. Watch videos, hear audio files, and more.

http://www.bbc.co.uk/education/languages/german/

German Lessons and Vocabulary

How good are you at color names—in German? "*Klicken Sie auf: grün.*" If you click the green ball you'll get this response: "*Richtig!*" otherwise, "*Falsch!*" If you enjoy that, try some crossword puzzles in German. There are multimedia audio and video exercises, plus text grammar lessons.

http://www.germanfortravellers.com/learn/

JAPANESE

The Japanese Tutor

This extensive guide to Japanese culture and language will let you hear everyday words and phrases, spoken by a native speaker. You'll also learn the polite way to count on your fingers and how to use chopsticks.

http://www.japanesetutor.org/

Kid's Window

This is a great site for children. Here, kids can visit a virtual library with stories and a picture dictionary, a restaurant filled with delicious Japanese dishes (and how to pronounce them), a school with language and crafts areas, and a gallery of art created by kids aged 3 to 18.

http://www.jwindow.net/KIDS/

LATIN

★ Latin Language

Wouldn't it be great to have a chat room in which to talk Latin declensions with people who really understood? A place where you could go to trade mnemonic devices for remembering stuff like which nouns are masculine? A place where you could find tons of resources, including fun stuff like a Latin crossword puzzle and maybe some trivia questions? Guess what? It's all at this site!

http://latin.about.com/education/latin/

Latin News

Most people already know some Latin. When you put P.S. at the bottom of a letter, that stands for *post scriptum*, Latin for "after writing." But as a spoken language, Latin's not in general use today. That means Latin students have to pore over dusty ancient texts and histories to learn Latin. Not anymore. CBC puts recent news into Latin for your reading pleasure. There's also a link to a Finnish radio station that delivers the news in Latin, too.

http://www.cbc4kids.ca/general/whats-new/
    latin-news/

Latin Weather

If you've ever wondered what the weather forecast might be like if we all spoke Latin, wonder no more. The Weather Underground has your meteorological *praedictiones*.

http://latin.wunderground.com/

SIGN LANGUAGES

ASL Finger Spelling

Finger spelling is one way to communicate with folks who can't hear. Or it's a secret language you and your friend can use when the teacher says, "No talking!" Here's an interactive finger spelling guide and a quiz. Type your name and see it returned to you in fingerspelling. See how fast you can "sign" your name!

http://www.where.com/scott.net/asl/

NET FILES

The Empire State Building in New York City often uses special colored building lights to celebrate holidays, wins by the New York Yankees, and other special occasions. How many different colors can be displayed?

Answer: The different colors are red, green, blue, yellow, and white. Additionally, a ring of high-pressure sodium vapor lights above the 103rd floor creates a golden halo effect around the top of the mast from dusk to dawn. Read http://www.esbnyc.com/html/tower_lights.html for more fascinating tower trivia.

ASL for Kids

This nice little introduction to American Sign Language features animated GIF images so you can see what a signed word actually looks like. Try the game—can you guess the name of the animal from its sign language equivalent? This site was created by students for the ThinkQuest Junior competition.

http://tqjunior.advanced.org/5875/

A Basic Guide to ASL

Parental advisory: please preview this site, there are loads of ads. If you have the QuickTime plug-in for your browser, you can see animations of many American Sign Language words. Every word is also described in text, so if the animation doesn't run, you'll still be able to learn that the sign for "home," for example, is made like this: "The closed fingers of the right hand are first placed against the lips (eat), then opened to a flat palm and placed on right cheek (sleep)."

http://www.masterstech-home.com/ASLDict.html

A
B
C
D
E
F
G
H
I
J
K
L
M
N
O
P
Q
R
S
T
U
V
W
X
Y
Z

A
B
C
D
E
F
G
H
I
J
K
L
M
N
O
P
Q
R
S
T
U
V
W
X
Y
Z

SignWritingSite

Did you know that there is a sign language alphabet? You may be familiar with finger spelling alphabets, but this one is different. It's an alphabet for the motion of the hands and body, as well as the facial expressions used in making the sign for a particular word. The result looks somewhat like hieroglyphics to someone seeing it for the first time! This type of notation has been around since the 1960s; the idea came from DanceWriting—a pictorial shorthand for writing down dance movements. Why not do the same type of thing for sign language movements? The results are here. Be sure to see if you can read "Goldilocks and the Three Bears" and the other children's stories (look in the Library): all the words are in SignWriting.

http://www.signwriting.org/

SPANISH

★ BBC Languages - Spanish

Whether you're a beginner or an advanced student, there's something here for you at this extensive site. Watch videos, hear audio files, and more. Follow along with Jenny as she tours Madrid, trying to shop, eat, and get a taxi. How many pairs of shoes will she buy?

http://www.bbc.co.uk/education/languages/spanish/

Quia - Spanish - Top 20 Activities

Can you put the months in chronological order—in Spanish? That's only one of the fun drill and skill practice quizzes here. Test your vocabulary recognition of Spanish words associated with food, members of the family, numbers, and more.

http://www.quia.com/dir/spanish/

> ## You know something the Net doesn't——create your own home page! Look in the INTERNET- WEB BUILDING AND HTML section to find out how!

Webspañol

Did you know that English and Spanish share many similar-sounding and similar-meaning words? For example, the English "delicious" sounds very like the Spanish word for "tastes good"—*delicioso*. Over a thousand of these are collected and explained at the Espanglés section of this page (look in the Cognates section). You can hear pronunciation sound files, puzzle over some riddles in Spanish, try some lessons and links, and even scratch your head over Beatles lyrics in Spanish.

http://www.geocities.com/Athens/Thebes/6177/

LATINO, LATINA, HISPANIC AMERICANS

See also HOLIDAYS—CINCO DE MAYO and HOLIDAYS—DAY OF THE DEAD

Ana's Quinceañera Web Page!

The quinceañera is how girls from Spanish cultures celebrate their fifteenth birthday. It is their most important birthday, because it heralds their arrival into womanhood. Think of it as a cross between a Sweet Sixteen party and a debutante's ball, which introduces a young girl to society. Learn about this widely celebrated tradition. You can also read personal accounts of how girls celebrated their own quinceañeras. See photos of another girl's celebration at *<http://www.wenworld.com/news/features/ 0808.html>*.

http://clnet.ucr.edu/research/folklore/quinceaneras/

CULTURE

Arte Latino

There's a rich history of Latino art, from paintings to sculpture, and the Smithsonian American Art Museum may be bringing some of it to a gallery near you. Discover 75 photographs of the works, which are traveling around the U.S. through 2003. We loved the wonderful carved animals of Felipe Archuleta, and the graffiti-inspired paintings of Bojórquez.

http://nmaa-ryder.si.edu/t2go/1la/

Celebrating Hispanic Heritage

All phases of Hispanic culture are highlighted here, including music. Explore the genres of tejano, salsa, even the special song forms, the *corrido* and the *canción-corrido*. There are also 50 biographies of famous Hispanic Americans, plus a time line of over 500 years of Hispanic history.

http://www.gale.com/freresrc/chh/

Hispanic Americans

More than 22 million people of Hispanic descent live in the United States. Learn about how their culture and history has shaped general American culture and politics. Check out biographies of famous Hispanic Americans such as Cesar Estrada Chavez and Lee Trevino. Don't miss the Cinco de Mayo links for further information.

http://www.worldbook.com/fun/cinco/html/
  hispanic.htm

Let's Play Lotería

Latinos like to play a fun game called *Lotería*. It's like bingo, but it has colorful pictures with Spanish names instead of numbers and letters. Would you like to play the game? This class of kids made their own game cards. There is also lots of information on the riddles on the cards, as well as a lesson plan for teachers. For even more on this game, try <*http://nmaa-ryder.si.edu/webzine/loteria1.htm*>.

http://nmaa-ryder.si.edu/webzine/loteria1.htm

Mexico for Kids

Did you know that in Mexico, they make cactus ice cream? There are lots of fun facts and things to do at this site, including learning how to make a maraca using a soft drink can. You can also read some folk tales and learn a lot about the history and culture of Mexico.

http://www.elbalero.gob.mx/index_kids.html

Canku Ota (Many Paths)

Don't miss this truly inspired site. It features biweekly fresh articles and features. Inside you'll find interesting cultural stories from many nations, a kids page, numerous quality links to resources on native interests, and even coloring book pages. Recent articles included one on Huichol Indian beadwork, a recipe for Cherokee Berry Bread, and many news stories involving native youth. The collection of suggested links is outstanding, easy to use, and contains complete annotations. *http://www.turtletrack.org/*

HISTORY
Celebrate Hispanic Heritage

The roots of Hispanic heritage stretch from the Caribbean to California and date back more than 500 years. At this site, use the map to trace Hispanic history in the Americas. You'll also learn about 25 Hispanic history makers, including golfer Nancy Lopez and singer Gloria Estefan.

http://teacher.scholastic.com/hispanic/

Hispanic Heritage Month

Hispanic Heritage month runs from September 15 to October 15. You can find out about the history of this celebration as well as Hispanic history here. Learn about Hispanics in the Civil War, discover "Cinco de Mayo, the Real Story," and explore a varied set of outside links.

http://www.hanford.gov/doe/hrm/hispanic/
  hispanic_heritage.htm

A B C D E F G H I J K L M N O P Q R S T U V W X Y Z

NET FILES

How many miles do the Cotter High School (Winona, Minnesota) marching band members march in a year? How many total bars of music are played by the Cotter band each year?

Answer: They march 105 miles, give or take a few, er, feet, and they play 21,434,058 musical bars. By the way, there are 130 members in the band. The number of hamburgers consumed by Cotter band members in an average summer is 6,510, and at least 12 T-shirts go unclaimed on the band's bus after every road trip. Find more funny facts about this band at *http://escargot.mps.org/~chsband/facts.html*

LAW

See also UNITED STATES—FEDERAL GOVERNMENT—JUDICIAL

Debate Central

Would you like to be able win an argument by deftly picking apart the other person's reasoning? Would you like to be able to persuade others to your point of view? Debating teaches you how to do that with logic and style. Learn about the art and craft of debating at this site. You can also watch college debating teams take each other on in competition.

http://debate.uvm.edu/

Inside the Courtroom

How does a Federal prosecutor decide what cases to bring to trial? What are the steps she needs to take to bring a criminal to justice? From the investigation through the appeal, you'll learn about the entire process. There's also a glossary of legal terms.

http://www.usdoj.gov/usao/eousa/kidspage/

LAW ENFORCEMENT AND FORENSIC SCIENCE
★ Evidence: the True Witness

Can you solve the crime? Or is it a crime that you call yourself a detective? Maybe you'd better take a few minutes to learn something about forensic sciences before you take on the case of the kidnapped Susie Van Konkel. Study how law enforcement officials investigate a crime scene and what high-tech tools they use to track down criminals. This site was created by students for the ThinkQuest competition.

http://library.thinkquest.org/17049/

FBI Kids & Youth Educational Pages

The Federal Bureau of Investigation has had a long history of helping to solve crimes in the United States. At their Web site you can find out about fingerprinting, polygraph (lie detector) testing, DNA analysis, and other methods of crime detection. You'll be fascinated by the information on real-life crime dogs. They look for explosives, perform search and rescue operations, and also can be trained to sniff out drugs. Check the games section for a fun little concentration matching challenge and a secret agent disguise game. There are two sites. The one listed below is for younger kids. Teens should visit *<http://www.fbi.gov/kids/6th12th/6th12th.htm>*.

http://www.fbi.gov/kids/k5th/kidsk5th.htm

You never lose the pieces to the online games in GAMES AND FUN!

Why surf the Internet when you can sail it in BOATING AND SAILING?

Police Work

At this site you can learn about what police officers do. Check out police tools (what's all that stuff hanging from their belts?) and take a look at the types of vehicles used for police work. Did you know they sometimes ride bicycles? This site was created by students for the ThinkQuest Junior competition.

http://library.thinkquest.org/J002921/

🦆 Super Trooper - My Car

It's exciting and scary to see a police car! You don't want to go too close to a real police car, but you can walk right up to this one on the Internet. Press the horn, work the siren, listen to the squeal of the tires and the roar of the engine. No one will mind—well, maybe your sister will if she's trying to concentrate on her homework.

http://members.bellatlantic.net/~louis2/

Who Dunnit?

Who took a bite out of the candy? Sticky fingers have been found on the broken aquarium glass. Wet footprints lead to the open window. What is that powdery substance next to the broken piggy bank? Answering these questions is what forensic science is all about. At this site, you'll learn how to solve crimes by exploring the world of the forensic scientist.

http://www.cyberbee.com/whodunnit/crime.html

LIBRARIES

Awards and Notables from the Association for Library Service to Children

There's no doubt that librarians know tons about books. Every year, children's librarians in the American Library Association give two awards to authors and illustrators of the best books for kids. The Caldecott Medal <http://www.ala.org/alsc/caldecott.html> goes to the best illustrator of a children's book, and the Newbery Medal <http://www.ala.org/alsc/newbery.html> is given to the author of the finest kids' book. See the winners at these Web sites; you'll find some librarian-tested and approved books, videos, music, and even Web sites.

http://www.ala.org/alsc/awards.html

Dewey Decimal Classification

How would you like to walk into a library and find all the books arranged by size, or color? It would be a little hard to find a book! That's why librarians (usually) organize books based on their subjects. One of the most popular systems for U.S. schools and public libraries is called the Dewey Decimal System. It was created by Melvil Dewey, and you can find out about him and his classification scheme here.

http://www.oclc.org/dewey/about/ddctour/ddc1.html

"Do We" Really Know Dewey?

By the way—are you confused about the difference between fiction and nonfiction? Just say to yourself, "I can only say 'No' once for each term." Then write out these little reminders: NOnfiction = True, and Fiction = NOt true. This site was created by students for the ThinkQuest Junior competition.

http://tqjunior.advanced.org/5002/

LITERARY CRITICISM

See BOOKS AND LITERATURE—LITERARY CRITICISM AND REVIEWS

A
B
C
D
E
F
G
H
I
J
K
L
M
N
O
P
Q
R
S
T
U
V
W
X
Y
Z

A
B
C
D
E
F
G
H
I
J
K
L
M
N
O
P
Q
R
S
T
U
V
W
X
Y
Z

MAGIC TRICKS

Can the Hall's of Magic Find Your Card?

Just pick a card, any card. Who will figure it out first? "Mojo: Using gut instinct and street smarts? The Sheik: Using psychic powers? Dr. Megabyte: Using cybernetic calculations?" Now remember whose hand the card is in and click on the appropriate illusionist. Unfortunately, they're none too smart, and you'll have to tell them again—and again. But by the third time they've got it right, and sure enough, the card they choose is the same one you picked. Try it again—it works!

http://www.hallsofmagic.com/cards/cards.htm

Conjuror

Learn to do the "coin though the elbow" trick, the "hypnotized handkerchief," and 13 more mystifying illusions. The history of magic section should, on the other hand, be previewed by parents.

http://www.conjuror.com/magictricks/

★ Hocus Pocus Palace

Dare to challenge The Great Mysto in a game of mind reading and clairvoyance. Through magical and as yet unexplainable Internet protocols, The Great Mysto will astound you with his long-distance feats. Doubters may scoff and say these are simple "magic square" tricks, but we're not so sure (how did he know we were thinking of Marge Simpson?). O Great Mysto, you have a truly fun site!

http://www.teleport.com/~jrolsen/

The Magic Secrets Basement - Magic for Beginners

Want to try your hand at magic? This is the place to start. The basic rules are important, but the card and coin tricks described at this site are a lot more fun! Remember that practice is the key to performing a trick that's believable.

http://www.spiderlink.net/users/ralcocer/basement/imc.html

Magic Show

Abracadabra! The magic trick amazes the people in the audience, who whisper to each other, "That's impossible! How do they do it?" Everyone loves a magic show. The only thing better than watching a magic show is being the magician. This Web magazine has articles about professional magicians who astound people, show after show. Each issue also contains the secrets of how to perform these magical feats yourself. There are even movie clips so you can admire the professionals (look in the Magic Theater). Whether you want to learn magic or you just enjoy watching it, this site has something for you. Don't forget the hat (and the rabbit).

http://allmagic.com/

Trendy Magic - Interactive Style

Check this one out! Here are some interactive tricks that are guaranteed to catch you off guard. We thought, hey, how mysterious can it be—it's only a rabbit. Wrong! It fooled us! Then we tried Color Theory. How'd they do that? Maybe we're just too susceptible. But after the Psycho Test, we just turned off the computer, backed away, and kept a safe distance for a while.

http://magic.trendy.org/interactivemagic.shtml

MAMMALS

★ Art Tales: Telling Stories with Wildlife Art

Pretend you're a frontier explorer with a story to tell. Select wildlife artworks to illustrate your tale, and add a soundtrack of animal sounds or music. You might also choose to be a field guide writer or a museum curator. When you've produced your story, or book, or your gallery guide, you can send it in for possible publication on the Net.

http://www.wildlifeart.org/ArtTales/

The Hall of Mammals

Take a tour to four major groups of mammals and discover the differences among them and how they are classified. One group, the *multituberculata*, is extinct. Once these pre-rodent creatures were widespread and successful, but our knowledge of them comes only from observation of their fossils. As you explore this site, try the occasional audio sound bite (it doesn't hurt!).

http://www.ucmp.berkeley.edu/mammal/
  mammal.html

Hinterland Who's Who

Learn about more than 80 animals native to Canada's hinterlands. Put on your snowshoes and follow the animal tracks across northern Canada to discover everything from moose to polar bears.

http://www.cws-scf.ec.gc.ca/hww-fap/eng_ind.html

Nature-Wildlife

Need a warthog illustration? Desperate to discover what a zebra looks like when he's threatening to bite? Want to see over 60 high-quality photos of elephants? This is a professional wildlife photographer's page, illustrated with his own photos. This site also contains lots of information about these and other African mammals.

http://nature-wildlife.com/mammals.htm

Sounds of the World's Animals

Everybody knows that a dog's bark is "woof-woof," right? Well, not everybody knows that! A French dog says, "*ouah ouah*," while a Japanese dog says, "*wanwan*." In Sweden, the dogs say, "*vov vov*," and in the Ukraine, you'll find them saying, "*gaf-gaf*." This is a Web page full of what the world thinks various animals sound like. There's an audio sound file for some animals, so you can hear and decide for yourself which language "says it best."

http://www.georgetown.edu/cball/animals/
  animals.html

NET FILES

Mastodon, mammoth, bison, and musk ox traveled one way, passing the camels, horses, and cheetahs going in the other direction. What were they doing?

Answer: They were migrating across the land bridge that connected Asia and North America during the Ice Age, when massive ice packs covered more of the Earth's surface than they do today. Falling sea levels exposed enough land to make the connection possible. The first group of animals came to North America from Asia, while the second group originated in North America. Behind both groups were humans, chasing their respective food sources! The chilling truth is out there at *http://www.tyrrellmuseum.com/tour/iceages.html*

World Wide Fund for Nature

This site offers photos, range maps, and facts on 17 different species, including the beaver, giraffe, bear, chimpanzee, elephant, and several more.

http://www.panda.org/kids/wildlife/idxalsmn.htm

ARTIODACTYLA (CLOVEN-FOOTED MAMMALS)
A–Z of the Arabian Camel

Source of transport, food, and clothing, the camel is an important part of desert life in many parts of the world, notably Africa and Asia. This site teaches many surprising facts about camels. They have two fleshy toes on each foot. When walking, the toes splay out against the sand, providing a snowshoe (sandshoe?) effect that keeps the camel from sinking. All camels shed their coats in the spring and grow new ones by the fall. Their hair is sought after for making fine artist's brushes, garments, and rugs.

http://www.arab.net/camels/welcome.html

A
B
C
D
E
F
G
H
I
J
K
L
M
N
O
P
Q
R
S
T
U
V
W
X
Y
Z

A
B
C
D
E
F
G
H
I
J
K
L
M
N
O
P
Q
R
S
T
U
V
W
X
Y
Z

Media Awareness Network—the Three Little CyberPigs

The Three Little Cyberpigs are learning about Internet safety the hard way. The first adventure is all about the Three Little CyperPigs and how they meet up with the Big Bad Wolf in "Privacy Playground." The second is called "Cybersense and Nonsense." It will teach you chat room safety, and convince you that you can't trust everything you read on the Internet.

http://www.media-awareness.ca/eng/med/kids/kindex.htm

Introduction to the Artiodactyla

Artiodactyla may seem like a strange name, but you're already familiar with many members of this group. It includes the split-hoofed mammals, such as sheep, goats, cows, camels, and giraffes. This site is also where the deer and the antelope play; join them!

http://www.ucmp.berkeley.edu/mammal/artio/
   artiodactyla.html

Mountain Sheep

Mountain, or bighorn, sheep have a varied lifestyle. Some of them live in the below-sea-level deserts of Death Valley, while others inhabit the steep alpine cliffs of the snowy Rocky Mountains. Their huge curving horns are never shed, and biologists can estimate a sheep's age by examining his horns. Mountain sheep are brown, not white like the domesticated ones you may have seen on farms. They are also very much larger, standing over three feet tall at the shoulder.

http://www.cws-scf.ec.gc.ca/hww-fap/mtnsheep/
   mtnsheep.html

North American Bison

Two hundred years ago, millions of bison, also called buffalo, roamed the Great Plains areas of North America. They were hunted by Native Americans and provided food, clothing, and shelter to the native people. In the 1800s, the animals were killed by the millions and hunted to near extinction. The activities of the commercial buffalo hide hunters, pioneers, and others may have opened up the grasslands for cultivation, but the native peoples were left with a bitter legacy. Now, bison are protected in national parks and other sanctuaries. They are the largest land animal in North America, and you can learn much more at this site.

http://www.cws-scf.ec.gc.ca/hww-fap/bison/
   bison.html

ARTIODACTYLA (CLOVEN-FOOTED MAMMALS)—DEER FAMILY

The Magnificent Moose Project

Students in Fairbanks, Alaska, couldn't help but notice the moose in their backyards and in their schoolyard. So they decided to create a classroom project with collected moose information. There are lighthearted parts of the site (the moose in comics and cartoons), but there is also a section on moose hunting, which might disturb sensitive kids. High on the "Yuck!" scale is the part of the site dedicated to the funky things you can make out of moose droppings.

http://www3.northstar.k12.ak.us/schools/awe/moose/
   moosepage.html

Moose

The moose is the largest member of the deer family, often as large as a saddle horse. Old antlers are shed each autumn and new ones are grown in the spring. An adult bull moose can have an antler spread as wide as six feet or more; usually, though, they are about four feet wide. Moose eat twigs, leaves, and water plants. They are often seen wading in shallow ponds, munching water lilies. They swim well and have been known to dive over 18 feet deep to reach a succulent plant!

http://www.cws-scf.ec.gc.ca/hww-fap/moose/
   moose.html

> **People are the true treasures of the Net.**

White-Tailed Deer

Find out about the life cycle of white-tailed deer at this site. Here at Pollywood Farm, we see a lot of deer. We see deer eating the arborvitae, deer eating the gold thread cypress, and deer eating the tender perennials. We also spot deer cleaning up seeds under the bird feeder. One year we tried buying actual deer food, because we thought that then they might be too full to eat our shrubs. Nah. So now we just enjoy them and try to plant things deer don't like to eat.

http://www.cws-scf.ec.gc.ca/hww-fap/deer/deer.html

ARTIODACTYLA (CLOVEN-FOOTED MAMMALS)—GIRAFFES

Giraffe

Tall and majestic, giraffes cruise the grasslands of Africa with grace and style. But don't even think of messing with them! These 15-foot reticulated wonders are into neck wrestling and head banging, and if threatened, they can kill a predator with a single kick. You definitely want to keep on the good side of this 4,000-pound animal. Even the babies are six feet tall at birth.

http://www.oaklandzoo.org/atoz/azgiraf.html

GiraffeCam at Cheyenne Mountain Zoo

You've got to see the giraffes at the Cheyenne Mountain Zoo in Colorado Springs, Colorado. Sometimes they are in, sometimes they are out, but keep tuning in and you're bound to see a giraffe or two eventually. We did! They are normally visible from 10 A.M. to 4 P.M. (mountain time). This zoo is famous for successfully breeding giraffes in captivity.

http://c.unclone.com/zoocam.html

CARNIVORES—BEARS

The Bear Den

This page says, "For bears everywhere, and for those humans who are on their side." We don't know how many bears are actually using the Internet. For one thing, there is the problem of getting a telephone line installed in their dens. For another, there is the difficulty of hitting the right keys when they type with their big, furry paws. However, we are sure that when bears finally get all those problems solved, they will love this Web page. You'll learn about eight species of bears, catch up on current news in the world of bears, and discover some tips on what to do if you ever meet up with a wilderness bear who doesn't act like Yogi and Boo-Boo.

http://www.nature-net.com/bears/

Black Bear

You're walking on a trail and see something up ahead. You can't decide if it's a black bear or a grizzly bear. So you dig into your daypack and bring out your laptop. Hooking it up to your cellular phone, you log onto your Internet account and visit this Web site to learn the distinguishing features of each type of bear. You also visit the grizzly page <http://www.cws-scf.ec.gc.ca/hww-fap/grizzly/grizzly.html>. By then the bear is sitting next to you, looking over your shoulder while eating your lunch. Maybe it's time to log off and move away quietly.

http://www.cws-scf.ec.gc.ca/hww-fap/blbear/blbear.html

Polar Bear

The scientific name for the polar bear is *Ursus maritimus*, which in Latin means "bear of the sea." Although polar bears are good swimmers, they are really large land carnivores. An average adult male weighs 1,100 to 1,300 pounds. Their fur is translucent, which allows sunshine all the way down the hair shaft to the black skin below. The black skin helps absorb heat from the sun. This helps keep the bear warmer.

http://www.cws-scf.ec.gc.ca/hww-fap/plbear/pbear.html

A B C D E F G H I J K L **M** N O P Q R S T U V W X Y Z

A
B
C
D
E
F
G
H
I
J
K
L
M
N
O
P
Q
R
S
T
U
V
W
X
Y
Z

Polar Bears

Do polar bears really like winter? You bet they do! In fact, polar bears would rather live on ice than on land. Discover more about their chilly lifestyle, and learn why you can't sneak up on a polar bear (for one thing, they can smell you coming up to 20 miles away). There are also some arctic activities, including how to make simulated ivory "scrimshaw" by carving a bar of soap with a plastic knife.

http://www.seaworld.org/polar_bears/pbindex.html

San Diego Zoo - Giant Pandas and Panda Cam

It's the panda cam! Is that one, over there by the cave? See what you spot when you tune in! (Hint: those things in the front of the picture are tourists.) So, is the giant panda a bear, or a raccoon, or what? According to this page, "The giant panda is a bear. It is different enough from other bears to be placed in its own subfamily, but it is still a bear." In the wilds of China, there are only about 1,000 giant pandas left. In captivity, there are another 110, again mostly in China. The San Diego Zoo has several pandas, and this is their home page. Read up on panda habitat, panda characteristics, and panda snacking behavior.

http://www.sandiegozoo.org/special/pandas/
   pandacam/

CARNIVORES—CAT FAMILY

Big Cats On-line

Here, kitty kitty! Almost 40 members of the cat family are curled up on this page, waiting for you to discover them. Want to see the big cats up close and *purrsonal*? This is the right place. What's the biggest cat of all? The smallest? How do cats see in the dark? Learn about the evolution of the cat family, as well as conservation efforts under way to save those that are endangered. There's also a litter of links that will make big cat lovers purr with pride.

http://dialspace.dial.pipex.com/agarman/bco/
   ver4.htm

Canada Lynx

The Canada lynx is a secretive creature. It is most active at night and is rarely seen in the wild. Its main food source is the snowshoe hare, and as hare populations go up, lynx numbers increase as well. The lynx has large, tufted feet, which act as snowshoes in the wintertime. This is good for the lynx, but bad for the hare.

http://www.cws-scf.ec.gc.ca/hww-fap/lynx/lynx.html

★ Cats! Wild to Mild

The Natural History Museum of Los Angeles County has a traveling exhibition all about cats. This companion site to the exhibit has encyclopedia-type entries for 19 feline species from around the world. Represented are jaguars, lions, tigers, leopards, bobcats, and wildcats, as well as house pets. You can see wonderful color pictures of the cats, plus range distribution maps for each. Many of them are endangered species; for example, only 50 Florida panthers are estimated to be left in the wild. Some still exist on the Web, though: you'll find a collection of links for each species. Do you have a cat? Chances are that you do or that you know someone who does. Garfield would be so pleased.

http://www.nhm.org/cats/

Cougar

Sometimes also known as a mountain lion, puma, or panther, this large cat's favorite prey is the white-tailed deer. It will also attack bighorn sheep, moose calves, and anything else below its link on the food chain. As solitary hunters, these cats inhabit a wide variety of forested foothills and mountains. Although adults have tawny to chocolate brown coats, kittens are spotted at birth. Their spots disappear by the time they become a year old.

http://www.cws-scf.ec.gc.ca/hww-fap/cougar/
   cougar.html

Pony up to HORSES AND EQUESTRIAN SPORTS.

★ Cyber Tiger @ Nationalgeographic.com

At this site, first you choose a name for your tiger; then you write in your own name (or a name you make up for yourself). Now it's time to become a zookeeper and raise this six-year-old Siberian male tiger. There's a lot of work involved in keeping this fellow alive and happy, and we want him to be happy. Otherwise, he might decide to jump out of his virtual cage (he can leap 10 feet off the ground), and that wouldn't be good for anybody! You're going to have a lot of fun—and learn something, too—as you build a home, feed, and care for your virtual tiger.

http://www.nationalgeographic.com/features/97/tigers/maina.html

★ Tiger Information Center

Why is this Web site's domain named "5tigers"? Because only five subspecies of tigers remain on Earth today. Three other subspecies have disappeared into extinction in the last 70 years. There are estimated to be only about 5,000 to 7,500 wild tigers left. This organization will teach you something about conservation efforts and how you can help. Take a quiz and see how much you already know about the natural history of tigers. Then play a fun adventure and listen to tiger sounds, scratches, and growls.

http://www.5tigers.org/Directory/kids.htm

CARNIVORES—DOG FAMILY

Coyotes

This is one of the few mammals whose range is increasing rather than decreasing, despite efforts to control the coyote population. The clearing of forests and the loss of wolves as a competitor has allowed coyotes to prosper. Here's another fact: the coyote can be a very fast runner, reaching speeds of 24 to 40 mph. This page says that greyhounds can catch up with coyotes, but it takes them quite a long time to do so.

http://www.cws-scf.ec.gc.ca/hww-fap/coyote/coyote.html

CARNIVORES— DOG FAMILY—FOXES

Adam's Fox Box III

When Fox went out on a chilly night, it was probably heading to this home page. Learn fox facts; view some great fox photos; and read stories, songs, and poems about foxes.

http://www.foxbox.org/

Red Fox

Here at Pollywood Farm we see foxes fairly often. Once a whole family of foxes moved into a den in the stone wall, and every day we were treated to an entertaining show of fox cubs rolling and tumbling on the lawn. Foxes eat small mammals, insects, eggs, and garbage. Find out more about their natural history at this Web site.

http://www.cws-scf.ec.gc.ca/hww-fap/redfox/redfox.html

NET FILES

It seemed like such a normal day. Suddenly, you turn around, only to discover that you're being chased by a Grizzled Skipper, a Red Admiral, and a Painted Lady!

What should you do?

Answer: Enjoy the beautiful sight! These are three types of butterflies found in New York State. You can see their pictures at this resource: http://www.npwrc.usgs.gov/resource/distr/lepid/bflyusa/ny/toc.htm. If you live somewhere else in the U.S., pick your state from the list at this level: http://www.npwrc.usgs.gov/resource/distr/lepid/bflyusa/bflyusa.htm

A B C D E F G H I J K L M N O P Q R S T U V W X Y Z

A B C D E F G H I J K L **M** N O P Q R S T U V W X Y Z

CARNIVORES— DOG FAMILY—WOLVES

Kids Only Wolf Information

Study the pictures at this site and see if you can tell a wolf's mood just by looking at his body posture and the position of his tail. There's also an animal tracks quiz, suggested books to read, and lots more. We had trouble with the jigsaw puzzle; it did not seem to function properly for us.

http://www.timberwolfinformation.org/kidsonly/
    kidsonly.htm

NOVA Online - Wild Wolves

What's in a howl? What are wolves trying to communicate? At this site, you can listen to a community howl and read a scientific explanation of what's going on. You'll learn a lot from an interview with one of the people responsible for reintroducing wolves to Yellowstone National Park, and then try a quiz to test your knowledge of how wolves and dogs are similar and different.

http://www.pbs.org/wgbh/nova/wolves/

NET FILES

How many miles of yarn can be spun from one pound of wool?

Answer: According to *http://www.cyberspaceag. com/woolfacts.html*, the answer is twenty miles of yarn from one pound of wool!

CARNIVORES—OTTERS

Sea Otters, California's Threatened Treasure

No wonder sea otters were prized for their warm, luxurious fur. A sea otter's coat has up to one million hairs of fur per square inch. That's more than the hairs on eight human heads! Its sought-after hide was the main reason why these cute, furry critters were almost wiped out. This fact-packed site will tell you more and enlighten you on the current dangers threatening the sea otter that was once so prevalent along the California coast. This site was created by students for the ThinkQuest competition.

http://library.thinkquest.org/J0111704/

CARNIVORES—RACCOONS

Raccoons

According to this site, "The name raccoon is derived from the Algonquin Indian word arakun, meaning 'he scratches with his hand.' The species name, *lotor*, refers to the raccoon's supposed habit of washing food with its front paws. This activity, however, is probably associated with the location and capture of aquatic prey such as crayfish." Read up on the rakish raccoon at this home page.

http://www.cws-scf.ec.gc.ca/hww-fap/raccoon/
    raccoon.html

The World Wide Raccoon Web

Who's that pack of bandits prying off the lid of your garbage can? It's a family of raccoons! Their nimble paws, black masks, and long, ringed tails make them unmistakable. Visit this home page to meet a true fan of raccoons and their natural—and unnatural—history. You'll find lots of photos, legends, and links, and in the News section you can read the incredible story of how one raccoon saved a student's life at Cornell University.

http://www.loomcom.com/raccoons/

CARNIVORES—SKUNKS

Skunk and Opossum Web Site

What would you do if your dog got sprayed by a skunk? Does a tomato juice bath really work? Sort of, but it may turn your dog pink for a while. You can also try a newer remedy; the recipe is below, and on this site. It turns the skunk scent into harmless oxygen. This is the recipe for deodorizing a skunked cat. For a dog you may need larger quantities. 1 Quart of 3% Hydrogen Peroxide (Use FRESH Hydrogen Peroxide). 1/4 cup of Baking Soda. 1 teaspoon of Liquid Soap. Wash animal while mixture is bubbling. Rinse off with tap water. At this site, there is also advice on keeping skunks as pets, plus loads of lore on both skunks and opossums.

http://granicus.if.org/~firmiss/m-d.html

Skunks

You know that skunks can spray a foul-smelling musk in order to deter a predator, but what else do you know about them? They are useful because they eat mice, shrews, grasshoppers, crickets, and insect larvae such as white grubs, army worms, and cutworms. According to this page, "They will even eat wasps and bees, which they kill with their front feet. It has been estimated that almost 70 percent of a skunk's diet constitutes a benefit to people and only 5 percent is harmful to human property."

http://www.cws-scf.ec.gc.ca/hww-fap/sskunk/
   skunk.html

CETACEANS

Cetacea

What's the *porpoise* of this Web site? All cetaceans. All the time. This encyclopedic resource covers all species of whales, dolphins, and porpoises. There is also detailed information about where to go to see whales around the world, and what time of year to do it.

http://www.cetacea.org/

The National Marine Mammal Laboratory's Education Web Site

There are over 70 species of whales, dolphins, and porpoises. You'll learn all about them at this Web site. If you just need a few facts, you can get that; otherwise, keep clicking and you'll soon be presented with encyclopedic knowledge about each species.

http://nmml.afsc.noaa.gov/education/

WhaleTimes SeaBed

Can you tell the difference between a shark and a whale? Many sharks have two dorsal fins; a whale has only one dorsal fin, if any at all. Also, a shark's tail is vertical, and a whale's tail is horizontal. If you're fishing for fishy (or marine mammal) facts, you can ask Jake the Sea Dog, who will answer questions. You can even help write an ocean story. Take a swim to this Web page and see for yourself.

http://www.whaletimes.org/

CETACEANS—DOLPHINS

Dolphins - The Oracles of the Sea

Learn about the evolution of various dolphin species and how scientists sort them all out. The section on anatomy of the dolphin dives right into basic body parts, physiology, and propulsion. There are sections on dolphin behavior and how dolphins and man interact, including the arguments on the pros and cons of captivity. This beautifully designed site was created by students for the ThinkQuest competition.

http://library.thinkquest.org/17963/

Leap into the World of Dolphins

Have you ever wondered how a dolphin lives? What it eats? How it communicates? You can find out some of that information here. If you take the quiz, you'll learn that not all dolphins are friendly like the dolphin in the movie *Flipper*. Dolphins have personalities (just like people), so some will be nicer than others. This site was created by students for the ThinkQuest competition.

http://library.thinkquest.org/J0110164/

A B C D E F G H I J K L M N O P Q R S T U V W X Y Z

A
B
C
D
E
F
G
H
I
J
K
L
M
N
O
P
Q
R
S
T
U
V
W
X
Y
Z

CETACEANS—WHALES

★ J. J.'s Adventure: A Baby Gray Whale's Rescue and Release

J. J. the gray whale made lots of news in 1997. In January, she was found on the beach at the tender age of seven days old. Although very sick, she was rescued, cared for, and eventually released back to her home in the Pacific Ocean. Three schoolgirls loved the story so much they decided to make a Web page and enter the ThinkQuest Junior contest. Guess what? They won Best of Contest for 1998! View lots of great photos and learn how J. J. got her name at this terrific site.

http://tqjunior.advanced.org/4397/

Keiko's Corner - Ocean Futures

How are plans progressing for Keiko (the *Free Willy* whale) to be released, now that he's been swimming around in a bay pen off Iceland? Slowly, Keiko is trying to learn skills he will need if he ever returns to freedom. Lately, he's learned to follow a boat and has been taken on short "ocean walks." At this site you can check his progress and find out more about orcas.

http://www.oceanfutures.com/keiko/

Whale Sounds, Cries, Howls, Whistles, and Songs

Do you think these whales sound like cows, pigs, or wolves? Turn up your speakers and enjoy the wonderful voices of singing whales. These were recorded off Hervey Bay, Queensland, Australia. You can listen to them individually or with an informative human narration. The streaming audio version is almost nine minutes long.

http://dkd.net/whales/wsounds.html

Staring off into space? Discover ASTRONOMY, SPACE, AND SPACE EXPLORATION!

WhaleNet

Have you ever wanted to go on a whale watch? So do lots of other people! Every day, big boats of whale seekers leave from port cities all over the world, in search of sighting one or more of the marine mammals. Now you can go on a whale watch right here! Climb aboard the boat and head out into the Atlantic Ocean. On this trip, you are guaranteed to see some whales. There's lots of great information about whales available at this site, too. Check the pictures of the kids who made a 55-foot long inflatable whale. Find out how to purchase the directions and make a whale at your school.

http://whale.wheelock.edu/

Zoom Whales - Enchanted Learning Software

You already know that a whale is a mammal, not a fish (otherwise you'd be reading about them in section "F"). Did you know the biggest whale of all is the blue whale? This whale can grow to 94 feet long—that's as high as a nine-story building. At this site you'll find information on whale behavior, whale songs, and lots of puzzles and links.

http://www.EnchantedLearning.com/subjects/whales/

CHIROPTERA—BATS

★ The Adventure of Echo the Bat

Follow the story of Echo, the baby bat, as he learns to fly, catch insects, and "see" with his ears. How is that possible? It's called echolocation, and you'll learn all about it right along with furry Echo. A sudden storm separates Echo from his mom, but he remembers she told him something about a big cave down south, where bats meet up to spend the winter. Can he find his way there? Turns out he also has a special tag that allows his route to be tracked by satellite. If you have a 4.0 or better browser, you can become a scientist and track Echo on his journey to find Mom.

http://imagers.gsfc.nasa.gov/

Bat Conservation International

Don't miss the BatCam at this site! What will you see hanging around? Did you know that the world's smallest mammal is the bumblebee bat? It weighs less than a penny does. Nearly 1,000 different kinds of bats account for almost 25 percent of all mammal species. Most bats are very good to have around. One little brown bat can catch 600 mosquitoes in just one hour. Visit this site to learn more about bats and bat houses, or stop in at North America's largest urban bat colony by clicking on "Congress Ave. Bridge"—that's in the Projects area. You can even "adopt" a bat at this most interesting site.

http://www.batcon.org/

Bat Echolocation Station

This site has some amazing bat facts that will make you glad you eat a home-cooked meal. If you were a bat, you'd eat insects, lots of them. So many that you would eat half of your weight in insects every night to stay alive and healthy. That's what bats do, and they use sound to find their prey. Now, what if you really were a bat? How many one-pound buckets of bugs would you need to eat each night? Simply enter your weight to find out. This site will do the math.

http://www.museumca.org/caves/onli_echo.html

The Buzbee Bat House Temperature Plot

At this batty site, you can check the temperature inside the Buzbee's bat house, and remember, bats like to be warm. After that, discover a whole colony of educational links about bats. You'll find pictures, facts, and even tours to bat caves.

http://www.batbox.org/

Goin' Batty

Do bats really want to suck your blood? You can find out here, and discover plenty of bat facts, pictures, and more. There are over 1,000 species of bats, and they live everywhere on Earth except for the poles (that would be one chilly bat). This site was created by students for the ThinkQuest Junior competition.

http://tqjunior.advanced.org/5813/

What baseball team was the first to continuously use numbers on their uniforms, and in what year did this happen?

Answer: In 1929, the New York Yankees became the first team to use numbers on their uniforms. The numbers corresponded to the batting order. Find out more at *http://cbs.sportsline.com/u/baseball/bol /chronology/1929JANUARY.html*

LAGOMORPHS—RABBITS AND HARES

House Rabbit Society

"Wanted: A patient human with a sense of humor who spends a lot of time at home and doesn't mind hanging out on the floor with me. I am a bunny rabbit in need of a good home. I am inquisitive, sociable, and litterbox trained, and would make a wonderful companion for the right person. I need to be protected from predators, poisons, temperature extremes, electrical cords, and rough handling. I may even purr when I am happy. Stop by to find out what life would be like if you adopted me. Please hurry, my friends and I need your help!" The House Rabbit Society has rabbits for adoption all over the U.S. You'll also find out a lot about rabbit care and handling, so hop on over!

http://www.rabbit.org/

A B C D E F G H I J K L M N O P Q R S T U V W X Y Z

A B C D E F G H I J K L **M** N O P Q R S T U V W X Y Z

Snowshoe Hare

Although brown in summer, snowshoe hares turn completely white in the winter. That's good, because it camouflages them in the snow. Their big furry feet help them stay on top of the snow rather than sink in, like a deer would. They have large ears with which to detect nearby predators, but the ears serve another purpose: they help regulate body temperature by dispersing excess heat.

http://www.cws-scf.ec.gc.ca/hww-fap/snowshoe/
  snowshoe.html

MARSUPIALS (POUCHED MAMMALS)

Red Kangaroo

Something we learned at this site is that kangaroos don't live in herds, they live in mobs. A mob of kangaroos includes one dominant male, several females, and baby kangaroos called joeys. If you take the link to the main floor of this site <*http:// home.mira.net/~areadman/aussie.htm*>, you'll find other pages on "kangaroo-like" animals.

http://home.mira.net/~areadman/red.htm

NET FILES

How do you make "Flubber"?

Answer: It's a silly-putty-like substance made of borax, Elmer's glue, and water. You can get the right recipe at *http://www.erbspalsy.org/craftrecipes.html*. Unfortunately, this isn't the cool stuff they had in the movie, but it's pretty neat!

MARSUPIALS (POUCHED MAMMALS)—KOALAS

Koala Foundation

Learn basic koala facts such as habitat and range, plus discover what they eat and how many are left. What surprised us most about this site was the audio file of the koala's "voice." Just click on the koala picture to hear it. Did you think a koala sounded like that?

http://www.savethekoala.com/koala.html

Koala's Page

What seldom drinks, has a big rubbery nose, large fluffy ears, and little or no tail, and looks like a cuddly toy? Why, a koala bear, of course! Koalas live in trees, eat eucalyptus leaves, and are categorized as marsupials because they nourish their young in abdominal pouches. A mother koala only has one baby at a time, and she carries it around in her pouch for seven months; after that, the baby clings to its mother's back until it is about one year old. An old Australian story tells how the first koala was created. Stop by this page and check it out.

http://www-oms.berkeley.edu/~jpeng/Koala/
  koala.html

MARSUPIALS (POUCHED MAMMALS)—OPOSSUMS

National Opossum Society

What animal gives birth only 13 days after mating? What animal has thumbs on its hind feet? What animal plays dead if unable to escape from a predator? Give up? Or are you just playing 'possum? Learn all about the amazing opossum at this home page. Did you just find an infant opossum? Emergency instructions are at this site.

http://www.teleport.com/~opossums/

Skunk and Opossum Web Site

Opossums are marsupials, meaning they carry their babies in a pouch. Another little-known fact is that a 'possum has 50 teeth—more than any other North American mammal. Track down facts on opossums and skunks at this critter-friendly page.

http://granicus.if.org/~firmiss/m-d.html

MONOTREMES— EGG-LAYING MAMMALS

Echidna

The momma echidna lays one egg directly into her pouch. It's about the size of a green grape. The baby hatches after about 10 days, and then it spends about 50 days nestled inside the pouch. By then it has started growing spines of its own (ouch!), so mom moves it into a special nursery burrow she digs in the earth. This page is part of a larger site on Australia's unique animals.

http://home.mira.net/~areadman/echidna.htm

Introduction to the Monotremata

All species of living monotremes come from either Australia or New Guinea. They include the duckbilled platypus and two species of echidna, sometimes called spiny anteaters. Like other mammals, these animals produce milk to nurse their young, but they lay eggs—setting them apart from all other mammal species. Learn about the fascinating monotremes at this page.

http://www.ucmp.berkeley.edu/mammal/
   monotreme.html

Platypus

It looks like a duck, but it doesn't walk or quack like one—it's the duckbilled platypus. At this site you'll learn all about these extreme monotremes, including the fact that the males have a spur on their hind legs that emits a toxic venom!

http://home.mira.net/~areadman/plat.htm

Infection, Detection, Protection

Meet the microbes! They are everywhere, and they are among the oldest life-forms on Earth. At this site you'll learn about bacteria, viruses, and protozoa. Some of these can cause diseases, but over 95 percent of them are harmless. Use the Size-o-Meter to get a sense of how small these critters actually are, and then go on a microbe quest in the school cafeteria and try to solve the microbe riddle. Learn how Lou got the flu, and try playing detective in the Case of the Mixed-Up Microbes.
http://www.amnh.org/nationalcenter/infection/

PERISSODACTYLA
World Wide Fund for Nature - Rhinos

Not very many of these animals exist on the planet today. Some people believe that the rhino "horn" has medicinal properties, so there's a market for it. Unfortunately, many animals are killed by poachers who want to harvest the horn. The rhino "horn" isn't attached to the skull, and it's made out of keratin (the same substance found in fingernails), so it is not a true horn at all. Some zoos, such as the San Diego Wild Animal Park, have had some success breeding these animals, but they will never return to the wild, since their habitat is mostly gone. Learn about all species of rhinoceros at this site.

http://www.panda.org/species/rhino.cfm

Visit the CHEMISTRY section periodically.

A B C D E F G H I J K L **M** N O P Q R S T U V W X Y Z

A
B
C
D
E
F
G
H
I
J
K
L
M
N
O
P
Q
R
S
T
U
V
W
X
Y
Z

PERISSODACTYLA— HORSES AND ZEBRAS

See also HORSES AND EQUESTRIAN SPORTS

African Savannah: Grant's Zebra

What are the stripes for? What sounds do zebras make? The answers to these questions are at this site for you to enjoy.

http://www.oaklandzoo.org/atoz/azebra.html

Zebra Home Page

Did you know there are really several different species of zebra? You can find out lots of information about them at this site. One extinct subspecies, the quagga, may someday be restored. Check out The Quagga Project at <http://www.mweb.co.za/ctlive/ museums/ sam/quagga/quagga.htm>.

http://www.imh.org/imh/bw/zebra.html

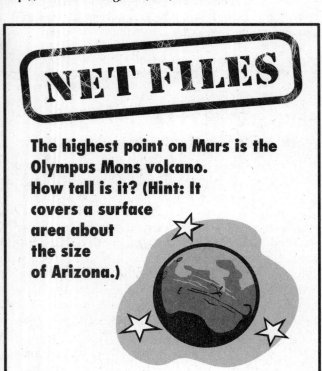

NET FILES

The highest point on Mars is the Olympus Mons volcano. How tall is it? (Hint: It covers a surface area about the size of Arizona.)

Answer: According to the Exploring Mars page, "this huge shield volcano is about 25 km (15.5 miles) high and 600 km (372 mi) across." You'll find more information at http://www.jpl.usra.edu/expmars/basicfacts.html

PRIMATES

African Primates at Home

Uh-oh. There's something moving in the trees overhead. It must be a grey-cheeked mangabey— that "whoop-gobble" call is unmistakable. How did Net-mom get so good at identifying the call of the ape, er, monkey? By listening to the sounds at this Web site, of course. It's really a swingin' place!

http://www.indiana.edu/~primate/primates.html

★ All About Apes

Learn about several great apes (gorilla, chimpanzee, orangutan) and the lesser apes (gibbon, siamang) via links to zoos, organizations, and other sources of information on the Web. There's also an excellent geologic time line so you can locate primate development in the scheme of things.

http://www.EnchantedLearning.com/subjects/apes/

The Gorilla Foundation

Koko the gorilla was born in San Francisco, California. Koko loves to eat corn on the cob, play with her pet kitten, and surf the Internet. OK, so we were kidding about that last part. But she does have her own computer, and she knows about 1,000 signs in sign language. In the wild, gorillas sleep about 13 hours each night and rest for several hours at midday. They build new sleeping nests every night by bending nearby plants into a springy platform, usually on the ground or in low trees. When not resting, they spend most of their time looking for food and eating it. Want to know more about these shy mammals? This is a great place to learn.

http://www.gorilla.org/

Gorillas Online

Quit monkeying around and swing by this site for in-depth gorilla information. We predict you'll go ape.

http://www.selu.com/bio/gorilla/

The Jane Goodall Institute

Chimpanzees are biologically close to humans; there is only a 2 percent genetic difference. This is why they are frequently used in research. The Jane Goodall Institute is committed to improving the lives of chimpanzees both in the wild and in captivity. Goodall's wildlife research in Africa is internationally known and respected. Find out how your school can get involved with her Roots & Shoots program, and enjoy reading about current research.

http://www.janegoodall.org/

Orangutan Foundation International

The current number of orangutans left in the wild is estimated at between 15,000–25,000. They are an endangered species and are the only big apes found in Asia. Unlike other primate species, they do not live in groups, preferring a solitary life. They feed on fruits; bark; leaves; and insects, such as ants, termites, and bees. Male orangutans feed at ground level; the females prefer staying in the trees. Stop by this page and meet the Orangutan of the Month and learn more about projects in support of orangutan rehabilitation and preservation around the world.

http://www.orangutan.org/

Primate Center (Lemurs) at Duke University

You can find all kinds of information on lemurs and lorises at this site. We were particularly interested in how captive lemurs like to play. Apparently they like plastic Easter eggs filled with live mealworms, balls sprayed with cologne, and—dolls.

http://www.duke.edu/web/primate/

PROBOSCIDEA—ELEPHANTS

★ Elephanteria

Do you love elephants? This is probably the site you'll like best. Not only can you find information on these precious pachyderms, but also there's an elephant dance and an elephant cake and cookies! (Look in the Elephant Day area.)

http://www.elephanteria.com/

National Zoo - African vs. Asian Elephants

In old Tarzan movies you sometimes see elephants with very unusual ears. That's because they are wearing ear "costumes." The movies were supposed to take place in Africa, but all the elephant wranglers had available were Asian elephants. Asian elephants have small ears while African ones have huge ones. Artificial ears were hastily constructed to make the Asian elephants fit into their "characters." They must have wondered what the heck was going on. The ears aren't the only differences. This Web site shows you side-by-side comparisons of the two species.

http://natzoo.si.edu/zooview/exhibits/elehouse/
      elephant/afrvsasn.htm

World Wide Fund for Nature - African Elephants

The African elephant is the largest living land mammal. They live in herds of 6 to 70 animals, and are led by a large female. Elephants live in a wide range of habitats, from the forest to the mountains to the seashore. Learn more about them here.

http://www.panda.org/species/eleph_african/

World Wide Fund for Nature - Asian Elephants

Asian elephants are smaller than African ones, and only some of the males have tusks. the females have small "tushes" that usually don't show. Some Asian elephants have been domesticated, and are trained as working animals, lifting logs and such in forestry operations.

http://www.panda.org/species/eleph_asian/

A B C D E F G H I J K L M N O P Q R S T U V W X Y Z

A
B
C
D
E
F
G
H
I
J
K
L
M
N
O
P
Q
R
S
T
U
V
W
X
Y
Z

RODENTS

Beavers

This site makes the case that the beaver has greatly influenced the development and settlement of Canada, from the 1600s on. Explorers and trappers pushed farther and farther into the wilderness seeking more beaver for their pelts, which could be sold at a high price. Beavers now appear on Canadian stamps and coins, as well as on North American wilderness lakes. This page shows beaver tracks, illustrates how they engineer their dams and lodges, and explains the many uses of those broad, flat tails.

http://www.cws-scf.ec.gc.ca/hww-fap/beaver/
   beaver.html

The Best Gerbil Links on the Web

One of the places kids learn about gerbils might be in their classrooms. Another place is right here at this page. A lot of sites about gerbils have been collected at this location. You can read about how to take care of gerbils, and you can even get to know gerbils owned by kids all over the world. We liked the gerbil role playing games, too. Will you conquer Chile the Chinchilla in your quest for a sunflower seed?

http://home.wtal.de/ehr/gerbils/links.htm

The Capybara Page

What would you get if you crossed a guinea pig and a hippopotamus? Probably something that looks like a capybara. These large, friendly rodents are rather vocal, making a series of strange clicks, squeaks, and grunts. Although they adapt easily to captivity, potential pet owners will have to pass this one by: capybaras are the largest living rodents on Earth, weighing in at 100 pounds or more! Great-grandma calls them "outdoor hamsters."

http://www.rebsig.com/capybara/

AMPHIBIANS! Visit them before you croak.

Chipmunks

Who can resist these friendly little striped creatures? They are fun to watch and can easily be tamed to take peanuts or seeds from your hand. They sit on your hand and push peanuts into cheek pouches, turning the nut over and over, trying it this way, then trying it that way, until they get the perfect fit. Then they run off to store the nuts in their burrows. They have "dominance areas" of territory usually ranging from one to three acres, which includes their burrow. They usually don't go into another chipmunk's territory, but if one trespasses, there is general chasing and chattering and lots of excitement.

http://www.cws-scf.ec.gc.ca/hww-fap/chipmunk/
   chipmunk.html

Lemmings

Is it true that arctic herds of these mouselike critters throw themselves into the sea if there's a lack of food available? Although there is no firsthand evidence of this, their numbers do fluctuate dramatically from year to year. Sometimes there are lemmings everywhere you look, while other years you'd be hard pressed to find a lemming for miles of treeless tundra. What's going on? The cycle seems to take four years from "lots of lemmings" to "Hey, did these guys just go extinct, or what?" This site takes some guesses as to the reasons. What do you think?

http://www.cws-scf.ec.gc.ca/hww-fap/lemming/
   lemming.html

Muskrat

It's not a beaver; it's not even a rat—it's really an overgrown field mouse that has adapted to life in and around wetlands all over North America. They don't build dams, but they do dig burrows in the soil along riverbanks. Muskrats have thick waterproof fur and can remain totally submerged for more than 15 minutes. This helps them dig underwater, root out tasty plants, and escape predators.

http://www.cws-scf.ec.gc.ca/hww-fap/muskrat/
   muskrat.html

Porcupine

How do you pet a porcupine? Very carefully, of course. His long brown guard hairs conceal barbed quills, which can be five inches long. Some people believe that porcupines can "throw" their quills, but that's not true. The porcupine's favorite foods include water lilies and other water-loving plants. Sometimes these creatures can be seen swimming (the air trapped in their quills helps keep them afloat). Learn more about this unusual rodent at this site.

http://www.cws-scf.ec.gc.ca/hww-fap/porcupin/
porcupin.html

★ Prairie Dogs @ Nationalgeographic.com

Wow! Did you know that prairie dogs live underground? They are burrowing rodents a foot or so in length, weighing from one to three pounds. They're related to squirrels, but some early settlers thought their barks sounded like those of dogs, thus the name. At this site, you can listen to that sound (and others—hear what a prairie dog chorus sounds like when they all bark at once), see what they like for dinner, and check out their tunnel.

http://www.nationalgeographic.com/features/98/
burrow/

Woodchuck

The woodchuck is one creature that has actually benefited from forests being cleared in order to plant pastures and crops. If the land is well drained, there is probably a woodchuck or two about somewhere. At this site you can see a cross section of an underground woodchuck burrow. In the winter, they hibernate, going into a deep sleep. They are able to lower their body temperature, reduce their heart rate, and reduce their oxygen consumption. In the spring, they awaken and come out to munch on the tender new vegetation—like the seedlings coming up in your garden! See also the HOLIDAYS—GROUNDHOG DAY section of this book.

http://www.cws-scf.ec.gc.ca/hww-fap/woodchuc/
woodchuc.html

The foil, the épée, and the sabre refer to what?

a) Essential items for your next barbecue
b) Those little bones in your ear
c) The three weapons of fencing

Answer: C. Fencing is that sport where the players, well, have a sword fight—you know, with those cagelike masks on their faces. Fencing is a sport and, to many, an art. Concentration, quickness, and agility are all very important to the fencer. At http://library.thinkquest. org/15340/tutorial.html, find out how fencing started, and how it is done, scored, and won. It's not just for swashbucklers!

RODENTS—RATS AND MICE

OMSI RatCam

From the Oregon *Mouseum*, er, Museum of Science, we present—the RatCam. View Dorothy, Sophie, Junebug, and Harriet in their home, sweet, rat home. There are also links to fine rat news and views such as The Rat Fan Club <http://www.ratfanclub.org/>.

http://web1.omsi.edu/explore/life/lab/ratcam/

Rat and Mouse Club of America

Move over, Mickey—it's the Rat and Mouse Club of America (RMCA). These pages are absolutely stuffed with more information and resources about mice and rats than you can ever imagine. Rat and mouse pet show standards, photos, pet info—this site is a pack rat's dream come true.

http://www.rmca.org/

A B C D E F G H I J K L M N O P Q R S T U V W X Y Z

RODENTS—SQUIRRELS

The Squirrel Almanac

Ever wonder what kind of squirrel that is, stealing all your birdseed? Visit this site, click on your state, and find out about the species that inhabit your area. Don't forget that some squirrels only come out at night.

http://spot.colorado.edu/~halloran/sqrl.html

★ SquirrelLand.com

We've seen a lot of odd webcams on the Internet over the years. This is one of them. Explore "squirreltopia"—a squirrel feeder complex that looks like a little Christmas village. It's even lit at night. You might see squirrels, blue jays, *nuthatches*, or the owner filling up the feeders. Check it out.

http://www.squirrelland.com/

SIRENIA—MANATEES

Kids Only Manatees and Dugongs

Beautiful undersea drawings of manatees at play contrast with an illustration of a 35-foot long dead sea cow, hunted in the mid-1700s. But there is still hope for the manatee, and it's outlined in this informative booklet, which doubles as a coloring book.

http://www.cep.unep.org/kids/kids.html

Save the Manatee Club

Have you ever heard of the manatee? Found in waters around Florida, throughout the Caribbean, and into South America, West Indian manatees are gentle vegetarians. They are, believe it or not, related to elephants, and some think the myth of mermaids may have come from sailors who saw these graceful creatures swimming. To learn more about manatees, dugongs, and sea cows, take a look at this page.

http://www.savethemanatee.org/

MATH AND ARITHMETIC

★ Coolmath.com

This is the greatest math site ever. Really, it has no equal. Want to multiply your fun on the Net—as far as arithmetic, geometry, algebra, trigonometry, or calculus goes? You can learn about tessellations and all kinds of other really neat math stuff here, including puzzles and math tricks. There are no limits to what you can do at Cool Math—or are there? See for yourself! We'd add more, but we don't want to take away the surprise.

http://www.coolmath.com/

★ Harcourt Math Glossary

For those who would rather look at a picture or animation rather than words when trying to understand the definition of a math-related term or concept—this site is for you. Arranged by grade level, it begins with simple first grade explanations of bar graphs, even numbers, and patterns. By the time you click on eighth grade, you'll be learning about algebraic expressions and trigonometric ratios.

http://www.harcourtschool.com/glossary/math/

★ History of Mathematics

Based on the most frequently requested biographies at this site, the most famous math guy of all time was Einstein, followed by Pythagorus. Click on any of the 1,350 names and you'll find facts about the person, as well as a brief biography and photo or portrait, if available. Other wonderful features of this site include information on female mathematicians, birthplace maps, and even a list of lunar craters named after mathematicians (search in "Societies, etc." under "lunar features").

http://www-groups.dcs.st-and.ac.uk/~history/

**Why is the sky blue?
Look in the WHY section.**

Manipula Math with Java

Did you know everyone learns in different ways? Some kids learn by hearing something explained; other kids have to see something in a drawing or model; still other kids have to manipulate something themselves to really understand it. These too cool Java applets let you manipulate geometric figures as never before. The Pythagorean theorem was never like this! Don't stop there—try clicking and dragging your way around some trigonometric functions. You'll also find applets in calculus, as well as that ever-popular category: miscellaneous.

http://www.ies.co.jp/math/java/

Math Archives

Looking for math shareware for the Mac or Win platforms? Maybe what you really want is a drill in multiplication, or a demonstration of fractals. It's all here, along with a fantastic section of links that math teachers and parents will love, too. Don't miss the classic math fallacy that "proves" 1=2. The direct path is <http://www.math.toronto.edu/mathnet/falseProofs/fallacies.html>.

http://archives.math.utk.edu/

★ Math.com

In ancient Rome, what did diners do when they needed to figure out the waiter's tip? They just pulled out their Roman numeral calculators, of course! Is there such a thing? On this site, there is! But that's not all. Math.com offers a clearinghouse of everything related to mathematics. Try "math in one minute" tutorials to brush up on the basics, or inspect the fractal of the day. There are math biographies and a history of math, plus formulas and even fun games. Whether it's information on pre-algebra, geometry, or algebra, or just a handy calculator to figure out how much garden mulch to buy, we figure you'll love math.com.

http://www.math.com/

★ The Math Forum: Student Center

Part of a larger forum devoted to geometry, this page focuses on links that could be useful or of interest to students. Lots of games, projects, and downloadable software can be found here. There is also a Problem of the Week and an Internet Hunt, where you can search for answers to math trivia on the Net. In addition, there is a whole archive of math tricks so you can beat a calculator any time you want!

http://forum.swarthmore.edu/students/

Math Goodies: Interactive Math Lessons

Check these interactive math lessons, such as understanding percentages or the circumference and area of circles. There are also message boards for both teachers and students, as well as math crossword puzzles and word searches. Check the link library for a carefully focused collection of pointers to more math on the Net.

http://www.mathgoodies.com/

NORAD Tracks Santa

Every Christmas eve, the good folks at the North American Aerospace Defense Command track Santa on their radar systems. At their Web site, you can find out the technical details of how they accomplish this feat (it involves the infrared signal given off by Rudolph's nose). There are also scientific explanations for how Santa manages to fly around the world so quickly, and how he manages to consume all those cookies. There are also specifications for both the Canadian CF 18 Hornet and Santa's sleigh. The former is 56 feet long, while the latter is 75 cc (candy canes)/150 lp (lollipops) long. *http://www.noradsanta.org/*

A B C D E F G H I J K L M N O P Q R S T U V W X Y Z

A
B
C
D
E
F
G
H
I
J
K
L
M
N
O
P
Q
R
S
T
U
V
W
X
Y
Z

Math in Daily Life

What's math good for, anyway? Plenty! What if you need to know how many rolls of wallpaper to buy to cover your wall space? What if you want to double a recipe? Imagine you want to buy a car on credit—how do you decide if the loan's interest rate is a good deal? Find out why learning all that math turns out to be a good idea.

http://www.learner.org/exhibits/dailymath/

MathPower

You don't need to see a psychiatrist to cope with your fear of fractions or other math anxieties. You need to see Professor Freedman. Her site will help you reduce your math anxiety (like "consider math a foreign language—it must be practiced"). You'll also learn basic math and algebra in an entertaining way. Sure, you'll find online math games. But the value in Professor Freedman's site lies in the tutorial lessons, math assignments, study skill tips, and links to free tutors. Hint: many pages at this site have automatic background music, without giving the user an on/off control. If you don't like this sort of thing just turn off your speakers before you visit.

http://www.mathpower.com/

★ Maths File - BBC Education

This math game show game is hosted by "your ancient mathematical hosts, Hypatia and Pythagorus." You can play at various levels but you need to know a little (or a LOT) about arithmetic, prime numbers, fractions, and multiples. Look for some help in Key Ideas or Tips. The Builder Bob game cracked us up. We even won a virtual Pythagorus doll in Late Delivery (about a postman in a rather odd town where all the house addresses are in algebraic terms). There are also games you can print. (Hint: Look in the Teacher's section for the answers.)

http://www.bbc.co.uk/education/mathsfile/

CATS are purrfect.

Explore underwater archaeology in SHIPS AND SHIPWRECKS.

★ Maths Year 2000 - Museum

Walk up the virtual steps and click on the door to visit this unusual museum. If you check the map you'll see there are three different galleries and three floors to explore. There are math and science-related objects to interact with, such as a set of nesting *matryoshka* dolls, or an abacus. Keep poking around the exhibits; you never know what you'll find.

http://www.mathsyear2000.org/museum/outside.html

National Library of Virtual Manipulatives

Wanted: Good problem-solving abilities and a knack for math. If you've got that, proceed to this site for some fun Java games. You'll use your computer mouse to manipulate objects, make shapes, solve problems, hide a ladybug under a leaf, and much more. Sometimes the game instructions could be a bit more clear, but don't let that stop you from playing these highly interactive math games.

http://matti.usu.edu/nlvm/enu/navd/

Online Math Applications

Here's a question for you: What does math have in common with investing? How about math's relationships to music, history, science, or travel? Some kids who wanted to enter the 1998 ThinkQuest Junior competition decided to create a Web page about math and its connections with each of these areas. It was so good that it was named one of the finalists. Stop by and learn if listening to Mozart can improve test scores. Find out more about scientific notation, compound interest, pattern recognition of routes between cities, and lots more. And you thought math was only 2 + 2!

http://tqjunior.advanced.org/4116/

ALGEBRA AND PRE-ALGEBRA

★ Absurd Math

The Powers2B are holding the DVine PImander in an unknown location. Members of the Society of the Half-closed Eye will appear to you and assist you in your quest to rescue the DVine PImander—an alien being with fabulous mathematical knowledge. You'll have to know (or learn) some pre-algebra skills, and the way is treacherous. Can you meet the challenge? (Don't forget to talk to the Vorpal Rabbit.)

http://www.learningwave.com/abmath/

Math for Morons Like Us

Ranging from pre-algebra to geometry to calculus, this site offers simplified explanations, tutorials, and quizzes for the math-challenged. Learn how to tell if lines are parallel, how to solve basic equations, and how to work with square roots. If you're really stuck, ask for help in the message board section, where people gather to discuss the fine points of parabolas and quadratic equations. This site was created by students for the ThinkQuest competition.

http://library.thinkquest.org/20991/

Mathcounts

Would you like to compete in an international math contest? Every year, over 28,000 seventh and eighth graders participate at the local level. There are many sample problems, warm-up exercises, and lots more information at the Web site. See if you can climb Math Mountain. The contest is sponsored by the National Society of Professional Engineers and others. The motto? "Go Figure!"

http://mathcounts.org/

BRAIN-TEASERS

Brain Teasers

If you're looking for some cool puzzles to stretch your brain cells, try this site. Every week you'll find new brain teasers, arranged by grade level. Typical puzzles include map reading, word problems, and puzzles that require a genuinely different outlook. Stumped? If you need a clue, the solutions are provided.

http://www.eduplace.com/math/brain/

Favorite Poem Project

Do you have a favorite poem? A lot of people do, and at this site, you will see and hear them read their special poem and tell why it has made a difference in their lives. President Clinton reads "Concord Hymn," while a student recites "Casey at the Bat." The stories (and poems) are fascinating. Perhaps you could organize a "Favorite Poem" reading at your school or public library. This site, sponsored by a grant from the National Endowment for the Arts, will tell you how.
http://www.favoritepoem.org/

Chapters of the MegaMath Book

Kids from 9 to 90 will have hours of fun playing the thinking games here, which involve flat and topological geometry, as well as other math and logical concepts. Everything is presented in a colorful, simplified manner, so you may be surprised by the complexity of thought that is needed for some of these games. The Most Colorful Math of All, Games on Graphs (which can be played on a table or playground), Algorithms and Ice Cream for All, and The Hotel Infinity are some of the activities awaiting you here.

http://www.c3.lanl.gov/mega-math/workbk/
  contents.html

Surf today, smart tomorrow.

A
B
C
D
E
F
G
H
I
J
K
L
M
N
O
P
Q
R
S
T
U
V
W
X
Y
Z

CALCULATORS

The Abacus

As early as 500 B.C., the Chinese were using calculators! Not battery or solar ones, as we have today. An abacus has a graceful hardwood frame, divided into upper and lower decks. Within these decks are beads, representing numbers, which may be moved up and down thin bamboo rods. You can perform addition, subtraction, multiplication, and division on an abacus. To learn how to use one, try this site. There are also directions on how to make your own abacus out of Lego blocks.

http://www.ee.ryerson.ca:8080/~elf/abacus/

Slide Rule Universe

If you have no idea what a slide rule is, check this site. Y3K compliant, elegant, and wireless, the slide rule is truly the calculating instrument of a gentler age. In fact, there's a 1928 manual reproduced here that will show you how to use one.

http://www.sphere.bc.ca/test/sruniverse.html

TI Calculators for Education

Some schools require kids to use a Texas Instruments (TI) graphing calculator when they start pre-algebra classes. It has a lot of neat functions and a nice little screen, but what everyone really wants to know is "Where do I get games and software for it?" You get them here.

http://www.ti.com/calc/

Vintage Calculators

Nobody seems to want an old calculator except collectors—and this site. Here you'll find an exhaustive list of photos of old calculators. You'll learn that the earliest calculators were not something you'd want to lug around in your backpack. They were big, heavy, and clunky. You'll also learn about the calculator industry and why they're less expensive these days.

http://www.vintagecalculators.com/

COUNTING

BaseTen

Against the beat of the bongos, your challenge is to drag the correct number of blocks into the counting square. You can choose to count in ones, tens, or hundreds. If you get it right, you'll see a high five (in this case, ten).

http://www.learningbox.com/Base10/BaseTen.html

Bluedog Can Count!

This site is a classic. Painter George Rodrigue's famous character, Blue Dog, has appeared in paintings, books, and an animated film. Now she will also solve simple math problems for you. Simply enter the problem on this page, and then listen to Blue Dog bark out the answer. Actually, your browser will download and play a sound file of Blue Dog—the more barks, the longer it will take to load. Make sure your cat isn't around!

http://www.forbesfield.com/bdf.html

Chisanbop

Here's a method of solving basic math problems on your fingers. You've probably been told to avoid counting this way, but with the chisanbop (or chisenbop) method, that's what you'll need to learn. Watch brief videos and practice with the chisanbop visual calculator until you get the idea.

http://klingon.cs.iupui.edu/~aharris/chis/chis.html

Counting on a Cloud

Rabbits can't fly, but you can make them appear on a cloud, in any number from one to ten. When you get tired of counting rabbits on a cloud, you can change the image to a frog, dog, egg, or a star, and the list goes on. It may sound elementary, but it's a fun way to teach young kids to count.

http://www.kaboose.com/shockWin2.cfm?infoID=
   cloud&shockType=sw

☙ Counting to Ten

Count along as the bananas appear on the screen. What happens when you get to ten? Oh-oh—you'll get a surprise!

http://www.totcity.com/totplaces/Activities/
school003/school003.html

☙ Cynthia Lanius' Lessons: Let's Count! Activities

Spinning cars, dancing frogs, bouncing puppies—can you count moving things? If that's too hard, try the other games: Which is more?, What comes next?, or Stars or Hearts? There's also a "counting machine" that shows you how to count by twos, threes, fives, and tens. The site is in English and Spanish.

http://math.rice.edu/~lanius/counting/

Large Numbers

Mathematician Edward Kasner's nine-year-old nephew coined the name for a very large number. That number—10 to the power of 100, otherwise written as a one with a hundred zeroes trailing it—was named a googol. While this was a very large number indeed, perfect for trotting out at parties to impress people, another mathematician was unimpressed and came up with something even more immense: googolplex, a 10 to the power of googol. But don't stop there. Other people have invented even larger numbers. Find out about how it all adds up here.

http://forum.swarthmore.edu/dr.math/tocs/
large.elem.html

★ Powers of Ten

Imagine a special camera that would take pictures of the same scene from ten meters away, 100 meters away, 1,000 meters (one kilometer) away, and so on. Not only that. This camera would be able to look at the scene microscopically, too. This site simulates that kind of a camera. Within a small number of photos, you'll see a flower bed from the perspectives of both the farthest reaches of the universe and the interior of a proton.

http://cern.web.cern.ch/CERN/Microcosm/P10/
english/welcome.html

NET FILES

How many gallons of orange paint does it take to paint one of those 48-foot long Allied moving van trailers?

Answer: According to the Allied site, it takes nine gallons! Find out more fun facts here. http://www.alliedvan.net/c_about_facts.html

The Prime Page

A prime number is one that can be factored only by itself and 1. The primes under 25 are 2, 3, 5, 7, 11, 13, 17, 19, and 23. How many prime numbers are there? An infinite number! Find out the history of prime numbers, get to know who's who in prime research, and enjoy prime number "music" <http://www.utm.edu/research/primes/programs/music/listen/>.

http://www.utm.edu/research/primes/

Roman Numerals 101

All those XX's and L's, V's, and I's. With that kind of alphabet soup, how did the Romans ever balance their checkbooks? If you need a refresher on the Roman numeral system, visit this site. Once you've mastered the basics, try some math problems. Don't miss the guessing game, where you'll pick a number and the computer guesses it. It's always right!

http://www.cod.edu/people/faculty/lawrence/
romans00.htm

Her name is Randy'L He-Dow Teton and her heritage is Shoshone-Bannock and Cree. Why is she famous? (Hint: look for a clue in your pocket change.)

http://www.ihs.gov/PublicInfo/heritage/Heritage2000/Randy'LBio.htm

Answer: She was the model for Sacagawea, pictured on the U.S. "golden dollar" coin. Find out more here.

DRILL AND PRACTICE

★ A+ Math

Loads of math drills are found at this site, and one of our favorites is Matho—it's like playing bingo except you have to know your multiplication tables and other math facts to win. You'll also find interactive flash cards and homework helper tips.

http://www.aplusmath.com/

BBC - KS2 Revisewise - Maths

Each section (numbers, shapes, mental math, and more) features a tutorial and activity, a fact sheet, and a quiz. In the shapes activity, various angles are demonstrated by a friendly crocodile. You won't believe it when he demonstrates an obtuse angle!

http://www.bbc.co.uk/education/revisewise/maths/

Click on Bricks

Those darn multiplication tables can be so difficult sometimes. It was a real relief to find this ThinkQuest Junior site, where different-colored bricks can help you learn multiplication from one to four. There are also links to other math sites; so if you need more help, click here. Now if we could only find someone who knows about long division.

http://tqjunior.advanced.org/3896/

★ Coolmath4Kids

If you think math is the most boring thing you've ever done, you haven't seen Coolmath4Kids, the "amusement park of math and more." Try the quick and friendly fraction lessons, and then stare the Number Monster right in the face and show him you can do it! Don't miss the tessellations, fractals, and our very favorite: the genius test! Sample question: "Some months have 31 days; how many have 28?" It's a trick question: the answer is that all of them do! That's not all—be sure to discover Spike's Game Zone with its more than 35 thinking games, plus jigsaw puzzles and counting coloring books for younger kids.

http://www.coolmath4kids.com/

Dave's Math Tables

Dave must be the smartest guy in the entire universe when it comes to math. He has written down just about everything you could possibly need to know, and he even helps you understand what it's all about. That's more than most mothers and fathers can do. In fact, your parents will probably be thrilled if you let Dave help you understand the solutions to your problems. General math, algebra, trigonometry, calculus—they're all here, and you can even download the information to study at your leisure. This site is in both English and Spanish.

http://www.sisweb.com/math/tables.htm

Volcanoes are an explosive subject. Find one in EARTH SCIENCE.

A B C D E F G H I J K L M N O P Q R S T U V W X Y Z

Discovery School Math

Try the Riddle of the Sphinx adventure game—only you and your superior math knowledge can save the ancient city of Thebes. If you think you need a little refinement of your skills first, you might get the answers you seek at the Webmath, with its cool math problem solver calculators. There are also loads of brain boosters, some of which don't even require math to solve. Here's one: A boat has a rope ladder hanging over the side. It just reaches the water. Its rungs are eight inches apart. How many rungs will be under the water when the tide rises four feet? Answer: When the tide rises four feet, the boat and its ladder will also rise, so no rungs will be under the water.

http://school.discovery.com/students/math.html

★ Figure This! Math Challenges for Families

It's good to work on a tough problem with someone else, because a second brain may be able to look at the problem in a whole new way. These family challenges involve interesting problems that encourage the whole family to do the math. There's also a list of questions that might help you to figure out your homework, and hints on how to get the most out of your math class.

http://www.figurethis.org/

Flash Cards for Kids!

This set of flash cards for math was originally developed for an elementary school tech fair. They had so much fun with the program that it was put on the Web so everyone could use it. If you are having problems with a particular aspect of simple mathematics, or if you just like practicing your addition or division or other math tables, stop by here and have some fun!

http://www.edu4kids.com/math/

> **I wonder what the QUEENS, KINGS, AND ROYALTY are doing tonight?**

Fraction Pairs

Take a circle and divide it into three parts. If you take away one piece, what portion of the circle is missing? The answer is one-third. Using an object to explain fractions helps to visually illustrate them. Using numbers like 1/3 is the more traditional way to write a fraction. Now that you know both, drop by this site and play a memory matching game about fractions.

http://www.numeracyresources.co.uk/pairsfrac.html

★ Fun Mathematics Lessons by Cynthia Lanius

So if a Bill Gates–type of guy walks into your classroom and offers you a job for thirty days, would you take it? What's the pay, you ask? Well, he's offering you a choice. A flat fee of one million dollars, or salary calculated with a special formula: one cent on the first day, two cents on the second day, four cents on the third day, etc. Assuming you wanted to take the job, which choice would you take? This site will make your choice clear, plus enthrall you with similar types of math problems and amazing feats of arithmetic.

http://math.rice.edu/~lanius/Lessons/

★ Go-Go Go-Karts

Pick your driver and head out to the racetrack. The object, of course, is to get to the finish line. You can choose your own speed, but be careful. Sometimes you will land on a red square that will actually move you backwards! Green squares tilt to give you a free ride ahead. This fun game teaches basic arithmetic skills and is a lot of fun for either one or two players.

http://www.kaboose.com/shockWin2.cfm?infoID=
    karts&shockType=sw

★ Math Cats

Practice with pattern building in "Tessellation Town," build a collection of paper polyhedrals, and try more math games as curious kittens follow you around the site. If you use the Microworlds plug-in, there are quite a few applications for you to enjoy, such as counting money, arranging polygons, and manipulating multipliers.

http://www.mathcats.com/

A B C D E F G H I J K L **M** N O P Q R S T U V W X Y Z

A
B
C
D
E
F
G
H
I
J
K
L
M
N
O
P
Q
R
S
T
U
V
W
X
Y
Z

Math for Kids - A Medieval Adventure in Problem-Solving

Two fourth graders developed this page, and it was a finalist in the 1998 ThinkQuest Junior competition. Using a medieval knights and castles theme, they offer lots of sample word problems, complete with step-by-step instructions on how to come up with the correct answer. They also have an area where you can determine the proper strategy for solving a word problem. "Sir Godfrey has been collecting gemstones for three years. His favorite gems are rubies. Out of his 233 gems, 75 are rubies. How many gems does he have that are not rubies, if there are three other types of gemstones?" Did you get it? No? Read all the help messages and try again. Then try some of the other problems.

http://tqjunior.advanced.org/4471/

The Math League

If this page had been around many years ago, Net-mom might have conquered long division when she was expected to! As it is, she still has trouble when it comes to fractions and decimals. But now that we have this page to practice with, there is renewed hope. There are lots of answers to lots of questions about mathematics here. There is also a great section explaining Math League contests and how to get involved in them. If you are a math whiz, you will love this place. In fact, even if you have problems with math, you're going to love this place!

http://www.mathleague.com/help/help.htm

Megamaths

All triangles have three sides, just as all squares and rectangles have four sides. That's a clue that's pretty hard to miss! But there are other properties that objects share, and you'll learn to recognize them at this site. Don't miss the fun multiplication table games in other parts of the site.

http://www.bbc.co.uk/education/megamaths/

Multiplication: An Adventure in Number Sense

Did you know that if you memorize only 13 "math facts" you'll be able to master the entire multiplication tables? Here's one example. To multiply a number by nine, first multiply it by ten and then subtract the number 6 from it! The number 6 times the number 6 is what? First multiply the number 6 times 10. The answer is 60. Then subtract 6 from 60, which is equal to 54. That's the right answer!

http://www.naturalmath.com/mult/

Multiplication Facts

In the song Inchworm, a little inchworm measures the marigolds using multiplication tables. This site has latched onto that idea—using rhyming words and music to teach you your times tables. Your new knowledge will be reinforced by stories and activities, as well as games, and you'll find lots of them. The site has even put a new twist on an old teaching method—flash cards. These flash cards are interactive, so there's nothing to print. But if you want some old-fashioned paper flash cards, you'll find them here, too.

http://www.multiplication.com/

Ohio Math Works

What's so mathematical about a chocolate chip cookie? Plenty, as it turns out. According to this site, "Making snacks is both a business and an art, and every aspect of it requires solid math skills. The right equipment has to be designed and must work with all other pieces of equipment on the production line." The same thing could be said for designing attractions at a theme park or patterns in fabrics and carpet. At this site, companies will take you behind the scenes to show you how professionals use mathematics on the job. You'll also get a chance to do the same math-based tasks.

http://www.ohiomathworks.org/

> There's some funny business going on in the CIRCUSES AND CLOWNS section!

★ Plane Math

It's not about mathematical planes, it's about airplanes. Find the shortest distance between two cities. How do you figure out capacity so you'll know how many people can board your plane? How do you convert 12-hour clock time to 24-hour clock time? There's also a section about aviation pioneers, complete with suggested activities. See if you can get Amelia Earhart's plane to Howland Island.

http://www.planemath.com/

Quia! Mathematics Activities

Featuring lots of little drills for basic math facts, Quia! is a dependable quiz site for almost any topic. Be sure to notice that you can create your own matching and other puzzles and post them on the site for all to use. You have to register with the site first, but it is free.

http://www.quia.com/math.html

Visual Fractions

When it comes to fractions, seeing is believing. So, if you find fractions difficult to understand, clarify your thinking with a visit to this comprehensive site. You'll use circles and lines to identify fractions. But the online lessons don't stop there. Comparing, calculating with, and writing fractions as mixed numbers are some of the many others. Hint: to find Grampy in the hedge, you'll have to know a lot about mixed fractions.

http://www.visualfractions.com/

FORMULAS AND CONSTANTS

See also HOLIDAYS—PI DAY

The Joy of Pi

Pi is that endless mathematical number that helps us understand the relationship between the circumference of a circle and its diameter. You may think of it as being about 3.14159 . . . , but the number keeps going and going and, well, you get the idea. Lots of people have experienced the Joy of Pi; now you can, too. Parental advisory: Not all links have been checked.

http://www.joyofpi.com/

NOVA Online - The Proof

Known as Fermat's Last Theorem, it stood unproven for centuries. No one, it seemed, could discover the solution. Then one day, Andrew Wiles came along and searching for a solution became his life's work. In the mid-1990s, he was finally triumphant. Read about his story here. In another part of the site, check the Shockwave proof that the Pythagorean theorem really works.

http://www.pbs.org/wgbh/nova/proof/

FRACTALS
Exploring Emergence

See the pattern "moving" across the screen? Well, it's really not moving, it's just that lights are turning on and off in order to create that appearance. Experiment with the starting pattern yourself and see what happens when you click Start. Does the pattern behave as you predicted? Or does it turn into a chaotic mess?

http://el.www.media.mit.edu/groups/el/projects/emergence/

A
B
C
D
E
F
G
H
I
J
K
L
M
N
O
P
Q
R
S
T
U
V
W
X
Y
Z

A
B
C
D
E
F
G
H
I
J
K
L
M
N
O
P
Q
R
S
T
U
V
W
X
Y
Z

IFSoft Home Page

Fractalina is a program for making fractals, and Franimate! is a program for animating fractals, and you will find them both right here. The programs were developed to allow middle school and high school students to illustrate problems dealing with fractals. Even elementary school students can try it if they wish, although it is beneficial to know at least a little about fractals before you begin using this site.

http://www.geom.umn.edu/java/IFSoft/

Sprott's Fractal Gallery

What is a "Julia set," a "strange attractor," or an "iterated function system"? They are all math equations that generate beautiful fractal images. A fractal drawing is the picture a computer makes as it maps out one of these equations. Sprott's Gallery includes sample programs to download and run on your computer so you can see fractals for yourself. There is a FAQ section and also lots of cool fractal pictures to download. Don't miss the animated GIF attractors! The "fractal music" is hard to dance to.

http://sprott.physics.wisc.edu/fractals.htm

GEOMETRY

The Fibonacci Numbers and the Golden Section

Leonardo of Pisa, Italy, was known as Fibonacci, the son of Bonacci. He was the greatest European mathematician of his time. In 1202, he wrote a book introducing the Hindu-Arabic number system to Europe. That is the base ten number system we use today, including the decimal point and zero. He also wrote about a sequence of numbers that could be found over and over again in nature. These later became known as Fibonacci numbers, and they describe the spirals of pine cones and the leaf growth patterns of plants. You can learn more about Fibonacci and his numbers here, as well as investigate where they appear in art, architecture, science, math, and nature. Closely related is the golden section, and you will see how it is used in everything from origami to flags of the world.

http://www.mcs.surrey.ac.uk/Personal/R.Knott/Fibonacci/fib.html

★ The Geometry Center

If you're looking for interactive geometry, you've come to the right place. Manipulate Java or other Web-based geometric drawing programs. You can also download many of them to play on your own computer. One of our favorites is KaleidoTile for the Mac, which lets you create geometric figures you've never heard of before and can't pronounce (fortunately, a voice tells you what they are). The interactive "math you can manipulate" programs have big names, but don't let that put you off. Check out the directions for building the world's largest 20-sided icosahedron. You probably need one for your room. Find the construction plans at <http://www.geom.umn.edu/docs/education/build-icos/>.

http://www.geom.umn.edu/

Geometry in Motion

Deepen your understanding of shapes that have curved lines, such as ellipses, hyperbolas, and parabolas. But bring along the JavaSketchpad. The Sketchpad makes these shapes spring to life on the computer screen. You get to drag and drop lines to form new shapes or see how they interact with each other. The aim of this site is to help visually illustrate key concepts of geometry.

http://www15.addr.com/~dscher/

Splat! Estimating Angles

Choose the right angle and Greg Gunk will rotate far enough around the circle to gunk one Sunny Jim, a smiley face. If you choose the wrong angle, Sunny Jim will get away. But he'll appear again, ready to be gunked again. This is a fun way to learn what angles are all about. This site works best with Internet Explorer.

http://www.numeracyresources.co.uk/sunny.html

The wonderful world of worms may be admired in the section called INVERTEBRATES.

★ StudyWorks! Online: Interactive Geometry

Can't fathom how to find the sum of the angles in a triangle? Or explain why a line always stays horizontal? Put down that pocket calculator and try out the interactive geometry activities at this site. You'll get a hands-on feel for some of the fundamental principles of geometry. This site works best with Internet Explorer.

http://www.studyworksonline.com/cda/explorations/
main/0,1023,NAV2-21,00.html

GRAPHS

Golf Transformations

And you think putt-putt is hard. If you can make par with this online golf game, then you must already know your X axis from your Y axis. This site simulates a golf course in the shape of a graph. Your job is to hit the golf holes. Each time you maneuver the ball into a hole, another hole appears in a different location on the graph. "Fore!" Or should we say "Four"?

http://www.numeracyresources.co.uk/golftrans.html

Grapher

If you think you need a ruler and paper to make a graph, think again. This site lets you create a customized graph with the click of your mouse button. Create columns, label the X axis, and enter a title for your graph. When you've finished, you can even print it.

http://www.ambleside.schoolzone.co.uk/ambleweb/
mentalmaths/grapher.html

MATH GAMES

★ Coolmath4kids - Games - Lemonade Stand

In this easy-to-learn simulation game of high finance, you start with a fistful of dollars, a dream, and a weather forecast. Balance the cost of paper cups, lemons, ice, and sugar into your sales price per cup. Can you squeeze out a lemonade empire or will everything go sour?

http://www.coolmath4kids.com/lemonade/

★ FunBrain.com - Numbers

Can you use your arithmetic and pre-algebra skills to help build a pyramid? Maybe you can guess a hidden pattern and discover the missing number in a series. Or maybe you just want to kick back and eat some fresh-baked fractions. Much more than drill and practice, these games are also fun!

http://www.funbrain.com/numbers.html

★ Math Advantage

Marvelous math games may be manipulated at this site, which offers learning for kids in kindergarten through eighth grade. Younger ones will enjoy sorting numbered bumper cars in Carnival Cars and playing tic-tac-toe with shapes. The eighth-grade challenges include solving extraterrestrial math problems in Cargo Bay and graphing coordinates to make a robot Elvis dance. In between are many more animated and talkative games to add interest.

http://www.harcourtschool.com/menus/
math_advantage.html

StarChild: A Learning Center for Young Astronomers

This is a wonderful beginner's guide to astronomy. It's written for younger children and is presented in easy-to-read text. This site includes sections on general astronomy, Earth, planets, stars, galaxies, the Sun, and more. Use these pages to introduce a child (or brother or sister) to the wonders of space. You may even learn some new stuff yourself. There are two levels; Level One is for younger kids, and you can choose to have the material read to you—or sung to you, in the case of the Doppler shift song! If the material on this level is too basic for you, just click into Level Two.

http://starchild.gsfc.nasa.gov/docs/StarChild/StarChild.html

A B C D E F G H I J K L M N O P Q R S T U V W X Y Z

How many rooms are there in Buckingham Palace, official residence of Britain's Queen Elizabeth II?

http://www.all-london-hotels.net/buckinghampalace.htm

Answer: According to this page, there are 600 palace rooms. That's a lot of dusting and vacuuming!

STATISTICS AND PROBABILITY
★ Cast Your Vote!

You are about to become a statistic. Before you can learn about how statistical data is developed, you will be asked to complete a survey. Once you've posted your last answer, you will be ushered to an area where you can learn how polls are taken and what factors are used in weighing the results. This is an excellent place to visit if you'd like to understand more about the electoral process and how public opinion affects the end result.

http://www.learner.org/exhibits/statistics/

Go climb a rock in OUTDOOR RECREATION.

You are your own network.

Ken White's Coin Flipping Page

The teacher gives an assignment: write a 20-page paper on statistical analysis in modern-day America, or flip a dime 100 times and see what the odds of heads versus tails ends up to be. The decision is fairly simple to make, since you don't have 20 pieces of paper. Unfortunately, a quick check of the pockets, lunch bag, and locker shows that you also don't have a dime. Thank heavens for the SHAZAM Econometrics Team, which is willing to do the flipping project for you. Just punch in the number of flips you need and click on the flipping button. It'll be done before your mother can say, "Sweetie, do you have any homework to do?"

http://shazam.econ.ubc.ca/flip/

Mighty M&M Math

It is important to purchase proper supplies for this math experiment page. Go to the store at once and buy two big bags of M&M candies. One bag is for the homework. The other is to eat. This lesson was developed by a California teacher who obviously knows a good way to teach fractions and percentages. Now this is our prediction: 100 percent of the students will enjoy 100 percent of the supplies when 100 percent of the work has been completed.

http://mighty-mm-math.caffeinated.org/main.htm

StudyWorks! Online: Probability and Statistics

How many people would have to be at a party in order for at least two of them to share a birthdate? Strangely enough, only about 60. The explanation behind this answer is at this site. You can also learn the math behind baseball statistics, study polling and randomness, and more. Will you enjoy this site? Probably.

http://www.studyworksonline.com/cda/explorations/main/0,1023,NAV2-76,00.html

A B C D E F G H I J K L M N O P Q R S T U V W X Y Z

TRIGONOMETRY

CTC's Trigonometry Explorer

This site offers a few Java demos from a larger CD-ROM about trigonometry. The easy-to-use applets include a little game of measuring angles with a protractor, as well as a brief introduction to angles and their functions and pi. There is a bit on sextants, navigation, and latitude and longitude, too.

http://www.cogtech.com/EXPLORER/

MEDIA LITERACY

See also INTERNET—MEDIA LITERACY; NEWS, NEWSPAPERS, AND MAGAZINES; and TELEVISION—MEDIA LITERACY

Media Literacy Clearinghouse

What is media literacy? It means that you learn to look at media critically. Who is speaking? What do they have to gain? Whose voice is not being heard, and why? These are just some of the questions you should ask when you're confronted with a news story, a commercial advertisement, a magazine story, a TV movie, or other media message. This site provides links to many other sources where you can hone your media smart skills.

http://www.med.sc.edu:1081/

MIDWAY ISLAND

See UNITED STATES—TERRITORIES

MILITARY AND ARMED FORCES

★ Air Force Link Jr.

Play games relating to planes (don't miss Math Mission), as well as have fun with the coloring book pages and word searches. In the Media section, you'll learn about the history of the Air Force and check out how they helped move Keiko, the *Free Willy* whale. Listen to music from Armed Forces Radio. You can also send friends electronic postcards featuring planes and images of the space shuttle.

http://www.af.mil/aflinkjr/

Arlington National Cemetery - The Final Post

This Virginia cemetery is America's special place of rest for many members of the U.S. armed forces, Medal of Honor and other award recipients, persons who have been elected to Federal office, astronauts, honored civilians, and others through the years. It has a rich history, some of which is detailed in this page, created by students for the ThinkQuest competition. For extensive official information, see the Arlington National Cemetery site at <http:// www.mdw.army.mil/cemetery.htm>.

http://library.thinkquest.org/2901/

Blow the Ballast!

In 1939, the *USS Squalus* submarine was the pride of the Navy. But it sank during a test dive off the coast of New Hampshire. The 33 men inside the stricken submarine were trapped in 240 feet of water. Thankfully, the men were rescued with a newly developed diving bell invented by Swede Momsen. This site provides insight into Momsen, a salvage and rescue expert, and his innovative technologies that saved the Squalus and her men. You can learn about this event in history plus all about submarines at this site.

http://www.onr.navy.mil/focus/blowballast/

A
B
C
D
E
F
G
H
I
J
K
L
M
N
O
P
Q
R
S
T
U
V
W
X
Y
Z

Oceanography: An ONR Science & Technology Focus Site

For the inside story on waves, currents, tides and more, this site from the Navy's Office of Naval Research is top class. In the resources section, you can try some experiments to learn why huge ships don't sink, how a submarine works, and our favorite—making desktop icebergs.
http://www.onr.navy.mil/focus/ocean/

Bugle Calls

In the early days of the military, when people didn't own watches and there were few clocks or other timepieces, the passage of time and calls to specific events were marked by special bugle calls. Reveille told the soldiers when to get up in the morning, and Taps sent them off to sleep. Various "Mess" calls announced meals, while other Water or Stables calls required cavalrymen to attend to their horses. Hear what a Fort Larned, Kansas, bugle player's day was like in 1868. For more on military bugling, try the American Civil War Bugler page at *<http://www.acwbugler.org/>*.

http://www.nps.gov/fols/bugle/

There's a real gem of a site in EARTH SCIENCE—GEOLOGY— GEMS AND MINERALS!

Lost your sheep? Find them in FARMING AND AGRICULTURE.

Quartermaster's Museum

The motto "Supporting Victory" belongs to the Quartermaster Corps, a branch of the U.S. Army. Its mission, not surprisingly, is to feed, clothe, and equip soldiers. So, if you want to know more about rations or how soldiers did their laundry in the line of duty, turn to this site. You'll also learn that the Quartermaster Corps was involved in selecting the body of the WW I soldier who now rests in the Tomb of the Unknown Soldier in Arlington, Virginia. Information about the Quartermaster Museum also awaits you here.

http://www.qmmuseum.lee.army.mil/

U.S. Naval Sea Cadet Corps

Sea Cadets is an organization open to kids aged 11–17. It is divided into two divisions, one is for younger kids 11–13 while the older kids have a division of their own. Special Navy uniforms are worn, and cadets learn military drill, seamanship, and lots about the maritime military forces. Is there a Sea Cadet unit near you? Check the map and see.

http://www.seacadets.org/

U.S. Navy: Welcome Aboard

On the flight deck of an aircraft carrier, you'll see a rainbow of uniforms. The Ships section (look in the Site Index under "S") provides a handy field guide to the colors and what they mean. For example, the "grapes" wear purple uniforms. They provide fueling services. The folks in blue move the planes around, while the brown-suited ones are air wing plane captains. Besides this, you'll learn about naval history, the SEALS special unit, the Blue Angels air show team, and lots more.

http://www.navy.mil/

A B C D E F G H I J K L M N O P Q R S T U V W X Y Z

United States Air Force Museum

The U.S. Air Force museum is in Dayton, Ohio. Take a virtual visit to it here. See hundreds of planes, missiles, and other exhibits in this cyberspace version. Of note is a special feature on presidential aircraft. The "Sacred Cow" was the nickname of Franklin Roosevelt's plane, built in 1944. Because the president used a wheelchair, the plane was equipped with an elevator behind the passenger cabin. This site offers fascinating facts and stories about planes throughout the history of the Air Force.

http://www.wpafb.af.mil/museum/

The United States Army

There is a lot of Army history collected here, from America's beginnings at Bunker Hill in 1775 to Army activities in today's news. Learn about Army battle monuments, insignia, and the "Old Guard," the Army's official ceremonial unit. Among many other duties, they can be seen providing a 24-hour vigil at the Tomb of the Unknown Soldier at Arlington National Cemetery. In case you've ever wondered what the inside of an Army barracks or the inside of a tank looks like, you're in luck. That's here, too, in glorious virtual reality.

http://www.army.mil/

United States Coast Guard

Learn about the history and heroes of the Coast Guard, which was formed in 1915 from several preceding services. Besides their well-known search and rescue operations, the Coast Guard is responsible for drug interdiction, international ice patrol, and almost everything related to navigation in the United States. There are also some fascinating links collected here, including instructions on how to purchase a retired lighthouse (look in the FAQ section). It's a little hard to find, but there is a Kid's Corner at <http://www.uscg.mil/hq/g-cp/kids/kidindx.html>. Follow the ship side reports from C.G. Bear, find out where Coastie the safety boat is, and print some coloring book pages.

http://www.uscg.mil/

MONEY

See also COLLECTORS AND COLLECTING—COIN COLLECTING; REFERENCE WORKS—CURRENCY CONVERTER

CollectPaperMoney.com

Most people like money. Most people like to spend money. Some people also like to collect it. At this site you can learn a lot about paper currency and what to look for when you begin a collection. Large denomination (that means how much the bill is worth) bills often have a watermark. That's a mysterious little pattern or portrait seen only when the currency is held up to the light. Lots of bills have a picture of someone famous on them, as well as a long serial number for identification. But in various countries, there may be many other interesting components in a bill—bar codes, the name of the printer, or colorful threads. Stop here and learn it all.

http://www.collectpapermoney.com/

NET FILES

What do music by Bach, Chuck Berry, Australian Aborigines, and a Mexican mariachi band have in common?

Answer: They are all recorded on special golden discs affixed to the Voyager spacecraft and sent out to find the farthest reaches of the solar system. Find out lots more about the disc at the Voyager mission home page.
http://vraptor.jpl.nasa.gov/voyager/record.html

A
B
C
D
E
F
G
H
I
J
K
L
M
N
O
P
Q
R
S
T
U
V
W
X
Y
Z

Euro

January 1, 1999, marked the beginning of a new unified currency in Europe—the euro. Eventually, there may be no more shillings, marks, or francs. Read about it at this site in the 11 languages of the European Union. This page is designed to help people make the switch from the previous currency to the new one and includes pictures of the new notes and coins.

http://europa.eu.int/euro/html/entry.html

★ Ithaca HOURS Local Currency

In Ithaca, New York, there's a local currency called "Ithaca Hours." The idea is simple. One hour of work is worth ten dollars. They print and issue special Ithaca dollars based on one hour of work and fractions of hours. The money looks really cool, too—check it out. The special dollars pay for goods and services locally. What can you buy with Ithaca Hours? The site says, "buy plumbing, carpentry, electrical work, roofing, nursing, chiropractic, child care, car and bike repair, food, eyeglasses, firewood, gifts, and thousands of other goods and services. People pay rent with Hours. The best restaurants in town take them, as do movie theaters, bowling alleys, two large locally-owned grocery stores, our local hospital, many garage sales, 55 farmer's market vendors, the Chamber of Commerce, and 300 other businesses." To learn more about this project and its benefits, and to find other local currency projects around the globe, spend some time here.

http://www.ithacahours.org/

KidsBank.Com

How does a checkbook work? What's interest? What does the bank do with the money in your account? Find out how banks work, how money is made, and even how electronic funds transfer takes place.

http://www.kidsbank.com/

The Sun never sets on the Internet.

Money Curriculum Unit

Money: you see it every day. You probably have some in your pocket right now. But how much do you know about its history and how it's made? Recently, the government has made many changes in U.S. money to make it harder to be copied. See what new tricks are being used to stop counterfeit cash. And if you don't know what all the symbols on U.S. bills mean and whose portrait is on each one, then you will by the time you finish with this site, offered by the Federal Reserve Bank of Minneapolis.

http://woodrow.mpls.frb.fed.us/econed/curric/money.html

Money Origami

You might want to practice these with sheets of paper the same size as a dollar bill. Otherwise, you'd really be throwing money away! Once you have enough practice to make a neat butterfly, a ring, or other figure, it would be a nice birthday gift for a small niece or nephew. There are also links to other "bill folds" around the Web.

http://www.umva.com/~clay/money/

NOVA Online - Secrets of Making Money

This is a fascinating look at the security features built into the U.S. $100 bill. You'll discover color-shifting ink made possible by the metallic flakes mixed into it. Check the special engraving techniques used to foil counterfeiters, as well as the special items embedded into the paper on which the bill is printed. These include the red and blue fibers, the microprinted security thread, and other items too secret to mention in print. But you can read about them on the Web! Then see if you can spot the bogus bill in the online quiz.

http://www.pbs.org/wgbh/nova/moolah/

Ron Wise's World Paper Money Homepage

Enjoy over 7,000 scans of paper currency from all over the world. Just click on the area you want to see, and then choose the country you want from there. There's a list of various denominations you can select. Do look into the souvenir "Antarctican dollars."

http://aes.iupui.edu/rwise/

The Royal Canadian Mint / Monnaie Royale Canadienne

In 1996, the Royal Canadian Mint introduced a two-dollar coin. The reasoning was simple: coins last longer than paper money. A metal coin can survive circulation for about 20 years. The two-dollar bill was very popular, but the government had to replace the bills every year as they wore out. It costs more to make a coin, but over the coin's lifetime, Canadians will save millions. The latest version is a very cool-looking coin, too. There is a smaller circle in the center, made of gold-colored aluminum bronze, while the outer ring is silver-colored nickel. You'll have to guess what animal is pictured, but here's a hint: it's big and it's white. Kids call these coins "twonies." Why? Just for fun, and to differentiate them from the one-dollar coins. The one-dollar coin has a loon on it, and those coins are called "loonies." Learn a lot about the Royal Canadian Mint and the history of currency at this site.

http://www.mint.ca/

The United States Mint - H.I.P. Pocket Change

That's not just change jangling around in your pocket—that's history! Take a trip on the Time Machine and see what stories coins can tell. Don't miss the games section, where you can use musical crayons to color in designs from the new state quarters.

http://www.usmint.gov/kids/

★ The U.S. Bureau of Engraving and Printing

Did you know that Martha Washington is the only woman whose portrait has appeared on a U.S. currency note? It appeared on the face of the $1 silver certificate of 1886 and 1891 and on the back of the $1 silver certificate of 1896. There are lots more interesting facts to learn when you visit the Bureau of Engraving and Printing (BEP). If you are in Washington, D.C., you can visit in person, or you can do it right here if you are surfing the Internet. The BEP also has a really neat area with games especially for kids. Did you know that if you had ten billion $1 notes and spent one every second of every day, it would require 317 years for you to go broke? Bill Gates had better start spending!

http://www.bep.treas.gov/

NET FILES

The famous Indianapolis 500 car race is held at the Indianapolis Motor Speedway each year. The track is 2.5 miles long. It was built in 1909 and its first surface was crushed stone and tar. When that broke down (after some early races), the speedway was paved with bricks. How many bricks did it take?

Answer: 3.2 million. Most are still there, sealed under the speedway's current driving surface of asphalt. This explains why the famed track is sometimes known as "The Brickyard." If you want to know more, check out *http://www.nascar.com/TRACKS/indianapolis/*

World Currency Museum

This site offers all banknotes, all the time. What currency would you like to view today? From British shillings to Tongan *Pa'anga*, you'll find them all here.

http://www.banknotes.com/images.htm

COUNTING MONEY

★ FunBrain Change Maker

See how good you are at making change for a dollar. How many pennies, nickels, dimes, and quarters should you give back after a certain purchase is made? This site has other fun games, too, including a concentration matching game and math baseball.

http://www.funbrain.com/cashreg/

A
B
C
D
E
F
G
H
I
J
K
L
M
N
O
P
Q
R
S
T
U
V
W
X
Y
Z

A
B
C
D
E
F
G
H
I
J
K
L
M
N
O
P
Q
R
S
T
U
V
W
X
Y
Z

Money Flashcards

Your dad says he'll give you the change that's in his pocket, up to two dollars' worth. Need some practice counting the value of loose coins? This is your site to visit.

http://www.aplusmath.com/cgi-bin/flashcards/money

☙ Sorting Money Practice with Pigs

Pig has left a lot of loose change out on the table. Can you drag and drop the half-dollars, quarters, nickels, and dimes into the right slots?

http://www.enteractive.com/store/shockpig.html

ECONOMY

Econopolis!

Let's join up with Mega Money and his pets Bill the horse and Dollar the dog. They're prepared to lead us on a tour through Econopolis, a ThinkQuest Junior Web page designed to help children learn about economics. There's a quiz at the end of each part of the tour, and an incorrect answer will take you back to the beginning.

http://tqjunior.advanced.org/3901/

The Inflation Calculator

Inflation is an interesting concept. Lots of times you will hear an older person talk about "the good old days" and how much—actually, how little—something cost back then. This inflation calculator lets you figure out just how much monetary values have changed over the years. A nickel candy bar in 1959 (yes, they did cost just five cents then!) would be priced at 28 cents today. Actually, they cost more than that, don't they? How do you explain that? Anyway, one of those '59 candy bars would be pretty stale by now. You can also explain to your dad that the $5 allowance he used to get should really be translated into $28 today!

http://www.westegg.com/inflation/

The Public Debt Online

What's the public (or national) debt? The U.S. government spends more money than it takes in. When this happens, it has to borrow money from someplace else. The amount it owes to other sources is called the national debt. This site tells you exactly how much the government owes—to the penny. Who will pay back all that money? The answer is your parents, all the other taxpayers, and, eventually—you! This site offers a look at the national debt through time as well.

http://www.publicdebt.treas.gov/opd/opd.htm

What's a Dollar Worth? CPI Calculation Machine

Did you know that, from day to day, week to week, and year to year, money is not always worth the same amount? The consumer price index is a way for us to compare the buying power of today's money to the money of yesteryear. Type in an amount and a base year; then put in this year and see the difference.

http://woodrow.mpls.frb.fed.us/economy/calc/
    cpihome.html

INVESTING

★ Investing for Kids

How can you use money to make more money? What's the deal with stocks, anyway? And what the heck are mutual funds? This page, developed by kids for other kids, will let you check your knowledge of the stock market, play some money games, and learn about the world of financial investments. Study this ThinkQuest entry; then give your parents some advice!

http://library.thinkquest.org/3096/

InvestSmart

This is another great investing site from another ThinkQuest team. This one follows along as one team member buys his first share of stock, invests in his first mutual fund, and decides what stocks should go into his portfolio. You'll learn about investment basics, take some lessons, and play a stock market simulation game.

http://library.thinkquest.org/10326/

> **What time is it, anyway? Check with the atomic clock in TIME.**

The Stock Market Game

The Stock Market Game has been played by over six million kids over the last 20 years. Get your teacher involved, and then get your team together. Play with a hypothetical $100,000, and see how much more pretend money you can make over the course of the game. Results are tallied once each week. There is a nominal registration fee.

http://www.smg2000.org/

PERSONAL FINANCE

Escape From Knab

First off, you have to pronounce it correctly. It's "ka-nabe" and it rhymes with "Abe." Second, although it's cleverly designed as a space adventure game, don't be surprised if you learn something about financial management. It's full of stuff like budgets, credit cards, and interest rates. Here's the deal. You're trying to get back to Earth, but a return ticket costs $10,000. Will you take a job in an oxygen canning factory, or the Hair Piece Harvesting company? One pays more starting out, but is slow to give raises. The other pays less to new employees, but the opportunities for advancement are better. You have six virtual months to play.

http://www.escapefromknab.com/

FDIC Learning Bank

Did you know that (subject to certain limits) the money you have in your bank account is insured by the Federal Deposit Insurance Corporation? That means if anything happens to your bank, the government will give you back your money. Find out how the FDIC program works, and how banks make money, and learn about events on a time line of banking history. Carmen Cents (a piggy bank) leads the tour.

http://www.fdic.gov/about/learn/learning/

NET FILES

When New York City's famous Rockefeller Center Christmas tree is taken down at the end of the holiday season, what happens to it?

Answer: It is donated to the U.S. Equestrian Team Headquarters and Olympic Training Center in Gladstone, NJ. They use it to construct cross-country jumps for the horses.
http://www.uset.com/html/goodies1.cfm

Kids' Money

Want to make some money? This site offers a list of jobs kids like you are doing around the house to earn extra cash. Better still, you will find out what the usual rate is for lawn mowing, dog walking, baby-sitting, and lots more tasks. And what are other kids getting as a weekly allowance? Check this site to see!

http://www.kidsmoney.org/

MoneyCents

After visiting this site, you just might think twice about putting your spare change in a piggy bank. After all, the pig will only give you the exact amount that you put in, and not a penny more. If you follow the advice here, you'll at least give your money a chance to grow. You'll also learn about how to earn money and—now the fun part—how to spend it.

http://www.kidsmoneycents.com/

A B C D E F G H I J K L **M** N O P Q R S T U V W X Y Z

A
B
C
D
E
F
G
H
I
J
K
L
M
N
O
P
Q
R
S
T
U
V
W
X
Y
Z

KODAK: Taken On The Road—American Mile Markers

Now here's an interesting site. The premise is this: drive coast to coast, from the Statue of Liberty in New York to the Golden Gate Bridge in San Francisco. Every mile, point your camera out the window and take a photograph. Put the whole thing up on the Web. Users will be able to retrace your trip and see the city morph into corn fields, the mountains rise up out of the plains, and the Pacific come into view.
http://www.kodak.com/US/en/corp/features/onThe Road/home/

Practical Money Skills for Life

Looked in your wallet lately? If you shout into it, do you hear an echo? Things looking a little empty in there? If you'd like to change all that, you'd better study this site. It's full of lessons and activities that will have you planning a budget, setting up a matching grant program with the Bank of Dad (or Mom), and playing funny games like Ed's Bank. For a similar eye-popping reality check and look at what lifestyles cost lately, try the Jump$tart Coalition page *<http://www.jumpstart.org/>*.

http://visa.edgate.com/visa/english/resources/ familyfun.html

MONSTERS

See also HOLIDAYS—HALLOWEEN

Monsters of Mystery

Here a monster, there a monster, everywhere a monster monster! Seems like every region of the world has a "pet" monster they like to tell stories about. Whether it's the Yeti of Asia or the Mokele-Mbembe of Africa, you can read some of those legends here.

http://www.nationalgeographic.com/world/9903/ monsters/

Nessie, the Loch Ness Monster

Mark Chorvinsky has put together a remarkable Web site exploring the controversies surrounding Scotland's world-famous Loch Ness Monster. Nessie, as the lake monster is affectionately known, has been the subject of numerous credible sightings over the past 60-plus years, even though extensive scientific efforts to track it down have been a lesson in frustration. This page presents well-researched and clearly written essays on the sightings, the searchers, and the debunkers, as well as investigations into other, lesser-known lake monsters from around the world. For example, ever heard of Canada's Ogopogo? He/she's been spotted regularly since 1926 in Lake Okanagan, British Columbia.

http://www.strangemag.com/nessie.home.html

NOVA Online - The Beast of Loch Ness

Learn about how the legend of Nessie got started, and then read (and hear) eyewitness accounts of sightings by local residents. Do you believe?

http://www.pbs.org/wgbh/nova/lochness/

The Official Monster Hunter's Site

It's a dark and stormy night as you enter Dr. Petrie von Dish's monster lab. Peek at his secret monster hunting files, create some e-cards of your own, and play a few ghoulish games. There seem to be sound effects connected to everything, if you're squeamish, don't visit after lunch!

http://www.goldenbooks.com/monsters/

MOVIES

See also DISNEY

Academy of Motion Picture Arts and Sciences

If you're a movie fanatic, don't miss the Official Guide to the Academy Awards, designed to help you explore Oscar nominees and winners, past and present. There are pictures and lots of information on many of them. You may be surprised to find out that the Academy of Motion Picture Arts and Sciences does a lot more than just give out awards. They have an amazing movie history library, too. They also sponsor Student Academy Awards, designed to recognize excellence among college students enrolled in film courses throughout the United States.

http://www.oscars.org/

★ Cinema - How Are Hollywood Films Made?

It's fun to see a movie in a theater, but have you ever wondered what it takes to bring a movie to the big screen? This site takes you through the whole process, starting with screenwriting and moving through producing; directing; acting; and, of course, editing. Along the way there are activities for you to try. For example, can you write a good comedy scene?

http://www.learner.org/exhibits/cinema/

Special Effects: Titanic and Beyond

It took hundreds of the greatest movie artists to create *Titanic's* spectacular effects, such as the view of the passengers strolling on deck against a background of the gorgeous sunset. For more examples, plunge into this site. You'll get the real scoop on how the effects were created and a chance to judge what's real (and what's not) from a scene in the movie.

http://www.pbs.org/wgbh/nova/specialfx2/

REVIEWS

Grading the Movies

Parental advisory: please preview this site. Despite the title, this site also grades music and games. Who cares? Well, your parents may want to see why a movie got a PG-13 rating before they agree to let you see it. Or you may want to get that information yourself *before* you ask your parents if you can see a particular movie. The reviewers grade movies and other media on violence, sexual content, language, and alcohol/tobacco references. Warning: If using a Mac, you must use Netscape to open this site. It will crash IE5.

http://www.gradingthemovies.com/

Kids-In-Mind: Movie Ratings That Actually Work

Parental advisory: please preview this resource. Parents can cut through the movie hype at this site. Movies are rated on their level of sex, violence, and profanity. Artistic merit isn't considered. Not as complete in its reviews as some of the other rating services we list here, but it's a very worthwhile site for parents to visit since the scope of its collection is so broad.

http://www.kids-in-mind.com/

Meta Critic

Parental advisory: please preview this site. Want to find out how real reviewers from major newspapers, magazines, and Web sites have rated movies, DVDs, music, and games? This is the site for you. Each review is ranked on a ten-point scale. Anything at seven or above gets a green background; below that, you'll find yellow and red (for a really bad review). You can easily scan movie titles to see what the critics' prevailing opinions are, and then read the full reviews for added insight.

http://www.metacritic.com/

A B C D E F G H I J K L M N O P Q R S T U V W X Y Z

A B C D E F G H I J K L **M** N O P Q R S T U V W X Y Z

The Movie Mom

Parental advisory: please preview this site. Nell Minow is an author and a critic, but, most important, she is a mom. She calls herself "Movie Mom" and gives lots of advice to kids and families on the best movies to see. Take a look at this site to read her reviews (she considers artistic merit as well as profanity, nudity/sex, language, alcohol/drug, violence/scariness, and tolerance/diversity issues). Movie Mom also recommends the All-Time Best Family Movies you must see.

http://www.moviemom.com/

Parent Guides at CinemaSpot.com

Parental advisory: please preview this site. CinemaSpot offers everything you could ever want to know about movies, but this is the link to information just for parents. You'll find other movie rating guides to help your parents choose the best movies for the family to see.

http://www.cinemaspot.com/categories/parent.htm

Screen It! Entertainment Reviews for Parents

Parental advisory: please preview this site. These movie, video, and DVD reviews are astonishingly complete, scoring each title in a variety of sensitive areas that might be of concern to parents. How much violence? How much bad language? How many instances of disrespectful behavior or nudity? This site helps parents "know before you go" so there will be no surprises later.

http://www.screenit.com/

SOUNDS AND THEMES

Newton's Apple: Movie Sound Effects

Grab your rubber bands, sandpaper, Popsicle sticks, and tape recorder and head over to this site to learn how to be a Foley artist. They decide which movie sounds need to be fixed, replaced, or just improved a little. They even invent sounds nobody's ever heard before, like the sound of a dinosaur egg hatching. They're named after Jack Foley, a film sound pioneer from the days when talking pictures were first invented.

http://www.pbs.org/ktca/newtons/12/movisnd.html

Skywalker Sound

Learn how movie sound tracks are made from the pros at Skywalker Sound, where the famous sounds of the *Star Wars* movies, *Jurassic Park*, and *Toy Story* were made. One of Skywalker's specialties is creature sounds, like the ones made by Imperial Walkers, Chewbacca, and other aliens. To make these characters sound sad, happy, or scary, sound artists use everything from bicycle chains dropping on concrete to the voices of lots of different animals mixed together.

http://www.thx.com/skywalker/skywalker.html

MUSIC AND MUSICIANS

All-Music Guide

Parental advisory: please preview this site. The All-Music Guide is a huge review archive for— guess what?—all music. That includes rock, folk, blues, jazz, country, gospel, holiday, and lots more. You can search for albums by artist, title, or record label. Learn a little bit about each artist and how his or her work fits into the great scheme of things.

http://www.allmusic.com/

Billboard.com

Parental advisory: please preview this site. If you want to know the top 200 songs and albums, the latest dish on the music scene, and everything else about your favorite bands and vocalists, this is the site you want. Like its print counterpart, it is a mainstay of the music industry.

http://www.billboard.com/

CultureFinder

Looking for a concert, opera, ballet, musical theater, or other cultural event? At this site you can find out what's happening in your town, and when. Going on vacation? You can make plans to attend a concert there, perhaps. Key in the city and see what's scheduled when you will be there. This site offers online ticket sales as well.

http://www.culturefinder.com/

The GRAMMY Awards

Music is a universal language. Everybody likes music, whether it's pop sounds, rock and roll, rap, or R&B. Most music we listen to is recorded, either on tapes, CDs, the radio, or TV. The National Academy of Recording Arts and Sciences is an organization of recording specialists who vote on the best recordings each year. The winning recording artists receive an award called a Grammy. To see (and hear) who has won in the past and who is nominated for the upcoming awards, take a look at this page. It's the place to look if you like music!

http://www.grammy.com/

K–12 Resources for Music Educators

You can show this page to your music teacher, and it will really make his or her day. Resources are collected in categories for band, orchestra, and choral music teachers, and there are links for classroom music teachers. The selection is interesting for the rest of us, too. You'll find composers' biographies, newsgroups, MIDI resources, and hints on how to really listen to music. There are also links to free piano lessons by Web, online sheet music, and lots more.

http://www.isd77.k12.mn.us/resources/staffpages/
   shirk/k12.music.html

★ Musi-Cal: Concert Calendar Search

So you want to go to a concert or a festival. You like acoustic music (or blues, or ska) and your dad is willing to travel up to 20 miles from your home. Musi-Cal's advanced search will pinpoint the very concert you seek. The site strives to provide easy access to current worldwide music information. Search by performer, city, venue, or event. It includes artist(s), event, city, radius around city (up to 200 miles, or 400 kilometers), dates, venue, musical genres, and even keywords. There are sometimes links to performers' Web pages as well.

http://www.musi-cal.com/search.shtml

BLUES
CD University - Blues

Blues is much more than just a category of music. It is a passionate expression of human feelings. So, when you think of blues music, think of truth, tradition, and personal expression. This site pulls together the history of blues and points you to the many different styles that have developed regional characteristics. The Chicago Blues, Country Blues, and West Coast Blues are some of them.

http://www.cduniverse.com/asp/University/bl/
   bl_home.asp?style=audio&afl=&cart=95593884

CHILDREN'S MUSIC AND CAMPFIRE SONGS
🦆 Arthur's Music Box

Arthur's got a great little boombox for you to listen to while you put together animated puzzles. You can choose a four- or nine-piece puzzle to work out. If you get everything in the right place, you'll get a special animated surprise as Arthur's dancing really speeds up.

http://www.pbs.org/wgbh/arthur/arthur/musicbox/

NET FILES

Georgia has an official state vegetable. What is it?

Answer: The Vidalia onion. Although the seed grows pungent onions everywhere else, when planted in the fields around Vidalia and Glennville it turns out sweet enough "to eat as an apple." It's true! Learn more at
http://www.sos.state.ga.us/museum/html/state%5Fvegetable.html

A
B
C
D
E
F
G
H
I
J
K
L
M
N
O
P
Q
R
S
T
U
V
W
X
Y
Z

Becky's Campfire Songbook

Every silly song you ever learned at camp is in this collection, plus a few yells, clapping games, and skits. This is a must before you go on a long road trip with your parents. They will love hearing these songs over, and over, and over, and . . . .

http://www.geocities.com/EnchantedForest/Glade/
    8851/

Children's Music Web

Want to know when your favorite performer is coming to a town nearby? Looking for a radio station that just plays music for kids? Want to find some online songbooks? Check here for an extensive collection of links about all this and more.

http://www.childrensmusic.org/

Delmont and Resica Falls Scout Reservation's 1996 Songbook

Summer camp is known as a great place for mosquitoes, strange food, and learning songs to annoy your parents! If you need the words to favorites like "Do Your Ears Hang Low?," this is the place. Simple skits are also included. Warning: some are gross!

http://cac.psu.edu/~jxm181/songs.html

♣ Fred Penner Jukebox

Did you know "There's a Hole in the Bottom of the Sea"? Find out all about it as Fred Penner sings this song and other favorites.

http://www.kaboose.com/shockWin2.cfm?infoID=
    jukebox&shockType=sw

**Visit the stars in
ASTRONOMY, SPACE,
AND SPACE EXPLORATION.**

Judy and David

This Canadian duo started performing in 1993. Are they the next Raffi(s)? Time will tell. In the meantime, they've put together a sweet home page. If you are in the audience when Judy and David perform, you'll find that every song they sing also has a part for you. Their online presence is similar. The Online Songbook includes the words of traditional children's songs and their original songs as well. There are suggested hand motions, activities, and more; so after you sing "Alice the Camel," go to the coloring page, print a picture of her, and color her to your liking.

http://judyanddavid.com/

Kid Songs

We bet your parents and grandparents will know many of these songs and teach them to you. The lyrics are here, as well as the MIDI tunes. Most of them are predictable titles ("Grandfather's Clock," "Thank Heaven for Little Girls," and "Mairzy Doats"). But you'll also find "Candle in the Wind" and— "Who Let the Dogs Out," which you may have to teach to your parents!

http://www.geocities.com/EnchantedForest/Glade/
    7438/

KIDiddles (TM) - Mojo's Musical Mouseum

Lots of old-fashioned and a few more contemporary songs for kids are collected here. You'll find the lyrics and sometimes a MIDI file so you can sing along, karaoke style.

http://www.kididdles.com/mouseum/

★ On Air Concert

Shhhh! It's time to listen to a musical performance featuring kids from all over the world. You'll hear Anne-Raphaelle (age nine, France) playing the piano, Max (age six, U.S.A.) playing his violin, and many others. Some kids have even sent in vocal performances. You can also share your own audio files if you want to join the band.

http://www.kids-space.org/air/air.html

If you can read this, good! Now check BOOKS AND LITERATURE.

Red Grammer

Red Grammer is a wonderful songwriter and singer who travels all across the country performing at schools and in concert. He and his wife, Kathy, have written a lot of great tunes, including "Teaching Peace." It won a Classic Children's Audio Recording Award from Parents' Choice, an award few albums ever achieve. The All Music Guide declared "Teaching Peace" to be one of the top five children's recordings of all time. You can listen to some of Red's songs (click on the Music Shop), learn movements to his songs, and see if he's coming to your school.

http://www.redgrammer.com/

Songs for Scouts and Scouters

Gather 'round the campfire and share some singing—here are silly songs, lots of gross songs, and songs that are just plain fun. If you want the definitive version of "Greasy Grimy Gopher Guts," look no further.

http://www.macscouter.com/Songs/

COMPOSERS AND CLASSICAL MUSIC

★ The Classical Archives

Take a musical tour of the greatest classical hits from the fourteenth century to the twentieth, sampling the tunes of more than 700 composers along the way. Go to the Site Map. You can choose to listen by time period or search for a composer's name. There's also a really interesting time line so you can see who might have been influenced by whom. Composers' biographies add the final flourish to this excellent site. Visit the Learning Center for some great tips.

http://www.prs.net/midi.html

The Anglo-Saxons

Try writing in Anglo-Saxon runes, see if you can guess the answers to some puzzling riddles, and help Hild find five objects she must bring to the village feast. Along the way, you will learn about daily life in A.D. 800. If you successfully gain entrance to the great hall, you can print several activity sheets. One gives instructions to make a musical lyre out of a shoe box.
http://www.bbc.co.uk/education/anglosaxons/

★ Essentials of Music

This terrific page outlines the six major periods in music history: the Middle Ages, Renaissance, Baroque, Classical, Romantic, and Twentieth Century. In each, you'll learn about cultural and other forces of the time period and discover the major composers of the era. There are more than 70 composer biographies included, many containing audio clips.

http://www.essentialsofmusic.com/

Hooked on Symphonics

Check this site if you need a quick introduction to the symphony orchestra. There's a little bit about many of the instruments, plus links to a glossary so you can look up unfamiliar terms. Read biographies of six famous composers. The best part of the site is the guided tour to the famous musical version of "Peter and the Wolf," by Sergei Prokofiev. Listen to each character's musical theme, and you'll soon be able to identify flutes, bassoons, French horns, and other instruments. This site was created by students for the ThinkQuest competition.

http://library.thinkquest.org/17321/

A
B
C
D
E
F
G
H
I
J
K
L
M
N
O
P
Q
R
S
T
U
V
W
X
Y
Z

A
B
C
D
E
F
G
H
I
J
K
L
M
N
O
P
Q
R
S
T
U
V
W
X
Y
Z

J. S. Bach Home Page

The home page of J. S. Bach really does lead you to his home. Under "Biography," a clickable hypermap shows you the relatively limited geographical space he inhabited from 1685 to 1750. You can travel through time and space from Eisenach, Germany, where he was born, to Leipzig, Germany, where he died. Either click on the map or go from link to link in the right order. You'll see portraits of significant people and photos of buildings. Also, check the entry for his birth in the official birth registry in Eisenach. It's quite a time capsule! You'll also find directory information on his complete works here: by catalog number, category, instrument, and title. There is a similar listing for Bach recordings and Web sites with Bach MIDI files.

http://www.jsbach.org/

Thinking Fountain!

From A to Z, you're going to find a lot of wonderful ideas and information at the Thinking Fountain. Allow us to demonstrate! A—Read about Anansi the Spider, and then find out how to make your own sliding spider toy. G—Golf-O-Rama, a book about miniature golf, complete with everything you need but the ball and the putter, and a story about some kids who made their own mini-mini golf course. N—Noodle-ing around: learn to build a structure out of spaghetti. (Don't believe it? The secret is in the mini-marshmallows.) Z—Zoo Machines: invent a machine to take care of all those animals. Keep going; you're sure to find lots more activities and ideas, galleries to show your work, books you can use, and surprises inspired by the Thinking Fountain.
http://www.smm.org/sln/tf/nav/tfatoz.html

★ Mozart's Magical Musical Life

What if your parents named you Johannes Chrysostomus Wolfgangus Theophillus Amadeus Mozart? Can you imagine writing that on the top of your paper in school? This great story, complete with audio clips, tells about "Wolfie," or Mozart as we know him today. Wolfie had a sister named Nannerl and a dog named Bimperl. He also had a tremendous talent for music and a father who realized that his son was a genius. Is there a genius in your family?

http://www.stringsinthemountains.org/m2m/
   1once.htm

★ The Symphony: An Interactive Guide

Learn about almost 20 different composers of symphonies at this slick site. It offers access by composer name and country. Why did so many famous composers come from Germany and Austria? (Isn't that the place where the hills are "alive with the sound of music"?) You can also explore a 200-year-long time line in the development of the symphonic form. What's the "symphonic form"? It's all explained here, from the sonata in the first movement, to the scherzos in the second and third movements, to the rondo in the fourth. Discover the guide to the instruments of the orchestra, complete with audio files. This site was created by students for the ThinkQuest competition.

http://library.thinkquest.org/22673/

Young Composers

If you think composers are all dead guys from long ago, think again. This site highlights composers who are not only alive today, but who are kids like you! Listen to all styles of music by teens: classical, rock, funk, reggae, and more. If you compose your own tunes, read how you can submit them to this online library. There is also a chat room; and if you're good at recognizing musical themes, try playing Music Match. Listen to the music and see if you can identify the composer.

http://www.youngcomposers.com/

COUNTRY MUSIC

Billy Gilman

At the age of twelve, singing sensation Billy Gilman became the youngest solo artist in history to appear on the country radio charts. His debut album "One Voice" features the title track, a moving story about gun violence in America. Find out news about Billy and his tour schedule here.

http://sonynashville.com/BillyGilman/

Country Music Association

The first three musicians to be inducted into the Country Music Hall of Fame were Jimmie Rodgers, Fred Rose, and Hank Williams. The first woman wasn't added until 1970, when the Carter Family (A. P. Carter, his wife, Sara, and sister-in-law, Maybelle) joined the others before them. Did you know that Elvis is in the Hall of Fame, too (1998)? Besides finding out about country music's past, find out about its present and future with information on the next series of awards and links to the fan club pages of many popular country entertainers.

http://www.cmaworld.com/

FOLK MUSIC

★ Folk Music of England, Scotland, Ireland, Wales, and America

Many of your favorite tunes are here, in wonderful MIDI versions. There are also a fair number of "sea shanties" and cowboy songs. Sing along, because the lyrics are provided for most of the titles.

http://www.contemplator.com/folk.html

★ Popular Songs in American History

Give a listen to this unique collection of audio files, lyrics, and historical notes. Find out what songs were popular during various periods in American History. Included are interesting historical details. "Greensleeves" was popular in sixteenth-century America. "The Drinking Gourd" was from the Civil War era. "I've Been Working on the Railroad" was what the forty-niners sang as they searched for gold in California. How many do you recognize?

http://www.contemplator.com/america/

INSTRUMENTS

★ Energy in the Air

Let the conductor be your guide as you stumble through the forest of music stands to meet various parts of the orchestra. Let's try the brass section. It says here that trumpets used to be over seven feet long! Thank goodness they changed that before they invented marching bands. You'll read about the history of each instrument, see its range on the musical scale, and even hear sound clips from famous works featuring the instrument. There's also a section on the science of sound. Did you know that sound waves look different for each instrument? This site was created by students for the ThinkQuest Junior competition.

http://tqjunior.thinkquest.org/5116/

Indian Musical Instruments

The music of India is unmistakable, but you may not be familiar with its instruments. At this site you can hear and learn about many string, wind, percussion, and other components of the Indian sound.

http://www.indianmusicals.com/

🦆 Match 'Em

Can you match the sound of an instrument with its picture? Click on the eye to find out what instrument is pictured, and then click on the ear to hear it. When you think you've made a match, click on the equal sign to see if you're right.

http://www.kaboose.com/shockWin2.cfm?infoID=matchem&shockType=sw

Musical Sand

Here's something unique: did you know walking on some types of sand makes "music"? Here's a Web page about it—don't miss the sound of sand audio files!

http://www.bigai.ne.jp/~miwa/sand/

A B C D E F G H I J K L M N O P Q R S T U V W X Y Z

A B C D E F G H I J K L M N O P Q R S T U V W X Y Z

NET FILES

On a merry-go-round, the horses usually follow one special leader, known as the "king horse." How do you tell which horse is the leader?

http://www.learner.org/exhibits/parkphysics/carousel2.html

Answer: Look carefully. There's usually one horse that's just a little bit bigger and just a little more elaborate in its decorations and trappings. Often it's a war horse wearing armor, and sometimes it has the logo of the company prominently displayed. For other clues, see

New York Philharmonic KidZone!

Meet the musicians and conductors of the New York Philharmonic Orchestra, and listen to some of their music. When you trek over to this site, you're in for a special treat. The Instruments Lab lets you invent your own instrument. Too bad you can't take it home with you. This info-packed site will also give you an earful on all of the different instruments the musicians play.

http://www.nyphilkids.org/

★ Play Music

Meet other kids involved in playing and writing music, learn parts of the orchestra, and take the suggested links to other musical sites. One is Creating Music *<http://www.creatingmusic.com/>*, where you can try out a musical sketch pad. Did you know you can "draw" in notes and tones?

http://www.playmusic.org/

Telephone Songs

No instrument to play? Try the telephone keypad. Call a friend FIRST, and then practice the tunes. Otherwise, you might make a long-distance call to Zanzibar by mistake!

http://www.jlc.net/~useless/telsongs.html

INSTRUMENTS—KEYBOARD

All About Pianos

The King of Instruments. That's what they call the piano, because its tonal range covers the full spectrum of all instruments in the orchestra, from below the lowest note of the double bassoon to above the top note of the piccolo. It is also the largest musical instrument (excluding the pipe organ), most versatile, and probably the most interesting. You can learn just about anything you want to know—or need to know—about a piano here. Then you can order a book and begin your lessons!

http://www.pianoworld.com/

★ Music Magic: A Piano Exploration

This great little tutorial features 15 interactive piano lessons with an onscreen piano you can play. Learn about rhythm, time signatures, and notes, and even try a few simple songs. The lessons feature numerous MIDI files so you can hear what you're supposed to sound like! There is also a glossary defining 1,000 different musical terms plus brief biographies of famous pianists and composers. This site was created by students for the ThinkQuest competition.

http://library.thinkquest.org/15060/

★ The Piano Education Page

Having fun while practicing the piano—isn't that a contradiction in terms? Maybe not. The Just for Kids section of this page features piano-related advice from Taz, tips for practice fun (really!), and an interview each month with a famous (sometimes dead) composer. There's a section on how to choose a piano teacher, one on studio etiquette, and lots of MIDI piano files.

http://www.unm.edu/~loritaf/pnoedmn.html

> ## Never give your name or address to a stranger.

★ Piano on the Net

Would you like to learn how to play the piano or maybe just how to read music? You can! The first few lessons don't even require a piano, but for later lessons you will want one. Even a small portable keyboard will do. This easy, reassuring series of modules includes QuickTime movies, audio files, and even online metronomes to keep you in time with the music.

http://www.pianonanny.com/

Steinway Factory Tour

It starts as 18 thin layers of hard rock maple, and ends up as a concert instrument worthy of the world's most accomplished musicians. Take the online factory tour and see how a piano is made. You will also learn about famous pianos and find out where you can continue your research on this instrument.

http://www.steinway.com/html/tour/tour.html

INSTRUMENTS—PERCUSSION

Bill Powelson's School of Drums

Have you ever wondered if you have the right stuff when it comes to playing drums? Sure, you may have been good at banging on pots and pans when you were little, but what if you were able to use a real drum set? Wonder no more. Visit this site and take the drummer's aptitude test. The author says you'll be drumming before the page loads completely. There are also some free drumming lessons, plus for-fee lessons if you become really hooked.

http://www.catalog.com/drummers/bphome01.html

Kids, Percussion, and STOMP

Is pure rhythm really music, or is it just a cacophony of noise? If you go to a performance of "STOMP," you will see and hear the cast members "play" Zippo lighters, push brooms, trash cans, newspapers, and other common objects. Visit this Web site to see and hear audio from the show and learn more about the science of rhythm. There are also some neat activities, like making a "rain stick" out of paper towel tubes, toothpicks, and lentils.

http://www.stomponline.com/percuss1.html

MIT Guild of Bellringers (Change Ringing)

Have you ever heard the sound of bells from a church and thought how much fun it would be to pull the bell ropes and work the levers yourself? If a church has several bells, sometimes a group of people can perform what is called change ringing. The object is to ring the bells in succession, according to specific patterns, which are often complex and lengthy. A change ringer needs to be very aware of timing in order to pull the bell through a ring and have it stop at the top of the arc, mouth up. If it stays there for a split second, the next bell in line becomes the "lead" bell, and the "round" starts with that bell. Each bell takes a turn at being the lead bell, and the others switch positions in the order of ring. According to this page, "Twenty-four changes [is called] Plain Bob Minimus, and twenty-four changes are all the permutations possible on four bells. It takes less than a minute to ring. If you add a bell, you have Plain Bob Doubles: 120 different permutations are possible on five bells. Each new bell brought into the pattern multiplies the number of changes which can be rung without repetition. Six bells offer 720 changes; seven: 5,040, and a peal. A peal entails five thousand or more changes without break, without irretrievable errors, and (when seven or more bells are being rung), without repetition. It takes six or more people working together coordinating hand and eye, minding permutations and bells for three hours or more." You will learn all about the history of change ringing here and find out where you might be able to hear it, learn it, and participate in it.

http://web.mit.edu/bellringers/www/html/change_ringing_info.html

A
B
C
D
E
F
G
H
I
J
K
L
M
N
O
P
Q
R
S
T
U
V
W
X
Y
Z

A
B
C
D
E
F
G
H
I
J
K
L
M
N
O
P
Q
R
S
T
U
V
W
X
Y
Z

★ Rhythmweb

You'll love this sampler of various drums and percussion techniques used in both solo drumming and drumming circles. There are free lessons, sample CDs to purchase, and lots more, including a look at and links to the language of drums in different cultures around the world.

http://www.rhythmweb.com/

★ Steel Drum

This is really extremely cool. You can bang on the virtual steel drum and hear all the notes, or you can listen to some recorded steel drum music. You can even record your own little melody and play it back.

http://www.mathsyear2000.org/museum/gallery1/
  steeldrum/

INSTRUMENTS—STRINGS

The Classical Guitar

Suppose you've been playing classical guitar since three weeks ago last Tuesday. Is there anyplace you can find quality guitar music with fingerings? Try the Classical Guitar Beginner's Page on this site. Whether you're a beginning or experienced classical guitarist, you'll have fun browsing here. The Beginner's Page suggests recordings, books, and videos to get you off to a great start. There's sheet music and the MIDI files to go along with it.

http://www.guitarist.com/cg/cg.htm

★ Dansm's Acoustic Guitar Page

So you have never picked up a guitar and you're not really sure what the word "acoustic" really means. This is the place where you belong. Dan Smith, a Cornell University student and guitar player, has developed one of the greatest Web pages—if not the greatest Web page—on the subject. He explains everything you need to know. Take some time first to let Dan help you choose the guitar meant just for you. Then get yourself an instrument and play. There are lessons online, including a fascinating tutorial on chord theory.

http://www.people.fas.harvard.edu/~desmith/guitar/
  acoustic/

From Frying Pan to Flying V: The Rise of the Electric Guitar

Whoever thought of adding a pickup sensor and an amplifier to an instrument that had been around for hundreds of years must have been a real visionary. People had been trying to figure out a way to make a louder guitar since the 1800s. Until engineers of the '20s and '30s figured out the magnetic pickup technology and how to hook it up to an amplifier, the electric guitar was only a dream. Once they became more commonplace, in the 1940s, people debated whether or not it was a "real" instrument! Find out about the history of the electric guitar at this site.

http://www.si.edu/lemelson/guitars/

Stringstuff Free Sheet Music

Exercises for strings, downloadable sheet music for all occasions, MIDI files, and lots more for the discriminating violin, viola, cello, and bass player.

http://www.geocities.com/Vienna/Studio/8745/
  freemusic.html

★ WholeNote - The On-Line Guitar Community

Guitar basics, free lessons, tablature, and lots more await you at this portal to the guitar-playing community. There's even an online tuner (just click on the tuning fork on the bottom left).

http://www.wholenote.com/

INSTRUMENTS—WOODWINDS

Bagpipes at Best

Where else but on a page devoted to the playing of bagpipe music could you hear a tune named "The Clucking Hen"? Bagpipes are interesting to listen to, and this page has more than two hours of bagpipe music. This can be useful. When you're trying to get everyone up early to go fishing, head to this site, choose "Scotland the Brave," and turn up the volume. Everyone will be very surprised.

http://www.bagpipesatbest.com/

Gemeinhardt Web Notes

A flute has 257 parts, and at this site you can see how they all fit together if you take the virtual factory tour; Also check the history of the flute; fingering diagrams; care of the instrument; and, of course, links.

http://www.gemeinhardt.com/

Ocarina Songbook

You know those four-holed oval clay whistles or flutes you see at craft fairs? Net-mom has bought several of them over the years, and has never been able to play more than an annoying shriek or two. But that's all changed now. That's because we've discovered the animated ocarina tutorial and songbook. There's hope for you and your ocarina, too.

http://www.clayz.com/songlist.html

Recorder Home Page

Nicholas Lander's site imparts information on history, technique, and repertoire of the recorder. His notes on fingerings and vibrato techniques are very complete. He also has links to recorder makers, catalogs, MIDI files, and references to journals and books.

http://members.iinet.net.au/~nickl/recorder.html

Saxophone Factory Tour

Did you ever wonder how saxophones are made? This site takes you through that process from the first computer-aided design to the final polish of the brass. The final part of the tour answers that burning question: "Why is a brass instrument considered a woodwind when it is made out of metal, not wood?"

http://www.yamaha.co.jp/edu/english/factory/sax/

JAZZ
Jazz Improvisation

How does jazz work? This site can tell you. Not for performers only, these lessons on jazz theory and practice fill you in on history, fundamentals, and playing with others. You'll get new insights into the heart of jazz. Also take a look at the shorter Jazz Improvisation Primer. The rest of this site is an entire jazz library. Other links are to Pop and Commercial Music, Jazz Education resources, and World Music, where you'll find Chinese, Russian, and Bulgarian sounds, and the Mbira Home Page.

http://hum.lss.wisc.edu/jazz/

Jazz Kids

What do Louis Armstrong, Duke Ellington, Billie Holiday, and Charlie Parker have in common? They were all great jazz musicians, and you can explore their lives at this site. When you learn more about them, you'll discover how jazz became America's music. If you feel like tapping your feet, the Repeat the Beat section will let you listen to a musical instrument.

http://www.pbs.org/jazz/kids/

2GOOD 2MISS

Where the Waves Are

Sure, you can surf the Internet, but can you build the perfect wave for a surfer? Juggle adjustments for the local weather, intensity, and distance of a storm, and then—surf it! Are you headed for a wipeout or a round of applause? Check this site on the physics of surfing and wave formation. *http://www.discovery.com/news/features/surfing/surfing.html*

A B C D E F G H I J K L M N O P Q R S T U V W X Y Z

LYRICS

Looking for lyrics to your favorite rock song? The best thing to do is to search on "lyrics" in Yahoo <http://www.yahoo.com/> and then try some of the general directories you will find. Lyrics sites go up and down and disappear quite rapidly, since many of them are breaking copyright law. You can also search for the official site of the band you want. The official site will often have lyrics, sound files, and lots more.

MARCHING BANDS

★ John Philip Sousa - American Composer, Conductor & Patriot

If you are listening to a band parading down the street, chances are good it is playing a tune written by John Philip Sousa. He wrote more than 130 marches during his lifetime. Although he died in 1932, Sousa is still known as the March King, and his pieces are played thousands of times each year by bands throughout the world. This site has some neat information about Sousa and sound clips of some of his more famous tunes. It also has lots of links, including ones to the bands of the U.S. military. Did you know that the United States Marine Corps band is called "The President's Own" and that it closes its weekly Washington, D.C., concert with a Sousa march? A few years ago, President Ronald Reagan named Sousa's "The Stars and Stripes Forever" as the national march. We guarantee you'll be humming his tunes and tapping your toes before you leave this page.

http://www.dws.org/sousa/

MP3

How MP3 Files Work

MP3 is actually shorthand for the audio level 3 compression standard developed by the Moving Picture Experts Group (MPEG). It's a way to compress audio files without degrading the quality of the sound. At this site, you can find out how it works and what you'll need to both download MP3 files to your own computer and also create your own files. Once you have a MP3 file, you can share it with others or carry it around on a portable MP3 player, if copyright rules allow.

http://www.howstuffworks.com/mp3.htm

MUSIC GAMES

★ Continental Harmony

The Sound Lounge will blow you away. Explore how we create and manipulate music "and how it manipulates us." In six interactive activities, you can experiment with melody, rhythm, instruments, and harmony, and play the role of composer.

http://www.pbs.org/harmony/soundlounge/

✿ Hop Pop Town

Preschoolers who love music, march right this way! Click on objects and animals to experiment with noises, sounds, and instruments. Record your own tune and play it back online. This rollicking site is fun and easy to use—with a little help from an adult or older brother or sister.

http://www.kids-space.org/HPT/

Mozart's Musikalisches Würfelspiel

Do you know anything about a minuet? Here's a hint: it has something to do with music, and it deals with timing. Play a game devised by the great composer Mozart. That's right, a game. He wrote the measures and instructions for a musical composition dice game. Tell your orchestra teacher about this. She will think you are crazy. Then show her the site, and she'll think you're a genius and promote you to first chair. Just follow the instructions and "compose" your own minuet.

http://sunsite.univie.ac.at/Mozart/dice/

Musical Illusions and Paradoxes

You know what an optical illusion is: a picture that can look like several different things all at once. (If you don't know, check the OPTICAL ILLUSIONS section in this book.) Are you ready for an audio illusion? Diana Deutsch's CD is called *Musical Illusions and Paradoxes*, and you can hear several samples at this Web site. Did you know that people hear sounds differently? Sometimes your brain can be tricked into hearing melodies that aren't really there. Sound impossible? Listen to the audio files here and see if you can identify the mystery tune.

http://www.philomel.com/

A
B
C
D
E
F
G
H
I
J
K
L
M
N
O
P
Q
R
S
T
U
V
W
X
Y
Z

MUSIC THEORY

Big Ears Online Ear Trainer

When you sing or play an instrument, it's important to have a good ear for pitch and being in tune. This page offers a drill so you can see how well you do at hearing whether the interval between two notes is a perfect fifth or a minor third or something completely different. Keep practicing!

http://www.ossmann.com/bigears/

Gary Ewer's Easy Music Theory

We've been looking for a site that teaches music theory, and now we've found one. From time signatures to triads, you'll explore 26 free lessons, quizzes, and more. Here comes the Maestro now!

http://www.musictheory.halifax.ns.ca/

NATIONAL ANTHEMS

National Anthems of the World

Choose the country, and then hear the anthem and (in many cases) read the lyrics. Take the anthem quiz and see if you can guess the name of the country by hearing its anthem. Hint: if you don't want to peek at the answer, don't have your status bar open! Did you know that even the Holy See (the Vatican) has its own national anthem?

http://www.emulateme.com/anthems/

OPERA

Opera Synopses/Composer Bios

Maybe you're looking for the plot summary for the opera your parents are taking you to this week. Maybe you are trying hard to remember the names of the characters in *The Mikado*. Or maybe you need a quick biography of a composer like Benjamin Britten or the original Engelbert Humperdinck. Remember this site!

http://www.nycopera.com/learn/resource/

Web Operas

Fourteen nineteenth-century light operas are presented here, from *Pirates of Penzance* to *H.M.S. Pinafore*. You'll find all the music, the lyrics, and the dialog of these Gilbert and Sullivan (and other) operas.

http://math.idbsu.edu/gas/midi/html/
    web_opera_home.html

REVIEWS

Grading the Movies

Parental advisory: please preview this site. Despite the title, this site also grades music and games. Who cares? Well, your parents may want to see why a CD got a parental warning sticker. Or you may want to get that information yourself before you ask your parents if you can buy a particular CD. The reviewers grade music, movies, and other media on violence, sexual content, language, and alcohol/tobacco references. The movie section is up-to-date but the music section is not. Warning: If using a Mac, you must use Netscape to open this site. It will crash IE5.

http://www.gradingthemovies.com/

NET FILES

Idaho has an official state horse. What breed is it?

Answer: It's the spotted Appaloosa. Possibly originating with the Nez Perce Indians, today you see Appys in parades, on ranches, and in horse shows. The coloring of the Appaloosa's coat is distinct in every individual horse and ranges from white spotted hips to a full all over leopard-look. Find more fascinating facts at
http://www2.state.id.us/gov/symbols.htm

A
B
C
D
E
F
G
H
I
J
K
L
M
N
O
P
Q
R
S
T
U
V
W
X
Y
Z

Meta Critic

Parental advisory: please preview this site. Want to find out how real reviewers from major newspapers, magazines, and Web sites have rated the latest music? This is the site for you. Each review is ranked on a ten-point scale. Anything at seven or above gets a green background; below that, you'll find yellow and red (for a really bad review). You can easily scan CD titles to see what the critics' prevailing opinions are, and then read the full reviews for added insight.

http://www.metacritic.com/music/

ROCK MUSICIANS AND MUSIC

★ The Beatles 1

This site's presentation, imagination, innovation, and class matches that of the music that inspired it. This site (literally) revolves around 27 Beatle songs, all of which "reached the top of the US or UK charts." Each song has its own page, complete with memorabilia, photos, record sleeve images, audio, video, and a "New Feature." Each New Feature section is a work of art in itself. And, oh yeah, each New Feature section is accompanied by its music.

http://www.thebeatles.com/

❧ Boom Thang

You won't win any song-writing awards, but you will have a lot of fun at this site while composing your own music. Simply click the record button, and select the instrument you want to play. You can choose from four different categories of sound: drums, bass, keyboard/guitar, and special effects. When you've finished, the site lets you play back your creation.

http://www.kaboose.com/shockWin2.cfm?infoID=
   boomthang&shockType=fl

Elvis.com - The Official Site

Ever heard of Elvisology? Neither had Net-mom until she dropped into this Web site to pay her respects to The King. It includes an official biography, a list of all the recordings and movies, and answers to frequently asked questions about Elvis.

http://www.elvis-presley.com/

The Internet Beatles Album

A splendid time is guaranteed for all! Look here for Beatles history, interviews (sometimes as audio files), lots of photos, and some gossip. The information is classified using Beatles song titles. For instance, the section called I Should Have Known Better debunks (or verifies) certain Beatles rumors. Is "Lucy in the Sky with Diamonds" about drugs? No. Four-year-old Julian Lennon's drawing of the same name gave John the inspiration, and you can look at the picture here. Eight Days a Week tells you what happened today in Beatles history.

http://www.getback.org/

Rock and Roll Hall of Fame and Museum

Look in the Exhibitions area, in the Permanent Collection. Are these really the 500 songs that shaped rock and roll? Well, it's a start. The Rock and Roll Hall of Fame and Museum is in Cleveland, Ohio, and it is a little bit like the Baseball Hall of Fame in Cooperstown, New York. Read profiles of the rock legends who have been inducted into the Hall of Fame. The oddest thing about the Rock and Roll Museum Web site is the lack of audio files and other multimedia.

http://www.rockhall.com/

The Top 100 Greatest Videos Ever Made

Parental advisory: please preview this resource. Part of the MTV site, this URL address is the direct path to the top 100 music videos ever made. See short clips from them all, from number 100 (Green Day's "Basket Case") to number 1 (Michael Jackson's "Thriller.") At the main level of the MTV.com site, you can see and hear current music video clips, explore music reviews, and download MP3 files.

http://www.mtv.com/mtv/tubescan/100videos/

★ Turntables

Think you'd make a phat DJ? Here's your chance to find out! Select a beat, choose a scratch, and rock on. Click to activate the lights and be sure to tell the "shouting man" what lyrics to yell. Hint: touch his sneakers to make him go backstage.

http://www.turntables.de/start.htm

SHEET MUSIC

The Free Sheet Music Guide

The growth of this site's huge database of links offering free sheet music proves the point that music on the Web keeps expanding. This guide to pop, rock, jazz, historical, classical, and patriotic music lists hundreds of sites where you can download free sheet music. The site can be browsed by topic or searched. Sign up for its free electronic newsletter, and it will alert you to new sheet music finds.

http://www.freesheetmusicguide.com/

Richard Robinson's Tunebook

Haul out your fiddle (or flute, sax, or tuba) and try some of these great tunes. This is real sheet music. If you hang out with acoustic or traditional musicians, you'll recognize some of these tunes. Jigs, reels, polkas, schottisches, and more were selected from France, Finland, Turkey, and Cape Breton, as well as lots from the British Isles. There's bound to be some bourrée or other you've never played before. The real fun comes when you share the tunes with other players. Anybody can play them. If you've been taking Suzuki method lessons for a while, try something new. It's the 32-bar pause that refreshes!

http://www.leeds.ac.uk/music/Info/RRTuneBk/
  tunebook.html

VOCAL

Charlotte Church

Charlotte Church, the Welsh teen singing sensation, is known for her signature song *Pie Jesu* from Andrew Lloyd Webber's *Requiem*, as well as other sacred and secular tunes. At her official Web site you can read her biography, listen to sound clips, and follow her tour diary. Her CD *Voice of an Angel*, is one of Net-mom's favorites.

http://www.charlottechurch.com/

Colleen Moore's Fairy Castle

The ultimate dollhouse is in the Chicago Museum of Science and Industry. It was created by Colleen Moore, a star of 1920s silent films, who decorated the interior with antiques, real gold, jewels, and other precious items. The dollhouse is located in a magic garden, with a weeping willow tree that really weeps! Who is to say fairies don't really live there? You'll see the Rock-a-Bye Baby cradle, Santa Claus' sleigh, and lots of other objects familiar from nursery rhyme lore and legend. The table is set in King Arthur's dining hall, and the Bluebird of Happiness sings in the princess' bedroom. Don't miss the attic—Rumplestiltskin's spinning wheel hangs from the rafters.
*http://www.msichicago.org/exhibit/fairy_castle/
fchome.html*

The Society for the Preservation and Encouragement of Barber Shop Quartet Singing in America

Check the Tutorials section to learn about barbershop harmony. It's a special kind of singing done without accompaniment. There are four vocalists: the lead sings the melody, the tenor harmonizes above, the bass sings harmony below, and the baritone fills in. As the singers "strike a chord," there is often heard a "fifth voice" of undertones and overtones that defines the magic of barbershop harmony. Listen to examples here, including audio of the world champions. The direct link to the Jukebox is hard to find. It's right here: *<http://www.spebsqsa.org/ jukebox/>*.

http://www.spebsqsa.org/

Lots of monkey-business in MAMMALS.

NATIVE AMERICANS AND FIRST NATIONS

Aboriginal Youth Network

Parental advisory: please preview this site. This resource is an example of how the Internet can bring people with similar interests or backgrounds together no matter where they live. It can also provide information for those of us interested in a particular native topic. The Aboriginal Youth Network was established in 1995 to unify aboriginal youth in Canada, but since then it has gone into all corners of the world. Check out all kinds of information available, as well as e-mail, chat lines, listings of events and programs, and more. We think you'll find it a very interesting place to spend some time.

http://ayn-0.ayn.ca/

Cultural Debates Online

The Mentawai tribe is facing some big changes. Should they embrace modern education or continue with traditional methods? Watch a brief videotape outlining this cultural issue, consider several sides of the argument, and vote for your own decision. There are six cultural challenges to experience and debate.

http://www.teachtsp2.com/cdonline/

Native Languages Page

Would you like to learn a little Navajo or a smattering of Quechua? Maybe you'd like to try using a Cherokee font or learn something about Mayan hieroglyphs. This page offers links to all of this and more.

http://www.nativeculture.com/lisamitten/natlang.html

AUSTRALIA
How to Play Digeridoo

Attend "Digeridoo University" to see and hear how to play this native instrument. After you master the drone, you can practice on other voices of the digeridoo: the kookaburra, the kangaroo, and more. Other parts of this site explain the Dreamtime and other facets of First Nations cultures. By the way, if you don't have a digeridoo, you can make one out of PVC pipe. The directions are available here <http://ctct.essortment.com/didgeridooshow_rkuc.htm>.

http://aboriginalart.com.au/didgeridoo/ dig_background.html

★ Stories of the Dreaming

According to this site, the Dreamtime is sometimes considered as the native Australian "time before time," or the "time of creation." The belief is that there were ancestor spirits who took human form. As they traveled throughout the country, they created landscape features like rivers and hills. There are often stories associated with these places, and some are collected here. You can view them in video form, hear just the audio, or read the text-only version.

http://www.dreamtime.net.au/main.cfm

CANADA
First Nations in Canada

Imagine yourself living thousands of years ago. You're traveling across a land bridge from Asia to North America and coming into the vast wilderness we now know as Canada. Maybe you would have hunted buffalo, moving your tipi and following the herds as they crossed the plains. Maybe you would have established a permanent village along the Pacific coast and fished for salmon and whales. Read all about the six distinct Canadian Indian cultures and the main tribes in each. Find out how they lived and hunted, what their dwellings looked like, and what they wore. This site takes you through the centuries of change the native populations have experienced, including progress in the last 30 years. The Kids' Stop section offers audio of several native languages, an interactive map of aboriginal place names, and more.

http://www.inac.gc.ca/pr/pub/fnc/index_e.html

First Peoples on Schoolnet

From the maritime provinces to Nunavut, you can learn about the First Nations of Canada from the links at this site. You'll find everything from Cree language lessons to creation stories if you spend some time exploring.

http://www.schoolnet.ca/aboriginal/menu-e.html

Native Musical Instruments

Music is fun to listen to and dance to, but it also has a place in sacred ritual and ceremony. Explore some special native instruments such as bullroarers, drums, calls, and rattles. You will also learn a little about the people who produced each artifact.

http://www.civilization.ca/membrs/fph/stones/instru/inmenu.htm

Wave Eaters - Native Watercraft in Canada

The boat-making skill of indigenous peoples is legendary. The Canadian Museum of Civilization's watercraft collection highlights kayaks, dugouts, bark canoes, and *umiaks* (an arctic skin boat, used for hunting whales). Learn how each was made, admire some wonderful pictures, and find out how the museum staff preserves the boats so they may be enjoyed for years to come.

http://www.civilization.ca/membrs/fph/watercraft/wainteng.html

NATIVE AMERICANS

Against the Winds: Traditions of Native American Running

Running is not just a way to get from place to place. It is also part of Indian spiritual practice. At this site you will read about native running and runners, past and present.

http://www.peabody.harvard.edu/mcnh_running/

NET FILES

Maryland has an unusual official state sport. What is it?

Answer: It's the equestrian sport known as jousting! Read why at http://www.inform.umd.edu/UMS+State/UMD-Projects/MCTP/Technology/School_WWW_Pages/pogs/Jason.html, an informative Web page created by fifth graders about Maryland's official symbols.

★ American Indian Radio on Satellite

Programming on this radio network is aimed at the interests of tribal communities, although anyone is invited to listen. Click on "Listen to Live Radio" to hear contemporary native singers and musicians, find out about current events from a native perspective, and hear live call-in shows.

http://www.airos.org/

★ Canku Ota (Many Paths)

Don't miss this truly inspired site. It features biweekly fresh articles and features. Inside you'll find interesting cultural stories from many nations, a kids page, numerous quality links to resources on native interests, and even coloring book pages. Recent articles included one on Huichol Indian beadwork, a recipe for Cherokee Berry Bread, and many news stories involving native youth. The collection of suggested links is outstanding, easy to use, and contains complete annotations.

http://www.turtletrack.org/

A B C D E F G H I J K L M N O P Q R S T U V W X Y Z

SquirrelLand.com

We've seen a lot of odd webcams on the Internet over the years. This is one of them. Explore "squirreltopia"—a squirrel feeder complex that looks like a little Christmas village. It's even lit at night. You might see squirrels, blue jays, nuthatches, or the owner filling up the feeders. Check it out. *http://www.squirrelland.com/*

Cradleboard

Presented by the Nihewan Foundation, which was founded by singer-songwriter Buffy Sainte-Marie, this site supports cross-cultural education using the Internet. The project links native schools with non-native classrooms via special chat rooms and e-mail. The object is to encourage self-esteem and especially to teach non-native kids that Indian culture is alive today.

http://www.cradleboard.org/main.html

Crazy Horse Memorial Foundation

Gazing up at the huge stone faces of Mt. Rushmore—all great American presidents—one man began to wonder why a native face wasn't up there on the cliff side. Korczak Ziolkowski spoke with Lakota Sioux about his dream to honor Crazy Horse, the famous Lakota Sioux leader, who died in 1877. He began his great work, sculpting a mountain in the Black Hills area of South Dakota. Although he died in 1982, his family continues his work. Get pictures and progress reports here. The year 1998 marked the 50th anniversary of the first rock blast on the mountain.

http://www.crazyhorse.org/

> We like the INVERTEBRATES best.—The Nields

★ The Double J Files

Try this fun detective game to learn about some of the inventions of the First Nations in North America. Some cases: Did the Inuit of the Arctic North invent sunglasses? Is Lacrosse a game invented by the Iroquois? Click on the right clues, and you'll discover the answers to these questions and more.

http://www.tvokids.com/doublej/

The Great Sioux Nation

In the nineteenth century, the Great Sioux Nation comprised 20,000 people in seven tribes. You might remember hearing about Sitting Bull and Custer's Last Stand, the battle of Little Bighorn (near Billings, Montana). You can read all about that famous battle here, and you'll also learn much more about the Sioux—but, by the way, that word means "enemy." They called themselves Lakota. That word means "people." This is part of the History Channel Web site.

http://www.historychannel.com/exhibits/sioux/

A Guide to the Great Sioux Nation

The people of the Sioux Nation prefer to be called Dakota, Lakota, or Nakota, depending on their language group. On this South Dakota home page, you can learn about the languages, legends, and rich cultural traditions of these proud peoples. You'll see beautiful costumes, and maybe you can attend one of the powwows. You'll find a calendar of annual events here, so go get yourself some fry bread and enjoy the music and dance!

http://www.state.sd.us/state/executive/tourism/sioux/sioux.htm

A B C D E F G H I J K L M **N** O P Q R S T U V W X Y Z

Homeland

PBS invites you to take a trip to the Pine Ridge, South Dakota Indian reservation and meet four Lakota families who live there. The documentary follows them as they struggle to overcome the harsh realities of reservation life—alcoholism, unemployment, and scarce housing. Every day they work to keep their cultural traditions strong and build a better life for their children and future generations. There's also a fry bread recipe and material on the legend of the white buffalo. If you want to share your thoughts, you can e-mail the families.

http://www.pbs.org/homeland/

Indian Country Today

What's news in Indian country? Find out at the online version of this highly respected native-produced newspaper. Keep up with sovereignty issues, reservation news, tribal government, and lots more.

http://indiancountry.com/

National Museum of the American Indian

The Smithsonian Institution's National Museum of the American Indian is in New York City, not in Washington, D.C. (like their other museums). Most of the one million objects in its collection represent cultures in the United States and Canada, although there are also items from Mexico and Central and South America. You can see many artifacts of ancient and contemporary culture through the online exhibits of clothing, baskets, beadwork, and other objects. This museum displays sacred materials only with the permission of the various tribes and returns these materials on request.

http://www.si.edu/nmai/

Native American Authors

At the time we visited this rich collection, there were almost 500 Native American authors listed. You can get information on their books, honors, and—in many cases—Web sites. A neat thing to try is to look up the tribe's name and see how many authors are listed from that nation. You can also browse by author or title.

http://www.ipl.org/ref/native/

Native American Shelters

The Minnesota State University has a wonderful online museum interpreting anthropology and archaeology for those who stop in via this cyberdoor. Learn about seven distinct areas of the United States, and see how ancient Native Americans lived centuries ago. From the pueblos of the southwest to the igloos of the far north, you'll learn how the structures were made and what functions were served by different types of dwellings.

http://www.anthro.mankato.msus.edu/prehistory/settlements/

Just before the justices enter the Supreme Court, they are announced by the marshall. What does the marshall say? (Hint: He repeats the word three times.)

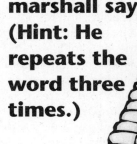

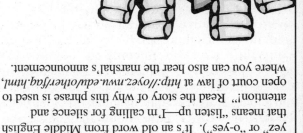

Answer: "Oyez, oyez, oyez!" (pronounced "o-yay" or "o-yez" or "o-yes"). It's an old word from Middle English that means "listen up—I'm calling for silence and attention!" Read the story of why this phrase is used to open court of law at *http://oyez.nwu.edu/other/faq.html*, where you can also hear the marshal's announcement.

It never rains in cyberspace.

Native American Sites

You have a report due on a Native American nation you've never heard of before. So you walk down to the public library to look for it. Trouble is, all the books on Native Americans have been checked out, and the reference books have only one paragraph on your topic! Now you can go straight to the source. Many nations have their own home pages, complete with historical and cultural information. They are listed here, at a site put together by a librarian who says she is "mixed-blood Mohawk urban Indian." You'll also find links to tribal organizations, colleges, businesses, powwows, singers, and more. This site is carefully tended and updated. We have not checked outside links.

http://www.nativeculture.com/lisamitten/indians.html

★ NativeTech: Native American Technology and Art

Learn about a lot of Native American art and technologies like beadwork, clay and pottery, leather and clothes, toys and games, and more. We started at beadwork because it seems so interesting. There is information about the kinds of beads and their meanings. Wampum beads were made from shells and often decorated clothing. Long, woven wampum belts were often exchanged at treaty signings or other formal occasions. You can find out how the beads were made—it was a very difficult process! Let's mosey on over to porcupine quillwork, perhaps the oldest form of Native American embroidery. Native American artists sometimes decorate their clothing and birchbark containers with quills. At this site, not only do you learn the history of these fascinating art forms, but you can also learn how to do many of these crafts. Maybe you should start with the cornhusk doll instructions, though, since corn's easier to find than porcupine quills. Look in the Plants and Trees section.

http://www.nativeweb.org/NativeTech/

Oneida Indian Nation

The Oneida were the first Native American nation to put up a Web page and claim territory in cyberspace. Net-mom was honored to have been a part of this history—see <http://www.cs.org/CSQ/csqinternet.html#Polly>. The Oneida homelands are located in central New York State, and they remain an unconquered nation. In fact, they were the only Native American tribe to fight on the side of the American colonists during the American Revolution. This fact, often left out of history books, is detailed on this site. In 1777–78, Washington's soldiers were enduring a hard winter at Valley Forge, Pennsylvania. Oneida people walked hundreds of miles south, carrying food and supplies, to come to their aid. Polly Cooper was an Oneida woman who helped the soldiers, and she taught them how to cook the corn and other foods the Oneida had brought with them. Although offered payment, she refused, saying it was her duty to help friends in need. She was thanked for her assistance by Martha Washington herself, who presented Polly with a fancy shawl and bonnet. The shawl has been a treasured Oneida relic since then, and you can see a photo of it here. You can also hear some Oneida words, take a tour of the cultural museum, read original treaties, learn why the cornhusk dolls have no face, and see some real wampum!

http://oneida-nation.net/

Pueblo Cultural Center

In the New Mexico desert, 19 Pueblo communities welcome visitors, both real and virtual. You can read descriptions of all of them here, as well as pick up maps to the pueblos, calendars of events, and even rules for attending dances (don't applaud—dance is a prayer, not a performance). Gaze at the stunning wall murals, with titles such as these: The One-Horned Buffalo Dance; The Sounds of Life and Earth as It Breathes; and Indian Maiden Feeding Deer. You can read biographies of the artists, too.

http://www.indianpueblo.org/

Everyone's flocking to BIRDS!

> ## Origami: the fold to behold!
> ## Check out CRAFTS
> ## AND HOBBIES.

Southern Native American Powwows

This site was created by kids for the ThinkQuest competition. In it, you'll learn where to sit (and where not to sit) to watch the dancing, and you'll know what to do if you are a dancer. Don't forget to honor the Head Man and the Head Lady and give respect to the Drum, which has probably traveled a long way to give you beautiful music. Listen to the audio files of various songs, and check out the various styles of dances for both men and women. There is even advice for the new dancer and someone wishing to get involved with this tradition.

http://tqd.advanced.org/3081/

Totem Poles of the Northwest

If you've ever seen a totem pole, you might wonder why there are various figures and objects carved into it. You'll usually see animals, such as the eagle, raven, frog, killer whale, grizzly bear, and others. They all have meanings, and you can learn more at this most interesting site. This site was created by students for the ThinkQuest Junior competition.

http://tqjunior.thinkquest.org/5160/

Wacipi PowWow

Everyone is welcome at Native American powwows. Please rise, as the flags and eagle staffs enter the arena. Learn about the dance, regalia, drum, and songs you'll hear. If you're thinking about attending a powwow, this page will teach you its customs. Learn more by reading the entries in the DANCE section of this book.

http://www.ktca.org/powwow/

Marconi Calling

Today, we think nothing of turning on the TV and seeing events happen, live, on the other side of the world. This was not always the case. Before the development of fast communication technologies, news often took months to work its way across the globe. One of these great technological breakthroughs was radio—wireless communications. December 12, 2001, marked the 100th anniversary of the first transatlantic radio signal, which was received in St. Johns, Newfoundland, by Guglielmo Marconi. The signal sent was the letter "S" in Morse code: "click-click-click." On December 15, 1902, Marconi sent the first wireless transatlantic message to Cornwall, England, thus making Glace Bay, on Cape Breton Island, Nova Scotia, the birthplace of transoceanic wireless communication. Read more and see historic photos, artifacts, and lots more at this outstanding site. *http://www.marconicalling.com/*

NATIVE AMERICANS—HISTORY

Archaeology at Crow Canyon - Castle Rock Pueblo

Located in what is now southwest Colorado, Castle Rock Pueblo was once a thriving community. Sometime around the year 1200 all that changed, and no one really knows why. It's now abandoned except for National Park Service employees and tourists. Take a virtual trip to the ruins and see if you can find any clues to what happened to its residents and culture. That's only one of the three mysteries for you to solve at this site.

http://www.crowcanyon.org/EducationProducts/ElecFieldTrip_CRP/

A
B
C
D
E
F
G
H
I
J
K
L
M
N
O
P
Q
R
S
T
U
V
W
X
Y
Z

A
B
C
D
E
F
G
H
I
J
K
L
M
N
O
P
Q
R
S
T
U
V
W
X
Y
Z

Camping with the Sioux: Fieldwork Diary of Alice Cunningham Fletcher

In 1881, photographer Alice Fletcher traveled to Dakota Territory to live with Sioux women. She photographed them and recorded their way of life in her diary. This site seeks to preserve Fletcher's work, much of which is fascinating to read now, over 100 years later. The photo gallery features portraits of many Sioux women and their families. A handy calendar lets you read Fletcher's diary, day by day. There are also a few folk tales, but they are somewhat grim.

http://www.nmnh.si.edu/naa/fletcher/fletcher.htm

The Cherokee Trail of Tears - 1838-1839

In 1838, the U.S. government (led by President Andrew Jackson) decreed that the Cherokee nation would be forcibly removed from their rich lands in North Carolina, Georgia, and Tennessee. Some left voluntarily, but 13,000 others were marched the 1,200 miles to Indian territory in Oklahoma. Many died along this "Trail of Tears." It is a tragedy of American history, and you can learn more about it, and the National Historic Trail that exists today, at this site.

http://rosecity.net/tears/

Edward S. Curtis's North American Indian

As noted at this Library of Congress Web site, Curtis' book "was one of the most significant and controversial representations of traditional American Indian culture ever produced." It was printed in a series of 20 volumes over the years from 1907–1930, and it continues to influence beliefs about Native Americans today. On this site you can view his historic images of more than 80 tribes. There is a warning message included: "Some captions and images portray ceremonial rituals and objects that were not intended for viewing by the uninitiated. No images have been excluded or specially labeled. They are included in this digital collection in order to represent the work fully."

http://lcweb2.loc.gov/ammem/award98/ienhtml/curthome.html

DID YOU KNOW WRITING IN ALL CAPITAL LETTERS IS CONSIDERED YELLING? See, isn't this nicer? Use upper and lower-case letters in mail and chat rooms.

Homes of the Past: The Archaeology of an Iroquoian Longhouse

What if you were an archaeologist and were exploring an ancient Iroquois village site? What could you learn about the culture from the clues left behind hundreds of years ago? This resource lets you imagine you are that scientist, trying to make sense out of hearths, post mould, storage pits, and pottery fragments. Based on a real dig site in Ontario, Canada, this page encourages you to make educated guesses based on the archaeological evidence.

http://www.rom.on.ca/digs/longhouse/

New Perspectives on the West

This is a companion site to the eight-part PBS television series The West. It is a history of the expansion of the American West, and we are including it because of the rich biographical information about famous Native Americans. Just click on People. You'll find short biographies about Sitting Bull, Chief Joseph, Chief Seattle, Crazy Horse, Sacagawea, and more.

http://www.pbs.org/weta/thewest/

Pomp - The True Story of the Baby on the Sacagawea Dollar

Have you seen the beautiful "golden" dollar coin? It features a portrait of the nineteenth-century Native American guide Sacagawea and her little baby boy, who was named Pomp. As this site points out, that trip with explorers Lewis and Clark was only the beginning of Pomp's adventures. Find out why Pomp is famous in his own right.

http://pompstory.home.mindspring.com/

Sipapu - Chetro Ketl Great Kiva

Over a thousand years ago, there was a great civilization in what is now northwestern New Mexico, in the southwestern desert of the United States. What remains now are cliff dwellings and other scattered hints about how these people lived and worked. One central part of their existence was the kiva, an underground enclosure used for sacred and other purposes. Young men would enter the kiva to learn secret languages and hidden lore of the tribe. The kiva was the central spiritual focus of the community. Large communities needed a Great Kiva, and this site reconstructs one for you to climb down in and visit virtually. It is based on the recently excavated Chetro Ketl Great Kiva, which is located in isolated Chaco Canyon, in northwestern New Mexico. You can choose the multimedia tour, with QuickTime VR, or you can try the less bandwidth-intensive version. The descendants of these ancient peoples now live in the various pueblos of the area. They also use kivas for ceremonies, and they are off-limits if you are a visitor to the pueblo.

http://sipapu.gsu.edu/html/kiva.html

NATIVE ARCTIC PEOPLES
Arctic Circle: History and Culture

You'll find information here about many people who are native to the Arctic Circle region of the world. You'll learn not only about the Cree of northern Quebec and the Inupiat of Arctic Alaska, but also about the Nenets and Khanty of Yamal Peninsula, northwest Siberia, and the Sámi of far-northern Europe. Find out why the concept of "wilderness" is unknown to these people, who live in harmony with their natural surroundings.

http://arcticcircle.uconn.edu/HistoryCulture/

Looking for the State Bird or the State Motto? It's in the UNITED STATES—STATES section.

NATIVE HAWAIIANS
Hawai'i Independent and Sovereign

In November 1993, President Bill Clinton signed into law U.S. Public Law 103-50, which is "To acknowledge the 100th anniversary of the January 17, 1893 overthrow of the Kingdom of Hawaii, and to offer an apology to Native Hawaiians on behalf of the United States for the overthrow of the Kingdom of Hawaii." Some native Hawaiians are trying to restore Hawaii to sovereign nation status. That means it would have its own leaders and could determine its own future. Read news about the Nation of Hawai'i, and find out about native island culture here.

http://hawaii-nation.org/

NAVASSA ISLAND

See UNITED STATES—TERRITORIES

On the Internet, nobody knows you're a frog. Craving some "Bee Grubs in Coconut Cream"? Where on Earth can a frog find a cookbook?

Answer: At Dr. Frog's Recipe Page, of course! "Marinate bee grubs, sliced onions, and citrus leaves in coconut cream containing some pepper. Wrap in pieces of linen and steam. Serve as a topping for rice." (It doesn't suggest where a frog might get some linen, though.) For more recipes, hop on over to http://www.frogsonice.com/froggy/recipes.shtml

NEWS, NEWSPAPERS, AND MAGAZINES

See also INTERNET—SEARCH ENGINES AND DIRECTORIES and TELEVISION—NETWORKS AND CHANNELS. Many sites, such as those found in INTERNET— SEARCH ENGINES AND DIRECTORIES, offer newspapers that you can easily customize yourself. One example is *<http://edit.my.yahoo.com/config/login>*, but almost all the search engines and directories have something similar.

E&P Online Media Directory

Editor & Publisher has been around for a long time, providing information for the news industry. Now they've got this great online media directory for you to use! You will find associations, city guides, magazines, newspapers, news services and syndicates, and radio and television Web sites listed both geographically and by media type. Check it out and find the newspaper in your community, the community where you used to live, or the community you're moving to. If you've got a homework assignment about current events in, say, Bermuda, you can read the daily news from local newspapers there.

http://emedia1.mediainfo.com/emedia/

NET FILES

Everyone knows frogs can jump pretty far. How far? What's the longest recorded length a frog has leaped?

Answer: According to the Exploratorium, a South African frog holds the record for leaping 33 feet 5.5 inches in a single jump. Hop to it!

http://www.exploratorium.edu/frogs/mainstory/

How to Analyze News

This page has a tremendous amount of very solid information, as well as suggestions on how to get kids thinking about news stories. Who gathered the information, who reports it, what's the slant, who sponsors the program—all these things and more should be evaluated when we hear a news story. Make sure you're media-aware! Visit the main level of this site for more.

http://www.media-awareness.ca/eng/med/class/teamedia/htan.htm

MAGAZINES

Highlights for Children

The first thing you need to do on this site is register, but it's free. Only then will you gain access to most of the site's features and online activities. You can, however, take a Guest tour of the site to see what it's all about. You'll see that it's about reading stories and creating your own, and making crafts like marble and bead jewelry. The Science Questions section is a good place to find out, for example, "Why do camels have humps?" There's much, much more once you start to explore this cool site.

http://www.highlightskids.com/

Ranger Rick Magazine

The National Wildlife Federation has a magazine for kids that's about nature, wildlife, and wilderness, and some of it is online. You can sample activities from past issues in Prowl the Past, such as making a detergent bottle bird feeder, or check articles in the Kids Zone, like the Cool Tour through a virtual wetland.

http://www.nwf.org/rangerrick/

Stone Soup Magazine

Stone Soup is a well-known magazine of stories, poems, and artwork by kids, for kids. Here at their Web site, you can peek at a sample issue, plus read some online stories and poems. Maybe you'll be able to send them some of your own work. There is nothing like seeing your name in print, next to something you wrote, whether it's printed in a magazine, a book, or on the Net!

http://www.stonesoup.com/

TIME for Kids

TIME is a very popular news magazine for adults, but now there is an online version for kids, and it is HOT! You'll find current news stories on the front page, but dig deeper for cartoons, multimedia, and an archive of past issues. Recent stories included information on Harry Potter's movie, buggy ice cream, and on a global warming agreement. There are three versions, one for K and first grade, one for second and third grades, and one for fourth through sixth grades.

http://pathfinder.com/TFK/

Weekly Reader Galaxy

How much do you know about this month's top news stories? Play the News Busters Game and see. You can also view top stories from the perspective of various grade levels, three through six. There are often fun games, quizzes, online polls, and other activities sprinkled throughout this site.

http://www.weeklyreader.com/

WORLD Magazine @ Nationalgeographic.com

National Geographic has been a family favorite for decades. They also have a magazine just for kids, called WORLD, and this is its online version. The contents of the issues vary, but we've enjoyed articles on the space station, pirates, and movies of an avalanche in action. What will you find when you check in?

http://www.nationalgeographic.com/media/world/

NEWS

ABCNews4Kids.com

Foreign policy? The plight of the unemployed? Alan Greenspan and Wall Street? Is that what kids want to know about? ABC News doesn't think so. So, it has put together a news site for kids. The news that makes news on this site is really useful stuff. As they say, "find out what's happening around the corner, around the country, and around the world."

http://abcnews.go.com/abcnews4kids/kids/

Children's Express WorldWide - News by Kids for Everybody

Kids from ages 8 to 18 report news stories from all over the world. CE articles appear in newspapers all over the world, and some of its reporters are also on TV and radio. About 750 kids are in the active press corps. Read some of their stories, and then find out how you can become involved.

http://www.cenews.org/

NEWSPAPERS

★ The New York Times Learning Network

This site is aimed at teachers, parents, and students in grades 3–12. You'll find age-appropriate current news stories, feature stories, quizzes, lesson plans, and lots more. As you're reading a story, you can turn on some helper applications. Need help with the vocabulary? Highlighted words are linked to a dictionary. Countries are linked to a world atlas. There's even a crossword puzzle.

http://www.nytimes.com/learning/

NORTHERN MARIANA ISLANDS

See UNITED STATES—TERRITORIES

A B C D E F G H I J K L M N O P Q R S T U V W X Y Z

A
B
C
D
E
F
G
H
I
J
K
L
M
N
O
P
Q
R
S
T
U
V
W
X
Y
Z

OPTICAL ILLUSIONS

★ EncycloZine: Optical Illusions

The wealth of patterns, shapes, and vivid colors makes this site a thoroughly enjoyable visual experience. "Impossible" objects, moving pictures, and vivid 3-D images are just a few of the optical illusions to view. But the site provides more than just images. You'll learn the scientific principles behind them. The animated optical illusions written in SVG (Scalable Vector Language) are the most unusual. They require the SVG plug-in for viewing.

http://encyclozine.com/Illusions/

IllusionWorks

Discover not only sight illusions but also sound illusions! Try to figure out the distorted puzzles or the camouflaged hidden pictures. Some of these require Shockwave or Java-enhanced browsers. A caution to parents: not all links leading off this site have been checked.

http://www.illusionworks.com/

Petfinder

This amazing site coordinates the availability of pets for adoption at U.S. animal shelters or rescue organizations. You can search for information about pets in your home town or across the country. Narrow your search by type of animal (dog, cat, bird, pig, horse, and more), breed, age, gender, or size. There are also terrific discussion forums for everything from emergency rescue needs to lost and found pets.
http://web2.petfinder.org/

Mark Newbold's Animated Necker Cube

Do not try this illusion at home. Remember, we warned you. OK, well maybe you can try it at home, but make sure you have your seat belts fastened first and your tray and seat backs are fully upright. Prepare for your brain cells to get messed up as your perception of this seemingly innocent cube switches around. According to this site, "The Necker Cube is named after the Swiss crystallographer Louis Albert Necker, who in the mid-1800s saw cubic shapes spontaneously reverse in perspective." But don't try the Counter-Rotating Spirals Illusion—unless you want to have fun!

http://dogfeathers.com/java/necker.html

★ Online Exhibits @ the Exploratorium

Don't look now. At this site there are illusions that will make you think your computer is spinning, your palm is squirming, and Mona Lisa is frowning. If that's not enough to convince you to go to this site, there's an audio short story called "Ladle Rat Rotten Hut" that will completely confuse you, and then amuse you. Remember, the moral of this very familiar story is "Yonder nor sorghum stenches shut ladle gulls stopper torque wet strainers."

http://www.exploratorium.edu/exhibits/

★ SandlotScience.com

They're all here: those illusional figures that leave you wondering. You'll see impossible illusions, like the animated triangle and the endless staircase. You'll also find camouflage illusions and hidden pictures, and, finally, our favorite: moiré patterns. They're caused when two transparent patterns overlap. You will enjoy visiting this site, but don't be in a hurry—these illusions are irresistible!

http://www.sandlotscience.com/

The truth is out there in UFOS AND EXTRATERRESTRIALS. Maybe.

Saskatchewan Science Centre - Optical Illusions

Are optical illusions magic? No, but they are clever ways of showing us how our eyes and brains work together. Run down the hall of illusion and see how far you get before your brain tells your eyes, "Enough!"

http://www.sciencecentre.sk.ca/optical.htm

The World of Escher

Waterfalls that flow up? Stairs that seem to keep going down, yet, suddenly, they're back on top of a building? These inexplicable drawings by M. C. Escher must be seen to be believed. There's a contest, too. Can you make a drawing like this?

http://www.worldofescher.com/

ORGANIZATIONS

Amazing Kids

Meet Amazing Kids from all over: a classroom of recording artists, a lab of young inventors, and kids who make their own videos. Enter contests (the current one seeks amazing poetry done by kids) and find your own place in this site that celebrates the achievements of children.

http://www.amazing-kids.org/

Children's Defense Fund

Being a kid can be tough. Poverty, abuse, and negligence are a few of the problems kids confront. The Children's Defense Fund (CDF) is an organization designed to help kids with some of the difficult problems they face. To learn more about how kids can get a Head Start, a Healthy Start, a Fair Start, a Safe Start, and a Moral Start—find out what the CDF is doing in order to (as their trademark says) "Leave no child behind."

http://www.childrensdefense.org/

Kids Can Make a Difference

Around the world, every day, there are very poor families who never get enough to eat. At this Web page you can learn how to assist kids who need a helping hand. There are lots of ideas: for example, you can write letters to politicians, newspaper editors, and others to alert them to the problems of hunger. You can hold car washes or bake sales to raise money for relief organizations. One class "adopted" a family at a local homeless shelter, while others held a "hunger banquet" and collected canned food to stock a local food pantry. Take a look now—it'll make you feel good to learn how you can do something positive for your community and your world.

http://www.kids.maine.org/

Make-a-Wish Foundation of America

Founded in the belief that lives are measured by memories and not by years, the Make-a-Wish Foundation has granted more than 83,000 wishes to children around the world who have terminal illnesses or life-threatening medical conditions. Since the first wish (granted in 1980 for a seven-year-old boy with terminal leukemia who wanted to be a policeman), many chapters have sprung up all over the globe. With the family's participation, the Foundation is committed to providing a memorable and carefree experience for these children, whose wishes are limited only by their own imaginations. If you know someone who would like to make a special wish, check the Chapter Listing to find the Make-a-Wish chapter nearest you. One of the most frequently requested wishes is to travel to Disneyland or Disney World, but many unusual wishes have been granted, and you can read about them here. Also, be sure to check out the story of Craig Shergold and other hoax chain mail wrongly attributed to Make-a-Wish.

http://www.wish.org/

It's hard to remember, but mnemonic memory tricks are in WORDS.

A
B
C
D
E
F
G
H
I
J
K
L
M
N
O
P
Q
R
S
T
U
V
W
X
Y
Z

A
B
C
D
E
F
G
H
I
J
K
L
M
N
O
P
Q
R
S
T
U
V
W
X
Y
Z

NET FILES

On a clear day, how many states can you see from the top of the Empire State Building in New York City?

Answer: Five. According to the official Empire State Building page, "On clear days visitors can see the surrounding countryside for distances up to 80 miles, looking into the neighboring states of New Jersey, Pennsylvania, Connecticut, and Massachusetts, as well as New York." http://www.esbnyc.com/html/facts.html

The Penny Boy: Matthew Nonnemacher

Ten-year-old Matthew had a dream. He wanted to help the poor. So he decided to collect one million pennies ($10,000). With the help of his community, and a lot of his own time, Matthew more than achieved his goal. This Web site tells you how you can start a similar project. Matthew's newest project: collecting one million dollars for charity!

http://www.pennyboy.org/

SERVEnet!

Parental advisory: this site contains links to many different types of organizations and their Web sites; please preview. Do kids care? You bet they do! Lots of kids find ways to volunteer their time with charitable organizations such as the Ronald McDonald House, the American Red Cross, and many homeless shelters. Do you want to show you care? Type in your ZIP code and search for volunteer opportunities in your city or region.

http://www.servenet.org/

USA Weekend's Make a Difference Day

What are you doing the last Saturday in October? That's National Make a Difference Day, and plenty of kids are getting involved. Visit this page for ideas on what projects might benefit your community. Maybe you'll hold a parade to build awareness of substance abuse. Or maybe you'll organize a wheelbarrow brigade to help make a wheelchair-accessible baseball field. Perhaps you can help elderly residents install smoke detectors, or collect old clothing for the homeless shelter, or . . . the list goes on and on. If you already have an idea, register it at this site. There are prizes for the best projects—find out more!

http://www.usaweekend.com/diffday/

★ Volunteer Match

Parental advisory: please preview this site, many organizations are involved. What's different about this award-winning resource? It matches volunteers with opportunities that can be temporary or ongoing. You can even become a virtual volunteer and participate without ever leaving your computer keyboard. Visit the site and you'll be hooked. We found out our local science museum wanted volunteers to help build a new door, catalog a small library, and run the planetarium show. Volunteer Match is so easy to use, and fun, too.

http://www.volunteermatch.org/

CLUBS

Boys & Girls Clubs of America

Where can you go after school and (usually) on the weekends? The local Boys & Girls Club, of course! There are 2,851 of them across the U.S., Puerto Rico, the Virgin Islands, and on U.S. military bases abroad. What can you do there? You can play games, attend a career counseling session, hang out in the teen center, learn crafts, explore the Internet, and even play a game of b-ball. What are you waiting for! Just type in the name of your city and find the address of the closest club.

http://www.bgca.org/

Camp Fire Boys and Girls

Camp Fire was originally founded as an organization for American girls. That was in 1910. In 1975, they decided to let boys join, too. Headquartered in Kansas City, Missouri, approximately 650,000 kids are now Camp Fire members. The organization stresses self- reliance, making friends, and helping one's community. You can visit this page to find out about Camp Fire programs in your area.

http://www.campfire.org/

Girls Incorporated

"Inspiring all girls to be strong, smart and bold" is this group's trademark. Organizations affiliated with Girls Incorporated serve 350,000 young people ages 6–18 at over 1,000 sites nationwide. Find out here if there is one in your city. If there isn't, you can learn how to start a club in your area. Meanwhile though, there are lots of online things for you to do at this site. Some help you explore the differences in the way women and girls are portrayed in the movies and on TV versus the real world of you and your friends.

http://www.girlsinc.org/

National 4-H Council

What does it mean to be a member of 4-H? It can mean learning how to give a great speech, or helping to save the environment. Maybe you'll get involved in raising animals, or work on another project with friends. From country lanes to city streets, kids are involved in 4-H activities, and 4-H kids are having fun and learning a lot. To get the inside scoop on 4-H, take a peek at this Web site.

http://www.fourhcouncil.edu/

YMCA of the USA

Why would you go to the "Y"—the YMCA? You could go for all kinds of reasons. You could go for a game of b-ball, swimming or judo lessons, or even classes in basketry. The Y is a fun place for everybody in the family, and there are more than 2,400 YMCA facilities all over the U.S.

http://www.ymca.net/

CLUBS—SCOUTING
Boy Scouts of America - National Council

You'll find lots of scouting information and a few games. For those, click on Youth Participants, then Family Fun. Try "Name That Merit Badge" or "What Knot Would You Use?" Parental advisory: please preview this site.

Http://www.bsa.scouting.org/

Girl Scouts

There are about 2.7 million Girl Scout members, including adults and girls ages 5–17. At this site you can learn about the cool things Girl Scouts do (it's more than selling cookies). You'll find clip art and logos (look in the About Us area), and links to the Web pages of almost 200 local troops (look in the Council Finder area). There's also a section called Just for Girls, offering links, activities, and feature stories for girls interested in science, sports, and a lot more.

Http://www.gsusa.org/

Scouter Interactive - Your Guide to Scout Out the Net

Your patrol is supposed to come up with a campfire skit or funny songs for Scout camp. No problem— just check some of the Meeting Activities links here. You'll also find resources on international scouting, times and places for the next Jamboree or other scouting event, fundraising ideas, discussion groups, and links to other pages for both Boy Scouts and Girl Scouts. Parental advisory: please preview this site and its discussion boards.

Http://scouter.com/

Did the groundhog see his shadow? Find out if it will be an early spring in HOLIDAYS.

A
B
C
D
E
F
G
H
I
J
K
L
M
N
O
P
Q
R
S
T
U
V
W
X
Y
Z

The Scouting Web

Strictly for Girl Scouts, the information here ranges from "Ceremonies and Flags" to "Songs, Skits, and Stories." You'll also be able to find links to some great ideas for making troop to troop "swaps." You can find more "swaps" ideas in the CRAFTS AND HOBBIES section of this book.

http://www.scoutingweb.com/scoutingweb/

OUTDOOR RECREATION

See also SPORTS

FISHING

See also AQUARIUMS and FISH

NET FILES

Who is credited with inventing the concept of computer programming?

Answer: Ada Byron Lovelace (1815–1851) is credited with the invention of programming, for her work with Charles Babbage's analytical engine. A military programming language, Ada, is named after her in commemoration. Read more about this mathematician at http://www.agnesscott. edu/lriddle/women/love.htm

---

Fun Fish and Fishing Facts

Hey! You caught a fish! NOW what? Is it big enough to keep? Will it be used as food? If not, this site shows you how to gently release it so you can catch it again when it's bigger. There's also a tackle box checklist and information on lots of fishy facts.

http://www.sarep.cornell.edu/Sarep/Kids/facts/ Facts.html

GORP - Fishing

Parental advisory: please preview this site. Looking for the right angle on fishing? GORP is where they're biting. This is no line—you'll find everything from general fishing to fishing gear to information on fishing trips. There are lots of links to fishing hot spots on the Web. Stop by and catch your limit today.

http://www.gorp.com/gorp/activity/fishing.htm

GOLF AND MINIATURE GOLFING

Caddie Training Manual

If you like golf, you might consider being a caddie. It's a big responsibility, though, so this online resource gives you advice and encouragement. You'll learn how to manage your golfer's golf bag, replace divots, rake sand traps, and look for lost balls, among other things.

http://www.teachingkidsbusiness.com/ caddietrainingmanual.htm

Golf, a Game for Life

Discover the world of golf: its history, the equipment used, the techniques needed, and—of course—the rules of play. Meet golf champions and read brief biographies. Tiger Woods won his first world golf title at age eight! His success has made him a multicultural hero—Woods is African American, American Indian, Chinese, European, and Thai. By the way, what's Tiger's real name? It's Eldrick.

http://www.worldbook.com/fun/golf/html/golf.htm

PGA Junior Golf

Would you like to improve your golf game? What? You don't even have a golf game? This site, from the Professional Golfers' Association, will give you beginner tips and help you get started. You can also find out about junior events, as well as initiatives like The First Tee, which aims to develop small kid-friendly golf facilities. There's also a program called Clubs for Kids, which is an equipment source for kids who can't otherwise afford golf gear.

http://www.pga.com/juniors/

HIKING, ORIENTEERING, AND BACKPACKING

See also TREASURE AND TREASURE HUNTING

Appalachian Trail Conference

The Appalachian Trail stretches from Springer Mountain, Georgia, to Mount Katahdin, Maine—a distance of 2,167 miles. If you started at one end and walked it straight through, it would take you between four and six months before you emerged at the other end. This official site will tell you everything you need to know about planning for such a journey. There are also volunteer opportunities to help with trail maintenance.

http://www.atconf.org/

GORP - Hiking

Parental advisory: please preview this site. This site covers trails all over the world. You can find tips on hiking equipment, as well as a multimedia collection of links, books, and videos. You can read other hikers' stories of the trails they have traveled or check the jawboning in the discussion areas. There is also a very interesting section on historic routes, such as the Oregon Trail, the Santa Fe Trail, and others. Look in National Scenic Trails, and then click on National Historic Trails.

http://www.gorp.com/gorp/activity/hiking.htm

Geocaching—The Official GPS Stash Hunt Site

Is there any treasure near your house? Worldwide, geocache game players have hidden small waterproof boxes filled with inexpensive gadgets and goodies. On this page, they give sketchy directions and GPS readings to assist would-be treasure hunters. Be sure to bring an adult along to help, as well as a trinket of your own to trade. http://www.geocaching.com/

How to Use a Compass

On a hike, a compass will help you find your way, but first you have to learn to use one properly. You can learn in your own backyard, or in a park, or in a school playground. This site gives you a guided tour to a compass and its use. There are also tips on how to find your way in very difficult conditions, like fog or snow whiteouts.

http://www.uio.no/~kjetikj/compass/

Orienteering

Does this sound like fun? You and your friends use a very detailed map and a compass to visit various checkpoint flags hidden in the forest. When you reach a checkpoint, you use a special hole punch (usually hanging by the flag) to verify that you found the flag. The punches make differently shaped holes in your control card. This fast-growing sport can be enjoyed as a simple family walk in the woods or as a competitive team race. Learn about getting started in orienteering here, and don't miss the explanation of international control symbols. Remember: a big asterisk means look for an ANTHILL!

http://www.williams.edu/Biology/orienteering/

A
B
C
D
E
F
G
H
I
J
K
L
M
N
O
P
Q
R
S
T
U
V
W
X
Y
Z

Vertical alphabet tab down left margin: A B C D E F G H I J K L M N O P Q R S T U V W X Y Z

Pacific Crest Trail Association

It's 2,650 miles long, stretching from Mexico to Canada and winding through three Western states. The Pacific Crest Trail is described at this site, along with tips for those willing to commit to the 5–6-month transit time. About 200 hikers start the journey each year, but only about 50–60 make it the whole way. The rest drop out for various reasons.

http://www.pcta.org/

ROLLER AND INLINE SKATING
Rollerblade

This is a commercial site, developed by the Rollerblade company. It has lots of info on how to get started in rollerblading and catch up with your friends (or your parents, as the case may be). You'll learn about the scenes, the moves, the equipment, even the lingo. There's lots on safety, too, because "asphalt bites"!

http://www.rollerblade.com/

NET FILES

HERE IS THE SAME SOUND DESCRIBED IN SEVERAL LANGUAGES. WHAT SOUND IS IT?

Arabic (Algeria): *couak couak*

Chinese (Mandarin): *gua gua*

Finnish: *kvaak kvaak*

Japanese: *gaagaa*

Russian: *krya-krya*

Turkish: *vak, vak*

Answer: It's the sound of a duck quacking! Hear the duck for yourself and see what language you think says it best at http://www.georgetown.edu/cball/animals/duck.html

---

SKATEBOARDING

Birdhouse Skateboards

Hey! How'd he do that? What's it called? A Backside Popshuvit? Watch slow-motion, close-up QuickTime movies of nine different tricks. 'Course when you attempt these tricks, please wear a helmet and padding!

http://www.b-house.com/

Skateboard History

Back in the day, it was called "Sidewalk Surfing." In fact, duo Jan and Dean had a Top 40 hit song all about it. The boards were little more than narrow planks of wood with roller skate wheels attached below. They weren't very safe, and no one thought of wearing helmets and pads. What a long way we've come. For a look at just how far, read up on skateboarding history at this page.

http://www.discovery.com/stories/history/toys/SKATEBOARD/shoulda.html

Skateboard Science

Sometimes it seems like skateboarders are breaking the laws—of physics! But it turns out they are just using them to their advantage. See some video of skateboard pros in action, and hear an interview with a skateboard designer. Then discover the physics behind ollies, nolies, and kickflips, among other tricks.

http://www.exploratorium.edu/skateboarding/

PALMYRA ATOLL

See UNITED STATES—TERRITORIES

PEACE

Bully Advice for Kids

What makes a bully act that way? More important, what can you, the victim, do about bullies? Plenty. You don't have to just take the abuse, and you are not alone. Visit this site to learn more.

http://hometown.aol.com/kthynoll/advice.htm

Bullying.org

This site makes the point that when dealing with a bully, it's not your fault! In the stories section, you can share your own "bully" stories and read what's happened to other kids. The Help section of the site offers many links to information about bullies for both children and parents. Bullying must be taken seriously—and stopped.

http://www.bullying.org/

Department of Justice Kid's Page

Your parents want you to say grace and thank the Lord before you eat lunch at school; but when you do, the other kids make fun of you and call you names. What should you do? You could stop saying grace, you could sit somewhere else, or you could talk to an adult about it. Each one of these choices has other consequences; compare them and see which is the right decision for you. The Attorney General of the United States presents this page about racial, religious, and other types of prejudice. Learn to recognize, and then do something, about hateful acts like these, whether it happens to you or to someone else.

http://www.usdoj.gov/kidspage/kids.htm

★ Get Your Angries Out

Are you always yelling at your sister? Is there a bully bothering you at school? Are you mad and cranky a lot? This site gives you some useful ways to get your anger out in constructive ways. For example: "Check your tummy, jaws and your fists. See if the mads are coming. Breathe! Blow your mad out. Get your control. Feel good about getting your control. Stop and think; make a good choice. People are not to be hurt with your hands, feet or voice. Remember to use your firm words, not your fists." There are many more good ideas here, and don't forget to check the links about peace while you're dealing with your angries!

http://members.aol.com/AngriesOut/

National Youth Violence Prevention Resource Center

If you are afraid that someone in your school is going to commit a violent act, there's no better place to get informed about this growing problem than at this site. You'll find articles discussing the latest trends in teen violence. You'll also get tips on how to peacefully end disagreements. The dozens of links under each section are also worth investigating.

http://www.safeyouth.org/teens/

Out on a Limb: A Guide to Getting Along

It's easy to yell at your parents or friends or ignore them when they do something that hurts your feelings or makes you angry. But that's not the best way to deal with problems like that. You have to learn to get along, and that's what this site will help you do. The advice it gives will also help later as you become an adult. So, take it. You'll be a happier person.

http://www.urbanext.uiuc.edu/conflict/

Bring an umbrella, we're going to explore **WEATHER AND METEOROLOGY** resources!

A
B
C
D
E
F
G
H
I
J
K
L
M
N
O
P
Q
R
S
T
U
V
W
X
Y
Z

A
B
C
D
E
F
G
H
I
J
K
L
M
N
O
P
Q
R
S
T
U
V
W
X
Y
Z

Peace Corps Kids World

Peace Corps volunteers share their skills with others by giving two years of service. They help communities in developing countries, often by teaching people how to obtain a safe water supply and prevent the spread of diseases. At this site you'll learn about the goals and history of the Peace Corps, and play a game called Pack Your Bags to see how much you have learned. Check the Food, Friends, and Fun section to see what people eat in Nepal, Ecuador, and many other places. Even if you can't join the Peace Corps until you're older, there are plenty of ideas here to help you make a difference now, where you live.

http://www.peacecorps.gov/kids/

The Peace Pilgrim Home Page

How far would you walk for peace? Maybe around the block? A mile? Five miles? How about 25,000 miles? That's what Peace Pilgrim did. "From 1953 to 1981 a silver haired woman calling herself only 'Peace Pilgrim' walked more than 25,000 miles on a personal pilgrimage for peace. She vowed to 'remain a wanderer until mankind has learned the way of peace, walking until given shelter and fasting until given food.' In the course of 28 years of walking she touched the hearts, minds, and lives of thousands of individuals all across North America. Her message was both simple and profound: 'This is the way of peace: overcome evil with good, and falsehood with truth, and hatred with love.'" You can read about her life, her journey, and her message at this site. Since her death in 1981, others have taken up similar quests, and you can read their stories here.

http://www.peacepilgrim.com/

Peace Process 2001

Who were the peacemakers throughout history? What can we learn from them? How can we move forward into the twenty-first century and make sure it will be a peaceful millennium? View poems and drawings about peace, created by children throughout the world. This site was created by students for the ThinkQuest competition.

http://library.thinkquest.org/3078/

OPTICAL ILLUSIONS: now you see them, now you don't!

Planet Tolerance

Kids who believe in unity and justice are joining together to create the largest mural on the Web dedicated to these ideals. How can you participate? Draw a picture or write words about what "One World" means to you, and upload your creation. It will be added to the mural, which you can then search to find your contribution.

http://www.tolerance.org/pt/

The Sadako Peace Project

Sadako and the story of the thousand cranes has touched hearts worldwide. An old Japanese legend says that anyone who folds 1,000 origami cranes can have a wish. Sadako was a survivor of the atomic bomb attack on Hiroshima, Japan, in 1945. The radiation made her very ill, and she wished to be well again. Though she never gave up, she died before completing all her cranes. Her friends completed them, and they were buried with her. Sadako's courageous story is not forgotten. Her inspiring statue stands today in the Hiroshima Peace Park. The year 1995 marked 50 years of peace between the U.S. and Japan, and many people around the world decided to fold cranes and send them to the Peace Park to honor Sadako and her gentle message of peace. Read the story of how many children's hands made these cranes, which flutter today over the park of peace. Find out what new projects are planned, and what you can do to become involved. For still more places to send paper peace cranes, try <http://rosella.apana.org.au/~mlb/cranes/destinat.htm>.

http://www.sadako.org/

Tutu and Franklin: A Journey To Peace

Take an online step toward a more peaceful world. At this site, you're invited to talk honestly about your perceptions of people of color and learn how two great men confront racism and racial differences. See what misconceptions African and American teens had about each other. But first, take the peace and history quiz. It will show you where to continue your education on racial equality and human rights.

http://www.pbs.org/journeytopeace/

Values: Making Good Choices for Life

We all have things we value. It may be a toy, or something else, like our families. We also value other things: honesty, playing fair, and friendship are just a few of these. If you've never really considered what values drive you to make choices in life, visit this site. Experience a simulation involving a new student at school. How will you react? You make the call. This site was created by students for the ThinkQuest Junior competition.

http://library.thinkquest.org/J001709/

Who Ya Gonna Call? The Teasebusters!

Teasing is the PITS! When kids make fun of your clothes, your looks, or the way you talk, it says more about them than it does about you. According to this site, "Bill Cosby recommends repeating the word, 'So?' in response to teasing. That must drive the teaser crazy after a while!" Learn lots of tips from the Teasebusters.

http://www.faculty.fairfield.edu/fleitas/teasing2.html

You Can Handle Them All

Shhh! This is a special site just for teachers. It gives them tips on handling all sorts of problems in the classroom. Over 100 behaviors are identified, such as The Bully, The Spoiled Darling, and The Tattletale. There are also suggestions to help teachers understand what may be behind the child's actions, and also ways to help the child change. Pick up some teacher tips you can use too!

http://www.disciplinehelp.com/

Great Lakes and Seaway Shipping

Whether you are looking for information on the Soo Locks, ocean freighters, or Great Lakes shipwrecks, you'll find a whole cargo of information at this site. There's a very complete story about the *Edmund Fitzgerald* disaster, including haunting Real Audio radio transmissions reporting the wreck. Did you know fleet vessels can be identified by the markings on their stacks? There are illustrations of 30 different ones at *http://www.lre.usace.army.mil/shipping/glshhmpg.html*. Another cool thing to try is in the Vessel Passage section. Click there and choose Current Vessel Locations or Real Time Vessel Locations—Seaway. You can zoom in on ships and find out where they are from and where they are going. *http://www.boatnerd.com/*

PEN PALS

Education World®: Keypals and Pen pals

Please be very careful when writing to either pen pals (through the regular mail) or keypals (e-mail). While it's often rewarding and fun to write to a "pen friend," you must be aware that some dangers do exist. Sometimes people are not who they pretend to be. Often it is safest to use a classroom to classroom pen pal or keypal exchange. This site offers many resources to help you set up this type of program at school, or participate in one as an individual. Look for sites that require registration. Even though it is free, it does provide more assurance that messages can be tracked to their source, should trouble arise.

http://www.education-world.com/a_sites/
  sites008.shtml

A B C D E F G H I J K L M N O P Q R S T U V W X Y Z

A
B
C
D
E
F
G
H
I
J
K
L
M
N
O
P
Q
R
S
T
U
V
W
X
Y
Z

2GOOD 2MISS

Letterboxing North America

Unravel clues, and then take a hike to locate hidden plastic "letterboxes" containing only a logbook and a unique rubber stamp. Use it to mark your own travel journal, and then "sign" the guest book with your personal stamp. Instructions teach a nifty way to make one from an eraser or pieces of foot cushion foam. *http://www.letterboxing.org/*

★ ePals Classroom Exchange

Would your whole class or homeschool like to write to another class of kids on the other side of the world? You can, just by adding your information to the database here. Almost 50,000 other kids have! Search for kids by city, state, country, grade/age, or language. There are also some real-time password-protected chat facilities offered. Your class and your keypals can have a private chat room for free.

http://www.epals.com/

A Girl's World - Penpal Club

Here's the good news: this site lets you safely exchange e-mail with girls aged 7 to 17 from around the world. Here's the bad news, guys: the site is for girls only! (See Keypal Club below for a coed pen pal exchange.) This system takes your e-mail and remails it, giving you a member number instead. Your pen friend writes back to your box number, the computer at A Girl's World matches your box number with your real e-mail address, and—poof!—your e-mail arrives at your regular mailbox. It sounds a lot more complicated than it is. Read some of these girls' descriptions: they sound really interesting and fun to get to know.

http://www.agirlsworld.com/geri/penpal/

★ Keypals Club

A part of the safe, fun Keypals Club, this is a good place to learn about others and the world around you as you practice the art of writing. If you're a student looking for keypals or a teacher looking for a classroom-to-classroom project, fill out a form with information about yourself, click a button, and ZAP! you've just joined the group. Well, almost zap. If you're a student, you do need parental permission. This site acts as a remailer and does not divulge your e-mail address.

http://www.teaching.com/keypals/

★ Penpal Box

Part of Net-mom's favorite site, Kids' Space, the Penpal Box offers kids aged 6 to 16 the opportunity to have an e-mail friend. Actually, there is more than one box: look through the box for six and under, the box for ages seven and eight, the one for nine and ten, and so on. There's also a box for classes that want to exchange e-mail. Remember to read the FAQ for safety tips, and remember not to give your home address to anyone.

http://www.ks-connection.org/penpal/penpal.html

PEOPLE AND BIOGRAPHIES

See also AFRICAN AMERICANS; ASIAN AMERICANS; INVENTIONS AND INVENTORS; LATINO, LATINA, HISPANIC AMERICANS; NATIVE AMERICANS AND FIRST NATIONS; QUEENS, KINGS, AND ROYALTY; REFERENCE WORKS; and UNITED STATES—PRESIDENTS AND FIRST LADIES

Stick to the beekeeping sites in FARMING AND AGRICULTURE, honey.

BBC Education - Centurions

Who are the century's greatest creative thinkers and doers? This site lists the 100 most significant writers, painters, architects, filmmakers, designers, sculptors, and poets of the twentieth century. The eclectic collection includes Francis Bacon, the Marx Brothers, Henri Matisse, and Arthur Miller. Get a glimpse into their lives and then see if you can ace the quiz.

http://www.bbc.co.uk/history/programmes/
centurions/

Biography.com

Got a name? Get the facts! Here's a searchable online database from A&E TV. Discover the who, what, and why of 25,000 of the greatest names, past and present. Find out about the "Top Ten Bios," and then take the biography quiz. There are also some neat features on entertainers and titans of technology.

http://www.biography.com/

Britannica's Lives

Ever wonder who shares your birthday? Sure, it might be your mom or your dad or even your twin brother. But was anyone famous born on your birthday? (Besides you, of course!) Find out at this useful site.

http://www.eb.com/bol/lives?

Famous Immigrants

Did you know that fashion designer Liz Claiborne was originally from Belgium? Sammy Sosa, the baseball player, was an immigrant to the United States from the Dominican Republic. Even Captain Kirk (William Shatner) is from Canada. Find out about more famous immigrants here.

http://www.wiltonlibrary.org/ya/school/
immigrants.htm

Gauche! Left-Handers in Society

Bill Clinton is one. So is Queen Elizabeth II. Paul McCartney. Phil Collins. Larry Bird. For somewhere between 2 percent and 30 percent of the world's population, life is challenging because it seems like everything is being done backward! This site will help all lefties to better understand "handedness." Also, solutions are provided for dealing with common everyday activities. Want to know who else is a famous lefty? Try <http://www.indiana.edu/~primate/left.html>.

http://www.indiana.edu/~primate/lspeak.html

HyperHistory Online

This site will teach you about important people from 1000 B.C. to the present. You'll find scientists, artists, musicians, authors, politicians, explorers, and many others. But that is not all: you can also trace events through history, as well as look at important maps of time periods and the spread of civilizations.

http://www.hyperhistory.com/online_n2/History_n2/
a.html

Lives, the Biography Resource

You won't find any "fan pages," but you will find links and pointers to biographies and primary source material such as photographs, memoirs, diaries, and interviews. Search by time period, profession, or region. There are also special collections on Canadians, women, African Americans, the Holocaust, the Civil War, and other topics.

http://amillionlives.com/

Man of the Year

Need biographies of famous people? Cruise over to this page for information about the man, woman, or idea considered by TIME magazine to be the biggest influence on events each year from 1997 back to 1927. In 1982, the computer was "Man of the Year." Check <http://www.time.com/time/time100/> for the 100 most important people of the twentieth century. Who was selected as Person of the Century? It was Albert Einstein. Learn about him here.

http://www.pathfinder.com/time/special/moy/
moy.html

A
B
C
D
E
F
G
H
I
J
K
L
M
N
O
P
Q
R
S
T
U
V
W
X
Y
Z

Zamboni

OK, hands in the air: how many of you really have the secret fantasy of driving the Zamboni around the ice rink? You know, that big machine that magically lays down a new layer of smooth ice for you and your friends to skate on. Net-mom usually plays "Slamboni" instead, at *http://www.sikids.com/ games/slamboni/slam_index.html*, but now she has discovered the official Zamboni site. You can learn the history of the company (they celebrated their 50th birthday in 1999), buy some cool Zamboni merchandise (including the fabulous "Zamboni Crossing" sign), and check out the trivia. For example, did you know that the top speed of a Zamboni ice resurfacing machine is 9 mph? There's also a neat diagram of how the machine actually works. *http://www.zamboni.com/*

BOYS

We regret we have not been able to locate suitable "boy empowerment" sites. Son of Net-mom is particularly annoyed by this turn of events. If you discover a great resource, please write and let us know!

GIRLS
Club Girl Tech

Did you ever hear of that sneaky but inept criminal Carmen Sandiego? Did you ever play with a Yak-back recording toy? If so, you're already acquainted with the inventor of this Web site. The site celebrates creative girls who like to think, whether it's about science or celebrities. There's also a fascinating section on women inventors.

http://www.girltech.com/Index_home.html

Girl Power!

You'll know you've got Girl Power after you visit this page! It offers activities, features, role models, and lots more. It's from the Department of Health and Human Services, and its mission is "to help encourage and empower 9- to 14-year-old girls to make the most of their lives." That means there are lots of fun things to do here, and important things to think and dream about.

http://www.health.org/gpower/

A Girl's World Online Clubhouse

Looking for the space that's totally girl-powered? Explore a "girls-only" clubhouse, find a pen pal (your e-mail address is kept private), see stories about famous women, and have all sorts of fun. You'll also find crafts, links, and even peeks into the diaries of other girls like you!

http://www.agirlsworld.com/

★ GirlSite

"Think you can't make a difference? Think again." This site launches you from your dreams into a real career. Learn about the planet, make some girl gear, explore your personal well-being, and join the club to participate in safe chat with other smart, funny girls like yourself!

http://www.girlsite.com/

PIRATES
Pirates!

Parental advisory: please preview this site. What's the story with pirates, anyway? Did they really act the way they do in the movies and in books? Compare the legend to the hard facts in this close-up look at pirates, their history, ships, customs, and lots more.

http://www.piratesinfo.com/

★ Pirates! @ Nationalgeographic.com

Can you solve these National Geographic adventures? You'll have to read clues and figure out which pirate, which ship, and which treasure star in each of the mysteries. Beware: if you get it wrong, you may have to walk the virtual plank and start all over again! There are also links to additional materials, books, and links about pirates.

http://www.nationalgeographic.com/features/97/
pirates/maina.html

WOMEN

Anne Frank House

Parental warning: there are several grim photos of concentration camps in one section of this resource. In 1942, 13-year-old Anne Frank and her family went into hiding in a house in Amsterdam. They were Jews, fleeing from Nazi terrorism. During her 24-month stay in "the Secret Annex," Anne kept a diary of her thoughts and ambitions. Ultimately, the secret hideout was discovered and Anne was captured; she later died at the age of 16. Her legacy remains. Her diary was published by her father, who survived the concentration camp experience. The diary has been translated into many languages and has sold millions of copies around the world. This site has photos of the Anne Frank House, as well as pictures of the original diary. See another Anne Frank site in the HISTORY—WORLD HISTORY—WORLD WAR II section of this book.

http://www.annefrank.nl/

Distinguished Women of Past and Present

The biographies of women writers, educators, scientists, heads of state, politicians, civil rights crusaders, artists, entertainers, and more are listed at this site. Some were alive hundreds of years ago and some are living today. Some are famous, and some are not as well known. No matter—their stories are interesting and would be a real plus for a school writing project. They're listed by name, as well as field of activity, so it is easy to find women in journalism, or architecture, or sports, or any other topic in which you're interested.

http://www.DistinguishedWomen.com/

The National Women's Hall of Fame

"Come Stand Among Great Women." That's the motto of the official home page of the National Women's Hall of Fame, which is located in Seneca Falls, New York. That town was the site of the first Women's Rights Convention, back in 1848. The convention led to the passage of the 19th Amendment to the Constitution, which granted U.S. women the right to vote. Visit this site to learn about women who have been inducted into the Hall of Fame. They include Sandra Day O'Connor, Ella Fitzgerald, Georgia O'Keeffe, Rosa Parks, and many others.

http://www.greatwomen.org/

The National Women's History Project

Let's celebrate! That's what the National Women's History Project is all about. It celebrates women's diverse lives and historic contributions to society. The background of Women's History Month (in March) is here, along with links to each of the states showcasing their activities. Here's one quick question from the Test Your Knowledge section. Name the First Lady who traveled the country and the world to gather information about the problems and concerns of workers, children, minorities, and the poor. She wrote a daily newspaper column and made frequent radio broadcasts. Time's up. Did you guess Eleanor Roosevelt? If you did, head to the quiz for more interesting questions. If you didn't guess right, go there anyway. You've got a lot to learn.

http://www.nwhp.org/

Not For Ourselves Alone: The Story of Elizabeth Cady Stanton and Susan B. Anthony

Explore the history of the women's rights movement in the United States through the lives of Elizabeth Cady Stanton and Susan B. Anthony, two of its early foremothers. Examine key events in the suffrage movement; delve into historic documents and essays. You can also find out where women stand today at this multimedia site from PBS.

http://www.pbs.org/stantonanthony/

A
B
C
D
E
F
G
H
I
J
K
L
M
N
O
P
Q
R
S
T
U
V
W
X
Y
Z

A
B
C
D
E
F
G
H
I
J
K
L
M
N
O
P
Q
R
S
T
U
V
W
X
Y
Z

Places Where Women Made History

This site takes you on a tour of New York and Massachusetts, stopping at famous women's homes and sites where history took place. You'll visit the tranquil garden pond at poet Edna St. Vincent Millay's home, Steepletop. And you'll see the infamous Triangle Shirtwaist Factory, scene of a devastating fire in 1911, fatal to 146 sweatshop garment workers, most of them women. Should you want to visit any of these sites in person, you'll find information about that, too.

http://www.cr.nps.gov/nr/travel/pwwmh/

★ The Quest Beyond the Pink Collar

Explore a time line of famous women throughout history. Take a closer look at portrayals of women in the media, and find out how unrealistic images of beauty may help to foster a psychological disorder called anorexia nervosa. There's a biography of Karen Carpenter, who died of its complications. Try the activity in Know Thyself to get closer to your best friend: yourself! There's also a great section on nontraditional careers for women, and much more. This site was created by students for the ThinkQuest competition.

http://library.thinkquest.org/21298/

NET FILES

If you took all the salt out of the ocean and piled it up on land, how much would you have?

Answer: According to the U.S. Geologic Survey, 50 quadrillion (50 million billion) tons of dissolved salts are in the sea. If you could get them out, the resulting pile would form a layer more than 500 feet thick, or about the height of a 40-story office building! Read why the ocean is salty at *http://oceanography.palomar.edu/salty_ocean.htm*

Become one with the Net.

★ The Quest for Equality: Women's History

Meet women trailblazers and pioneers in science, the arts, aviation, politics, education, sports, and other fields. Learn about the struggle for equality in the 1700s and 1800s as women sought the right to become full citizens and vote. More recent movements sought equity in employment opportunities and wages. This excellent site is presented by *World Book* encyclopedia.

http://www.worldbook.com/fun/whm/home.html

★ Victorian Women

Pick a door, any door, and the animated Victorian lady will knock on it. You'll get a question about women's rights in the reign of Queen Victoria of England. You'll be asked about when women won, for example, the right to get a job, earn a college degree, vote, and keep their children after a divorce. The answers may surprise you! This is a fun game that's reinforced with a summary at the end.

http://www.bbc.co.uk/history/games/
victorian_women/

Women in American History

This *Encyclopedia Britannica* collection covers famous American women in four time periods: Early America, the Nineteenth Century, At the Crossroads, and Modern America. It is presented in a time line beginning in 1587, with the birth of Virginia Dare, the first child in America born of English parents. It ends with the opening of a contemporary museum dedicated to the works of Georgia O'Keeffe in Santa Fe, New Mexico. Many of the items in the time line have links to more information about the woman or the event.

http://women.eb.com/women/

Women in Canadian History

Many women played important parts in Canada's history. Dr. Emily Jennings Stowe was the first woman to practice medicine in Canada. Lucy Maud Montgomery became known worldwide as the author of *Anne of Green Gables* and other books. Madeleine Jarrett Tarieu single-handedly defended an entire fort against invaders. And there are others. The stories here are very interesting!

http://www.niagara.com/~merrwill/

Women Mathematicians

These pages are an ongoing project by students at Agnes Scott College in Decatur, Georgia. You'll find brief comments on over 140 women in mathematics, and expanded biographies, photos, and more information on at least ten of them. There are also extensive links to pages about women scientists, computer scientists, and others.

http://www.agnesscott.edu/lriddle/women/women.htm

PETS AND PET CARE

See also AMPHIBIANS; ANIMALS; AQUARIUMS; BIRDS; CATS; DOGS AND DOG SPORTS; FARMING AND AGRICULTURE; FISH; HORSES AND EQUESTRIAN SPORTS; INSECTS AND SPIDERS; MAMMALS; REPTILES

The American Animal Hospital Association's Healthypet Page

The American Animal Hospital Association's pages include frequently asked questions on many types of pets, from birds to dogs, from felines to ferrets. There are also coloring book pages, as well as a pet care library. If you own a pet or are thinking of getting one, the advice here is a must-see.

http://www.healthypet.com/

AVMA Care for Pets

The American Veterinary Medical Association offers a super page on selecting a pet—and selecting a veterinarian to take care of it. Included are sections on dogs, cats, horses, and general pet information. Learn how to keep your pet healthy, discover the best way to travel with your pet, and pick up some safety tips on how to behave around animals. There's also a very sensitive section on how to know when it's time to say good-bye to your pet and how to handle the sadness that comes after that decision is made.

http://www.avma.org/care4pets/

Bow Wow Meow - Need a Perfect Name for a New Pet?

Here you'll find names for all kinds of pets. Search for names by letter, gender, or category (or "dog"egory). Find out what the most popular names are, and read why you might not want to name your dog Joe.

http://www.bowwow.com.au/

★ Classroom Animals and Pets

Go way beyond the typical classroom guppy tank and find out why millipedes, twig insects, and snails make fabulous pets. Learn their housing and feeding needs, as well as what you will learn from watching these unusual creatures. There are also tips for the goldfish tank, as well as other more common animals.

http://www.teacherwebshelf.com/classroompets

Kyler Laird's Animal Rescue Resources

If you want a particular breed of dog, but can't afford a puppy, you might try to adopt an older dog that has been "rescued" from an animal shelter or given up for adoption by its owner. There's a rescue club for most breeds; you'll find a list of them at this site. If none seem to be nearby, try contacting a distant one anyway; dog people usually have a network of other dog people who are willing to help dogs find great homes. This site lists rescue organizations for cats, birds, horses, rabbits, and other animals.

http://www.ecn.purdue.edu/~laird/animal_rescue/

A B C D E F G H I J K L M N O P Q R S T U V W X Y Z

A
B
C
D
E
F
G
H
I
J
K
L
M
N
O
P
Q
R
S
T
U
V
W
X
Y
Z

★ Petfinder

This amazing site coordinates the availability of pets for adoption at U.S. animal shelters or rescue organizations. You can search for information about pets in your home town or across the country. Narrow your search by type of animal (dog, cat, bird, pig, horse, and more), breed, age, gender, or size. There are also terrific discussion forums for everything from emergency rescue needs to lost and found pets.

http://web2.petfinder.org/

INSTANT PETS

Sea-Monkey Central

It's "Instant Life"—it's "Sea-Monkeys"—it's a great marketing gimmick! Take the lowly brine shrimp (also known as live fish food) and develop a foolproof way to raise herds of them in a tiny plastic "zoo" aquarium. Advertise in the backs of comic books and sell the little critter eggs for a really cheap price. Everything you'd ever want to know about these fun but tiny pets is here, including terrible jokes, such as this one: Question: What do you call a Sea-Monkey tank that's been spilled on your sister's favorite doll? Answer: Shrimp on the Barbie.

http://www.sea-monkey.com/

The Florida State Fire College Kids Site

Follow Li'l Boots into the firehouse as he explains the features and uses of various kinds of firefighting vehicles, including pumpers, ladder and aerial trucks, and special-use equipment. How has fighting fires changed over the years? Find out at this site. Don't miss the Home Hazard Hunt. If you can locate all the hazards, you get to print a cool certificate. *http://www.fsfckids.ufl.edu/*

The Triops Information Page

Which one is better: the little horseshoe crab-like triops, or the ever popular brine shrimplike Sea-Monkey (see previous entry)? Compare and contrast these weird little creatures and decide for yourself. Here at Pollywood Farm we did raise a nice flock of triops about a year back. They were a whole lot of fun, so now we're going to try some Sea-Monkeys, too.

http://www.uakron.edu/biology/triops.html

VIRTUAL PETS

★ SwineOnline

Now don't get too attached to your little virtual piglet. You only have about a week to raise him to a hog; and at the end of the week, well, he'll either win a ribbon or wind up as pork chops. Think of this more as a game of luck, strategy, and fun. Can you beat out the other farmers and get high score of the week? Be sure to take really good care of your pig (he'll e-mail you if he's not happy). New games start every week.

http://www.swineonline.com/

PHILOSOPHY

"Here, Madam": An Exploration of Inspiration

Philosophy means "love of wisdom," and it deals with the basic questions of life: what is truth, what is our purpose on earth, what is beauty, and other puzzles. There have been many famous philosophers through time, starting with Greeks such as Sophocles and Plato. Other notable deep thinkers include Kant and Nietzsche. Meet them all here and learn about their answers to some of these questions. Other parts of the site explain the five main divisions of philosophy: metaphysics, epistemology, logic, aesthetics, and ethics. You'll get an overview of each one. This site was created by students for the ThinkQuest competition.

http://library.thinkquest.org/3075/frames.htm

PHOTOGRAPHY

★ Eastman Kodak Company

You would expect Kodak to have an active home page, and they do indeed. You can find all sorts of valuable information on photography here, whether your interests lie in producing professional-quality photographs or simple snapshots. One example is the Taking Great Pictures section featuring the Top Ten Techniques for photographers to take and make good pictures <http://www.kodak.com/US/en/ nav/ takingPics.shtml>. You'll also find advice for preserving family albums there. A new section allows you to upload pictures from your computer and manipulate them so it looks like your mom's coming out of a flower and your little brother is an ape. It's in the Picture Playground section—check it out.

Http://www.kodak.com/

★ Exposure - A Beginner's Guide to Photography

Photography—is it technology or magic? Even if you have a nonadjustable camera, you can try some of these tips and tricks to jazz up your photos. If you do have a camera with a lot of controls on it, you can really change how the picture looks. You can learn how to set the camera so that the background blurs out of focus. This puts more emphasis on your main subjects in the foreground of the picture. On the other hand, you might want to make sure that as much of the scene as possible stays in focus. There is a special way to set the camera for that, too. You can try it all using Sim-Cam, a way-cool applet that will teach you the mysteries of f-stops and aperture by letting you set a virtual camera, take a picture, and see immediate results!

Http://www.88.com/exposure/lowrez_i.htm

Expect a miracle in RELIGION AND SPIRITUALITY!

George Eastman House

Explore the history of photography and view some very interesting early cameras and photographic experiments. George Eastman was the founder of the Eastman Kodak company. This site also contains a tour of his house and gardens in Rochester, New York, which has been preserved as a photographic museum.

http://www.eastman.org/

Konica

Have you always wondered how film is made? Here's a clue: it's made in the dark! At this site, you can take a virtual factory tour and see the steps of its manufacture. There's a nice little introduction to color photography and lots of tips and tutorials from Konica.

http://www.konica.co.jp/english/e_menu.html

Make a Color Photograph

Take two black-and-white photographs. Expose one with a green filter, and the other with a red filter. The result: a color photograph. This online activity demonstrates that process, which is similar to that used by Eastman Kodak's original Kodachrome. That two-step film developing process is now outdated. But modern film developing relies on the same principles.

http://www.pbs.org/wgbh/amex/eastman/sfeature/ color_kodachrome.html

Oatmeal Box Pinhole Photography by Stewart Lewis Woodruff

Shhh . . . don't tell the manufacturers of expensive photographic equipment: you can make pictures using an old oatmeal box. This page provides step-by-step detailed instructions on how to make a pinhole camera, load it with paper film, develop the film, and make prints. Just remember to eat the oatmeal first. By the way, Kodak offers its own pinhole camera, film, and processing page <http://www.kodak.com/global/en/consumer/ education/lessonPlans/pinholeCamera/>.

http://www.nh.ultranet.com/~stewoody/

A
B
C
D
E
F
G
H
I
J
K
L
M
N
O
P
Q
R
S
T
U
V
W
X
Y
Z

A
B
C
D
E
F
G
H
I
J
K
L
M
N
O
P
Q
R
S
T
U
V
W
X
Y
Z

StudyWorks! Online: Photography: Composition

Point an automatic camera and press the button. It's just that easy. Or is it? Today's cameras may be easy to use, but it doesn't guarantee a well-composed picture. For that, it helps to understand some of the techniques for taking good pictures. This site promises to help you do that. You'll learn about the math, science, lighting, art, and technology that have given rise to modern photography. Most of this material focuses on 35mm photography, but other formats are also explored.

http://www.studyworksonline.com/cda/content/ explorations/0,1035,NAV2-6_SEP16,00.html

PHYSICS

See also COLOR AND COLORING BOOKS; ENERGY; ENGINEERING; INVENTIONS AND INVENTORS; SCIENCE—EXPERIMENTS; SCIENCE—SCIENCE FAIRS; and WHY

Einstein - Image and Impact

Lots of people think Albert Einstein was the greatest physicist ever. His famous theory of relativity includes the equation $E = mc^2$. He even had an element named after him! Einsteinium, element 99, was discovered in 1952. Einstein won the Nobel Prize for physics in 1921. Although he urged President Roosevelt to consider making an atomic bomb (the letter is at this site), he believed in peace. This site is presented by the American Institute of Physics.

Http://www.aip.org/history/einstein/

Do you know the way to San Jose? If not, check a map in GEOGRAPHY.

★ Internet Plasma Physics Education

If you want the latest info on nuclear fusion as an energy source, visit this site, where you'll learn about magnetism, matter, electricity, and lots more. One of the unusual interactive experiences you can try is the Virtual Tokamak. (That's a new word made from the Russian words *toroid-kamera-magnit-katushka*, meaning "the toroidal chamber and magnetic coil.") Basically, it's a containment device to keep the fusion reaction and the plasma safely buttoned up. That's good, because the plasma is hotter than the core of the sun. (Don't try to build one of these at home!)

http://ippex.pppl.gov/ippex/

★ Miami Museum of Science - The Atoms Family

How many times can you cut a 28-centimeter piece of paper in half? If you could do it 31 times, that would be the size of one atom! Most people can't get beyond cutting 10 times, but go ahead, give it a shot. The directions are here. This wonderful site leads you through the rather odd world of the Atoms Family: Frankenstein's Lightning Lab, Dracula's Library (he wants to read all he can about light, so he can avoid it, we guess), and the Phantom's Portrait Parlor (matter, atoms, that paper cutting activity, and molecules).

http://www.miamisci.org/af/sln/

Multimedia Physics Studios

Even little kids will understand Newton's Laws of Motion when they see these animated GIF images. There's a detailed explanation if you have to know the science behind the illustration. Other physics principles demonstrated are work and energy, momentum and collisions, and many more.

http://www.glenbrook.k12.il.us/gbssci/phys/mmedia/

★ Physics 2000

Featuring a neat collection of Java applets, this site lets you interact with polarized lenses, virtual marshmallows in a microwave, brightness controls on a TV screen, and many more demonstrations.

http://www.colorado.edu/physics/2000/

ELECTRICITY

AC/DC: What's the Difference?

AC/DC. What does it stand for? A rock group? A form of electricity? Answer: Both. But this site is not about the rock group. Instead, it's a simple explanation that shows the difference between AC, which stands for alternating current, and DC, or direct current. To find out more about electric currents, and two ways that the currents can be produced, check the interactive illustration.

http://www.pbs.org/wgbh/amex/edison/sfeature/acdc.html

Cleco: Fun and Educational Electric Information

Follow the path of electricity from the power plant to town, to your neighborhood, to your house, and finally to your room lights. Learn some very cool facts about electricity, its early history, and important inventors. Be sure to visit the safety zone to discover how to be safe around electricity in the bathroom, kitchen, and outside.

http://209.141.118.23/

The Electric Club

You'll want to visit this site to check out a great list of neat experiments to try, like creating lemon power. We know that the news may be shocking, but it's true: you can make a lightbulb light using lemons as the source of energy. There is another experiment called "charge it," which uses a comb, some bits of paper, and a head of hair (not a credit card)!

http://www.schoolnet.ca/general/club-electrique/e/

Electricity Around the World

Although the general principles of electricity are the same everywhere, electrical plugs and voltages are different all over the world. If there's foreign travel in your future, check this site first to discover what type of converter plugs you'll need so you can use your stuff. Even if you're not going on a trip, you'll be interested in the great variety of wall plugs you'll see here.

http://kropla.com/electric2.htm

NET FILES

Besides a state bird, a state tree, and a state flower, Wyoming has a state dinosaur—which one is it?

Answer: The triceratops. More Wyoming dinosaurs may be found at http://www.trib.com/WYOMING/dino.shtml

Electricity Online

Explore the history and properties of electricity at this award-winning ThinkQuest site. There's a lot to learn about magnetism, electrochemistry, and electronics. Don't miss the resistor calculator applet.

http://library.thinkquest.org/28032/

★ The Internet Guide to Electronics

Do you know the difference between a parallel electrical circuit and one that is in series? You will within moments of opening this Web page and clicking on Theory. It's a real beginner's guide to the topic and includes many illustrations and clear explanations. There are also some cool calculators for Ohm's law and yet another type of resistor calculator, plus a guide to multimeter use and a handy chart of schematic symbols.

http://webhome.idirect.com/~jadams/electronics/

A
B
C
D
E
F
G
H
I
J
K
L
M
N
O
P
Q
R
S
T
U
V
W
X
Y
Z

Internet Anangram Server

Do you know what an anagram is? Take all the letters in a word or phrase, scramble them, and come up with a new word or phrase! For example, "Inert Net Grave Near Mars" is an anagram for "Internet Anagram Server." Type in ten or less letters and see what mysterious phrase you'll get.
http://www.wordsmith.org/anagram/

The Shocking Truth About Electricity

How much do you depend on electricity? It powers your alarm clock, your hair dryer, your TV, and your lights. It may also make your water hot, cook your food, and wash your clothes. Did you ever wonder where electricity comes from? What's the deal with watts, anyway? Find out at this site, created by students for the ThinkQuest Junior competition.

http://tqjunior.thinkquest.org/6064/

Theater of Electricity

Scientists who need a lot of static electricity for an experiment use a Van de Graaff generator, which makes electricity from a revolving belt inside one of its towers. Read about its history and construction, and all about lightning and electricity. You can see the huge original generator, built by Dr. Robert J. Van de Graaff, in the Theater of Electricity at the Museum of Science in Cambridge, Massachusetts, and on this Web site. You probably won't have a generator like this at home, but at this site you'll find some experiments you can do with balloons, paper bunnies, and static electricity.

http://www.mos.org/sln/toe/toe.html

EXPERIMENTS
★ Little Shop of Physics

Welcome to the Little Shop of Physics: nothing here will harm you (well, you might want to stay away from that disreputable-looking plant over in the corner!). They have concocted some interesting demonstrations using everyday objects that might amuse you and teach you something about physics. There are optical and auditory illusions, plus lots of special effects you can try right on your computer screen. Come closer!

http://littleshop.physics.colostate.edu/

Physics Experiments You Can Do at Home

How quickly do you react when someone throws you a ball or when a book drops from a table? Reaction time is one of several home experiments you can try, developed by a University of Wisconsin professor as part of a program he calls Wonders of Physics. Learn about the Doppler effect, take a "random walk," or try a vortex experiment. You'll soon be discovering lots of interesting new things.

http://scifun.chem.wisc.edu/WOP/HomeExpPhys.html

FORCES
★ Amusement Park Physics

As your free-fall car rises to the top of the drop, you think, "I hope the designer of this ride got an 'A' in physics." As you practice your driving skills on the bumper cars, do you ever take time to thank Newton's third law of motion? Learn the physics behind many popular rides, and you'll never look at an amusement park the same way again.

http://www.learner.org/exhibits/parkphysics/

Bad Coriolis

Does draining water really turn one way in the northern hemisphere and the opposite way in the southern hemisphere? You'll learn a lot about Coriolis force science—good and bad—at this site. Also, check how you can fake out your class into believing the equator runs right through your classroom.

http://www.ems.psu.edu/~fraser/Bad/BadCoriolis.html

A B C D E F G H I J K L M N O P Q R S T U V W X Y Z

Not everything on the Net is true.

★ From Apples to Orbits: The Gravity Story

Here are some weighty questions. What is gravity? Was it really "discovered" when an apple hit Isaac Newton on the head? What are the large and small scale effects of gravity, and can anything be done about it? Maybe. Head to the lab and try some of the simulations. Some of them are out of this world. This site was created by students for the ThinkQuest competition.

http://library.thinkquest.org/27585/

★ Funderstanding Roller Coaster

Only on the Internet can you play roller coaster designer with no lives at stake! You see, there are two hills and a loop in this prototype thrill ride. Your mission is to pick the right degree of forces to get the car from the beginning all the way to the end—without getting embarrassingly stuck part-way through. If you can meet that challenge, try changing the shape of the hills.

http://www.funderstanding.com/k12/coaster/

★ Interactive Physics Modules

Learn all about the properties of matter and the differences among atoms, ions, elements, and molecules. Once you've got all that straight, check the section on Electricity and Magnetism. Watch animations and participate in interactive experiments—rub a balloon across a virtual wool sweater, and then see if you can make it cling to the virtual wall. That's static electricity. There are many other things to try in this engaging resource. But be careful—you might learn something about physics before you know it!

http://ippex.pppl.gov/ippex/PhysicsModules.html

Magnetism

What's the attraction? Magnetism helps us find our way with a compass. It's what makes electric motors run. Did you know it's also responsible for the northern lights—the aurora borealis? Read about the history of magnetism and how it works. Drawings show how magnetic fields are made up of invisible field lines. There are also facts about the contributions of Michael Faraday and James Maxwell to the field of magnetism. May the force be with you!

http://www-spof.gsfc.nasa.gov/Education/Imagnet.html

The Science Behind a Home Run

Time to grab a bag of peanuts, crank up the radio or TV, and listen to the sweet sound of the baseball bat against the ball as another one flies out of the park. Did you ever wonder how a person holding a narrow wooden bat could hit a baseball so hard that it could fly several hundred feet? It happens every day all across the country during the baseball season, and now you can read how physics and forces make it all happen. Remember the magic words "viscosity" and "density," take a gulp of fresh air, and read on.

http://www.exploratorium.edu/learning_studio/news/september97.html

NET FILES

How many people are on Earth?

Answer: Quite a few—over six billion! For the latest estimate, check the world population clock at http://www.census.gov/cgi-bin/ipc/popclockw/

Soap Bubbles

Have you ever noticed that bubbles are always round, no matter what shape the wand you blow through is? Is that because your breath is shaped like a circle as it comes out of your lips? No. A bubble is round because of physical forces you can learn about here. You'll also learn that when a bubble looks gray or black, it is about to pop. Why does it lose its pretty colors? Find out at this site, and don't miss the Internet Resources section for more good, clean fun.

http://www.exploratorium.edu/ronh/bubbles/
   bubbles.html

Toys in Space

In 1993, the space shuttle *Endeavor* took off with an interesting payload: a high-tech communications satellite and a chest full of toys! The idea was to see how the familiar toys performed in orbit, without the force of gravity. This site compares normal Earth operation of the toys with the orbit results. You'll be very surprised.

http://observe.ivv.nasa.gov/nasa/exhibits/toys_space/
   toyframe.html

WaterWorks

Oh, the magic of water fountains. Some are tall, some are wide, and others squirt in many directions at once. Discover what makes a fountain work and the forces it takes to make water do its tricks. Pictures of different types of fountains are shown, along with some that were made by students. There are even movies and sounds of the different fountains available. (Caution: The files are big!)

http://www.omsi.edu/explore/physics/ww/

LASERS
Holography, Lasers, and Holograms

Lasers can do some pretty amazing things. Did you know they are used to make interesting 3-D pictures that allow you to "look inside" and see around objects? That's called holography. Although lasers are needed to make a hologram, you don't need a laser to view one. Think it's all too complicated? Not at the HoloKids area!

http://www.holoworld.com/

Laserium

The word "laser" is really an acronym, that stands for "light amplification by the stimulated emission of radiation." Lasers are used in many scientific and medical applications, but everyone agrees the most fun you can have with lasers is at a "laserium" show. Often held in planetarium buildings and performed to music, the laserist is a true artist, as he or she "plays" the laser controls to draw fabulous light effects on the domed ceiling. This page tells about the history of laser shows and explains the science behind the vibrant colors overhead.

http://www.laserium.com/

★ Overview of the Lasers Site

How many lasers do you think you encounter in a day? Go to the checkout line at the grocery store: lasers read the prices coded on those zebra-striped labels. Climb into the car and crank up some tunes on the CD player—lasers again. Every CD player has a tiny laser in it to read the digital code on the CD. Visit this site for more close encounters of the laser kind.

http://www.thetech.org/hyper/lasers/overview.html

LIGHT
Bob Miller's Light Walk

This site will really illuminate your knowledge of light and shadow. In fact, it's a bright idea to check it out if you have a science fair project due, since there are project directions for building your own pinhole camera, making your own "light walk," and performing more tricks of light. You'll find a whole spectrum of stuff here and a fascinating look into shadows. Don't be scared, just lighten up!

http://www.exploratorium.edu/light_walk/
   lw_main.html

NOVA Online/Einstein Revealed

What would happen if you could travel at the speed of light? Einstein had his own theories, now you can formulate your own, based on the Time Traveler game at this site.

http://www.pbs.org/wgbh/nova/einstein/

Optics for Kids

Why should we care about controlling light, anyway? It's pretty important when you consider how your own eyes work. It's also critical for eyeglasses, binoculars, telescopes, microscopes, even CD players. They all work by controlling light in various ways. Learn about the optics of reflection and refraction at this site. There's also a nice section on how lasers work.

http://www.opticalres.com/kidoptx.html

The Science of Light

This site will shed some light on . . . light. Without it, information from the world could not be carried to our eyes and brains. We wouldn't be able to see color, shapes, or shadows. While there's plenty on this site to read, head for the activities. One of them answers some questions about Fun House mirrors. What makes you tall in one and look short in another?

http://www.learner.org/teacherslab/science/light/

MACHINES

BrainPOP: Simple Machines

Ramps and levers are two examples of simple machines. 'Nuff said. Not quite. How do they work? Where can you find them? How difficult are they to use? Do you know the answers? Tim and his sidekick Moby the Robot do, and they'll tell you if you play the movie. If you do know the answers, you can jump ahead and take the quiz. It's just that simple.

http://www.brainpop.com/tech/simplemachines/

Simple Machines

Did you ever think of a wedge—or a screw—as a simple machine? What about a pulley? A simple machine is a tool to make the work of a job easier. You can even try some demonstrations that will prove how machines help make life easier.

http://www.fi.edu/qa97/spotlight3/spotlight3.html

Life Beyond Earth

"Absence of evidence isn't evidence of absence" says this Web site. That means just because we haven't found any proof of extraterrestrial life, it doesn't mean that none exists. "Drive" along a five-kilometer time line of the Earth's history and notice that all of human history lies within the last half-meter. Watch a fascinating animation showing the difficulties of communicating with alien cultures across time and space. And don't miss the Infosphere to hear what residents of the environs of Alpha Centauri, Capella, and other places are hearing from us right now. That is, if there are any residents to listen.
http://www.pbs.org/lifebeyondearth/

NUCLEAR PHYSICS

Accelerate a Particle!

How on Earth do you steer a teeny little subatomic particle you can't even see? Turns out you can herd it with magnetic forces. Get your particle driver's license right here.

http://cern.web.cern.ch/CERN/Microcosm/RF_cavity/ex.html

Antimatter: Mirror of the Universe

Attend Antimatter Academy and find out what play dough and mirrors have to do with the concept of matter and antimatter. Be reminded of *Star Trek* episodes starring "Anti Matter" herself. And don't miss the fascinating questions answered by real physicists, such as, "If you've got some antimatter, how do you store it?"

http://livefromcern.web.cern.ch/livefromcern/antimatter/

A B C D E F G H I J K L M N O P Q R S T U V W X Y Z

A
B
C
D
E
F
G
H
I
J
K
L
M
N
O
P
Q
R
S
T
U
V
W
X
Y
Z

The Heart of the Matter

Find out the difference between a proton and a positron. Learn what antimatter is . . . and isn't. Discover why you are made of matter that's as old as the universe. Scientists at CERN, the European Consortium for Nuclear Research, use some of the biggest tools in the world—accelerators—to look at the tiniest pieces of all. Check it out at this most interesting resource.

http://www.exploratorium.edu/origins/cern/

SOUND

Do You Know What These Sounds Are?

Do your ears have what it takes? Try guessing some strange sounds at this site. You'll hear sounds made by pretty neat and useful inventions, like the sound of Velcro peeling apart. Listen and take a guess! A right answer tells you all about the invention. So if you're ready, turn up the audio for some noisy fun.

http://www.cbc4kids.ca/general/kids-club/slf/

Medieval Women - An Interactive Exploration

For a woman, life in the Middle Ages was anything but the usual image of a damsel in distress being rescued by a knight in shining armor. A woman during these times was more likely to be a nun, or someone who cared for the sick and poor, or a mom, raising a family. At this site, you can explore the life and times of a young woman during the fifteenth century. The journey she will take you on is filled with colorful graphics, music, and video. There is a lot to explore. If you get lost, the Timeline section will set you straight.
http://mw.mcmaster.ca/intro.html

★ Online Experiments

Part of a larger site called Little Shop of Physics (see earlier entry under PHYSICS—EXPERIMENTS), this lets you experience two weird Shockwave demonstrations. The first is an illusion in sound—pure sound, that is. Do you hear the notes as going up or going down? Check the science behind this very strange auditory foolery! The second demonstration explains how they make that emergency broadcast signal sound so annoying. Check it out.

http://littleshop.physics.colostate.edu/Online.html

Sound Site

Close your eyes. Listen. Dad clearing his throat in the living room. Footsteps down the hall. The steady click of the clock on the wall. Distant thunder outside. There's a lot more sound around us than we think. This page engages you to think creatively about sound. Listen to composers talk about their works, and help kids "sample" sounds for use in a special performance.

http://www.smm.org/sound/

★ The Soundry

This site uses wonderful interactive demonstrations to demonstrate how we hear what we hear. Start off with the structure of the ear, move into physics and the characteristics of a sound wave, and learn about the history of recorded sound. Don't miss the applets in the Sound Lab. Create a sound "scene" or movie using only sounds arranged in a particular order. Listen to a few of the samples, such as "Tarzan Has an Accident." You'll get the idea. Other applets include the Doppler effect, harmonics, waves, and beats. In fact, no one could beat this site. The 1998 ThinkQuest Grand Prize winner was created by kids!

http://library.thinkquest.org/19537/

If you forgot the words to "gopher guts" try lyrics in MUSIC AND MUSICIANS.

PLANTS, TREES, AND GARDENS

See also FARMING AND AGRICULTURE

The Amazing Story of Kudzu

Love it or hate it, you can't ignore kudzu—the vine that ate the South! It's not a native plant, but it now covers millions of acres, climbing up and over everything in sight. How did it all start? Where did kudzu come from, and, more important, where is it going? (What's that climbing up your leg?) Is there any use for the stuff? Find out here.

http://www.cptr.ua.edu/kudzu/

Fun with Lichens

Lichens are a combination of a fungus and an alga that combine to form a unique third type of organism. You see lichens growing on rocks, on trees—pretty much everywhere. The lichen needs sunlight in order to manufacture food for itself, and they won't grow where the air pollution is bad. There are lots of useful things to know about lichens, including the fact that they are used to make medicine and dye wool. Some of them grow only a teeny bit each year. At this site you'll learn all about lichens and their diversity around the world. For more on lichens, check the BIOLOGY—FUNGI section of this book.

http://mgd.NACSE.ORG/hyperSQL/lichenland/

★ The Great Plant Escape

Bud and Sprout are on hand to help Detective Le Plant solve some of the great mysteries of plant life. Case by case, you will check the clues, try experiments, and solve problems as Bud and Sprout journey into the world of plants. The detective promises lots of fun, but the outcome will remain a mystery until your investigative duties are completed. You can also find your way to some other great "green links." Get the dirt on soil—it's much more than you think. Do you know the difference between a daffodil bulb and a potato? Bud and Sprout will help you find out about a lot of plants, fruits, and vegetables, and they will even show you how to grow your own mango!

http://www.urbanext.uiuc.edu/gpe/

Kids World - Plant Nutrition

You know that a plant needs light and water—but what other sorts of nutrients help a plant to grow? There are 16 of them, divided into those that are mineral and nonmineral. Nonminerals needed are hydrogen, carbon, and oxygen. Minerals include nitrogen, phosphorus, and potassium, among many others. Find out what each does to grow a healthy plant. There's also information on how to read a fertilizer label. Don't miss the game, quiz, and coloring book.

http://www.agr.state.nc.us/cyber/kidswrld/plant/

The Last Straw Project

Plants need to eat, just like you do. But they don't get their food from the grocery store. They make their own from minerals absorbed from the soil, water, and carbon dioxide in the air. They also use different tactics for collecting water in a dry, drought situation. Want to learn how? Visit the Virtual Lab. It lets you experiment with and compare the growth of plants in different climate conditions.

http://cycas.cornell.edu/ebp/projects/laststraw/ise.info.html

★ Plants and Our Environment

If you don't know a sepal from a cotyledon, this is the place for you! Learn all about plants at this site, which was one of the finalists in the 1998 ThinkQuest Junior competition. The handy A-to-Z glossary reveals that the cotyledon is the hard outer case of the seed, which holds the embryo (baby part of the plant) and gives it a food supply, whereas the sepals are the outer green parts of the base of the flower. Sepals protect the flower bud before it opens. The entire process of growth is explained, and the site includes lots of great graphics.

http://tqjunior.thinkquest.org/3715/

Go climb a rock in OUTDOOR RECREATION.

A
B
C
D
E
F
G
H
I
J
K
L
M
N
O
P
Q
R
S
T
U
V
W
X
Y
Z

A B C D E F G H I J K L M N O **P** Q R S T U V W X Y Z

Poisonous Plants

You may have heard about poison ivy and poison oak, but did you know that some of the prettiest flowers are also harmful in some way? While some have mild irritating effects, others are deadly, even in small doses. Be safe and learn which plants to pick and which ones to avoid. There are also links to information on plants poisonous to pets. The page listed here has pictures. Another page, without pictures but with easy-to-understand information, is at *<http://aggie-horticulture.tamu.edu/ plantanswers/ publications/poison/poisonlinks.html>*. Be sure to see the page under HEALTH AND SAFETY—SAFETY in this book as well.

http://www.ansci.cornell.edu/plants/plants.html

GARDENING (INDOOR AND OUTDOOR)

Aggie Horticulture Just for Kids

This is a treasure trove of gardening links and projects just for kids and families, brought to you by Texas A & M. Whether growing a salad on your windowsill or sprouts in an eggshell, you'll find easy-to-understand projects here.

http://aggie-horticulture.tamu.edu/kindergarden/

The Bonsai Primer

This excellent primer explains what bonsai is, and isn't. It is a small tree and pot, grown in visual harmony to give the impression that you're looking at an ancient tree, not a shrub. It is not a dwarf tree. The tree's branches have been trimmed carefully, sometimes wired and trained, in order to give the impression that you're looking at a very old tree, or in the case of *saikei*, an entire tiny landscape. You can learn the basics of this gardening hobby at this site, including which trees and shrubs lend themselves best to the art of bonsai.

http://www.bonsaiprimer.com/

Bonsai Web - Beginner's Guidelines

This page shows you step by step how to take a throwaway nursery plant and start it on the path to becoming a beautiful bonsai—a miniature tree in a lifelike setting. There is a list of special tools you'll need if you want to take up this intriguing hobby.

http://www.bonsaiweb.com/forum/articles/begin/
    begin.html

Bulb.com

After a long winter, there's nothing so cheerful to see as tiny crocuses blooming in the sun. Did you know that most spring-flowering bulbs are planted in the fall? At this site you can find out everything you'd ever want to know about bulbs, including how to "force" bulbs to bloom out of season, how to keep squirrels from eating all your bulbs, and the latest in the quest to develop a black tulip.

http://www.bulb.com/

FastPlants

If the science fair is coming up and you need a plant that grows really fast, this is it. *Brassica rapa* goes "from seed to seed" in 35–40 days. Find out how to get seeds (or plants) here.

http://www.fastplants.org/

★ The Garden Gate

This great jumping-off point is blooming with links to help you figure out how to make your garden grow. You'll find resources on pest control, plant identification, wildflowers, water gardens, deer-resistant plants, composting, perennials, and much more. Be sure to visit this site when you've got time to smell the roses, because there's enough here to keep you busy all day!

http://garden-gate.prairienet.org/

★ GardenGuides - Come Garden with Us

Asparagus, beans, beets, broccoli, Brussels sprouts, cabbage, carrots, cauliflower, Chinese cabbage, corn, cucumbers, eggplant, garlic, greens, leeks, lettuce, onions, parsnips, peas, peppers, potatoes, tomatoes, and zucchini. You can grow 'em all, and you can find out how at this site! But that's not all you'll find. There are all kinds of facts on flowers, hints on herbs, and information on everything from compost to winter protection. Speaking of winter, that reminds us of Santa Claus. Did you know he really loves to garden all summer? It must be true because he always says to his elves, "Hoe, hoe, hoe!"

http://www.gardenguides.com/

Junior Master Gardener Program

If you and at least four friends would like to learn more about growing beautiful flowers and tasty vegetables, grab a willing adult and stop in here. Register your group and complete various fun activities (for example, learn about soil using peanut butter, candy bits, and cereal), and become a certified Junior Master Gardener. The program is free, but watch out for the bees on the home page!

http://jmgkids.com/

★ Kid's Valley Webgarden

Growing flowers and vegetables takes more than a few seeds and some dirt. It all begins with developing a plan and choosing the right place to plant. The people at Kid's Valley Webgarden will tell you when to plant (depending on the climate in your part of the world), what to plant, and how to do it. Then you have to maintain the garden, but don't worry—they're ready to help. Water, fertilize, mulch, weed; water, fertilize, mulch, weed. Just when you get the bugs all worked out, the fruits of your labor will be ready to enjoy! You will love to visit this gardening bonanza.

http://www.raw-connections.com/garden/

KidsGardening.com

Besides tons of family and classroom gardening info, you can find out how to get a Youth Gardening Grant. Every year, the National Gardening Association awards Youth Garden Grants to 400 schools, neighborhood groups, community centers, camps, clubs, treatment facilities, and intergenerational groups throughout the United States. Each grant consists of tools, seeds, and garden products. To be eligible, an organization must plan to garden the following spring with at least 15 children between the ages of 3 and 18 years. Selection of winners is based on the "demonstration of a child-centered plan that emphasizes children directly learning and working in an outdoor garden. Selection criteria include leadership, need, sustainability, community support, innovation and educational, environmental and/or social programming." Check the details here and prepare to plant! Also inspect the extensive information database—there must be something you need to know here.

http://www.kidsgardening.com/

NET FILES

When you touch something hot, your brain makes you say "OUCH!" right away. How fast does information travel within the human nervous system?

Answer: It depends on which type of neuron is sending the message. According to the Neuroscience for Kids - Explore the NS page, "Transmission can be as slow as 0.5 meters per second or as fast as 120 meters per second. That's the same as going 268 miles per hour! Check the math out yourself." Speed over to *http://faculty.washington.edu/chudler/what.html* for more fun facts from the world of neuroscience.

A
B
C
D
E
F
G
H
I
J
K
L
M
N
O
P
Q
R
S
T
U
V
W
X
Y
Z

A
B
C
D
E
F
G
H
I
J
K
L
M
N
O
P
Q
R
S
T
U
V
W
X
Y
Z

★ Michigan 4-H Children's Garden

What's in a children's garden? Well, it would definitely have a treehouse, and a pond, and maybe a garden planted in a maze. And how about a pizza garden? Take a tour of a place in Michigan where all this, plus imagination, grows.

http://www.4hgarden.msu.edu/main.html

★ Partners For Growing

These neat activities include a virtual field trip to a temperate rain forest, a feature about how to grow a school garden, a game to see how well you can match an insect's name with a close-up view of its mouth parts, and a description of how they work and what it eats.

http://www.mobot.org/PFG/samples/

Every year the Worshipful Companies of the Vintners and Dyers participate in an unusual and ancient ritual on the River Thames in London. What is it?

Answer: This group is charged with the royal duty of rounding up and taking a census of all the swans. For many centuries, mute swans in Britain were raised for food, like other poultry. Individual swans were marked by nicks on their webbed feet or beak, which indicated ownership. Somewhat like cattle brands in the American West, these markings were registered with the Crown. Any unmarked birds became Crown property. The swans are rounded up at a "swan-upping," and although they are no longer used for food, the Queen's Swan Marker continues the tradition to this day. For more information, check *http://www.thamesweb.co.uk/windsor/windsor1999/upping.html*

Rittners School Floral Education Center

You've spent the summer hoeing, pulling weeds, and watering, and now you have lots of beautiful flowers. Congratulations! Now pick some for the house and come inside. You are about to learn how to make arrangements that will make the neighborhood florists jealous of your talents. Well, maybe you're not ready to put them out of business yet, but several of the arrangements described at this Web site are simple to do. Ask your mom or dad to give you a hand and prepare to create an arrangement of beauty.

http://www.tiac.net/users/stevrt/RittnersGallery.html

School Gardens

Why grow a garden at school? For one thing, the cafeteria can use the vegetables! But it's also a great source of learning for the kids. Find out how to plan your school garden, care for it, and benefit from the experience.

http://aggie-horticulture.tamu.edu/nutrition/
    schoolgardens/schgard.html

Seeds of Change Garden

What's a Seeds of Change garden? It's a combination of green thumb and cultural exchange. Before Columbus arrived in the New World in 1492, there were "Old World" plants native to Europe and "New World" plants native to the Americas. People's food choices were limited to what grew nearby; if oranges didn't grow in their village, for example, they would never get to taste one. Exploration and trade with other nations changed all that. Read about how schools are growing Old World and New World gardens and a third garden based on seeds from traditional fruits and vegetables saved from their home kitchens. This terrific site will tell you all about the history of food crop plants and how you can create your own Seeds of Change garden! You'll find recipes here, too.

http://www.mnh.si.edu/garden/

**Computers are dumb,
people are smart.**

TREES AND FORESTS

See also EARTH SCIENCE—LAND
FEATURES—RAIN FORESTS

Ancient Bristlecone Pine

Imagine a tree that is nearly 5,000 years old! Back
in the 1950s (that seems like a long time ago, but not
when compared to the age of the tree), a man named
Edmund Schulman was studying bristlecone pine
trees in the White Mountains of California. He and
fellow researchers discovered "Methuselah," which
was found to be 4,723 years old. That was in 1957.
Today, it remains the world's oldest known living
tree. Read more here.

http://www.sonic.net/bristlecone/intro.html

★ Brockman Memorial Tree Tour

This neat site offers a clickable map around the
University of Washington in Seattle. You can pay
a virtual visit to 80 different tree species, including
the bristlecone pine, the sierra redwood, and the
monkey puzzle tree, among others. Most offer
photos of the trees, as well as information about
how and where it grows.

http://www.washington.edu/home/treetour/

★ Explore the Fantastic Forest @
Nationalgeographic.com

You may want to tell people to *leaf* you alone while
you trek through this fantastic forest, picking up clues
along with maple leaves. We encountered a deer, a
woodchuck, and some running buffalo clover. You
can learn a lot about the forest and its inhabitants by
spending an afternoon here. Remember to pack out
your trash, if you have any.

http://www.nationalgeographic.com/features/96/
forest/html/forest.html

Forest Puzzles

The Oregon Museum of Science and Industry presents
this site about the various stages of forest growth.
While everyone agrees that forests are valuable,
differences of opinion abound. Is the forest more
valuable as a source of forest products like lumber, or
as a habitat for wildlife and as a recreational resource?

http://www.omsi.edu/explore/life/forestpuzzles/

★ Georgia-Pacific: Educational in Nature

Could your school or neighborhood use a little
"sprucing" up? This site explains how you can
make a landscape map of the area and experiment
with adding shrubs, trees, and other improvements
on paper. You might site a basketball hoop or a small
fish pond. Once your plan is complete, you can submit
it to your school—maybe they will like your ideas!
Besides teaching you what foresters do and what
forest management is, this site offers close-up looks
at five different types of forest, a flock of informative
tidbits on birds, and many activities, recipes,
and games.

http://www.gp.com/educationalinnature/

❧ Seussville's Lorax "Save the Trees" Game

"I am the Lorax, I speak for the trees!" Even very
little children will have fun trying to catch seeds in
this Shockwave game inspired by Dr. Seuss. Use your
mouse to position your basket just right. If you catch
ten seeds, you'll be able to replant the Truffula Forest,
and the Truffula Forest is what everyone needs.

http://www.randomhouse.com/seussville/games/lorax/

Shades of Green: Earth's Forests

Learn about all different types of forests: tropical
and temperate rain forests, broadleaf forests, and
coniferous forests. Find out what types of trees,
plants, and animals live in them. Explore a virtual
forest walk and examine diagrams such as a cross-
section of a tree. What threatens these forests today?
Pollution, fire, deforestation, erosion, and climate
change are only a few of the problems you can learn
about here. This site was created by students for
the ThinkQuest competition.

http://library.thinkquest.org/17456/

A B C D E F G H I J K L M N O P Q R S T U V W X Y Z

A B C D E F G H I J K L M N O P Q R S T U V W X Y Z

NET FILES

What are the Cissoid of Diocles, the Pearls of Sluze, and the Witch of Agnesi?

Answer: They are all famous mathematical curves, drawn from notable historic equations. They do look something like their namesakes; for example, the Witch of Agnesi does look like a witch's hat. According to this site, Maria Agnesi studied this equation in 1748 and wrote about it in her mathematics book—and more than 250 years later, Net-Mom mentions it in her book! Be sure to find more famous curves at http://www-groups.dcs.st-and.ac.uk/~history/Curves/Curves.html

Teaching Youth About Trees - The National Arbor Day Foundation

Trees provide us with shade, lumber, food, and fuel. Trees are great! *Wood* you ever think there's some way for you to get inexpensive trees? There is. What a *releaf*. The Arbor Day Foundation folks will send you ten seedlings—just send them ten dollars for membership, shipping, and handling.

http://www.arborday.org/programs/
    TeachingYouth.html

Thank a Tree

When it's sunny and hot, you thank a tree for the shade it provides. But there are a lot of other reasons to thank a tree. Just ask wild animals like squirrels and raccoons, caterpillars, birds, and insects. When you play this online game, they'll tell you why trees are important for their survival.

http://www.nwf.org/kids/games.html

❧ Treehomes - Who Lives Here?

Trees are beautiful for us to see, but they are also homes for many animals and birds. Explore this small grove and see what you find hidden among the trees. We found at least 13 things, including a red-headed woodpecker and a little mouse.

http://www.lhs.berkeley.edu/shockwave/
    treehomes.html

Trees

Did you ever wonder why trees have different shapes? You can tell a palm tree from a pine tree, but what makes them look so dissimilar? Read about tree shapes, and then try designing your own tree based on the clues you are given about the environment in which it will grow. Other sections include lessons on the ways trees spread their seeds.

http://miavx1.muohio.edu/~dragonfly/trees.htmlx

Treetures

Let the Treetures fill you in on everything you need to know about trees. These little acorns stand ready to help you plant and take care of a real tree. They'll also tell you why trees are important. You can also write the Treetures about a tree you've adopted, or send them some *poet-tree*.

http://www.treetures.com/

★ What Tree Is That?

Identify common trees by name or by leaf, fruit, or nut. Learn what they look like and how they grow. Another way to learn about even more types of trees (and cacti!) is to check the Audubon Field Guides at <http://www.enature.com/guides/
select_trees.asp?curGroup=Trees>.

http://www.oplin.lib.oh.us/products/tree/

POLLUTION

Environmental Defense

You can learn a lot about our environment at this home page of the Environmental Defense Fund. Do take the link to Hog Watch to learn about pollution caused by hog farm runoff. Parts of the site are not for the sensitive, so go on back to the EDF site and visit the Kids area. It has lots of neat things—like an Alpha Bestiary. Don't know what that is? Then check this site. Don't miss the animal concentration game called Kokoto—it's fun to play, and you'll learn something about the birds and beasts as you make your match.

http://www.edf.org/

★ U.S. EPA Explorers Club

Do you know what the EPA is? It's a governmental entity (how's that for a big word!) called the Environmental Protection Agency, and it makes sure everyone works to keep the air, land, and water safe and pure. We headed to the recycling section and found a lot of neat things about how we can reuse and recycle materials. There are a lot of other sites on this page that can help you understand the environment and our impact on it. This place is guaranteed to make you more aware of your surroundings so you and others can grow up in an environment that is safe for everyone.

http://www.epa.gov/kids/

AIR POLLUTION

Acid Rain

It takes years for acid rain to cause problems, so its existence remained unknown for a long time. It can cause acid levels in lakes to increase so that fish and plant life cannot survive. Acid rain can also slowly eat away at buildings and structures, causing long-term damage. Where does it come from? What can be done about it? This page, from the Acid Rain Program of the Environmental Protection Agency, answers those questions and more.

http://www.epa.gov/airmarkets/acidrain/

★ Air Junk

Ever wondered about all those dust particles you see floating around in the air? Here's some news—it's probably not just dust, but animal and human skin flakes and dandruff, sand, pollen, and mold. Build some particle traps—the directions are here—and use your magnifying glass and this page to identify that "dust."

http://www.hhmi.org/coolscience/airjunk/

Air Pollution Activities

According to this site, "Americans make the equivalent of 3 million trips to the moon and back each year in cars, using up natural resources and polluting the air." Find out about the major kinds of air pollution and what you can do to help. There are lots of classroom activities, too—how about putting on a play about pollution? Maybe you can get the part of reporter Connie Lung!

http://www.nwf.org/animaltracks/resources/airactiv.cfm

GARBAGE AND RECYCLING

★ Dumptown Game

Welcome to Dumptown! Look around—there's litter and pollution, lots of garbage cans and dumpsters, but no way to recycle. You can save Dumptown. You can make things better, but you've got to do so in a cost-effective way. It won't be easy, but you can discover how proper management of resources can make a difference in saving this community. There will be lots of help, because this site is run by the Environmental Protection Agency.

http://www.epa.gov/recyclecity/gameintro.htm

Environmental Defense: Get the Facts on Recycling

You don't even need rubber gloves to paw through this garbage! Just click on items in the virtual waste can to learn astounding facts. Among them: did you know that we throw away enough iron and steel to continuously supply all U.S. car manufacturers?

http://www.environmentaldefense.org/clickable_gcan/

A
B
C
D
E
F
G
H
I
J
K
L
M
N
O
P
Q
R
S
T
U
V
W
X
Y
Z

A
B
C
D
E
F
G
H
I
J
K
L
M
N
O
P
Q
R
S
T
U
V
W
X
Y
Z

Garbage

The average American generates about four pounds of solid waste each day. We are generating waste products faster than nature can break them down. We're also using up resources faster than they can be replaced. At this site you can learn about the various types of waste and how we can begin to turn the tide. Don't miss the links on this site (which, by the way, is made from 100 percent recycled electrons).

http://www.learner.org/exhibits/garbage/

★ Rotten Truth (About Garbage)

When you throw something "away," where does it go? This site makes the point that there is no such thing as "away" when we have only one planet to live on. Learn the rotten truth about garbage, and then do something about it. Make a worm bin. Construct a soda bottle bioreactor. Organize a local landfill tour. There are lots of ideas and activities here.

http://www.astc.org/exhibitions/rotten/rthome.htm

NOISE POLLUTION
Noise Pollution Clearinghouse

A jet aircraft taking off. A loud "boom car" driving by. Lawn mowers. Leaf blowers. All of these can produce noise pollution. So what? So it can damage your hearing! Studies also show that test scores go down when there is lots of noise in the environment. What can you do to reduce noise pollution? Choose quieter toys, turn down the volume on your CD player, and follow this site's advice for dealing with noise problems in the neighborhood. You'll also find a current listing of many articles, studies, and other information on noise pollution.

http://www.nonoise.org/

Earthquakes are only part of what's shakin' in EARTH SCIENCE.

WATER POLLUTION
Nonpoint Source Pollution

Point source pollution is easy to see. It's a stream of chemicals dripping from an industrial pipe, or smoke billowing from a dirty smokestack. Nonpoint source pollution is another way of saying polluted runoff. This could be water running from a farm where fertilizers have been overused. Or water in the street that has picked up oil and gas from the pavement. Eventually, nonpoint source pollution ends up in our waterways just the same, but it's sometimes hard to identify where it came from. This site offers an impressive set of activities and links to resources about drinking water and how it is kept safe.

http://www.epa.gov/OWOW/NPS/kids/

Ocean Planet: Oceans in Peril

Did you know U.S. sewage treatment plants discharge more oil into the ocean than spills from oil tankers do? Medical waste, plastics, and other debris threaten not only water quality but also sea creatures' lives. You can learn more facts about pollution of the ocean and waterways by taking a look at this exhibit, presented by the Smithsonian Institution as part of a larger Internet exhibition on the ocean. You'll never think the same about water draining from your kitchen sink!

http://seawifs.gsfc.nasa.gov/OCEAN_PLANET/HTML/
ocean_planet_oceans_in_peril.html

Water Quality Activities

From the National Wildlife Federation, these fun K–8 activities teach the sources of pollution, the reach of a watershed, and the problems of discarded plastics in the sea. Can you solve the mystery of who is polluting the neighborhood's water? There's also a quick tutorial on water pollution. Sure sounds like a fun way of learning!

http://www.nwf.org/animaltracks/resources/
watactiv.cfm

PRESCHOOLERS

See also BOOKS AND LITERATURE—PICTURE BOOKS; FAMILY FUN; GAMES AND FUN—ONLINE GAMES; TELEVISION. Also, look for the rubber ducky symbol throughout this book, which means the site is best for young children. There is also a special Preschooler's Hotlist in the hotlist section at the front of the book.

🦆 Arnott's Adventures

Here's an odd little selection of games. One involves tiny teddies on safari while another requires you to create a tall sandwich of stacked luncheon meats and cheeses. Or you might attempt to Bake a Biscuit using an old shoe, rubber ducky, and other unusual ingredients.

http://www.arnotts.com/Fun/FunForKids.asp

🦆 BBC Education - Snapdragon

Practice your colors and counting with a Welsh dragon, and learn Welsh at the same time.

http://www.bbc.co.uk/wales/snapdragon/

🦆 BBC Online - Little Kids

In Picture Perfect, you need to identify shapes in a picture of a boat, a house, and a castle in order to win fish, flowers, and swans. Play the "easy" version until you get the idea. In another game, try to remember where Postman Pat has delivered packages (Mac users, this crashed IE 5 but was OK in Netscape 4.x). Try Apple Antics—but watch out! You need to catch apples in a bushel basket while avoiding the apple cores. There are also Teletubbie games, painting and coloring activities, and several audio storybooks.

http://www.bbc.co.uk/littlekids/

🦆 BlackDog's Games for the Younger Crowd!

Match colors and shapes with BlackDog; then stick some pictures on the virtual refrigerator or paint on the graffiti wall. Don't forget to visit the farm to hear all the animals.

http://blackdog.net/games/tots/

University of Delaware Graduate College of Marine Studies

Wow! There's a lot of neat stuff here. Prowl along the interactive coastal habitat and learn how important horseshoe crabs and other species are; then hop into a submersible submarine and take a Voyage to the Deep. If you're not too water-logged after that, settle down to look at a picture book: Denizens of the Deep. Hint: don't look if you frighten easily!
http://www.ocean.udel.edu/neatstuff/neatstuff.html

🦆 Bob the Builder

Explore Bob the Builder's town and see what needs to be fixed. Maybe it's a broken vase, or radiator pipes that need to be put back together. When you're through, Bob's got other things for you to do. He might want you to help him clean up his tool shed, or help Mr. Dixon pick up packages. As long as you've got Flash, you've got the right tool to help Bob and learn something about the construction business.

http://www.bobthebuilder.org/

🦆 Build-a-Monster

This is a sweet little game to amuse the little kids in your family. Pick a head for your monster—how about that frog? OK, now choose a body—do you like that chicken? Now, which feet should you select? Yikes, that makes a very strange-looking monster, but it won't scare anyone.

http://www.rahul.net/renoir/monster/monster.html

A B C D E F G H I J K L M N O **P** Q R S T U V W X Y Z

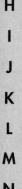

SandlotScience.com

They're all here: those illusional figures that leave you wondering. You'll see impossible illusions, like the animated triangle and the endless staircase. You'll also find camouflage illusions and hidden pictures and, finally, our favorite: moiré patterns. They're caused when two transparent patterns overlap. You will enjoy visiting this site, but don't be in a hurry—these illusions are irresistible!
http://www.sandlotscience.com/

🦆 Chateau Meddybemps

On the island of Meddybemps, jelly beans grow on vines, like grapes. You can learn all about the ritual and lore of gourmet bean tasting (yes, they sell them here, too). But that's not the best part. You can check out some wonderful and imaginative stories, such as "Frogwart and the Tooth Fairies." But that's not the best part either. Visit the Learning Games section in Fun and Games. Pat a Prairie Dog and move animals around to experiment with "in," "on," and "beside," and then see if you can find the biggest rutabaga on the train. And that's the best part!

http://www.meddybemps.com/

🦆 Children's Storybooks Online

Explore these stories with your little baby sister or brother, who will be delighted by the busy animations and funny "animal" noises, and enchanted by the tales themselves. There are stories for older kids, too.

http://www.magickeys.com/books/

🦆 Children's Storybooks Online - Alphabet Letters

Is your brother or sister just learning his or her ABCs? This series of alphabet pages will surely help. Each letter is illustrated with a cute animation. The "B is for Bear" winks and stretches, the "H is for Helicopter" hovers around the computer screen, and the "N is for Nest" hatches out some baby birds. Can you guess what "Z" is for?

http://www.pacificnet.net/~cmoore/alphabet/

🦆 Clever Island - Free Games

This area gives you a few sample games from the subscription-based site. When we visited, we counted and matched ants, searched for lost Australian animals, and watched an interactive movie about dinosaurs.

http://www.cleverisland.com/free_games/

🦆 Clifford the Big Red Dog

Now you can read online stories about Clifford the Big Red Dog, plus play matching games with sounds and letters. Don't miss the link to Birdwell Island for more Big Dog fun. Who's under the sand castle? Click and see!

http://teacher.scholastic.com/clifford1/

🦆 DragonTales

"I wish, I wish with all my heart . . . To fly with dragons in a land apart." Follow the clues to hidden treasure in a secret maze. Play shape matching with mushrooms, sing and dance with the Singing Springs, and even bake a real "dragonberry cake."

http://www.pbs.org/dragontales/

🦆 Dress Caillou

Caillou wants to get dressed up to go outside and play. Can you figure out the weather based on the costume choices you're given?

http://pbskids.org/caillou/dresscaillou/

Edy's Cone Factory

Some of these games may be too hard for little kids, so you may have to help your younger sibling toss ice cream into moving cones, collect ice cream sundae ingredients in the right order, and smash the ice cream containers into one gooey mess. How strangely satisfying.

http://www.conefactory.com/GamesArea/

🦆 Fun with Spot

Everyone likes to play with Spot, the friendly puppy from the Eric Hill books. Be on the lookout to "spot" matching animals on the farm and count starfish and crabs on the sandy beach. At the party, there are so many presents! Can you find a pattern of three matching objects?

http://www.funwithspot.com/

🦆 Gamequarium

This Web site might be underwater, but don't let that stop you. Just select the pre-K to 2 wading pool or the 3 to 6+ shallow end. Then click on the friendly fish to splash into safe waters all around the Internet. Learn about colors, shapes, ABCs, numbers, counting money, and lots more.

http://www.gamequarium.com/

🦆 Help Rusty Move In

Snug as a bug in a . . . teapot? Just click and drag to arrange and rearrange Rusty's furniture until you feel comfortable and right at home.

http://www.worditude.com/kids/rustyshome.html

🦆 If You Give a Pig a Pancake: Games

Pig is hiding somewhere under the clothes on your closet floor. Pick up each article of clothing until you find her. (Hint: you'll find a lot of other things, too!)

http://www.harperchildrens.com/pigpancake/htm/
   pig_game.htm

🦆 Julia's Rainbow Corner

We were charmed by this site, designed for pre-readers and anyone else who wants to have fun. We loved the bright colors, audio narration, and enchanting games and stories. Help Julia the octopus find her crown, help decorate the day, and then try the night—how many stars can you put in the sky? There is so much to do here, you'll want to return to this rainbow often.

http://www.juliasrainbowcorner.com/

🦆 Kids Play Safe: Boowa and Kwala Games

The games here change from time to time, so you may have to look around a bit to find a flower arranging game, a "Where is the cow hiding?" guessing game, and a fish bone-a-phone xylophone.

http://www.boowakwala.com/games.htm

🦆 KidsPsych - Games for Children Ages 1 to 9

Sort shapes, paint an online circus picture, or decide which way to go around a maze if you're a very young visitor to this site. Older kids can try to repair a space station with a secret code, or sort out mixed-up faces, or play I Spy. There's also a brain-teasing puzzle involving a fox, a chicken, and a bag of grain. You have to get them all across the river, but your boat will only hold one at a time. Don't leave the chicken alone with the grain, or the fox alone with the chicken. Can you figure it out? If you can there's a surprise!

http://www.kidspsych.org/

Kindergarten Kafe

Each issue of this online newsletter offers a finger play, a story, suggested books, crafts, activities, and more. For example, one issue features the theme "Apples." There's a little apple poem, a couple of suggested Web sites, and a tasty snack made of apple slices, peanut butter, and a few mini-marshmallows. Scrolling down, we find an apple-printing craft and picture books with an apple flavor. Look through back issues for holiday crafts and other activities.

http://www.kkafe.net/

A B C D E F G H I J K L M N O P Q R S T U V W X Y Z

A
B
C
D
E
F
G
H
I
J
K
L
M
N
O
P
Q
R
S
T
U
V
W
X
Y
Z

🦆 Kokoto

Even little kids will be able to click on the stones and see what animal hides behind them. Can you find two matching animals? If yes, the pictures are circled, and you'll learn some facts about that creature. If no, the pieces are turned back over, and you can select two more. This game takes concentration, which is another name for it.

http://www.earth2kids.org/Kokoto/

🦆 Literacy Center - The Early Childhood Learning Place

There are several letter recognition and matching games at this site to help young readers improve their skills. Unfortunately, the site offers little in the way of directions. If you are confronted with a screen of the entire alphabet, just click a letter on your keyboard and listen!

http://www.literacycenter.net/

🦆 The Little Animals Activity Centre

Follow Foxy Dancer onto the dance floor and see if you can imitate his musical steps, and then play a rhyming word game with Digby Mole (hope you like to eat worms). Mike Maker offers craft and activity suggestions, while other Little Animals hop up and down and try to get you to play with them, too!

http://www.bbc.co.uk/education/laac/

🦆 Nick Jr.

Click on Play Now and decide which snowflakes match, or guess the identity of the hidden picture in the Race Against Time. Blue has many games here for curious preschoolers—see which ones you like! Don't miss Dora the Explorer, either. She has lots of cool friends who teach her Spanish!

http://www.nickjr.com/

🦆 Noddy

Try matching musical patterns or following clues to find Noddy, the impish wooden toy from Toyland. There are sing-along songs, coloring book pages, and loads of suggested activities to try on your own.

http://www.pbs.org/kids/noddy/

🦆 Paw Island

It's shaped like a paw print, it's inhabited by dogs and cats, and it's called—can you guess?—Paw Island! We landed at Howlin' Hills, but your arrival may be at a different spot; just click on the map to explore. Wherever you go, be sure to look for (and click on) hidden smiley faces in each picture. There are online games, coloring pages, activities, and lots more fun on this tropical isle.

http://www.pawisland.com/

🦆 Sesame Street Games

Shall we play a game with Bert, Cookie Monster, Big Bird, or—hmm, let's play a game with Elmo! Let's go on a road trip to the farm. Can you help Elmo find the sheep? That was easy, but how about the chicken? If you find all the critters, go back and choose another game. All your favorite *Sesame Street* friends are waiting for you!

http://www.sesameworkshop.org/sesamestreet/games/

🦆 Seussville Games

Just pick up the clover containing the entire Who civilization and place it back in Horton's trunk. Seems easy, right? Not when the screen is dark! Then scramble your brains with the Cat in the Hat's concentration game, or see if you can match the right kooky teacher with her classroom in Diffendoofer School. Try to sort out Sneetches with stars on their bellies from those without them, and then play Net-mom's favorite, the Lorax's Save the Trees game.

http://www.randomhouse.com/seussville/games/

🦆 St. Charles Public Library - The Miss Mouse Game

Where is Miss Mouse? She's gone into one of these colorful houses, but which one? Let's try the orange house. Oops, there's a fire truck in there. How about the green house? Nope, just an old shoe. Keep clicking until you find her. Every game is different.

http://www.st-charles.lib.il.us/low/missmouse.htm

🦆 Teletubbies Playground

Who Spilled the Tubby Custard? Can you put the jigsaw puzzle back together? Want to try some online coloring? Don't forget to wave bye-bye to the Tubbies!

http://www.bbc.co.uk/education/teletubbies/playground/

🦆 Toddler Activities

Challenge your mom to a one-on-one cow race, and make sure you pick the red cow, not the blue one. You see, the red cow moves forward with every key press. The blue cow moves forward with every FOUR mouse clicks. In other games you can count bananas, listen to animals sounds, and practice dialing a phone. Parental advisory: please preview the arcade link from this site.

http://www.totcity.com/totplaces/Activities/activities.html

🦆 The Toy Box

Jim-Jim is a frog with three things going for him. He catches flies, he can jump as well as Michael Jordan, and—get this—he changes color. Strangely relaxing to play with, Jim-Jim was our favorite until we looked around the site some more and saw Milkshakes the Bouncing Bovine.

http://www.sun-sentinel.com/graphics/entertainment/toybox.htm

NET FILES

Why do bees buzz?

Answer: Bees buzz because their wings are moving up and down more than 11,400 times per minute. This motion produces that distinctive drone.
http://www.honey.com/kids/facts.html

🦆 Wimzie Activities

Rearrange the furniture in the living room as many times as you want. Then try to unscramble the tops, middles, and bottoms of each character until they all look right. Find out what's making noise in the garden and then make some noise yourself with Play Music.

http://www.pbs.org/wimzie/kc_1.html

🦆 Zini's Activity Page

Print these 36 activity pages for some offline fun. Circle the biggest flower. Put an X on the smallest one. See if you can follow a tricky maze. Mark the shape that doesn't match the others. You can color the pages, too.

http://www.incwell.com/Zini/

A
B
C
D
E
F
G
H
I
J
K
L
M
N
O
P
Q
R
S
T
U
V
W
X
Y
Z

A B C D E F G H I J K L M N O **P** Q R S T U V W X Y Z

♨ Zoboomafoo

Can you match the animal to the snack he prefers? Can you guess the mystery animal? Try the Going to the Closet adventure: take a jungle raft tour and see if you can find five different animals hidden in the foliage. After that, relax with some coloring pages from this PBS television series.

http://www.pbs.org/zoboo/

PUERTO RICO

See UNITED STATES—TERRITORIES

PUPPETS AND MUPPETS

The Jim Henson Company

The main Henson page is a hoot. There's an online look at the Creature Shop, a biography of Henson himself, and a trip to various Henson-related links around the Web. But be sure to take the Muppet World link to visit <http://www.muppets.com/>. Before this site opened, while it was under construction, this was the message displayed on the screen: "Hi Ho, Kermit the Frog here. We are busy building Muppets.com, the first Virtual Reality, 5D, secured-socket, fully encrypted, dynamically interactive, bearly browserable, community based, Java-enabled, highly compliant, platform independent, frog-functional, scalable, backwardly compatible, indefinitely online, gif-animated, e-deliverable, sequentially tagged, third generation, CGI reciprocal, porcine promoted, plug-and-play, state of the art Web site. Unfortunately, last night Animal ate our hard drive. We're working hard to get that fixed. But for now, you can read all about us." Check out what they came up with after Animal coughed up the hard drive.

http://www.henson.com/

★ Lights, Puppets, Action!

Don't miss this activity! You're the director: choose your performers, tell them what to do, and then sit back and enjoy your play. Will you write a drama, a documentary, a comedy, or a rock video?

http://www.childrensmuseum.org/artsworkshop/ puppetshow.html

★ The Puppetry Home Page

Looking for a place to buy fake fur, foam rubber, and neoprene to build your own original puppets? Check the resources listed here. If your puppet-making aspirations are more along the old sock variety, you'll find links and patterns to help with that, too. Explore puppetry traditions around the world, from the Punch and Judy shows of France to the shadow puppetry of Asia. There are also links to ventriloquism resources on the Web, so you can learn to throw your voice in cyberspace, where no one can see your mouth move!

http://www.sagecraft.com/puppetry/

Strings, Springs, and Finger Things

Here's the scoop on puppets—some string, some spring, some finger things! That's not all. You will learn about the various methods of puppetry and see examples of each. There are puppets from many countries. For example, bunraqu is a traditional form of Japanese puppetry, native to Osaka. Very large and elaborately jointed and costumed figures are operated in full view of the audience. It takes a whole team of people to manipulate these puppets. Then there are water puppets, which originated in Imperial China. A water puppet consists of two parts: the body, which stands out of the water, and the support, which acts as a floater. The entire production takes place in the water, and the puppeteer stands up to his waist. Want to learn more? Let your fingers take you to this site.

http://www.civilization.ca/membrs/arts/ssf/ ssf00eng.html

QUEENS, KINGS, AND ROYALTY

Heraldica

Wondering if you have a coat of arms? This site gives hints on how you might find out, as well as discover something about your family tree. Learn about chivalry, royal families, the Society for Creative Anachronism, and much more at this site. One oddity is the heraldry of car logos, like Porsche and BMW. Another section is on famous Americans and their coats of arms. For example, John F. Kennedy's arms are described as follows: "In 1961, the Chief Herald of the Republic of Ireland granted arms to John F. Kennedy, then President of the United States. The arms are: Sable three tilting helms in profile or lined gules and a bordure per saltire gules and ermine. The crest is an arm proper, armed argent, holding four arrows proper." What does that mean? Use the information on this site to puzzle it out. Don't miss the Alt.talk.royalty FAQs for information on current monarchs.

http://www.heraldica.org/

King Ludwig II of Bavaria - His Life and Art

Ludwig II was known as "the Mad King," as well as "the Dream King." You have probably seen his fairy-tale castle, Neuschwanstein, on many a travel poster. They say it even inspired one of the Disney castles. Net-mom and family visited this castle while on vacation in Germany. It is pretty, and it has many unusual features in it. For example (as Net-mom recalls), in the ceiling over the king's bed were many pinprick holes. The floor above was lit with many lanterns, so the king could look up at his ceiling and pretend it was illuminated by stars. There is also a room decorated to look like a cave and a ballroom with a silent, smiling audience painted on the walls. This site offers details on the life of Ludwig II, who reigned in Bavaria from 1864 until he was deposed in 1886. An account of his mysterious death is also included.

http://www.geocities.com/Paris/LeftBank/4080/

Queen Liliuokalani

Did you know that Hawaii was once a sovereign nation with its own monarch? The last queen of Hawaii was Lydia Liliuokalani, who was illegally deposed in 1893 by the American "Committee of Safety." Though briefly restored, the monarchy was over by 1894, when the queen was arrested and imprisoned inside Honolulu's beautiful Iolani Palace. You can read about her life and history here.

http://www.uic.edu/depts/owa/history/
     liliuokalani.html

NET FILES

What does a Van de Graaff generator generate, anyway?

The story is **shocking!**

Answer: The Van de Graaff generator makes static electricity from a huge revolving belt inside one of its towers. Read about its history, construction, and all about lightning and electricity. You can see the original generator, built by Dr. Robert J. Van de Graaff, which now lives in the Theater of Electricity at the Museum of Science in Cambridge, Massachusetts, and on this site at http://www.mos.org/sln/toe/construction.html

A
B
C
D
E
F
G
H
I
J
K
L
M
N
O
P
Q
R
S
T
U
V
W
X
Y
Z

A
B
C
D
E
F
G
H
I
J
K
L
M
N
O
P
Q
R
S
T
U
V
W
X
Y
Z

The Double J Files

Try this fun detective game to learn about some of the inventions of the First Nations in North America. Some cases: Did the Inuit of the Arctic North invent sunglasses? Is Lacrosse a game invented by the Iroquois? Click on the right clues, and you'll discover the answers to these questions and more. *http://www.tvokids.com/doublej/* them in video form, hear just the audio, or read the text-only version.

The Royal Court of Sweden

This is the official Web site of the Swedish monarchy. Carl XVI Gustaf, who ascended the throne in 1973, is the 74th king of Sweden. The monarchy goes back over a thousand years. You will learn about the king, Queen Silvia, and the rest of the royal family here. Check the information on the royal palace and why it has a different architectural style on each of its four sides.

http://www.royalcourt.se/eng/

Royal Families of the World

This resource has collected official (and not so official) home pages of royalty in Europe, the Middle East, the Far East, and even—Canada (it's OK, it's all about Queen Elizabeth II). By the way, if you ever meet the queen and her husband the duke, here's what to do. "The Queen is called 'Your Majesty' initially and 'Ma'am' (rhymes with 'jam') as the conversation continues. The Duke of Edinburgh is called 'Your Royal Highness' initially and 'Sir' as the conversation continues."

http://www.royalfamily.com/

UNITED KINGDOM
★ The British Monarchy

This is the official Web site of the British monarchy. Here you will learn about the monarchy as it exists today, as well as its historic past. You'll visit the palaces and the Crown Jewels, and follow along on a typical day in the life of Her Royal Highness. You'll even find out why Elizabeth II keeps corgis as pets! There is also a special section on the life of Diana, Princess of Wales.

http://www.royal.gov.uk/

The Prince of Wales

The Prince of Wales is wired! At his Web site you'll find his daily appointment book; an online forum; his biography; many speeches (on everything from genetically altered food to architecture); and, of course, lots of photos. Did you know that as a student the prince once got a C in French? Or that he paints wonderful watercolor landscapes? You can learn more about the prince here and see his paintings (look in About the Prince). There's also quite a bit on Prince William and his brother Prince Harry.

http://www.princeofwales.gov.uk/

Royal Palaces

Why bother standing in long lines to tour Britain's historic royal palaces when you can browse them from the comfort of your desktop. Visit Kensington Palace; Hampton Court Palace; the Tower of London, home to Crown Jewels; and more. That's not to say that a trip to see the palaces wouldn't be worthwhile. Indeed it would. Check out the Events page for info on special tours and attractions.

http://www.hrp.org.uk/

**Attention everyone.
The Internet is closing.
Please go play outside.**

QUOTATIONS

Bartlett, John. Familiar Quotations

Project Bartleby, from Columbia University in New York, is an easy way to look for "phrases, proverbs, and passages" from works of literature. Keep in mind that you won't find anything contemporary here, just things prior to 1901. You can search for specific words or for entries from various authors. Want to know some famous Ben Franklin sayings? Just click on his name. Hmmm—"Early to bed and early to rise, makes a man healthy, wealthy and wise." And you thought your dad made that up! According to the notes, Franklin didn't make it up, either, but he helped popularize it.

http://www.bartleby.com/100/

★ Quotations

"A child of five could understand this. Fetch me a child of five." The comedian Groucho Marx said that. To find all kinds of quotes, from long ago and just yesterday, be sure to try this page. You'll find quotes by everyone from Miss Piggy to David Letterman here. There's a collection of the world's most annoying proverbs ("Haste makes waste"), as well as "miscellaneous malapropisms" and student bloopers ("The Egyptians built the Pyramids in the shape of a huge triangular cube"). Don't miss The Best of Anonymous either ("Remember, a day without sunshine is like night"). This site is highly recommended!

http://www.geocities.com/~spanoudi/quote.html

Simpson's Contemporary Quotations

From 1950 through 1988, 4,000 people said over 10,000 quotable things, which have been collected here for your use.

http://www.bartleby.com/63/

UM Weather

Do you think you could predict the weather better than the guys on TV? You may be able to, once this terrific site from the University of Michigan pops up on your radar. It's so hot, it's cool. We forecast a heavy download from the weather-related software tools area. There's also an incoming front of live weather cams from around the world. How many states and provinces can you visit today? *http://cirrus.sprl.umich.edu/wxnet/*

It's stored in Washington, D.C., inside a heavy-gauge stainless-steel container, which is pumped full of argon gas instead of plain air. The container is kept in a carefully controlled environment at 49.5 degrees Fahrenheit and 49 percent relative humidity. Special quarter-inch Plexiglas sheets filter out ultraviolet light.

What on earth is inside?

Answer: Actually, two items are inside, both of them drafts of Lincoln's Gettysburg Address, in the Library of Congress collection. You can see the storage containers and read about the rare documents inside them at
http://www.loc.gov/exhibits/G.Address/gapres.html

A
B
C
D
E
F
G
H
I
J
K
L
M
N
O
P
Q
R
S
T
U
V
W
X
Y
Z

RADIO

Broadcasting History

Can you imagine riding in a car without hearing tunes on the radio? Car radios weren't introduced until 1930. Radios were expensive back then, and not every home had one. In 1929, home radios were $120 each, which was a fortune! Before 1935, most radios broadcast only live music. After that, stations got record players and began spinning 33 1/3 or 78 rpm records. You say you don't remember records? Ask your parents about them. Radio plays were big, too: one of the biggest early successes was a western called *The Lone Ranger*, and one of its sponsors was Cheerios. Follow the amazing history of broadcast radio from the 1920s through the 1950s at this site.

http://www.people.memphis.edu/~mbensman/
history1.html

The CanOz Connection

Your whole class might not be able to visit a faraway country, but why not send an ambassador instead? First you need to find another classroom willing to participate. Some classes exchange a stuffed animal, like a teddy bear. They send it along with a bag full of accessories. Each night the bear goes home with a different student, who writes in the bear's diary or fills out a simple form detailing the bear's activities. After a short stay, the bear ambassadors go home, each with a diary full of new experiences to share with their classes. This page explains the whole process. Check out Monty Moose's New York visit to Net-mom! Net-mom is interested in participating with your class, too; please contact her at feedback@netmom.com.
http://www.teacherwebshelf.com/canozconnection/

★ Marconi Calling

Today, we think nothing of turning on the TV and seeing events happen, live, on the other side of the world. This was not always the case. Before the development of fast communication technologies, news often took months to work its way across the globe. One of these great technological breakthroughs was radio—wireless communications. December 12, 2001, marked the 100th anniversary of the first transatlantic radio signal, which was received in St. Johns, Newfoundland, by Guglielmo Marconi. The signal sent was the letter "S" in Morse code: "click-click-click." On December 15, 1902, Marconi sent the first wireless transatlantic message to Cornwall, England, thus making Glace Bay, on Cape Breton Island, Nova Scotia, the birthplace of transoceanic wireless communication. Read more and see historic photos, artifacts, and lots more at this outstanding site.

Http://www.marconicalling.com/

★ Oatbox Crystal Set Project

It's easy and fun to build your own "crystal" radio set using only some simple components. You will need a soldering iron, some stuff from Radio Shack or your favorite electronics parts store, a Quaker oatmeal box (or other round, tall box), and some time. All the directions are explained at the URL listed here. If you want a more elaborate project, you can find an old cigar box and build a radio with a simple tuner. Cigar stores may have empty boxes; just ask. The directions for that project are at <http://www.midnightscience.com/cigar.html>.

http://www.midnightscience.com/project.html

Ask not what the Net can do for you, ask what you can do for the Net.

Whoooooooo will you find in BIRDS?

★ Old Time Radio

Many years ago, before cable TV, even before any TV, there was radio—not just talk and music on the radio, like today, but radio "shows." Radio shows were like today's TV shows, without the pictures. People enjoyed listening to comedies, dramas, mystery thrillers, and variety shows. It was a whole different kind of radio, at a whole different time, and now it is known as "old-time radio." This page is entertainment and history all rolled into one, and it is packed with information, pictures, and sounds. In the OTR Sounds and Sound Snippets area, hear clips from such radio greats as Captain Midnight. In the Kids' Shows section you can hear favorites like Chandu the Magician and Smilin' Ed's Buster Brown Gang. In another section, you can take a fascinating virtual tour of the old NBC radio studios in <http://www.mcs.net/~richsam/>, Chicago's Merchandise Mart. Don't turn that dial!

http://www.old-time.com/

Very Low Frequency Radio Project

It's a good thing our ears aren't sensitive to very low frequency sounds. If we could hear them, it would be a very noisy world indeed! Natural "sferic, tweek, whistler, and chorus" sounds are produced by such things as lightning and far-off sources in space, while man-made VLF emissions come from satellites and other spacecraft. There's a way for you to amplify and listen to these sounds, and the whole experience is described here. You will also be able to hear some recordings of the sounds. This site was created by students for the ThinkQuest competition.

http://library.thinkquest.org/2784/

AMATEUR RADIO

See also CODES AND CIPHERS

AA9PW's Amateur Radio Exam Practice Page

You know ham radio is another name for amateur radio, don't you? You didn't imagine knobs and buttons and an antenna sticking out of a ham, we hope. Ham radio is fun and exciting, and people of all ages have found it to be a useful hobby as well. You need to be licensed to operate a ham rig, and to get a license you have to take a test. At this site, you can take sample amateur radio licensing exams. How well can you do? This site will check your exam and suggest areas where you need more study.

http://www.aa9pw.com/radio/exam.html

The American Radio Relay League

The American Radio Relay League, or ARRL, has been helping amateur radio enthusiasts since 1914. They now have over 160,000 members. At the ARRL site, you can tune in to lots of information on getting started in the hobby. It's best to find a local radio club to help guide you, and there's a convenient directory at this site. You'll also learn about licensing rules, upcoming testing in your area, and lots more.

http://www.arrl.org/hamradio.html

★ Ham Radio Online

Licensed ham radio operators use high-tech radios for communications with others (it's sort of like using a cellular phone, but without the cost of airtime charges). Hams meet new friends and "visit" with hams in countries all over the globe. They have even talked with astronauts orbiting Earth. Many U.S. and Russian astronauts are also licensed hams, and they make contacts from space for educational uses and sometimes just for fun. If you're not already an amateur radio operator, get into the Education section. If you are a ham, here's where you'll keep up on all the newest amateur radio news and latest technological developments. Since hams often provide emergency communications in the event of a disaster (some systems even have 911 emergency access), this site also has real-time links to earthquake and other disaster-monitoring sites all over the globe. Other unusual features are real-time forecasts for auroral, solar, and meteor shower activity. Don't forget to bring an umbrella if you're going out in a meteor shower!

http://www.hamradio-online.com/

A B C D E F G H I J K L M N O P Q R S T U V W X Y Z

NET FILES

Where would you look for a tiger's pug mark?

Answer: On the ground. It's another word for a footprint or track. Its actual size is 5.5 inches by 4.5 inches (10.8 cm by 8.75 cm)! You can see a tiger's pug mark at http://www.5tigers.org/pug.htm

How to Build a Simple Telegraph Set

What's the good in learning Morse code if you don't have a telegraph key to practice sending it? Sure, the stores are full of cell phones and palm-size computers, but have you tried to find a telegraph set lately? The good news is that it's easy to build one; and if you can get to a hardware store, you're going to be all set—telegraph set, that is.

http://www.chss.montclair.edu/psychology/perera/perbuild.html

RADIO STATIONS

★ BBC World Service

The British Broadcasting Corporation's site offers world news in 43 different languages, and you can hear them all through this site. There are also lots of audio features, including a large section on "Learning English."

http://www.bbc.co.uk/worldservice/

NPR Online - National Public Radio

Many people think National Public Radio (NPR) gives us the best news, feature stories, and music on the radio. This site gives you a lot of all these and lets you know where you can find NPR on your local radio dial. Like PBS on television, NPR is federally and privately funded programming. It's also commercial free. This Web site has the same "News Now Highlights" as the NPR radio broadcasts. Yes, you can actually listen to the most recent NPR news report right on your computer. You can also listen to past broadcasts of favorite NPR shows. Tune in and see what public radio has to offer.

http://www.npr.org/

Radio Locator

Who needs a boom box when the Internet will let you crank up the music. Use this comprehensive search engine for finding radio stations, and you'll discover more than 2,500 audio streams. The music comes from radio stations in the United States and around the world. Listen to Reggae, Rock, and Blues, to name a few. The engine also links to more than 10,000 radio station Web pages.

http://www.radio-locator.com/

Voice of America

"The news may be good. The news may be bad. We shall tell you the truth." That's what announcer William Harlan Hale said during the first VOA broadcast, February 24, 1942. In some places around the world, news and information is controlled by the government. Sometimes it is hard for citizens to find out the truth of a situation, in the face of broadcasts and newspapers from controlled news media. The Voice of America broadcasts have a regular listenership of more than 91 million people. One interesting thing to do is to listen to news broadcasts in other languages. We listened to Hindi, Creole, Greek, and Swahili, among the many others that were available. To do this, click on "Times and Frequencies" and then select a language. On the next page that opens, you may see a broadcast time followed by the words "Real Audio." That's where you need to click to hear the broadcast.

http://www.voa.gov/

Yahoo! Radio

It's always fun to listen to a radio station that's far away. Sometimes it's hard to pick up a signal though. You don't need a powerful antenna to pick up these broadcasts—all you need are the right plug-ins and your Net connection. Search for live, mostly U.S. broadcasts by station location, call letters, or format. You can also listen to air traffic control and police scanners at this site.

http://radio.yahoo.com/

SHORTWAVE

Numbers Stations on Shortwave Radio

"So this is one of those special shortwave radios. What do you guys listen to on these things? Wait, turn the knob the other way, slowly. Right there—stop! What in the world is THAT? It sounds like counting in a foreign language. What is that?" Could it be a math lesson in Russian? A language class in the U.K.? A spy sending secret code from some remote island? Or maybe someone in the U.S. is giving someone in Germany a company e-mail address? Hmmm, the spy answer is definitely the most fun—and it just might be the right one. The so-called numbers stations heard on shortwave radio make a fascinating topic. For many years, listeners came across them now and again, never really sure of their purpose. Even today, their origin and meaning are mysterious. Can you find the signals? What might they really be? This page helps you track them down and uncover the truth. Listen in! If you're really interested, visit <http://www.spynumbers.com/> as well.

http://havana.iwsp.com/radio/numbers.html

Shortwave/Radio Catalog - Radio Services

What is shortwave radio? Technically, that's the name for radio frequencies between 2.3 and 30 MHz. Shortwave broadcasts can be received over long distances, making it possible to communicate internationally—yes, without the Internet! You can tune in radio broadcasts from around the world. Questions, anyone? The answers are here. Be sure to pay special attention to the links marked "Newbies take notice!"

http://havana.iwsp.com/radio/RadioCatalogRS.html

WWW Shortwave Listening Guide

Shortwave radio enthusiasts can find out what programs are on right now, today. You can also follow the instructions to find programs on various topics, such as language lessons. Learn Arabic, Korean, German, and many other languages via shortwave radio. Many of these broadcasts are also available over the Internet.

http://www.anarc.org/naswa/swlguide/

RAILROADS AND TRAINS

Central Pacific Railroad Photographic History Museum

You can almost hear the ring of tools on the rails at this unique site. Stunning photos offer a rare glimpse into the effort that went into building the first U.S. railroad to link the East with the West. They are also all that remain of the United States' first transcontinental railroad. In 1942, the rails were taken up to support the war effort.

http://www.cprr.org/

☙ Fun with Trains

See the train coming? Do you think it is a short train or a long train? Scroll to the right and see what happens! Now here comes the rutabaga train. Its first car has some pretty big vegetables. But there are some bigger ones coming up. How good are you at rutabagaspotting?

http://www.meddybemps.com/9.411.html

Kids Corner

Learn how to become a train engineer, scratch your head over some weird railroad phrases, try and figure out railroad nicknames, view some extinct route maps, and check the history of the U.S. Railroad Retirement Board.

http://www.rrb.gov/teachers.html

A
B
C
D
E
F
G
H
I
J
K
L
M
N
O
P
Q
R
S
T
U
V
W
X
Y
Z

★ North American Steam Locomotives

While a rarity today, steam trains have not entirely vanished from the American landscape. This page provides information about steamers of the past and today's survivors, including schedules of currently running steam excursions, specifications of steam trains, and sections on trains that are "Lost Forever (but not forgotten)." There is also information on rail fairs, rail museums, and a special piece on the annual reenactment of the Golden Spike ceremony in Utah, featuring some terrific photographs—look for it in the Regional Tours area. In the FAQ you can see a cutaway diagram of a steam engine and find out how it works.

http://www.steamlocomotive.com/

Operation Lifesaver, Inc.

Trains are fascinating but dangerous. Did you know that a big, 100-car freight train traveling at 55 mph can take more than a mile to come to a complete stop? In the U.S., about 3,500 deaths and injuries per year involve trains and cars, or pedestrians. Here's something interesting: a train sticks out three feet from either side of the tracks. So, on a trestle, or bridge, there's only room for the train, not a pedestrian. Operation Lifesaver educates adults and kids on trains and train safety. There are loads of handouts and lesson plans for your teacher, too. Make tracks to visit here soon.

http://www.oli.org/for_kids/

RailCams at RailServe

Interested in spotting a few real trains yourself? Visit this collection of train cams! For example, you might check Trainorders trains on the Tehachapi Hill, "the busiest single tracked mainline in the world." It's one of the main north-south routes for rail traffic in California, and the RailCam is situated on a stretch featuring a 2.2 percent grade. That's nothing for a car, but it's a big deal for a train. The cam shows pictures of the last few trains spotted by the camera. Be sure to click on the button to find out more about what you can see in the photos.

http://www.railserve.com/RailCams/

TGVweb

A TGV (*train à grande vitesse*) is a high-speed system launched in the 1960s, comprising train, track, and signaling technologies, that when combined make high speeds possible. The TGV system is owned and operated by the French national railways, and it is an integral part of French rail travel. There are directions for "railfanning," or watching these trains as they whoosh by. But don't blink, or you'll miss it. A typical top speed is 186 mph. This site offers a scale model train for you to print and put together. If you assemble the whole thing, it will be five feet long. Younger kids will need adult help; each car takes about 40 minutes to build and a whole trainload of patience.

http://www.trainweb.org/tgvpages/tgvindex.html

Union Pacific Railroad - Facts, Figures, & History

This site offers everything from a history of railroading in the U.S. to a roster of freight car types. Find out whatever happened to cabooses and delight in some wacky railroad lingo.

http://www.uprr.com/aboutup/

Webville and Hypertext Railroad Company

If you've ever wondered "How to Boot a Steam Locomotive," or what those railroad signal lights mean, or wished you had lots of audio samples of train engine horns—this is your site! It has loads of links and some of the best material we've seen on trains both large and small.

http://www.spikesys.com/webville.html

MODEL RAILROADS
All-Gauge Model Railroading Page

Get imaginative, and re-create the operations of a big railroad yard, such as the Hoboken Shuttle or the Jersey Shore. Or, stick with something simple, and choose one of the basic track layouts. Either way, at this site you'll learn a thing or two about building model railroads. Extensive resources will show you how to buy, build, and operate model trains. Some of the videos require the Vivo Player.

http://thortrains.hypermart.net/

A B C D E F G H I J K L M N O P Q R S T U V W X Y Z

Be swampwise in EARTH SCIENCE.

The Lionel Station

The Lionel Manufacturing Company was founded in New York on September 5, 1900. In 1901, they sold animated display trains called "The Electric Express" to draw customers to store windows. A year later, they published a 16-page catalog, but it wasn't until 1906 that their product line included steam locomotives, trolleys, passenger cars, freight cars, and a caboose. Since then, Lionel has become a name famous in model railroading. You can check out their history, catalogs, cool accessories, and tips for hobbyists. Many track layouts are suggested in the Central Station Resources area.

http://www.lionel.com/

National Model Railroad Association

In the World Wide Rail Sites links area, there are more than 4,000 sites listed. Information is collected here on everything from garden trains—larger than O scale (1:48) but smaller than the trains that are large enough to ride on—to tiny Z gauge (1:220) trains. Want a track layout that does more than go around a Christmas tree? It's probably here. All aboard—the track's clear as far as you can see on the Net!

http://www.nmra.org/

Trains.com

Some people like to collect precision-made miniature railroad cars, accurate down to the last bolt. Others like to build elaborate layouts, with running water and real plants for their model trains to roll past. Lots of people are in between. If you're just getting started in model railroading, you'll find an online introduction here. There are also a couple of very active webcams you can control.

http://www.trains.com/story/story_list.asp

READING AND LITERACY

🦆 Food Jumble

Learning how to spell? Forget the flash cards, and surf over here. This fun spelling game will teach you how to spell with virtual fridge magnets. All that's required is your knowledge of spelling and a Shockwave-enabled browser. Use your mouse to place the letters in the right order, and then click on the picture it spells.

http://www.kaboose.com/shockWin2.cfm?infoID= jumble&shockType=sw

Read Across America

What does singer Garth Brooks have to do with the Cat in the Hat? Both lead in the 2002 Read Across America promotion sponsored by the National Education Association. It is an annual reading promotion that culminates on March 2 (that's Dr. Seuss' birthday). Find out what events are planned and how you can get involved. One activity is to try to read 50 books—one that takes place in each of the 50 states. There are booklists here so you can get started!

http://www.nea.org/readacross/

Building a School Web Site

This site's teacher, Wanda Wigglebits, proclaims: "If you can follow a recipe, you can build a Web site!" Although the title mentions school Web sites, this tutorial works for any kind of Web page. Go from rank beginner to a creator of animated GIFs in just a few short, free lessons! Wanda, you go, girlfriend! *http://www.wigglebits.com/*

A B C D E F G H I J K L M N O P Q R S T U V W X Y Z

A
B
C
D
E
F
G
H
I
J
K
L
M
N
O
P
Q
R
S
T
U
V
W
X
Y
Z

Teacher2Teacher

Kids aren't the only ones who need help learning. Teachers need help, too, and this site is designed for them. Here you'll find many free flip charts, classroom activities, and training guides for grades K–5 and Special Education. Resources are designed to reinforce basic skills in spelling and reading, as well as math.

http://www.createdbyteachers.com/

PHONICS

★ BBC Education - Words and Pictures

Throw some sounds together in the virtual blender, mix them all up, and what does it make? If you've chosen the right sounds, it spells a word. That's how the Wordblender works. This fun-packed site also offers reading and writing activities you can print. If you want to practice writing letters, the magic pencil will show you how to shape them.

http://www.bbc.co.uk/education/wordsandpictures/

IKnowThat.com

"The grumpy troll is being rather MEAN." That's one of the sentences we got when we decided to practice "long 'e'" sounds in the reading and phonics section of this site. What other words can we make that have the same sounds? If we drag over this "b" we'll hear a child's voice say "Buh. Ean. BEAN. On a towering stalk grows a giant BEAN." Check the reading area for loads of phonics *phun*, er, fun.

http://www.iknowthat.com/

TampaReads.com

The menu includes dozens of colorful and creative worksheets for learning how to spell using phonics. No online activities here; just lots of materials for teachers to print and use in the classroom. Most worksheets are designed for Grades 1 through 4, but there is some kindergarten material.

http://www.tampareads.com/

REFERENCE WORKS

See also WHY

Ask an Expert

Got a question no one seems to know how to answer? Maybe you need to call in an expert. Experts are people who know a lot about a certain topic—so much, in fact, that they often write the textbooks themselves! Many scientists and others have offered to answer questions about science, math, medicine, history, and other topics. You won't usually get an answer overnight, though, so think ahead.

http://njnie.dl.stevens-tech.edu/askanexpert.html

★ e-nature

Wow—it's the Audubon Field Guides online! There are over 4,800 animals and plants pictured on these Web pages, drawn from the well-known print guidebooks. The content includes Amphibians, Birds, Butterflies, Fishes, Insects, Mammals, Reptiles, Seashells, Seashore Creatures, Spiders, Trees, and Wildflowers. Each specimen is pictured in a small thumbnail photo. If you click on it, you'll get a larger picture plus lots of information on the creature or plant.

http://www.enature.com/

Electric Library Personal Edition

The Electric Library indexes newspaper and magazine articles, maps, television and radio transcripts, and photos and images. There's also an encyclopedia and a fair number of reference books. You can search topics for free; but if you want to read the full text of the articles, you must become a member. There's a 10-day free trial offer.

http://ask.elibrary.com/

Read any good Web sites lately?

ICONnect - KidsConnect

You've got a question, and no one seems to have an answer. Can you wait two more days? Just head to this site and pose your question to one of the school library media specialists throughout the world. They provide direct assistance to any student looking for resources. They'll help you learn how to use the Internet effectively for your class work. But don't use it for tonight's homework, because it usually takes two school days to get an answer. There's a chance someone else has asked the same question, so check the FAQ <http://www.ala.org/ICONN/kcfaq.html> first.

http://www.ala.org/ICONN/AskKC.html

★ LibrarySpot

You may not need this today, but believe Net-mom, you'll need it in the future, as term paper season approaches. Acronym dictionaries, biographical dictionaries, inventions, useful calculators (how much grass seed to buy, how to convert cooking measurements)—all are here for your use. There are also links to hundreds of library card catalogs all over the world. Explore numerous magazines and newspapers, phone books, mapping programs, and more. If you like Library Spot, you'll love its sister site, Book Spot <http://www.bookspot.com/> with links to the bestseller lists, authors, publishers, and what's new and old in award-winning books for kids and adults.

http://www.libraryspot.com/

MuseumSpot

Find an online gallery, splash into an online aquarium, browse through an online history museum, or peek into the live webcams of some of the nation's best zoos. You can do all this and more at MuseumSpot.

http://www.museumspot.com/

The Seven Wonders of the Ancient World

Everyone's heard about them, but who can name them? Well, there are the Pyramids, of course, and uh . . . hmmm. Luckily, there is a list of all of them here, along with pictures and links. Since there are not many of the ancient wonders of the world around anymore, you'll also find a list of the Modern Wonders of the World, as well as the Natural Wonders of the World. There are also pictures and links for wonders such as these: the Great Wall of China, Victoria Falls, and the Eiffel Tower.

http://ce.eng.usf.edu/pharos/wonders/

Study Web

Whatever your homework assignment is, this site is sure to have something you can use, with "over 162,000 research-quality" links, listed by subject category. The Reference Shelf is a good place to start, but the brief reviews of each entry will also help you select just the right place to look. Tell your parents and teachers about this, too, because there is some neat stuff for them here as well.

http://www.studyweb.com/

Interactive Weather Maker

Who said you can't fool with Mother Nature? At this site you can try your hand at weathermaking. Turn a sunny day into a windy day. Or, stir up a rainy day. If you create the correct conditions, you can make a blizzard—complete with a snow whiteout. The site also links to Weather Central, which explains how weather works. The Flash plug-in is required to create your own weather. *http://teacher.scholastic.com/activities/wwatch/winter/blizzard/*

A B C D E F G H I J K L M N O P Q **R** S T U V W X Y Z

A
B
C
D
E
F
G
H
I
J
K
L
M
N
O
P
Q
R
S
T
U
V
W
X
Y
Z

Xrefer

Is it a search engine? Is it a reference tool? It's both! It offers "free access to over 50 reference titles containing more than 500,000 entries." What good is it? Just try typing in a name, place, or phrase. If you're lucky, you'll not only get an answer, but cross-references to other articles relating to your original question.

http://w2.xrefer.com/

ALMANACS AND GAZETTEERS

★ CIA World Factbook

Did you know that Kenya (582,650 square kilometers) is twice the size of Nevada? Did you know that in Denmark five languages are spoken (Danish, English, Faroese, Greenlandic, and German)? If you ever wanted to know facts like these about countries around the world, this is the place to look. You'll also find a section on oceans of the world. By the way, did you know that, as of 1997, there were an estimated 219 million TV sets in the United States?

http://www.odci.gov/cia/publications/factbook/

The Food Timeline

Ever wonder what medieval knights ate at their farewell meal before setting off to the crusades? Did you ever need to write a report on cookery in the 1800s? Maybe you just have to know some good recipes from Civil War times. Remember the food time line! Stretching from information on grains back in 17,000 B.C. to the details on foods of the 1990s, this site provides entertaining and educational fare.
http://www.gti.net/mocolib1/kid/food.html

★ Fact Monster

This is great! We typed in "highest waterfall" and up came a list starting with Angel Falls, about 3,212 feet high. Then we tried typing "Britney Spears birthday." BAM! She was born December 1, 1981. You can build your vocabulary with Word of the Day and find out whose birthday is celebrated today. How stupendous will your score be on the Harry Potter quiz? (We got a few wrong.) Don't miss this site.

http://www.factmonster.com/

★ How Far Is It?

In the not-too-distant past, finding the distance from one part of the globe to another took a fair amount of work. It involved using complicated tables and converting map scales. Now, we have an alternative. On this page, all you need to know is the name of two locations, and the distance between the two is calculated for you. This service provides distance for almost all places in the United States and a good number of major cities elsewhere. If a city doesn't appear to be in the database, just put in the name of the country and see what cities are available.

http://www.indo.com/distance/

The Old Farmer's Almanac

The Old Farmer's Almanac has been published ever since George Washington was president. This almanac gives the best time to plant crops, helps to determine the weather long in advance, and has lots of cool old sayings (these are called aphorisms). People have used and enjoyed the Old Farmer's Almanac throughout history. Now, parts of this publication are available on the Internet. You can see weather predictions, read some old-timey quotes, and find a great history of the almanac. Whether you live on a farm or in a city high-rise apartment, you'll like this site.

http://www.almanac.com/

Friends don't ask friends for their passwords.

> ## Strike up the bandwidth in MUSIC AND MUSICIANS.

AWARDS

See also BOOKS AND LITERATURE; MOVIES; MUSIC AND MUSICIANS; and TELEVISION

ALSC: The Randolph Caldecott Medal; The John Newbery Medal

There's no doubt that librarians know tons about books. Every year, children's librarians in the American Library Association give two awards to authors and illustrators of the best books for kids. The Caldecott Medal goes to the best illustrator of a children's book, and the Newbery Medal is given to the author of the finest kids' book. See the Caldecott winners at this Web site; then scroll to the bottom and click on the Newbery page for those winners. You'll find some librarian-tested and approved books!

http://www.ala.org/alsc/caldecott.html

The Nobel Foundation

Alfred Nobel was a Swedish-born inventor and international industrialist, most famous for the invention of dynamite. He died in 1896. His will founded the Nobel Prizes in the fields of physics, chemistry, literature, physiology/medicine, and peace. Since 1901, they have been presented to the winners (called Nobel laureates) at ceremonies on December 10, the anniversary of Alfred Nobel's death. Most of the prizes are awarded in Stockholm, Sweden, while the Nobel Peace Prize is awarded in Oslo, Norway. Since 1969, the Sveriges Riksbank (Bank of Sweden) Prize in Economic Sciences in memory of Alfred Nobel has been awarded in Stockholm at the same time. You can get a list of all the winners and pictures of the medals awarded, plus a biography of Nobel and a history of his prizes at this site.

http://www.nobel.se/

The Pulitzer Prizes

Joseph Pulitzer was an American newspaper publisher known for his innovative ideas and bold reporting style. When he died, his will established the Pulitzer Prizes. The first ones were awarded in 1917. Each year, achievements in American journalism, letters, drama, and music are recognized. Fourteen prizes are given in journalism. The prizes in "letters" are for fiction, history, poetry, general nonfiction, and biography or autobiography. There are also prizes for drama and music. At this site, you can read about the winners from 1917 through the present.

http://www.pulitzer.org/

CURRENCY CONVERTER

FXConverter - 164 Currency Converter

When is a dollar not a dollar? Wait a minute! Where did you get that dollar? Is that a U.S. dollar, or an Australian dollar, or a Namibian dollar? If it's a Namibian dollar, then it is likely worth less than half the U.S. dollar. The Australian dollar is worth more than the Namibian dollar but is still not worth as much as the U.S. dollar. Confused yet? What about the German mark, the Japanese yen, or the Slovenian tolar? Whoa! This stuff can get confusing. Luckily, at this site, with just a couple of clicks you can compare 164 currencies all over the world, from their values in 1990 through today. Try it!

http://www.oanda.com/converter/classic

DICTIONARIES

🦆 Little Explorers by Enchanted Learning Software

Try this on very little kids. They can click on any letter in the alphabet and link to lots of Web sites and activities that begin with that letter. This is an interactive picture dictionary, with hours of fun just waiting behind the letters. This page also has English-French, English-German, English-Portuguese, and English-Spanish versions.

http://www.EnchantedLearning.com/Dictionary.html

A B C D E F G H I J K L M N O P Q R S T U V W X Y Z

★ Merriam-Webster's Collegiate Dictionary

Sure, you can look up words online and get the definitions from this famous dictionary publisher. You can even hear the word pronounced for you. One of the coolest online features is that if you spell the word wrong, it quickly gives you a list of possible alternative spellings. But you can also read some of the fascinating features about interesting words and scratch your head over some perplexing word puzzles. See what words Shakespeare coined at *<http://www.m-w.com/lighter/shak/ShakHome.htm>*, or trace the history of the word "phat" at *<http:// www.m-w.com/lighter/flap/ flaphome.htm#Phat>*. Find out how words get into the dictionary, too. This page explains how Merriam-Webster does it, and they should know the best way, because they have been doing it since the 1880s.

http://www.m-w.com/netdict.htm

NET FILES

Where on Earth can you climb *inside* a huge elephant and live to tell your friends about it?

Answer: Lucy is a famous elephant-shaped building in Margate City, New Jersey. She dates back to 1888, built by a realtor to advertise his business development plans! It took one million pieces of lumber for the structure and 12,000 feet of tin for the elephant's skin. You can climb up spiral staircases inside the legs to get to the rooms inside. See a picture of Lucy at *http://www.levins.com/lucy.htm*

OneLook Dictionaries

Parental advisory: please preview this site, as it contains links to street, drug, and rap slang. Did you know that a lot of specialized online dictionaries are scattered all over the Net? There are dictionaries for medicine, sports, religion, art, music, and more. This site has cobbled together 751 of them to create a huge dictionary you can search with just one look (can you guess what it is called?).

http://www.onelook.com/

Spellweb

N'Sync or Backstreet Boys? Hot dogs or hamburgers? Let the Net decide which is more popular. Based on the number of search engine hits on each name, you can reach a popularity poll, of sorts. You can also use this to check on the most frequently used spelling of a word, for example, "nettiquette" or "netiquette." The latter wins by a landslide.

http://www.spellweb.com/

★ A Web of On-line Dictionaries

Parental advisory: Remember, some dictionaries may contain profanity and obscenity. This exceptional resource collects links to hundreds of specialty online dictionaries and word lists in 270 different languages. You'll also find other reference sources, such as thesauri, rhyming dictionaries, grammars, and more.

http://www.yourdictionary.com/

★ Word Central

Don't miss the winner of the year 2000 Webby Award for the best educational Web site for kids. It's a dictionary, but it's so much more than that. Just enter the hallway and look around. Straight ahead, stop in at the Daily Buzzword. Expand your vocabulary (listen to how the word is pronounced), and then move to the second floor and try experimenting with words in the Science room. Turn a word into Morse code, or send it through the vowel monster to see what happens.

http://www.wordcentral.com/

Curl up with a good Internet site.

ENCYCLOPEDIAS

★ Encyclopædia Britannica Online

The *Encyclopædia Britannica* is available on the Internet. All those great articles on science, history, and geography are obtainable by point and click—the whole enchilada is here! However (and this is a big however), it costs money to subscribe to this service. You can, though, sample the Britannica Online to see if you want to purchase access. Use the Sample Search area to get partial information in answer to any question; sometimes that's enough. Try the link to Britannica.com for an excellent list of annotated links on all sorts of subjects: *<http://www.britannica.com/>*.

http://www.eb.com/

HOW-TO

eHow - How Things Get Done

Parental advisory: please preview this site. If you've ever wanted to know how to organize a scavenger hunt, plan a teddy bear picnic, build a sand castle, or find a Pikablu (also known as Marril or Mariru) Pokémon card, this is your site. You can also learn to do hundreds of other useful or fun things.

http://www.ehow.com/home/

Learn2.com

Parental advisory: please preview this site. Do you know how to use chopsticks, or clean a freshly caught fish? Could you use a lesson in putting a golf ball or breaking in a new baseball mitt? How about tips on folding a shirt or cleaning up a stain? This truly great site will teach you all of the above and thousands of more skills.

http://www.learn2.com/learn2_everyday.asp

POPULATION
U.S. Census Bureau

Do you know what Obi-wan Kenobi said to Luke Skywalker in Star Wars, when he had a question about the population of the United States? "Use the Source, Luke!" For such questions, go right to the source: the U.S. Census Bureau. How do they count the number of people in the U.S.? Find out here; plus learn lots of statistical info on jobs, housing, health, crime, income, education, marriage and family, race and ethnicity, aging, transportation and travel, and recreation.

http://www.census.gov/

U.S. POPClock Projection

The current estimated U.S. population is found at this site. The U.S. Census Bureau starts with the most recent census and adds the births and subtracts the deaths. Then they factor in their best guesses about trends and come up with this estimated result. In case you wondered, only residents in the U.S. and the District of Columbia are counted, and not families of military serving overseas or others living abroad.

http://www.census.gov/cgi-bin/popclock/

World POPClock Projection

Quick! If you wanted to send a letter to everyone in the world, how many stamps would you need? See an estimate of the world's current population at this site.

http://www.census.gov/cgi-bin/ipc/popclockw/

THESAURI
Merriam-Webster's Collegiate Thesaurus

Sometimes words can be so frustrating. Have you ever had a homework assignment and found you were using the same word over and over again? You just couldn't think of another word that meant the same thing. To solve this problem, use a thesaurus. All you have to do is type in a word and you'll get a list of similar words. Now you'll be able to impress your teachers with your growing—expanding, increasing, enlarging—vocabulary.

http://www.m-w.com/thesaurus.htm

A B C D E F G H I J K L M N O P Q R S T U V W X Y Z

A B C D E F G H I J K L M N O P Q R S T U V W X Y Z

★ Plumb Design Visual Thesaurus

This resource offers a Java-based way to see relationships in English words. Imagine the starting word at the center of the screen, floating in space. Around it are the various synonyms of that word, arranged like spokes on a wheel. If you click on one of those words, you will see that word drift to the center, while new spokes for it appear. The link to the original word is still there for you to see, too. It's a visual dictionary. No, it's a flight simulator. No, it's just fun!

http://www.plumbdesign.com/thesaurus/

The Wordsmyth English Dictionary - Thesaurus

Why no one on the Web ever thought of this before, we don't know. This resource combines a dictionary with a thesaurus, so you can find synonyms and antonyms, as well as definitions. There are also regular contests, interesting word lists, and other diversions from folks who are obviously in love with language.

http://www.wordsmyth.net/

You Be the Historian

This site invites you to find out all you can about an American family's life in the 1700s. By examining artifacts and documents at this site, you may be able to get a fairly good picture of what life was like for Thomas and Elizabeth Springer's family in New Castle, Delaware, 200 years ago. Compare your guesses to what historians have concluded. What could future archaeologists and historians learn about your family from what's on the floor of your closet, under your bed, or in your trash? *http://americanhistory.si.edu/hohr/springer/*

WEIGHTS AND MEASURES
Online Conversion

When this site says it can convert just about anything to anything else, it means it. Here you'll find more than 30,000 conversions and calculators. So, if you want to convert Celsius to Fahrenheit or vice versa, drop by this site. With so many conversions, you won't get bored. But if you do, check out Fun Stuff. One of the calculators will let you calculate your age in dog years. Arf!

http://www.onlineconversion.com/

Unit Converter

This great resource will convert distance (such as miles to kilometers), mass (or weights, including pounds to kilograms), temperature (for example, Celsius to Fahrenheit), speed (such as kilometers per hour to miles per hour), and other types of measurements.

http://www.webcom.com/~legacysy/convert2/
    convert2.html

UnitWiz - Convert Inches, Feet, Meters, and Other Length Units

If you don't like the interface for the preceding sites, you may like this one better. It performs about the same set of conversion calculations for length, area, mass, temperature, and a lot more measurements.

http://www.unitwiz.com/

WORLD RECORDS

See name of sport or subject under SPORTS

ZIP AND POSTAL CODES
ZIP Code Lookup

This is a very useful U.S. ZIP code lookup service. This site will provide, in most instances, a ZIP code for towns you provide. This service is provided by the U.S. Postal Service. If you don't know your nine-digit ZIP code, this site *<http://www.usps.gov/ncsc/lookups/ lookup_zip+4.html>* will tell you, based on your address.

http://www.usps.gov/ncsc/lookups/
    lookup_ctystzip.html

RELIGION AND SPIRITUALITY

See also ARCHITECTURE; HOLIDAYS.

There are many ways people show reverence to a higher power. We list only some of them here. Please note that many religious and spiritual traditions don't yet have Web pages with material aimed at a youthful audience. We keep looking! If you would like to suggest a page for consideration, please write to feedback@netmom.com.

BeliefNet Teen Channel

Parental advisory: please preview this site. If you're looking for other Hindu teens to talk to, or other Christian teens, or Pagan teens, or atheist teens (the list goes on and on), you might visit this site's discussion boards and look around. There are also interviews with young people you'll be interested to know, like the teenage Buddhist nun in Nova Scotia and the Teens-4-Christ group in Ohio. There's a young woman making the Hajj pilgrimage to Mecca who is currently sharing her online journal. For good measure, there are interviews with Bono, and you can find out what N'Sync, Britney Spears, Faith Hill, and others have in common with the Pope.

http://www.beliefnet.com/index/index_608.html

Creation Stories

On this page, you'll find creation stories and traditional wisdom as told by schoolchildren. Included are animal legends, creation stories, tales about the environment, and other stories from Australia, Iceland, Canada, Alaska, and Israel. There is also a collection of links for further study.

http://www.internet-at-work.com/hos_mcgrane/
   creation/cstorymenu.html

Visit the stars in ASTRONOMY, SPACE, AND SPACE EXPLORATION.

Faith and Reason

This site makes the point that faith and scientific reason have not always been in conflict, but have in fact always been entwined. Some scientists and theologians believe that faith and reason can even support each other. The issues considered here are evolutionary biology, cosmology, genetics, and technology. PBS offers its usual excellent multimedia presentation of this topic.

http://www.pbs.org/faithandreason/

★ God Speaks

You've seen them on the highway. Gigantic black billboards with stark white lettering. They say "What part of 'you shall not' didn't you understand?" and "Don't make me come down there." They are signed, simply, "God." Who's behind these messages? Find out here. There's also an even better site for kids, called WuzupGod at <http://www.wuzupgod.com/>.

http://www.godspeaks.org/

Religious Movements

Every year, students taking this professor's course are required to create an entry in what's become an encyclopedia of religions. Each profile contains a basic overview of the religion plus worthy links and print resources to consult for further information. There are more than 200 of these profiles now listed.

http://religiousmovements.lib.virginia.edu/

StudyWeb: History & Social Studies: Religion

Gain a general overview of the diversity of religious Web sites available. Notice that each selected site is briefly annotated, and sometimes there are little red apples next to the best ones. Locate "research-quality" sites on everything from the Amish to Wicca.

http://www.studyweb.com/History__Social_Studies/
   relig_toc.htm

A B C D E F G H I J K L M N O P Q **R** S T U V W X Y Z

Table Graces and Blessings

This little collection of table graces and prayers ranges from very reverent to something you might hear at summer camp. Some of the prayers come from a Christian perspective while the majority are nonsectarian. For Jewish, as well as Christian prayers and table graces, try this site <http://www.bedtime.com/html/prayers.html>.

http://homiliesbyemail.com/graces.html

★ Virtual Religion Index

From the Religion Department at Rutgers University, this annotated selection of links provides a convenient shortcut to quality sites about various religions, beliefs, and practices. Hint: if you can't find the subject heading you're looking for, try the Confessional Agencies section.

http://religion.rutgers.edu/vri/

Your Guide to the Religions of the World

Learn about the beliefs and practices of six major religions: Islam, Judaism, Hinduism, Sikhism, Buddhism, and Christianity. You'll study how each faith began, discover a little about its prophets and leaders, and find out how the faith is put into practice today. There is also a list of links for each section.

http://www.bbc.co.uk/worldservice/people/features/world_religions/index.shtml

APPARITIONS AND MIRACLES

Apparitions of the Virgin Mary in Medjugorje

The apparitions of Mary in Medjugorje (in Bosnia Herzegovina, the former Yugoslavia) are well known, and many pilgrims travel there each year to experience this special place on a personal level. If you can't take a trip there, you can learn about it at this Web site. Please explore this site with a trusted adult.

http://www.medjugorje.org/

Catholic Online Angels

Many people believe that angels, while invisible to the human eye, may be felt by the human heart. This site is a good introduction to angels. Did you know there are nine different kinds of angels? Most are described on this page, but not all. For the rest, visit this page as well: The Holy Angels at <http://www.ocf.org/OrthodoxPage/reading/angels.html>. Parental advisory: this site also contains information on fallen angels.

http://www.catholic.org/saints/angels.html

The Miracles Page

Crosses of light, weeping statues, healing waters, the Hindu milk miracle, the white buffalo—are these events hoaxes or real? One thing is sure: it's next to impossible to find information about them in a book (except this book!), since so many of them are new and facts are sketchy. Check the info at this site, and see if you can make up your own mind from the information as it is presented. You might want to ask a parent or other trusted adult what he or she thinks about it all.

http://www.mcn.org/1/miracles/

The Shroud of Turin

In a cathedral in Turin, Italy, sits a silver chest. Inside the chest is the mysterious Turin Shroud, which many believe to be the burial cloth that covered Jesus Christ. You'll view amazing photographs and research about the famous shroud. Examining the evidence, what do you see?

http://www.shroud.com/

BAHÁ'Í
Bahá'í Faith

One of the world's fastest growing religions, Bahá'í was founded in the mid-nineteenth century by Bahá'u'lláh, a Persian nobleman. He gave up a comfortable and secure lifestyle for a life of persecution and deprivation. Learn more about his life and teachings here, and at the official U.S. Web site <http://www.us.bahai.org/>.

http://www.bahai.com/

The Bahá'í World

Could many of the world religions be rolled into one? The Bahá'í believe that there have been many messengers from God, each one arriving during a different age. This online archive will show you other teachings, texts, sacred sites, and where to find more on the Bahá'í faith.

http://www.bahai.org/

BIBLE STUDY

★ Audio-Bible

Would you like to have the entire Bible read aloud to you? The version here takes 72 hours, but you don't have to listen to it all at one time. Alexander Scourby recorded the King James version back in the 1940s. It was a "talking book" for the blind, but now it is available to everyone over the Internet.

http://www.audio-bible.com/

★ Bible Gateway

Can't seem to recall that Bible verse about the "lilies of the field"? Just visit this site. Type the target word, phrase, or verse into the search box and hit Lookup. Here it is, Matthew 6:28, "And why are you anxious about clothing? Consider the lilies of the field, how they grow; they neither toil nor spin." That's not much, so click on the button that lets you see the complete chapter for the context of the quote. If you want to see a different translation, you have your choice of several. And if you'd like to hear the Bible (in several versions) you can select it in English, Chinese, Italian, Portuguese, or Spanish.

http://bible.gospelcom.net/bible?

Bible Quizzes

Do you know how long Noah's ark was? Do you recall who ended up in the fiery furnace? What was Jesus' teaching about prayer? Try these illustrated quizzes and see how much you know about the Bible.

http://www.twopaths.com/biblequizzes.html

Blue Letter Bible

This resource combines a King James Version Bible and other research tools. It's very extensive, and if you're into Bible study, this site is powerful. The Blue Letter Bible features "over 3,560,000 links onsite to over 165,000 pages of concordances, lexicons, dictionaries, commentaries, images, and Bible versions!"

http://www.blueletterbible.org/

The Unbound Bible

Search ten English versions of the Bible, plus Greek and Hebrew versions, ancient versions, and 42 variants in other languages. If that's not enough, explore Bible commentaries, dictionaries, and more. If the Bible seems like a huge undertaking to read, this site encourages you to take a whole year, and read it one or two chapters at a time. See what chapter they recommend for today. You can read it right at this Web page.

http://www.unboundbible.org/

BUDDHISM
★ Buddha Mind

"The light of wisdom dispels the darkness of ignorance. Light the candles." And enter the meditation room. After you experience that, you may think that's pretty much it in Buddhist practice. But you haven't seen the Right Brain side of the site yet. Good luck. If you get too confused, try the Left Brain section instead.

http://www.BuddhaMind.cjb.net/

What's a Humuhumunukunukuapua'a?

http://oldhawaii.com/igd/keiki/games/humu.htm

Answer: Also known as the trigger fish, it's the official state fish of Hawaii, and you can see a drawing of one at

A
B
C
D
E
F
G
H
I
J
K
L
M
N
O
P
Q
R
S
T
U
V
W
X
Y
Z

A B C D E F G H I J K L M N O P Q R S T U V W X Y Z

★ BuddhaNet: Buddhist Information Network

The principles of Buddhism explained, Real Audio meditation lessons and chanting, and the top ten Buddhist URLs are only a few of the resources at this extensive site. Don't miss the "Ten Oxherding Pictures," which symbolize the spiritual quest, at <http://www.buddhanet.net/oxherd1.htm>. There are even Buddhist crossword puzzles! Be sure to see the kids' pages, too, at <http://www.buddhanet.net/mag_kids.htm> for Buddhist children's stories, interactive pictures, and more.

http://www.buddhanet.net/

Healing the Earth: A Sacred Art by the Tibetan Lamas of Drepung Loseling Monastery

This site follows the creation of a Tibetan sacred sand painting from the beginning to its end. Considered a healing ceremony, the area for the sand painting is claimed and blessed. Local spirits are asked for permission before construction begins. The monks draw an intricate geometric mandala on the floor. Colored grains of sand are painstakingly placed with precise movements. The process takes several days. The mandala's patterns have significance on many different levels: learn about them at this site. After the painting is complete, there is a dismantling ceremony. All the sand is swept up and deposited in a nearby body of water. Find out why.

http://www.civilization.ca/membrs/traditio/mandala/
    mandalae.html

Zen

You're trying to meditate, concentrating on your breathing, and all of a sudden a really annoying fly lands on your nose. What do you do? Experience the first step of Zen.

http://www.do-not-zzz.com/

Zen@MetaLab

Zen Buddhism is based on a philosophy of life taught by Gautama Buddha, who lived and taught in northern India in the sixth century B.C. The Buddha was not a god—Buddha means "enlightened one" or "one who is awake." The teachings of Buddhism have one aim: to relieve beings from suffering. This meta-resource includes art, philosophy, meditation, and many fascinating links. Parental advisory: not all links have been checked.

http://metalab.unc.edu/zen/

CHRISTIANITY

All About Jesus - Ongoing Bible Study for Children

Even preschoolers can learn about the Bible with these age-appropriate verses, pictures, and animations. The studies offer additional links and sometimes a few suggested activities. For those who want even more, there's a newsletter and plenty of Christian links.

http://www.geocities.com/~perkinshome/
    childrennew.html

★ Children's Chapel - What's Here?

Gather 'round for 54 Bible stories, told in such a way that even little children will be anxious to hear the outcome. You'll find stories of Joseph, Moses, and Jesus. Each story comes with a Bible memory verse, a short prayer, and a question, "Can you find this story in the Bible?" The citation is given, so you won't be confused very long. There is also a wonderful selection of Christian children's links at this site.

http://www.misslink.org/children/bibstory2.html

NET FILES

What plants attract butterflies?

Answer: Many flowering plants attract butterflies, and others help feed their caterpillars. Some of these are milkweed, lantana, lilac, cosmos, goldenrod, and zinnia. If you flutter by, you can find out more at http://www.butterflies.com/guide.html

★ The Cyber Hymnal

This site has more than 2,900 Christian hymns from many denominations. They are available in MIDI format for your listening pleasure. Don't remember the words? The lyrics are here, too, and you can sing right along. You can also view hymns by topic, for example, Children's Hymns. In the trivia section you can find hymns appearing in movies or sung at celebrity funerals and other events. Usually there is a biography of the hymnist, as well as a picture or photo.

http://www.cyberhymnal.org/

Danielle's Place

Wow! Danielle is full of terrific craft ideas for vacation Bible school, Sunday school, or any time. There are also games and selected activities to go along with Bible stories. How about making your own armor of God, or a "prayer rock" to remind you to say your prayers.

http://www.daniellesplace.com/

Ecclesiastical Calendar: Enter a Year

Easter is a movable feast. That means it's on a different day each year, based on a special formula explained at this site. You can find the dates for both the Western Easter and the Orthodox Easter, through the year 2124. It also calculates the dates of many Christian holy days for any year you please.

http://www.smart.net/~mmontes/ec-cal.html

Joyful Noise Christian Music for Kids

Karaoke Christian music? For kids? You betcha. Don't miss the one that teaches you all the names of all 66 books of the Bible. It has a very familiar tune that you will recognize right away.

http://www.ajoyfulnoise.net/kidspage.htm

★ Kids 4 Truth

Hover over the control buttons and see what's in store for you at this site. There are Creation and Nativity coloring pages, missionary multimedia, and lots more. The really outstanding part of this site is in the Dynamation section. Watch stunning multimedia presentations called Creation, One, The Arrival, and Chosen. Parents should preview them first.

http://www.kids4truth.com/

Virtual Church Kids!

This virtual church has a youth room just for kids. You'll find Bible stories with colorful graphics to go along with them. If you want to read an exciting one, try "The Men in the Fiery Furnace." If you're a younger kid, you can ask a parent to download coloring pages. Explore the other rooms in this church, too. The library, for instance, contains crossword puzzles, trivia quizzes, and word jumbles. Don't miss a peek at the skeletons in the closet!

http://www.virtualchurch.org/kids.htm

Who Is Jesus?

This page, offered by the Campus Crusade for Christ, asks who is the most outstanding personality of all time? Their answer is Jesus, but some wonder if he was a liar, a lunatic, or truly the Son of God. Explore this question as you look at a detailed life of Jesus, through words of the Bible.

http://www.ccci.org/whoisjesus/

CHRISTIANITY—AMISH, MENNONITE

The Amish and "The Plain People"

If you've ever been curious about the Amish, Mennonites, the Brethren, or the other "Plain People" of the Pennsylvania Dutch country, visit this page. You'll learn a little about their beliefs, their mode of dress, and their customs. Did you know that an Amish bride wears a blue wedding dress, or that kids attend school only through the eighth grade?

http://www.800padutch.com/amish.html

A B C D E F G H I J K L M N O P Q R S T U V W X Y Z

Discovery Online, Amish Online

What happened when a reporter stayed with an Amish family for a week? She got a lesson in baking shoofly pie, quilt-making, and cow management. She also learned a lot about how the Amish really live. Read this fascinating tale, punctuated by recipes that look delicious.

http://www.discovery.com/area/exploration/amish/amish1.html

CHRISTIANITY—CATHOLIC
Chant

In New Mexico is a Benedictine monastery called Christ in the Desert. The Brothers chant the Divine Office daily. It is a series of seven prayer sessions throughout the day and one at night. They have recorded some of their sacred chants so you can learn about them. This is a beautifully designed site.

http://www.christdesert.org/noframes/chant/chant.html

Volunteer Match

Parental advisory: please preview this site, many organizations are involved. What's different about this award-winning resource? It matches volunteers with opportunities that can be temporary or ongoing. You can even become a virtual volunteer and participate without ever leaving your computer keyboard. Visit the site and you'll be hooked. We found out our local science museum wanted volunteers to help build a new door, catalog a small library, and run the planetarium show. Volunteer Match is so easy to use, and fun, too. *http://www.volunteermatch.org/*

Holy Year 2000 - The Great Jubilee

Holy Year has been celebrated every 25 years from 1450 until the present time. People flock to Rome to ask forgiveness for their sins. They visit the great basilicas of St. Peter, St. Paul, St. John Lateran, and St. Mary Major. Catholics believe that participating in these special ceremonies will grant them indulgences, which remove the penalties for their past sinful behavior. Each basilica has a holy door, which is sealed except during the term of the Holy Year. Pilgrims pass through the holy doors, and at the end of the year, the doors are walled up to await the next jubilee. Learn the history of this holy event at this site.

http://www.annosanto2000.com/ENGLISH/

Lectio Divina, Centering Prayer, and the Contemplative Tradition

According to this site, "*Lectio Divina* aims at giving an awareness of God's presence through a fourfold process, *lectio*, *meditatio*, *oratio*, and *contemplatio*. Lectio is receiving the word of God, meditatio, allowing the Word to be present in the awareness giving rise to oratio, prayer, and contemplatio, resting in the presence of God." See what high school students have written as part of this process. There's also a section on "centering prayer," which is using one word to help you meditate and reflect, letting go of your other thoughts.

http://www.lectiodivina.org/

The Marian Hour

Many Catholics around the world pray using a special set of beads called a rosary. They use the beads to count the various prayers they have said. You can learn about the mysteries of the rosary at this well-designed site, as well as hear the various prayers for yourself. The organization will send a free rosary to anyone who wants one. This site has audio files in French as well as English, and text files in many languages.

http://www.marianhour.ca/

The Mary Page

Mary, the mother of Jesus, is also known as Mary, the Blessed Virgin; Our Lady; Madonna; Notre Dame; Domina, and more. Learning more about Mary, some believe they may acquire a fuller knowledge of Christ. Check the FAQ to find out why Mary is not always pictured wearing light blue.

http://www.udayton.edu/mary/

Patron Saints

You can find the patron saint for just about any occupation or country or organization at this site. Did you know there's a patron saint for broadcasters? And comedians? Check it out here!

http://www.catholic.org/saints/patron.html

Vatican Radio

Vatican Radio first went on the air in 1931, and at this site you can read its history and discover that Marconi himself (the telegraphy pioneer and Nobel laureate) was its first director. Staff from 61 countries prepare hours of broadcast material every week in 40 different languages. Radio Vatican broadcasts on radio, satellite, and the Internet. You can listen to streaming Real Audio features in several languages. As they say, "Listen, for heaven's sake!"

http://www.vaticanradio.org/inglese/enindex.html

Vatican: The Holy See

The Vatican has established an official and attractive Web site under its own top-level country domain, ".va." There's a tremendous amount of material about the pope, the structure of the Roman Catholic Church, history of the church and previous pontiffs, and information about the Vatican museums. This site is well worth checking—and you can do it in several different languages!

http://www.vatican.va/

> ### Have an order of pi in MATH AND ARITHMETIC.

CHRISTIANITY—CHRISTIAN SCIENCE
The Church of Christ, Scientist

Here is a quote from this page: "Christian Science is based on the words and works of Christ Jesus, and draws its authority from the Bible. Its teachings are set forth in Science and Health with Key to the Scriptures by Mary Baker Eddy. Although a distinctive part of Christian Science is the healing of disease by spiritual means alone, its higher purpose is universal salvation from every phase of evil—including sin and death (see Matthew 10:8)." The site offers a convenient FAQ about specific beliefs, a VR (virtual reality) tour of the mother church, and much more.

http://www.tfccs.com/

CHRISTIANITY—EPISCOPAL
The Episcopal Church Welcomes You

This is the official site of the Episcopalian Church. It gives a concise version of church beliefs, church history, what to expect at a worship service, and more.

http://www.episcopalchurch.org/welcome/

CHRISTIANITY—GREEK ORTHODOX
Greek Orthodox Archdiocese of America

Click on "About Orthodox Christianity" to find out the beliefs of this faith. According to the site, "Orthodox Christianity begins with the first Pentecost in Jerusalem and the outpouring of the Holy Spirit on Christ's small circle of disciples. It is then that the Orthodox Church was born—the second largest organized body of Christians in the world."

http://www.goarch.org/

A B C D E F G H I J K L M N O P Q R S T U V W X Y Z

Earth and Moon Viewer

This isn't really a clock, but it will show you where it's day and where it's night—right now—all over the planet. When it's 10 A.M. and bright and sunny in Florida, what's it like in Japan? Stop by this site and ask the server, which will show where it's light and dark anyplace in the world. You can choose the satellite location from which to view, or you can tell it to look at Earth from the Sun's or Moon's perspective. You can even create a custom request and specify the desired longitude and latitude you want to see; the computer then picks the best viewpoint.
http://www.fourmilab.ch/earthview/vplanet.html

CHRISTIANITY—JEHOVAH'S WITNESSES

Jehovah's Witnesses: Watchtower Society Official Web Site

Learn about the beliefs and practices of the Jehovah's Witnesses through an online Bible study pamphlet and numerous articles from The Watchtower and other publications.

http://www.watchtower.org/

CHRISTIANITY—PRESBYTERIAN

Presbyterian Church (U.S.A.)

Find out about beliefs, ongoing missions, and events sponsored by the Presbyterian Church. There's also a special youth site at *<http://pyc.pcusa.org/>* with links to other Presbyterian youth pages.

http://www.pcusa.org/pcusa/welcome.htm

CHRISTIANITY—RELIGIOUS SOCIETY OF FRIENDS

Friends General Conference

Also known as Quakers, the Religious Society of Friends has had a long history of working for social justice. This site says, "Quakers do not win acceptance because they are numerous or because they are growing in numbers. What does distinguish the Quakers from many other Christians is their personal commitment to God and humanity. The Quaker worships God by serving Him through society. Although decidedly mystical, Quakerism does not understand a purely interior religion. It believes that the Christian faith must express itself in action and service." Learn more here.

http://www.quaker.org/friends.html

CHRISTIANITY—SEVENTH-DAY ADVENTIST

Adventist World Church Official Website

This official site explains the church's name this way: "The name Seventh-day Adventist includes two vital beliefs for us as a Church. 'Adventist' reflects our passionate conviction in the nearness of the soon return ('advent') of Jesus. 'Seventh-day' refers to the Biblical Sabbath which from Creation on has always been on the seventh day of the week, or Saturday." You can easily find the church's beliefs regarding more than 25 subjects. There is also a link called Bible Info, *<http://www.bibleinfo.com/>*, where you can learn more.

http://www.adventist.org/

CHRISTIANITY—TAIZÉ

The Taizé Community

This contemplative community was founded in France in the 1940s. Its simple style of worship, utilizing prayer and song, has since spread around the world. Learn about Taizé practice and listen to lovely audio clips.

http://www.taize.fr/

CHRISTIANITY—THE CHURCH OF JESUS CHRIST OF LATTER-DAY SAINTS

All About Mormons

Visit this reflective site for information on the distinctive beliefs of the Latter-day Saints, also known as Mormons. This is not an official Church site, so parents should preview the opinions stated here.

http://www.mormons.org/

American Prophet: The Story of Joseph Smith

This PBS documentary traces the life of Joseph Smith, founder of the Church of Jesus Christ of Latter-day Saints. You'll also learn about Church history and beliefs and find a select list of links for further research.

http://www.pbs.org/americanprophet/

The Church of Jesus Christ of Latter-day Saints

The Church of Jesus Christ of Latter-day Saints was officially organized on April 6, 1830, with six members. Today, congregations of the church are found all over the world. With millions of members, it is one of the fastest growing religions in the world and one of the largest Christian churches in the United States. Neither Protestant nor Catholic, the Church of Jesus Christ of Latter-day Saints is "a restoration of the ancient Church as established by Jesus Christ." This site outlines the beliefs of the church, as well as the worldwide programs it offers. A detailed history of the church is also offered, and the Pioneer Trail Story section at <http://www.lds.org/gospellibrary/pioneer/ pioneerstory.htm> is particularly interesting.

http://www.lds.org/

LDSWorld

This is the place to go to find numerous sites of interest to the Latter-day Saints. There's an interactive tour to the faith's historic sites, an audio version of The Book of Mormon, and even links to LDS specialty products you can purchase online. Don't miss Kids World at <http:// www.ldsworld.com/kidsworld/> for LDS games, simplified articles of faith, and more.

http://www.ldsworld.com/

Temple Square Tour

The Deseret News offers a stunning tour of the landmarks of Temple Square in Salt Lake City, Utah, home of the Church of Jesus Christ of Latter-day Saints. You'll see the temple, the tabernacle, and various monuments around the grounds. Be sure to take a peek at the world-famous pipe organ in the tabernacle. It has 11,623 pipes!

http://deseretnews.com/confer/sqtour/tour.htm

CHRISTIANITY—UNITED METHODIST

Official Website of the United Methodist Church

This official Web site for the United Methodist Church includes information about the various departments within the church structure, as well as links to hundreds of resources for individual churches across the country. Find historical origins of the church and doctrinal beliefs in the About section.

http://www.UMC.org/

There's a real gem of a site in EARTH SCIENCE— GEOLOGY—GEMS AND MINERALS!

A
B
C
D
E
F
G
H
I
J
K
L
M
N
O
P
Q
R
S
T
U
V
W
X
Y
Z

CREATION STUDIES

Creation Science

How did life on Earth begin? Some scientists believe life evolved over millions of years. Others believe there are some real problems with the theory of evolution. For instance, how did life originate from dead chemicals? How could man have come from the apes? To see the arguments against the theory of evolution, go to this site, and follow up on the many links suggested. Parental advisory: please preview this site.

http://emporium.turnpike.net/C/cs/

Creation SuperLibrary - ChristianAnswers.Net

Some people believe that dinosaurs are mentioned in the Bible, and that man and dinosaurs once lived during the same geologic time period. If you would like to learn more about these ideas, visit this Web resource. Parental advisory: please preview this site.

http://www.christiananswers.net/creation/

★ Kids4Truth Creation

View this amazing portrayal of the seven-day Biblical Creation story. It will take a while to load, but it's worth it. If you have questions about the presentation, just click on the link to the FAQ at the end.

http://www.kids4truth.com/creation.htm

Theory of Evolution and Creation Science

Have you ever thought about how Earth began? Or how all the plants and animals came to be? "Creation scientists" are those who believe that it all came about as described in the Bible. To help form your own theories, investigate this page, which is part of a larger site. Parental advisory: please preview this resource.

http://www.religioustolerance.org/evolutio.htm

HINDUISM

★ Hindu Kids Universe

Learn about Hindu prayers, songs, and alphabets, and download coloring pages. Older kids will prefer the Hindu Youth pages <http:// www.hinduyouth.com/> although some of the information is the same. Unfortunately the comics section no longer works. But the official *Amar Chitra Katha* comics site is supposed to launch soon <http:// www.amarchitrakatha.com/>.

http://www.hindukids.org/

The Hindu Universe Resource Center

Parental advisory: please preview this site. At this resource page, you can explore the Hindu universe: art, music, dance, philosophy, sages, gurus, scriptures, and more. You will see many wonderful photos of Hindu temples and learn about Hindu festivals.

http://www.hindunet.org/

Hinduism Today

This site offers an introduction to Hindu belief and practice, including a link to "How to Become a Hindu." Check out *Hinduism Today*, the monthly magazine "Affirming the Sanatana Dharma and Recording the History of a Billion-Strong Global Religion in Renaissance." Back issues include a June 1998 article about saris, the lovely draped garment many Indian women wear.

http://www.hinduismtoday.kauai.hi.us/

Hinduism Online

In this resource from Gurudeva's ashram on Kauai, you'll find lots of information on Hindu beliefs, as well as a link to the magazine Hinduism Today. The resources section includes links to sites on yoga, ayurvedic medicine, and more.

http://www.himalayanacademy.com/

Crack open CODES AND CIPHERS.

★ Meeting God - Elements of Hindu Devotion

These powerful and extraordinary photographs illustrate daily devotional ritual for Hindus, Sikhs, and Jains. The exhibit has been in the Houston Museum of Natural History and is in the American Museum of Natural History in New York from September 28, 2001, to February 10, 2002.

http://kaladarshan.arts.ohio-state.edu/exhib/meetgod/hp.htm

Nine Questions About Hinduism

On July 4, 1990, the youth meeting of the Hindu Temple of Greater Chicago had a special visitor: Gurudeva, Sivaya Subramuniyaswami. He was asked to give "official" answers to nine questions, ranging from "Are Hindus idol worshippers?" to "What's this reincarnation thing?" to "Why do Hindu women wear the dot on the forehead?" It's a revealing look at what kids want to know about Hinduism. Hindu gods are described and illustrated in one link from this page (scroll to the bottom), and the top level at this site includes numerous outside links. Parental advisory: Links from this page have not been checked.

http://www.spiritweb.org/Spirit/nine-questions.html

TempleNet - Indian Temple Information

Hindu temples are designed to reflect the beliefs of that religion, and to symbolize the meeting of the real world with the eternal one. Entrances face east, towards the rising sun, and temples are often constructed to look like mountains, because Hindu gods like them. At this site you can not only learn about temple architecture and decoration, but also explore many Hindu temples in India.

http://www.templenet.com/

NET FILES

If you were to go fishing for a glacier, what kind of bait would you use?

http://www.execpc.com/~washman/iceworms.htm

Answer: Ice worms, of course! These little critters are the only animals that live inside glacial ice. You can read a bit more about them and see a picture of one at

INTERFAITH AND NONSECTARIAN

Gobind Sadan: House of God

There is a place in India where the holidays of all faiths are celebrated with reverence. It is a farm-based spiritual place of pilgrimage for all people, under the guidance of Baba Virsa Singh Ji, known simply as Babaji. He asks for no charity, he recruits no followers, yet people from all over the world, and all walks of life, come to this place to see him, hear his teachings, and perform short periods of voluntary service. The place, in South Delhi, is called Gobind Sadan, "House of God." There is a similar site in the U.S. near Central Square, New York. Babaji says, "All the Prophets have come from one Source. They did not come to build religious institutions as walled forts, they came to change our consciousness. They came to teach us how to live. Sectarian divisions have been created by religious 'authorities,' out of self interest. Ignore them—we are all sisters and brothers, with one parent." Babaji emphasizes that religion is not a matter of outer rituals. It is a loving inner surrender to God's eternal teachings. His farm communities, built on former wastelands, are now fertile and thrive with abundance. They are self-supporting and do not seek monetary donations.

http://www.GobindSadan.org/

A B C D E F G H I J K L M N O P Q R S T U V W X Y Z

A
B
C
D
E
F
G
H
I
J
K
L
M
N
O
P
Q
R
S
T
U
V
W
X
Y
Z

ISLAM

CyberSalat - A Multimedia Islamic Prayer Simulator

Running under Windows, this free download (actually, "charityware") program teaches Islamic prayer to young and old alike. Learn the body postures used, and what the Arabic sounds like, and receive English instructions at the same time.

http://www.ummah.net/software/cyber/

Islam: Empire of Faith

Explore the interactive time line of the Islamic faith, politics, and culture. There's also information about beliefs, Islamic art and architecture, and lots more.

http://www.pbs.org/empires/islam/

The Islamic Center of Blacksburg

The Islamic Center of Blacksburg offers numerous audio files of prayers and other texts. Listen to the Arabic, and then take the link to Salat: The Prayer Page to read the illustrated guide to the prayer ritual practiced by Moslems around the world.

http://www7.bev.net/civic/icb/

The Smallest Page on the Web

A drop of green pond water hides a tiny microscopic world. In it, you might find water bears, hydra, and beautiful crystalline diatoms. This page in praise of protozoa offers a quick identification guide to what's on your slide as you look through the lens. If you'd like to farm your own paramecium, or enjoy a little aquarium of protozoa, the directions are here: http://www.microscopy-uk.org.uk/mag/wimsmall/smal1.html

Islamic Texts and Resources MetaPage

This is an excellent jump station to introductory material, scriptures, Islamic art and culture, and many other resources on the Net. According to this site, "Islam is derived from the Arabic root *salaama* [meaning] peace, purity, submission, and obedience. In the religious sense, Islam means submission to the will of God and obedience to His law." Muslims believe there have been 25 messengers and prophets. These include Noah, Abraham, Ishmael, Isaac, Moses, Jesus, and Muhammad. Their messages were all the same: Submit to God's will and obey His law. Explore more at this fascinating site.

http://wings.buffalo.edu/student-life/sa/muslim/isl/isl.html

Islamic Virtual School

Learn Arabic vocabulary and the alphabet by playing several games; then get out your virtual crayons and try the coloring book. Parents should look at the articles about Muslim schools and parenting in general. There's also an extensive directory to help you find Islamic pages of interest.

http://www.islamicschool.net/

IslamiCity.com

This wide-ranging resource offers many links, including one to a video and audio presentation of the prayer rituals. There's also audio from Radio Al-Islam, and in the Virtual Mosque, a biography of the Prophet Muhammad and many resources about the faith. There are also detailed sections about the Hajj—the sacred pilgrimage to Mecca that all Muslims must take in their lifetimes.

http://www.islamicity.com/

DINOSAURS AND PREHISTORIC TIMES are in the past, but they are under "D."

Sacred Places: Dome of the Rock, Israel

Built in A.D. 692, the Dome of the Rock is one of the great Muslim monuments. The building looks like an enameled, multicolored jewel, capped by a shining, golden dome. The Dome protects and houses the Sacred Rock of Jerusalem sandstone at the summit of Mount Moriah. Muslims believe that the prophet Muhammad, guided by the archangel Gabriel, traveled to Jerusalem and rose to the presence of God from this Rock. The area is also sacred to other faiths, as it was formerly the location of the Temple of Solomon. This site also details other sacred places around the world.

http://www.arthistory.sbc.edu/sacredplaces/
   domeofrock.html

What Do We Say: A Guide to Islamic Manners

This simple picture book asks questions like "What do we say when someone sneezes?," and "What do we say after we have finished eating?" You'll know all the right Arabic answers after you've explored this resource.

http://www.soundvision.com/kids/wesay/

JUDAISM

See also HOLIDAYS—JEWISH HOLIDAYS

Aish HaTorah's Window on the Wall

The Western Wall is the last remaining structure from the holy temple in Jerusalem, destroyed in A.D. 63. It is a place of sacred pilgrimage to those of the Jewish faith. At this site you will see a live photo of the wall and those who pray before it. The site offers a guide to what you can see in the video screen, and many resources about the wall and Judaism in general. For a donation, you can send e-mail to the wall; your prayer will be printed and delivered there by a student of Aish HaTorah.

http://www.thewall.org/

Akhlah: The Jewish Children's Learning Network

You may know your ABCs, but do you know your *Aleph's*, *Bet's*, and *Gimmel's*? Those are some of the letters in the Hebrew Aleph-Bet (alphabet), and you can learn them here. Explore this site some more, and you can also learn about Israel, Jewish holidays, and Torah heroes. Other activities: listen to the Hebrew Phrase of the Day, or color some coloring pages.

http://www.akhlah.com/

Bar Mitzvah, Bat Mitzvah, and Confirmation

The bar/bat mitzvah ceremony (bar mitzvah for boys, bat mitzvah for girls) is celebrated when a Jewish boy turns 13 or a Jewish girl turns 12. The child embraces the Jewish tradition and assumes adult responsibility for fulfilling Jewish law. This page explains it all. It is part of a much larger resource on Jewish belief and customs, reviewed below.

http://www.jewfaq.org/barmitz.htm

Dwelling Place

Welcome to the land of knowledge in the ocean of Torah. Start the adventure by clicking on the map. You might choose to explore the wheel of Jewish celebrations, but you'd better know a little bit beforehand or you'll have to press the "cheat" button. Puzzle over a jigsaw of the flag of Israel, and try to sort through what's kosher and what's not in the Wiz Quiz. (Hint: pepperoni pizza is not kosher!)

http://members.aol.com/dwelplace/

★ Hebrew for Me

You may not know how to dress the Torah. You will if you drop by this site. Enhance your knowledge about Judaism in general with lots of fun online activities. You can also transform your keyboard into a Hebrew keyboard and learn Hebrew letters and words. The best thing about this site is that it won't make you feel intimidated to learn a little bit about Judaism.

http://www.zigzagworld.com/hebrewforme/

A
B
C
D
E
F
G
H
I
J
K
L
M
N
O
P
Q
R
S
T
U
V
W
X
Y
Z

Why is the left side of a boat called the "port" side?

Answer: According to BoatsafeKids.com, no one really knows. However, the other side of a boat—the right side—is called the "starboard" side. Before the invention of rudders, boats were steered by use of a steering board that hung over the right side of the ship. Only the left side remained free of obstruction with the ability to tie up to the dock when coming into the seaport, or "port." http://boatsafe.com/kids/portkidsques.htm

Judaism 101

Providing a broad overview of the Jewish faith, this site also offers information on prayers and blessings, holidays, and even Jewish cooking. Find out what's inside the *mezuzah* on the doorpost of a Jewish home, and what to do if you own one and have to move.

http://www.jewfaq.org/

★ Nurit Reshef: Funland

This site is chock-full of fun little Java games to help you practice Hebrew. For example, check out Word Match. There are four pictures of common objects. Click on English and match the words with the pictures. Now click on Hebrew and see if you can do as well! (Hint: Play the audio of each word, listen to how it sounds, and match the picture to the word that looks like what you heard.) Press Score to see how well you did; then click on New to get four new words to try.

http://www.bus.ualberta.ca/yreshef/funland/
   funland.html

Nurit Reshef: Shabbat

The Jewish Sabbath, or *Shabbat*, begins just before sunset on Friday night. It can't begin until one lights the Sabbath candles, and the lighting is usually done by a woman. She lights the candles, covers her eyes, and says a special blessing in Hebrew. Only then does she open her eyes to look at the Sabbath light. Learn the traditions of the Shabbat at this site. Other pages by the same author: From Pesach to Shavuot <*http://www.bus.ualberta.ca/yreshef/pesach/index.html*> and Jewish Funland <*http://www.bus.ualberta.ca/yreshef/funland/funland.html*>.

http://www.bus.ualberta.ca/yreshef/shabbat/
   index.html

Torah.org: The Judaism Site

Project Genesis works to establish a strong Jewish identity, expand Jewish knowledge, and encourage its participants to become more involved with Judaism and the Jewish community. A variety of classes are offered online, and additional information regarding Judaism is available. There are also links to other sites of Jewish interest.

http://www.torah.org/

★ Torah Tots

This site is a must if you're looking for coloring pages, games, and educational fun for Jewish kids of all ages. All holidays are represented. Other links will take you to some catchy music files and to related sites.

http://www.torahtots.com/

PAGANISM

See also HOLIDAYS—PAGAN HOLIDAYS

Circle Sanctuary

According to this site, the myth that witches worship the devil is "wrong, wrong, wrong." Learn more about this "earth religion" and its holidays: Samhain, Beltane, Lammas, and many more. This site will answer many of your questions about this religion. The "Religious Tolerance" section is particularly good.

http://www.circlesanctuary.org/

A B C D E F G H I J K L M N O P Q R S T U V W X Y Z

Teenagers and Young People Discovering Paganism

This site from the Pagan Federation of Canada is explicit in its list of Do's and Don'ts. Here's number one on the list: "Don't load yourself down with silver jewelry, pentacles, black makeup and clothes because that's how you think Pagans dress. It is great for shock value, but it doesn't represent the way Pagans dress. If you want to be taken seriously, dress in your own personal style. Don't change your clothes because you want to change your religion. You might risk those who have been practicing Pagans for years to just look on you as Pagan wannabe's and they will probably tell you to go away and come back when you are serious." The rest of the list is equally direct. Non-pagan parents should read the help page at *<http://www.pfpc.ca/family/conpar.html>*.

http://www.pfpc.ca/family/dearteen.html

SACRED SITES

Pictures of Places of the Bible

If you have the IPIX viewer, you can experience 360-degree views of various places in Egypt, Israel, and other regions. You can download the viewer for free if you don't already have it. Zoom in to see the area of Jesus' Sermon on the Mount. Sit on the steps of Jerusalem's Damascus Gate. There are many sites to visit; try them all!

http://www.mustardseed.net/html/places.html

★ Places of Peace and Power

Anthropologist and photographer Martin Gray has visited over 1,000 places of religious and spiritual pilgrimage. This resource offers many of his photos and writings about the sites, as well as a calendar listing of Gray's upcoming slide shows and appearances. See and read about Stonehenge, Mount Olympus, the Golden Temple, places in Jerusalem, and many more. Be sure to read what you'll have to go through if you want to kiss the Blarney Stone in Ireland!

http://www.sacredsites.com/

Fetch some fascinating info in DOGS AND DOG SPORTS.

Sacred Places

Learn all about sacredness of place, including caves, stones, trees, mountains, water, and other landscape forms. Visit more than 15 sacred places around the world, such as Chartres in France and Bodh Gaya in India. Besides photos, you will find suggested links for further exploration.

http://www.arthistory.sbc.edu/sacredplaces/ sacredplacesintro.html

SIKHISM

The Sikhism Home Page

The Sikh religion, founded over 500 years ago, today has a following of over 20 million people worldwide. Sikhism "preaches a message of devotion and remembrance of God at all times, truthful living, [and] equality of mankind . . . . [It] denounces superstitions and blind rituals." The Sikh scripture is called the Sri Guru Granth Sahib, and it is considered a Living Guru, or spiritual teacher. It contains devotional hymns and poetry from many faiths.

http://www.sikhs.org/

TAO

Taoism Information Page

Taoism began about 2,500 years ago, in China. The Tao, or Way, is illuminated by several texts, one of which is the Tao-te-Ching. It is among the shortest of all sacred scriptures, containing only 5,000 words. Here are a few of them: *It is not the clay the potter throws, which gives the pot its usefulness, but the space within the shape, from which the pot is made.* This site offers a good introduction to Taoism.

http://www.clas.ufl.edu/users/gthursby/taoism/

A
B
C
D
E
F
G
H
I
J
K
L
M
N
O
P
Q
R
S
T
U
V
W
X
Y
Z

A B C D E F G H I J K L M N O P Q R S T U V W X Y Z

UNITARIAN UNIVERSALIST

Unitarian Universalist Association

According to the information at this official site, "Unitarian Universalism is a liberal religion born of the Jewish and Christian traditions . . . . We believe that personal experience, conscience, and reason should be the final authorities in religion. In the end religious authority lies not in a book, person, or institution, but in ourselves. We put religious insights to the test of our hearts and minds. We uphold the free search for truth. We will not be bound by a statement of belief. We do not ask anyone to subscribe to a creed. We say ours is a non creedal religion. Ours is a free faith." Learn more here.

http://www.uua.org/main.html

REPTILES

See also PETS AND PET CARE

Melissa Kaplan's Herp Care Information Collection

Everything you need to know about snakes, amphibians, lizards, turtles, and iguanas is here, at least we think so. Learn how to treat your turtle and how to coddle your chameleon. Whether you want to soothe your snakes or animate your amphibians, this page will surely be of use. Looking for a reptile for your classroom? Advice is here. And think again about getting an iguana—read the facts first!

http://www.sonic.net/~melissk/

You never lose the pieces to the online games in GAMES AND FUN!

CROCODILES AND ALLIGATORS

Crocodilians: Natural History & Conservation

Have you ever heard the threatening hiss of a cranky crocodile? Neither had we until we visited this site! Listen to audio of threat calls, distress calls, and hatching calls. There are 23 species in the crocodile family. Learn about them all here. You'll find range maps, information on diet, how endangered or widespread the species is, and plenty more.

http://www.crocodilian.com/

The Gator Hole

Much maligned and misunderstood, alligators have existed since the time of the dinosaurs. Hunted almost to extinction, they have made an astounding comeback. You will find an amazing collection of gator myth and fact lying around this virtual gator hole. Find out here if the stories you hear about alligators are true.

http://home.cfl.rr.com/gatorhole/

NOVA Online - Crocodiles

They look so . . . prehistoric. How did crocodiles survive when the dinosaurs did not? Was it because they are water-dwellers? Because they can go without eating for long periods? or was it something else entirely? Speculate along with the experts as you discover even more about the crocodile species.

http://www.pbs.org/wgbh/nova/crocs/

St. Augustine's Alligator Farm

Chomp, chomp! Be careful, don't get too close. Visit the St. Augustine Alligator Farm, and remember: you should never feed wild animals. There is lots of alligator info at this site, along with FAQs on other reptiles. Don't forget to pick up your discount admission ticket at this Web site, too, should you ever visit the real zoological park in Florida.

http://www.alligatorfarm.com/

Watch your steps in DANCE.

LIZARDS

Heatherk's Gecko Page

Interested in geckos? So is Heatherk, and she's got some care sheets for several different breeds. Although the cost of buying a pet lizard may be low, check out all the other stuff you have to have to house one properly. Be sure you can afford it!

http://www.geckopage.com/

SNAKES

American International Rattlesnake Museum

Did you know that the rattlesnake was a serious contender for our national symbol? It's true. The bald eagle won out, of course. If you found that fact about rattlesnakes amazing, slither over to this site for more. Learn about venom, rattles, fangs, and view some snake-related artwork, posters, and memorabilia.

http://www.rattlesnakes.com/

King Cobra @ Nationalgeographic.com

The king cobra is one snake you don't want to go messing with; but if you check him out here, it will be relatively safe. Consider these facts about Mister KC: It has a head as big as a man's hand and can stand tall enough to look you straight in the eye. Its venom can stun your nervous system and stop your breathing. Ready for more? Its fangs are a half-inch long, and a little bite will deliver venom from glands attached to the fangs. Within minutes, neurotoxins stun the prey's nervous system, especially the impulses for breathing. Other toxins start digesting the paralyzed victim. We've had enough, but if you'd like more information, there's plenty available!

http://www.nationalgeographic.com/features/97/
 kingcobra/index-n.html

Snakes of Massachusetts

You've found a snake you don't recognize sunning itself on your deck, and you want to know if it's safe to move it. Answer a series of questions, and you can quickly identify that suspect snake. If you already know the snake's name and want to know more about its lifestyle and habits, you can also find that here. But once you make an identification, remember: usually it's best to let a sleeping snake lie.

http://www.umass.edu/umext/nrec/snake_pit/

TURTLES

Adventures of Lilo the Green Sea Turtle

Follow along as Lilo the green sea turtle makes her way throughout the islands of Hawaii. To help her continue the journey, you will have to answer questions about sharks, pollution, ghost nets, and many more topics. Luckily, there are lots of resources to help you find the answers. This site was created by students for the ThinkQuest Junior competition.

http://tqjunior.thinkquest.org/6067/

NET FILES

Where is the smallest area administered by the National Park Service? (Hint: It is a national memorial.)

Answer: It's in Pennsylvania. The Thaddeus Kosciuszko National Memorial is 0.02 of an acre. He was a Polish-born Revolutionary War patriot and helped to fortify both Saratoga and West Point. Read more about him at *http://www.nps.gov/thko/*

A B C D E F G H I J K L M N O P Q **R** S T U V W X Y Z

A
B
C
D
E
F
G
H
I
J
K
L
M
N
O
P
Q
R
S
T
U
V
W
X
Y
Z

California Turtle and Tortoise Club

When Net-mom was little, she read her King James Version of the Bible and saw in Song of Solomon 2:12 the following verse about spring: "The flowers appear on the earth; the time of the singing is come, and the voice of the turtle is heard in our land." Well Net-mom could not understand it, because her pet turtles never seemed to make any noise. (Years later, Net-mom figured out it was supposed to be an abbreviation for the turtledove, and the Revised Standard Version bears this out. Duhhh.) However, should you want to hear the real voices of real turtles, just visit this page, click on Tortoise Calls, and turn up your speakers. There is also an exhaustive selection of links and care sheets.

http://www.tortoise.org/

Discovery Online - Love and Death on Turtle Beach

Scientists estimate that only one in 2,500 turtle hatchlings makes it to maturity. That means a lot of others are eaten by predators, entangled in nets, or don't survive for other reasons. Learn all you can about leatherback turtles at this site and associated links; then try the quiz to see if you can get all five of your hatchlings safely to the water. If you get a question wrong, one baby turtle is removed from the game.

http://www.discovery.com/exp/turtles/turtles.html

Reslider's Swamp

This site has extensive information on caring for pet red-eared sliders, a common type of turtle for sale in pet stores. You'll learn that they need cuttlefish bones to sharpen their "beaks," that raw meat is bad but live crickets and guppies are OK, and that it's important to filter the water in which your turtle is kept. There's a lot more to visit here in Reslider's Swamp, including links to info about other species of turtles. Slide on in, the water's fine!

http://www.altern.com/reslider/res.html

★ Turtle Trax

Did you know that all species of marine turtles are either threatened or endangered? That's right, and a major reason for this is danger to their nests. These dangers include increased numbers of people on the beaches where the turtles dig their nests. Also, some people dig up the nests and sell or eat turtle eggs. Another problem is artificial lighting around beaches, which has a disorienting effect on little turtles—they can't find the safety of the sea. In addition to the nesting threats, don't forget about the environmental threats to turtles, which include water pollution and getting stuck in floating trash. These are just some of the most serious threats. For more information about marine turtles, their environment, and ways you can help, visit this page. The Kidz Korner has some wonderful true stories. And don't miss the series of pictures from the Amazingly Way Cool BogusCam™. (Hint: Keep loading them—you'll get a surprise!) To find these treasures, click the Contents page.

http://www.turtles.org/

RIGHTS AND FREEDOMS

See also AFRICAN AMERICANS—HISTORY

Children's Rights

Parental advisory: please preview this site. Around the world, many children are forced to work, become soldiers, or become heads of their own families. They are called children of conflict and you will learn much about them at this site. Thank goodness this grim resource also outlines ways you can help.

http://www.bbc.co.uk/worldservice/people/features/
    childrensrights/

How is Kwanzaa celebrated? Find out in HOLIDAYS!

A School for Iqbal - A Bullet Can't Kill a Dream

If you think kids don't have much power, visit this page. Here are the main points you should know about the tragic story of a Pakistani child named Iqbal, as quoted from this site: "Iqbal was sold into child bonded labor at four years of age for the equivalent of $12. He escaped at age ten and began to speak out against child slavery and for freedom and schools for all Pakistani children. Iqbal won the Reebok Human Rights Youth in Action Award 1994. Easter Sunday, 1995, he was murdered. In response, students at Broadmeadow Middle School (Quincy, Massachusetts) formed a campaign in order to help fight for Iqbal's Dream." There's good news. In the last few years, the school has been built. Read updates about the school, and find out what you can do to help end child slavery.

http://www.digitalrag.com/iqbal/

★ Stand Up for Your Rights

Religious freedom. Voting rights for women. School desegregation. Explore the history of these rights in interactive feature stories, games, and engaging graphic presentations. In Buzz, you can read interviews with people who were there and experienced these events firsthand. For example, meet Melba Beals, one of the "Little Rock Nine"— the first African American kids to attend Central High School. That was in 1957. There's much more— visit and see!

http://www.pbs.org/wgbh/amex/kids/civilrights/

ANIMAL RIGHTS

Animal Protection Institute

Whether it's trying to end elephant acts in circuses, or attempting to stop the illegal exotic animals trade, the Animal Protection Institute is an activist organization that helps all kinds of animals. Find out about their work here.

http://www.api4animals.org/

Just for Kids at the American Humane Association

If you want to know what's new (or old) in animal rights, this is the site for you. Find out how you can help animals at your school, in your neighborhood, or as a career. There's a link to Volunteer Match to help you find even more opportunities to be an animal's best friend. A similar site is Humane Teen from the American Humane Association <http://www.humaneteen.org/>, although much of the information is not for young children.

http://www.americanhumane.org/kids/

ROBOTS

Aibo, the Robotic Dog

Meet Aibo, Sony's robotic dog. It has amazing lifelike movements! According to the product information, it is also capable of artificial intelligence: it thinks, feels, and "grows up." Learn about what it does, how it works, and how you can get one. (Hint: You'd better have lots of money.)

http://www.world.sony.com/aibo/

New York Underground @ Nationalgeographic.com

Below the streets of New York City are lots of telephone and electrical cables, subway tunnels, sewers, and huge water tunnels that bring fresh water to the city from reservoirs far away. Learn all about what's underground as you explore a cross section. Do albino alligators really live in the New York sewers? The answer is here.
http://www.nationalgeographic.com/features/97/nyunderground/

A
B
C
D
E
F
G
H
I
J
K
L
M
N
O
P
Q
R
S
T
U
V
W
X
Y
Z

Why is ROY G. BIV important?

http://tinyelabs.kcts.org/teach/eg_print/eg16.html
Read more about light at
bottom: red, orange, yellow, green, blue, indigo, and violet.
them remember the colors of the rainbow, in order from top to
Answer: ROY G. BIV is the name scientists made up to help

American Visionary Art Museum

Scroll down until you see "Make Your Own Robot" and click there. Then drag robot pieces over to the power grid and build away. Is everything touching? You want your circuit to work! OK, throw the power switch to the "on" position and watch them dance!

http://www.avam.org/brainfood/

BattleBots

If you've ever wondered how to build a battlebot robot and compete with the big boys on the TV show, this is the site you want. It covers everything from essential parts to how to find a sponsor. Are there rules? Of course.

http://www.battlebots.com/

★ The Computer Museum - Introduction to the Robots Gallery

If you were going to build your own robot to explore Mars, or maybe creep into a live volcano, or perhaps entertain humans at a party, what would you need to consider in your design? You'd need to figure out how it gets power; how it moves around; and, of course, how it looks. This Shockwave simulation allows you to try out various choices in a robot lab and get feedback on your choices.

http://www.tcm.org/html/galleries/robots/

Cool Robot of the Week

The robot universe is getting larger all the time. Luckily, NASA is on top of it all. See what's new and cool in the world of robotics, and then take the link at the bottom of the page to visit real robots you can actually control over the Web.

http://ranier.hq.nasa.gov/telerobotics_page/
  coolrobots.html

Get a Grip on Robotics

There are five parts to a typical robot arm. There's the elbow of course, and the wrist, and the fingers—no wait, that's the typical human arm. A robotic arm includes a controller, an arm, a drive, an end effector, and a sensor. Find out how all the pieces work together to give robots their dexterity. Most robotic joints can move in at least six different directions. This online exhibit from The Tech museum will show you the moves. You'll also learn about robots in the workplace and in science fiction.

http://www.thetech.org/exhibits_events/online/
  robots/teaser/

Robot Maxamilian

If you have about $600, a computer, and four months on your hands, you can build a robotic android head to impress everyone at the science fair. It does look pretty cool, and the two video camera eyes make the thing useful, too.

http://www.howtoandroid.com/

San Francisco Robotics Society of America

Snake robots, bots from NASA, spiritual robots—new robots are big invented all the time. Luckily, the San Francisco Robotics Society of America club is on top of it all. Check their page for what's new and cool in the world of robotics, including robots you can control over the Web.

http://www.robots.org/

SCHOOLS AND EDUCATION

ABCTeach

Next time you want to find a worksheet, report planner, book report form, or flash card, head over to this site. Make sure your printer is turned on, because what you'll find here are many pages suitable for printing. Also included are decorative papers and borders for stationery and invitations.

http://abcteach.com/

Free Worksheets & Activities

Thousands of free worksheets on everything from phonics to weather are available at this site. But there's even more. Every day there are two new treasure hunts. One leads to a craft and the other leads to a movie. Can you find the hidden gold? If you do, you'll discover special activities selected just for today. You might have to match pictures of horses, or decide which months are in summer and which ones are in winter. The treasure hunts are archived if you'd like to look through past selections.

http://www.schoolexpress.com/fws/

HomeworkSpot

Whether you're a fourth-grader writing a report on elephants or a high-school student reading a Jane Austen novel, this site will help you mine the Web for more information. Go to practically any academic subject, and you'll find links to the greatest homework help sites on that subject. If you need a study break, the site offers some online games. But they'll still make you think!

http://www.homeworkspot.com/

You won't believe how the PLANTS, TREES, AND GARDENS section grew!

BIBLIOGRAPHIES AND COPYRIGHT

★ Citing Electronic Resources

Using the Net to find information for research projects is great, but how do you give credit to, or cite, all those electronic resources? This useful list of guides from the Internet Public Library will show you the way. If the style sheet you need is not mentioned, try Karla's Guide to Citation Style Guides at <http://bailiwick.lib.uiowa.edu/journalism/cite.html>.

http://www.ipl.org/ref/QUE/FARQ/netciteFARQ.html

Copyright with Cyberbee

It's OK to copy anything that's on the Internet and use it in your homework, right? WRONG. Learn all about the Ten Big Myths About Copyright, and how you can avoid breaking the law.

http://www.cyberbee.com/cb_copyright.swf

★ NoodleBib - The MLA Bibliography Composer

Creating a bibliography for your school paper is a breeze with this free bibliography generator. A handy pull-down menu lets you select the type of reference you need to cite (book, magazine, Web page, etc.). A template prompts you to fill in the blanks. Once you press submit, presto—your bibliography citation is created online and in the proper format. It couldn't be easier.

http://www.noodletools.com/noodlebib/

Sources

You had a brilliant idea and decided to write about it in your school paper. Then you decided your article needed to be a little longer. So you found a similar idea in a magazine and figured you'd just add that paragraph in, too. Do you try to pass off the magazine quote as your own original work? Or, do you acknowledge your source? Unsure? Turn to this site for the answer. It will tell you when you should credit your sources and why it is important to do so. It also explains plagiarism and spells out the consequences for stealing other people's ideas.

http://www.dartmouth.edu/~sources/contents.html

A B C D E F G H I J K L M N O P Q R S T U V W X Y Z

A
B
C
D
E
F
G
H
I
J
K
L
M
N
O
P
Q
R
S
T
U
V
W
X
Y
Z

Rotten Truth (About Garbage)

When you throw something "away," where does it go? This site makes the point that there is no such thing as "away" when we have only one planet to live on. Learn the rotten truth about garbage, and then do something about it. Make a worm bin. Construct a soda bottle bioreactor. Organize a local landfill tour. There are lots of ideas and activities here.

http://www.astc.org/exhibitions/rotten/rthome.htm

EDUCATIONAL LINK DIRECTORIES

B.J Pinchbeck's Homework Helper

"Beege" is 14 years old and has collected over 700 resources that he uses with his school homework. Maybe they will work for you, too. You'll find everything from biographical dictionaries to flags of the world.

http://school.discovery.com/students/homeworkhelp/
   bjpinchbeck/

★ Blue Web'n Learning Sites Library

This site collects the cream of the crop of learning-oriented Web sites. All sites are rated and categorized by area, audience, and type. Each subject category has links to related tutorials, activities, projects, lesson plans, and more. You can also use their keyword search to explore their collection. Want more? Join the free mailing list for weekly updates. We found the sites listed here to be excellent resources for eager learners, as well as educators looking for teaching materials.

http://www.kn.pacbell.com/wired/bluewebn/

The Busy Educator's Guide to the World Wide Web

Marjan Glavac has been a teacher for 20 years, so he knows how busy it can get in the classroom. There's not enough time to correct homework, let alone seek out great Web sites to support the curriculum. He's written a book to help teachers with that problem. This site has information on ordering the book, and also how to get his free newsletter, as well as some of his favorite educational picks.

http://www.glavac.com/

EdGate: The Copernicus Educational Gateway

Visit this nice clearinghouse of projects, lesson plans, daily education news, and links. There's a section on scholarships and contest opportunities, too.

http://www.edgate.com/

The Gateway to Educational Materials

The Gateway to Educational Materials is also known as GEM. Although it's really aimed at teachers and homeschooling parents looking for lesson plans, kids can use it to find great Internet resources, too. It's sponsored by the U.S. Department of Education and the ERIC Clearinghouse on Information & Technology. More than 21,000 resources are currently contained in the collection, which is fully searchable by word, grade, or subject.

http://www.thegateway.org/

Kathy Schrock's Guide for Educators

This site says it's for educators, but it's also for kids! The links in this guide are organized according to subject area. In History, for instance, you'll get a breakdown of Web pages, from "American History" to "World History." Each month, a list of new resources will point you to the latest and greatest.

http://school.discovery.com/schrockguide/

AMPHIBIANS! Visit them before you croak.

Multnomah County Library - Homework Center

This well-organized collection of links will pay off for you when the library's closed, when your CD-ROM encyclopedia won't load, and when your dad's taking a nap and can't help. The brief annotations help you find that diagram of the human eye you need, for example, or information on what kinds of foods were eaten by the Incas. Remember to check here—this site was built by librarians.

http://www.multnomah.lib.or.us/lib/homework/

Surfing the Net with Kids

Barbara Feldman's syndicated column, "Surfing the Net with Kids," runs in numerous newspapers. Each week, she picks five great Web sites on a favorite topic, such as mazes, paper money, robots, and more. You can read her excellent column at her Web site and even subscribe to the e-mail edition for free.

http://www.surfnetkids.com/

HISTORY

The History of Education and Childhood

Parental advisory: please preview this site. Someday you're going to have to write a paper on a typical childhood day in colonial America; or child labor in the nineteenth century; or the history of education in, say, China. When you get that assignment, remember this site!

http://www.socsci.kun.nl/ped/whp/histeduc/

The One-Room School Homepage

Mom of Net-mom went to school in a one-room schoolhouse in Terre Haute, Indiana. When she was little, Net-mom heard all kinds of tales about what it was like to have six kids in your grade, and all the grades in the same room. Now, you could write to Mom of Net-mom and ask her to tell you all those stories, too, or you could visit this Web page. Hear it all from a former one-room schoolhouse teacher! Remember the beloved nursery rhyme "Mary Had a Little Lamb"? See the picture of the one-room schoolhouse that may (or may not) have inspired the tail, er, tale. Follow this link: <http://www.wayside.org/research.html>.

http://www.msc.cornell.edu/~weeds/SchoolPages/welcome.html

HOMESCHOOLING

★ Homeschooling Information

Visit this excellent selection of homeschooling resources for an overview of what's current and what's useful. You'll find thoughtful, briefly annotated links to homeschooling associations, magazines, newsgroups, and more. Some of the most interesting are the Real Audio files with interviews of interest to homeschooling families. For example, you can listen to Susannah Sheffer, author of *A Sense of Self: Listening to Homeschooled Adolescent Girls*. Don't miss the links to selected high-energy homeschooling families, and scroll to the bottom to find some great software to support homeschooling (and other) families.

http://www.dimensional.com/~janf/homeschoolinfo.html

★ Jon's Homeschool Resource Page

Do homeschooled kids fit into the "real world"? Will you be able to get into college? Research shows that the answer to these questions is a loud "Yes!" This site also has a collection of home pages and photos from families; check out what they're doing and learning.

http://www.midnightbeach.com/hs/

A B C D E F G H I J K L M N O P Q R S T U V W X Y Z

NET FILES

On a merry-go-round, the horses usually follow one special leader, known as the "king horse." How do you tell which horse is the leader?

Answer: Look carefully. There's usually one horse that's just a little bit bigger and just a little more elaborate in its decorations and trappings. Often it's a war horse wearing armor, and sometimes it has the logo of the company prominently displayed. For other clues, see *http://www.learner.org/exhibits/parkphysics/carousel2.html*

LEARNING GAMES

See also GAMES AND FUN—EDUCATIONAL GAMES; and names of the various subjects, like HISTORY, MATH AND ARITHMETIC, and more.

★ Harcourt School Publishers - The Learning Site

Enter this site for a spectacular collection of entertaining and educational games for all age levels. In Science, for example, go to the Activities and Resources student area. Scroll to the third grade section and take a walk on The Resource Trail. Move the ant from start to finish based on your answers to questions like "What resource is used to produce forests?" Is it mineral, plant, animal, air, water, or some other resource? There are spelling, reading, math, social studies, art, health, and other games and activities that you can use for free.

http://www.harcourtschool.com/

★ Quia!

Quia's one of our favorite educational sites. Anyone can create a quiz or an activity to be enjoyed by others. You can take a quiz about French verbs, computer systems, or state capitals. Try Science Stumpers if you like Jeopardy-style games. For a few more quizzes, try Quizhub *<http://quizhub.com/>*.

http://www.quia.com/

PROJECTS

See also GEOGRAPHY; and PEN PALS

Boomerang Box

What's the Boomerang Box? It's a 40-foot long container box, used to transport cargo via ship, truck, and rail. You can follow the movements of the brightly decorated box as it travels from port to port. Sometimes it is carrying airplane parts, other times it might be toys or paper goods. You can learn about geography, world trade, and the people behind the scenes who make it all work. There's even a Boomerang Box Junior that makes school visits, if you're interested. Teachers can download lesson plans here, too.

http://www.apl.com/boomerangbox/

★ The CanOz Connection

Your whole class might not be able to visit a faraway country, but why not send an ambassador instead? First, you need to find another classroom willing to participate. Some classes exchange a stuffed animal, like a teddy bear. They send it along with a bag full of accessories. Each night the bear goes home with a different student, who writes in the bear's diary or fills out a simple form detailing the bear's activities. After a short stay, the bear ambassadors go home, each with a diary full of new experiences to share with their classes. This page explains the whole process. Check out Monty Moose's New York visit to Net-mom! Net-mom is interested in participating with your class, too, please contact her at feedback@netmom.com.

http://www.teacherwebshelf.com/canozconnection/

★ CIESE Online Classroom Projects

The collaborative projects at this site encourage classrooms to make their own observations of the world and contribute to a real-time database in order to show global trends. Some ongoing projects include one designed to find out how much water we use, a quest to discover the boiling point of water around the world, and the ever-popular Noon Day project measures the circumference of the Earth.

http://k12science.stevens-tech.edu/currichome.html

Co-nect Teleprojects

Although the classroom-to-classroom teleprojects change from time to time, one of the current ones your class could join is creating a biography library of famous scientists, engineers, and astronauts in collaboration with Space Camp and the U.S. Astronaut Hall of Fame. Other classes are participating in an online cultural exchange with a class in Buenos Aires, Argentina. There are projects for all grade levels, so check it out and get involved.

http://exchange.co-nect.net/Teleprojects/

★ Cybersurfari

Join the Cybersurfari and search the Net for hidden treasures. The more clues you solve, the better your chances are of winning prizes like waist packs and T-shirts. There are also cash prizes! Just go to this site and register (it's free). Decide if you want to register as an individual child, an individual adult, a family team, or a school team in one of several categories. Then get going and chase down the first clue.

http://www.cybersurfari.org/

★ Flat Stanley Project

He's been on the space shuttle *Discovery*. He's visited the Eiffel towel, met President Clinton, and had adventures all over the world. Who is he? Flat Stanley, of course. A normal kid until squashed by a falling bulletin board, Stanley's two-dimensional lifestyle has positive features. He fits into an envelope and can be mailed to his friends. Hundreds of classrooms are making their own Flat Stanleys and sending them to other kids around the globe. How can you participate? Find out here. Net-mom is interested in participating with your class; please contact her at feedback@netmom.com.

http://flatstanley.enoreo.on.ca/

★ The Global Schoolhouse

The folks in charge of GSN just keep collecting and coming up with more terrific ideas all the time. You can host or join a virtual field trip; participate in the GeoGame; or search through a database of collaborative projects like a worldwide cookbook, a travel buddy exchange, or a study to determine dominant genetic traits worldwide.

http://www.gsn.org/

★ I*EARN

The best way to understand people of a different nationality or race or religion is to get to know them. Basically, that's what the developers of this nonprofit site are doing, and it is a concept that has won them praise from all kinds of sources. Simply put, classrooms of children from kindergarten through secondary school work together in developing projects on a variety of subjects, using telecommunications to pave the way. School classes are invited to participate in a project already in progress or to begin something new. Like the idea? Read more about it and talk to your teacher. Soon your "classmates" could be kids from halfway around the world!

http://www.iearn.org/

A B C D E F G H I J K L M N O P Q R S T U V W X Y Z

Intercultural E-Mail Classroom Connections

One of the great aspects of the Internet is that it provides children with the opportunity to reach well beyond their community to kids just about anywhere. This site provides listserv discussions for teachers to find other teachers and classes interested in a pen pal exchange. If you are a teacher, definitely take a look. If you are a student, parent, or caregiver, mention IECC to a teacher. A whole new way of communicating may open up, since at last count more than 7,600 teachers in 82 countries were participating. IECC provides connections for students of all ages, from grade school through college. Do you know someone over 50 who likes to send and receive e-mail? The Intergenerational Exchange allows kids to interact with the wisdom of the elders!

http://www.iecc.org/

Eastman Kodak Company

You would expect Kodak to have an active home page, and they do indeed. You can find all sorts of valuable information on photography here, whether your interests lie in producing professional-quality photographs or simple snapshots. One example is the Taking Great Pictures section featuring the Top Ten Techniques for photographers to take and make good pictures *http://www.kodak.com/US/en/nav/takingPics.shtml*. You'll also find advice for preserving family albums there. A new section allows you to upload pictures from your computer and manipulate them so it looks like your mom's coming out of a flower and your little brother is an ape. It's in the Picture Playground section—check it out.
http://www.kodak.com/

★ International Schools CyberFair Competition

The International Schools CyberFair invites schools to participate in a collaborative project to create world-class Web sites. Projects should "exploit the unique abilities of the World Wide Web to build relationships and alliances with different people and groups within their local community." One of the goals is to promote an "Internet style of learning" that encourages participants to reach out and use the Web for information gathering. There are prizes and incentives to encourage participation. Check out the list of prizes, rules, and past winners' sites. Be the hero who gets your school started in the CyberFair competition.

http://gsh.lightspan.com/cf/

The JASON Project

Ever heard of The JASON Project? It was founded in Massachusetts in 1989, and here's how it got started. Dr. Robert D. Ballard had just discovered the wreck of the *RMS Titanic*. When he got back, he was overwhelmed by the letters he received from interested kids. He decided to develop a way for kids to interact with real science and take part in global field trips. Past JASON projects have let kids control deep-sea submarines and make other real observations. You never know what JASON's going to do next! To participate in the real-time projects, there is a fee involved. But anyone can look over the past expeditions for free.

http://www.jasonproject.org/front.html

KIDLINK: Global Networking for Youth Through Secondary School Age

You know the world's got some big problems: pollution, hunger, poverty. Why not talk to other kids and see if you can help solve some of them? Make new friends, and have some fun with kids from 137 different countries on the KIDCAFE discussions. Take a look at the KIDLINK mailing list page, and start e-mailing new friends. Show this to your teacher and parents, too. They'll find lots of good information about how to share a project with a class in another country. Many of the discussions are held in languages other than English, too.

http://www.kidlink.org/

> **Volcanoes are an explosive subject. Find one in EARTH SCIENCE.**

MindsEye Monster Exchange Project

This is a site that everyone is going to love—students, parents, teachers—you name it, stop here! It's simple. Your class draws a monster, but then you have to describe it well enough so that another class can re-create the monster just from the written description. Then both monsters are scanned and put on the Web so everyone can compare. Teachers, take a tour of the site and see how your classes can discover new excitement in creative writing.

http://www.monsterexchange.org/

MontagePlus

Searching for another school to partner with on a shared learning experience? Montage allows you to find another school or project by its country, or subject, or target age group. Some of the ongoing experiments in collaboration include weather, trees, dreams, and lots more.

http://www.montage.edu.au/

Odyssey of the Mind

Learn to solve problems. Become a creative thinker. Combine those two life skills, and you've got the foundation of this international program. Students form local teams to solve problems that fall into five general categories. They include everything from building mechanical vehicles to writing another chapter to a literary classic, such as *Moby Dick*. Interested in getting your mind involved? Visit the site for a rundown on this year's problems, contest rules, and local contacts.

http://www.odysseyofthemind.com/

Online Expeditions

One of the amazing strengths of the Internet is to overcome what's called the "tyranny of distance" so that you can connect easily with far away people and events. At any time, there are numerous real-life expeditions you can track online. Sometimes you can pose questions to the participants, too. This site offers a collection of some of the most interesting adventures happening right now. When we visited, we saw a chance to talk to a guy who is rowing around the world. Other opportunities involved expeditions to Africa, Australia, and more.

http://www.lightspan.com/teacher/pages/onlineadv/
default.asp?_prod=LS&_nav=t3_proj_onlineadv

★ ThinkQuest

Would you like to win thousands of dollars? Do you have a great idea for a new Web resource? You might be a fabulous C++ programmer, but you can't write interesting English prose very well. Or maybe you're terrific at graphics but can't code. Maybe you're not a computer nut at all, but you really know how to research a topic. There is a place for all of you at ThinkQuest. First, you have to create a team to work on your project. Advertise your skills and your ideas at the Team Maker part of the site. Typically, teams are formed with two or three kids from all over the world; they have usually never met, and they usually come from schools or homeschools with widely varying levels of technology. You also need a coach or three—usually teachers or parents, but it could be someone else. You decide how to tackle the project, and then spend many months building your Web resource on the server space provided by ThinkQuest. You and your team members use chat rooms to discuss the project, as well as e-mail and other forms of communication. Eventually, the contest deadline rolls around, and your project is frozen in time so that the judges can take a look. There are several contests: one for elementary grades, called ThinkQuest Junior, and the original one for older kids. At this site, you can explore past winners' sites and get information about the latest ThinkQuest competition schedule.

http://www.thinkquest.org/

A
B
C
D
E
F
G
H
I
J
K
L
M
N
O
P
Q
R
S
T
U
V
W
X
Y
Z

Tomatosphere

Rarely does a tomato seed circle the Earth 170 times while it travels on a space shuttle for eleven days. But when it does, it qualifies for a research project involving Canadian school children. This project for Grades 3 to 6 allows students to compare the growth of tomatoes that have flown in space to those have stayed on Earth. Their findings will help them learn about science, space exploration, food, and nutrition.

http://www.tomatosphere.org/

★ Traveling Buddies

It's always more interesting to learn about a far-off place from someone who has actually been there. How would you like to learn about geography from a stuffed animal? Lots of toys are now traveling the world and sending back reports. Classes take the animals on local field trips, write in journals about the animal's experiences, and send pictures and postcards back to the animal's home school. Then the toy is packed up and sent on to the next destination. Maybe your school or family can host one of them in the future. This page explains how you can get started.

http://www.siec.k12.in.us/~west/article/travbud.htm

STUDY SKILLS

★ The Big6 Skills - Information Problem-Solving Approach

Would you like to be able to answer any question? Try this methodical approach. There are six steps: 1. Define the problem; 2. Brainstorm how you might find answers; 3. Figure out where the resources might be, and get them; 4. Read the information and take notes; 5. Organize your information and present it; and 6. Evaluate your product and how effective it is in communicating the answers to the problem. Sounds so simple, doesn't it? It's amazing how many people can't even get started on a project. This method lets you break down your research into manageable steps. At the official site, you'll find lots more detail, examples, and sample lesson plans. Forget study tricks: go Big6!

http://www.big6.com/

"I Think . . . Therefore . . . M.I."

"It's not how smart you are, it's how you are smart," says this site. Did you know that people learn and think differently? Howard Gardner of Harvard University came up with this theory of "multiple intelligences"—and so far he has identified nine different ways people learn. These include kids who learn visually, or through activity, music, or other mode. How do these multiple intelligences work? This site offers ten links per intelligence category so you can get a feeling for each one. In which categories do you fit?

http://www.surfaquarium.com/im.htm

★ Learning to Learn

What's your learning style? If you said "sitting," we'll give you points for humor, but that's not exactly what we meant. You might like to visualize a problem, act it out, talk about it, or draw a diagram. This site will help you analyze how you like to learn best, and give you ideas and strategies for maximizing your memory, reading, writing, problem solving, and creative skills. Hint: click on the red words to open the next screens.

http://snow.utoronto.ca/Learn2/modules.html

Notetaking Strategies

Have you noticed you can't just listen to the teacher or read a book and expect to remember EVERYTHING? Learn how to take notes! Notes are good because you can refer to them later when you are studying, both to refresh your memory about what you learned and to help you prepare for a test. This site will help you learn how. Be sure to take the link back to General Purpose Learning Strategies for many other tips on learning to learn.

http://muskingum.edu/~cal/database/notetaking.html

★ Study Buddy: Your School Survival Connection

A wonderful collection of tips on everything from memorizing lines in a play to dealing with procrastination is in store for you at this site. You'll find lots of study "survival" information here, too.

http://studybuddy.com/

A B C D E F G H I J K L M N O P Q R S T U V W X Y Z

★ Study Guides

How would you like to think like a genius? This site says anyone can learn to do it. Think in unusual ways. Think in opposites, suspending your logic. Find resemblances in different fields of thought, and prepare yourself for chance. Besides learning to think like a genius, you can learn about note-taking, study systems, taking tests, self-assessment, making yourself heard in class, and lots more.

http://www.iss.stthomas.edu/studyguides/

Techniques to Manage Procrastination

Procrastination! What does it mean? It means we put off doing that term paper, report, or science project until it's too late to complete it! Why do we do that? There are lots of theories, but one thing's for sure: we all want to get over it! For techniques on how to conquer procrastination, check this site without waiting another minute. Here is one tip: "Break the task down into little pieces. Not: There's so much to do, and it's so complicated. I'm overwhelmed by my English term paper. Instead: I don't have to do the whole project at once. There are separate small steps I can take one at a time to begin researching and drafting my paper."

http://students.berkeley.edu/slc/CalRen/
   procrastechniques.html

★ Virtual Presentation Assistant

Do you have to stand up in front of your whole class and give an oral report? Swat those tummy butterflies by trying the tips at this site. Learn how to organize your presentation in a variety of different ways so that you keep your audience's attention.

http://www.ukans.edu/cwis/units/coms2/vpa/vpa.htm

Wanniassa Hills Information Skills Project

This is another way to look at The Big 6 (see the earlier entry). Follow along with the Hello, Kitty cat as you select a project, learn what information you need to find (and just as important, what to leave out!), and choose a method of presenting your findings. Will you make a model? Prepare an audiovisual presentation? Or write a paper?

http://www.whps.act.edu.au/WHISP/whisp.html

NET FILES

How many mosquitoes can one little brown bat catch in one hour?

Answer: It can catch 1,200 mosquitoes! Read more fascinating bat trivia at http://www.batcon.org/discover/trivia.html

★ You Don't Have to Play Football to Score a Touchdown

Although this study skills page was designed for high school and college students, anyone can learn from these short tips. Did you know that the best time to study is right after class? Have you heard that when taking a test you should skip the hard questions, do the easy ones, and then return to spend time figuring out the more difficult problems? This page will help you take notes, manage your time, and learn to do your best to make and meet your goals. Be sure to take the link to Study Skills Help Page for more.

http://www.mtsu.edu/~studskl/hsindex.html

WEBQUESTS

iWebQuest

Is your teacher into Web Quest? Tell her or him about this site. The Hotlist section is an invaluable resource. It links to articles offering a nuts-and-bolts explanation of these online lesson plans and projects, including how to plan one and how to make the best use of them. It also points to some of the best Web Quests on the Net, so you can see what other schools have done.

http://www.iwebquest.com/

A B C D E F G H I J K L M N O P Q R **S** T U V W X Y Z

A
B
C
D
E
F
G
H
I
J
K
L
M
N
O
P
Q
R
S
T
U
V
W
X
Y
Z

Palmyra Atoll: Rainforest of the Sea

It's one of the most remote areas on Earth, and that makes it a perfect place to study an untouched ecosystem. Scientists are examining the old growth forests and coral reefs around Palmyra Atoll, and this site invites you along, too. View stunning underwater photography, video, and other multimedia.
http://www.oneworldjourneys.com/palmyra/

WebQuest - Kathy Schrock's Guide for Educators

What in the world is a WebQuest? According to Kathy Shrock's excellent introductory page, "A WebQuest is defined, by Bernie Dodge at San Diego State University, as 'an inquiry-oriented activity in which some or all of the information that learners interact with comes from resources on the Internet.'" Explore some of the best WebQuests around, and learn how you can prepare your own. There's a 16-slide Powerpoint presentation to help! For more details on creating WebQuests, try Ozline at *<http://www.ozline.com/learning/>*.

http://school.discovery.com/schrockguide/webquest/
webquest.html

The WebQuest Page

Some teachers let kids create a Web Quest instead of writing a traditional paper. You'll find a list of training materials, examples, and tips to help you create your own Web Quest or problem-solving activities. By using these tools, you'll learn critical thinking skills.

http://edweb.sdsu.edu/webquest/webquest.html

SCIENCE

See also under name of specific subject discipline throughout the book; DINOSAURS AND PREHISTORIC TIMES—EVOLUTION; WHY

60 Second Scientist

Got a couple minutes? Then you've got time to learn some science! Watch brief QuickTime video on such topics as bats, hand washing, pollen, fireworks, and something remarkable—a replica of Stonehenge made from junked cars. It's appropriately called "Car Henge."

http://tc.unl.edu/rbonnstetter/60ss.htm

BBC Education - Dynamo's Lab - Science Splat Quiz

Have you ever wondered how you'd do on that *Who Wants to be a Millionaire?* show? This game is sort of like that. You're in the hot seat, all right. You won't win any money—but if you get a question wrong, you'll be SLIMED.

http://www.bbc.co.uk/education/dynamo/lab/quiz/

BBC Education - Science - Litmus Test

If you think other science quizzes are too easy, try the Litmus Test. If you're a UK resident, you might win a prize, but science nerds everywhere will enjoy the questions.

http://www.bbc.co.uk/science/playground/litmus/

★ BBC - Science in Action

Try some great online activities and explore air, forces, light, microbes, and mixtures. In Mixtures, learn about the Bonneville salt flats, and then try mixing up some virtual "solutes and solvents" yourself in the Action Lab.

http://www.bbc.co.uk/sia/

Try actual reality.

★ Bill Nye the Science Guy's Nye Labs Online

It's Bill Nye the Science Guy, and is he loaded with science goodies to show you! Check out the Demo of the Day or visit the Home Demos section to see what's cool in Bill's world o' science. Lots of experiments and lessons on things scientific can be found here—plenty of fodder for your next science fair project.

http://nyelabs.kcts.org/

★ BrainPOP

Watch over 130 entertaining and educational animated cartoons that explain lots of scientific things, such as how your eyes work and how your sense of smell operates. There are other topics, too, such as the water cycle, electricity, and rainbows. Try some experiments with "Bob, the Ex-lab Rat" or register (it's free) to ask questions of your own. The more activities and features you read, the more "points" you can get. Collect enough points and you win a T-shirt and are entered in other prize drawings.

http://www.brainpop.com/

★ Explore Science

People learn in different ways—some people like to hear explanations, other people like to read them. Still others like to physically interact with a problem, and this page is for those folks (and anyone else who wants to have fun!). We hope you have Shockwave, because most of these little science demonstrations require that plug-in. Examine physics, mechanics, waves, optics, and much more. If you do nothing else, try the various snowflake designers in Fun and Games.

http://www.explorescience.com/

NET FILES

Pretend you have a special light switch in your bedroom and it is connected (with a really l o n g cord) to a lamp on the Moon. If you switch it on, how long will the delay be before the bulb lights?

Answer: It would take only 1.26 seconds for it to light up, shining over 238,857 miles away. Find out more at http://209.141.118.23/jfk_fun.html

Extreme Science

This one is all about scientific extremes: the highest and lowest elevation on Earth, the biggest mountain, the deepest cave, the greatest earthquake, and—well, you get the idea. Don't forget to check the Creature World section for the largest snake, deadliest creature, and more records from those that creep, swim, walk, and fly. You can also meet cool scientists, have some online adventures, and explore many fun science links.

http://www.extremescience.com/

Frank Potter's Science Gems

This treasure chest of science gems includes links to resources on physical sciences, earth science, life science, engineering, and math. There are over 14,000 science and math links here, which makes one wonder what Frank's life is like! The Web pages are arranged by subject and ordered by grade level. In some sections, a handy list shows which sites are popular and are most often "clicked."

http://www.sciencegems.com/

A
B
C
D
E
F
G
H
I
J
K
L
M
N
O
P
Q
R
S
T
U
V
W
X
Y
Z

A
B
C
D
E
F
G
H
I
J
K
L
M
N
O
P
Q
R
S
T
U
V
W
X
Y
Z

★ MadSciNet: The 24-hour Exploding Laboratory

Do you have a question about science that is stumping everyone you ask? Or maybe you have a really simple question you're too embarrassed to bring up in class. Look no further. You have just stumbled onto the solution. This site is a collaborative effort of scientists around the world, who have gathered to answer your questions. You can search the archives and see if your question, or one like it, has already been answered. There's also a library of experiments you can try (don't miss the section on Edible/Inedible Experiments), as well as links to more resources.

http://www.madsci.org/

The One Inch Square Project

What if you don't have a microscope and a lot of fancy equipment? You can still do real science using only one square inch of "something interesting," and your observation and recording skills. Cut out a one-square-inch window (the directions are at this site), and print the observation form. Now take your "window" and hold it against a tree trunk, a flower, the ground, even your dad. Then write down details about what you see. Being able to describe your observations is a big part of learning to become a scientist.

http://www.hhmi.org/coolscience/inchsquare/

★ Revisewise Science

Predict whether various virtual electrical circuits will light up a bulb, discover the five processes of all living things, and figure out how to separate sugar from sand. There's a brief review of each lesson, an activity, and a quiz. This is part of a larger site covering math and English skills.

http://www.bbc.co.uk/education/revisewise/science/

Royal Science Site

Click on Projects to find out what Mr. Royal's class is up to this year. You'll find a lot of interesting collaborative science projects, but that's not all. Click on Ken's Konnections or Mr. R's articles to get some great tips on putting technology to work in schools.

http://www.newtown.k12.ct.us/~royalk/

★ A Science Odyssey

Just visit this site. You will not be disappointed. Check out the Shockwave simulations in the You Try It section. In the Technology at Home area, scroll through the decades of the twentieth century and see what changes in the living room and kitchen. Old iceboxes disappear, to be replaced by modern refrigerators. Telephone equipment improves—what else will you notice? You can mouse over each item and see some facts about it: what it is, who invented it, and when it came into vogue or went out of style. Now try the other explorations: human evolution, radio transmission, probe the brain, atomic structure, and several more. When you get done with those, read the On the Edge comic books about various scientists and their discoveries. Did radio astronomer Jocelyn Bell really think she received a message from little green men in outer space? Find out here. Don't miss the hit game show That's My Theory! You can question the three contestants to see which one is the real Einstein, the real Freud, and the real ENIAC.

http://www.pbs.org/wgbh/aso/

★ Thinking Fountain!

From A to Z, you're going to find a lot of wonderful ideas and information at the Thinking Fountain. Allow us to demonstrate! A—Read about Anansi the Spider, and then find out how to make your own sliding spider toy. G—Golf-O-Rama, a book about miniature golf, complete with everything you need but the ball and the putter, and a story about some kids who made their own mini-mini golf course. N—Noodle-ing around: learn to build a structure out of spaghetti. (Don't believe it? The secret is in the mini-marshmallows). Z—Zoo Machines: invent a machine to take care of all those animals. Keep going; you're sure to find lots more activities and ideas, galleries to show your work, books you can use, and surprises inspired by the Thinking Fountain.

http://www.smm.org/sln/tf/nav/tfatoz.html

Become one with the Net.

★ Try Science

The content at this site changes from time to time as it is all contributed by science museums around the Web. You might try to build and test a paper bridge, investigate the best way to clean up an oil slick, or measure your own lung capacity. If you click on Field Trips you can check out live cams at science centers all over the world. Don't miss the Adventures section with the Star Trek Starfleet Academy simulation. If you explore all the activities you can graduate as an ensign!

http://www.tryscience.com/

★ Who Wants to Win $1,000,000? - The Science Game

The questions and answers are real, but the money is not. In this version of *Who Wants to Be a Millionaire?*, you answer questions to test your knowledge of science and math. As you work your way to the million-dollar level, you can answer the question or get some help, just like on the real television show. The questions are different each time you play.

http://education.jlab.org/million/

YES Mag

Canada's science magazine for kids has an electronic version. It includes book and software reviews, in-depth articles, and science news and projects. We particularly liked the How Does That Work? section, where we learned lots about telescopes, cameras, submarines, and other inventions.

http://www.yesmag.bc.ca/

EXPERIMENTS

Edible/Inedible Experiments Archive

Can you learn about earth science by observing cracks in cheese? Can you chew light? Is it possible to learn anything about static electricity from Rice Krispies? Absolutely. And the best part is that after the experiment is over, you can eat it.

http://www.madsci.org/experiments/

Home Experiments

What do you mean there's nothing to do. Why, with Mom or Dad and a few simple household ingredients, you could bend water, collapse an aluminum can, float soap bubbles in an aquarium full of carbon dioxide, or even remove tarnish from silver! Is it magic? No, just chemistry, physics, or both. There are also links to even more home experiments to try.

http://scifun.chem.wisc.edu/HOMEEXPTS/
    HOMEEXPTS.html

Hunkin's Experiments

Tim Hunkin is an engineer turned cartoonist. At his site, you'll find hundreds of cool cartoon experiments and activities that use food, light, sound, clothes, and more. This site just might inspire you to come up with your own cartoon experiment. If it does, e-mail Hunkin. If your entry wins, he'll turn it into a cartoon and feature it on the site.

http://www.hunkinsexperiments.com/

The Official Harry Potter Web Site

This is it! The one, the only official Harry Potter site! Step right up and enroll; then go through the sorting hat ritual (Net-mom's in Gryffindor!). Look over the list of books and magical items you'll need for your first year at Hogwarts; then head off to Ollivander's wand shop to select your . . . oops, we mean, let your wand select you! Dawdle at Bertie Botts and choose an Every Flavor Bean (will you get ice cream or smelly feet?), and then head back to campus. Are you ready for some quidditch? You can also download the trailer for the new Harry Potter movie!
http://harrypotter.warnerbros.com/home.html

A
B
C
D
E
F
G
H
I
J
K
L
M
N
O
P
Q
R
S
T
U
V
W
X
Y
Z

A
B
C
D
E
F
G
H
I
J
K
L
M
N
O
P
Q
R
S
T
U
V
W
X
Y
Z

Iron Science Teacher

If you've seen the cable TV show, *Iron Chef*, you know what to expect! Take some science teachers and give them a commonly found "secret ingredient" such as kitty litter or baking soda. Then ask them to cook up their best science experiment using that item. The most creative experiment wins, and the victorious teacher earns the coveted title of "Iron Science Teacher." So, who are the winning teachers and what experiments did they create? Tune in to this site with your Real Player plug-in to find out.

http://www.exploratorium.edu/iron_science/

Real Time Experiments

Amazing physics experiments you can do with common household items, things to try right on your computer, and amazing tricks with Shockwave— these things and more are waiting for you, courtesy of the Little Shop of Physics.

http://littleshop.physics.colostate.edu/ Experiments.html

Miss Maggie's Earth Adventures

The big red button holds the key to joining Miss Maggie as she travels around the world to protect the environment. Click it and join her on a mission, such as saving dying coral reefs in the Pacific Ocean. Each mission has lots of creative, interactive tools designed to make you environmentally smart. When you've completed a mission, watch some of the movies, or learn a fascinating fact about a wild animal. This neat site is animated like a comic book, so keep the audio turned up. *http://www.missmaggie.org/*

★ Reeko's Mad Scientist Lab

It sure is dusty here in Reeko's basement science lab. Better put on this lab coat to keep your clothes clean, and a pair of goggles might not be a bad idea, either. Fun educational experiments in astronomy, chemistry, physics, and earth science are categorized by subject and level of difficulty. Reeko has a fun sense of humor, too. Consider the description for Rocket Powered Pennies: "O.K., so maybe the term rocket powered is taking it a little too far. But we still get to propel an object. All we need for this simple experiment is an empty soda bottle and a penny (unless you are getting your Mad Scientist supplies from Dad, in which case—ask for a quarter)."

http://www.spartechsoftware.com/reeko/

Science Experiments for Kids

Would you like to demonstrate the iso-trophic and thixo-trophic properties of certain emulsions? Or would you just like to play with SLIME, the greatest polymer of them all? That's only one of the experiments you can try at this gooey site that also explains paper airplanes, Cartesian divers, air pressure, and more.

http://www.fatlion.com/science/

Science Lab

Did you know some rocks can absorb liquid like a sponge? This site has a science experiment that will show you how. The Science Lab section is filled with many more experiments you can try at home or in the classroom. There are also plenty of science articles to read; and if you've got a question about something scientific, you can ask an expert from this site.

http://www.slb.com/seed/lab/

★ Science Playwiths

Get your hands dirty, have fun, and learn something about science. That's what this site wants you to do. It's got intriguing sections on bubbles, kitchen chemistry, zoology, surface tension, living things, physics, magnetism, building cool stuff, and more. You'll also find almost 2,000 ideas for science fair projects. This guy is the Harry Potter of science.

http://members.ozemail.com.au/~macinnis/scifun/

Whelmers

Before we go further, answer this: Is there iron in your cereal? Can a penny dance on the top of a soda bottle? Want to find out? Try these "whelmers"—activities that catch the mind and the eye of every student. At this really cool site, you can open up 20 different whelmers and have a lot of fun while actually learning some useful information! It will require gathering some simple materials and then reading instructions on how to complete the task. Remember, you can never be too whelmed by science, although you can be overwhelmed with homework.

http://www.mcrel.org/whelmers/

★ Wondernet - Your Science Place in Cyberspace!

Here are some activities aimed at the very youngest chemists. For example, try some experiments with soda pop. Do you think you could put a can of diet soda and a can of regular soda into a bucket of water and be able to pick out which is the diet can—while blindfolded? That's chemistry! Read about this trick, plus several others; then go ask Dad or Mom to help. Be sure to check out the tour to how soda is made, too. It's in the past issues area under the Science of Sodapop.

http://www.acs.org/wondernet/

SCIENCE FAIRS
Agricultural Ideas for Science Fair Projects

What affects the speed of ripening fruit? What results can you expect from different fertilizers? Does seed size matter? These are only a few of the great science fair ideas for those interested in things that grow. Learn how to prepare a great science fair project with an agricultural theme.

http://www.ars.usda.gov/is/kids/fair/ideas.htm

Find your roots in GENEALOGY AND FAMILY HISTORY.

Do Science!

This page offers "things to do while waiting for the food to come" in a restaurant; but Net-mom suggests you try these at home, because some involve a possible mess if done the wrong way. You'll find lots of annoying things you can do with straws, how to make a lava lamp (sort of, see Density Drips), and plenty of fodder for science fair magic.

http://www.doscience.com/

Exploratorium Learning Studio Science Fairs

Net-mom's favorite hands-on museum offers tips for your science fair project. Besides a general overview of the Scientific Method, you will find resources for teachers (who run the science fairs), students (who create projects), and parents (who try to keep calm). There's also a handy section on where to get slime mold spores, beakers, and other important supplies. For more great ideas for demonstrations, try the Exploratorium's Science Snack area at <http://www.exploratorium.edu/snacks/>.

http://www.exploratorium.edu/ls/pathfinders/scifairs/

Helping Your Child Learn Science

OK, it's really a brochure for parents, but you should check out the experiments here, because some of them would make neat science fair projects. You'll find lots of kitchen chemistry tricks and fun with static electricity, and don't miss "celery stalks at midnight"!

http://www.ed.gov/pubs/parents/Science/

How to Make a Great Poster

The biggest problem with science fair posters is that the print isn't large enough to be seen from a few feet away. Don't make the judges squint! Make BIG letters. Also, don't make your poster too "busy" with material and information that's not of primary importance. This Web site explains it all and suggests many ways to make your poster the best ever.

http://www.aspb.org/education/poster.cfm

A B C D E F G H I J K L M N O P Q R S T U V W X Y Z

A
B
C
D
E
F
G
H
I
J
K
L
M
N
O
P
Q
R
S
T
U
V
W
X
Y
Z

Have you written to your PEN PALS lately?

Intel Science Talent Search

Now you can earn serious money for that science fair project. Every year, the Intel Corporation sponsors a prestigious science competition for high school seniors. The top prize is $100,000. The runners-up also receive thousands of dollars. Find everything you need to participate here. Get tips on starting early, pore over the rules and guidelines, and examine past projects.

http://www.intel.com/education/sts/

IPL Science Fair Project Resource Guide

This is your first science fair project, and you're not really sure where to begin. The folks at the Internet Public Library can help: they have collected a lot of good information to get you going.

http://www.ipl.org/youth/projectguide/

Science Explorer: An Exploratorium-At-Home Book

You might be able to use these little science show-stoppers at a science fair, but they are probably better to amuse your visiting cousins. Make a glitter globe, discover secret colors in a black marker, or learn how to construct a flying paper hoop.

http://www.exploratorium.edu/science_explorer/

Science Fair Central at DiscoverySchool.com

Maybe you're a science fair veteran but don't want to make yet another volcano model. You need some new ideas! This resource is a great place to start. There are sections aimed at students, teachers, and parents with everything you need to know to participate in—or organize—a science fair.

http://school.discovery.com/sciencefaircentral/

★ Science Lessons by Subject

Even preschoolers can have a science fair with the ideas at this site. Light up a bulb using only a lemon ("Lemon Power"). Make a spider web you can keep ("Why Don't Spiders Stick to their Own Webs?"). Middle and high school kids will be intrigued by the Solar Hot Dog Cooker and other more elaborate demonstrations. There are many more in this collection, so spend some time when you visit.

http://www.eecs.umich.edu/mathscience/
funexperiments/agesubject/subject.html

The World-Wide Web Virtual Library: Science Fairs

Is there a science fair near you? If your school doesn't run one, try your local science museum. No museum? Your state may offer regional fairs. There may also be special fairs put on by industry. You can find out about all of them at this resource.

http://physics1.usc.edu/~gould/ScienceFairs/

SCIENCE MUSEUMS

★ Exploratorium: ExploraNet

Do you know what makes a fruit fly grow legs out of its head? How would you like to take a "light walk" and explore the world of shadows? The Exploratorium, in San Francisco, California, is a huge hands-on science laboratory for kids of all ages. Discover the many interesting wonders that they have ported to the Web!

http://www.exploratorium.edu/

MuseumSpot

Want to see a picture of the world's most complete *T.rex*? Peek through the webcams at some of the world's best zoos? Splash into an online aquarium? Thanks to this site, you can do all of the above and more. This site links to museum sites and their exhibits from all over the world. Read, learn, enjoy.

http://www.museumspot.com/

★ Questacon

Australia's National Science and Technology Centre has a fabulous online museum. Explore virtual galleries of interactive exhibits, head-scratching puzzles, challenging games, and more. Dinosaurs, meteors, optical illusions, and clever science activities abound here. It's one of the best sites on the Net for kids interested in science.

http://www.questacon.edu.au/

SHARKS

See also FISH

NOVA Online - Island of the Sharks

According to this NOVA site, there are more than 400 species of sharks. But are they really the vicious creatures people say they are? Find out from the sharkmasters here, and learn all about shark tagging, shark anatomy, life cycle, and more.

http://www.pbs.org/wgbh/nova/sharks/

Zoom Sharks - Enchanted Learning Software

Did you know that sharks have no bones? Their skeletons are made of thick, fibrous cartilage. There are all sizes of sharks, too, from a shark that would fit on your hand to a shark as big as a bus—the whale shark can be over 50 feet long! At this site you can learn about types of sharks found around the world, how they are classified, what they eat, what their teeth look like, and more. You can also print shark coloring pages to make a souvenir shark booklet.

http://www.EnchantedLearning.com/subjects/sharks/

SHIPS AND SHIPWRECKS

See also AFRICAN AMERICANS—HISTORY; BOATING AND SAILING; MILITARY AND ARMED FORCES; TREASURE AND TREASURE HUNTING; and WEATHER AND METEOROLOGY—SNOW AND ICE

NET FILES

The Empire State Building in New York City often uses special colored building lights to celebrate holidays, wins by the New York Yankees, and other special occasions. How many different colors can be displayed?

Answer: The different colors are red, green, blue, yellow, and white. Additionally, a ring of high-pressure sodium vapor lights above the 103rd floor creates a golden halo effect around the top of the mast from dusk to dawn. Read http://www.esbnyc.com/html/tower_lights.html for more fascinating tower trivia.

California Shipwrecks

There's a neat database at this site that lets you search for shipwrecks off the California coast. Say you're looking for wrecks off Mendocino. Plug in that county name and BAM! You'll find records on more than 200 shipwrecks. It tells how they went down, too, from a "monster wave" to a collision. Other parts of the site tell the stories of several famous (and not so well-known) shipwrecks, and suggest links to maritime museums on the Net.

http://shipwrecks.slc.ca.gov/

The Diving Game

Explore the perils of the deep, and discover the secrets of shipwrecks. In this online game, you need to locate the treasure on the ocean floor. It seems accessible: only ten questions below the surface. But you'd better know something about marine archaeology, because if you get one question wrong, you must return to the surface and start over. Beware of the sharks.

http://www.bbc.co.uk/history/ancient/archaeology/marine_diving_game.shtml

A
B
C
D
E
F
G
H
I
J
K
L
M
N
O
P
Q
R
S
T
U
V
W
X
Y
Z

A
B
C
D
E
F
G
H
I
J
K
L
M
N
O
P
Q
R
S
T
U
V
W
X
Y
Z

Kids Snow Page

If you lived in the frozen North, you might have as many different words for snow as the Inuit do. There are words that mean falling snow, ground snow, smoky snow, and wind-beaten snow. Do you live in a snowy climate? Go on a scavenger hunt activity! Use the list of all the different kinds of snow and see how many you can find where you live. If you'd like to keep your snowflake finds, learn how you can do it with a piece of glass and some hair spray. Make an edible glacier, cut and fold paper snowflakes, and learn that soap bubbles won't pop if you blow them outside when it's minus 40 degrees Fahrenheit, as it is pretty often where the Teel family kids live—in Alaska.
http://www.teelfamily.com/activities/snow/

Edmund Fitzgerald Bell Restoration Project

You may have heard the Gordon Lightfoot song commemorating the wreck of the *Edmund Fitzgerald*. On November 10, 1975, the 729-foot freighter was hauling a heavy cargo of iron ore pellets across Lake Superior and was caught in a severe storm that sent the ship suddenly to the bottom, killing its 29 crew members. This page describes the search for the wreck, the salvage effort, and the restoration of the ship's bell. Surviving family members asked that the bell be recovered as a memorial to the sailors who gave their lives in the maritime accident. A duplicate bell, inscribed with the names of the sailors, was left in the pilot house of the ship. The original bell was brought to the surface and dedicated on July 7, 1995. At the ceremony, the bell was rung 30 times: once for each of the 29 Fitzgerald crew members, and once for all mariners who have lost their lives at sea.

http://web.msu.edu/bell/

★ Great Lakes and Seaway Shipping

Whether you are looking for information on the Soo Locks, ocean freighters, or Great Lakes shipwrecks, you'll find a whole cargo of information at this site. There's a very complete story about the *Edmund Fitzgerald* disaster, including haunting Real Audio radio transmissions reporting the wreck. Did you know fleet vessels can be identified by the markings on their stacks? There are illustrations of 30 different ones pictured at *<http://www.lre.usace.army.mil/ shipping/glshhmpg.html>*. Another cool thing to try is in the Vessel Passage section. Click there and choose Current Vessel Locations or Real Time Vessel Locations—Seaway. You can zoom in on ships and find out where they are from and where they are going.

http://www.boatnerd.com/

The Legend of Steamboatin' the Grand Old South

Listen to the eerie trumpet of several old steam whistles, and imagine the time when these big boats trolled the Mississippi and other river systems. Much of this site is broken (try the "this page without Javascript" option where available if you have problems), but the calliope audio and video files are unique, so we are listing this site anyway.

http://www.steamboats.org/

Lightship Huron

Where it was too deep or impractical to build a lighthouse, but a navigation aid was still needed, a lightship like the *Huron* was often used. They displayed a light at the top of the mast and offered bells, whistles, foghorns, and other warning sounds as well. Take a virtual tour of this historic vessel, and learn all about the uses of lightships on the Great Lakes. There is also an extensive list of maritime links

http://www.oakland.edu/boatnerd/museums/huron/

People are the true treasures of the Net.

Everyone's flocking to BIRDS!

Lost Liners

The *Titanic*, *Lusitania*, *Empress of Ireland*, *Britannic*, and the *Andrea Doria*. What do they all have in common? They are the greatest lost ocean liners in maritime history. Discover why they sank and what remains of them, and learn about the science of deep-ocean archaeology and what it really means to go down under.

http://www.pbs.org/lostliners/

The Mary Rose

July 19, 1545: On the flagship, the Tudor king, Henry VIII, was having a lavish dinner. The *Mary Rose*, a four-masted warship built between 1510 and 1511, sailed nearby. French ships appeared and fired on the fleet. A little while later, the *Mary Rose* was lying at the bottom of the Solent, a body of water between Portsmouth, England, and the Isle of Wight. Most of the 500-person crew drowned. The ship was rediscovered in 1971 and was raised to the surface in 1982. This site takes you on a tour of the museum artifacts found on board, as well as a dry dock containing what is left of the ship itself. You'll be fascinated at the technology used to raise the ship and the stories of shipboard life during those times.

http://www.maryrose.org/

★ NOVA Online - Submarines, Secrets, and Spies

View detailed QuickTime VR pictures inside a submarine. Notice how the cursor changes as you mouse over the periscope, for instance? If you click on it, another window opens with information about that particular piece of equipment. Read what life on a submarine is really like, and find out what happens when you finally "earn your dolphins" as a qualified submariner.

http://www.pbs.org/wgbh/nova/subsecrets/

NOVA Online - Voyage of Doom

Take a tour to French explorer Robert Cavelier Sieur de La Salle's ship, *La Belle*, as it was excavated by the Texas Historical Commission. Then visit the Commission's page to see even more at <http://www.thc.state.tx.us/belle/>, including some of the over 700,000 blue glass beads that are found. They are still fashionable today!

http://www.pbs.org/wgbh/nova/lasalle/

The Official Site of the Hunley

The *Hunley* was a Confederate submarine in the Civil War. On February 16, 1864, it became the first sub in history to engage and sink a warship. Unfortunately, it sunk, too. In 2000, it was raised from its location in Charleston harbor. It now sits in a lab in South Carolina where scientists are excavating its interior. Human remains have been found and more are likely. Keep up-to-date on the latest findings and learn more about the recovery process when you visit this site. For more on the history of this vessel, see <http://www.history.navy.mil/branches/ org12-3.htm>.

http://www.hunley.org/

Polynesian Voyaging Society

The Polynesian Voyaging Society has built two replicas of ancient canoes—*Hokule'a* and *Hawai'iloa*—and conducted many voyages in the South Pacific to retrace ancient migration routes and recover traditional canoe-building and wayfinding (non-instrument navigation) arts. Discover this voyaging tradition at their official Web page.

http://leahi.kcc.hawaii.edu/org/pvs/

The Soo Locks

The four shipping locks at Sault Saint Marie, Michigan, help about 10,000 vessels a year transit from Lake Superior to Lake Huron, or vice versa. At this site you can learn about the history of the locks, see an animation of how one works, and take a link to several webcams to check on boat traffic right now <http://www.crrel.usace.army.mil/ ierd/ webcams/soo/>.

http://huron.lre.usace.army.mil/SOO/soohmpg.html

A B C D E F G H I J K L M N O P Q R **S** T U V W X Y Z

A
B
C
D
E
F
G
H
I
J
K
L
M
N
O
P
Q
R
S
T
U
V
W
X
Y
Z

Wayfinding in the Middle of the Pacific

Journey back through time to the days of the early Hawaiians, and see how they voyaged across the sea without instruments or a compass to guide them. They had only the stars and other natural "signposts" to show them the way. Some young people from several elementary schools in Hawaii thought that was really unusual and cool. So they did a lot of research about the early settlers of Hawaii and entered their Web page in the ThinkQuest Junior competition. You'll enjoy reading about how the original Hawaiians traveled and how they used stars to navigate. You can even play a game that will prove just how much you have learned.

http://tqjunior.advanced.org/3542/

RMS TITANIC

★ Discovery - On Board the Titanic

Assume the role of one of five real passengers on the *Titanic*. What will be your fate? Will you be one of the survivors or one of many who lost their lives that night in 1912? You won't know whose role you're playing until it's all over. (Hint: read the "date of death" carefully. If it's not 1912, you survived the wreck.) Don't miss the *Titanic*'s final hours, at the same site <*http://www.discovery.com/stories/science/ sciencetitanic/sciencetitanic.html*>.

http://www.discovery.com/guides/history/titanic/
    Titanic/titanic.html

★ Titanic

You'll find lots of artifacts; annotated Web links; and facts, lore, and legend at this *Titanic* offering from *Encyclopedia Britannica*. Even if you think you've read everything about the *Titanic*, give this site a try, too. One good thing that came out of this disaster was the establishment of an International Ice Patrol. About 1,000 icebergs are tracked each year during the iceberg season, from March to August. The U.S. Coast Guard broadcasts their locations twice daily via satellite and high-frequency radio facsimile.

http://titanic.eb.com/

SPORTS

See also BOATING AND SAILING; DOGS AND DOG SPORTS; HORSES AND EQUESTRIAN SPORTS; OUTDOOR RECREATION

CBS Sportsline - Kids Zone

Scanning for up-to-the-minute scores and team news, and the latest on athletes and other figures in sports? CBS Sportsline covers the NBA, NFL, baseball, NHL, golf, tennis, soccer, volleyball, skiing, boxing, and even horse racing events such as the Kentucky Derby. In the Kids Zone, you can get all kinds of player profiles, listen to audio and see video clips, check sports news for kids, and play sports-related games.

http://www.sportsline.com/u/kids/

College Nicknames

Teams usually pick a nickname to describe themselves, like the Wolverines or the Wildcats. Which names go with which U.S. colleges? Find out here. Did you know there's even a team nicknamed the White Mules? They're at Colby College, in Waterville, Maine.

http://www.smargon.net/nicknames/

★ The Locker Room . . . . Sports for Kids!

Do you need basic information on how to hold a bat, kick a football, serve a volleyball, or shoot a hockey puck? Get it here. Besides "skills and drills," you'll find the rules of these sports and many others, their histories, fun facts about them, and a glossary of terms. There is also advice on how to do warm-up exercises and how to deal with team problems. If you don't have a big brother or sister to teach you this stuff, this page is the next best thing.

http://member.aol.com/msdaizy/sports/locker.html

★ Sports ID Instructional Videos for Every Sport

Wouldn't it be great to have a personal trainer—somebody who would be available to you all the time? This site offers something like that—video instruction in sports like bodyboarding, bowling, fly fishing, football, hockey, martial arts, and on and on. Your favorite sport is probably listed. Choose from movies in several different formats, based on your Internet connection speed.

http://www.sportsid.com/sid2000/

★ Sports Illustrated for Kids

When was the last time you sailed around the world, or picked up some tips from the world's best skateboarders—all without leaving your computer? This online magazine is all about athletic challenges. If you've been wanting to try your hand at a new sport, this is where you can find out all about the moves, the lingo, and the equipment. Don't miss the interviews with sports heroes, games, and a whole lot more. Hint: Buzz Chat isn't, really.

http://www.sikids.com/

Yahoo! Broadcast

You missed the big game? Check here to see if an audio broadcast is available. Some are live; others are archived here to be enjoyed whenever you tune in. You'll also catch online shows with coaches and players, as well as special reports. Just about every sport you can think of is listed here.

http://www.broadcast.com/Sports_Events/

BASEBALL

America's Pastime - The Men Who Made the Game

Who's on the All-Century All-Star team? Find out here! See photos, read stats, and try a fun trivia game. This site was created by students for the ThinkQuest Junior competition.

http://library.thinkquest.org/J002612/home.htm

The American President

This companion guide to the PBS series of the same name offers a spectacular game called The War Room. Could you manage a presidential campaign all the way from the New Hampshire primaries to the November election? Try the simulation! Also see another companion guide to this series under UNITED STATES—PRESIDENTS AND FIRST LADIES.
http://www.americanpresident.org/

Baseball Cards - Hall of Famers

The creator of this Web page collects baseball cards from the 1960s, and he presents them for all to enjoy. Click on a card and find information and stats about famous players like Mickey Mantle, Don Drysdale, and others. For more on this topic, see COLLECTORS AND COLLECTING—SPORTS AND OTHER TRADING CARDS.

http://www.primenet.com/~jpmill/bball/

★ Baseball: The Game and Beyond

Baseball, apple pie, and motherhood: three American traditions. Everyone understands what motherhood is, and everyone knows how to eat an apple pie, but a lot of people don't really understand how baseball is played. Or why a pitcher throws a curve ball one time and a fastball the next, or how physics is involved in this age-old sport. Well, wonder no longer. This ThinkQuest finalist team has come up with a lot of the answers. If they could only tell us when the Red Sox will win the Series! There's also a very interesting section about the official announcer and what his day is like.

http://library.thinkquest.org/11902/

A
B
C
D
E
F
G
H
I
J
K
L
M
N
O
P
Q
R
S
T
U
V
W
X
Y
Z

NET FILES

How tall is the Oscar award, and how much does it weigh?

Movies

Answer: The Academy Awards statuette, known as "Oscar," is 13 1/2 inches tall and weighs 8 1/2 pounds. The statuettes are made from gold-plated alloy called britannium. Learn more about the awards and the winners at
http://www.oscars.org/academyawards/awards.html

Black Baseball's Negro Baseball Leagues

Among the many great African American baseball players were Satchel Paige and Josh Gibson. Did you know there was a time in American history when major league teams didn't allow African American players on the same team with white players? It seems impossible to believe now. These fantastic players competed in what was called the Negro Baseball Leagues. You can find out all about their history and greatest athletes at this excellent site.

http://www.blackbaseball.com/

★ Exploratorium's Science of Baseball!

Do you think you could hit a 90-mph fastball, coming straight for you? You can test your reaction time online. There are more activities for you to try, and don't miss the scientific slugger and his quest for a home run. There's also a nice history of baseball equipment—then and now—and a look at women players and baseball in Japan (*besuboru*). Also, did you know weather conditions can affect your hits?

http://www.exploratorium.edu/baseball/

Joe DiMaggio: Beat the Streak

How would you like your name added to the Beat the Streak Hall of Fame? If you can get a hit in at least 40 straight baseball games, your name will be added to the list. But don't run out of the house just yet. For this game, you'll be playing on your computer. So, step up to the plate, and give it a try. If you can get a hit in 56 virtual straight games, you'll tie Joe DiMaggio's record, set in 1941.

http://www.pbs.org/wgbh/amex/dimaggio/sfeature/
    game_intro.html

Kids Domain Baseball Fun

Do you love baseball and hate when the season is over? Then this is the site for you. It's full of online baseball-related games and fun. Many are online Java and Shockwave games, while others are downloadable to play offline.

http://www.kidsdomain.com/sports/baseball/

Louisville Slugger

This maker of legendary baseball bats has a factory in Louisville, Kentucky, but also has a virtual museum in cyberspace, and you can visit it online. In business since 1884, they have supplied bats to Babe Ruth, Ty Cobb, and a host of other well-known baseball greats. Players can be very particular about their bats. Some like wood with a narrow grain, while some like a wider grain. They like different weights, different wood stains, and different dimensions. Ted Williams once said his newly received bats didn't feel right. They weren't. When measured, they were 5/1000ths of an inch off his specifications!

http://www.slugger.com/

★ Mudball

Austin "Mudball" Taylor's dream is to play baseball in the major leagues. At his Web site, you can follow his personal stats and his training progress through his early high school career. Check his secret training weapon—but make sure you have your parents' and coach's approval before you try it, and always remember to stretch and warm up first.

http://www.mudball.com/

★ The National Baseball Hall of Fame

Visit the Baseball Hall of Fame in Cooperstown, New York. Get information on exhibits and tours, and check the online versions. You'll read about Babe Ruth's bat, Mickey Mantle's locker, and the special displays on women in baseball. You can also read about the baseball greats who have been inducted into the Hall of Fame, as well as see pictures of this year's class of inductees. Don't miss the list of new acquisitions in the research library. When we checked, they had recently received a uniform worn by the batboys of the House of David baseball team, c. 1930s, and the costume worn by "The San Diego Chicken."

http://baseballhalloffame.org/

Official Site of Little League Baseball International Headquarters

Do you play Little League baseball? Did you know that the Little League baseball organization has a Web site? This site gives you answers to frequently asked questions about Little League and its history. You'll also find summer camp information, Little League World Series news, and access to the Little League gift shop. No Little League near you? Talk Mom and Dad into starting one for you and your friends—contact names for starting the procedure are here.

http://www.littleleague.org/

★ The Official Site of Major League Baseball

All the information you'd ever need to settle any World Series argument is here: all the stats, all the teams, everything but the hot dogs. Hotlist this site right away, because you'll need it all season. Here, you'll find official information on all the major league teams, expanded box scores for all the games, live audio broadcasts, and a great photo gallery! A baseball team shop is here, too.

http://www.mlb.com/

Who's on First

"Who's on First?" is one of the all-time great routines by Bud Abbott and Lou Costello, a pair of comedians known for their radio show in the 1940s and 1950s. You can hear their rendition if you visit the Baseball Hall of Fame in Cooperstown, New York. If you can't get there, you can check it out at this Web site.

http://www.city-net.com/abbottandcostellofc/
   whoscrip.htm

BASKETBALL

FinalFour.net

So, who are the four final teams in the NCAA championship games? Stop scratching your head and head over to this site. You'll find all the information you'll need to not only name the teams, but also learn about the players and what they do both on and off the court. If you really want to bone up on your NCAA history, go to the Trivia section and play the video trivia game. You'll get to watch live action clips of some of the greatest moments in NCAA Final Four history and predict the outcome.

http://www.finalfour.net/

Harlem Globetrotters Online

One sports team has played before more people and has won more consecutive games over the last 70 years than any other: the Harlem Globetrotters, of course! Check out these funny athletes at their Web site.

http://www.harlemglobetrotters.com/

National Wheelchair Basketball Association

This site tells you all about the sport of wheelchair basketball: what are the rules, how to get started, and where to play or see a game. Did you see the L.A. Sparks women's wheelchair team on the front of the Team Cheerios box? They won the 1999 Women's National Championship. Way to go!

http://nwba.org/nwbaindx.htm

A
B
C
D
E
F
G
H
I
J
K
L
M
N
O
P
Q
R
S
T
U
V
W
X
Y
Z

A
B
C
D
E
F
G
H
I
J
K
L
M
N
O
P
Q
R
S
T
U
V
W
X
Y
Z

NBA.com

The official NBA Web site really lets you interact with the players and teams. You can't go one-on-one (yet), but they do have live chat sessions with all your favorite players. Don't worry, if you miss one, you can go back and read the transcript. This site offers all the teams, all the players, and all the multimedia you could ever want.

http://www.nba.com/

Women's National Basketball Association

Step aside, Michael. Move over, Shaquille. The women have made their mark in basketball history, and you can read all about it right here. The two-division, 16-team league features top names from college and Olympic play. This site has you sitting courtside, with highlights of the players and their teams. Ask a question, read the stats, and learn the history of the league and of women in basketball. You can even find out how to order a shirt or hat from your favorite team—but check with your parents before you do that!

http://www.wnba.com/

NET FILES

What U.S. president once invited all of Washington, D.C., into the White House to help him eat a 1,400-pound (636-kilogram) wheel of cheese?

Answer: According to the White House at *http://www.whitehouse.gov/history/presidents/aj7.html,* "Anyone could come to Andrew Jackson's public parties at the White House, and just about everyone did! At his last one, a wheel of cheese weighing 1,400 lbs. was eaten in two hours. The White House smelled of cheese for weeks."

BICYCLES AND BICYCLING

Bicycle Helmet Safety Institute

Bicycle helmets make good sense. Many parts of the U.S. and Canada, plus all of Australia, require helmets. Other places are studying such laws and may require helmets as well. This all-volunteer organization tells you what types of helmets meet safety standards and where you can get inexpensive ones. According to this site, a round, smooth helmet is better than one with points that can snag on pavement. Visit this site for much, much more about bike and helmet safety.

http://www.helmets.org/

Exploratorium's Science of Cycling

Sure, you'll find information on the history of cycling here, but you'll also find out about the science behind those little skinny wheels you see on road bikes and those big fat wheels you notice on mountain bikes. And did you ever wonder why tires are spoked that way? It's all about tangents. You'll never look at a bicycle the same way again after you've visited this site.

http://www.exploratorium.edu/cycling/

Propelled by Pedals: A Fun Guide to Bikes

Learn about how a bicycle works and check out safety equipment and laws concerning bikes and their use. There's a section on choosing a bike, the history of bicycling, and the current bike racing and long distance riding scene. This site was created by students for the ThinkQuest Junior competition.

http://library.thinkquest.org/J002670/

ROMP - Beginner's Guide

This site has everything you need to take your first mountain bike ride. Not only will you learn the techniques and check out the equipment needed, but you'll also cover the trail etiquette necessary to make your ride a pleasure—for everyone else!

http://www.romp.org/rides/beginnerguide.html

Le Tour de France

The classic bicycle race called the *Tour de France* started in 1903. It was in six different stages as it made its way around France. The 2001 race had 21 stages and traversed 3,462 kilometers (2,151 miles). Check the Flash version of the entire route using an interactive map of France that shows details of each location and more. You can follow the ups and downs of the most recent race at this site.

http://www.letour.fr/

USA Cycling Online

Whether you're interested in BMX, mountain, track, road, or CX (cyclo-cross) cycling, you'll find results, upcoming race calendars, pro bios, and so much more at this site.

http://www.usacycling.org/

BOOMERANGS

Aboriginal Steve's Boomerang Page

This should be called Boomerangs for Dummies, because the instructions are very simple and easy to follow. Even Net-mom holds out hope that she might finally get a 'rang to return to her, by close adherence to these rules of thumb, er, wrist, er . . . .

http://www.vcnet.com/abosteves/booms.html

BOWLING

Complete Bowling Index

At this site, you can get bowling news from around the world, tournament dates and results, plus links to other bowling sites. But there's so much more: equipment, lists of bowling organizations (including those for the disabled), and the history of bowling. You'll also find a link to information for beginners.

http://www.bowlingindex.com/

Professional Bowler's Association Tour

You're going to love this Web site. Are you having a hard time finding the latest news stories and results from the PBA tour? At this site, you can get the latest results, tour schedules, and the history of the PBA. The PBA is popular all over the world: tournaments have been held in Canada, Puerto Rico, Japan, South America, France, and England. Chat with other bowling enthusiasts in the real-time chat emporium. Maybe you'll even get to talk to a pro!

http://www.pbatour.com/

COACHING
Coaching Youth Sports

You ask your mother to coach your basketball team this year. She says, "Yes." As the season gets closer, she starts wondering about what she should do. How can you help? Check out this site, which offers some basic tips about coaching kids in sports.

http://www.tandl.vt.edu/rstratto/CYS/

EXTREME SPORTS
Eco-Challenge

It's a 24-hour-a-day, more than 300-mile race for teams over extremely demanding territory. It may involve running, hiking, scaling cliffs, canoeing, swimming, bicycling, or riding horseback. One of the unusual parts of this competition is that the entire team must finish together. If one team member can't go on because of injury or fatigue, the entire team is disqualified. This grueling race attracts worldwide media attention for environmental concerns, which are highlighted for each region where the race is held. Be there, or be here to find out more.

http://www.ecochallenge.com/

Ultramarathon World

What is an ultramarathon? Imagine people running races of 50 miles, 100 miles, even more! Consider the Sri Chimnoy ultramarathon: 1,300 laps around a 1-mile loop. Or how about the Trans America Footrace, from Los Angeles to New York? Find out all this and more at this site.

http://fox.nstn.ca/~dblaikie/

A
B
C
D
E
F
G
H
I
J
K
L
M
N
O
P
Q
R
S
T
U
V
W
X
Y
Z

> Trick roping secrets are revealed in KNOTS.

FENCING

Advance Lunge

Find out about the history of fencing, the equipment used, and basic techniques. There's a tutorial, lots of links, and an online "grudge match" duel between two seasoned players. Who will win? This site was created by students for the ThinkQuest competition.

http://library.thinkquest.org/15340/home.html

U.S. Fencing

Everyone likes a great sword fight in the movies: Peter Pan, Zorro, a party of pirates, or a platoon of shiny knights, all jumping here and there, swiping at the opponent, all the while avoiding the other person's sharp sword. Sometimes it's scary, but it's always exciting. The sport of fencing is exciting, too. Fencing is an Olympic sport that is practiced almost everywhere. This is the site for the U.S. Fencing Association.

http://www.usfencing.org/

FIGURE AND SPEED SKATING

Amateur Speedskating Union of the United States

When you take up the sport of speed skating, you are guaranteed to be hanging out with some cool people! Is it fast? You'd have to be crazy to go this fast. How crazy? Well, let's see: ice, blades, power, speed—sounds just crazy enough to be fun. And it is fun, for everyone from kids to seniors. If you're just thinking about starting, this page fills you in; if you're already a die-hard skater, you'll get advanced details on clubs and special events. It's great exercise, and it makes those long winters (and you) go really fast.

http://www.speedskating.org/

Figure Skater's Website

The life of a figure skater isn't as simple as it may seem. Many young people decide they're willing to devote the time and energy this sport demands, though. This Web site is especially for them. It lists the rules and regulations of competition, the judges' perspective, a calendar of upcoming events, and a lot more. There is a ton of how-to articles, exercises for skaters, and links to other skating pages.

http://www.sk8stuff.com/

Recreational Figure Skating FAQ

What's the difference between a crossover and a progressive? Do you need to know how to execute a closed mohawk? How do you know when your skates need sharpening? At this site, you'll find the answers to these questions. In fact, chances are you'll find answers to most of your skating questions here. There's even advice on how to make your own outdoor rink.

http://www.cyberus.ca/~karen/recskate/

US Figure Skating Online - USFSA

Looking for reliable figure skating news, results, and rule changes? This is your site! There are also athlete profiles, and a skater' museum with some online exhibits.

http://www.usfsa.org/

FOOTBALL

The Football Archive

Close your eyes. Breathe deeply and savor the smell of fall. It's football season, and it's time to read up on some of the history of the game, some of its greatest players, and a few of the plays used by your favorite team. You can also read about the top 50 players in the history of football. You can ask the questions you have and search the site for a particular team or moment in football history. It's all here, football fans, and this site was built by kids for the ThinkQuest contest. Enjoy!

http://library.thinkquest.org/12590/

NFL Internet Network

The official NFL site provides the latest headlines and league statistics and everything you'd ever want to know about the teams and the players. If you're looking for records, history, and rules, they are hard to find. Here's the direct link: <*http://www.nfl.com/fans/rules/*>. On the main page, try the Kids Play Football choice to visit a special area just for kids, reviewed next.

http://www.nfl.com/

Play Football - The Official NFL Site for Kids

Learn football basics; track the latest scores; and play some challenging (but goofy) arcade games, such as Trainer Terror. In this one, the trainer tries to cross the field avoiding players, marching bands, lawnmowers, and other hazards. In other sections of this site, check out video highlights, learn to play your position like a pro, and get the info on the next Punt, Pass, and Kick contest.

http://www.playfootball.com/

Pop Warner Football

Pop Warner football involves more than 300,000 kids in 38 states and several foreign countries. The organization prohibits tryouts and has a mandatory play rule. That means if you are on the team, you get to play in every game. But you have to keep your grades up. They also need cheerleaders, so get involved!

http://www.dickbutkus.com/dbfn/popwarner/

GYMNASTICS

Girls Gymnastics by Bela Karolyi

Just can't get the hang of that full-twisting back flip? Come to this site for training tips and advice from one of the great Olympic gymnastic coaches, Bela Karolyi. If you need more hands-on training, Karolyi has a gymnastics camp, and this site will tell you how to enroll. You can also read inspirational stories, peek at some rising stars, and post questions. Former Olympic gymnasts sometimes answer questions.

http://www.girlsgymnastics.com/

NET FILES

The Hubble Space Telescope orbits the Earth at five miles per second. If your car went that fast, how long would it take you to drive from New York to Los Angeles?

Answer: About ten minutes! Find out more fun facts about the Hubble here. *http://hubble.stsci.edu/fun_and_games/where.a.s_hubble_now/where_is.html*

Gymn, an Electronic Forum for Gymnastics!

Know the results of the gymnastics world championships and other current events by tumbling over to this site! Do you like to read articles about gymnasts? Would you like a list of famous gymnasts with their own home pages? Find them here. You can take gymnastics trivia tests, too. Did you ever wonder about the "chalk" you see gymnasts rub on their hands? It's magnesium carbonate, and they use it to absorb sweat so that they won't lose their grip on the equipment.

http://www.gymn-forum.com/

USA Gymnastics Online

When the U.S. women's gymnastics team appeared at the 1996 Summer Olympics, it was truly a magical event. Their skill and courage inspired many kids. Where are they now? Find out here. Keep up with who is who on the current U.S. teams and other events in gymnastics at this site. There's a lot on men's gymnastics, trampoline, and tumbling as well.

http://www.usa-gymnastics.org/

ICE HOCKEY

★ The Exploratorium's Science of Hockey

There you are—center ice at the San Jose Arena. Join the San Jose Sharks as they explore the science of one of the most exciting sports. You will soon learn a lot about the game, starting with the surface it's played on. For example, did you know there is a difference between fast ice and slow ice? Fast ice is harder and colder with a smoother surface, while slow ice is warm and soft, and may have a rough surface. Follow the Sharks as you learn about the ice, the skills, the equipment, and more. And when your mom tells you to be careful with your teeth, listen—she knows what she's talking about!

http://www.exploratorium.edu/hockey/

NHL.com - The National Hockey League

Read the rules for competition and find links to all your favorite National Hockey League teams here. You can see the latest hockey news, too. Be sure to take the Kids link to NHL for Kids site, for games, polls, and loads of fun.

http://www.nhl.com/

Dinofish.com - Coelacanth:
The Fish Out of Time

In 1938, fishermen off the coast of South Africa found the first living coelacanth in recent history; and there was another reported find in 1952, off the Comoro Islands (to the northeast, in the Mozambique Channel). This isn't just another fish story, either. The coelacanth (pronounced "see-la-kanth") is a 400-million-year-old "living fossil" fish, once thought to have become extinct long ago. This account of its amazing discovery reads like a mystery novel. *http://www.dinofish.com/*

The Official Site of the NHLPA

You and a friend are talking hockey, but you disagree on the number of goals your favorite player has scored this season. Where do you go for the answer? The National Hockey League Players' Association site provides player stats for each NHL player, and these stats are updated each day. You can find pictures, personal information, stats for this season, and stats from past seasons—just like online hockey trading cards. And there's more. The NHLPA Young Players' Zone has lots of cool stuff, including games and online Wayne Gretzky playing tip videos!

http://www.nhlpa.com/

★ Zamboni

OK, hands in the air: how many of you really have the secret fantasy of driving the Zamboni around the ice rink? You know, that big machine that magically lays down a new layer of smooth ice for you and your friends to skate on. Net-mom usually plays "Slamboni" instead, at *<http://www.sikids.com/games/slamboni/slam_index.html>*, but now she has discovered the official Zamboni site. You can learn the history of the company (they celebrated their 50th birthday in 1999), buy some cool Zamboni merchandise (including the fabulous "Zamboni Crossing" sign), and check out the trivia. For example, did you know that the top speed of a Zamboni ice resurfacing machine is 9 mph? There's also a neat diagram of how the machine actually works.

http://www.zamboni.com/

MARTIAL ARTS

Taekwondo - A Dream Becomes Reality!

This great introduction to taekwondo explains the history of the martial art, including its philosophy and spirit. You'll discover the symbolism of the belt and uniform, and check out some important stances and techniques. There are videos of sparring and information on legal and illegal actions, but this site stresses that you need an instructor to help you learn and practice. This site was created by students for the ThinkQuest competition.

http://library.thinkquest.org/16082/

OLYMPICS

The Ancient Olympics

When you think of the Olympics, chances are you picture brightly colored uniforms, and men and women competing in many different events. The ancient Olympics were much different. There were fewer events, and only free men who spoke Greek could compete, instead of athletes from any country. Also, the games were always held at Olympia instead of moving around to different sites every time. This site tells you a lot about all of the Olympics and has very interesting information.

http://www.perseus.tufts.edu/Olympics/

The International Olympic Committee

Here is the official site for the Olympics, where you can explore the past, present, and future of the games. When new Olympic cities are announced, you can read news and updates here first. There is lots of information on the Salt Lake City games of 2002, and the 2004 Summer Games in Athens, Greece. You can keep track of progress in all of them at this site. Don't miss the Olympic Museum for historic footage, artifacts, and information from past games.

http://www.olympic.org/

Official Site of the Sydney 2000 Olympic Games

In the year 2000, athletes gathered in Sydney, Australia. This is the official Sydney Olympics 2000 site. You'll find a lot of info here, including an explanation of what the logo means. It's called The Millennium Athlete. It uses shapes of a boomerang, the Sydney opera house, and color to evoke the Australian landscape and spirit.

http://www.olympics.com/

Origami: the fold to behold! Check out CRAFTS AND HOBBIES.

Have a whale of a time in MAMMALS.

The Real Story of the Ancient Olympic Games

A lot of people think the Olympic Games have gone way overboard when it comes to commercialization and marketing. They long for the old days of the ancient Olympics, when it was all about athletics. Was that really the case? This site invites you to discover the answers and find out whether or not ancient Greek athletes actually trained and competed for no other reason than the love of physical exercise and fair competition.

http://www.upenn.edu/museum/Olympics/olympicintro.html

★ Salt Lake Organizing Committee for the Olympic Winter Games of 2002

The XIX Olympic Winter Games will be held in Salt Lake City, Utah, February 8–22, 2002. This site gives information on where the events will be held and where the Olympic Village will be located. If you live in the Salt Lake City area, there is information on how to join the volunteer program for the 2002 Olympics. Get to know the 2002 mascots—their names are Powder, Copper, and Coal. Can you guess what animals they are?

http://www.slc2002.org/

★ United States Olympic Committee

This is a comprehensive site on all Olympic sports. Find each sport's history, rules, equipment needs, and even a specialized glossary of terms. Connect to team headquarters for each sport to learn the latest on the athletes. If there's a sport new to you and you just want to check it out, watch brief informative slide shows on U.S. team participation in that discipline.

http://www.olympic-usa.org/

A B C D E F G H I J K L M N O P Q R S T U V W X Y Z

A B C D E F G H I J K L M N O P Q R **S** T U V W X Y Z

NET FILES

How many miles of yarn can be spun from one pound of wool?

Answer: According to http://www.cyberspaceag.com/woolfacts.html, the answer is twenty miles of yarn from one pound of wool!

SKIING

U.S. Ski Team

If you are a fan of the U.S. ski team, you can follow the standings, write to your favorites, and pick up the latest news about the slopes and competitions worldwide at this site. You'll also learn about the different styles of ski competition (Alpine, Nordic, disabled, freestyle, snowboard) and find out how you can get your own official team gear.

http://www.usskiteam.com/

SKIING—NORDIC SKIING

Cross Country Ski World - XC Junior

Are you interested in cross-country skiing but don't know how to start? This site is packed with information on the world's oldest skiing sport, in a special section just for junior skiers. You'll find out how to choose equipment, how to wax for various conditions, and competition results from around the world.

http://www.xcskiworld.com/junior/

SNOWBOARDING

Jump into Snowboarding

Just when you think they've done just about everything crazy on snow, up comes a new sport. This one is called snowboarding, and we thought we'd slide on over to this ThinkQuest Junior site (built by kids) and see what it's all about. The sport began in the early 1960s when an eighth grader in shop class decided to try a new way of heading down a snowy hill. The first snowboard was made of plywood; now they're fiberglass. This site tells you all about the special language used by snowboarders—try an "Indy Grab on a Halfpipe, Dude"—as well as the six snowboarding events in the Olympics.

http://tqjunior.thinkquest.org/3885/

SOCCER

American Youth Soccer

Still wondering why the sport is called "soccer" in some countries and "football" in others? OK, we'll tell you. The sport started as football in England. By the time it became popular in other parts of the world, some countries already had sports known as football: the U.S. had American football, and Australia had Australian rules football. In countries where football was already played, the sport became known as soccer, short for "association football," the original name for the sport in England. Visit the American Youth Soccer Organization here.

http://www.soccer.org/

Federation Internationale de Football Association

Federation Internationale de Football Association (FIFA) is the organization behind all the World Cup and other official international soccer competitions. You'll find authoritative team standings, a history of FIFA, and lots of soccer news at this site. You'll also be able to read the official rule book, called the Laws of the Game (there are only 17 rules). Soccer, football, whatever you call it—what a kick!

http://www.fifa.com/

MLSnet.com - The Official Site of Major League Soccer

In North America, it's called soccer, but elsewhere in the world it's called football. Confused? Don't be—it will all become clear to you if you visit this site. From here, you can link to team pages, check standings, news, and more. You'll be able to see video highlights of great plays, hear interviews, and enjoy other multimedia treats if you have the right browser plug-ins.

http://www.mlsnet.com/

The Soccer Patch

Does your soccer team have a patch? Or maybe you've gotten a different patch for each tournament in which you've participated. Is your team patch displayed on this page? If not, send it in. They have over 1,200 patches now, from all over the world! There are also lots of links to kids' soccer pages, team pages, and news and information about the sport.

http://www.soccerpatch.com/

SPECIAL OLYMPICS
Special Olympics

"Let me win, but if I cannot win, let me be brave in the attempt." This is the oath of the Special Olympics. What great inspiration this is for all athletes, not just "special" kids with mental and physical challenges! The first International Special Olympic Games was held in 1968, at Soldier Field in Chicago, Illinois. It was organized by Eunice Kennedy Shriver. Since then, the Special Olympics have become the world's largest year-round program of physical fitness, sports training, and athletic competition. In the U.S., games at the local and chapter levels are held every year, with special summer and winter events held every four years.

http://www.specialolympics.org/

Pony up to HORSES AND EQUESTRIAN SPORTS.

SURFING
Let's Go Surfing!

No one knows who first thought of surfing, but at this site you can learn quite a bit about its early history and lore. In the early days of Hawaiian surfing, boards for royalty were different from those for commoners. And specific beaches were reserved for the royal family's sole use. Aren't you glad it's not like that today? At this site you can learn about different types of surfboards and how they are made, as well as learn a little about wave mechanics. This site was created by students for the ThinkQuest Junior competition.

http://tqjunior.thinkquest.org/5282/splash.shtml

★ Where the Waves Are

Sure, you can surf the Internet, but can you build the perfect wave for a surfer? Juggle adjustments for the local weather, intensity and distance of a storm and then—surf it! Are you headed for a wipeout or a round of applause? Check this site on the physics of surfing and wave formation.

http://www.discovery.com/news/features/surfing/surfing.html

SWIMMING AND DIVING
All About Swimming

Ms. Daizy's beginner's tips for swimming really make a splash. Be sure to dive in and learn the moves, the breathing, and most of all the water and pool safety rules you need to know. There is also information on synchronized swimming.

http://members.aol.com/msdaizy/sports/swim.html

Swimnews Online

Do you swim? We're not talking about an occasional wade through the baby pool. We're talking about competitive swimming. You know: pruny looking fingers, webbed toes, red eyes, and gills. If that's you, then you need to see this online magazine. Virtually every major swim meet in the world is here, and the results are updated regularly. You'll find features on the world's best swimmers, and all the world records are here, too. Links? You bet. This is the diving platform for your lane.

http://www.swimnews.com/

A B C D E F G H I J K L M N O P Q R S T U V W X Y Z

A
B
C
D
E
F
G
H
I
J
K
L
M
N
O
P
Q
R
S
T
U
V
W
X
Y
Z

TENNIS

All About Tennis

According to this site, the name of this sport came from the French word *tenetz*, which means "take heed" or "watch out!" That's what players yelled as they served the ball. In the early days, people didn't have tennis rackets; they used their bare hands. If this is true, it's amazing the game of tennis isn't called "OUCH!" At this site, you'll get a fine introduction to tennis rules, fun facts, and drills and skills.

http://members.aol.com/msdaizy/sports/tennis.html

The Tennis Server

Would you like free tips from a tennis pro? Would you like to know how to avoid tennis elbow? Would you like information on tournaments, players, rankings, and equipment? How about links to other tennis sites? You get all this and more when you go to the Net for this Tennis Server.

http://www.tennisserver.com/

TRACK AND FIELD

Around the Track and Back

Can you all hear me OK out on the field? Great! Will everybody go into the warm-up area first, and learn some of those stretches and flexibility exercises coach is always harping on? There's a big long list, so you ought to be able to find a few you can do. After that, meet us on the bleachers for training tips on nutrition and general health. Pick up your gear and move on to the events area, which is why we are all here, right? Learn tips and strategies for dealing with all the track and field events you want. What's that? No, Jerry, I don't know where you put your discus. Use a pizza from the lunchroom instead. I have one more announcement! This field event was created by students for the ThinkQuest Junior competition.

http://tqjunior.thinkquest.org/5043/

Athletics Home Page

Who is the world's fastest Norwegian? Who is the best overall Italian athlete? What's the Moroccan record in the high jump? If you are a track and field statistics nut, this is the site for you. It lists world records, indoor and outdoor, for men and for women, as well as track and field records for many nations.

http://www.hkkk.fi/~niininen/athl.html

The Official Boston Marathon Web Site

What is the world's most well-known race? A lot of folks would argue it's the Boston Marathon. Learn its history and facts about the next race at this official site. You'll view some winners, see a map of Boston's 26-mile, 385-yard course, and more! The first race was in 1897.

http://www.bostonmarathon.org/

USA Track & Field

USA Track and Field is the governing body for track and field competition in the United States. This site gives you news on the latest happenings in track and field, with links to other sites. You'll really enjoy reading about record performances and the athletes who made them. This is a great source for short sports biographies, too. Youth results in regional and international competitions are also covered.

http://www.usatf.org/

WRESTLING

Sumo Wrestling

Sumo wrestling has been practiced for over 1,500 years. Its origins stem from religious rites, which were matches performed to please the gods. Many ritual elements remain, including the symbolism of the *dohyo*, or wrestling ring. Above the ring there is always a roof resembling a Shinto shrine. Four giant tassels hanging from each corner signify the seasons of the year. At this site, you can learn about sumo wrestling history, culture, and champions.

http://www.sumo.or.jp/index_e.html

STAR TREK, STAR WARS, AND SPACE EPICS

2001: Destination Space - 2001 at The Tech

When the film *2001: A Space Odyssey* came out in 1968, it offered a glimpse into the world of the future. How accurate were its projections? What comparisons can we draw between the science and technology of today to what was depicted in the film? San Jose's The Tech museum has the answers.

http://www.thetech.org/2001ds/at_the_tech/

The 2001 Internet Resource Archive

"Good afternoon, gentlemen. I am a HAL 9000 computer. I became operational at the H.A.L. lab in Urbana, Illinois, on the 12th of January, 1992." Long before we had Picard and Kirk and before we had Luke Skywalker and Princess Leia, we had HAL, the killer computer on the spaceship in *2001: A Space Odyssey*. This movie was released in 1968, and it explored the differences between humanity and technology. The story is told in a free-form kaleidoscope of images and sounds, and years later, people are still arguing about what it all means. This site gives you a lot of famous audio clips from the movie, as well as pictures and links to other resources about the film, including a HAL birthday Web site featuring the book's author, Arthur C. Clarke.

http://www.palantir.net/2001/

★ Ask Yoda

Be cool you must. And also chill out you should. Only the truth does Yoda speak. Carefully you must listen, important things tell you he will. Come to him sooner you should have.

http://www.sun-sentinel.com/graphics/entertainment/yoda.htm

Why is the sky blue? Look in the WHY section.

Make-A-Hero

Just choose the gender of your hero, and select a skin color and background picture. Then start clicking on the picture you just made. You'll find you can change headgear, as well as upper and lower articles of clothing. Each time you change something, you'll get a little information about that item's legendary background. All done? Print your hero or heroine; then try some of the suggested activities. It's mix and match heroes, and it's fun!
http://www.lucaslearning.com/myth/flash/myth.html

The Klingon Language Institute

How many languages do you speak? Have you checked the batteries in your universal translator? If you saw a snarling Klingon warrior, what would you say? Are you worried that your opportunities on the Klingon homeworld are limited because of the language barrier? If so, then this site is the place for you!

http://www.kli.org/

★ Star Wars Kids

Themed and written expressly for the youngest *Star Wars* fans, this site offers games, trivia, and news about the much-anticipated *Episode II* and other *Star Wars* movies. There are also some interesting polls, like "Who would you rather hang out with: Princess Leia or Queen Amidala?" The results showed a distinct preference for Queen Amidala.

http://www.starwarskids.com/

A B C D E F G H I J K L M N O P Q R **S** T U V W X Y Z

A
B
C
D
E
F
G
H
I
J
K
L
M
N
O
P
Q
R
S
T
U
V
W
X
Y
Z

Expect a miracle in RELIGION AND SPIRITUALITY!

★ Star Wars: The Official Web Site

Who is your favorite character in the *Star Wars* saga? Is it Jedi Knight Luke Skywalker, or do you prefer that scoundrel Han Solo? Maybe you'd like to be like courageous Princess Leia and have a couple of happy-go-lucky droids like C-3P0 or R2-D2 to give you a hand. Whether you like the old or the new digital version of these sci-fi classics, you're really going to like this Web site! Let's not forget *Episode I*. Do you like Jar Jar Binks or hate it/him/her? Results have been mixed. Net-mom thinks he/she/it is OK, but doesn't care enough to buy the action figure. Visit the National Air and Space Museum's Star Wars: The Magic of Myth site at <*http://www.nasm.edu/StarWars/*>.

http://www.starwars.com/

Starbase 907 - Starfleet Ship Registry Database

Can't tell a Galaxy-class ship from a Miranda-class ship? Have you always wondered where the *USS Bozeman* went for 80 years? This site lists over 20 classes of Starfleet ships. Within the classes, you'll find descriptions, Starfleet ship registration numbers in that class, and some ship histories. Also check out photos of the Sovereign Class Enterprise-E from the movie *Star Trek: Insurrection*.

http://www.webzone.net/rowan/sb907/ssrd/

★ StarTrek.com: The Official Star Trek Web Site

This is the best site on *Star Trek* you're going to find, outside of the Starfleet Academy library itself. Chats with cast members, crew data, games, contests, news on the shows—it's all here.

http://www.startrek.com/

Warp Theory

The *U.S.S. Enterprise* teaches you all about warp theory. Just type in your initials and click "engage." The only problem is that in the early twenty-first century, this has not been invented yet. We have to wait around for Zefram Cochrane's flight of the Phoenix in 2061.

http://www.sun-sentinel.com/graphics/science/warp.htm

SUMMER CAMPS

Peterson's - Summer Camps and Jobs Channel

Get your older brother or sister to apply for a job at camp! Peterson's (the educational directory publisher) posts lists of summer jobs here, mostly at summer camps, for both older teenagers and young adults. Phone numbers and e-mail contact addresses are included, making this a good place to look for that first-time job. There are also links to the American Camping Association's Directory of Accredited Camps, and lots of information for international students. Your parents may want to explore the rest of the items at this comprehensive educational directory. They will find everything from K–12 schools to colleges, and from studying abroad to career information.

http://www.petersons.com/summerop/

★ U.S. Space Camp

It's light-years away from any other camp experience! You can visit Space Camp here on the Web and see pictures of some of the things kids (and adults) get to do there. How would you like to ride a space shuttle simulator or build your own satellite? Beam yourself up to this site—you'll definitely find intelligent life here. Son of Net-mom was able to take the Space Academy training. (He was on the Coke team. Here's their yell: "OHH-OHH COKE *clap* Whoosh!!!) He can't wait to go back.

http://www.spacecamp.com/

TELEPHONE

★ AT&T: Brainspin

Ever wonder how your telephone works? This site gives you an overview of what takes place when you make that call to your great-grandparents in Cleveland. You did remember to thank them for sending those cool handkerchiefs for your birthday, right? You'll also learn about fiber optics, Alexander Graham Bell, and what the phone company's going to do when they run out of phone numbers. There are also some fun interactive games to try.

http://www.att.com/technology/forstudents/
brainspin/

TELEVISION

★ Digital TV

Just about everything is going digital these days—television, music, cameras, telephones. There must be something about digital sound and pictures that make it better. To find out the pros and cons of digital television and its future, tune in to this site. You'll also learn to decode a digital picture. You might know that the small rectangular dots that make up a television image are called pixels. But did you know that pixel stands for Picture Element?

http://www.pbs.org/opb/crashcourse/

Emmy® Awards - Academy of Television Arts & Sciences

Academy of Television Arts and Sciences members select the best TV performances and programs every year. The winning shows and actors receive an award called an Emmy. To see who the current winners are, check out this Web page. To see winners of past years' competitions, go to the "Advanced Search" screen in the Emmy Awards section, and then type in the year you want and click the box that says "Display Winners Only." This site also has multimedia archives of past award presentations.

http://www.emmys.org/

MZTV Museum of Television

At the 1939 World's Fair in New York City, it was a big deal to have a TV camera pointed at you and to watch your image turn up on a nearby monitor. In fact, they gave everyone a little souvenir card to mark the event; it read "This is to certify that (your name here) was televised at the RCA exhibit building New York World's Fair . . . ." Why was this so unusual? In 1939, most people had never seen television before. NBC's first broadcast was on April 30, 1939. TV sets were expensive ($2,000 to $6,000 in the equivalent of today's dollars) and bulky. Find out all about the early history of TV in the Gallery section of this online museum.

http://www.mztv.com/

Exposure - A Beginner's Guide to Photography

Photography—is it technology or magic? Even if you have a non-adjustable camera, you can try some of these tips and tricks to jazz up your photos. If you do have a camera with a lot of controls on it, you can really change how the picture looks. You can learn how to set the camera so that the background blurs out of focus. This puts more emphasis on your main subjects in the foreground of the picture. On the other hand, you might want to make sure that as much of the scene as possible stays in focus. There is a special way to set the camera for that, too. You can try it all using Sim-Cam, a way-cool applet that will teach you the mysteries of f-stops and aperture by letting you set a virtual camera, take a picture, and see immediate results!
http://www.88.com/exposure/lowrez_i.htm

A
B
C
D
E
F
G
H
I
J
K
L
M
N
O
P
Q
R
S
T
U
V
W
X
Y
Z

A
B
C
D
E
F
G
H
I
J
K
L
M
N
O
P
Q
R
S
T
U
V
W
X
Y
Z

MEDIA LITERACY

Media Smarts

Can you talk back to your television? Maybe not, but you can learn something about how television talks to you, and the messages it is sending. What's the story with commercials? Do you feel pressured to wear a certain kind of clothing, or buy a certain type of music? Are you being manipulated by what you see on TV? Find out about some kids who spoke up and made a difference, learn to avoid "sneaky speak" on TV, and learn what five things you should remember when you're watching TV.

http://www.media-awareness.ca/eng/med/kids/
    medsmart.htm

WARNING! WARNING! WARNING!: Television Violence

Whether it's an anvil falling on a cartoon character or an armed conflict out in the streets, kids see a huge amount of violence on TV every day. According to this site, "young children watch 8,000 murders and 100,000 acts of violence before leaving elementary school." This Web site starts from the premise that this isn't a Good Thing and that it should be stopped. Created by students for the ThinkQuest Junior competition, the site offers arguments against violence on TV and suggests plans to stop it, including what one person can do to help.

http://tqjunior.thinkquest.org/5676/

NETWORKS AND CHANNELS

C-SPAN.org

If you want to see the U.S. government at work, you'll see it here. Hearings, meetings, legislative sessions: this site will tell you what C-SPAN will be showing, and when. You can watch right over the Internet, or on regular TV. C-SPAN also covers other events of national interest. There are also classroom activities and lesson plans for teachers and others interested in seeing comprehensive program guides.

http://www.c-span.org/

Strike up the bandwidth in MUSIC AND MUSICIANS.

Cartoon Network

Road Runner, Scooby-Doo, Tom and Jerry, the Flintstones, Bugs Bunny, and plenty more of your favorites appear here on their own Web pages. You can play games, find out about the shows, and even see some exclusive video clips.

http://cartoonnetwork.com/

CNN.com

CNN, the 24-hour news channel, has made it easy and fast to get the news of the moment over the Internet. And it's in a multimedia format that brings you lots more than words. Don't forget that CNN covers entertainment, sports, style, and other fun stuff. In Entertainment, you'll find the top ten movies, albums, and TV shows, plus reviews of all the latest releases.

http://www.cnn.com/

Discovery Online

You'd expect to find background articles on many of the Discovery Channel's programs here, and you'd be right. There are stories and pictures from shows on history, nature, science, and people. And there's more: links to the Learning Channel and Animal Planet programming and a way to search the archives of past fascinating stories! A new area is DiscoveryKids, at <http://kids.discovery.com/ KIDS/>, which highlights features of particular interest to kids.

http://www.discovery.com/

Nickelodeon

Ooze into this Web site, but please avoid the mess the Rugrats made! All your favorite shows are here, and some have special "Super-sites" with sounds, pictures, screen savers, and other goodies. Download some cool games for Macintosh or Windows, and make sure the rest of your family notices the links to Nick Jr. and Noggin. Other sections include tunes: streaming audio of four different Nick-flavored radio stations. On the playlist when we listened were Britney Spears, Li'l Romeo, and the Backstreet Boys. The best part is, if you absolutely can't stand to hear "Baby One More Time" one more time, just hit the fast forward control to skip it. You can't do that on regular radio! Hint: Mac IE is not supported, use Netscape instead. Parental advisory: please preview the games area.

http://www.nick.com/

★ Noggin

Noggin is . . . a TV network. No, it's also a Web site. No, it's . . . well, maybe YOU can figure it out! And it's from the folks at Nickelodeon and Sesame Workshop, who put their heads together and came up with the concept of Noggin. There are online places for you to explore and loads of fun games (try Flood Control). You can make your own soundscape and your own animation, which might be added to the animation "quilt." There's also a special Noggin just for little kids, look for it and click on that button.

http://www.noggin.com/

🦆 PBS Kids

If it's on PBS, it's educational, entertaining, excellent, or all three. See what's new with the *Teletubbies*, *Mister Rogers*, *Barney*, *Arthur*, and many more of your favorites. Check out the fun games associated with each show, such as the animal games in *Zoboomafoo*.

http://www.pbs.org/kids/

TV Land Online

Everyone loves this stuff: *Leave it to Beaver*, *Get Smart*, *My Favorite Martian*, *The Mary Tyler Moore Show* . . . good ol' classic TV. It's fun TV, and now you can visit those wacky characters on the Web. Check the clever and funny ads and listen to nostalgic theme songs.

http://www.tvland.com/

PROGRAMS

See also BOOKS AND LITERATURE—CONTEMPORARY FAVORITES

🦆 Arthur: The World's Most Famous Aardvark

Arthur's got a terrific site going for him here. We particularly liked his boombox and its great tunes, as well as D.W.'s Art Studio, where we rubber-stamped paw prints all over Mr. Ratburn's suit. Don't miss Grandma's recipes (hope you get there before the health department does!).

http://www.pbs.org/wgbh/arthur/

🦆 Barney and Friends

It's here: a site that celebrates Barney and all his pals! You'll find activities, audio, games, coloring pages, and more.

http://www.pbs.org/barney/

🦆 Between the Lions

Early readers, right this way! Watch an animated story right over the Internet, and then see if you can answer questions about it. Every story is followed by about a dozen fun games, all of which will help you learn to read. There are songs, things to print and color, and loads of tips for parents and caregivers of new readers.

http://www.pbs.org/wgbh/lions/

A
B
C
D
E
F
G
H
I
J
K
L
M
N
O
P
Q
R
S
T
U
V
W
X
Y
Z

NET FILES

What country "spans 11 time zones, 2 continents, and comes within 50 miles of North America"?

http://www.interknowledge.com/russia/

Answer: Russia, of course! The Official Guide to Russia ought to know, and it will show you more at

🦆 Bookworm Bunch

Can you find Corduroy bear? He's hiding somewhere in the street scene, you'll just have to keep clicking until you find him. He moves around each time, so you can play again. The Seven Little Monsters section offers finger puppets you can print, and a fun addition game you can play online. Timothy challenges you to a jigsaw puzzle (he lets you know if you're right or wrong), and George Shrinks so you can play hide 'n' seek with him. You need a magnifying glass, of course. Marvin, the Tap-dancing Horse competes in a race game, but we like this Marvin site better <http://www.nelvana.com/main/ kids.html>.

http://www.pbs.org/bookwormbunch/

🦆 Mister Rogers' Neighborhood

This beloved TV show has entertained three generations of neighborhood visitors and has won every broadcast award there is. Kids have fears, dreams, hopes, and feelings—just like everyone else. Fred Rogers has always understood that, and his Web site shows that care and detail. There's a nice virtual neighborhood for you to explore (don't forget to feed the fish in the kitchen!), as well as the neighborhood of make-believe. There are games, recipes, and coloring book pages for you to discover as you travel.

http://www.pbs.org/rogers/

🦆 Sesame Street Central

Home to the Sesame Street cast of lovable characters, you'll find an interactive storybook, online games, and coloring pages. The Music section offers Sesame Street Radio (Mac surfers use Netscape). Click on the Site Map to make sure you don't overlook something on this (peanut butter and) jam-packed site!

http://www.sesameworkshop.org/sesame/

🦆 Teletubbies

If you love Tinky Winky, Dipsy, Laa-Laa, and Po, you'll love a visit to this site. The games offered include simple matching and sequencing fun. Want more activities? (Or, as the Tubbies would say, "Again! Again!") Teletubbies are on in the United Kingdom, too. In fact, there are three Teletubbies sites to choose from, all accessible from this one address. We like the BBC one. Which Teletubbie site do YOU like better?

http://www.teletubbies.com/

🦆 Theodore Tugboat at PBS Online

Color online pictures of Theodore and all his friends in the big harbor. You can also help him decide what to do in the interactive stories, and listen to episodes, boat whistles, and more at this fun interactive site. Be sure to look for *Theodore Too*, a real tugboat that may be visiting a harbor near you soon. The travel schedule is online.

http://www.pbs.org/tugboat/

🦆 Wimzie's House

Can you help the gang play music? Click and drag the correct instrument to each musician; and when you get it right, it will stay in place. Otherwise, the cymbals, horn, and microphone will slide back to the bottom and you can try again. In other games, rearrange the living room furniture any way you like, and see what's making all the noise in the garden.

http://www.pbs.org/wimzie/m1.html

A B C D E F G H I J K L M N O P Q R S **T** U V W X Y Z

★ ZOOM

Zoom is a wonderful show for kids of all ages. That's not surprising, because kids help produce the show! Play offline games, try some crafts, read embarrassing moments stories, review recent books and movies and see what other kids said, and more. Then there are the jokes. Ah, the jokes. Example: What goes in one hole and out three holes? A person putting on a T-shirt. Get it? Try clicking on the Site Map to make sure you don't miss anything.

http://www.pbs.org/wgbh/zoom/

REVIEWS AND RATINGS

Parents Television Council

What's on TV tonight that's suitable for family viewing? You know, TV that doesn't glorify violence, doesn't contain trashy language, and that does make sure every viewer in the room feels comfortable watching. The Parents Television Council rates each evening's shows based on their use of violence, bad language, and sexual themes. Look for their easy-to-use traffic signal so you'll know where to "GO."

http://www.parentstv.org/

TV Guide

This site offers a wide spectrum of television reviews, but what we recommend that you do is this: Click on TV Listings, and then enter your ZIP code. Follow the instructions, and then look for the control that lets you choose to see selections for Children Only. Click on the name of the show to see its rating and to get a brief review.

http://tvguide.com/

TV-Turnoff Network

If you can't imagine a whole week without TV, then it's really time for you to see this Web site! These folks sponsor TV-Turnoff Week (the next one is April 22-28, 2002), an opportunity to unplug the tube and learn a craft, read a book, discover the outdoors, or just spend time together as a family. Browse through the research here and see what science has to say about too much TV.

http://www.tvturnoff.org/

V-Chip Education Project

Have you heard of the V-Chip? No, it's not a new flavored snack product, but it may improve your "taste" in television viewing. Since January, 2000, all TV sets manufactured in the United States contain a "V-Chip." When activated, it can be used to block programming by content or age recommendation. Some sets also allow blockage of individual shows or entire channels. To learn about the V-Chip and the criteria used to rate shows, check this site. What's behind that little content symbol at the beginning of TV shows? Find out what the letters and codes mean here.

http://www.vchipeducation.org/

TIME

Sunrise/Sunset Computation

Sometimes you have to get up awfully early to watch the sun rise. Exactly when the sun or moon rises or sets depends on where you live and the time of year. You can take the mystery out of when old Sol (that's another name for the sun) takes off in the morning by using this page from the U.S. Naval Observatory. All you have to do is plug in a date and a place; and through the magic of computers, the time of sun (and moon) rise and set is provided. For fun, enter your birthday and birthplace or pick an interesting date. You'll also find out when the solstices and equinoxes are through the year 2005.

http://aa.usno.navy.mil/AA/data/

★ Tempus Fugit

Is your concept of time the same as everyone else's? Probably not. "Time flies when you're having fun," as they say, but it seems to drag when you're bored. What can we learn about time from gazing at artworks throughout history? As it turns out, quite a bit. This visually stunning site will show you, if you have time for the download.

http://www.nelson-atkins.org/tempusfugit/

A B C D E F G H I J K L M N O P Q R S T U V W X Y Z

A B C D E F G H I J K L M N O P Q R S **T** U V W X Y Z

CALENDARS
★ A Base for Calendar Exploration

"Thirty days hath September, April, June, and November. All the rest have thirty-one, except . . . ." Except what? And when? It's about time someone came up with a site devoted to calendars! You will learn some fascinating information here, including the origins of the seven-day week, leap year, calendar structures and changes, and much more. By the way, what began above ends like this: ". . . excepting February alone: which hath but twenty-eight, in fine, till leap year gives it twenty-nine." Click on "An introduction to calendars" and learn all about the "Thirty Days" rhyme.

http://www.greenheart.com/billh/

Build Your Own Stonehenge

Stonehenge is a mysterious circle of standing stones on Salisbury Plain in England. It is thousands of years old and no one is sure for what purpose the circle was used. Some believe it is an ancient astronomical calendar. You can build one yourself, but it will take you a year to do it. Get started with the directions at this site.

http://familyeducation.com/article/
   0,1120,1-4200,00.html

Fun With Spot

Everyone likes to play with Spot, the friendly puppy from the Eric Hill books. Be on the lookout to "spot" matching animals on the farm, and count starfish and crabs on the sandy beach. At the party, there are so many presents! Can you find a pattern of three matching objects?
http://www.funwithspot.com/

Calendar Zone

Are you looking for a new calendar, or maybe an old one? This page has calendars that will calculate moon phases, holidays, and many other types of date-watching delights. You'll also find Islamic, Hebrew, Chinese, and other cultural or religious calendars. There is downloadable software and links to pages of interest, including one on Calendar Reform (click on "reform"). Did you know that some people think we should have 13 months in the year? Others propose 12 equal months, with "blank days" that don't belong to any month at all and are celebrated as world holidays. One result of this plan is that you wouldn't need a new calendar every year, because the dates would always fall on the same days of the week. Calendar manufacturers are probably not happy with the idea.

http://www.calendarzone.com/

Calendars: Counting the Days

Before people had calendars on their walls, they looked up in the sky to check the passage of time. The position of the sun, phase of the moon, and visible constellations told them all they needed to know. However, time marched on, and now we have all sorts of ways to figure out what time it is. This very interesting site from *World Book Encyclopedia* teaches you about ancient as well as modern calendar systems. There is even a section on future calendars!

http://www.worldbook.com/fun/calendars/html/
   calendars.htm

Calendars Through the Ages

If you're just looking for a comparison between various calendar systems, or a few choice facts about time, visit this site. Isn't it interesting to know that when you ask someone to "wait a second," that the second is actually defined as the "time it takes for 9,192,631,770 oscillations of the Cesium atom at zero magnetic field."

http://webexhibits.org/calendars/

Have you written to your PEN PALS lately?

This Day in History - From the Archives of the History Channel

The date is May 4. The year is 1979. Do you know what was happening in world history? Margaret Thatcher was being elected prime minister of England. This Day in History will let you time-travel anywhere you want. In 1626 on this day, Governor Peter Minuit made a great deal on his purchase of a 20,000-acre island—what is now Manhattan, New York City. The price was $24 worth of cloth and brass buttons. Just punch in any date and year, and see what bit of history you can learn.

http://www.historychannel.com/tdih/

Time and Date.com

If you've ever needed a quick calendar, for, say, the year 1753, or maybe the year 3000, or anything in between, you'll love this site in Norway. Key in the year you want (try the year you were born), and, like magic, a calendar is generated.

http://www.timeanddate.com/calendar/

CLOCKS

Biological Timing Online Science Experiment

Did you ever hear of a biological clock? That's what helps you go to sleep at night and wake up in the morning. At this site, there's a fascinating article called The Mystery of Sleepy Adolescents. Do you have trouble waking up for school? You're not alone. These kids decided to investigate the whole problem. This is their Web page about biological clocks, circadian rhythms, and how plants and animals tell time.

http://www.cbt.virginia.edu/Olh/exp.html

Daylight Saving Time - Saving Time, Saving Energy

Spring forward, and Fall back. That's how we remember which way to set our clocks in order to be "on time." What's the idea behind Daylight Saving Time, anyway? Does it really save anything? This site explains the history of DST and the rationale that keeps it going. There's also a handy little calendar with the dates of the time changes through 2004.

http://www.energy.ca.gov/daylightsaving.html

★ Earth and Moon Viewer

This isn't really a clock, but it will show you where it's day and where it's night—right now—all over the planet. When it's 10 A.M. and bright and sunny in Florida, what's it like in Japan? Stop by this site and ask the server, which will show where it's light and dark anyplace in the world. You can choose the satellite location from which to view, or you can tell it to look at Earth from the Sun's or Moon's perspective. You can even create a custom request and specify the desired longitude and latitude you want to see; the computer then picks the best viewpoint.

http://www.fourmilab.ch/earthview/vplanet.html

🦆 Interactive Judy Clock

If you need some practice in figuring out what time it is, try this site. Click the big red button to see a target time on the digital clock. Then use your mouse to move the analog clock hands until they match that time.

http://www.troll.com/product/features/
   judygame.html

★ Lemelson Center Invention Features: Quartz Watch

These days, only 13 percent of the world's watch-wearing wrists have mechanical windup watches on them. The rest of us are wearing these newfangled ones with the liquid crystal displays. Have you ever wondered how your quartz watch works? What's inside it? How does that blue indiglo work? Find out here!

http://www.si.edu/lemelson/Quartz/

A
B
C
D
E
F
G
H
I
J
K
L
M
N
O
P
Q
R
S
T
U
V
W
X
Y
Z

A B C D E F G H I J K L M N O P Q R S **T** U V W X Y Z

The Martian Sundial

There's a planned landing on Mars coming up in 2002, and one thing it will do is place a sundial on the red planet. Now the Martians will always know what time it is. Find out what the thing will look like and how it will work at this site.

http://www.washington.edu/newsroom/news/
  1999archive/04-99archive/k042199.html

The Official U.S. Time

Here it is! The definitive answer to not only "What time is it on the east coast?" but also the correct time for Alaska, Hawaii, and every other U.S. time zone. You'll even find the accurate time for U.S. territories, like Guam and the Northern Mariana Islands. There are also fascinating exhibits and links about time, clocks, and timekeeping.

http://www.time.gov/

Canadian Heritage Information Network

The Virtual Museum of Canada includes online exhibits from many different Canadian museums. We loved the multimedia look at "Hockey: A Nation's Passion" with its hockey puck cursor and animated Zamboni ice machine. The "Endangered Species in Endangered Spaces" is very informative, and you can even play the virtual musical instruments at this exhibit *http://www. virtualmuseum.ca/Exhibitions/Instruments/Anglais/ composition_musicale.html*. (Hint: move your mouse to where the arrows point, don't just click on the arrows. You will find you are able to strum each string of the guitar, for example.) *http://www.chin.gc.ca/*

Sundials on the Internet

Before we had digital clocks—even before we had analog clocks with hands—we had sundials. They didn't work very well when it was raining, and they also didn't work very well unless they were precisely "tuned" to your latitude. Since commercial sundial companies pretty much standardized on latitude 45, that left the rest of the world scratching their heads and asking each other, "Hey, anybody got the time?" This Web page changes all that. There are four projects that explain how to make your own sundial. Remember, sundials "count only sunny hours."

http://www.sundials.co.uk/home3.htm

Teaching Time

OK, when the little hand is on six and the big hand is on twelve, what time is it? How about when the big hand is on six, no, the little . . .? Having trouble telling time, or explaining it? Why use words when you can use pictures to teach kids how to tell time. At this site, you'll find online games and exercises, and printable worksheets.

http://www.teachingtime.co.uk/

★ Time Service Dept

The U.S. Naval Observatory in Washington, D.C., is the official timekeeper for the United States. This site is tied into the master clock—clocks, actually. U.S. Naval Observatory timekeeping is based on several unusual clocks: cesium beam and hydrogen maser atomic clocks. You can find out more about these at this site. They also use a network of radio telescopes to make sure they are always right on time. Why is that so important? Well, if a rocket engine burns a second too long, the rocket may end up miles from where it should be. Or, if one computer sends a message but the other computer isn't "on" to receive it yet, that's a problem. These clocks are correct to the nanosecond level, which is a billionth of a second! At this site, you can also calculate the sunrise, sunset, twilight, moon rise, moon set, and moon phase percentages and times for a U.S. location.

http://tycho.usno.navy.mil/time.html

Virtual Globe

Here's the Earth, spinning along in space. See exactly where it's still daytime and where night has fallen. Then click on any point on the globe and it will be redrawn with your selection in the center of the screen. This visualization is updated every five minutes to keep up with the rotation of the Earth.

http://members.aol.com/edhobbs/applets/vglobe/

A Walk Through Time

Until about 5,000 or 6,000 years ago, there was no need to know the exact time. When the sun rose, people woke up and worked at getting food, fuel, and shelter. When it got dark, people went to bed. Nobody needed to ask, "Is it time for my favorite TV show yet?" or "Am I late for school?" At this site, you can follow the evolution of timekeeping and clocks, from the Sumerians right up until today.

http://physics.nist.gov/GenInt/Time/time.html

★ The World Clock

Hey, what time is it, anyway? Are you curious about the clocks in Copenhagen? Or maybe you want to make inquiries in Istanbul. This page gives you the current time in over 130 locations on the globe! If you keep watching it, the page will automatically update every minute.

http://www.timeanddate.com/worldclock/

MILLENNIUM

The 21st Century and the Third Millennium

Many people think we celebrated a new millennium on January 1, 2000. Don't be fooled by false millennia! This site explains why that wasn't true and why those who got out the party hats on December 31, 2000 were correct. Take the link to the Royal Observatory for fascinating facts.

http://aa.usno.navy.mil/AA/faq/docs/millennium.html

Greenwich Prime Meridian

In 1884, the International Meridian Conference decided to designate the Prime Meridian, longitude zero, at a spot in Greenwich, England. Since world time is designated as so many hours plus or minus Greenwich Mean Time, you could say that Greenwich is just next door to where Time runs out and the location where Time begins again. Learn more about the Prime Meridian, the millennium, and the story of time.

http://www.rog.nmm.ac.uk/mill/

TOYS

See also GAMES AND FUN; KITES

🦆 Fisher-Price

Sure, you can find out about Fisher-Price products and news about the company, but the best part is the section called Fun! Try to see if you can help a little puppy guess who is at the door. Listen for the clues, examine the two choices, and then click on "the friend who works on the farm." The door swings open—were you right? Of course, in real life, you shouldn't open the door unless an adult says it is OK. Other games include shape and color recognition, as well as an alphabet game. There are also activity sheets to print.

http://www.fisherprice.com/us/fun/

Kids Stuff with Magical Balloon-Dude Dale

For a beginner's guide to twisting balloons, try this site. You can learn how to make an airplane, a cobra, a dog, and several other objects. Don't miss the balloon sculptures in the gallery for some wonderful inspiration! Mac users will have best results with Netscape, not IE5.

http://www.mbd2.com/kidsstuff.htm

Pokémon

Pokémon can be found in the VIDEO AND COMPUTER GAMES section of the book.

A
B
C
D
E
F
G
H
I
J
K
L
M
N
O
P
Q
R
S
T
U
V
W
X
Y
Z

A
B
C
D
E
F
G
H
I
J
K
L
M
N
O
P
Q
R
S
T
U
V
W
X
Y
Z

★ Rumpus Games

Here's the deal. These games are terrific. So much fun, that the company hopes to sell you toys based on the games. Don't worry. You can just click back to the original game window and choose another game. And what games they are! The spitting gallery is wonderfully gross. The Skwertz family tries to take out the arcade ducks by—ahem—spitting at them. The sound effects are particularly juicy. Along the same line, Gus Guts . . . has quite a digestive problem. If you'd like something a little more refined, try Herschel Hopper, who needs you to clear a path to the Easter eggs, or Benny Blanket who'll take you back to the '60s in search of flower power.

http://rumpus.com/news_games.html

Silly Putty University

Learn about the history of Silly Putty ("the toy with one moving part!"). About 4,500 tons of the stuff have been sold since 1950 when it first oozed onto the American toy scene. What can you do with it? Find out here.

http://www.sillyputty.com/

Timeline of Toys and Games

Sometimes the hot toys of today end up in a clothes basket tomorrow, collecting dust in the back of the closet. Other times, they become a children's classic. Crayons, Lincoln Logs, Raggedy Ann dolls, and yo-yos are a few toys that have endured generations. There are many others, and they're captured in a time line at this site.

http://www.historychannel.com/exhibits/toys/
    timeline.html

Toy Manufacturers of America

At this site from the Toy Manufacturers of America, you can discover fascinating trivia, such as the fact that Mr. Potato Head was the first toy to be advertised on television. You'll also be able to link to online games and find toy safety information. Take a peek at the Industry side of the site to see into your future: what was hot at the toy fair this year?

http://www.toy-tma.org/

CONSUMER INFORMATION
Consumer Product Safety Commission Recalls

Is that toy safe? This site lists all toys and infant products that have been recalled since 1974. You'll usually be able to see a picture of the toy, find out what's wrong with it, and learn what to do to get a replacement or a refund.

http://www.cpsc.gov/cpscpub/prerel/category/
    topic.html

★ Dr. Toy's Guide

Quick quiz: What toys are appropriate for a two-year old? What toys are sure-fire winners for vacation travel? Do you know the best classic toys, audiotapes, or videotapes for children? Stuck scratching your head? Not to worry. Dr. Toy has it all figured out for you. The Institute for Childhood Resources presents this toychest packed with facts, reviews, and sage advice. Dr. Toy, also known as Dr. Stevanne Auerbach, is a well-known expert on toys, child development, and parent education. Her site is a must for busy families!

http://www.drtoy.com/

DOLLS AND DOLLHOUSES
About Cornhusk Dolls

Have you ever wanted to make a cornhusk doll but didn't know how to get started? It only takes a few simple materials, which are listed here along with the easy-to-follow directions. Then, get creative in decorating your dolls. You'll be surprised at how quickly and easily you can grow your own personal cornhusk doll collection. You can dress your doll as a man or a woman, but remember that cornhusk dolls have no faces. Read the native legend about why this is so.

http://www.nativetech.org/cornhusk/corndoll.html

American Girl

Have you already met toy dolls Kit, Felicity, Josefina, Kirsten, Addy, Samantha, and Molly? They "lived" long ago, and you can explore their worlds through a wonderful series of books. This site tells you all about each of these heroines and their stories, but that's not all. There is an American Girls Trivia game and an American Girls Picture Pieces game, a Daily Trivia game, and more. If you're ever in Chicago, visit American Girl Place, with exhibits and performances galore! Until then, you can peek at photos of it online.

http://www.americangirl.com/homepage2.html

★ Barbie.com

Barbie's come a long way from that perky teenage fashion model in the striped bathing suit. Now she's a dentist, a veterinarian, and a teacher, and she even rides a Harley-Davidson motorcycle! At this site you can learn all about the many faces of Barbie and play fun Barbie games. There are also links to Barbie Collectibles at <http://www.BarbieCollectibles.com/>, containing tips, trivia, and information for collectors.

http://www.barbie.com/

★ Colleen Moore's Fairy Castle

The ultimate dollhouse is in the Chicago Museum of Science and Industry. It was created by Colleen Moore, a star of 1920s silent films, who decorated the interior with antiques, real gold, jewels, and other precious items. The dollhouse is located in a magic garden, with a weeping willow tree that really weeps! Who is to say fairies don't really live there? You'll see the Rock-a-Bye Baby cradle, Santa Claus' sleigh, and lots of other objects familiar from nursery rhyme lore and legend. The table is set in King Arthur's dining hall, and the Bluebird of Happiness sings in the princess' bedroom. Don't miss the attic—Rumplestiltskin's spinning wheel hangs from the rafters.

http://www.msichicago.org/exhibit/fairy_castle/
fchome.html

NET FILES

What do **Gerald Ford, Ronald Reagan, George Bush, and Bill Clinton all have in common** (besides the fact that they have all been U.S. presidents)?

Answer: They are all left-handed! Find out more about famous lefties at http://www.indiana.edu/~primate/left.html

★ Everything You Wanted to Know About Dollhouses but Didn't Know Who to Ask

From types of dollhouses, to how to build one—including supplies needed—this site really does give you everything but the doll! There are instructions on wiring your dollhouse, wallpapering and decorating, and even exotic details like how to make realistic-looking soapsuds for the bathtub.

http://www.miniatures.com/scripts/oneweb.nl/
global?UID=MVULULNP37BDU67B&Page=Article_
Display&312=3485&333=4254

CATS are purrfect.

A
B
C
D
E
F
G
H
I
J
K
L
M
N
O
P
Q
R
S
T
U
V
W
X
Y
Z

A
B
C
D
E
F
G
H
I
J
K
L
M
N
O
P
Q
R
S
T
U
V
W
X
Y
Z

★ Liana's Paper Doll Boutique

Would you like a new doll? Do you have access to a printer, either color or black-and-white? If so, you can have a whole new paper doll collection right away, to say nothing of a complete wardrobe of doll casual clothes, formal clothes, princess gowns, and even fantasy costumes like a faery dress! If you don't have a color printer, just print the outline drawings and use colored pencils for the details.

http://www-personal.umich.edu/~lsharer/paperdolls/old/

★ Marilee's Paperdolls Page: Printable Paperdolls, Links, Books

This is the mother lode of printable paper doll pages! You can discover links to Civil War dolls; dolls featuring royalty, pets, children; and even international dolls. Parents, not every link has been checked.

http://www.ameritech.net/users/macler/paperdolls.html

KALEIDOSCOPES

Kaleidoscope Heaven

Did you ever sit in your bedroom on a cloudy afternoon, wishing you could think of something to do that could brighten up the day? Well, grab a kaleidoscope and start twirling. Don't have one? Look here to find out how to make one from some tape and mirrors. You'll also find some links to online virtual kaleidoscopes and more fun.

http://kaleidoscopeheaven.org/

LEGOS

LEGO

Your dog chewed all the little pieces, and now you need some new ideas for other Lego projects to make with what's left! On the LEGO Information page, you can see pictures of other people's creations, and discover how to make and play Lego games. You'll also find fun online games, screen savers, and other things to download for Legomaniacs everywhere. Some of the games are especially for preschoolers.

http://www.lego.com/

Lugnet

Locate lots of Lego enthusiasts and let them all loose on a Web site, and what do you get? Probably something that looks very much like this one. It has Lego instructions, Lego collectibles, Lego news, Lego movies, Lego crossword puzzles—pretty much everything you'd ever want to know about those colorful little bricks.

http://www.lugnet.com/

🦆 The Minifig Generator

This neat interactive site uses Lego body parts and JavaScript so you can have fun choosing heads, torsos, and legs to create your own mini-figure. How about a pirate's head on a doctor's lab coat, with skeleton legs? You can make your own selections or let the computer randomly pick its own. Name your creation and print a copy. Cool, huh?

http://www.baseplate.com/toys/minifig/

TEDDY BEARS

Bear Story

Germany and the United States each have laid claim to the fame of originating the teddy bear, back in the early 1900s. Check out both stories and decide for yourself which one was bear first.

http://www.qvc.com/bearstry.html

★ The Teddy Bear Project

The folks at I*EARN have a fabulous idea. They team pairs of schools around the world and have them exchange special teddy bear "ambassadors." The bears keep detailed diaries of their travels and often e-mail back home. Want to join in on the fun? This site will tell you how. Some schools have similar projects involving bears with accompanying backpacks full of postcards, coins, and other souvenirs for the other classroom. What a great way to learn about life in another part of the world. Other projects like this may be found in the SCHOOLS AND EDUCATION—PROJECTS section of this book.

http://www.iearn.org.au/tbear/

WATER GUNS

SuperSoaker

Net-Mom has run away from more Super Soaker water play than she cares to remember. Seems like every year, Son of Net-Mom just HAS to have the latest, greatest, and newest model. Luckily, he hasn't discovered this Web site yet. And don't YOU tell him! He'd be drooling over the CPS 1-3-5. No, Net-Mom's going to keep this site a secret.

http://www.supersoaker.com/

YO-YO

American Yo-Yo Association

Three-Leaf Clover. Brain Twister. Reach for the Moon. Atom Smasher. These are all master yo-yo tricks. At the American Yo-Yo Association page, you'll see a world of yo-yo info, including tips on tuning your yo-yo, tricks, museums, and clubs.

http://www.pd.net/yoyo/

Getting Ready to Yo-Yo

For complete beginners, this site is tops. Learn everything from how long the yo-yo string should be to how to hold the yo-yo. Study the drawings and instructions to perform both spinning and non-spinning tricks.

http://www.yo-yoguy.com/info/yoyo/

Learn Yo-Yo Tricks

Listed in order of difficulty are complete instructions for performing several yo-yo tricks. Master the Sleeper and move right in to Walk the Dog, Creeper, Eddie Spaghetti, and more.

http://www.windwizards.com/windwizards/
learyoytric.html

National Geographic Try This: Yo-Yo

This site offers basic yo for the yo-yo challenged. Learn how to rock the baby and walk the dog, among other tricks. Just say "Yo!"

http://www.nationalgeographic.com/world/trythis/
tryyoyo1.html

TRAVEL

See also CANADA; COUNTRIES OF THE WORLD; UNITED STATES—STATES

Car Trip Games

What we liked about this selection of road games was that some of them can be played at night. We think "Restaurant Takeover" sounds nicely competitive, and the "Electric Night Light" seems like it would be fun too.

http://www.homestead.com/lynx87/
cartripgames.html

History Channel - Traveler

How about a tour that re-creates the Civil War? Or one that helps you understand the Klondike gold rush in Alaska? This site will help you plan a vacation you'll remember forever. Once you have the plans made, better tell Mom and Dad that you will need them to drive you there!

http://www.historytravel.com/

2GOOD 2MISS

Genetic Science Learning Center

You don't need fancy equipment to extract DNA from cells. This site shows you a method using only a test tube (or jar), a little detergent, and some rubbing alcohol. (Hint: extract the DNA from wheat germ, not your big toe.) This resource also explains gene mapping and reveals what scientists do for fun: they think up clever names for genes! Surely you can do better. Give it a try here.
http://gslc.genetics.utah.edu/students.html

A
B
C
D
E
F
G
H
I
J
K
L
M
N
O
P
Q
R
S
T
U
V
W
X
Y
Z

A
B
C
D
E
F
G
H
I
J
K
L
M
N
O
P
Q
R
S
T
U
V
W
X
Y
Z

Interactive Suitcase

Pick a trip: there's a beach trip, a business trip, and a ski vacation. Now choose things you need to pack for that particular journey. Hint: although you want to pack light, you don't need to bring your own bulb.

http://www.phxskyharbor.com/kids/suitcase/
    suitcase.html

John and Michael's Travel Games

You'll never be bored in the back seat again when you've got this cool collection of travel games. They are kid tested and approved by both John and Michael, so you know they are tops. There are games to play with license plates, words, or cow-spotting. You might even want to go on a road trip so you can try some of these!

http://home.southwind.net/~oyer/T_GAMES.HTM

Klutz - Travel Games

You are on a 1,000-mile cross-country trip to visit Aunt Mabel. Your kid brother is singing "Do Your Ears Hang Low" for the umpteenth time, and your dad keeps going on and on about how he walked to school barefoot through the snow. In other words, you're bored out of your skull. Fight road boredom with some great travel games from this site. See license plates from around North America so you can quickly recognize which state cars are from (before anyone else). Print off some matching games that'll keep your brother quiet and give you both fun times. You may even look forward to going to Aunt Mabel's now!

http://www.klutz.com/coolstuffpages/roadgames.html

National Traffic and Road Closure Information

Before you head out on a road trip, check this site! It links you to each state's road conditions, construction delays, and more. Knowing where the construction areas are ahead of time will allow your parents to avoid them, and minimize delays in getting the right answer to "Are we there yet?"

http://www.fhwa.dot.gov/trafficinfo/

US State Department Travel Warnings & Consular Information Sheets

Have you ever fantasized you were an international spy? This site has links to all sorts of cool stuff! There are travel advisories and maps of all the different countries. Check out the Central Intelligence Agency (CIA) publications and handbooks. Look at what's going on in different countries, what is necessary to get across the border, and what to take with you to be safe (besides your passport and your parents, that is).

http://travel.state.gov/travel_warnings.html

World's Largest Roadside Attractions

Want to plan a summer vacation trip that will allow you to visit the World's Largest Clam, the World's Largest Ukrainian Easter Egg, and the World's Largest Cuckoo Clock? No problem. This Web site has all the details you'll need! (By the way, you'll be visiting Pismo Beach, California; Vegreville, Alberta; and Wilmot, Ohio.)

http://www.infomagic.net/~martince/

TREASURE AND TREASURE HUNTING

See also CODES AND CIPHERS; PEOPLE AND BIOGRAPHIES—PIRATES; and SHIPS AND SHIPWRECKS

★ Geocaching - The Official GPS Stash Hunt Site

Is there any treasure near your house? Worldwide, geocache game players have hidden small waterproof boxes filled with inexpensive gadgets and goodies. On this page, they give sketchy directions and GPS readings to assist would-be treasure hunters. Be sure to bring an adult along to help, as well as a trinket of your own to trade.

http://www.geocaching.com/

★ Letterboxing North America

Unravel clues, and then take a hike to locate hidden plastic "letterboxes" containing only a logbook and a unique rubber stamp. Use it to mark your own travel journal, and then "sign" the guest book with your personal stamp. Instructions teach a nifty way to make one from an eraser or pieces of foot cushion foam.

http://www.letterboxing.org/

Oak Island

Did you ever dig a hole? What if you dug a hole and found beams of wood? What if you then found a buried shaft? You'd probably be excited! That's exactly what happened to a young man years ago on Oak Island, just off the coast of Nova Scotia, in Maritime Canada. What's really intriguing is that many people have dug deeper into the shaft since then and found inscribed stones, coconut fiber, an iron plate, and oak wood, just as might be found in treasure chests. Problem is, the shaft is booby-trapped to flood with water, and no one has made it to the bottom. Is there treasure? No one knows. See more about this mystery at this Web page, or at <http://unmuseum.mus.pa.us/oakisl.htm>.

http://www.activemind.com/Mysterious/Topics/
    OakIsland/

The Riddle of the Beale Treasure

The Beale ciphers hold the key to one of the greatest unsolved puzzles of all time. The story goes that around 1820, a fellow named Beale hid two wagon loads of silver, gold, and jewels someplace near Roanoke, Virginia. He left three coded letters, supposedly detailing the location of the treasure, with a trusted friend. Then he left for the West and was never seen again. One of the letters, describing the treasure, has been deciphered. It is in a code based on the Declaration of Independence. It is believed the other letters are similarly coded to the same document or other public documents. You can read about the status of the Beale ciphers, and you might want to try solving them yourself (if you find this treasure, please let us know!).

http://www.unmuseum.org/beal.htm

NET FILES

What is Earth's oldest living tree?

Answer: As far as we know, it's a bristlecone pine tree named "Methuselah," in the White Mountains of California. It is more than 4,700 years old. Read more at http://www.sonic.net/bristlecone/intro.html

Silver Bank @ Nationalgeographic.com

"Spanish galleon Nuestra Señora de la Pura y Limpia Concepción set sail from Havana, Cuba, in September 1641. Eight days later a hurricane thrashed the ship. Leaking, she began a month-long limp toward Puerto Rico for repairs. Just short of salvation, the Concepción struck a shallow reef and began sinking slowly. Three hundred hapless passengers and crew perished, and a fortune in silver tumbled into the Atlantic, inspiring the reef's shiny new name: Silver Bank." That's the background. This site allows you to explore the last days of the ship, the wreck itself, and salvage efforts over the years. Treasure hunter Tracy Bowden is the most recent explorer of the Silver Bank, and you can see many artifacts at this site. There are links to other marine archaeology and treasure Web sites, too.

http://www.nationalgeographic.com/features/98/
    silverbank/

Treasures of the World

There are seven wonders of the world, and, according to this site, six treasures. The Hope Diamond and the *Mona Lisa* are two of the six treasures. Do you know the others? Discover what they are with a visit to this site. You'll learn that eggs form the basis for one of the others, and that a mural by Picasso holds the key to another.

http://www.pbs.org/treasuresoftheworld/

A B C D E F G H I J K L M N O P Q R S **T** U V W X Y Z

TRUCKS AND HEAVY EQUIPMENT

❧ The Great Picture Book of Construction Equipment

Looking for a field guide to construction equipment? Dig into this one and learn how to distinguish (for example) a mud bulldozer from one that works better in a wood lot. There are QuickTime movies so you can watch them move, too! The picture book includes dump trucks, hydraulic excavators, bulldozers, cranes, front loaders, and lots of other things that dig, move, shovel, and tow.

http://www.komatsu.co.jp/kikki/zukan/e_index.htm

❧ Make a Strange Truck

Click on the cab, middle, or back section of the fire truck to make an all-new vehicle with a strange name. How about an ambu-garbage-van or a moving-dump-engine? How many real trucks can you match? This is perfect for preschoolers!

http://www.enchantedlearning.com/Slidetrucks/
   Slidetruck.html

Terry the Tractor

Terry the Tractor starts out as a frame in a factory. Gradually, he gets sprockets, an engine, and more parts, until he emerges from the factory as a shiny new bulldozer. His new owner treats him roughly, and it looks like the scrap heap is going to be Terry's next home. But someone realizes there's still a lot of work left in Terry, if only the damage can be repaired. See what happens to this little dozer with the big heart.

http://www.butler-machinery.com/kids.html

Find your roots in GENEALOGY AND FAMILY HISTORY.

Truckworld Online

Parental advisory: please preview this site. Interested in monster trucks, 4x4s, sport utility vehicles, and all kinds of street and off-road equipment? You'll love this site. Check the QuickTime video of the world record monster truck jump—see a 10,000-pound truck fly as Team Bigfoot clears a distance of 141 feet, 10 inches. Do visit the Team Bigfoot Web site, too, at <http://www.bigfoot4x4.com/>.

http://www.truckworld.com/

FIRE TRUCKS

❧ Fire Truck Home Page

Visit the fire truck gallery to see lots of different kinds of fire and rescue vehicles. Be sure to click on the different types of sirens and see which ones seem most effective. Explore the parts of Sparky's fire truck and play an excellent fire truck driving game at this site for those who think fire trucks are hot!

http://www.sparky.org/firetruck/

The Firehouse Museum

Did you ever wonder how fires were fought in your grandparents' day? They didn't have the sleek, powerful fire trucks we have now. See some historic photos and memorabilia from this museum in San Diego, California, dedicated to firefighters all over the world. Check the steam fire engines and old fire extinguishers, and don't miss old La Jolla #1, a hand-drawn chemical fire truck.

http://www.globalinfo.com/noncomm/firehouse/
   Firehouse.HTML

★ The Florida State Fire College Kids Site

Follow Li'l Boots into the firehouse as he explains the features and uses of various kinds of firefighting vehicles, including pumpers, ladder and aerial trucks, and special-use equipment. How has fighting fires changed over the years? Find out at this site. Don't miss the Home Hazard Hunt. If you can locate all the hazards, you get to print a cool certificate.

http://www.fsfckids.ufl.edu/

A B C D E F G H I J K L M N O P Q R S T U V W X Y Z

U.S. VIRGIN ISLANDS

See UNITED STATES—TERRITORIES

UFOS AND EXTRATERRESTRIALS

The Bermuda Triangle

There are two sides to every story, and this page takes the skeptic's side of the mysteries of the Bermuda Triangle. This page explains, in factual terms, why many of the mysterious events attributed to the Bermuda Triangle may be no more than products of "overactive imaginations."

http://blindkat.tripod.com/triangle/tri.html

FBI - Unidentified Flying Objects

Here are some of the Federal Bureau of Investigation's real X-Files! Released under the Freedom of Information Act, you can pore over 1,600 pages of UFO reports dating back to 1947, as well as one solitary page on the Roswell incident. You'll need the free PDF reader to look at the documents. Parents: All reports may not be suitable for your kids.

http://foia.fbi.gov/ufo.htm

★ Life Beyond Earth

"Absence of evidence isn't evidence of absence" says this Web site. That means just because we haven't found any proof of extraterrestrial life, it doesn't mean that none exists. "Drive" along a five-kilometer time line of the Earth's history and notice that all of human history lies within the last half-meter. Watch a fascinating animation showing the difficulties of communicating with alien cultures across time and space. And don't miss the Infosphere to hear what residents of the environs of Alpha Centauri, Capella, and other places are hearing from us right now. That is, if there are any residents to listen.

http://www.pbs.org/lifebeyondearth/

NET FILES

Where is the world's largest bell?

Answer: The Tsar Bell, weighing 210 tons, is in Moscow, Russia. It stands 20 feet high and has a diameter of 22 feet at the base. A fire swept Moscow in 1737, including the bell's location in the Kremlin. When water was poured on the hot bell, it cracked, and a huge piece broke off. The bell now rests on a special granite stand at the foot of the Ivan the Great bell tower. See a picture of it at *http://www.online.ru/sp/comin/kremlin/english/31.html#*

★ SETI@home: The Search for Extraterrestrial Intelligence

Now you can use your Win, Mac, or Unix computer to help look for alien signals! Just download the free screen saver (gee, it looks really cool while it is running). Then leave your computer on when you are not using it, and the SETI@home screen saver will come on and do its work. It does not need to be connected to the Internet. It uses your spare computer cycles to check the backlog of radio astronomy data sets, looking for signals that seem odd. When it completes a data set, it does need to connect to the Internet to transfer results. It's all explained in the FAQ. Here at Pollywood Farm, we are part of the SETI project, and you might consider joining too. You'll be doing some real science, and wouldn't it be cool if YOUR computer found the signal pattern that means off-Earth intelligence?

http://setiathome.ssl.berkeley.edu/

A B C D E F G H I J K L M N O P Q R S T U V W X Y Z

A
B
C
D
E
F
G
H
I
J
K
L
M
N
O
P
Q
R
S
T
U
V
W
X
Y
Z

★ Unnatural Museum - Hall of UFO Mysteries

Parental advisory: please preview this site. Look up in the sky. What's that weird light? Is it a reflection from a high-flying plane? Maybe Venus rising? Or— could it be an Unidentified Flying Object? Learn about the history of UFOs, including famous hoaxes.

http://www.unmuseum.org/ufo.htm

Who's Out There? A SETI Adventure

What if you were hired to search for life out there in the universe? How would you go about planning your investigation? What types of signals would you try to find? Where would you look? Try this adventure game to find some answers, but beware— it may open still more questions in your mind.

http://www.seti-inst.edu/game/

UNITED STATES

FirstGov

This site is a portal to Federal and State government Web sites. Use it to contact officials, find out about highway safety, track down statistics, and lots more.

http://www.firstgov.gov/

★ GovSpot

What are the most popular baby names? How do you get a flag that's been flown over the Capitol building? Where can you find a list of foreign embassies? Where are the best government sites for kids? Why not visit GovSpot and find out?

http://www.govspot.com/

Students.gov

If you've ever wondered how to get a passport or apply for student aid, this site provides a convenient clearinghouse for government information. There's a section on military service, as well as community service, and a short overview course called Government 101.

http://www.students.gov/

FEDERAL GOVERNMENT

★ Ben's Guide to U.S. Government for Kids

Founding father Ben Franklin is your guide to how the United States government works. Just choose your grade level, and you're off to learn about national symbols, the three branches of government, historical documents, citizenship, and lots more topics. There are also links to other sites on a variety of topics. This excellent resource starts with the needs of kindergartners and finishes up at the high school level.

http://bensguide.gpo.gov/

The Library of Congress

The U.S. Library of Congress is the world's largest collection of library materials anywhere. It would be great if everything in the library were available to be viewed on the Internet, but that hasn't happened yet. However, the folks at the Library of Congress have made a large amount of information available here. From this site, you can view beautiful graphic images of exhibits, such as original photographs from the U.S. Civil War, and you can see replicas of documents from Columbus' voyages to America. There's much more here to discover and explore.

http://lcweb.loc.gov/

USA Government

What are "checks and balances"? What is a democracy, anyway? And do you ever graduate from the "electoral college"? This excellent tutorial on the U.S. government will answer all those questions and plenty more. There are also suggested projects to go along with what you learn about each branch of government. For example, put on a skit about a Supreme Court case, or pretend you have to make up a new cabinet department—what would it be?

http://pittsford.monroe.edu/Jefferson/CALFIERI/ GOVERNMENT/GovFrame.html

Read any good Web sites lately?

May the force be with you in PHYSICS.

FEDERAL GOVERNMENT— EXECUTIVE

See also HEALTH AND SAFETY—HEALTH; MILITARY AND ARMED FORCES

Bureau of Engraving and Printing

Did you know that Martha Washington is the only woman whose portrait has appeared on a U.S. currency note? It appeared on the face of the $1 silver certificate of 1886 and 1891, and on the back of the $1 silver certificate of 1896. There are lots more interesting facts to learn when you visit the Bureau of Engraving and Printing (BEP). If you are in Washington, D.C., you can visit in person, or you can do it right here if you are surfing the Internet. The BEP also has a really neat area with games especially for kids. Did you know that if you had ten billion $1 notes and spent one every second of every day, it would require 317 years for you to go broke? Bill Gates had better start spending!

http://www.bep.treas.gov/

CIA Kids Page

Do you know what the Central Intelligence Agency does? People there collect and analyze all kinds of information from all over the world, and they do it in the name of national defense. Besides men and women, the agents include spy dogs and even spy pigeons! Don't miss the Try on a Disguise Shockwave game. We particularly like the way you can disguise the dog to look like a cat. You'll know a lot more about the CIA when you've finished spying on this site. Did we say spy? Shhhh!

http://www.odci.gov/cia/ciakids/

The Department of Health and Human Services Kids Page

The Department of Health and Human Services includes the Centers for Disease Control and Prevention, the Food and Drug Administration (FDA), and the National Institutes of Health, among other agencies. Their kids' page has a food safety coloring book, as well as information about smoking and drug abuse. There are some bizarre things collected on this page of links, though. We're not sure what holiday and brain teaser links have to do with the subject.

http://www.hhs.gov/kids/

Department of Justice Kids and Youth Page

The Department of Justice (DoJ) oversees everything from the FBI to the DEA (these are Federal Bureau of Investigation and the Drug Enforcement Administration, for those who aren't familiar with the acronyms). Visit the FBI link to learn which criminals are on the Ten Most Wanted list. You can also see what happens inside a courtroom as you trace a case from its initial investigation through its appeals process. Older kids will learn a lot from the civil rights information.

http://www.usdoj.gov/kidspage/

NET FILES

What do Julius Caesar, Annie Oakley, Betsy Ross, and Leonardo da Vinci have in common?

Answer: According to the Chinese Zodiac's twelve-year cycle, these famous people were all born in years of the Monkey. The Chinese belief is that people born in the year of the Monkey are very intelligent and always well liked. Find out more at http://www.lausd.k12.ca.us/Haskell_EL/ calendar%20past%20events/chinese new%20year%20gifs/chinesenewye ar.htm

A
B
C
D
E
F
G
H
I
J
K
L
M
N
O
P
Q
R
S
T
U
V
W
X
Y
Z

Sesame Workshop Sticker World

Everybody likes stickers—big ones, little ones, animated ones. Yes, that's right, at this site, you can collect online stickers that do things. Lions roar, flowers bloom, dragons breathe fire, test tubes boil, machines run—you get the idea. You begin with a limited number of starter stickers. Create your own free home page and decorate it with your stickers. Visit other kids' pages to "trade" stickers with them and play games. Collect points by visiting other kids' pages, and then "buy" more stickers for your collection. It's fun, free, and fabulous!
http://www.sesameworkshop.org/stickerworld/

Department of Labor Educational Resources

If you're thinking about dropping out of school, DON'T. This site explains what you will be facing in the world of work without a high school diploma. Did you know that dropouts earn an average of 27 percent less than teens with a diploma? You will also find out about child labor laws and youth employment laws, and be able to explore many careers at this site.

http://www.dol.gov/dol/asp/public/fibre/main.htm

The Department of the Interior Kid's Page

The Department of the Interior is in charge of the U.S. Fish and Wildlife Service, the National Park Service, U.S. Geological Survey, and the Bureau of Indian Affairs, among other things. At the kids' version of their home page, you can visit the Hoover Dam, learn how coal is mined, and download some great American landmarks to color.

http://www.doi.gov/kids/

Catch a ride on a Carousel in AMUSEMENT PARKS.

FBI Kids Page - Kindergarten Through 5th Grade

Did you know that dogs can be trained to sniff out drugs or explosives? They are also used as search-and-rescue helpers when the FBI is looking for a lost child, or a dangerous criminal. At this page, you'll learn all about working dogs, as well as other ways the Federal Bureau of Investigation solves crimes. There's a special page for kids in grades 6 to 12 *<http://www.fbi.gov/kids/6th12th/6th12th.htm>*. It includes the "Special Agent Challenge," which will take you all over the FBI Web site in search of information.

http://www.fbi.gov/kids/k5th/kidsk5th.htm

Housing and Urban Development - Kids Next Door

Arrange buildings to create a simulated city, unscramble words to help keep your community safe, and find out about helpers in your community. There's also a series of online field trips to some cool places: a park, city hall, and a public library. You can take the picture tour or the animated tour.

http://www.hud.gov/kids/

Social Security for the Young

It is red, white, and blue, and you should have one. No, it's not an American flag. It's a Social Security card. While everybody in the United States has to have one to get a job, a Social Security card serves other purposes. Turn to this site to understand the role Social Security cards play in our lives. And, if you don't have a card yet, this site will show you how to apply.

http://www.ssa.gov/kids/

State Department: The Geographic Learning Site

The Department of State is responsible for carrying out our diplomatic policies and relationships with other nations of the world. They oversee U.S. embassies abroad and our ambassadors to those countries. The Department of State is also the custodian of the Great Seal of the United States, which is used on treaties and very important official documents. Learn about it in the Historian's area at *<http://www.state.gov/www/about_state/history/faq.html>*. At this site you can also learn what the secretary of state does, and check his frequent flyer mileage. This site provides information on several different grade levels, but if you decide you have picked one that is too young or too old, you can easily change to another level at any point.

http://geography.state.gov/htmls/plugin.html

U.S. Department of Agriculture for Kids

From this vantage point, you can meet Smokey Bear, Woodsy Owl, Thermy, Rus the Surfin' Squirrel, and S. K. Worm. You'll also learn a lot in the History of U.S. Agriculture (1776–1990) and Agriculture for Kids sections, and a whole bushel of information about the food pyramid. Did you know there are really two nutritional pyramids? One is for young children and one is for Everyone Else. No, Twinkies are not on either one.

http://www.usda.gov/news/usdakids/

U.S. Patent and Trademark Kids Pages

"Can you get a patent for a smell?" This is just one of the intriguing questions asked and answered at this official government site (look in the Trademark Treasure section). Choose content geared to K–6, 6–12, or teachers and parents. Check the contest area to see what curriculum projects are suggested for an inventive experience at school.

http://www.uspto.gov/go/kids/

The White House

Now that there's a new administration in the White House, the White House for Kids site has undergone some changes. The information is still there, but the presentation just isn't the same (see what we mean for yourself, here's the old one: *<http://clinton4.nara.gov/WH/kids/html/home.html>*). At this site, you'll learn how the White House was built (bricks were made on the front lawn), tour the rooms, and find out about the First Family pets that have lived there (don't miss President Harrison's goat or Caroline Kennedy's pony). Did you know the president's desk was once part of a ship, abandoned north of the Arctic circle in 1854? The *HMS Resolute* was later found by the crew of an American whaling ship. It was repaired and refitted, and then sent to Queen Victoria as a gesture of goodwill. Later, when the ship was taken out of service and dismantled, a desk was made from some of its timbers. Queen Victoria presented the desk to President Hayes in 1880. The desk has been used by most presidents since then.

http://www.whitehouse.gov/kids/

FEDERAL GOVERNMENT— JUDICIAL

Anatomy of a Murder: A Trip Through Our Justice System

Even if you've never thought very much about the American justice system, you can learn all about it at this Web page. Follow a mysterious fictional murder case through the court system as you encounter grand juries, indictments, and plea bargains. You'll also explore famous Supreme Court decisions. Tied up in legal red tape and jargon? Just click on the Glossary for the Baffled!

http://library.thinkquest.org/2760/

HAY! Gallop over to HORSES AND EQUESTRIAN SPORTS.

The Federal Judiciary

Order in the court! Hmmm, but which court? Supreme Court, Court of Appeals, bankruptcy court—more courts than a tennis tournament! This site is a clearinghouse of information on the U.S. federal judiciary system, and the hypertext links will give you a brief overview, plus contact information for more in-depth help.

http://www.uscourts.gov/

Oyez Oyez Oyez

At this site from Northwestern University, you can research many (not all) Supreme Court cases by subject, date, or title. Sometimes there will be Real Audio of the actual arguments in Court. Meet the justices who have been appointed to the Court throughout its history. Take a virtual panoramic tour to the Supreme Court building in Washington, D.C. And visit the FAQ to find out what "oyez" means!

http://oyez.nwu.edu/

Supreme Court Collection

Prepared by the Cornell University Law School in New York, these hypertext Supreme Court decisions date from 1990. Also included are numerous famous cases that took place before this time.

http://supct.law.cornell.edu/supct/

Supreme Court of the United States

It's the official Supreme Court Web site, but why, oh why couldn't they have had the "About" files in plain text rather than PDF (Portable Document Format) files. Almost everything on this site requires Acrobat, a free PDF reader. (There's a link to get the free Acrobat reader, if you don't already have it.) Net-mom says this site is guilty of putting unnecessary complexity between the user and the information. If you think this site is hard to use, please tell them.

http://www.supremecourtus.gov/

> ## VIDEO AND SPY CAMS let you look in on interesting parts of the world.

FEDERAL GOVERNMENT—LEGISLATIVE

Congress.Org - Your Link to Congress

Did you know that you have representatives in Washington? They are supposed to be working for you, but they are so far away, how can you check up on them? One way is to use the Internet. Type in your ZIP code and find out how your representatives voted on recent legislation. You'll also find address books here, so you can write to your congresspeople (and local media!) and express your opinions. If you're a little hazy about how all this government stuff works, this site will get you up to speed.

http://www.congress.org/

CongressLink

If you need to know who's who in the Congressional leadership, or just want the short version of how our laws are made, or want some lesson plan ideas—then this is your site. Soon, they promise Congress for Kids *<http://www.congressforkids.net/>*; but at press time, it was not yet available.

http://www.congresslink.org/

★ THOMAS - U.S. Congress on the Internet

It's Congress at your fingertips—you'll find lots of information at this resource. Fnd out what happened during the last Congress, or get the scoop on the hot bills now under consideration at this Congress. The full text of the U.S. Constitution is also available here, as well as other important historic documents. Hint: if you receive e-mail about a bill "602P" or "602p" regarding a tax on Internet services—it's a hoax. Find out more here *<http://thomas.loc.gov/tfaqs/18.htm>*.

http://thomas.loc.gov/

U.S. Senate

Why are there two legislative houses, rather than just one? According to this resource, "The two houses of Congress resulted from the 'Great Compromise' between large and small states reached at the Constitutional Convention in 1787. Membership of the House of Representatives is apportioned according to a state's population, while in the Senate each state has equal representation. The Constitution assigns the Senate and House equal responsibility . . . ." At the Web site you can track senate activity, write to your senators, and take a virtual reality tour of the senate chambers. In the Senate FAQ <http://www.senate.gov/learning/learn_faq.html#history> you can find out about the "Candy Desk" and the recipe for Senate Bean soup!

http://www.senate.gov/

United States House of Representatives

The main function of Congress isn't to make headlines; it's to make laws. The whole process is outlined at this site (look in the Educational Links area). Put your newfound knowledge into action immediately by checking out what the House of Representatives considered today and what they will talk about tomorrow. Find out who voted; how they voted; and, best yet, how your own representative voted. Do you agree with what your representative did? Why not write a letter or e-mail—the addresses are available here, too. There's also a twist on amendments to the Constitution in the Educational Links area of this site. Besides the ones that did pass and have become law, there is a section on the six amendments to the Constitution that have been proposed but never ratified (which means approved by 75 percent of the states).

http://www.house.gov/

Know your alphabet? Now try someone else's in LANGUAGES AND ALPHABETS.

NET FILES

TIME magazine's annual "Man of the Year" isn't always male. Who was the first woman to be honored this way? (Hint: A king loved her so much that he gave up his throne to marry her.)

Answer: Wallis Warfield Simpson was *TIME* magazine's first "Woman of the Year" for the year 1936. Find out more at *http://www.pathfinder.com/time/special/moy/1936.html*

NATIONAL PARKS
ParkNet

Hosted by the U.S. National Park Service, this resource is loaded with facts! It includes visitor information, statistics, conservation practices, and park history. You can find information on a specific park or historic site in a variety of ways. Try the alphabetical list, or use a clickable map to select from a list of sites for that state.

http://www.nps.gov/

USDA National Forest Recreation

America's national forests belong to you, but when was the last time you visited one? To find out where they are and how to visit them, check the U.S. Department of Agriculture Forest Service guide, which lists every national forest, grassland, and park in the country. Click on any one of them to learn all about the area, including what kind of wildlife you can see and what there is to do, whether it's fishing, skiing, biking, kayaking, or camping. Once you've decided where you'd like to go, reserve your spot by downloading a reservation application.

http://www.fs.fed.us/recreation/

A
B
C
D
E
F
G
H
I
J
K
L
M
N
O
P
Q
R
S
T
U
V
W
X
Y
Z

A B C D E F G H I J K L M N O P Q R S T U V W X Y Z

NET FILES

YOU'VE MADE IT INTO THE FORBIDDEN CITY, HOME OF CHINESE EMPERORS OF LONG AGO. NOW, CAN YOU FIND YOUR WAY OUT? HOW MANY ROOMS ARE THERE?

Answer: Beijing is the capital city of China. At its center is the Forbidden City, which was the home and audience hall of the Ming and Qing Emperors. The Forbidden City contains 9,999 rooms! It was originally built in the early 1400s. Read more at http://www.museumca.org/exhibit/exhib_forbiddencity.html

POLITICS

The :30 Second Candidate

Political ads can either make or break a candidate. Here you can explore the step-by-step creation of an ad campaign. Learn how a political idea is transformed into a 30-second commercial. Discover how production details work together to convey a particular mood. You can also experiment and create your own ad.

http://www.pbs.org/30secondcandidate/

★ The American President

This companion guide to the PBS series of the same name offers a spectacular game called The War Room. Could you manage a presidential campaign all the way from the New Hampshire primaries to the November election? Try the simulation! Also see another companion guide to this series under UNITED STATES—PRESIDENTS AND FIRST LADIES.

http://www.americanpresident.org/

BrainPOP Election Movie

The President isn't elected by direct popular vote, but by ballots cast by people in the "Electoral College." Did you know that? Moby the Robot didn't! Tim (the smart human) uses a clever animation to explain the whole election process to him. Can you (or your parents) pass the quiz?

http://www.brainpop.com/specials/election/

Choose or Lose

The presidential election of 2000 was one of the most unusual ever held. Not often does a candidate win the popular vote but ultimately lose the election. Although this site is closed, its home page remains open for you to relive the wild events that took place. News, analysis, commentary, and opinion polls are some of the finds awaiting you here.

http://www.mtv.com/nav/intro_chooseorlose.html

CNN - AllPolitics

No matter where you live, your life is affected by politicians. They are everywhere! Politicians make laws about a lot of different things every day. CNN, one of the world's most trusted news sources, offers these pages dedicated to political news. From the federal budget to the presidential elections, look here for great leads on today's top stories.

http://cnn.com/ALLPOLITICS/

Copernicus Election Watch: The 2000 U.S. Presidential Election

The 2000 U.S. presidential election is over, but studying it is not. People will argue about it for years to come. Be informed! Here you can explore the how's and why's of this historic election. This site will also help you understand the process of choosing the president and vice president.

http://www.edgate.com/elections/inactive/

The Electoral College

The Electoral College is not a place of academic learning. This cartoon video will explain it all in an easy-to-understand way. You'll learn why some states have more electoral votes than others, how a candidate earns these votes, and why they determine the winner of a presidential election.

http://www.fraboom.com/BoomToons/election2000/

Issues 2001

Would you like to know where political power shakers stand on the issues? What is their position on the death penalty, abortion, or health care, to name a few? At this site, you get a snapshot of their thinking. It also discloses the views of commentators and business leaders, such as Microsoft chief executive Bill Gates. Do you know if your views classify you as a liberal or a conservative, or something else? Take the quiz and see *<http://www.govote.com/ votematch/index2.asp>*.

http://www.issues2000.org/

PBS Kids Democracy Project

Understanding government is more than just learning about candidates. It's also about laws and services provided in your community. At this site, you can take a tour of a virtual city and explore the role government plays. You can also be President for a Day and decide which election issues are most important to kids. Lesson plans are also included.

http://www.pbs.org/democracy/kids/

Project Vote Smart

Have you ever wondered how the U.S. government works? Vote Smart keeps track of what politicians are doing. If you are writing a paper about a candidate or a political issue, try this site. It has links to campaigns, educational material, and lots more. If you don't know who your elected officials are, just type in your ZIP code, and Vote Smart will tell you. You'll also learn about their voting records and how to contact them to tell them they are doing a good job, or to complain if you don't agree with their stand on the issues so far.

http://www.vote-smart.org/

TIME for Kids Election Connection

It's you against Dirk Soundbite, and he's ahead in the polls. But don't worry. Every Presidential history quiz question you get right convinces more voters to join your campaign. There's more: don't miss The Great Debate section of this site. "Debate" the two major party candidates, as well as . . . Britney Spears!

http://www.timeforkids.com/TFK/electconnect/

PRESIDENTS AND FIRST LADIES
Abraham Lincoln Online

Most of us know a few things about Abraham Lincoln, 13th president of the United States. But the facts found at this site go far beyond what we might learn in the average history book. Many of his speeches and letters are available, as are FAQs, historic sites, and links to other Web sites on Lincoln. The Quizzes About Lincoln Events (in the "Students" section) provides a lot of great questions, for example, "Which two things would Lincoln not want you to know?" The answers are here, too.

http://www.netins.net/showcase/creative/ lincoln.html

The American Experience - The Presidents

This site has a time line of U.S. presidents running across the top of the page, in the Presidential Record area. You can see who served when and for how many years. Click on any name to get more information. Look at the "Snap Shot" for a picture and a brief overview. Then use the menu of choices on the left to find out more about the historical era and events of the times. You'll get a sense of what the president's domestic and foreign relations policies were as well. Some presidents rate expanded feature stories where you can learn a lot more. The material is presented in an appealing and interesting way; see what you think.

http://www.pbs.org/wgbh/amex/presidents/frames/ record/record.html

Everyone's flocking to BIRDS!

A B C D E F G H I J K L M N O P Q R S T U V W X Y Z

The American President

This PBS series profiles all of America's past chief executives, with an unusual twist. You won't find them in chronological order. Instead, explore the presidents related by a common theme. For example, episode six is called "The World Stage," and deals with presidents challenged by world events and foreign policy. Monroe declared war on Spain after the American battleship *Maine* mysteriously exploded off Cuba in 1898. Wilson swept America into World War I. And George H. W. Bush went to the Persian Gulf to liberate Kuwait. Each episode guide is illuminated with multimedia and historical documents. Also see another companion guide to this series under UNITED STATES—POLITICS.

http://www.thirteen.org/amerpres/

The First Ladies

In recognition of the significant contribution to American history made by many of the presidents' wives, the First Ladies Web site has been added to the official White House Web site. From Martha Dandridge Custis Washington to Laura Welch Bush, read about their upbringing, their education, their courtships, their marriages, their children, and many interesting facets of their lives.

http://www.whitehouse.gov/history/firstladies/

Grolier Online's - The American Presidency

Who was the thirteenth president? Which president was involved in Watergate? What was Watergate? Links to all the Presidents' official sites may be found here. Grolier offers an outstanding presidential resource, which will teach you everything from elections to scandals, from impeachments to how a voting machine works. Some sections cater to lower elementary grades, while others are for teens and adults. Don't miss the presidential sound clips in the Gallery section.

http://gi.grolier.com/presidents/preshome.html

Inaugural Addresses of the Presidents of the United States

George Washington's second-term inaugural speech remains the shortest on record, requiring only 135 words. William Henry Harrison delivered one of the longest, speaking for an hour and 45 minutes in a blinding snowstorm. He then stood in the cold and greeted well-wishers all day; he died a month later, of pneumonia. Read the speech here, but make sure you keep your hat on! Project Bartleby, at Columbia University in New York, houses this site containing the inaugural addresses of the presidents. Also included is an article about presidents sworn in but not inaugurated, and the Oath of Office itself. This is a good site for finding inaugural factoids, such as the revelation that Geronimo, the great Apache, attended the inauguration of Teddy Roosevelt and that attendees at Grover Cleveland's second inaugural ball were all agog at the new invention: electric lights!

http://www.bartleby.com/124/

Inauguration 2001

On this day, speeches and ball gowns go together like butter and popcorn. It's inauguration day, and it happens almost every time a president is sworn into office. Speeches, fashion, and tradition are all part of the day's events, and you'll find a bevy of information on each at this site. Also, check out the inauguration quiz. You'll learn that George W. Bush isn't the only president to follow in his father's footsteps.

http://www.pbs.org/newshour/inauguration/

★ Inside the White House @ Nationalgeographic.com

Imagine you've just been elected president of the United States! What would your first decision be? What can people expect of your presidency? You can let your imagination soar and get an idea of what it's like to sit in the president's Oval Office right here at this Web page. Best yet, you'll learn loads about presidents and U.S. history while having fun. Be careful of those pesky newspaper reporters and radio talk show hosts!

http://www.nationalgeographic.com/features/96/whitehouse/whhome.html

Mount Rushmore

Who are "the four most famous guys in rock"? Well, it's not the Beatles; it's the four American presidents carved into the granite of Mount Rushmore, South Dakota. At this site you can find out why the faces of George Washington, Thomas Jefferson, Teddy Roosevelt, and Abraham Lincoln are sculpted there, and how the feat was accomplished.

http://www.travelsd.com/parks/rushmore/

POTUS - Presidents of the United States

This site is loaded with information about all of the U.S. presidents. You'll find a picture or photo, information about their elections, inaugurations, terms of office, and cabinet members. There are also links to other resources around the Net; for example, learning about Thomas Jefferson, we can take a virtual visit to his home, called Monticello. There are also links to biographies, historical documents, and trivia. Did you know that Jefferson wrote his own epitaph and did not mention that he had served as president of the United States?

http://www.ipl.org/ref/POTUS/

President Game

Can you click and drag all the U.S. Presidents into their correct locations on the time line? Position them near the dates; and if you are right, they will lock into place. Clicking on a "locked" President will bring up some information about him. If you get them all right, you'll hear the stirring sounds of "Hail to the Chief."

http://www.sprocketworks.com/shockwave/
  load.asp?SprMovie=presidentgame

The Presidents of the United States

For some kids growing up in the United States, becoming president is the highest ambition. So far, only a few people have achieved that goal, and the job of president is a tough one. At this site, you can read quick facts about each president, find links to other informative Web pages, and get a sense of the times and struggles of each leader of the U.S. Who knows, maybe some day you'll grow up to be president, and your picture will be on these Web pages!

http://www.whitehouse.gov/history/presidents/

Get Your Angries Out

Are you always yelling at your sister? Is there a bully bothering you at school? Are you mad and cranky a lot? This site gives you some useful ways to get your anger out in constructive ways. For example: "Check your tummy, jaws and your fists. See if the mads are coming. Breathe! Blow your mad out. Get your control. Feel good about getting your control. Stop and think; make a good choice. People are not to be hurt with your hands, feet or voice. Remember to use your firm words, not your fists." There are many more good ideas here, and don't forget to check the links about peace while you're dealing with your angries!
http://members.aol.com/AngriesOut/

U.S. Presidents of the Twentieth Century

Listen to Real Audio or MP3 sound files of 20 U.S. presidents. You'll hear campaign speeches, inaugural speeches, and more. Test: Teddy Roosevelt has left the building . . . he has left the building!

http://www.lib.msu.edu/vincent/presidents/

STATES

Do you need information about a U.S. state? We've found it for you! The "official" home page of each state's government, a direct link to each state's symbols, and the best tourism site we could find are all included. General information about each state can usually be found at either the "official" or the "tourism" site, and often at both. Expect to find information here on each state's history, culture, statistics, travel, and more.

A
B
C
D
E
F
G
H
I
J
K
L
M
N
O
P
Q
R
S
T
U
V
W
X
Y
Z

A B C D E F G H I J K L M N O P Q R S T U V W X Y Z

50States.com - States and Capitals

Pick a state, any state. Or pick a territory; they are here, too. You'll get a page with lots of information about each area. For example, look at Nebraska, the Cornhusker State; its capital is Lincoln. See the state flag, the bird, the flower, the song, even links to other information about the state. Hey, did you know Nebraska was the birthplace of President Gerald R. Ford? You do now!

http://www.50states.com/

The Life of a Bill in Mississippi

Governments have lots of laws and rules for people and businesses to follow. When a new law is needed, it goes through a maze of committees and meetings. The proposed new law is called a bill. This page contains a nice chart that shows all the steps necessary for a bill to become a law in Mississippi. Many states have similar procedures.

http://www.peer.state.ms.us/LifeOfBill.html

If you were to place every Oreo cookie ever made in a tall stack, one on top of the other, how high would the pile reach?

Answer: Since the beginning of time (1912), more than 362 billion Oreos have been made. The pile would reach all the way to the moon and back more than five times. Placed side by side, they would encircle Earth's equator 381 times! Find out more fun facts about the Oreo, America's favorite sandwich cookie, at http://www.oreo.com/Oreo/or_info.htm

RAILROADS AND TRAINS are on track.

Postcards from America
50 State Travel Adventure

See all 50 states through daily postcards sent directly to your e-mail box or viewed online. Visit this entertaining travel site that includes beautiful photos, special postage stamps, fun facts, travel tips, and more. Read the diary of Ken and Priscilla. They're the "postcard people" who travel around the country to show you what life is like across America.

http://www.postcardsfrom.com/

Quia Java Games - U.S. State Capitals

Do you have to memorize the state capitals for school? This neat site offers you online flashcards, concentration games, and other ways for you to commit to memory everything from Montgomery, Alabama, to Cheyenne, Wyoming.

http://www.quia.com/jg/4.html

State and Local Government on the Net

Hear ye, hear ye! Citizens that be among you wishing to partake of information from the category of state, federal, and tribal governments, assemble freely here. Delve ye deep within diverse agencies and departments. What ye find may astound you. Here be thy taxes at work.

http://www.piperinfo.com/state/

Stately Knowledge

This site offers information on every state (and Washington, D.C.). There are basic facts about each state, comparative statistics, and suggested books and other resources. You can play a state capitals game or a state flags game, too.

http://www.ipl.org/youth/stateknow/

Yahoo! Get Local

Yahoo! has just about everything available when it comes to U.S. states. If you don't mind wading through lots of links to find just what you're looking for, try here. To your advantage, though, each state's links are also sorted by category. You can ask for just the links on education, sports, outdoors, cities, government, and more. There's also a search field that you can use to narrow down your selection.

http://local.yahoo.com/

ALABAMA

Located in the Deep South, Alabama is the 22nd state. Alabama is an Indian name for "tribal town." The state bird is the yellowhammer, and the flower is the camellia.

Official State Home Page:

http://www.state.al.us/

State Symbols:

http://www.archives.state.al.us/kidspage/kids.html

State Tourism:

http://www.touralabama.org/

ALASKA

Alaska is the largest state, in area, and is home to the tallest mountain in the United States, Mount McKinley (20,320 feet). It's both the westernmost and easternmost state! This curiosity is possible because, technically, part of the Aleutian Island chain of Alaska is located in the Eastern Hemisphere, while the rest of Alaska is in the Western Hemisphere. Alaska gets its name from an Inuit word for "great lands." It is the 49th state, and some of it lies above the Arctic Circle.

Official State Home Page:

http://www.state.ak.us/

State Symbols:

http://www.dced.state.ak.us/tourism/student.htm

State Tourism:

http://www.dced.state.ak.us/tourism/

ARIZONA

The 48th state, Arizona, is home to the largest gorge in the U.S.: the Grand Canyon. It is more than 200 miles long and 1 mile deep. The name is from the Aztec word *arizuma*, meaning "silver bearing." The official state bird is the cactus wren, and the flower is the saguaro cactus. This western desert state has lots of cactus!

Official State Home Page:

http://www.az.gov/

State Symbols:

http://www.lib.az.us/museum/symbols.htm

State Tourism:

http://www.arizonaguide.com/

ARKANSAS

Rice grows in much of the lowlands of the 25th state. Midlands Arkansas is home to Hot Springs National Park, where people come from miles around to relax and soothe their tired muscles in the hot mineral baths. The name is from the Quapaw language and means "downstream people." The official state bird is the mockingbird.

Official State Home Page:

http://www.state.ar.us/

State Symbols:

http://www.sosweb.state.ar.us/about_ark.html

State Tourism:

http://www.arkansas.com/

Why surf the Internet when you can sail it in BOATING AND SAILING?

A
B
C
D
E
F
G
H
I
J
K
L
M
N
O
P
Q
R
S
T
U
V
W
X
Y
Z

A B C D E F G H I J K L M N O P Q R S T **U** V W X Y Z

Surf today, smart tomorrow.

CALIFORNIA

California, the 31st state, was once part of Mexico. It is known for its national park, Yosemite. Also, The lowest point of land in the United States is Death Valley, at 282 feet below sea level. Located on the West Coast, California's nickname is the Golden State. The state tree is the California redwood, and its flower is the golden poppy.

Official State Home Page:

http://www.state.ca.us/

State Symbols:

http://www.library.ca.gov/history/cahinsig.html

State Tourism:

http://gocalif.ca.gov/

COLORADO

One of the Rocky Mountain states, Colorado has the highest average elevation of all the states, and over 50 of the highest mountain peaks in the U.S. are found there. Yes, skiing is popular in Colorado! The 38th state has had over 20,000 years of human habitation. Its state flower is the graceful Rocky Mountain columbine.

Official State Home Page:

http://www.state.co.us/

State Symbols:

http://www.archives.state.co.us/arcembl.html

State Tourism:

http://www.colorado.com/

CONNECTICUT

Settled by the Dutch in the early 1600s, Connecticut was one of the original 13 colonies. It is the fifth state. The name of this East Coast state comes from a Mohican word meaning "long river place." The official state song is "Yankee Doodle."

Official State Home Page:

http://www.state.ct.us/

State Symbols:

http://www.kids.state.ct.us/

State Tourism:

http://www.tourism.state.ct.us/

DELAWARE

Delaware was the first state, becoming one in 1787. It's the second smallest state in area, ahead only of Rhode Island. Delaware was named after Lord De La Warr, a governor of Virginia. The motto of this eastern seaboard state is "Liberty and independence."

Official State Home Page:

http://www.delaware.gov/

State Symbols:

http://www.state.de.us/gic/facts/history/delfact.htm

State Tourism:

http://www.visitdelaware.net/

Attention everyone.
The Internet is closing.
Please go play outside.

DISTRICT OF COLUMBIA

Although it's not a state at all, the District of Columbia is well known for its city of Washington, D.C. It's the special place where the United States government buildings and leaders are. The president of the U.S. lives there, and you can visit the White House and other historic buildings either in person or over the Net. The District of Columbia has its own "state" motto, "Justice for all," as well as an official flower (American beauty rose), tree (scarlet oak), and bird (wood thrush).

Official Home Page:

http://www.washingtondc.gov/

State Symbols:

http://www.factmonster.com/ipka/A0108620.html

State Tourism:

http://www.washington.org/

FLORIDA

Florida has the distinction of being the flattest state. It is also home to the southernmost spot in the continental United States. Its peninsula divides the Atlantic Ocean from the Gulf of Mexico. Florida was named by Ponce de León in 1513; it means "flowery Easter." Lots of oranges and grapefruit grow here due to the mild, sunny climate. The 27th state's official flower is the orange blossom.

Official State Home Page:

http://www.myflorida.com/

State Symbols:

http://dhr.dos.state.fl.us/kids/

State Tourism:

http://dlis.dos.state.fl.us/fgils/tourism.html

BBC Languages - French

Maybe you have taken a little bit of French in school but you'd like to brush that up a little and know more. Or maybe you're a French whiz and you'd just like to learn some cool French student slang to jazz up your street credibility. Or perhaps you're a complete beginner and just want to try this language on for size. It doesn't matter what your level of skill is, this multimedia-rich site has something for you.
http://www.bbc.co.uk/education/languages/french/

GEORGIA

Georgia is named after King George II of England. The Cumberland Island National Seashore is a coastal wilderness area located in Georgia, also famous for its sea islands. The 1996 Summer Olympics were held in Atlanta. The fourth state's official tree is the live oak.

Official State Home Page:

http://www.state.ga.us/

State Symbols:

http://www.sos.state.ga.us/state_capitol/
education_corner/state_symbols.html

State Tourism:

http://www.georgia.org/tourism/

A
B
C
D
E
F
G
H
I
J
K
L
M
N
O
P
Q
R
S
T
U
V
W
X
Y
Z

A
B
C
D
E
F
G
H
I
J
K
L
M
N
O
P
Q
R
S
T
U
V
W
X
Y
Z

HAWAII

Hawaii's Mount Waialeale, on the island of Kauai, is the rainiest place in the world, with an average rainfall of over 450 inches a year. Also within this tropical state is the southernmost spot in the U.S., at Ka Lae on the Big Island of Hawaii. Hawaii comprises over 130 Pacific islands, but there are eight main islands. Its name is believed to have come from the native word *Hawaiki*, meaning "homeland." It is the 50th state, and its state tree is the candlenut. Some people in Hawaii are trying to return the state to sovereign nationhood. Please see the entry, "Hawai'i Independent and Sovereign," in the NATIVE AMERICANS AND FIRST NATIONS—NATIVE HAWAIIANS section.

Official State Home Page:

http://www.state.hi.us/

State Symbols:

http://www.gohawaii.com/hokeo/school/report.html

State Tourism:

http://www.gohawaii.com/

IDAHO

Idaho is known for its farming and its most famous crop, the Idaho potato. The deepest gorge in North America is in Hells Canyon, along the Idaho-Oregon border, measuring 7,900 feet deep. This Rocky Mountain state's official bird is the mountain bluebird. It is the 43rd state.

Official State Home Page:

http://www.state.id.us/

State Symbols:

http://www.state.id.us/aboutidaho/history.html

State Tourism:

http://www.visitid.org/

Curl up with a good URL in BOOKS AND LITERATURE!

ILLINOIS

Illinois is the Algonquin word for "warriors." The 21st state is also known as the Land of Lincoln, in homage to the 16th president, who lived and is buried in the Springfield area. The official bird of this Midwest state is the red cardinal.

Official State Home Page:

http://www.state.il.us/

State Symbols:

http://www.state.il.us/kids/learn/

State Tourism:

http://www.enjoyillinois.com/

INDIANA

The 19th state, Indiana means "land of the Indians." Indianapolis, its capital and largest city, is where the Indianapolis 500 auto race is held every year. This Midwest state's official tree is the tulip tree.

Official State Home Page:

http://www.state.in.us/

State Symbols:

http://www.state.in.us/sic/kids/

State Tourism:

http://www.enjoyindiana.com/

You can always
count on the info in MATH
AND ARITHMETIC.

IOWA

A major producer of corn and soybeans, Midwest state *Iowa* is a Native American name for "beautiful land." It is the 29th state. Its state bird is the colorful and jaunty eastern goldfinch.

Official State Home Page:

http://www.state.ia.us/

State Symbols:

http://www.traveliowa.com/iowa_facts.htm

State Tourism:

http://www.traveliowa.com/

KANSAS

The geographical center of the lower 48 states is located near Lebanon, Kansas. *Kansas* is a Lakota word meaning "south wind people." Famous for farming and wheat fields, the 34th state is also known as the mythical home of Dorothy and Toto of The Wizard of Oz.

Official State Home Page:

http://www.accesskansas.org/

State Symbols:

http://www.kansascommerce.com/0100facts.html

State Tourism:

http://www.state.ks.us/visitors.html

KENTUCKY

Kentucky, the "land of tomorrow," has one of the largest cave systems in the world, Mammoth Caves. The 15th state is also known for its many thoroughbred horse farms. Its state flower is goldenrod.

Official State Home Page:

http://www.kydirect.net/

State Symbols:

http://www.kdla.state.ky.us/links/symbols.htm

State Tourism:

http://www.kytourism.com/

NET FILES

What lighthouse is also one of the Seven Wonders of the ancient world?

Answer: The Lighthouse of Alexandria, on the island of Pharos, off Egypt, is one of the Seven Wonders of the ancient world. Built around 300 to 220 B.C., it was as tall as a modern-day 40-story building, making it the tallest structure in the world at that time. It had a miraculous mirror lit by the sun during the day and by fires at night. The light could be seen 35 miles away. By the mid-1300s it was in ruins, and for a long time its exact location was not known. Have pieces of the ancient lighthouse now been found? Discover more at http://unmuseum.mus.pa.us/pharos.htm

LOUISIANA

This southern state is where the mighty Mississippi River enters the Gulf of Mexico. Its largest city, New Orleans, is famous for its Mardi Gras celebration, held every year on the last day before Lent. The 18th state's bird is the brown pelican, which also appears on the state flag.

Official State Home Page:

http://www.state.la.us/

State Symbols:

http://www.crt.state.la.us/crt/sbcover.htm

State Tourism:

http://www.crt.state.la.us/crt/tourism.htm

MAINE

This is the state where the lobster rules. It's also the easternmost point of the U.S. mainland. The 23rd state is also famous for Acadia National Park and its rugged coastline. The state bird is the playful black-capped chickadee, and the official tree is the eastern white pine.

Official State Home Page:

http://www.state.me.us/

State Symbols:

http://www.state.me.us/sos/kids/

State Tourism:

http://www.visitmaine.com/

MARYLAND

The east coast of Maryland is near the District of Columbia, the capital of the United States. The national anthem, "The Star Spangled Banner," by Sir Francis Scott Key, was inspired by a battle in 1814 at historic Fort McHenry. Surrounding the Chesapeake Bay, much of eastern Maryland is known for its fishing industries, particularly for soft-shelled crabs. You may have read the horse story, *Misty of Chincoteague*, by Marguerite Henry. These stories were set at the Assateague National Seashore, which Maryland shares with neighboring Virginia. The seventh state, Maryland's state bird is the northern oriole.

Official State Home Page:

http://www.mec.state.md.us/

State Symbols:

http://www.mec.state.md.us/mecall.html

State Tourism:

http://www.mdisfun.org/

MASSACHUSETTS

The Pilgrims landed at Plymouth Rock, near Boston, on December 21, 1620. They later started one of the most traditional American feasts, Thanksgiving. Native Americans helped them survive. Famous folks from Massachusetts include John F. Kennedy and Louisa May Alcott. The sixth state's official flower is the mayflower.

Official State Home Page:

http://www.state.ma.us/

State Symbols:

http://www.state.ma.us/sec/cis/cismaf/mafidx.htm

State Tourism:

http://www.massvacation.com/

A B C D E F G H I J K L M N O P Q R S T U V W X Y Z

MICHIGAN

Henry Ford's Detroit auto factory began an industry that has made Michigan the center of U.S. car manufacturing. Michigan gets its name from *mici gama*, the Chippewa words meaning "great water." Michigan is in two parts, the Upper and Lower Peninsulas. It has shoreline on four of the Great Lakes: Lake Michigan, Lake Huron, Lake Erie, and Lake Superior. The 26th state's official bird is the robin.

Official State Home Page:

http://www.michigan.gov/

State Symbols:

http://www.sos.state.mi.us/kidspage/

State Tourism:

http://travel.michigan.org/

MINNESOTA

The Mississippi River starts here! Minnesota is from the Lakota word meaning "cloudy water," but it referred to the Minnesota River. This northern border state has over 15,000 lakes, left there by glaciers. The 32nd state's official bird is the common loon, and its flower is the pink-and-white lady's slipper.

Official State Home Page:

http://www.state.mn.us/

State Symbols:

http://www.state.mn.us/aam/

State Tourism:

http://www.exploreminnesota.com/

NET FILES

The foil, the épée, and the sabre refer to what?

a) Essential items for your next barbecue
b) Those little bones in your ear
c) The three weapons of fencing

Answer: C. Fencing is that sport where the players, well, have a sword fight—you know, with those cagelike masks on their faces. Fencing is a sport and, to many, an art. Concentration, quickness, and agility are all very important to the fencer. At *http://library.thinkquest. org/15340/tutorial.html,* find out how fencing started, and how it is done, scored, and won. It's not just for swashbucklers!

MISSISSIPPI

Southern state Mississippi's history dates back to the 1500s, when Spanish explorers visited the area. The French were first to settle it, however, in 1699. The 20th state was a center of attention in the 1960s with the activities of the civil rights movement. The state flower is the sweetly scented magnolia.

Official State Home Page:

http://www.state.ms.us/

State Symbols:

http://www.senate.gov/~cochran/facts.htm

State Tourism:

http://www.state.ms.us/its/msportal.nsf/WebForm/ Tourism?OpenDocument

A B C D E F G H I J K L M N O P Q R S T U V W X Y Z

An Atlas of Cyberspaces

You're not likely to take this atlas with you on your next road trip. But you may find it fascinating if you do much traveling on the Web. It's a funky collection of maps that visually depict various digital territories. Some look like a traditional real-world map, while others are much more abstract, like the one showing the structure of Web sites connected by their hypertext links. A must-see! *http://www.cybergeography.org/atlas/atlas.html*

MISSOURI

Two major rivers, the Missouri and the Mississippi, meet in the 24th state. Samuel Clemens, also known as Mark Twain, lived in Hannibal, Missouri, on the Mississippi River. The Ozark Mountains in this state contain more than 400 caves. A dam on the Osage River holds back the Lake of the Ozarks, one of the largest man-made lakes in the world. The hawthorne is the official state flower.

Official State Home Page:

http://www.state.mo.us/

State Symbols:

http://www.visitmo.com/d2k/servlet/
    internet.Static?page=dynamic/u/root/facts/
    default.html

State Tourism:

http://www.missouritourism.org/

MONTANA

Montana is "Big Sky Country," a nickname that came from the wide-open spaces that dominate the eastern grasslands. However, the Rocky Mountains in the west are responsible for its name, the Spanish word for "mountains." The 41st state's official tree is the ponderosa pine.

Official State Home Page:

http://www.state.mt.us/

State Symbols:

http://kids.state.mt.us/facts.htm

State Tourism:

http://travel.state.mt.us/

NEBRASKA

Nebraska's name is from the Omaha word meaning "broad water," referring to the Platte River. The Agate Fossil Beds National Monument contains bones from animals over 22 million years old. This Great Plains state is known for farming and grazing land. The official tree of the 37th state is the cottonwood.

Official State Home Page:

http://www.state.ne.us/

State Symbols:

http://visitnebraska.org/nefacts/quickref/

State Tourism:

http://visitnebraska.org/

What did grandma do when she was a kid? There is a list of questions to ask in GENEALOGY AND FAMILY HISTORY.

A B C D E F G H I J K L M N O P Q R S T **U** V W X Y Z

NEVADA

Hoover Dam, on the border between Nevada and Arizona, is one of the tallest dams in the world. Tourists from around the world visit Las Vegas for its gambling and entertainment. The official flower of the 36th state is the pungent sagebrush.

Official State Home Page:

http://silver.state.nv.us/

State Symbols:

http://www.travelnevada.com/nevada_info.asp

State Tourism:

http://www.travelnevada.com/

NEW HAMPSHIRE

This state's motto is "Live free or die." Although New Hampshire was the ninth state to be admitted into the United States, it was the first colony to declare its independence from Britain. Its state flower is the sweetly scented purple lilac.

Official State Home Page:

http://www.state.nh.us/

State Symbols:

http://www.state.nh.us/nhinfo/

State Tourism:

http://www.visitnh.gov/

NEW JERSEY

The third state admitted to the Union was New Jersey. Northeastern New Jersey is densely populated, with close ties to New York City. It is also known for Atlantic City, a popular seaside resort. The state flower is the purple violet.

Official State Home Page:

http://www.state.nj.us/

State Symbols:

http://www.state.nj.us/hangout/yourworld.html

State Tourism:

http://www.state.nj.us/nfvisitnj.html

NEW MEXICO

The 47th state has many natural wonders. Carlsbad Caverns National Park contains one of the world's largest cave systems. This western desert state claims the yucca as its official flower and the roadrunner as its bird.

Official State Home Page:

http://www.state.nm.us/

State Symbols:

http://www.state.nm.us/state/FastFacts/

State Tourism:

http://www.newmexico.org/

NEW YORK

From New York City to the Adirondack Mountains to Niagara Falls, New York has a diverse array of sights. Its history dates back to the 1620s, when the Dutch colonized Manhattan Island. The Baseball Hall of Fame is located in Cooperstown. The 11th state's official tree is the sugar maple. This state also has an official muffin!

Official State Home Page:

http://www.state.ny.us/

State Symbols:

http://www.iloveny.state.ny.us/facts.htm

State Tourism:

http://www.iloveny.state.ny.us/

A B C D E F G H I J K L M N O P Q R S T U V W X Y Z

A
B
C
D
E
F
G
H
I
J
K
L
M
N
O
P
Q
R
S
T
U
V
W
X
Y
Z

NORTH CAROLINA

Orville Wright made his historic first flight at coastal Kitty Hawk, North Carolina. The first English settlement in the Americas was made on Roanoke Island in 1587, but three years later, the village was found abandoned and in ruins. What happened to these people remains a mystery to this day. The 12th state's official tree is the long-leafed pine.

Official State Home Page:

http://www.ncgov.com/

State Symbols:

http://www.secretary.state.nc.us/kidspg/
    homepage.asp

State Tourism:

http://www.visitnc.com/

Carbon Is 4 Ever

Your name is Bond . . . Carbon Bond. Your mission is to learn about carbon and its components. So, spend some time doing that before playing Atom Casino and the other games. If you don't, you won't be able to pit your skills against the final game. Every mission will teach you something new about carbon, and the game that follows tests your knowledge. If you complete a mission, you get a code word. Once you've finished all four missions, you're ready for Mission Omega, the final challenge. Don't try to skip ahead. You need the code words to play Mission Omega. This site was created by students for the ThinkQuest competition. *http://library.thinkquest.org/C005377/*

> There's some funny business going on in the CIRCUSES AND CLOWNS section!

NORTH DAKOTA

This state is famous for its uneven territory known as the Badlands. The Badlands were justly named by early travelers, because they are almost impossible to cross. *Dakota* is a Lakota word, meaning "friend." North Dakota's official flower is the wild prairie rose. It is the 39th state.

Official State Home Page:

http://discovernd.com/

State Symbols:

http://www.ndtourism.com/info.html

State Tourism:

http://www.ndtourism.com/

OHIO

Ohio is an Iroquois word, meaning "good river." Ohio was one of the ancient homes of the Mound Builders, who built thousands of earthen burial and ceremonial mounds, many of which can be seen today. The Pro Football Hall of Fame is located in Canton. The 17th state's official tree is the buckeye.

Official State Home Page:

http://www.state.oh.us/

State Symbols:

http://www.oplin.lib.oh.us/products/ohiodefined/
    message.html

State Tourism:

http://www.ohiotourism.com/

OKLAHOMA

Oklahoma gets its name from a Choctaw word, meaning "red man." The 46th state's official tree is the redbud. Yahoo! The National Cowboy Hall of Fame is in Oklahoma City.

Official State Home Page:

http://www.state.ok.us/

State Symbols:

http://www.otrd.state.ok.us/StudentGuide/

State Tourism:

http://www.otrd.state.ok.us/

OREGON

The deepest lake in the United States is Crater Lake, in Crater Lake National Park, with depths to 1,932 feet. This lake is located inside an ancient volcano and has no water flowing in or out. Oregon's west coast is known for its dense woods and beautiful, mountainous scenery. Its state tree is the Douglas fir. It is the 33rd state.

Official State Home Page:

http://www.state.or.us/

State Symbols:

http://www.econ.state.or.us/kidrptf.htm

State Tourism:

http://www.traveloregon.com/

Safeguard your privacy online! Don't give anyone your name, address, or other identifying information without reading the site's privacy policy.

NET FILES

What extremely well-known science fiction movie was partially filmed in a place where it is so hot that people live underground?

Answer: The movie saw *Star Wars*, and Tunisia was the site of Luke Skywalker's uncle's moisture farm on Tatooine. Find out more at http://imdb.com/Trivia?0076759

PENNSYLVANIA

Pennsylvania was settled by Quakers from Great Britain in the 1680s. In 1863, during the Civil War, a famous battle was fought in Gettysburg. You'll also find the Liberty Bell in Philadelphia. Pennsylvania, which is the second state, has a small border on one of the Great Lakes, Lake Erie. Its official bird is the ruffed grouse.

Official State Home Page:

http://www.state.pa.us/

State Symbols:

http://www.state.pa.us/kids/

State Tourism:

http://www.experiencepa.com/

A
B
C
D
E
F
G
H
I
J
K
L
M
N
O
P
Q
R
S
T
U
V
W
X
Y
Z

A
B
C
D
E
F
G
H
I
J
K
L
M
N
O
P
Q
R
S
T
U
V
W
X
Y
Z

2GOOD
2MISS

The Locker Room . . . Sports for Kids!

Do you need basic information on how to hold a bat, kick a football, serve a volleyball, or shoot a hockey puck? Get it here. Besides "skills and drills," you'll find the rules of these sports and many others, their histories, fun facts about them, and a glossary of terms. There is also advice on how to do warm-up exercises and how to deal with team problems. If you don't have a big brother or sister to teach you this stuff, this page is the next best thing.
http://member.aol.com/msdaizy/sports/locker.html

RHODE ISLAND

Rhode Island is the smallest state in the U.S. It is also the 13th of the original 13 colonies and the 13th state. The first factory in the U.S. was built there in the 1790s. This East Coast state's official bird is the Rhode Island red chicken.

Official State Home Page:

http://www.info.state.ri.us/

State Symbols:

http://www.visitrhodeisland.com/facts/facts_fr.html

State Tourism:

http://www.visitrhodeisland.com/

Lots of monkey-business in MAMMALS.

SOUTH CAROLINA

The Civil War started in South Carolina, at Fort Sumter, in Charleston harbor. This historic East Coast city is very well-preserved. Hilton Head and Myrtle Beach are well-known and popular seaside vacation sites. The eighth state's official bird is the Carolina wren.

Official State Home Page:

http://www.myscgov.com/

State Symbols:

http://www.state.sc.us/histro.html

State Tourism:

http://www.discoversouthcarolina.com/

SOUTH DAKOTA

Famous Mount Rushmore is located in the Black Hills of South Dakota. Four 60-foot heads of U.S. presidents have been sculpted on the side of a mountain. The Black Hills look "black" from a distance because they are covered with dense pine forests. The 40th state's official bird is the ring-necked pheasant.

Official State Home Page:

http://www.state.sd.us/

State Symbols:

http://www.state.sd.us/state/sdsym.htm

State Tourism:

http://www.travelsd.com/

TENNESSEE

Tennessee, the 16th state, is known for the Great Smoky Mountains National Park. Nashville is famous as a world center for country music. The official state flower is the iris.

Official State Home Page:

http://www.state.tn.us/

State Symbols:

http://www.state.tn.us/education/mstudent.htm

State Tourism:

http://www.tourism.state.tn.us/index.html

TEXAS

Cattle and oil dominate the economy of Texas. It's the second-largest state in area, after Alaska. A famous battle in 1836, between thousands of Mexicans and a few hundred Texans, took place at an old Spanish mission called the Alamo, located in San Antonio. "Remember the Alamo" is a famous battle cry. Texas is the 28th state, and its flower is the bluebonnet.

Official State Home Page:

http://www.state.tx.us/

State Symbols:

http://www.state.tx.us/texasinfo/

State Tourism:

http://www.traveltex.com/

Let balloonists take you to new heights in AVIATION AND AIRPLANES.

UTAH

Utah comes from a Navajo word, meaning "upper." Salt Lake City is the spiritual center of the Church of Jesus Christ of Latter-day Saints (Mormon) religion. The Great Salt Lake in Utah is eight times saltier than the ocean. Utah is the 45th state, and its official bird is the seagull.

Official State Home Page:

http://www.utah.gov/

State Symbols:

http://www.utah.gov/about/symbols.html

State Tourism:

http://www.state.ut.us/visiting.html

NET FILES

Which large, plated dinosaur is known for having a brain the size of a walnut?

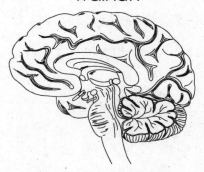

Answer: The stegosaurus. Its brain power was so limited that the animal needed a "second brain" in its hips in order to control its legs. Check out all the dinos at http://kids.infoplease. com/ipka/A0770763.html

A
B
C
D
E
F
G
H
I
J
K
L
M
N
O
P
Q
R
S
T
U
V
W
X
Y
Z

VERMONT

Vert and *mont* are French for "green" and "mountain," respectively. The Green Mountains are located in Vermont. One interesting fact about Vermont is that it has no major cities. This makes it the most rural state in the country. Its official flower is the red clover, and it is the 14th state.

Official State Home Page:

http://www.state.vt.us/

State Symbols:

http://www.1-800-vermont.com/travelvt/abtvt/aboutvermont.shtml

State Tourism:

http://www.1-800-vermont.com/

Who is credited with inventing the concept of computer programming?

Answer: Ada Byron Lovelace (1815–1851) is credited with the invention of programming, for her work with Charles Babbage's analytical engine. A military programming language, Ada, is named after her in commemoration. Read more about this mathematician at http://www.agnesscott.edu/lriddle/women/love.htm

VIRGINIA

Virginia has been home to both George Washington and Thomas Jefferson, and you can tour their historic homes today. Jamestown became the first permanent English settlement in 1607. It is the tenth state, and the dogwood is both its official tree and flower.

Official State Home Page:

http://www.state.va.us/

State Symbols:

http://legis.state.va.us./vaonline/v.htm

State Tourism:

http://www.virginia.org/

WASHINGTON

Coastal Washington state is known for its many natural features. The Cascade Range is where Mount St. Helens erupted in 1980. Olympic National Park contains vast sections of ancient rain forest. It is the 42nd state, and the rhododendron is the official flower.

Official State Home Page:

http://access.wa.gov/

State Symbols:

http://access.wa.gov/kids/

State Tourism:

http://www.tourism.wa.gov/

WEST VIRGINIA

West Virginia's natural features are dominated by the Appalachian Mountains. Mining in these mountains is a major industry, and coal is the main product. The 35th state's official bird is the brilliantly colored cardinal.

Official State Home Page:

http://www.state.wv.us/

State Symbols:

http://www.callwva.com/facts/wvfacts.cfm

State Tourism:

http://www.callwva.com/

WISCONSIN

Wisconsin is a state with over 8,000 lakes, carved out by glaciers long ago. Milk and cheese are major products. Bordered by two Great Lakes, Lake Superior and Lake Michigan, Wisconsin is the 30th state. Its official flower is the wood violet.

Official State Home Page:

http://www.wisconsin.gov/

State Symbols:

http://www.wisconsin.gov/state/core/
   wisconsin_state_symbols.html

State Tourism:

http://www.travelwisconsin.com/

> You know something the Net doesn't——create your own home page! Look in the INTERNET- WEB BUILDING AND HTML section to find out how!

WYOMING

Wyoming means "large prairie place" in Algonquin. Yellowstone National Park is famous for its geysers and hot springs (fictional "Jellystone Park" is where Yogi Bear and Boo-Boo live). This rugged Rocky Mountain state was the 44th to be admitted to the Union. Its official flower is the Indian paintbrush.

Official State Home Page:

http://www.state.wy.us/

State Symbols:

http://www.state.wy.us/kids.html

State Tourism:

http://wyomingtourism.org/tourism/index.cfm

TERRITORIES

AMERICAN SAMOA

American Samoa

Congressman Eni Faleomavaega is American Samoa's delegate to the House of Representatives. *Talofa* is the traditional greeting. At his home page, you can read his statements before the House, see legislation he has sponsored and cosponsored, and catch up on current American Samoa news.

http://www.house.gov/faleomavaega/

American Samoa Office of Tourism

This official site offers a history of the islands, information on language and culture, maps, and even a link to today's weather forecast. Should you need to experience sunny, 80-degree beaches, this site offers everything you need to plan your family's vacation, too.

http://www.amsamoa.com/tourism/

A B C D E F G H I J K L M N O P Q R S T **U** V W X Y Z

A
B
C
D
E
F
G
H
I
J
K
L
M
N
O
P
Q
R
S
T
U
V
W
X
Y
Z

National Park of American Samoa

This 76-square-mile island group sits in the middle of the South Pacific Ocean, 2,600 miles from Hawaii. Its citizens are considered U.S. nationals and can freely enter the United States. American Samoa has a large tuna fishery; other exports include coconuts, taro, yams, bananas, and breadfruit. You can't make a sandwich out of breadfruit, by the way. Well, maybe you can in the Sandwich Islands, but not in American Samoa! If you go to this site, you'll learn all about the national park and the animals and plants you'd see there.

http://www.nps.gov/npsa/home.htm

BAKER ISLAND

The World Factbook - Baker Island

This is a teeny, low-lying atoll in the North Pacific Ocean, about one-half of the way from Hawaii to Australia. It was mined for its guano deposits until 1891. The birds are still there, the guano is still there, but you'll need a permit to visit. Only offshore anchorage is possible, and be advised that there are no malls or fast-food restaurants. This island is also a national wildlife refuge. For a brief history of Baker Island, try the U.S. Department of the Interior's Fact Sheet at <*http://www.doi.gov/oia/ oiafacts.html#page7*>.

http://www.odci.gov/cia/publications/factbook/geos/ fq.html

NET FILES

The comic strip "Peanuts" was first printed on October 2, 1950. In what year did Snoopy the beagle first appear standing on two legs instead of four?

Answer: Snoopy first stood on two legs in 1958. You'll find more Snoopy facts at http://www.snoopy.com/ comics/peanuts/d_history/html/date/1958.html

---

GUAM

Guam's Official Congressional Web Site

Robert A. Underwood is Guam's delegate to the House of Representatives, and he has a terrific Web site. Find out about Guam's history, view some maps, check out the current time in Guam, and read current news. There is up-to-date information on Guam's quest to become a commonwealth with the right of self-determination.

http://www.house.gov/underwood/welcome.html

Legends of Guam

Sirena loved to swim in the sea. One day, she forgot her chores and spent the day swimming. When she did not come home, her angry mother said she should just become a fish if she loved the sea so much! Sirena's godmother quickly said, "But let the part of her that belongs to me remain." Sirena, still swimming, suddenly felt strange. She looked down and realized the lower part of her body had become a fish. The legend of Sirena is from Guam. Read more about the story and see a statue of Sirena.

http://ns.gov.gu/legends.html

The Official Guam U.S.A. Web Site

Hafa Adai! Located near the international date line, Guam is "where America's Day Begins." This island is in the West Pacific, 3,700 miles from Hawaii. Around Guam, there are more than 300 varieties of coral, which supports a rich diversity of fish— great for snorkeling. Scuba experiences include World War II shipwrecks for experienced divers, as well as plenty of spots for beginners. Many pages contain video clips, including clips on Chamorro songs, Chamorro culture, and local wildlife.

http://www.gov.gu/

HOWLAND ISLAND

The World Factbook - Howland Island

This tiny, sandy island is in the North Pacific Ocean, about one-half of the way from Hawaii to Australia. It's a national wildlife refuge, and you need permission from the U.S. Department of the Interior to visit it. The island is famous because of someone who never made it there. In 1937, an airstrip was constructed there as a refueling stop on the round-the-world flight attempt of Amelia Earhart and Fred Noonan. They had left Lae, Papua New Guinea, for Howland Island, but something happened, and they were never seen again. Their disappearance is one of the world's great unsolved mysteries—or is it? You can read about recent developments at The Earhart Project at *<http://www.tighar.org/Projects/Earhart/AEdescr.html>*. Earhart Light, on the island's west coast, is a day beacon built in memory of the lost aviatrix. The airfield is no longer serviceable.

http://www.odci.gov/cia/publications/factbook/geos/hq.html

JARVIS ISLAND

The World Factbook - Jarvis Island

This tiny coral island is in the South Pacific Ocean, about one-half of the way from Hawaii to the Cook Islands. It is a favorite nesting and roosting area for seabirds, and until the late 1880s, guano was mined there. Bird droppings are a rich source of fertilizer, but it seems like a long way to go to get some. You can't visit Jarvis Island without permission of the U.S. Department of the Interior, since it is considered a national wildlife refuge. They offer a little bit more information here: *<http://www.doi.gov/oia/oiafacts.html#page23>*.

http://www.odci.gov/cia/publications/factbook/geos/dq.html

Explore underwater archaeology in SHIPS AND SHIPWRECKS.

NET FILES

What's the most common mineral on Earth?

Answer: Quartz. It occurs in many different forms and colors. Find out more at http://www.minerals.net/mineral/silicate/tecto/quartz/quartz.htm. Some people classify water as a mineral, so we'll accept that answer, too. See http://www.minerals.net/mineral/oxides/water/water.htm for an explanation of this.

JOHNSTON ATOLL

The World Factbook - Johnston Atoll

This strategically located atoll group is in the North Pacific Ocean, about one-third of the way from Hawaii to the Marshall Islands. It's closed to the public and has been used for testing nuclear weapons. About 300 people work there on military and other projects. All food and other equipment has to be imported, but they do have excellent communications through an underwater cable link and satellites. Maybe they will get a home page on their own server soon! The U.S. Department of the Interior offers a bit more information here at *<http://www.doi.gov/oia/oiafacts.html#page24>*.

http://www.odci.gov/cia/publications/factbook/geos/jq.html

A B C D E F G H I J K L M N O P Q R S T **U** V W X Y Z

KINGMAN REEF

The World Factbook - Kingman Reef

We're talking very tiny: only one square kilometer of land area. This reef is in the North Pacific Ocean, about one-half of the way from Hawaii to American Samoa. It's only about one meter in elevation, so it's often awash with waves! If you go, bring your boots, but you'll need permission from the U.S. Navy. This reef was used as a way station by Pan American flying boats in 1937 and 1938. Now, it's basically known as a maritime hazard. You can find a few more details here at the U.S. Department of the Interior's Fact Sheet at <*http://www.doi.gov/oia/ oiafacts.html#page26*>.

http://www.odci.gov/cia/publications/factbook/geos/ kq.html

MIDWAY ISLANDS

Midway Atoll National Wildlife Refuge

If you read the most interesting history of this remote island, you'll know why it has been in the possession of the U.S. Navy for many years. However, on April 3, 1997, Secretary of the Navy John Dalton presented the "key to Midway" (in the shape of a Laysan albatross) to Department of the Interior Assistant Secretary Bonnie Cohen. Now Midway Atoll National Wildlife Refuge is managed by the U.S. Fish and Wildlife Service and visitors are welcome. This site explains how to get there and what to expect.

http://www.r1.fws.gov/midway/

The World Factbook - Midway Islands

This is an atoll group in the North Pacific Ocean, about one-third of the way from Hawaii to Tokyo, Japan. Over 400 U.S. military personnel are stationed there, and the area has recently been opened to the public. This is a famous World War II battle site, with many sunken wrecks in the area. For a view from those who served there, try the Past Residents of Midway Island page at <*http:// www.silverlink.net/midway/*>.

http://www.odci.gov/cia/publications/factbook/geos/ mq.html

NAVASSA

Navassa Island

The webmaster must be a fan of Navassa Island, because he's created a page with maps, photos, and information that rivals many. Gaze at the lighthouse, rising more than 160 feet off the hillside. View the lighthouse keeper's house, now abandoned and in ruins. Access to Navassa is hazardous (check the photos: rope ladders going up the rocky cliffs) and is allowed only by permission from the U.S. Department of the Interior.

http://members.aol.com/davidpb4/navassa.html

The World Factbook - Navassa Island

This Caribbean island is strategically located, about one-fourth of the way from Haiti to Jamaica, south of Cuba. Haiti disputes the U.S. claim to the territory. Haitians fishing there often camp on the island, which has steep cliffs and is populated by goats and cactus. There's a little more information at the U.S. Department of the Interior's Fact Sheet at <*http://www.doi.gov/oia/oiafacts.html#page29*>.

http://www.odci.gov/cia/publications/factbook/geos/ bq.html

NORTHERN MARIANA ISLANDS

Commonwealth of the Northern Mariana Islands

Between Guam and the Tropic of Cancer lie the 14 volcanic islands that make up this commonwealth. At this official site, you can read about them all. The island's inhabitants are U.S. citizens, and tourism is a major industry.

http://www.mariana-islands.gov.mp/

A B C D E F G H I J K L M N O P Q R S T U V W X Y Z

Curl up with a good Internet site.

Marianas Visitors Authority

Saipan is the largest island in this group, and it's famous for its crystal-clear, warm waters, perfect for viewing the coral reefs. Tinian is still partially used by a U.S. military presence, but on the rest of the island they expect large casinos to be built soon. Rota, a third island, offers exciting diving opportunities, as well as golf. The U.S. Department of the Interior gives a bit more information here at *<http://www.doi.gov/oia/oiafacts.html#page9>*.

http://www.visit-marianas.com/

PALMYRA ATOLL

★ Palmyra Atoll: Rainforest of the Sea

It's one of the most remote areas on Earth, and that makes it a perfect place to study an untouched ecosystem. Scientists are examining the old growth forests and coral reefs around Palmyra Atoll, and this site invites you along, too. View stunning underwater photography, video, and other multimedia.

http://www.oneworldjourneys.com/palmyra/

The World Factbook - Palmyra Atoll

Administered by the U.S. Department of the Interior, this atoll group lies in the North Pacific Ocean, about one-half of the way from Hawaii to American Samoa. It has only 12 square kilometers in land area, and its many tiny islets are densely covered with vegetation and coconut palms. The U.S. Department of the Interior's Fact Sheet at *<http://www.doi.gov/oia/oiafacts.html#page31>* offers a history of the atoll.

http://www.odci.gov/cia/publications/factbook/geos/lq.html

PUERTO RICO

Bioluminescent Bay - Vieques Island

One of the natural wonders of the world is "Bio Bay," home to magical glowing waters. Actually, it's not much of a mystery: each gallon of bay water contains up to 720,000 nontoxic dinoflagellates. When they are disturbed—by a boat paddle, or a hand in the water—they emit a soft eerie blue light, like a firefly. People come from all over the world to witness this phenomenon. Unfortunately, the bay is threatened by pollution and other development. Find out how you can help!

http://www.biobay.com/

Escape to Puerto Rico

The island of Puerto Rico is the smallest and the most eastern island of the Greater Antilles, in the Caribbean. *Puerto Rico* is Spanish for "rich port." Puerto Ricans are U.S. citizens. You may have heard of these famous Puerto Ricans: musician Pablo Casals, sports figure Roberto Clemente, and actress Rita Moreno. This site offers a good overview to the people and culture of the island, its government, and, of course, travel tips.

http://escape.topuertorico.com/

Interactive Model Railroad

This one is pretty cool. You get to give commands to an actual model train at the University of Ulm in Germany! You pick the train you want to control, tell it which station to go to, and if you're quick (and lucky) enough, you're in charge. A box on the page gives the domain name of whoever happens to be controlling the train at the time.
http://rr-vs.informatik.uni-ulm.de/rr/

A
B
C
D
E
F
G
H
I
J
K
L
M
N
O
P
Q
R
S
T
U
V
W
X
Y
Z

A
B
C
D
E
F
G
H
I
J
K
L
M
N
O
P
Q
R
S
T
U
V
W
X
Y
Z

Where the Waves Are

Sure, you can surf the Internet, but can you build the perfect wave for a surfer? Juggle adjustments for the local weather, intensity, and distance of a storm, and then—surf it! Are you headed for a wipeout or a round of applause? Check this site on the physics of surfing and wave formation.
http://www.discovery.com/news/features/surfing/ surfing.html

The Puerto Rico Statehood Web Site

Explore the various choices for Puerto Rico's future: commonwealth, sovereignty, or statehood. Check it out—there is even a picture of a U.S. flag with 51 stars! If you favor the independence route, there are links that support that view as well.

http://www.puertorico51.org/

U.S. VIRGIN ISLANDS

Congresswoman Donna Christian-Christensen

As the elected delegate to the House of Representatives, Congresswoman Christian-Green sits on several House committees. She holds a medical degree and works for many children's and environmental issues. At her site, you can track her statements in Congress, as well as learn more about the U.S. Virgin Islands. There is also a background history of the area illustrated with many beautiful photos.

http://www.house.gov/christian-christensen/

> ## Nothing to do?
> ## Check CRAFTS AND HOBBIES
> ## for some ideas.

The U.S. Virgin Islands Tourist Guide

This tourist guide to the Virgin Islands contains links to the islands of St. Croix, St. Thomas, St. John, and Water Island. Find information here on the islands' history and fishing, plus pictures and more.

http://www.usvi.net/usvi/

The World Factbook - United States Virgin Islands

The Caribbean islands of St. Thomas, St. John, and St. Croix are known as the U.S. Virgin Islands, and their residents are U.S. citizens. Columbus stopped there in 1493. Tourism has become a huge industry; there is a national park on St. John, an island famous for its coral reefs.

http://www.odci.gov/cia/publications/factbook/geos/ vq.html

WAKE ISLAND

The World Factbook - Wake Island

This almost flat volcanic island group is in the North Pacific Ocean, about two-thirds of the way from Hawaii to the Northern Mariana Islands. About 300 people live there, and a U.S. military base is located there. It is also used as an emergency stopover for transpacific commercial aviation. Also known as Wake Atoll, the U.S. Department of the Interior offers a bit more information here *<http:// www.doi.gov/oia/oiafacts.html#page44>*.

http://www.odci.gov/cia/publications/factbook/geos/ wq.html

VIDEO AND COMPUTER GAMES

Cheat Code, Hints, and FAQ

This huge archive of pointers will help you get past that last dragon, find the sole remaining treasure, and discover the end of the rainbow in games made for everything from game consoles to Macs and PCs. There's also information on GameShark, Game Genie, and more. Do see Son of Net-mom's Top Sites hotlist at the beginning of the book for his recommendations.

http://vgstrategies.miningco.com/library/misc/blcheats.htm

GameFAQs

In the old days, the game puzzles were pretty simple. You went west three moves, then south until you came to the rattlesnake, then east until you came to the wizard who gave you something of value. These days, though, you have to remember multiple plot lines, memorize a whole library of magical items, and become a veteran of hours of game play before you can come out a winner. No wonder everyone wants to find the hidden cheat codes, the back doors the designers used when they were play testing the games. Many of them are collected here.

http://www.gamefaqs.com/

The Good, the Bad, and the Pong; a Site on Video Games and Kids

This site briefly covers the history of video games and then launches into a study of how gaming affects kids and their schoolwork. Follow the survey methods to the results pages and see what happened when kids gave up video games for two weeks. This site was created by students for the ThinkQuest Junior competition.

http://tqjunior.advanced.org/5153/home.htm

Staring off into space? Discover ASTRONOMY, SPACE, AND SPACE EXPLORATION!

Mario Party 3

You're invited to a party! A party with Mario and his friends is happening right now, online, and you can play 70 "mini-games" inspired by this quirky cast of characters. Most are memory games or games of skill, and all are fun!

http://www.marioparty3.com/

Nintendo

Visit this site for the latest games, news, and inside information on dozens of Nintendo games. Yes, indeed, the site has cheat codes for N64, Game Boy, Game Cube, Super NES, NES, and Virtual Boy. Just look in the code bank. Coming soon: compare scores and get hints from other players—just click into the NSider area.

http://www.nintendo.com/

Pokémon School of Tech

"I was thinking to myself, 'Well this should be rather easy.' I thought wrong, she brought back the Squirtle, brought up the Magikarp and evolved it into a Gyrados while I had a Hitmonchan out. I was doing very little damage when I did damage, and then she got out her Blastoise. It looked like I was pretty much gone, but then I brought out my Mewtwo, used Energy Removals on her Blastoise and took out her Gyrados. I kept denying her energy and she eventually lost." Do you understand what the player is talking about? If you play Pokémon cards, this is your site for hints on decks, strategy, tournament results, and lots more. In the Links section, find your way to the official rules and a tutorial or two.

http://www.pokeschool.com/

A B C D E F G H I J K L M N O P Q R S T U **V** W X Y Z

A B C D E F G H I J K L M N O P Q R S T U **V** W X Y Z

Pokémon World

It's a game! No, wait, it's a cartoon! Hold on—it's a trading card game! Well, the only thing everyone agrees on is that Pokémon is a phenomenon! Look almost anywhere and you'll see Pokémon clothing, toys, even a breakfast cereal! Keep track of who's who in Pokémon World by consulting the Pokédex, an online encyclopedia detailing everything you need to know. This is the official Pokémon site, so you are assured that the information is correct. For official rules, league competition, and more, you want The Wizards of the Coast at *<http://www.wizards.com/pokemon/>*.

http://www.pokemon.com/

Sega.com

Is it a computer? Is it a game console? Is it both? It comes with a 56Kbps modem, so you can play a global game, and you can even get a fishing pole controller for it! It's Dreamcast, the latest and greatest video gaming system. Visit this site to learn all about it and other Sega products, such as the VMU (Virtual Memory Unit). Trade hints and tips on the community bulletin boards. You have to sign up, but it is free.

http://www.sega.com/

Sign the Declaration of Independence

Would you have signed the Declaration of Independence? It meant you were a traitor to the King. Find out what else it meant, and (if you still want to), select a quill and "sign" the document yourself. If you have a printer handy, you can keep a copy for your wall.
http://www.archives.gov/join_the_signers/sign_the _declaration/sign_the_declaration.html

REVIEWS

Kids Video Game Reviews

Video game sites are usually full of games for adults, but this one reviews games that are age appropriate for kids. Games for kids are rated by staff on a 1-to-10 score. A "1" means "Lame, don't even rent it" while a "10" means "Wow! Get it now!" There are also previews, feature stories, and—of course—links.

http://www.kidsvideogames.com/html/reviews.html

Meta Critic - Games

Find out which games are worth the money, and which ones are best left on the shelf. This site combines reviews from more than 30 gaming publications into one convenient spot.

http://www.metacritic.com/games/

National Institute on Media and the Family

This site makes the point that when a child watches TV, he's an observer. But when he plays a video or computer game, he's a participant. That's why it's critical that he doesn't "participate" in games that will desensitize him to violence. Kids should also avoid those games with themes that are "too old" for him. Parents can check out this site for video and computer game reviews, as well as movie and TV recommendations.

http://www.mediafamily.org/

VIDEO AND SPY CAMS

See also BIRDS; CATS; COMPUTERS—SOFTWARE ARCHIVES; FARMING AND AGRICULTURE; GAMES AND FUN—ONLINE GAMES; HOLIDAYS; INSECTS AND SPIDERS; MAMMALS; and RAILROADS AND TRAINS

AfriCam

Would you like to see wild animals in Africa? You can, right now, via a live camera network. Select any of 15 different views of water holes, grasslands, and other likely viewing vantage points. Some areas have lights so you can see the animals at night. You might spot a leopard or *zee* a zebra. *Remane* calm if you see a lion.

http://www.africam.com/

Bay Area Live Cameras

Ah, the City by the Bay, where every nightclub crooner always manages to leave his or her heart. Now you can visit San Francisco over the Net and see a new view every five minutes. Station KPIX has a camera high atop the Fairmont Hotel on Nob Hill. Since the camera pans from the Golden Gate Bridge to the Bay Bridge, you may be able to catch video of both bridges, plus views of downtown, the famous Coit Tower, Fisherman's Wharf, the Marina district, and other attractions. Better hold onto your heart, though! If you miss the sunset, don't worry: you can view a series of time-lapse photos and relive the whole thing.

http://www.kpix.com/live/

CamZone

You might decide to check out the panda cam, enjoy the surf with some swimmers at a California beach, or just kick back and watch planes land. Is the Net too cool, or what?

http://www.camzone.com/

Corn Cam

Everyone needs a little peace and quiet now and then. Here's a good place to get it. Sit back and watch the corn grow in an Iowa field. Check the archive to see how far it's come. Be sure to keep an eye out for any famous baseball players.

http://www.iowafarmer.com/corncam/corn.html

★ Discovery Online - Live Cams

The view of the world varies here. As we look at the selection of cams on the Web today, we see weddings in Las Vegas, a California beach, puppies, and naked mole-rats. So many cams, so little bandwidth.

http://www.discovery.com/cams/cams.html

Ghost Cam

Is there a ghost in the Willard Library? The cameras are kept on all night so people can watch for evidence of "The Lady in Grey." Some people have spotted lots of other things—be sure to check the "spoof" section of this site in Evansville, Indiana.

http://www.courierpress.com/ghost/

Giraffe Cam

You've got to see the giraffes at the Cheyenne Mountain Zoo in Colorado Springs, Colorado. Sometimes they are in, sometimes they are out, but keep tuning in and you're bound to see a giraffe or two eventually. We did! They are normally visible from 10 A.M. to 4 P.M. (mountain time). This zoo is famous for successfully breeding giraffes in captivity.

http://c.unclone.com/zoocam.html

How to Set Up a Webcam

Here at Pollywood Farm, Net-mom has visions of a webcam on the pond, so everyone can see what water lilies are in bloom today. Then there was the idea of the cat cam, to see which cats are napping on the deck at any given time. This Web site tells you how to broadcast your own video to the Net.

http://www.zdnet.com/zdhelp/stories/main/
  0,5594,2412377,00.html

A
B
C
D
E
F
G
H
I
J
K
L
M
N
O
P
Q
R
S
T
U
V
W
X
Y
Z

A
B
C
D
E
F
G
H
I
J
K
L
M
N
O
P
Q
R
S
T
U
V
W
X
Y
Z

Bread Bag Nightmares

Explore the exciting world of molds by experimenting with various types of bread and common household items, like lemon juice and sugar water. Soon, a colorful and fuzzy mold farm will be yours. Other cool projects at this site include Fun with Fomites, Biosphere in a Bottle, and Yeast on the Rise. You can also help Sam Sleuth Stalk the Mysterious Microbe.
http://www.microbe.org/experiment/nightmares.asp

★ Interactive Model Railroad

This one is pretty cool. You get to give commands to an actual model train at the University of Ulm in Germany! You pick the train you want to control, tell it which station to go to, and if you're quick (and lucky) enough, you're in charge. A box on the page gives the domain name of whoever happens to be controlling the train at the time.

http://rr-vs.informatik.uni-ulm.de/rr/

★ Iowa State Insect Zoo Live Camera

If you don't like creepy-crawlies, don't even bother connecting to this Web site! When we visited, the giant walkingsticks were on display. Eventually, we gained control of the webcam (you have to wait your turn) and explored the display using the remote controlled camera. Wow! We saw two of the insects right away. Most will love this site even though it may "bug" others.

http://zoocam.ent.iastate.edu/

★ Mawson Station, Antarctica

It's extremely "cool" to get a live image of Antarctica. This picture is usually updated automatically each hour. The date/time on the picture shows local Mawson time, which is six hours ahead of Universal Coordinated Time, or UTC (previously known as Greenwich Mean Time, or GMT). Gee, it's 1 A.M. there and the sky's pretty bright! Also, it's extremely depressing to find out that it's warmer at Mawson Station than it is outside our window. :-) To find out how your local temperatures compare, use the Celsius/Fahrenheit conversion entries listed in the REFERENCE WORKS—WEIGHTS AND MEASURES section.

http://www.antdiv.gov.au/stations/mawson/
    video.html

Old Faithful Geyser Webcam

Watch this famous geyser erupt via the magic of Yellowstone National Park's webcam. According to this site, the average interval between eruptions is about 76 minutes. You might have to wait a while to see the plume of steam and boiling water, but it's worth it! If you "visit" at night, check the archive of recent daytime pictures.

http://www.nps.gov/yell/oldfaithfulcam.htm

Swiss Cams

View cows, trains, mountains, and city centers throughout Switzerland via live cams. We keep looking for Heidi but haven't seen her so far.

http://sunsite.cnlab-switch.ch/livecam/swisscam.html

Traffic to Russia at the Vaalimaa Border Crossing Point

There's something satisfying about watching traffic waiting to cross the Finnish border into Russia. Check the map to see where this particular crossing is located. What's in that truck? Hey, that lady in the car—she looks just like Carmen Sandiego! What stories can you make up about the people and vehicles you see? This picture is only updated twice an hour, so don't hang around—someone might ask to see your passport!

http://www.tieh.fi/evideo.htm

Be dazzled by the laser shows in PHYSICS.

Yahooligans! Web Cams

Find out what the top ten webcams are. The day we visited, we looked at a street in Spain, a mountain in Scotland, a view of the Pacific Ocean of California, a coral reef, and a dairy barn. What will be popular when you visit?

http://www.yahooligans.com/content/wc/

VIOLENCE

See PEACE

VIRTUAL REALITY

There are two ways to think of virtual reality, or VR. The first is a continuous panoramic picture of something real. You can explore it by clicking and dragging your mouse. You are usually "standing" in the middle of the scene and can usually "look" at least right and left, sometimes all the way around you—up and down, too. You can sometimes click on something you see, and you'll "walk" towards it to get a better view. The second type of VR lets you "walk" around in a virtual world—one that doesn't exist anywhere but inside the computer. You may be represented in this world by something called an avatar. Sometimes, programs let you select what your avatar will look like, so you might be a smiley face, a big spotted dog, or even a monster! The VR world you may explore is computer created, so anything can happen! The following selected links give you a small sampling of both types of virtual reality. To find more, look in your favorite search engine under VRML (Virtual Reality Modeling Language), virtual reality, QuickTime VR, photo bubble, and similar terms.

★ The Geo-Images Project

Click on any of the Virtual Reality Panoramas, and prepare to be amazed as you travel from Death Valley, California, to Moraine Lake in the Canadian Rockies. Through the magic of QuickTime VR, you'll feel as if you are really there!

http://www-Geoimages.berkeley.edu/GeoImages.html

★ Greatest Places Virtual Reality

All you'll need is QuickTime to explore 360-degree photos from Iguazu Falls in Brazil. Hope you're not afraid of heights. Hold onto the handrail! (For the squeamish, try the solid ground views of Greenland.)

http://www.sci.mus.mn.us/greatestplaces/medias/
media_html/qtvr.html

★ PIX - Internet Pictures Corporation

You will need to download the IPIX plug-in for this one to work. But after you have it, you'll be able to walk around sports stadiums, real estate, famous landmarks, even sharks. Just check the gallery area and start your exploration. One place not mentioned here is the IPIX interactive tour to Westminster Abbey, which was created by CNN for the sad occasion of Princess Diana's funeral. Visit it. Check the Poets' Corner at <http://cnn.com/WORLD/9708/diana/london.pix/route.html>. Be sure to look up over your head and beneath your feet to see memorials to famous authors.

http://www.ipix.com/

"Use the source, Luke!" and look it up in REFERENCE WORKS.

A B C D E F G H I J K L M N O P Q R S T U V W X Y Z

WAKE ISLAND

See UNITED STATES—TERRITORIES

WEATHER AND METEOROLOGY

AccuWeather

Your picnic basket's packed, and you've got your Frisbee, but your mom's trying to make you wear your raincoat. Will it rain or not? Fast and reliable weather forecast service for many U.S. cities and summary data from many locations around the world are at this site. You can also get a free "weather by e-mail" service, travel weather for all over the world (and your local interstate), and many additional resources. Don't miss the "weather for aliens" at <*http://www.accuweather.com/adcbin/alien_index?nav=home*>, which tracks not only the temperature and wind speed but also the number of black helicopters sighted!

http://www.accuweather.com/

Automated Weather Source

Thousands of schools worldwide participate in this weather monitoring network. Is yours one of them? The WeatherNet AirWatch system hardware senses temperature, humidity, wind speed and direction, light intensity, barometric pressure, and other measurements. The weather station can run without a computer, it just needs to connect to the Internet occasionally to post its instrument readings. At this site you can see live data for current weather, and take a look back at famous weather events in recent history (see Greatest Hits).

http://www.aws.com/

People are the true treasures of the Net.

Bay Kids' Weather Page

It's summer, and the sky decides it's time to cook up some fun. Here are some interesting recipes; how about whipping up a nice afternoon thunderstorm? Let's see, check the ingredients: water vapor, dust particles, rising air, electricity potential. Yes, we seem to have all of those, now all we need to do is follow the instructions (and remember, really good lightning is shaken, not stirred). This ThinkQuest Junior entry, built by kids, will teach you all about weather events, jokes, myths, and much more.

http://tqjunior.advanced.org/3805/

BrainPOP - Rainbows

The spectacular light shows known as rainbows are really just spread-out sunlight. Tim knows that, but Moby the Robot seems a little confused. Learn all about the optics behind the magic of rainbows as you watch the cartoon and try the activities. Did you know that you can't really walk to the end of the rainbow to look for the leprechaun's pot of gold? Better tell Moby that!

http://www.brainpop.com/science/light/rainbow/

Cloud Types: Common Cloud Classifications

If you can say "cumulonimbus" or "cirrostratus" and point out these kinds of clouds in the sky, you can call yourself a cloud expert! If you'd like to be one, check out the University of Illinois Cloud Catalog. There are some really great pictures to go along with all these huge words. You may be surprised to find out how much difference there is between clouds close to the ground and clouds much higher in the sky.

http://ww2010.atmos.uiuc.edu/(Gh)/guides/mtr/cld/cldtyp/

Dan's Wild Weather Page

Do you want to know how clouds are formed or what to do if you are caught in a lightning storm? Just see Dan! He has info on almost any weather occurrence. From hurricanes to air pressure, Dan has it covered with colorful diagrams and graphics. Teachers and parents might learn a thing or two, as well.

http://www.wildwildweather.com/

FEMA - Preparedness for Severe Weather Safety

Would you know what to do if you heard a tornado was approaching? (Hint: Go to the basement or an interior room away from glass. Get out of cars and mobile homes. Lie flat in a ditch, if necessary.) What if there were flash flood warnings, or a winter blizzard, hurricane, or other severe weather forecast? This site from the Federal Emergency Management Agency offers lots of information on how to prepare for, and survive, these disasters and more, including nuclear power plant emergencies.

http://www.fema.gov/pte/prep.htm

GOES Project Science

GOES is an acronym. It stands for Geostationary Operational Environmental Satellite, and it's one of the high tech tools used by weather forecasters. Geostationary means it stays in the same place above Earth, moving along with Earth but always looking at the same view of the ground. The GOES system oversees the U.S. (among other scenic spots), but that is not all it does. It can also measure atmospheric temperature, moisture, and winds. It even receives and retransmits signals from marine buoys and "roving bears." If you want to see the view of Earth GOES sees, try this site. For more GOES imagery, visit <http://www.goes.noaa.gov/>.

http://rsd.gsfc.nasa.gov/goes/

★ Interactive Weather Maker

Who said you can't fool with Mother Nature? At this site, you can try your hand at weathermaking. Turn a sunny day into a windy day. Or, stir up a rainy day. If you create the correct conditions, you can make a blizzard—complete with a snow whiteout. The site also links to Weather Central, which explains how weather works. The Flash plug-in is required to create your own weather.

http://teacher.scholastic.com/activities/wwatch/
winter/blizzard/

Jupiter, the Weather Computer You Can Call

Want to experiment with talking to a computer over the phone? Call Jupiter at the Massachusetts Institute of Technology, and ask about the weather in more than 500 cities (mostly in the U.S.). You don't just have to ask about today's weather, you can ask about tomorrow. Or ask Jupiter to "find a sunny place in the Caribbean." Read the FAQ page first, and then call the toll-free number 1-888-573-TALK (1-888-573-8255). If you wish to call Jupiter from outside North America, the number is 617-258-0300. This is not a toll-free number, and you will be responsible for the (international) long-distance charges. This site is working on fielding questions and answers in many different languages. Note that this system is very active and you may have to keep trying to get through. We did! The call is recorded for research purposes.

http://www.sls.lcs.mit.edu/sls/whatwedo/
applications/jupiter.html

NET FILES

If you were stuck in a room with only a calendar, how would you survive?

Answer: Eat the dates and the "sundaes" and drink from the spring! Visit the Calendar Zone at *http://www.calendarzone.com/* for calendar poetry, lore, and jokes—of course.

A
B
C
D
E
F
G
H
I
J
K
L
M
N
O
P
Q
R
S
T
U
V
W
X
Y
Z

Discovery - On Board the Titanic

Assume the role of one of five real passengers on the *Titanic*. What will be your fate? Will you be one of the survivors or one of many who lost their lives that night in 1912? You won't know whose role you're playing until it's all over. (Hint: read the "date of death" carefully. If it's not 1912, you survived the wreck.) Don't miss the *Titanic's* final hours, at the same site.
http://www.discovery.com/stories/science/ sciencetitanic/sciencetitanic.html.
http://www.discovery.com/guides/history/ titanic/Titanic/titanic.html

Make Your Own Weather Station

You don't need fancy weather instruments to collect data. You can make your own barometer, hygrometer, rain gauge, and weather vane out of simple household materials. For example, to assemble the barometer, you need a glass, a ruler, some water, a foot of clear plastic tubing, and a well-chewed stick of chewing gum! Find out the instructions here.

http://sln.fi.edu/weather/todo/todo.html

Meteorology Guide: The Online Guides

This resource includes lots of interesting weather material, including classifying clouds and predicting precipitation. But we want to focus your attention on the Light and Optics section, which starts at *<http://ww2010.atmos.uiuc.edu/(Gh)/guides/mtr/opt/>*. Find out how particles of dust, water, and ice crystals combine to make spectacular sunsets, resplendent rainbows, and silver linings. Photos and drawings will help you understand each effect.

http://ww2010.atmos.uiuc.edu/(Gh)/guides/mtr/

NCDC Climate Visualization

Was this the rainiest April ever in your city? What was the weather like the day you were born? You're just a few clicks away from finding out, when you cruise over to the National Climatic Data Center (NCDC), the world's biggest collection of weather information. In seconds, you can create graphs showing what the weather's been like just about any time or anywhere in the world. Some of the weather statistics go all the way back to the 1700s. Choose Inventory to see what choices you have in displaying the information.

http://www.ncdc.noaa.gov/onlineprod/drought/ xmgr.html

NOAA - Owlie Skywarn's Weather Book

Tornadoes, flash floods, hurricanes, lightning, winter storms. Such severe weather conditions can be life threatening. Would you know what to do if, say, lightning strikes, and you're outside? At this site, Owlie Skywarn, the official mascot of the National Weather Service and the Federal Emergency Management Agency, will tell you. He's got a list of do's and don'ts so you'll know what to do if severe weather heads your way.

http://www.crh.noaa.gov/mkx/owlie/owlie.htm

NOAA Photo Collection

Need some great tornado photos for your report? This is the spot to find pictures of all kinds of weather and other natural images. The National Oceanic and Atmospheric Administration offers "thousands of weather and space images, hundreds of images of our shores and coastal seas, and thousands of marine species images ranging from the great whales to the most minute plankton." Search for big hailstones, photos of the great blizzard of 1966, and some of the most spectacular lightning photos you'll ever see (search on Eiffel tower, check your spelling).

http://www.photolib.noaa.gov/

Computers are dumb, people are smart.

North American Drought

When it rains, it pours. When it doesn't, it's dry. But how many rainless days does it take before scientists declare dry weather a drought? Turn to this site for the answer to this question and others. You'll also discover how scientists can pinpoint when droughts occurred during the last 2000 years.

http://www.ngdc.noaa.gov/paleo/drought/

One Sky, Many Voices

Join this eight-week program to learn about weather in your region and share observations with other classrooms around the world. The University of Michigan hosts this classic collaborative project.

http://groundhog.sprl.umich.edu/

★ Operational Significant Event Imagery

What's a "significant" event? Oh, something like a volcano's eruption, or a hurricane. It could even be something like a huge forest fire, or even a big iceberg breaking off from Antarctica. Not to worry. The satellite imagery folks have it all covered. Peek over their shoulders here, and see images and video loops of current and historical events.

http://www.osei.noaa.gov/

★ UM Weather

Do you think you could predict the weather better than the guys on TV? You may be able to, once this terrific site from the University of Michigan pops up on your radar. It's so hot, it's cool. We forecast a heavy download from the weather-related software tools area. There's also an incoming front of live weather cams from around the world. How many states and provinces can you visit today?

http://cirrus.sprl.umich.edu/wxnet/

> **Brother reading your diary again? Learn to encrypt in CODES AND CIPHERS.**

United States Climate Page

Get an up-close view of weather patterns in U.S. cities and states using a wide variety of weather data. Plot graphs, or make bar charts. You can also create a colorful map of the United States that shows, for example, where it rained the most since 1895. Average daily high and low temperatures, rainfall, and snowfall are some of the data available.

http://www.cdc.noaa.gov/USclimate/

★ USA Today Weather

This site is the best-kept secret on the Net for weather information! You'll find a ton of special articles, fun facts, and lots of other goodies at this site, from information on tornadoes and hurricanes to tips on weather forecasting. Check the Topics list at the left of the page. If you have a weather-related report due or if you're just interested in things meteorological, do not miss this excellent site.

http://www.usatoday.com/weather/wfront.htm

USWX - Weather

See at a glance where U.S. weather advisories have been issued today. Locate where the rivers are flooding, the clouds are thundering overhead, and the thermometers are threatening to burst from the heat. Color-codes make it easy to see where the weather's good, and where it's dismal. Other tools let you predict the weather for your birthday (or other notable date) years into the future. The almanac section features the phase of the Moon, temperature records, sunrise and sunset times for your locale, and loads of other predictable (and unpredictable) information. And don't miss the weather "gadgets" you can place on your home page.

http://www.uswx.com/us/wx/

A B C D E F G H I J K L M N O P Q R S T U V W X Y Z

A B C D E F G H I J K L M N O P Q R S T U V **W** X Y Z

Weather and Climate

Net-mom is a real fan of teacher Mr. Bowerman and his extensive pages on all sorts of topics. But right now, let's look at his collection of sites on climate and weather. You will discover fascinating links on the water cycle, monsoons, aurora borealis, El Niño, how the seasons work, and many other topics.

http://members.aol.com/bowermanb/weather.html

★ The Weather Classroom

Serious weather watchers and meteorologist wannabes should head over to the Weather Channel's education home page. There are lesson plans, experiments, and lots of hands-on activities to help you learn about weather. For today's forecast, just enter your city or ZIP code.

http://www.weather.com/education/

The Weather Dude

"Weather Dude" Nick Walker, a weathercaster for *The Weather Channel*, specializes in making weather fun. Our favorite part of this site is Weather Songs, where you can download audio clips and sing along with songs from Nick's "Weather Dude: A Musical Guide to the Atmosphere." Don't miss his tips on how to get free stuff, like the Winter Survival Coloring Book and hurricane tracking charts. It's in the Stuff for Teachers /Parents section.

http://www.wxdude.com/

Weather Gone Wild

Sometimes the weather gets a little out of hand. Tornadoes, hurricanes, tidal waves, and floods are just a few of the extreme weather situations detailed at this site. Each entry is easy to read; but if you don't understand some of the words, don't worry because there is a glossary. There's a nice tutorial on how to read a weather chart, with an explanation of all those weird symbols used by weather guys and gals. This site was created by students for the ThinkQuest Junior competition.

http://tqjunior.advanced.org/5818/

The Weather Rock

Build your very own weather station using— a Rock. This site explains how your observations of the Rock can reveal current weather conditions. For example: if the Rock is wet, it's raining out. There are many more observations you can make, guided by this funny site. Remember: if the Rock is bouncing up and down, it's an earthquake!

http://www.usscouts.org/profbvr/weather_rock/

WeatherEye

Aimed at the needs of teachers, this weather education site is designed to be used in the classroom. It includes weather lessons, projects, and more, for Grades 2 through 12. Younger kids will learn how clouds are formed and how to make their own cloud in a fun experiment. Some of the lessons for older kids cover weather phenomena like El Niño and how to handle a hurricane.

http://weathereye.kgan.com/

★ Web Weather for Kids

Can you make a thunderstorm in your kitchen, or construct a tornado in your breakfast nook? The "recipes" are here, along with slick animations and lots of multimedia. We can't wait to try making our own lightning!

http://www.ucar.edu/40th/webweather/

EL NIÑO AND LA NIÑA

★ El Niño - A Child of the Tropics

Learn all about the warm current phenomenon known as El Niño. As this site warns, "We are in hot water now!" Separate fact from fiction as you explore the hype and the science behind both this weather event and its cold-water sister, La Niña. There's also an interactive time line and a solid section on prediction methods. This multimedia-rich resource was created by students for the ThinkQuest competition.

http://library.thinkquest.org/20901/

Whoooooooo will you find in BIRDS?

NOAA El Niño Page

What kind of winter will you have this year, and how does the unusual combination of winds and currents known as El Niño affect the weather in your area? No one knows, but chances are that this site provides the best information. See impressive climate visualization data graphics, as well as real-time marine buoy readings.

http://www.elnino.noaa.gov/

HURRICANES

Hurricane Names

Have you ever wondered how hurricanes get their names? Nineteenth-century hurricanes were named after saints! Later, meteorologists "honored" their girlfriends or wives with the distinction of having their very own namesake hurricane. These days, things are a bit different. What are this year's planned names? This site lists the names of the storms we'll hear about through the 2006 season.

http://www.nhc.noaa.gov/aboutnames_text.html

Hyper Hurricanes, Create a Hurricane

Create a hurricane on your computer screen by manipulating the slider controls for water temperature, wind shear, and other variables. Then compare your meteorological creation to the statistics of historical storms. How well do they match? Learn about some monster storms, and then dive into coral reefs to find out how scientists uncover clues to ancient hurricanes.

http://www.discovery.com/stories/science/
  hurricanes/create.html

Learning to Learn

What's your learning style? If you said "sitting," we'll give you points for humor, but that's not exactly what we meant. You might like to visualize a problem, act it out, talk about it, or draw a diagram. This site will help you analyze how you like to learn best, and give you ideas and strategies for maximizing your memory, reading, writing, problem solving, and creative skills. Hint: click on the red words to open the next screens.
http://snow.utoronto.ca/Learn2/modules.html

Miami Museum of Science - Hurricane Storm Science

During Florida's Hurricane Andrew in 1992, the Benitez family huddled together in a closet while their whole farm was destroyed in 150-mph winds. "The part I thought was the worst was when we heard the windows break," says 11-year-old Patrick, whose family had nothing to eat for two days! Read this family's story and find out how they survived. Or maybe you'd like to try making your own weather station instruments. The directions are here.

http://www.miamisci.org/hurricane/

If you can read this, good! Now check BOOKS AND LITERATURE.

A
B
C
D
E
F
G
H
I
J
K
L
M
N
O
P
Q
R
S
T
U
V
W
X
Y
Z

★ The Tropical Prediction Center - National Hurricane Center

For the latest warnings and advisories regarding rough weather in the Atlantic and eastern Pacific regions, this site should be your first stop. There's also historical data and lots of reference material, such as descriptions of the various hurricane categories on the Saffir-Simpson Hurricane Scale. Want to know if the "Hurricane Tracker" weather reconnaissance planes are out today? Their schedule is posted here.

http://www.nhc.noaa.gov/index_text.html

Tropical Twisters

At this multimedia-rich site, you can closely examine a hurricane using virtual reality, watch time-lapse movies of storm development, and take a peek at one of the GOES weather satellites used to take those tracking photos you see on TV—and on the Net.

http://kids.earth.nasa.gov/archive/hurricane/

SNOW AND ICE

Current Snow Cover

So you think you're sick of shoveling the snow out of your parents' driveway? See where kids have it worse than you do! Check out how deep the snow is today, all over the U.S., with this snow cover map. Hint: this map is very boring to look at in the summer.

http://weather.unisys.com/surface/snow_cover.html

Discovery Online: Build Your Own Avalanche

According to this site, there's no such thing as a "typical" avalanche. Nevertheless, you can try to create a virtual one by altering the slope of the mountain, the snow depth, the tree cover, and even the weight of the skier. Look out, below!

http://www.discovery.com/exp/avalanche/build.html

★ Kids Snow Page

If you lived in the frozen North, you might have as many different words for snow as the Inuit do. There are words that mean falling snow, ground snow, smoky snow, and wind-beaten snow. Do you live in a snowy climate? Go on a scavenger hunt activity! Use the list of all the different kinds of snow and see how many you can find where you live. If you'd like to keep your snowflake finds, learn how you can do it with a piece of glass and some hair spray. Make an edible glacier, cut and fold paper snowflakes, and learn that soap bubbles won't pop if you blow them outside when it's –40 degrees Fahrenheit, as it is pretty often where the Teel family kids live—in Alaska.

http://www.teelfamily.com/activities/snow/

National Snow and Ice Data Center

These scientists really know snow. Come explore the digital drifts of their site. You'll discover where the polar ice caps are today, why snow looks white, and how people deal with snow removal when there's a blizzard. Learn about historical storms, weather records, avalanches, and lots more. For a photo gallery of snowflake images, try <http://www.its.caltech.edu/~atomic/snowcrystals/>.

http://nsidc.org/NSIDC/EDUCATION/

NOVA Online - Avalanche

An avalanche—the sudden shift and slide of tons of snow—can be deadly to those in its path. How can you stay away from trouble in avalanche-prone areas? If you're caught in an avalanche, what should you do? NOVA, the award-winning TV series, dug deep into the science of avalanches to bring you the answers. There's a transcript of the show, links, and plenty of video clips.

http://www.pbs.org/wgbh/nova/avalanche/

Never give your name or address to a stranger.

Not everything on the Net is true.

Snow Crystals

A snowflake is usually not seen in its newly formed pristine crystal state for very long. That's because it melts or is compressed into other snowflakes as they pile up. Caltech grows snowflakes in the lab, and photographs them to preserve their beauty for all to enjoy. Visit this site to see both natural and lab-grown snowflakes.

http://www.its.caltech.edu/~atomic/snowcrystals/

U.S. Coast Guard International Ice Patrol

According to this site, "10,000 to 15,000 icebergs are carved each year, primarily from 20 major glaciers between the Jacobshaven and Humboldt Glaciers" in west Greenland. These drift south, melting as they go. Sometimes they reach the shipping lanes, and in the old days this was a cause for great concern. Historical reports indicate that the iceberg that sunk the *Titanic* was 50 to 100 feet high and 200 to 400 feet long. These days, icebergs are located by radar and carefully tracked, and one of the organizations responsible for that is the U.S. Coast Guard. North Atlantic icebergs are tracked only during the "season" (it's variable, but it's usually 100 to 200 days in spring to midsummer), so you may not see a current map (for southern hemisphere, try *<http://www.natice.noaa.gov/icebergs.htm>*).

http://www.uscg.mil/lantarea/iip/

U.S. Coast Guard Polar Star

To see a real Coast Guard icebreaker vessel, try the *Polar Star* and its link to the *Healy* site. A kindergarten teacher has been traveling on the *Polar Star*; see what she's been studying in the Bering Sea.

http://www.polarstar.org/

THUNDERSTORMS AND LIGHTNING
Lightning

San Francisco's Exploratorium brings you the story of lightning, chock-full of trivia that will amaze you. Did you know that a lightning bolt has enough energy to lift a 2,000-pound car 62 miles high into the air? Or that a lightning flash jumps from the ground up to a cloud at 61,000 miles per second? You won't want to miss the story of Roy "Dooms" Sullivan, a former park ranger who holds the world's record for being zapped by lightning more than any other person: seven times. Now that's an electrifying personality!

http://www.exploratorium.edu/ronh/weather/
    weather.html

Lightning Explorer

The National Lightning Detection Network constantly monitors lightning discharges to ground within the mainland United States. Where is lightning striking right now? This page will show you what's happened in the last two hours. We'd write more in this annotation, but according to the map, there's a big thunderstorm coming our way!

http://www.lightningstorm.com/lightningstorm/gpg/
    lex1/mapdisplay_free.jsp

NET FILES

In what sport would you find the following terms: bump and run, fried egg, and smothered hook?

Answer: They are all golfing terms. Find out what they mean at http://www.pga.com/instruction/glossary/

A B C D E F G H I J K L M N O P Q R S T U V **W** X Y Z

Lightning @ Nationalgeographic.com

National Geographic brings you the whole shocking story: lightning is striking the Earth about 100 times a second. Read what it's like to be hit by lightning, told by people who have survived the encounter. And, when you've found out everything you've always wanted to know about lightning, this page says, "Don't bolt—take a quiz and win the hottest prize in cyberspace."

http://www.nationalgeographic.com/features/96/
    lightning/

TIDES

Make a Tide Prediction

You're going to St. Petersburg, Florida, and you want to know when low tide is because you really want to find some shells and go beachcombing. When you get to St. Petersburg, tide tables will be easy to locate; in fact, they are often printed in the local newspapers. However, your family lives in New York. What morning should you beachcomb and what morning should you go to a theme park? You need to be able to plan your trip! This site predicts high/low tides months in advance for places as diverse as the Florida coast, Alaska, Honolulu, and all up and down the east and west coasts of the U.S. Tide info for many Pacific islands is also available. For other places, try the WWW Tide/Current Predictor <http://tbone.biol.sc.edu/tide/ sitesel.html>.

http://co-ops.nos.noaa.gov/tp4days.html

TORNADOES

The Online Tornado FAQ

All the tornado facts you'd ever need are here, plus sources of free online tornado pictures. See what happens to a car during a tornado and why it's a bad idea to stay in one when these violent storms come around. Some of them have winds of up to 300 mph! Be sure to read the *USA Today* weather information on tornadoes, at <http://www.usatoday.com/ weather/tornado/wtwist0.htm>.

http://www.spc.noaa.gov/faq/tornado/

WHY

See also SCIENCE

Ask Dr. Universe

Do frogs sleep? Why are flowers colored the way they are? Why does electricity shock? These are some of the questions answered by a cat named Dr. Universe. She hunts down the answers to questions from people all over the world. Many times she has to pounce on a University expert to help her understand the question as well as the answer! The results of her labors are here.

http://www.wsu.edu/DrUniverse/

Ask Science Theatre Archive

Why does ice float? Where does helium come from? Why do we lose our tans in the winter? How does a match work? These are just a few of the hundreds of questions answered at this site, sponsored by Michigan State University.

http://www.pa.msu.edu/~sciencet/ask_st/
    date_index.html

Victorian Women

Pick a door, any door, and the animated Victorian lady will knock on it. You'll get a question about women's rights in the reign of Queen Victoria of England. You'll be asked about when women won, for example, the right to get a job, earn a college degree, vote, and keep their children after a divorce. The answers may surprise you! This is a fun game that's reinforced with a summary at the end.
http://www.bbc.co.uk/history/games/victorian_women/

★ Earth and Sky

Earth and Sky is a daily radio feature about science, heard on 950 stations around the world. Their topics range from deep-ocean vents to the farthest-flung star nurseries in deep space. They also answer intriguing listener questions, some of which have been collected on this Web site. Why is the sky blue? Are soap bubbles round in weightless conditions? Why do leaves change color in the fall? Earth and Sky knows! Now there's a special Earth and Sky for kids, too. See it here: <http://www.earthsky.com/Kids/>.

http://www.earthsky.com/

How Are Fireworks Made?

Learn the secrets of the pyrotechnician's art, as you "Ooh!" and "Aah!" your way around this site. What makes those burning star effects, and how do they get Roman candles to work? Is this kind of work any fun? According to the folks who do it, "It's a blast!" Be sure to try the Name That Boom game. Just click on a firework silhouette on the left, wait for the color picture to load on the right, and choose the best answer in the middle.

http://www.nationalgeographic.com/world/0007/fireworks/

★ How Stuff Works

Have you ever wondered how your television set works? Or how cell phones get a message from here to there without any wires? And CDs—how does all that music get written onto those shiny discs? Don't forget those See 'N' Say toys—how do they keep talking without using batteries? And while we're at it, let's look at How Airplanes Work, and How Toilets Work. There's even a dissection of the crazy Singing Fish. Haven't you always wanted to know what's inside?

http://www.howstuffworks.com/

Get on board, little children, in RAILROADS AND TRAINS.

How Things Work

Have you ever questioned some aspect of the science of physics? A professor of physics at the University of Virginia has listed answers to many questions, some of which are part of the basic physics courses he teaches at the university. A guide lists previous questions, as well as a place where you can ask a new question. The search button will help you find whether one of the previously asked questions is one you might also pose.

http://Landau1.phys.Virginia.EDU/Education/Teaching/HowThingsWork/

★ New Scientist: The Last Word Science Questions and Answers

Are you puzzled why penguins don't get frozen feet? Do you wonder how many times you can recycle paper? How about frozen carrots in a microwave—is it true they sometimes produce sparks during the cooking process? Wait, there's more: Are we ever going to run out of words? Why do some people sweat when they eat cheddar cheese? Why do onions make us cry? How were battery cell sizes named? The answers to these and hundreds of other questions can be found at this site.

http://www.newscientist.com/lastword/

OMSI Science Whatzit!

You name the topic, the Oregon Museum of Science has the info. Is there wood so dense it won't float? Why is the Earth round? How many stars are out there? How do fireflies light up? If you have a question, see if it's been answered at this site. If not, go ahead and ask it here.

http://www.omsi.edu/online/whatzit/

The Skinny On . . .

This site offers "the skinny on" a lot of unusual subjects. Why does bright light make you sneeze? How do sonic booms work? Why do you twitch sometimes when you're falling asleep? Why does eating beans give you gas? What color is snow (the answer will surprise you!).

http://www.discovery.com/area/skinnyon/skinnyon.html

A B C D E F G H I J K L M N O P Q R S T U V W X Y Z

A
B
C
D
E
F
G
H
I
J
K
L
M
N
O
P
Q
R
S
T
U
V
W
X
Y
Z

Smart Stuff with Twig Walkingstick

Did you ever wonder if fish have ears? Why rabbits like carrots? Where the water goes during low tide? What causes heartburn? This Twig guy has the answers to these and a lot more questions in a wide variety of topics. Check it out, and you'll learn why the sea is blue in some places and green in others, among other things.

http://www.ag.ohio-state.edu/~twig/

Why Do Cat's Eyes Glow in the Dark?

At night, if you shine a beam of light into a cat's eyes, they seem to glow back at you. You can also get this effect if you take a flash photo of a cat's face. What gives the eyes this spooky appearance? Find out at this site!

http://dialspace.dial.pipex.com/agarman/faq3.htm

The Why Files

Your coach has really gone crazy this time. He's climbed to the top of the backboard, and he's dropping a round basketball and a flat basketball (with no air in it) at the same time. Which one will hit the floor first? Everybody guesses one or the other, but the answer is that they will strike the floor at the same time. Why? The answer is at <http://whyfiles.news.wisc.edu/sports/basketball/>, a site that is funded by the National Science Foundation. You'll also find current science news for kids, as well as archives of past whys (and wise) answers!

http://whyfiles.news.wisc.edu/

Why Is the Sunset Red?

Did you ever wonder how a blue sky can have a red sunset? This site has a really neat experiment that will help you understand the phenomenon. All you need is a flashlight, a container of water (a fish tank is ideal), and a glass of milk. Hint: the colors of the sky and the sunset have to do with particles of dust in the air. The rest of the answer is here!

http://scifun.chem.wisc.edu/HOMEEXPTS/
   BlueSky.html

SEASONS

Autumn Leaves - Why Do Leaves Change Color in Fall?

Do you know the answer to this perennial question? Chlorophyll gives leaves their green color, but it goes away in the autumn. Then we see fiery red, orange, and yellow colors. They were there all summer, but the green covered them up!

http://www.sciencemadesimple.com/leaves.html

BrainPOP Autumn Leaves

In the fall, you may wonder, "Why do the trees turn beautiful colors?" What is actually happening to their leaves? Why do some leaves turn yellow and others red? As Tim and Moby will tell you, the mixture of red, yellow, and other colors is the result of a chemical process. Watch the movie, and discover how trees sense when to change colors. You'll also learn how trees know when to grow new green leaves again.

http://www.brainpop.com/science/ecology/
   autumnleaves/

What Causes the Seasons

At this Web site, you can learn how the weather is related to the tilt of the Earth and how it moves around the Sun. Did you know Earth is actually closer to the Sun in January (winter in the Northern Hemisphere) than it is in July? Find out all about it, and don't forget to click on the names of the seasons on the right side of the screen for more.

http://www.worldbook.com/fun/seasons/html/
   seasons.htm

Why Do Leaves Change Color in the Fall?

Ever wondered why leaves change color and why it always happens in the fall? There's a good explanation of it here, and it's not too technical. You'll also learn what happens to all those fallen leaves and why evergreens stay green. If you want a heads up on where to view the best fall color, the site provides the phone number of the U.S. Forest Service's Fall Color Hotline.

http://www.na.fs.fed.us/spfo/pubs/misc/leaves/
   leaves.htm

A B C D E F G H I J K L M N O P Q R S T U V **W** X Y Z

WORDS

See also LANGUAGES AND ALPHABETS—
ENGLISH; READING AND LITERACY;
REFERENCE WORKS—DICTIONARIES;
SCHOOLS AND EDUCATION—
LEARNING AND STUDY; WRITING

★ A.Word.A.Day

Do you love words? Then you'll want to get on the A Word A Day (AWAD) mailing list. It's free! Each day you'll get a new word, definition, and brief quote showing how the word is used. Net-mom's on the AWAD list, along with 433,000 other people! The home page has sample words from today and yesterday, or you can look through the archives to see what the list is like.

http://www.wordsmith.org/awad/

Common Errors in English

Plenty of people use common words and phrases the wrong way, and this page aims to set them all straight. Learn when to use "its" and when to rely on "it's." Discover why being "very unique" is impossible. Is it "loose" or "lose"? "Immigrate" or "emigrate"? Could you "care less"? Find out here.

http://www.wsu.edu/~brians/errors/

Fake Out!

OK, give this multiple-choice quiz a try. The word "otalgia" means: (a) A bacteria that grows on rainforest trees causing them to rot; (b) An earache; or (c) An eighteen-sided shape. If you said "b," you'd be right, and a winner at this definition guessing game. The object of the game is to come up with word definitions so believable you fool other players into picking the wrong one.

http://www.eduplace.com/dictionary/

NET FILES

What are the six major food groups? (Isn't one of them chocolate?)

Answer: The Food Pyramid lists six food groups:

❖ Bread, cereal, grains, pasta
❖ Fruit
❖ Vegetables
❖ Meat, poultry, fish, dry beans
❖ Milk, cheese, yogurt
❖ Oils, fats, sweets (yes, that's chocolate, but eat only a little!)

Find out more at http://www.nal.usda.gov:8001/py/pmap.htm

Gaggle

Did you know there are special words to use when there is a group of animals? You know that several cows make a "herd," and that a few chickens make a "flock." You may have heard of a "gaggle" of geese or a "pride" of lions. If you've ever been curious about the other "collective nouns," you can learn more in a fun game format.

http://www.LearningKingdom.com/gaggle/

Gry, Gry, Everywhere, and Not a Clue in Sight

Have you heard this puzzle? Quick—name three words that end in "gry." Having a hard time? Here are a list of "gry" words, but the solution to the puzzle may be that the question is just phrased the wrong way! Read it and see what you think.

http://www.word-detective.com/gry.html

Knotting - Resources, How to, and More

This terrific collection of tips and tricks includes directions for tying a friendship knot, among others. You can also learn how to tie a knot that looks like a dragonfly, and another one that makes a perfectly wonderful zipper pull. Don't forget the "trucker's hitch," which comes in handy for securing your kayak/Christmas tree/surfboard to the top of the family car.
http://www.dfw.net/~jazzman/knotter/knot.htm

★ Internet Anangram Server

Do you know what an anagram is? Take all the letters in a word or phrase, scramble them, and come up with a new word or phrase! For example, "Inert Net Grave Near Mars" is an anagram for "Internet Anagram Server." Type in ten or less letters and see what mysterious phrase you'll get.

http://www.wordsmith.org/anagram/

Scripps Howard National Spelling Bee

Are you a good speller? Are you under 16, or in eighth grade or below? Every year there's a contest to find out who's the best speller of all; but to get to the finals, you first have to win your local sponsor's contest. There are 240 sponsors in the United States, Europe, Guam, Mexico, Puerto Rico, the U.S. Virgin Islands, the Bahamas, and American Samoa. This site gives all the rules, explains what happens at the National contest level, and offers study hints on how you can get there.

http://www.spellingbee.com/

Spelling

This site has a secret. Your mom and dad will think you're just practicing your spelling. But the truth is, these spelling games are fun! First, pick your level. There are different lessons for first through sixth grade. First-graders can try to spot the misspelled word in this rhyming group: "pat-rat-st." Click the word that's wrong and then type the correction in the box: "s-a-t." Each time you get one right, you'll get one more turtle to stack up so a squirrel can reach a bag of nuts stashed on a high shelf. Sixth-graders have more of a challenge with their spelling games, but they are just as much fun to play.

http://www.harcourtschool.com/menus/
  harcourt_brace_spelling.html

★ Vocabulary University

Sam Mantics, Dean of Admissions and Directions at Vocabulary University®, guides you through several levels of puzzles as you search for the meaning of words and in the limitless quest of vocabulary acquisition. Don't get the idea this is very easy— start with the lowest level first and work up. Cinny Nym and Auntie Nym are available to give you hints, and there are clues everywhere. After you do a few of these, you'll catch on quickly!

http://www.vocabulary.com/

The Wacky World of Words

Can you actually do math with letters in words? Sure! Try taking the first 1/2 of "what" + the last 3/5 of "there," and you get the word "where." That's only one of the word puzzles offered for your wordplay pleasure. You'll love scratching your head over "numbletters," also known as word equations. Here's an example: "26 = L of the A." The answer? Twenty-six letters of the alphabet. Try this one: "0 = D C at which W F." The answer? Zero = Degrees Celsius at which Water Freezes. Try them all!

http://www.members.home.net/teachwell/

The Word Detective

The Word Detective answers readers' questions about the English language and its odd words and phrases, such as "busting chops," "lame duck," or "eyes peeled," and he does this cleverly, with wit and humor. His newsletter "aims for the large grey area between the Oxford English Dictionary and Monty Python." It's great, check it out!

http://www.word-detective.com/

Word Dragon

Do you like word games? Do you want to practice your language skills? At this site, you will find lots of puzzles: word scramble, sentence scramble, and word match. You can even create your own puzzles and add to the collection. It's best to try one of the puzzles before creating your own, however. A Java-enabled browser is required.

http://www.worddragon.org/

Word.Net's Ambigram.Matic

It's a flipped out, backwards world at this site, the world's only ambigram generator. Ambigrams are words or phrases that can be read in at least two different ways, such as right side up and upside down. To find out how, cruise over to this silly site and try typing in your name.

http://ambigram.matic.com/ambigram.htm

The Word Police Academy

Would you like to be a member of the Word Police? You must pass an entrance exam, but successful word police officers are empowered to bestow grammar citations to those who abuse the English language. Try the test, it's fun; and you get a really cool certificate to print if you pass, to say nothing of the handy grammar tickets you may print and distribute to offenders.

http://www.theatlantic.com/unbound/wordpolice/

MNEMONICS
The Mnemonic Number Alphabet

Mnemonics are handy little devices for jogging our memories. For example, the first letters of "My Very Educated Mother Just Served Us Nine Pickles" gives the initials, in order, of the nine planets. "Lucy Can't Drink Milk" provides the Roman numerals in order for 50, 100, 500, and 1,000. Some of these mnemonics have been helping students breeze through tests for years; now it's your turn to use them! Do you have trouble remembering dates in history class? Try the mnemonic alphabet system, which replaces numbers with consonants. Maybe you can make up some of your own, too. There's even more on memory systems at <http://www.jersey.net/~mitchell/page3b.htm>.

http://www.curbet.com/speedlearn/chap10.html

TONGUE TWISTERS
Tongue Twisters

Parental advisory: please preview this site. You'll find quite a few tongue twisters here, from the banal "How much wood could . . ." to the short and clever "Unique New York" and "Truly Plural." Go ahead—say them a few times.

http://www.geocities.com/Athens/8136/tonguetwisters.html

WRITING

See also INTERNET—WEB BUILDING AND HTML; LANGUAGES AND ALPHABETS—ENGLISH; READING AND LITERACY; SCHOOLS AND EDUCATION—LEARNING AND STUDY; WORDS

ABC's of the Writing Process

Writing doesn't just start when you pick up a pen or sit down at the computer. First, you need an idea and some inspiration. Where can you get ideas? How can you organize your random thoughts into an essay, story, or poem? There are some great tips here.

http://www.angelfire.com/wi/writingprocess/

A
B
C
D
E
F
G
H
I
J
K
L
M
N
O
P
Q
R
S
T
U
V
W
X
Y
Z

A
B
C
D
E
F
G
H
I
J
K
L
M
N
O
P
Q
R
S
T
U
V
W
X
Y
Z

BBC Education - Listen & Write

You won't just be whistling "Dixie" at this site. You'll be listening to a pretty crazy rap about dancing sheep, and then writing your own rap story. If rap music isn't your thing, try one of the other activities, such as writing a poem. Before you write something original, remember to check out the activities first. It will make you a better writer.

http://www.bbc.co.uk/education/listenandwrite/
    home.htm

★ BBC - KS2 Revisewise English

Can you solve the mystery of the missing jewelry? You'll have to read very carefully, and then question the witnesses. Who is telling the truth and who is lying? Can you shed some light on the real thief? Other parts of this rollicking good fun site teach you how to write a great story, spell well, and more.

http://www.bbc.co.uk/education/revisewise/english/

The Five Paragraph Essay Wizard

Writing a five-paragraph essay doesn't seem so hard once you've discovered this site. It takes you through the entire process, sentence by sentence. There are also prompts to help you break that "writer's block" when you get stuck.

http://www.geocities.com/SoHo/Atrium/1437/

★ Mag-o-Matic

Start the presses, the virtual presses that is. Here's your chance to be a magazine editor and photographer. Just pick the pictures you want to use and write headlines for them. Then, enter some more of your ideas, and submit everything. When you do, you'll instantly create a magazine cover that looks like the cover of TIME, only this one's for kids. It's really fun.

http://www.timeforkids.com/TFK/yourturn/white/
    0,6405,53275,00.html

Magnetic Poetry

Unscramble familiar nursery rhymes by clicking on words and dragging them into the right places. Once you have mastered the idea, try to straighten out the other poems, some of which may be new to you. If you become completely stuck, the answers are available, too.

http://home.freeuk.net/elloughton13/scramble.htm

★ The Neverending Tale

Help kids and "young at heart" adults add to the stories here. Maybe you'd like to choose your own path through the 6,000 pages of The Haunted Castle. Or maybe the Space Station Delta story (1,000 pages) is more to your liking. Just start reading a story, and when you get to the bottom of the page, you'll find a number of choices about what to do next. You can follow a path someone else has written, or you can easily add your own series of choices. The site is monitored for appropriate family content. One thing is for sure—there are two words you'll never find in any of these stories: The End.

http://www.coder.com/creations/tale/

Only a Matter of Opinion?

If you feel strongly about something, you should express yourself. Perhaps your school newspaper has an "Opinion" section, and you could write an editorial article for it. This site helps you formulate your ideas and execute a persuasive argument supporting your point of view. This site was created by students for the ThinkQuest competition.

http://library.thinkquest.org/50084/

Plagiarism Theme Page

Stealing someone else's writing or ideas is wrong, wrong, wrong. It's OK to quote from books and magazine articles, as long as you cite the real author and source of the article. What are the limits? How can you avoid plagiarism? If you're a teacher or parent, how can you help students steer away from the temptation of using the "new plagiarism" of cut and paste from online resources?

http://www.cln.org/themes/plagiarism.html

★ Poetry Pals Internet Poetry Publishing Project for K–12 Students

Do you like to write poetry? If the answer is "Yes!" then by all means visit this site and share your poems with other kids from all over the world. If you've never written a poem in your life and you'd like to give it a try, take a look at the ideas here.

http://www.geocities.com/EnchantedForest/5165/

Tips for Young Poets

Poet Kristine O'Connell George offers advice to kids who long to string words and ideas into poetry. Clever animations illustrate her on-target suggestions. In other parts of the site, you can listen as she reads some of her own favorite works.

http://64.77.108.137/kids_tips_1.htm

The UVic Writer's Guide

Your teacher assigns you a choice: you can write either an expository essay or a persuasive one. Huh? She explained it, but you still don't understand. This Web site introduces various types of essays, and then gives advice on how to get started writing an essay, how to proofread it, and how to solve common writing problems. If you're not up to writing a whole essay yet, there's a section on how to write paragraphs. Can't write a whole paragraph? Stick to the part about how to write a good topic sentence. There is something here for everyone! You'll also find a huge glossary of literary terms, as well as grammar basics.

http://www.clearcf.uvic.ca/writersguide/Pages/StartHere.html

★ Write on Reader

This great little writing grab-bag was created by students for the ThinkQuest Junior contest! Learn about the history of writing, the writing process, and how you can make and "publish" your own book. There are also some fascinating interviews with authors, librarians, and editors, as well as kid-approved book reports.

http://library.thinkquest.org/J001156/

GRAMMAR
Big Dog's Grammar

This bare bones grammar guide shows you how to identify the different parts of a sentence. The topics covered are the things that English teachers love to comment on in your papers—subject-verb agreement, dangling modifiers, and the like. The explanations are easy to understand, and there are lots of examples. Take the short, interactive exercises to reinforce what you've just learned.

http://www.gabiscott.com/bigdog/

The Elements of Style

This little book of grammar was written a long time ago, but writers use it to this day, often referring to it as their "bible." You might be interested in checking the list of words and phrases commonly misused and misspelled.

http://www.bartleby.com/141/

NET FILES

Every August, kids from all over the world can't wait to get to Akron, Ohio, and go as fast as they can down a 954-foot hill.

Why?

Answer: They're in the World Championships of the All-American Soap Box Derby. You won't find any motorized vehicles here—these are gravity powered! Three division winners get to wear the traditional gold championship jackets at the end of Derby Day. Read more about it at *http://aasbd.org/*

A B C D E F G H I J K L M N O P Q R S T U V **W** X Y Z

A
B
C
D
E
F
G
H
I
J
K
L
M
N
O
P
Q
R
S
T
U
V
W
X
Y
Z

DID YOU KNOW WRITING IN ALL CAPITAL LETTERS IS CONSIDERED YELLING? See, isn't this nicer? Use upper and lower-case letters in mail and chat rooms.

Grammar and Style Notes

Are you a little shaky on the parts of speech? Can you tell a preposition from a present participle? The names may be strange, but you use these elements in everyday conversation. A preposition usually describes the object of the sentence and its location in time, space, or relationship to the rest of the sentence. For example, in the next sentence, the prepositions are capitalized: BEFORE the alarm rang, the cat was ON the table. A present participle just adds "ing" to the rest of the verb: singing, sitting, walking. This resource teaches the parts of speech in a fun and easy way. You'll also learn about punctuation, building sentences and paragraphs, and yes—even spelling! Knowing the correct names for these grammatical terms becomes very important when you begin to learn another language. You'll want to know what the teacher means when talking about French subjunctives and superlatives! Just click on "Content" and explore.

http://andromeda.rutgers.edu/~jlynch/Writing/

Grammar Bytes

Using "lie" and "lay" correctly can be tricky. At this site, get a clear explanation of the proper usage of these verbs. Other grammar rules are also covered, and there's a big index of grammar terms and their definitions. The site also includes online exercises and handouts for teachers to print and use in the classroom.

http://www.chompchomp.com/menu.htm

OWL: Grammar, Spelling, and Punctuation

Are those commas confusing? How about nouns, verbs, and adjectives—do they puzzle you? Are apostrophes getting you mixed up every time? And what's a preposition, anyway? Come to this writing lab to figure out how you should use all these things. Your reports, letters, and tests will look impressive! There are also many resources aimed at writers who want to be published authors.

http://owl.english.purdue.edu/handouts/grammar/

Study Web Language Arts

To colon or semicolon, that is the question. For the answer, dash over here and capitalize on the grammar tips and tricks that punctuate this site. A variety of sources will help you organize your paragraphs, straighten your sentences, check your spelling, and keep those too-common commas and rogue apostrophes from running amok across the pages of your next assignment.

http://www.studyweb.com/Language_Arts/langtoc.htm

HANDWRITING

Handwriting

Whether you're looking for Zaner Bloser or D'Nealian print alphabets, or cursive style practice, here's a great source for blackline or dotted practice sheets.

http://www.abcteach.com/DNealian/DNealianTOC.htm

Handwriting Page Maker

So what letter would you like to form today? Use this utility to create any letter, word, or page of text. Once you do, you can print it and let your little brother copy the characters by joining the dots. This site's a great help for improving handwriting skills at any age!

http://www.argosphere.net/writing/

XYLOPHONE

Xylophone by David Kaplan

This xylophone requires that you click on a virtual mallet to play a note. Keep playing notes and you'll notice you're writing music on the tablature below. Click the Play button to hear your creation.

http://www.mathsyear2000.org/museum/gallery1/xylophone/

What makes a good password? Something that's not your name and won't be found in a dictionary. Instead, try a combination of letters and numbers.

YOGA

★ Yoga Studio

If you have Shockwave, you can create your own animated yoga class from the list of postures at this site. Whatever you pick will be demonstrated for you by the student on the screen. The virtual class takes place on a beach, accompanied by the sounds of waves, relaxing music, and crying seagulls. There are also many links to yoga magazines, associations, and Web sites.

http://www.timages.com/yoga.htm

ZOOLOGY

See also ANIMALS, plus species of animals, such as BIRDS, CATS, DINOSAURS AND PREHISTORIC TIMES, DOGS AND DOG SPORTS, FISH, HORSES AND EQUESTRIAN SPORTS, and SHARKS. Also see animal categories such as AMPHIBIANS, ENDANGERED AND EXTINCT SPECIES, FARMING AND AGRICULTURE, INSECTS AND SPIDERS, INVERTEBRATES, MAMMALS, PETS AND PET CARE, REPTILES, and ZOOS. Check the animal's name in the index at the back of this book if you're not sure which category to look in.

The Bioluminescence Web Page

We're going to give this page a "glowing" report. Bioluminescence is a chemical light produced by fireflies, fish, even fungus! This site concerns the mysteries of how this light is produced. It offers wonderful photos and explains why most bioluminescent deep-sea organisms flash blue lights more than any other color. Another site on this topic is Bio Bay at <http://www.biobay.com/>.

http://lifesci.ucsb.edu/~biolum/

National Wildlife Federation - Keep the Wild Alive

Did you know that up to 100 species become extinct every day? Visit this site and find out how you can get involved in a project or organization working to save endangered wildlife.

http://www.nwf.org/wildalive/

NET FILES

When was the first camera made available to consumers?

Answer: The first consumer camera was marketed all the way back in 1888. The Kodak camera was priced at $25 and included film for 100 exposures. It was a little inconvenient to get your pictures developed, though. The whole camera had to be returned to Kodak in Rochester, New York, for film processing. For more on the history of photography, click over to
http://www.eastman.org/5_timeline/1899.htm

A
B
C
D
E
F
G
H
I
J
K
L
M
N
O
P
Q
R
S
T
U
V
W
X
Y
Z

A
B
C
D
E
F
G
H
I
J
K
L
M
N
O
P
Q
R
S
T
U
V
W
X
Y
Z

CLASSIFICATION
Classifying Critters

You may know that you're a mammal, and have more in common with a moose than a snake. How good are you at classifying other animals? Sort five different critters into their correct groups. You'll need to know what cold-blooded and warm-blooded mean before you begin. Cold-blooded means that the animal's body temperature changes based on environmental conditions. For example, a snake may have to sit on a sunny rock because he needs to be warm and can't regulate his body temperature himself. You're warm-blooded, meaning that, unless you're sick, your body stays pretty much at a constant temperature.

http://www.hhmi.org/coolscience/critters/
  critters.html

Zoology Resource Guide

Did you know that you're a *Homo sapiens*? That's the scientific classification name for humans. All life can be organized and classified this way, using a system of scientific naming or nomenclature. Visit this site, where you'll find information on the ordering of organisms into groups based on their relationships. You'll find the order, class, and kingdom for everything here, from people to dinosaurs. In addition, you'll find reports containing the symbol, scientific name, common name, and family for each member of the animal kingdom.

http://www.biosis.org/free_resources/classifn/

NET FILES

How fast is a "snail's pace"?

Answer: According to the Conchologists of America, "*Helix aspersa*, a common garden snail, can travel about two feet in three minutes. At that rate, it would travel one mile in five and a half days!" For more on snails, read
http://coa.acnatsci.org/conchnet/facts.html

MIGRATION
Journey North

Migration occurs every year with all kinds of animals, birds, and insects (even some grandparents like to go south for the winter). Journey North is a project where the Internet really shines. Each year, monarch butterflies migrate from Canada and the U.S. to their wintering grounds in Mexico and California. In the spring, they start their journey north again. Where are they now? Go outside—see any monarch butterflies? OK, now go back inside, and log on to this site to report your findings. Click on Help Track Spring's Journey North. Your results will be combined with other reports from all over the U.S., and a map will be created to show where the migratory monarchs have landed. Butterflies aren't the only things monitored here. Besides tracking various animals and birds, this site knows when the ice goes out of various lakes and rivers, where the tulips are blooming, and where the spring frogs are peeping.

http://www.learner.org/jnorth/

Satellite Tracking of Threatened Species

Certain traditional bird migration routes, used for years, have become unsuitable for one reason or another, usually because habitat along the way has been destroyed. The key is to teach these threatened birds new routes. Meet the sandhill cranes who have been trained to migrate by riding in the back of a pickup truck! Check out other birds who follow ultralight aircraft, as seen in the movie *Fly Away Home*. You'll also learn about tiny transmitters worn by birds, and the NOAA satellites that receive their signals and transmit them back to the ground stations for data analysis. Many examples are given of birds that have been tracked all over the world. Watch their animated movements on the maps.

http://outside.gsfc.nasa.gov/ISTO/satellite_tracking/

**What time is it, anyway?
Check with the atomic clock
in TIME.**

ZOOS

The Bronx Zoo

The Bronx Zoo, near New York City, is home to over 6,000 animals, including many endangered species. Visit the spectacular multimedia online exhibit called Congo Gorilla Forest, and you'll get a preview of the animals and other creatures in this 6.5-acre African rain forest. Be sure to Play a Congo Game before you leave this area. Also visit the special site for kids called Kids Go Wild <*http://www.kidsgowild.com/*>.

http://www.bronxzoo.com/

The Brookfield Zoo

Chicago's Brookfield Zoo is world-famous for its exhibits and educational initiatives. Don't hesitate to enter the "Go Wild" section and play the Ways of Knowing Trail game. It's an exciting adventure the whole family can enjoy. Should you eat the grubs? Should you follow the hogs? Who knows?

http://www.brookfieldzoo.org/

★ The National Zoo

Check out the National Zoo in Washington, D.C. Admission is free. The only rule: Don't feed the animals—and don't smudge the computer screen with your nose! When we visited, the famous pandas and the naked mole-rats were visible on the live cams. There are loads of animal pictures and facts, and don't miss the multimedia demonstrations (we loved the annual elephant pumpkin stomp!).

http://www.si.edu/natzoo/

★ San Diego Zoo, San Diego Wild Animal Park

The San Diego Zoo is one of Net-mom's favorite travel destinations. The zoo started in 1916 with only 50 animals. Now the 100-acre park contains thousands of creatures! Besides wandering around in Tiger River, Polar Bear Plunge, and Hippo Beach, Net-mom loves the beautiful landscaping and exotic plants around the park. You can see some of the attractions at this site, as well as play a few games and send some electronic postcards.

Http://www.sandiegozoo.org/

Sara's Zoo Keeper Page

Want to see a lady and her tiger? Meet Sara Bratcher, zoo keeper to carnivores at the Nashville Zoo. She takes care of about 40 big cats, including tigers, lions, Siberian lynx, clouded leopards, snow leopards, servals, African leopards, ocelots, and cougars. Also, she's the keeper for two bears. Sara is known as "Cat Mom" (no relation to Net-mom), because she raises the baby kittens if their own moms can't take care of them for some reason. At her very informative page, Sara displays lots of photos of her charges and tells what it is like to be a zoo keeper. Want to know how to become an animal specialist like Sara? Visit this page!

Http://www.mindspring.com/~mbratcher/zookpr.htm

ZZZ

The End of the Internet

This is the end of the book, and so we present a page located at the end of the Internet. Well, sort of. There's not a real end to the Net, of course, but this is pretty close. Ansd it's a good excuse to turn off your computer. Go play outside now. :-)

Http://www.opaldata.com/the_end/

A B C D E F G H I J K L M N O P Q R S T U V W X Y Z

Index

Alphabetical List of Sites